JOSHUA RAY

WHITE-COLLAR CRIMINAL PROSECUTIONS IN THE U.S. AND U.K.

A COMPARATIVE TREATISE FOR PRACTITIONERS

ABA
AMERICAN BAR ASSOCIATION
Judicial Division

Cover design by ABA Design

Printed in the United States of America.

26 25 24 23 22 5 4 3 2 1

Library of Congress Cataloging-in-Publication Data

Names: Ray, Joshua L. (Lawyer), author. | American Bar Association.
Judicial Division, sponsoring body.
Title: White-collar criminal prosecutions in the U.S. and U.K. :
a comparative guide for practitioners / Joshua Ray.
Description: Chicago, Illinois : American Bar Association, [2022] |
Includes index. | Summary: "The content in this book, focuses on just
the most important points that financial crime lawyers in London,
New York, Los Angeles, or Washington are likely to encounter. The rationale
for writing this book was to create a resource that many may have wished
existed when they began a cross border practice: a holistic, easy-to-follow
explanation of the American and British statutes and procedural rules that
govern the investigation and prosecution of white collar crime, along with their
key differences. The author has sought to present this information objectively,
and hopes that it may be equally useful to those in law enforcement and other
lawyers in private practice"--Provided by publisher.
Identifiers: LCCN 2022020445 (print) | LCCN 2022020446 (ebook) |
ISBN 9781639051779 (paperback) | ISBN 9781639051786 (epub)
Subjects: LCSH: White collar crimes--Law and legislation--United States. |
White collar crimes--Law and legislation--Great Britain. |
Prosecution--United States. | Prosecution--Great Britain.
Classification: LCC K5215 .R39 2022 (print) | LCC K5215 (ebook) |
DDC 345/.0268--dc23/eng/20220729
LC record available at https://lccn.loc.gov/2022020445
LC ebook record available at https://lccn.loc.gov/2022020446

Contents

About the Author

Joshua L. Ray is a partner at CANDEY, an international litigation firm based in London. A member of the New York bar and a solicitor in England and Wales, he represents individuals and corporations in cross-border criminal and civil litigation, investigations, and contentious regulatory matters. He also advises international corporations on compliance with anti-money laundering, sanctions, and antibribery regulations in the United States and the United Kingdom. Josh has extensive experience defending individuals in enforcement proceedings brought by British and American law enforcement agencies including the Department of Justice, Securities and Exchange Commission, Commodity Futures Trading Commission, and Serious Fraud Office.

Josh received an undergraduate degree in government from Cornell University and his law degree with honors from Cornell Law School.

Author Acknowledgments

This book would not have been possible without the support of my parents, Larry and Debbie, and my fiancée, Colleen. I would also like to express my deepest gratitude to Hon. Mary-Margaret Anderson (Ret.), Jeffrey Salyards, and everyone else at the American Bar Association who helped guide the writing and editing process. Special thanks too to my contributing editors and my many other colleagues who practice in white-collar crime for their advice and insight. I am also grateful to my clients, who have trusted me with their cases and given me the opportunity to work in this fascinating field of law. Any mistakes are my own.

Contributing Editors

Vannina Ettori (call: 2009 [New York]; 2016 [England and Wales]; and 2019 [Paris]) is a Principal Investigative Lawyer at the Serious Fraud Office who develops cases at the pre-investigation stage in collaboration with foreign and domestic law enforcement agencies and manages a senior investigation team. She has been involved in a number of complex fraud and international corruption matters. Prior to the SFO, she was a legal advisor to the Chancellor of the United Kingdom High Court. Vannina earned undergraduate law degrees from the University of Cambridge and Université Paris II, Panthéon-Assas, and an LL.M. from Cornell Law School.

Alex Haines (call: 2007 [England and Wales]; 2019 [New York]; and 2020 [Ireland]) is a specialist in international organizations and international fraud and corruption at Outer Temple Chambers in London. He was appointed to the Attorney General's Panel of Counsel to the Crown in 2019 and as Sanctions Officer at the Caribbean Development Bank in 2020. He regularly advises the U.K. government and appears before international tribunals including in Washington, DC. He co-authored the chapter on U.K., UN, and EU sanctions for *Smith, Owen and Bodnar on Asset Recovery (Criminal Confiscation and Civil Recovery)* and he authored the chapter on the Sanctions Regimes of Multilateral Development Banks for *Lissack and Horlick on Bribery and Corruption* (3rd edition, Lexis Nexis).

Aziz Rahman is a solicitor-advocate whose practice focuses on defending individuals and companies in financial crime cases brought by law enforcement agencies in the United Kingdom.

Table of Key Statutes

United States

Statute	Abbreviation
Bank Secrecy Act	BSA
Clarifying Lawful Overseas Use of Data Act	CLOUD Act
Code of Federal Regulations	C.F.R.
Commodity Exchange Act	CEA
Electronic Communications Privacy Act	ECPA
Foreign Corrupt Practices Act	FCPA
Federal Rules of Appellate Procedure	Fed. R. App. P.
Federal Rules of Civil Procedure	Fed. R. Civ. P.
Federal Rules of Criminal Procedure	Fed. R. Crim. P.
Money Laundering Control Act	MLCA
Stored Communications Act	SCA
Sentencing Reform Act	SRA
Title III of the Omnibus Crime Control and Safe Streets Act of 1968	Title III/Wiretap Act
United States Code	U.S.C.

United Kingdom

Statute	Abbreviation
Bail Act 1974	BA
Bribery Act 2010	BA
Crime and Courts Act 2013	CCA
Civil Procedure Rules	CPR
Criminal Justice and Police Act 2001	CJPA
Criminal Procedure (Attendance of Witnesses) Act 1965	CPA

(Continued)

United Kingdom

Statute	Abbreviation
Crime and Disorder Act 1998	CDA
Crime (International Co-operation) Act 2003	CICA
Crime (Overseas Production Orders) Act	OPO
Criminal Appeal Act 1968	CAA 1968
Criminal Finances Act 2017	CFA
Criminal Practice Directions 2020	CPD 2020
Criminal Procedures Rules 2020	CrimPR
Criminal Justice Act 1967	CJA 1967
Criminal Justice Act 1987	CJA 1987
Criminal Justice Act 1993	CJA 1993
Criminal Justice Act 2003	CJA 2003
Criminal Law Act 1977	CLA
Criminal Procedure and Investigations Act 1996	CPIA
Economic Crime (Transparency and Enforcement) Act 2022	ECA
Extradition Act 2003	EA
European Convention on Human Rights	ECHR
Financial Services Act 2012	FSA
Financial Services and Markets Act 2000	FSMA
Fraud Act 2006	FA
Investigatory Powers Act 2016	IPA
Magistrates' Courts Act 1980	MCA
Police and Criminal Evidence Act 1984	PACE
Proceeds of Crimes Act 2002	POCA
Prosecution of Offences Act 1985	POA
Sentencing Act 2020	SA
Serious Organized Crime and Police Act 2005	SOCPA

Table of Government Enforcement Agencies

United States

Agency	Abbreviation
Department of Justice	DOJ
U.S. Attorney's Office	USAO
Securities and Exchange Commission	SEC
Commodity Futures Trading Commission	CFTC
Federal Bureau of Investigation	FBI
Bureau of Prisons	BOP
U.S. Marshals Service	USMS
Internal Revenue Service	IRS
Federal Trade Commission	FTC
Office of Foreign Asset Control	OFAC

United Kingdom

Agency	Abbreviation
Crown Prosecution Service	CPS
Her Majesty's Courts and Tribunal Service	HMCTS
Her Majesty's Prison and Probation Service	HMPPS
Her Majesty's Revenue and Customs	HMRC
National Crime Agency	NCA
Prudential Regulatory Authority	PRA
Serious Fraud Office	SFO

Preface

The phrase "white-collar crime" was reportedly coined by American sociologist Edwin H. Sutherland following the Great Depression of the early 1930s. In his view, white-collar crimes were the offenses typically committed by "the upper or white-collar class, composed of respectable or at least respected business and professional men."[1] Commenting on the rampant financial misconduct that contributed to the 1929 Wall Street Crash and subsequent economic devastation, Sutherland was the first to analyze crimes like financial misrepresentations, market manipulation, bribery, embezzlement, and securities fraud as a distinct category of social phenomena characterized by social status.

In 1977, the U.S. Department of Justice (DOJ) drafted an updated definition that stressed the nature of the criminal conduct instead of the societal status of the perpetrators: "White-collar offenses shall constitute those classes of non-violent illegal activities which principally involve traditional notions of deceit, deception, concealment, manipulation, breach of trust, subterfuge or illegal circumvention." As explained by a DOJ official at the time, this reformulation was driven by a recognition that Sutherland's preoccupation with status failed to take account of the demographic range of those who typically commit these crimes:

> The traditional academic approach does not accurately reflect the type of offenses and offenders encountered by the criminal justice system. Our experience has demonstrated that white-collar offenses are regularly committed by members of all social classes and are not the exclusive domain of the rich and powerful.[2]

White-collar crime is an imprecise concept, and there continues to be no single, unambiguous legal definition of the term.[3] In the United Kingdom, the conduct that is usually called white-collar crime in the United States is more often referred to simply as "financial crime." To lawmakers and lawyers in London, financial crime is generally understood to mean any

1. Edwin H. Sutherland, *White-Collar Criminality*, 5 AM. SOCIOLOGICAL REV. 1 (Feb. 1940).

2. Tony G. Poveda, *White-Collar Crime and the Justice Department: The Institutionalization of a Concept*, 17 CRIME L. & SOCIAL CHANGE 235, 242 (1992) (quoting Hearings on White-Collar Crime Before the Subcomm. on Crime of the House Comm. On the Judiciary, 95th Cong. 65 (1979)); *see also* JULIE R. O'SULLIVAN, FEDERAL WHITE COLLAR CRIME 4–5 (3rd ed. 2007).

3. *See, e.g.*, Lucian E. Dervan & Ellen S. Podgar, *"White Collar Crime": Still Hazy After All These Years*, 50 GA. L. REV. 711, 712–15 (Spring 2016); Stuart P. Green, *The Concept of White Collar Crime and Legal Theory*, 8 BUFF. CRIM. L. REV. 1, 3–13 (2004); KAREN HARRISON & NICHOLAS RYDER, THE LAW RELATING TO FINANCIAL CRIME IN THE UNITED KINGDOM 3–5 (2d ed. 2017).

offense involving fraud, misconduct related to financial markets, money laundering, and terrorism financing.[4] Like the DOJ's definition, the British perspective emphasizes crimes that involve moving or obtaining assets through deceit and misuse of the financial system.

In this book, white-collar crime and financial crime will be used interchangeably to refer to nonviolent crimes that involve deception, concealment, or a violation of trust, and that are primarily motived by a desire for monetary gain or professional advancement. These crimes are usually, but not always, committed by individuals who are not professional criminals or members of organized crime groups. Instead, the perpetrators typically work in a corporate setting and their crimes usually relate to, and are made possible by, their employment and professional expertise.[5] White-collar crimes also often "take place in benign social settings in which the only difference between crime and commerce may be the defendant's state of mind. For example, to commit fraud is to do a usually innocuous act—such as to make a representation of fact in a business transaction—with a prohibited state of mind, namely, the specific intent to defraud the counterparty."[6]

Whatever the exact definition, the effects of white-collar crime are undoubtedly significant: in terms of direct monetary losses, studies suggest that white-collar crime causes more harm than all other types of criminal offenses combined. Current estimates are that financial crimes cost the U.S. and British economies more than $500 billion and £190 billion, respectively, each year.[7]

Yet just as the business cycle fluctuates between expansion and recession, the public's interest in cracking down on mischievousness in the business world follows a similar ebb and flow. As explained by the former U.S. Attorney in Chicago, Anton Valukas, "In calculating where to devote our prosecutorial resources during boom times, we tend not to focus on complex white-collar crimes. The general thought seems to be, 'Why tinker with a system that is working?'" But when the "economy turns sour, revelations of criminal conduct and excessive practices that appear to have contributed to the downturn often lead the public to demand a swift and forceful response."[8]

Valukas notes, for example, that during the 1980s the bulk of law enforcement resources in the United States was "committed to drug task forces created to fight drugs, gangs, and street violence. It was only after the scandals on Wall Street and the Savings and Loan (S&L) crises, that the government put significant resources into financial fraud." Similarly, in "the wake of 9/11, vast resources were understandably shifted to fighting terrorism." But following the 2008/2009 economic crisis, the U.S. government rushed "to plug the holes left by that shift, moving agents, resources, and prosecutors back to prosecuting complex white-collar crime." As the crisis subsided, federal enforcement statistics for white-collar crime again

4. Financial Conduct Authority Handbook (Financial Services and Markets Act 2000 s.1H).

5. Paul M. Klenowski & Kimberly D. Dodson, *Who Commits White Collar Crime, and What Do We Know About Them? in* The Oxford Handbook of White-Collar Crime 101 (Shanna R. Van Slyke, Michael L. Benson, & Francis T. Cullen eds., Oxford University Press, 2016).

6. Samuel W. Buell, *Is the White Collar Offender Privileged?*, 63 Duke L.J. 841 (January 2014).

7. Roomy Khan, *White-Collar Crimes—Motivations and Triggers*, Forbes, Feb. 22, 2018.

8. Anton Valukas, *White-Collar Crime and Economic Recession*, Univ. Chic. Legal Forum, Iss. 1 Article 2 (2010), *available at* https://chicagounbound.uchicago.edu/uclf/vol2010/iss1/2.

began to trend downward. According to one study, the annual number of white-collar crime prosecutions brought by the DOJ dropped more than fifty percent between 2011 and 2020.[9]

Financial crime regulation in the United Kingdom reveals a similar dynamic. During an era of financial deregulation under Prime Minister Margaret Thatcher in the 1980s, London began to attract foreign criminals, including American mafia figures, who came to take advantage "of the new climate of enterprise, offering securities scams, commodity futures trading frauds and other forms of investment rip-offs."[10] "Almost overnight, London became the fraud capital of Europe and every con-man, snake-oil salesman, grafter and hustler turned up."[11] In response, alarmed British lawmakers passed the Criminal Justice Act 1987 which, among other things, created a dedicated financial crime prosecutor, the Serious Fraud Office (SFO). After the 2008/2009 financial crisis, Parliament responded once again by reorganizing Britain's regulatory agencies and creating two new ones: the Financial Conduct Authority (FCA) and the National Crime Agency (NCA).

But despite the massive investments made by the U.S. and British governments toward identifying and punishing financial crimes in the decade since the last financial crisis, a recent study of crime data since 2000 suggests that white-collar crime rates are at an all-time high.[12] If history is any guide, investigations and enforcement activity targeting white-collar crime is likely to increase in the near future. Indeed, data indicate that a renewed focus on identifying and prosecuting financial crime is already underway. In the first year of the Biden administration, for example, the number of new federal white-collar crime prosecutions reached nearly five thousand, an increase of more than ten percent over 2020.[13]

As the world economy slowly recovers from the COVID-19 pandemic, it is therefore unsurprising that law enforcement agencies on both sides of the Atlantic and throughout the world are intensely focused on white-collar crime.[14] In the same way that previous economic slowdowns drew attention to the "excessive practices" that became pervasive during the preceding "boom" stage of the economic cycle, this most recent upheaval will accelerate efforts to expose illicit financial schemes occurring during the relatively prosperous 2010s and the still-ongoing pandemic era itself.

As these crimes come to light in the coming years, U.S. and British law enforcement agencies will no doubt continue to cooperate closely on white-collar crime investigations and prosecutions. And as with many of the major cross-border white-collar crime cases over the past ten years—the London Interbank Offered Rate (LIBOR) and foreign exchange (FX) scandals, the Unaoil and Airbus foreign bribery cases, the collapse of tech firm Autonomy, and the "Flash

9. Stewart Bishop, *Wire Fraud Prosecutions Up Sharply in 2021*, Law360, Sept. 27, 2021.

10. Harrison & Ryder, *supra* note 3, at 97.

11. *Id.*

12. Dorothy S. Lund & Natasha Sarin, *Corporate Crime and Punishment: An Empirical Study* (University of Pennsylvania Institute for Law & Economics, Feb. 17, 2020).

13. Stewart Bishop, *Wire Fraud Prosecutions Up Sharply in 2021*, Law360, Sept. 27, 2021.

14. *See, e.g.*, Lisa Osofsky, *Ensuring Our Country Is a High Risk Place for the World's Most Sophisticated Criminals to Operate* (Serious Fraud Office, Sept. 3, 2018); Patricia Hurtado & Christopher Yasiejko, *White Collar Crime Probes Likely to Intensify Under Biden's DOJ*, Bloomberg, Nov. 11, 2020.

Crash" to name just a few—the next generation of cross-border financial crime litigation will include many cases involving aspects of both the U.S. and U.K. criminal justice systems. As the DOJ has acknowledged, "large scale economic crime conspiracies that harm U.S. markets, such as LIBOR rigging and the manipulation of the foreign exchange spot [price], often occur, in large part, overseas and successful prosecutions of these matters frequently rely on evidence provided by witnesses who live in foreign countries."[15] In 2017 the DOJ announced that it had detailed one of its anticorruption prosecutors to work at the U.K.'s FCA, the first time the Criminal Division made an overseas posting to cooperate with a foreign regulator on white-collar crime issues. In another cross-Atlantic exchange, Lisa Osofsky, the current head of the SFO, is an American and former senior lawyer for the Federal Bureau of Investigation. The SFO has also recently begun to employ DOJ prosecutors on secondment.

Although the two systems share a common heritage and a number of basic similarities, there are many significant differences that can have a decisive impact on legal outcomes. In *United States v. Allen*, for example, the fraud convictions of two British bankers in Manhattan's federal court were thrown out on appeal after it was revealed that the DOJ's main witness reviewed transcripts of testimony that the defendants were compelled to give to British law enforcement—a common practice in England but a violation of the U.S. Constitution's Fifth Amendment that was determined to have tainted the entire proceedings. "In order to be admitted into [U.S.] courts," the Second Circuit Court of Appeals wrote, "inculpatory statements obtained overseas by foreign officials must have been made voluntarily."[16]

The *Allen* case demonstrates why it is often advantageous—if not critical—for lawyers involved in cross-border criminal proceedings to have a thorough understanding of the relevant laws and procedures in each implicated jurisdiction. As stated by Mary Jo White, the former U.S. Attorney for the Southern District of New York, "To be truly effective, a lawyer must know the rules, all of the available tools, and the full range of issues that do or may arise in a criminal case."[17] The objective of this book is to give a foundational overview of criminal practice in the United States and United Kingdom, and to provide a practical guide to some of the nuances specific to white-collar crime cases in both jurisdictions.

This is obviously a very broad topic, and I have not attempted to comprehensively address every one of the numerous possible legal issues that can arise in complex white-collar crime matters. Rather, I have focused on just the most important points that financial crime lawyers in London, New York, Chicago, or Washington, D.C., are likely to encounter. My rationale for writing this book was to create a resource that I wish existed when I began my cross-border practice: a holistic, easy-to-follow explanation of the U.S. and British statutes and procedural rules that govern the investigation and prosecution of white-collar crime, along with their key differences. Although my practice focuses on defense, I have sought to present this information objectively, and hope that it may be equally useful to those in law enforcement and other lawyers in private practice.

---

15. United States v. Allen, 864 F.3d 63, 90 (2d Cir. 2017).

16. *Id.* at 80.

17. Gordon Mehler et al., Federal Criminal Practice: A Second Circuit Handbook xvii (20th ed. 2020).

1 The Fundamentals of White-Collar Practice

The differences in how white-collar crimes are investigated and prosecuted in the United States and the United Kingdom reflect the underlying system of government used in each country. To provide context for the chapters that follow, this chapter gives an overview of these systems and a description of the government enforcement agencies primarily involved in financial crime enforcement cases.

I. GOVERNMENT STRUCTURE

A. The U.S. Federal Government

Since coming into force in 1789, the Constitution has been the fundamental framework for how the U.S. government functions. It is the ultimate authority from which all other laws and regulations are derived and, by its own terms, is the "supreme Law of the Land" in the sense that all laws and government activity must comply with it.[1] The Constitution establishes three coequal branches of the national (or "federal") government: the Executive, which is led by the president and includes federal law enforcement and regulatory agencies; Congress, comprised of the House of Representatives and the Senate; and the Judiciary, comprised of the Supreme Court and the lower federal courts. At a basic level, the Constitution divides governance responsibility between the branches to ensure that no branch becomes too powerful or exceeds the bounds of its constitutionally dictated areas of responsibility: put simply, Congress creates federal laws, the Executive executes and enforces those laws, and the Judiciary interprets and applies them. Although the lines between these theoretically distinct roles have shifted over time, the separation of powers model remains the foundation of American government.[2]

Under the Constitution's 10th Amendment, political power in the United States is divided between the federal government in Washington and the fifty constituent states: "The powers

1. U.S. Const. art VI.

2. *See, e.g.*, Mistretta v. United States, 488 U.S. 361, 381 (1989) ("While the Constitution diffuses power the better to secure liberty, it also contemplates that practice will integrate the dispersed powers into a workable government. It enjoins upon its branches separateness but interdependence, autonomy but reciprocity.") (quoting Youngstown Sheet Tube Co. v. Sawyer, 343 U.S. 579, 635 (1952)).

not delegated to the United States by the Constitution, nor prohibited by it to the States, are reserved to the States respectively, or to the people." This has been interpreted to mean that the federal government has the power to regulate interstate and international activities pursuant to Congress's powers set forth in Article I, while the jurisdiction of the state governments is limited to localized conduct occurring within their borders. For example, bribery of a foreign official is principally a federal matter, whereas robbery and murder are most often dealt with at the state or city level. Reflecting this structure, the U.S. justice system is two-tiered, with the federal government and the states empowered to create and enforce their own independent criminal laws.[3] The same conduct can therefore violate both state and federal laws, and state and federal authorities can initiate simultaneous or successive prosecutions against a single defendant.[4] Certain states, most notably New York, have their own regulatory agencies with robust capabilities to target white-collar crime that rival those of the federal government.

While state and federal laws pertaining to white-collar crime function in parallel, there are significant differences in how the state and federal governments define certain crimes and the procedures used for adjudicating and punishing violations. This book is concerned only with federal crimes, most of which are defined in Title 18 of the U.S. Code, and the mechanics by which such crimes are prosecuted and defended under the Federal Rules of Criminal Procedure (Fed. R. Crim. P.).[5] There are more than 4,500 federal criminal statutes and an even larger number of regulatory offenses that carry criminal penalties.[6]

While there are some crimes in the U.S. Code, such as securities fraud or foreign bribery, that are clearly of the white-collar variety, other crimes, such as conspiracy, obstruction of justice, and violations of the Racketeer Influenced and Corrupt Organizations (RICO) statute, can be either white-collar or more traditional "street crimes." The statutes most commonly implicated in federal white-collar prosecutions are examined in detail in chapter 4.

---

3. Setser v. United States, 566 U.S. 231, 241 (2012).

4. United States v. Wheeler, 435 U.S. 313, 316–17 (1978); Abbate v. United States, 359 U.S. 187, 194–95 (1959); United States v. Coonan, 938 F.2d 1553, 1562 (2d Cir. 1991).

5. Cornell Law School's Legal Information Institute (https://www.law.cornell.edu) maintains a comprehensive public database that contains updated versions of the full U.S. Code, the Code of Federal Regulations, Federal Rules of Criminal Procedure, and Federal Rules of Appellate Procedure. It also publishes a guide explaining the rules of legal citation in the United States (https://www.law.cornell.edu/citation) and WEX, a free legal dictionary and encyclopedia (https://www.law.cornell.edu/wex).

6. This enormous statutory framework has been regularly criticized as unnecessarily dense and labyrinthine. *See, e.g.*, Julie R. O'Sullivan, *The Federal Criminal "Code" Is a Disgrace: Obstructions Statutes as Case Study*, 96 J. Crim. L. & Criminology 643 (2006) ("There actually is no federal criminal 'code' worthy of the name. . . . What the federal government has is a haphazard grab bag of statutes accumulated over 200 years, rather than a comprehensive, thoughtful, and internally consistent system of criminal law."); Frank O. Bowman III, *Pour Encourage Les Autres? The Curious History and Distressing Implications of the Criminal Provisions of the Sarbanes-Oxley Act and the Sentencing Guidelines Amendments that Followed*, 1 Ohio St. J. Crim. L. 373 (2004) ("[T]he substantive federal criminal law is a ghastly mess, with hundreds of overlapping and often oddly drafted provisions and no system for classifying the relative seriousness of offenses.").

Because federal laws typically deal with activities that have effects on a national or even international scale, most major white-collar crime cases are handled by federal prosecutors working for the Department of Justice (DOJ). Thus, even though federal courts hear significantly fewer white-collar crime cases than state courts, the cases they hear tend to be of greater significance and complexity. And because federal criminal statutes generally have greater extraterritorial reach than comparable state laws, the vast majority of cross-border white-collar crime prosecutions are brought within the federal system.

B. The Central Government in the United Kingdom

There is no single written document comparable to the U.S. Constitution in the United Kingdom.[7] Rather, the British government's overarching principles are dispersed throughout numerous agreements, treaties, legislation, court decisions, historical documents such as the Magna Carta (1215) and the Bill of Rights (1689), and unwritten constitutional conventions. It is a constitutional monarchy led by the prime minister with the support of the Cabinet and ministers selected from Parliament to run the bureaucracy. In contrast to the U.S. president, who is head of an independent branch of government, the British prime minister oversees government agencies while also leading the lower house of Parliament, the House of Commons. Parliament's upper house, the House of Lords, has nearly eight hundred members who are either appointed to their position by the Crown (on the advice of the prime minister) or assume a lordship via heredity or senior status within the Church of England. While the House of Lords generally cannot veto acts passed by the House of Commons, its members play an important oversight role in British lawmaking. The presiding monarch has limited practical powers but must nominally agree to all bills passed by Parliament before they become law and give (mostly ceremonial) approval to certain other government functions.

Reflecting the fact that each of the United Kingdom's four constituent countries were once independent, the U.K. government is "devolved," meaning that its powers are split between the central government in Westminster, London, and the quasi-autonomous governments of Wales, Scotland, and Northern Ireland. The Crown Dependencies of the Bailiwick of Guernsey, the Bailiwick of Jersey, and the Isle of Man are closely linked to, but not a part of, the United Kingdom and are self-governing, as are the fourteen British Overseas Territories (which include Gibraltar, Bermuda, the Cayman Islands, and the British Virgin Islands). As the revelations in the Panama and Pandora Papers confirmed, several of these territories are well-known tax havens, with bank secrecy rules that make them attractive to those seeking to hide the proceeds of financial crimes and are often implicated in international financial crime investigations.[8] Despite their close historical links, law enforcement in the United Kingdom has an arms'-length relationship with its counterparts in the Crown Dependencies and Overseas Territories, just as it has with regulators in any other country.

---

7. The formal collective name of the four countries is the "United Kingdom of Great Britain and Northern Ireland." For convenience, this book will be referring to it as the United Kingdom.

8. *See, e.g.*, Will Fitzgibbon, *US Lawmakers Call for Crackdown on Financial 'Enablers' after Pandora Papers*, ICIJ (Oct. 7, 2021); Nicholas Shaxson, *The City of London Is Hiding the World's Stolen Money*, N. Y. Times, Oct. 11, 2021.

Within the United Kingdom proper, Scotland and Northern Ireland operate their own independent criminal justice systems, while England and Wales operate a unified one. The scope of this book is limited to the criminal laws and procedures used in England and Wales, and references to the United Kingdom—which technically encompasses all four countries—should generally be understood as pertaining only to these two countries.

There is a single criminal code in England and Wales, and all criminal laws except for local misdemeanors are passed by both houses of Parliament (the House of Commons and House of Lords) and given Royal Assent by the Crown. These laws are enforced by central government agencies under the ultimate leadership of the prime minister in accordance with the Criminal Procedure Rules 2020 (CrimPR).[9] The Acts of Parliament that are most often implicated in financial crimes are contained within the Proceeds of Crime Act 2002, the Fraud Act 2006, various iterations of the Criminal Justice Act, the Bribery Act 2010, and the Financial Services and Markets Act 2000.

II. THE CRIMINAL COURT SYSTEM

A. The Federal Court System in the United States

Federal courts have exclusive jurisdiction over all cases involving alleged criminal violations of federal law. The federal court system has three tiers: the district courts, the circuit courts of appeals, and the U.S. Supreme Court. There are also bankruptcy and tax courts within the federal system that essentially function like specialist district courts. All federal judges—known as "Article III" judges because they are governed by Article III of the Constitution—are selected by the president and confirmed by majority vote of the Senate. Once in office, all federal judges except for magistrate judges are entitled to hold their positions "during good behavior," which generally means for life or until voluntary retirement; for serious misconduct, they can be removed upon impeachment by the House of Representatives and conviction by the Senate. Impeachment of a federal judge is exceedingly rare: to date, there have been fifteen judicial impeachments in the country's history, only eight of which have resulted in a conviction.[10] Magistrate judges, who assist district court judges in preparing cases for trial, are selected by district court judges and serve for a specified term.

1. *The District Courts*

District courts are the starting point for all white-collar crime cases: they are where grand juries sit, arrest warrants are issued, bail is decided, and preliminary legal motions are ruled upon. District courts are also where federal criminal trials are conducted and defendants' sentences are determined. Unlike the inquisitorial systems used in France and other European countries, district court judges play no active part in criminal investigations. While their

---

9. Updated versions of all legislation in the United Kingdom, including the Criminal Procedure Rules, are available through https://www.legislation.gov.uk.

10. FEDERAL JUDICIAL CENTER, IMPEACHMENTS OF FEDERAL JUDGES, *available at* https://www.fjc.gov/history/judges/impeachments-federal-judges.

approval is generally needed before government agents can execute arrest warrants and employ investigatory tools like search warrants and wire taps, district court judges are otherwise limited to making legal and factual determinations with respect to cases brought independently by federal prosecutors. Chief Justice John Roberts explained a judge's role during his Senate confirmation hearings using a baseball analogy: "Judges are like umpires. Umpires don't make the rules, they apply them. The role of an umpire and a judge is critical. They make sure everyone plays by the rules."[11]

There are currently 670 district court judges sitting in ninety-four district courts spread throughout the country and four overseas U.S. territories (Guam, Puerto Rico, the Northern Marian Islands, and the U.S. Virgin Islands). In criminal cases, magistrate judges will usually oversee preliminary case matters such as discovery, bail, and the issuance of search and arrest warrants, while district court judges will decide on more substantive legal motions and preside over the trial and sentencing.

All district courts are bound to follow the Federal Rules of Criminal Procedure, the Federal Rules of Evidence, and the Federal Rules of Civil Procedure (in noncriminal matters). In addition, many district courts and individual judges prescribe their own unique local rules governing practices and procedures regarding things like page limits for briefs, filing deadlines, and jury selection. Except in certain limited circumstances, district courts must also follow the decisions of the court of appeals in their region, as well as the decisions of the U.S. Supreme Court.[12] Opinions issued by district court judges are often used as reference points for later decisions, but they are generally not binding even on judges within the same district court.[13] This general rule is subject to various exceptions.[14]

Federal criminal trials are managed by a single district court judge. While the Constitution's Seventh Amendment gives all defendants facing felony charges the right to demand a trial by jury, defendants have the option of choosing to be tried without a jury in what is known as a "bench trial" so long as the prosecution and the judge both consent.[15] In a bench trial, the factfinding function of the jury is replaced by the district court judge. Depending on

11. *Confirmation Hearing on the Nomination of John G. Roberts, Jr. to Be Chief Justice of the United States Before the S. Comm. on the Judiciary*, 109th Cong. 55 (2005) (statement of John G. Roberts, Jr., Nominee to be Chief Justice of the United States).

12. *See, e.g.*, Olson v. Paine, Webber, Jackson & Curtis, Inc., 806 F.2d 731, 734 (7th Cir. 1986) (district courts are bound by higher federal courts unless circumstances indicate that the higher court would repudiate a previous decision at the earliest possible opportunity).

13. Colby v. J.C. Penney Co., 811 F.2d 1119, 1124 (7th Cir. 1987).

14. *See, e.g.*, United States v. Quintieri, 36 F.3d 1217, 1225 (2d Cir. 2002) (explaining that the "law of the case doctrine" requires district courts to adhere to their own decisions in a particular case); United States v. Alcan Aluminum Corp., 990 F.2d 711, 718–19 (2d Cir. 1993) (collateral estoppel doctrine precludes reopening of "an issue of law or fact actually litigated and decided by a court" in a subsequent suit between the same parties); United States v. Bhatia, 545 F.3d 757, 759 (9th Cir. 2008) (under res judicata doctrine "a final judgment on the merits bars further claims by parties or their privies based on the same cause of action").

15. Fed. R. Crim. P. 23; *see also* Singer v. United States, 380 U.S. 24, 34–35 (1965) (explaining bench trials and related issues); United States v. Preston, 751 F.3d 1008, 1029 (9th Cir. 2014) (noting defendant's consent to a bench trial does not carry over to any later retrial).

the type of charges involved, a bench trial can have distinct advantages and disadvantages over a jury trial. Choosing between the two can thus be a decision of critical strategic importance for the defense.[16] The conventional wisdom is that defendants generally fare better in front of a jury, but detailed studies of this phenomenon suggest that in fact the opposite may be true.[17]

The parties in a federal criminal case are the U.S. government—which is always represented by a DOJ prosecutor—and one or more defendant. The defendant is presumed innocent, and the government bears the burden of proving its case "beyond a reasonable doubt," meaning that the prosecution's evidence must establish that there is no reasonable doubt that the defendant committed the crime charged.[18] Defendants have no obligation to testify or to present evidence on their own behalf.[19] But if a defendant raises an affirmative defense, such as a claim that he or she withdrew from a conspiracy outside of the applicable statute of limitations, it is the defendant's burden to adduce evidence in support.[20]

a. Public Access to Court Proceedings and Records

Unlike in the United Kingdom, in the United States nearly all court opinions and orders, and most motions and supporting memoranda filed by the parties are open public records. Although sensitive materials such as grand jury transcripts and warrant applications are only available to attorneys for the government,[21] there is a presumption that all other filings and court proceedings will be open and available to the public.[22] The reasoning behind this is to maintain the justice system's credibility. As explained by the Supreme Court, public scrutiny of a "criminal trial enhances the quality and safeguards the integrity of the factfinding process," "fosters an appearance of fairness . . . and public respect for the judicial process," and permits the public to participate in and serve as a check upon the judicial process."[23]

Federal court dockets are electronically available for a fee through Public Access to Court Electronic Records (PACER) (www.pacer.gov), a government-run online service. Public access to case dockets of the U.S. Supreme Court since 2001 are available through the Supreme Court's website (www.supremecourt.gov/docket/docket.aspx).

---

16. United States v. Gabriel, 125 F3d 89, 94–95 (2d Cir. 1997) (discussing factors that may lead a defendant to choose a bench trial).

17. *See, e.g.*, Andrew D. Leipold, *Why Are Federal Judges So Acquittal Prone?* 83 Wash. U. L. R. 151–54 (2005).

18. United States v. Hughes, 389 F.2d 535, 537 (2d Cir. 1968) ("The jury is still required to acquit even though it is less likely that the defendant is innocent than guilty, so long as the jury is not convinced of that guilt beyond a reasonable doubt.").

19. United States v. Okatan, 728 F.3d 111, 121 (2d Cir. 2013).

20. *See, e.g.*, United States v. Kozeny, 493 F. Supp. 2d 693, 702 (S.D.N.Y. 2007).

21. Kamakana v. City & County of Honolulu, 447 F.3d 1172, 1178 (9th Cir. 2006).

22. United States v. Edwards, 672 F.2d 1289, 1294 (7th Cir. 1982); United States v. Turner, 367 F. Supp. 2d 319, 320 (E.D.N.Y. 2005) (parties in a criminal matter may file documents under seal "to the extent that such exceptions to the public filing requirement are supported by good cause").

23. Globe Newspaper Co. v. Superior Court, 457 U.S. 596, 606–07 (1982); *see also* Smith v. Daily Mail Publishing Co., 443 U.S. 97, 101–03 (1979); NAACP v. Button, 371 U.S. 415, 437 (1963).

Although court filings in criminal cases are more freely accessible in the United States than in the United Kingdom, the reverse is true with respect to other forms of media. Federal courts are prohibited from allowing "photographs in the courtroom during judicial proceedings or the broadcasting of judicial proceedings."[24] The many well-known broadcasts of high-profile criminal trials such as the O.J. Simpson and George Floyd murder trials all occurred in state court.

2. *The Circuit Courts of Appeals*

The ninety-four district courts are organized into twelve regional circuits, each of which has its own court of appeals (figure 1.1).[25] For example, the Second Circuit Court of Appeals—one of the most important courts for white-collar crime issues—hears appeals from the district courts located in New York, Connecticut, and Vermont. Each circuit court has a distinct number of judges, ranging from six on the First Circuit to twenty-nine on the Ninth Circuit, that reflects the population size within its jurisdiction. The procedural rules used in appeals to the circuit courts are set forth in the Federal Rules of Appellate Procedure (Fed. R. App. P.).

Criminal defendants who have been found guilty at the district court level have an automatic right to appeal their case to the relevant circuit court of appeal.[26] Because of

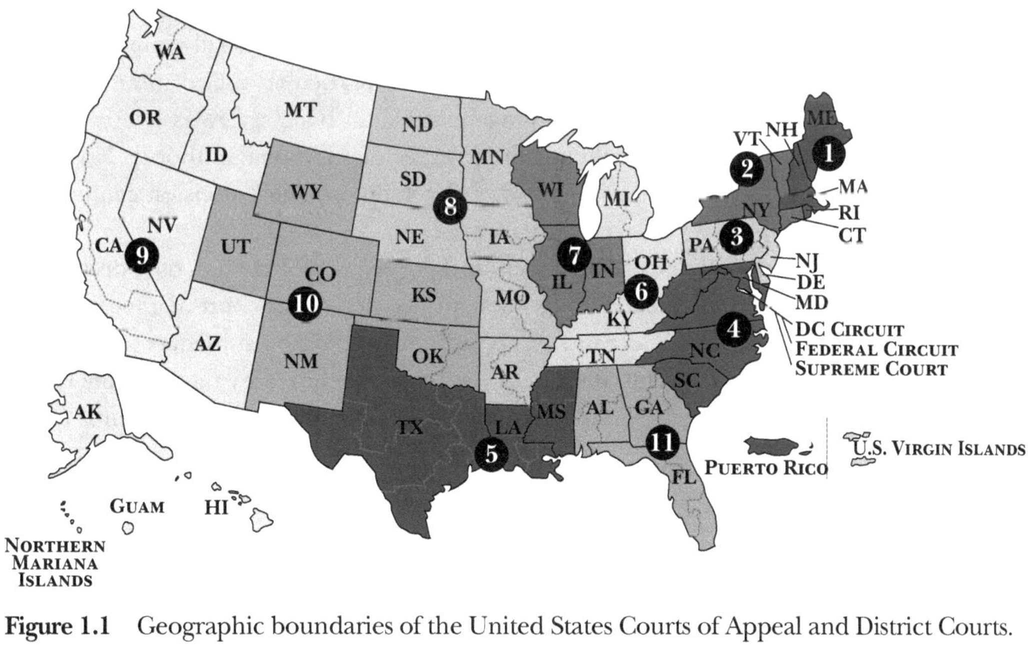

Figure 1.1 Geographic boundaries of the United States Courts of Appeal and District Courts.

24. Fed. R. Crim. P. 53; *see also* Cara Salvatore, *Donzinger Can't Get Livestream of Upcoming SDNY Trial*, Law360 (April 7, 2021).

25. Note that the Court of Appeals for the Federal Circuit, located in Washington, D.C., has nationwide jurisdiction but only over cases involving certain specific issues like patents and civil cases against the United States government. It also serves as the appellate court for criminal cases brought in the D.C. district court.

26. Fed. R. App. P. 4(b).

constitutional protections against double jeopardy, the government has no right to appeal a "not guilty" verdict in a criminal case, nor can it retry a defendant for the same conduct.[27] Federal prosecutors can, however, seek appellate review of a defendant's sentence or any pre-verdict ruling by a district court judge that effectively terminates or otherwise seriously impedes a particular prosecution.[28]

In certain very limited circumstances, parties to a criminal litigation may circumvent the usual limits on the types of district court orders that may be appealed by submitting a petition directly to the relevant circuit court "for a writ of mandamus."[29] To successfully obtain mandamus review, the requesting party must show a "compelling need."[30] This is a "demanding condition" that requires the petitioner to show there are no other adequate means to attain the relief it desires, its right to issuance of the writ is clear and indisputable, and the writ is otherwise appropriate under the circumstances.[31]

As explained in more detail in chapter 8, appeals are heard initially by a panel of three judges who reach decisions by majority vote. The circuit courts generally must accept the factual findings of the lower court and so do not hear additional evidence; if additional facts are necessary to reach a decision, the case will be remanded to the lower court for further proceedings. Otherwise, the panel either affirms or reverses (in whole or in part) the lower court's decision in a written order or opinion.

After a circuit court panel issues a ruling, either party may seek a rehearing before the same three judges if there is "a point of law or fact that the petitioner believes the court has overlooked or misapprehended."[32] In cases that raise novel or unusually important legal issues, all judges within a circuit may vote to consider a particular appeal in an "en banc hearing" to review the decisions of a three-judge panel.[33] En banc review is relatively rare, so when it does occur, the resulting ruling gains a degree of additional authority. No circuit court panel can overrule the decisions of another panel, but a panel's decision can be overruled in an en banc hearing.

Both the prosecution and defense may seek further review of a circuit court decision by the Supreme Court. If the Supreme Court declines, the decision of the court of appeals is considered final. All final decisions of a court of appeals are binding on subsequent panels and the district courts within that circuit. Because so few cases are heard by the Supreme Court, the courts of appeals are the de facto highest authority in virtually all federal criminal cases.

---

27. Blockburger v. United States, 284 U.S. 299, 302 (1932).

28. United States v. Hoskins, 902 F.3d 69, 76 (2d Cir. 2018) (permitting prosecution to appeal dismissal of any portion of an indictment); United States v. Moskowitz, 702 F.3d 731, 733 (2d Cir. 2012) (noting prosecutors may appeal orders suppressing or excluding evidence); 18 U.S.C. § 2518(10)(b) (allowing government to appeal orders suppressing wiretap evidence); 18 U.S.C. § 3731 (allowing government to appeal orders granting defendant's release on bail).

29. *See* 28 U.S.C. § 1651.

30. United States v. Dooling, 406 F.2d 192, 198 (2d Cir. 1969).

31. Cheney v. U.S. Dist. Court, 542 U.S. 367, 380–81 (2004) (describing a writ of mandamus as a "drastic and extraordinary remedy reserved for really extraordinary causes").

32. Fed. R. App. P. 40(a)(2).

33. Fed. R. App. P. 35(b).

3. The U.S. Supreme Court

The Supreme Court is the highest court in the U.S. judicial system, and is the only court specifically created by the Constitution.[34] It has the power to decide appeals from all cases brought in federal court, as well as those originating in the state courts that implicate federal law (for example, a criminal case brought in state court in which the defendant alleges a violation of the Fourth Amendment's protections against unreasonable searches and seizures). Certain types of cases, such as suits between the states, can be brought directly to the Supreme Court. In all cases before the Supreme Court where the interests of the federal government are implicated, the United States is represented by the Office of the Solicitor General, a division of the DOJ.

The primary function of the Supreme Court is not correcting errors made by judges in the lower courts, but rather to decide on important constitutional issues and resolve conflicting interpretations of federal laws between one or more of the circuit courts of appeals (referred to as "circuit splits"). Unlike circuit courts, which generally must hear appeals in criminal cases, the Supreme Court has virtually complete discretion over which appeals it selects to hear. Individuals or entities seeking a decision by the Supreme Court must file a writ of certiorari (informally called a "cert petition") explaining why review of their case is justified.[35] The vote of at least four justices is needed before the appeal can proceed. The chances of certiorari being granted are extraordinarily slim—of the seven thousand to eight thousand writs filed each year, only about eighty (one percent) are granted. When certiorari is denied, the lower court decision gets the justices' implicit approval and is left to stand as is.

There are currently nine justices on the Supreme Court (eight associate justices and one chief justice), and their decisions are made by majority vote. If a given opinion is not unanimous on one or more issues raised by the appeal, the Court will issue a split decision. While any part of a split decision that garners a majority will have binding legal effect, split decisions are considered less stable and more prone to being overturned by a different lineup of justices. The majority opinion is written by one of the justices who voted in favor; any dissenting justices have the option of writing a separate dissent explaining their reasoning for rejecting the majority position. Dissenting opinions can be relevant to later cases but have no binding effect.

Supreme Court cases are typically heard by all nine justices, except in situations where a justice must recuse themself due to a conflict of interest or some other issue. Because the judicial disqualification statute (28 U.S.C. § 455) permits sitting justices to determine whether their own recusal is required, controversy has arisen when a justice has declined to do so in the context of a case in which they are perceived to have a personal interest.[36] The Court's annual term begins on the first Monday in October and generally lasts until late June or early

34. *See* U.S. CONST. art. I Figure II, § 1.

35. Citations to a circuit court opinion will specify if the opinion was brought to the Supreme Court for review but certiorari was denied. For example, the case citation United States v. Cox, 34 F.2d 167, 189 (5th Cir.) (*en banc*), *cert. denied*, 381 U.S. 935 (1965) indicates that an en banc decision of the Fifth Circuit Court of Appeals was denied certiorari. While indications of subsequent appellate history such as the denial of certiori should generally be included in court filings, they are not included in this book.

36. *See, e.g.*, Debra Lyn Basset, *Recusal and the Supreme Court*, 56 HASTINGS L.J. 657 (2005).

July. The procedures that must be followed by appellants to the Supreme Court are set forth in the Rules of the Supreme Court of the United States.[37]

B. Criminal Court Structure in England and Wales

The court system in England and Wales is administered by Her Majesty's Courts and Tribunals Service (HMCTS), an executive agency within the Ministry of Justice. Unlike the unified federal court system in the United States, the United Kingdom has separate first-level courts to handle civil and criminal cases. There are two criminal first-instance courts where defendants are tried and sentenced—the magistrates' court and the Crown Court. Both courts share the same three appellate courts: the Divisional Court, Court of Appeal, and U.K. Supreme Court (but note that the Crown Court also hears appeals from the magistrates' court—figure 1.2).[38]

Whereas all federal and state judges in the United States wear the same standard black robe in court and are generally addressed as "Your Honor" or simply "Judge" (except for Supreme Court Justices), British courts use an elaborate code of colors and titles to specify different seniority levels among judicial officers.

Judge Type	Address in Correspondence	Address in Court	Dress Code in Court
Supreme Court Justice	The Right Honourable Lord/Lady Justice . . .	My Lord/Lady Your Lordship/Ladyship	Normal business attire
Court of Appeal Judge	The Right Honourable Lord/Lady Justice . . .	My Lord/Lady Your Lordship/Ladyship	Black robe with gold tabs
High Court Judge	The Honourable Mr/Mrs/Ms Justice . . .	My Lord/Lady Your Lordship/Ladyship	Red robe (when hearing a criminal case)
Circuit Judge	His/Her Honour . . .	Your Honour Judge	Purple sash over black robe (when hearing a criminal case)
Recorder	His/Her Honour . . .	Your Honour Judge	Black robe
District Judge	District Judge . . .	Sir/Madam	Normal business attire
Magistrates	Magistrate . . .	Your Worship Sir/Madam	Normal business attire

37. *The Federal Court System in the United States*, Administrative Office of the U.S. Courts (4th ed. 2016).

38. *See* University of Oxford Guide to U.K. Law, https://libguides.bodleian.ox.ac.uk/c.php?g=422832&p=2887371 (public database containing comprehensive overview of the U.K. legal system and a guide explaining U.K. case citation conventions).

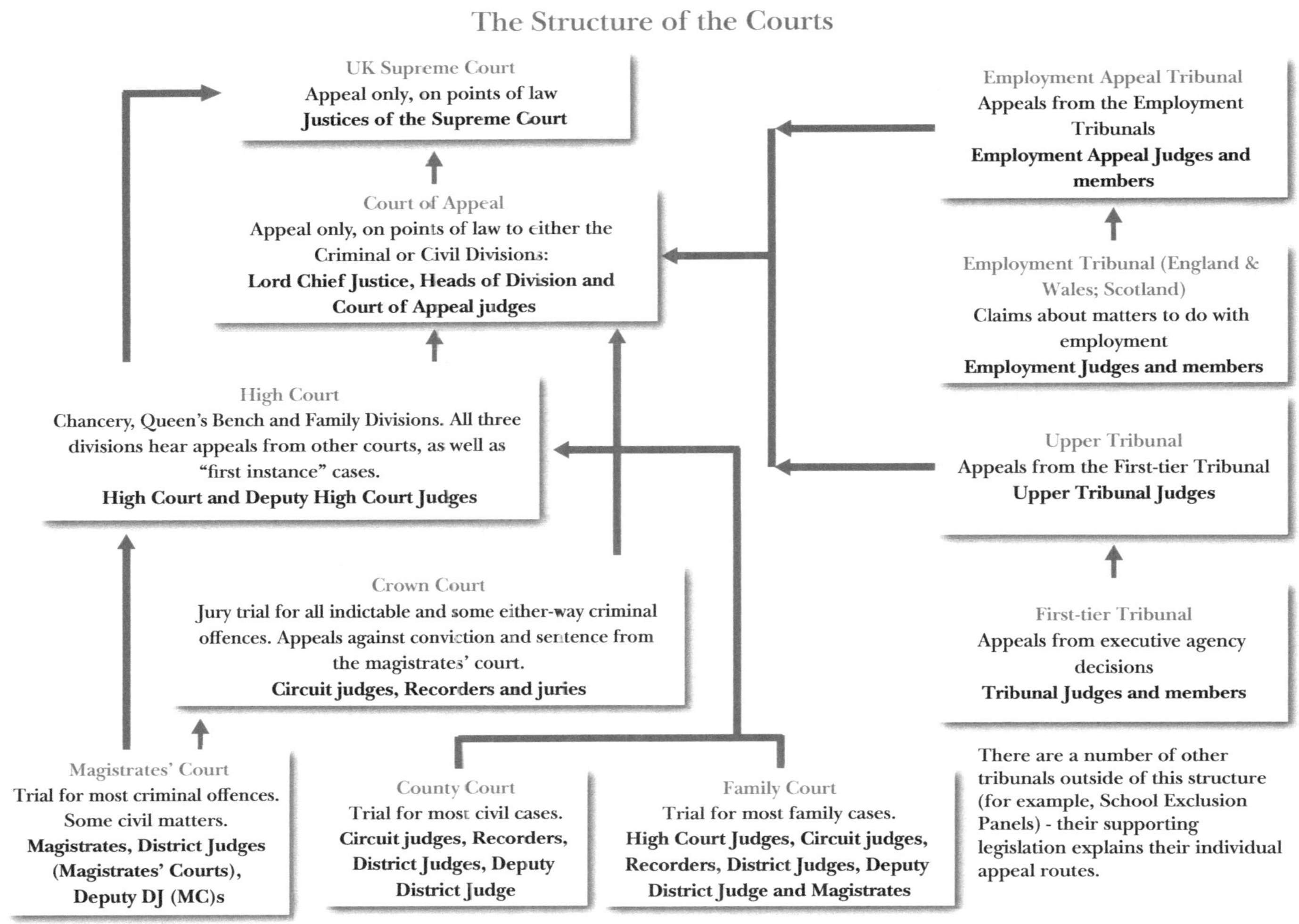

Figure 1.2 Structure of the U.K. Courts.

1. *Magistrates' Court*

Virtually all criminal cases start in magistrates' court. Depending on the severity of the offense and how a defendant pleads, criminal cases will either stay in magistrates' court or be sent to the higher-level Crown Court.

Criminal offenses in the United Kingdom are categorized as "summary only," "either-way," or "indictable only." Each classification reflects the seriousness of the offense and determines the level of court in which the matter will be handled. Summary-only offenses are dealt with in the magistrates' court. "Either-way" offenses, such as violations of the Fraud Act 2006, are resolved in either the magistrates' court or the Crown Court depending on their complexity, seriousness, and how the defendant pleads.[39] If a defendant in a low-value fraud case indicates an intention to plead guilty at initial appearance, for example, the case will remain in magistrates' court and the defendant will be summarily sentenced. Conversely, if the court determines that the case is not suitable for magistrates' court or if the defendant wishes to have the case heard before a jury, it will be transferred to the Crown Court. Otherwise, the trial will proceed in the magistrates' court.

Because magistrates' courts are only authorized to impose sentences of up to one year in prison,[40] if the presiding magistrate determines that a more severe sentence is warranted, the case will be referred to Crown Court for sentencing. This prevents defendants from effectively capping their sentencing exposure simply by pleading guilty in magistrates' court.

Trials in magistrates' court are informal, take place without a jury, and generally last no more than a few hours. The procedures governing criminal proceedings in magistrates' court are contained in the Magistrates' Courts Act 1980 and the Criminal Procedure Rules 2020.[41] The International Jurisdiction Office (IJO) within the Westminster Magistrates' Court in the Marylebone neighborhood of London is often involved in cross-border white-collar crime cases as it is where extradition cases are heard (see chapter 3).

Proceedings in magistrates' court are presided over by either a panel of three lay justices of the peace or a single district judge. Lay magistrates volunteer their time and are not required to have any formal legal qualifications. When a trial is being conducted by lay magistrates, they will be assisted by a qualified legal advisor. District judges are salaried and legally qualified. District judges are nominated by the independent Judicial Appointments Commission and formally appointed by the Crown. There are currently four hundred district judges in England and Wales.

2. *Crown Court*

All serious "either-way" offenses that are deemed unsuitable for magistrates' court and "indictable-only" offenses are tried in Crown Court, almost always before a jury and single judge. Prosecutions in Crown Court are technically brought on behalf of the monarch, referred

---

39. Crime and Disorder Act 1998, s.51.

40. Note that until recently, magistrates could only impose sentences of up to six months. This limitation was revised upwards in May 2022 to remove a backlog in Crown Court sentencing hearings created in part by the COVID-19 pandemic. *See* Emily Atkinson, "Sentencing Powers Doubled For Magistrates to Tackle Case Pile-Up," THE INDEPENDENT (May 2, 2022).

41. These statutes as well as all U.K. legislation related to criminal law and procedure are made publicly available by the British government (https://legislation.gov.uk).

to in case citations as either "Regina" (for a queen) or "Rex" (for a king) (e.g., *R v. Johnstone* [2003] 2 Cr App R 33).

Unlike the Federal Rules of Criminal Procedure, which give defendants the ability to have their case heard in front of only a judge if both the judge and prosecution consent, in the United Kingdom, this option is given only to the government. Under the Criminal Justice Act 2003, the prosecution can apply for a trial to be conducted without a jury in situations where there is a danger of jury tampering or where it is suspected that jury tampering has already occurred.[42] Prosecutors can also make an application[43] to proceed without a jury in serious fraud cases where "the complexity of the trial or the length of the trial (or both) is likely to make the trial so burdensome to the members of a jury hearing the trial that the interests of justice" may be impeded.[44] If an application for a bench trial is refused by the Crown Court, prosecutors can appeal it to the Court of Appeal if granted leave to do so.[45] Where a trial is held without a jury, the trial proceeds as usual except that the judge acts as fact finder.[46]

In addition to holding trials, Crown Courts hear appeals against convictions and sentencing decisions in magistrates' court. There are seventy-seven Crown Court locations across England and Wales. Due to their location in the U.K.'s primary financial center, London, the Southwark Crown Court and the Central Criminal Court of England and Wales (commonly known as the "Old Bailey") hear the majority of serious white-collar crime cases.

There are several different types of judges who preside in Crown Court: High Court judges, circuit judges, and recorders. High Court judges handle the most serious criminal cases. They are appointed by the Crown on the advice of the lord chancellor (a cabinet-level officer who is the approximate equivalent of the U.S. attorney general). Circuit judges sit in the Crown Court as well as the civil county courts. Recorders are similar to circuit judges but sit part time and generally handle less-complex matters.

Regardless of which type of judge is presiding over a particular case, if the proceedings are in Crown Court, they all have identical power and authority. In practice, the only difference between High Court judges, circuit judges, and recorders is the duration of their tenure and the complexity of the cases they are typically assigned. The role of a judge in a Crown Court trial is essentially the same as a district court judge in the United States: he or she makes rulings on evidence and other legal issues, instructs the jury on how the law should be applied, manages case schedules, and imposes sentences. When hearing appeals from the magistrates' court, the composition of the Crown Court will always be a circuit judge who sits with two lay magistrates.

---

42. Criminal Justice Act 2003, ss. 44–50; see *R v. T (R v. H, R v. C, R v. B)* [2009] EWCA Crim 1035 (finding that Crown Court judges should apply the criminal standard of proof (i.e., beyond a reasonable doubt) in deciding whether the conditions allowing a bench trial have been met); see also *R v. Twomey, Blake, Hibberd and Cameron* [2011] EWCA Crim 8; *KS v. R* [2010] EWCA Crim 1756.

43. Note that court filings in the United Kingdom are generally referred to as "applications." Equivalent filings in the United States are called "motions."

44. Criminal Justice Act 2003, s. 43.

45. *Id.*, ss. 47(1), (2).

46. *Id.*, s. 48(3).

As in the United States, U.K. courts follow the common law principle of *stare decisis* (Latin for "to stand by things decided"), which makes the rulings of higher courts binding on all lower courts.

a. Barristers and Solicitors

Since at least the 1400s, the legal profession in the United Kingdom is split between barristers and solicitors, and these terms are almost always used instead of the more generic "lawyer" or "attorney" used in the United States.[47] Barristers and solicitors are all lawyers in the sense that they are licensed to practice law throughout England and Wales, but their roles and training are different. In the United States, all lawyers receive the same type of legal training and, following law school, become admitted to the bars of particular states. To participate in litigation outside of states in which they are barred, American lawyers can seek to be admitted in the relevant district court on a *pro hac vice* basis (i.e., for that particular case only). There is no requirement to be physically located in a certain state to litigate cases there, although the rules in some states require *pro hac* lawyers to engage locally based counsel.

In modern practice in England, the exact dividing line between the responsibilities of barristers versus solicitors has become slightly less clear, but their respective roles nevertheless remain a critical part of criminal litigation.[48] Solicitors typically handle all phases of a criminal case that take place outside of a courtroom. This includes producing and obtaining discovery, interviewing the client and prospective witnesses, filing preliminary documents with the court, and providing overall strategic advice. Criminal defendants will usually first instruct a solicitor to manage their case, and the solicitor will then hire a barrister to help craft a trial strategy and conduct the in-court advocacy (although solicitors can also represent their clients in court if granted rights of audience by the Solicitors Regulation Authority). In the same way, barristers now often take on work, such as interviewing witnesses and conducting internal corporate investigations, that was historically considered exclusively within the solicitors' realm.

With certain exceptions, barristers can only be hired by solicitors or the government, not the general public.[49] Somewhat like "trial lawyers" in the United States, who specialize in courtroom advocacy, barristers are specialist legal advisers who devote the bulk of their practice to courtroom proceedings. Because of this, there is a strong focus on oral advocacy in the United Kingdom; written advocacy plays a much smaller role in the United Kingdom than in the United States, where legal issues are primarily decided through the submission of competing legal briefs (with oral argument rendered optional or simply a way for judges to probe questions raised by the briefs). Unlike solicitors, who usually work within a law firm, most barristers are self-employed, independent lawyers "called to the Bar." Groups of barristers may join together to form a "barristers' chambers," but each individual barrister is still considered independent. Just as American lawyers must be admitted to the bar of at least one state in order to practice, English barristers must join one of four Inns of Court (Lincoln's Inn, Inner

---

47. J. H. Baker, *Counsellors and Barristers: An Historical Study*, 27 CAMBRIDGE L.J. 205–29 (1969).

48. Marialuisa Taddia, *Solicitor-Advocates: Raising the Bar,* LAW SOC'Y GAZ. (Sept. 22, 2014).

49. In a relatively recent innovation, certain barristers who have elected to participate in the "direct access scheme" and completed a special training program can now be hired directly by end clients. *See* Bar Standards Board, "Public & Licensed Access Schemes," *available at* https://www.barstandardsboard.org.uk/for-barristers/public-and-licensed-access.html.

Temple, Middle Temple, and Gray's Inn), which function like bar associations in the United States (but with a more clubby, social atmosphere). The Inns of Court are based in ornate buildings clustered around Chancery Lane and the Royal Courts of Justice in central London.

While in the U.S. system only government prosecutors can prosecute criminal cases,[50] barristers in private practice are routinely hired by the British government to prosecute criminal cases against fellow citizens. Thus, most prosecutors working within British law enforcement function as solicitors who initially develop the factual bases of a case, while complex financial crime cases that reach trial are ultimately handled by barristers in private practice who are hired to represent the Crown in court. Even so, law enforcement retains ultimate control over the course of the prosecution and instructs the barristers in a principal/agent capacity. Because conflict of issues rules are substantially relaxed as between individual barristers at the independent bar, a prosecuting barrister can be within the same set of chambers as counsel for the defense.

Barristers can also be instructed by solicitors on behalf of private citizens to pursue criminal cases against others in what are known as "private prosecutions" (see the discussion of "Private Prosecutions" in section III.B later in the chapter). In fulfilling these roles, barristers are obliged to follow the Bar Standards Board (BSB) Handbook, which requires barristers to act as independent legal experts with a primary duty of assisting the court in the administration of justice and acting with honesty and integrity.

Like members of the British judiciary, barristers—but not solicitors—wear a specific type of wig and gown when in court and use formal titles: for example, fellow barristers will typically address one another as "My Learned Friend." Senior barristers can be awarded the title of Queen's Counsel (or King's Counsel during the reign of a king), to serve as "Her/His Majesty's Counsel in the law." QCs/KCs or "Silks" as they are known, wear a distinctive-style silk gown while in court, but otherwise serve the same functions as a normal barrister.

There are far more solicitors than barristers in England and Wales: there are approximately 140,000 solicitors but only about 16,000 barristers (a ratio of 8.75:1).

3. *Court of Appeal (Criminal Division)*

The Court of Appeal (Criminal Division) is based at the Royal Courts of Justice in central London and serves as the main appellate court for criminal matters heard in Crown Court. Like the circuit courts of appeals in the United States, appeals in the Court of Appeal are initially heard by a panel of judges (usually three). There is no automatic right of appeal in criminal cases, meaning that all prospective appellants must be granted leave to appeal by the Court of Appeal. When a conviction is challenged, the Court of Appeal will consider if the verdict was "unsafe" because of a material error in the trial process or because of the

50. Leeke v. Timmerman, 454 U.S. 83, 85–86 (1981). There is an exception to this general rule in cases concerning criminal contempt of court, a crime that can be charged, tried, and punished by a federal district court judge without the involvement of DOJ prosecutors. *See* 18 U.S.C. § 401. Although the Federal Rules of Criminal Procedure require a judge in such a situation "to request that the contempt be prosecuted by an attorney for the government," if the government declines, the court can then appoint an attorney in private practice to step in as prosecutor. *See* Fed. R. Crim. P. § 42. This happens only rarely, but there has been at least one high-profile instance in recent years. *See* United States v. Donzinger, 11-cv-00691 (S.D.N.Y.).

discovery of new evidence after trial. If the Court of Appeals determines a verdict to be unsafe, it can remove the verdict and remand the case back to Crown Court for retrial.

There currently are thirty-nine Lord and Lady Justices of Appeal. In addition, High Court judges and circuit judges may also sit on the Court of Appeal by designation in certain cases. Appeals in the Criminal Division are typically heard by a panel consisting of one Lord or Lady Justice and two High Court judges. The procedural rules used by the Court of Appeal are discussed in further detail in chapter 8.

4. The Supreme Court

The Supreme Court is a relatively new creation in the United Kingdom. Pursuant to the Constitutional Reform Act 2005, in October 2009 the Supreme Court replaced the Appellate Committee of the House of Lords as the country's highest court. It was established to achieve complete separation between the British judiciary and Parliament, since under the previous system the "Law Lords" of the upper house of Parliament (the House of Lords) not only heard appeals but were also involved in the legislative process.

There are twelve justices of the Supreme Court. The justices are officially independent from the rest of government, but they are appointed by the Crown upon nomination by the prime minister. Because it deals with issues throughout the entire United Kingdom, the Supreme Court is legally separate from England (where it sits).

The court hears appeals on significant points of law and other issues of great public importance. Its jurisdiction extends to the whole of the United Kingdom in civil cases, but only to England, Wales, and Northern Ireland in criminal cases. The Supreme Court also hears issues related to the devolution of powers between the central government in England and the governments of Scotland, Wales, and Northern Ireland.

The protocols used by the Supreme Court are listed in the Rules of the Supreme Court 2009. Unlike the U.S. Supreme Court which, by default, sits with all nine justices present, appeals to the U.K. Supreme Court are usually heard by a panel of five justices. A greater number of justices sit for a particular appeal only if the case involves a request to reverse an earlier Supreme Court decision, is of exceptionally high legal or public importance, or raises an important issue relating to the European Convention on Human Rights (ECHR).

Contrary to the prevailing rule in U.S. federal courts, almost all proceedings of the U.K. Supreme Court are filmed (and sometimes broadcast live on major television and radio networks).

III. LAW ENFORCEMENT AGENCIES

A. Federal Law Enforcement Agencies in the United States

1. The Department of Justice

With more than 100,000 attorneys, the DOJ has been described as the "world's biggest law firm" and acts as the primary enforcer of federal criminal laws. It sits within the executive branch of the federal government and is headed by the attorney general (AG), a political appointee who reports to the president. The AG supervises the administration and operation of the entire DOJ, which encompasses dozens of subsidiary agencies, including the Federal Bureau of Investigation (FBI), the Bureau of Prisons (BOP), each of the U.S. attorneys and their respective offices, the U.S. Marshalls Service, the Bureau of Alcohol, Tobacco, Firearms and Explosives (ATF), and the Drug Enforcement Administration (DEA).

Immediately below the AG is the deputy attorney general (DAG), who functions as the DOJ's chief operating officer, with broad authority over a range of legal, policy, and operational issues. Below the DAG is the associate attorney general and several assistant attorney generals in charge of DOJ's various divisions (including the Criminal Division—see figure 1.3).

DOJ headquarters in Washington, D.C., is known as "Main Justice." Main Justice prosecutors (referred to as "Trial Attorneys") handle cases in district courts throughout the country, often in partnership with prosecutors from the local U.S. attorneys' office. Main Justice houses a number of units that focus on specific types of white-collar crimes: the Money Laundering and Asset Recovery Section (MLARS), the Public Integrity Section (PIN), and the Fraud Section (which consists of a Foreign Corrupt Practices Act Unit, a Market Integrity and Major Frauds Unit, and a Health Care Fraud Unit). There are also other specialty divisions that handle prosecution of crimes such as tax, antitrust, and environmental offenses.

a. U.S. Attorneys' Offices

Every domestic judicial district has its own U.S. Attorneys' Office (USAO) headed by a U.S. Attorney appointed by the president to act as the chief federal law enforcement officer in his or her respective jurisdiction. All USAOs consist of a criminal and civil division, and many criminal divisions have specialized units that focus specifically on certain important categories of white-collar crimes (e.g., securities fraud, cybercrime, and public corruption).

Each U.S. Attorney oversees his or her office's prosecutors, known as assistant U.S. attorneys or AUSAs. AUSAs in the criminal division are responsible for directing investigations into violations of federal laws, deciding who to prosecute and on what charges, and for presenting criminal cases on behalf of the federal government in court. They also play an important role in the plea-bargaining process and in determining the sentences that violators receive (although ultimate responsibility for sentencing rests with the district court). The policies and procedures governing AUSAs and Main Justice trial attorneys are set out in the *Justice Manual* (https://www.justice.gov/jm/justice-manual—which was formerly called the *U.S. Attorney's Manual*).

Because of their location in the country's main financial hubs, the USAOs in Manhattan, Brooklyn, Chicago, San Francisco, and Los Angeles have an outsized influence on how federal white-collar crime laws are interpreted, prosecuted, and punished. This book, therefore, will focus generally on the decisions of the Supreme Court (which apply throughout the country) and the district courts and circuit courts of appeals in these cities (i.e., the courts within the Second, Seventh, and Ninth Circuits). It is important to remember, however, that the interpretation of federal law is not always consistent among the different circuits. While this book will typically present the majority position in these circumstances, practitioners will, of course, need to consult the unique case law within the specific circuit where a particular legal matter is pending when providing legal advice.

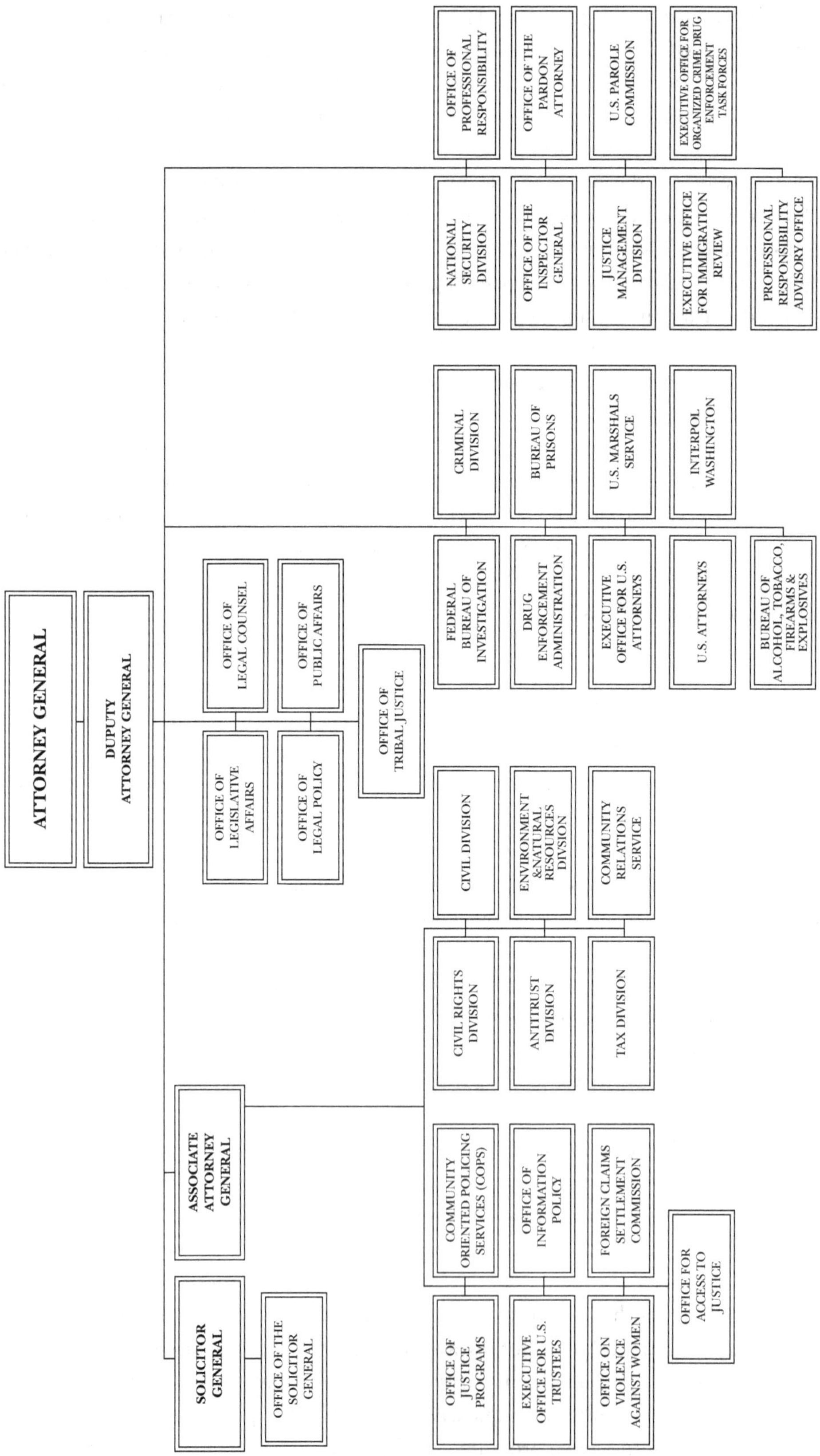

Figure 1.3 Structure of the U.S. Department of Justice.

2. *The Federal Bureau of Investigation*

The FBI, headquartered in Washington, D.C., is the principal investigative arm of the DOJ. It has the authority to investigate all violations of the federal criminal code, regardless of whether the conduct at issue occurs domestically or abroad. FBI investigators, known as "special agents," work closely with DOJ prosecutors to build cases and see them through verdict: they gather and analyze evidence, execute search warrants, interview potential witnesses, and at least one case agent will usually testify for the government during grand jury proceedings and at trial (if a case proceeds that far). The FBI has more than ten thousand special agents scattered throughout fifty-six field offices in the United States and sixty-three liaison posts overseas (including one at the U.S. embassy in London).

In October 2021, the FBI announced the creation of a specialized team focused on white-collar crime and corporate enforcement actions that will work directly with DOJ prosecutors at Main Justice in Washington.

3. *Federal Regulatory Agencies*

Many white-collar offenses are subject to both criminal and civil penalties (e.g., fines, disgorgement of ill-gotten gains, and injunctions). Only the DOJ is authorized to pursue criminal cases in the federal system, but various federal regulatory agencies have the power to launch civil enforcement actions targeting the same conduct.[51] The standard of proof in cases brought by civil regulators—preponderance of the evidence—is much lower than the "beyond a reasonable doubt standard" applied in the DOJ's criminal cases.[52]

The agencies most often involved in pursuing white-collar crimes are the Securities and Exchange Commission (SEC) and the Commodity Futures Trading Commission (CFTC). Other agencies such as the Internal Revenue Service (IRS) and the Federal Trade Commission (FTC) enforce tax and antitrust crimes that are properly characterized as "white collar," but because these are highly specialized areas, this book will not examine them in any detail. Nor will it address the sanctions and export control regulations enforced by the Treasury Department's Office of Foreign Assets Control (OFAC), or the banking regulations overseen by the Financial Crimes Enforcement Network (FinCEN), also within the Treasury.

DOJ prosecutors and enforcement attorneys at the SEC and CFTC routinely coordinate their investigations and combine their resources to pursue parallel criminal and civil actions.[53] Parallel proceedings are a critical component of white-collar crime enforcement tactics and courts generally find that "there is nothing improper about the government pursuing simultaneous criminal and civil investigations" so long as the proceedings and associated

---

51. Standard Sanitary Mfg. Co. v. United States, 226 U.S. 20 (1912).

52. SEC v. Lowy, 396 F. Supp. 2d 225, 240 (E.D.N.Y. 2003).

53. Standard Sanitary Mfg. Co. v. United States, 226 U.S. 20 (1912) (acknowledging that a single course of conduct could become the subject of both criminal and civil proceedings either "simultaneously or successively"); Anthony O'Rourke, *Parallel Enforcement and Agency Interdependence*, 77 Md. L. Rev. 985 (2018).

investigative tools are used for their proper purposes and in appropriate ways.[54] In other words, the government must not pursue parallel proceedings merely to increase pressure and litigation risk on a defendant or to gain a tactical advantage.

Because of the significantly more expansive means of discovery available to parties in a civil litigation,[55] the civil component of parallel enforcement proceedings is generally stayed—at either the defendant's or DOJ's request—pending the outcome of the criminal case. For a criminal defendant, a stay protects them from having to provide evidence under compulsory civil discovery mechanisms (interrogatories, requests for admission, and depositions) that are unavailable in criminal cases. For prosecutors, stays are advantageous because they prevent a criminal defendant from being able to access evidence (especially that held by third parties) that they would otherwise not be entitled to under the Federal Rules of Criminal Procedure (see chapter 5).

Whether a discovery stay is ordered in a parallel civil case is up to the discretion of the district court. Where a full stay is not appropriate, the district court can grant limited civil discovery, delay it until the criminal proceedings reach a particular point, or impose protective orders that limit how evidence obtained through the civil process can be used. In exercising this discretion, the district court should ordinarily consider (i) the extent to which the defendant's Fifth Amendment rights are implicated, (ii) the civil plaintiff's interest in proceeding expeditiously with its litigation, (iii) the potential burden on the criminal defendant, and (iv) the interest of the public in the pending civil and criminal litigation.[56]

a. The Securities and Exchange Commission

The SEC was created by Congress during the height of the Great Depression to "correct the evils of over-speculation and financial racketeering occurring on organized security exchanges, and to prevent as far as possible another major stock market crash with its attendant grief and destruction."[57] The agency's primary function is to enforce compliance with the 1933 Securities Act and the 1934 Exchange Act, which together create a comprehensive framework for governing the issuance and exchange of stocks, bonds, and other financial instruments.

Headquartered in Washington, D.C., the SEC is led by five presidentially appointed commissioners with staggered five-year terms. One of the commissioners is designated as

54. United States v. Kordel, 397 U.S. 1, 10 (1970); United States v. Stringer, 535 F.3d 929, 933 (9th Cir. 2008); SEC v. Dresser Industries, Inc., 628 F.2d 1368, 1374 (D.C. Cir. 1980).

55. In civil cases, discovery is governed by the "fundamental maxim" that "mutual knowledge of all the relevant facts gathered by both parties is essential proper litigation." "To that end, either party may compel the other to disgorge whatever facts he has in his possession." Hickman v. Taylor, 329 U.S. 495, 507 (1947). This principle is embodied in Federal Rule of Civil Procedure 26(b)(1), which permits parties to "obtain discovery regarding any nonprivileged matter that is relevant to any party's claim or defense." The range of discovery in criminal cases is far more limited.

56. Fed. Sav. & Loan Ins. Corp. v. Molinaro, 889 F.2d 899, 902 (9th Cir. 1989); *see also* Keating v. Office of Thrift Supervision, 45 F.3d 322, 324 (9th Cir. 1995) (discussing Fifth Amendment issues in relation to parallel proceedings).

57. James Wm. Moore & Frank W. Wiseman, *Market Manipulation and the Exchange Act*, 2 U. CHI. L. REV. 46 (1934–1935).

chairman, and by law no more than three of the commissioners may belong to the same political party. The SEC's Division of Enforcement investigates and prosecutes violations of the federal securities laws and the various attendant regulations created by the SEC itself. The same misconduct will often simultaneously violate a federal law and an SEC rule. Securities fraud, for example, is prohibited by both Section 10(b) of the 1934 Exchange Act and SEC Rule 10b-5. The Division of Enforcement can bring civil charges in either federal court or in administrative proceedings before its own in-house administrative law judges.

Administrative proceedings are controversial because they are assumed to give the SEC a "home court" advantage and allow it to effectively act as the prosecution, judge, and jury all at once.[58] Studies have shown, for instance, that the SEC wins well over ninety percent of its administrative proceedings but only around sixty percent of the cases it brings in federal court.[59] Defendants have repeatedly challenged administrative proceedings as unconstitutional, but so far with little success.[60] Under the 2010 Dodd-Frank Act, the SEC gained expanded authority to use the administrative process to impose civil penalties on essentially anyone who violates the federal securities laws, regardless of whether they are registered securities professionals. This has led to a substantial increase in the SEC's use of administrative proceedings in recent years.[61]

The SEC's administrative proceedings, governed by the SEC's Rules of Practice, are generally resolved much more quickly than cases in federal court, do not involve juries, and are more lenient in terms of the types of evidence that can be considered. There is also no provision for defendants to make a motion to dismiss, assert counterclaims, or move for summary judgment. There is very limited discovery during an SEC administrative proceeding and, in general, neither interrogatories nor depositions are allowed.[62]

As a check on the SEC's power, the liability and penalty decisions made by its administrative law judges are subject to an appellate review process. Initial decisions can be appealed first to the five SEC commissioners, whose decisions can then be appealed to a circuit court of appeals. Because the SEC is part of the executive branch, its decisions are given a significant degree of deference by the circuit courts, making the odds of a defendant successfully overturning an adverse SEC ruling in federal court slim. For example, the SEC's findings of fact are

---

58. Blake Edwards, *The SEC Is Doubling Down on Its Home Field Advantage, Report Says*, Bloomberg BNA (Jan. 14, 2016), https://bol.bna.com/the-sec-is-doubling-down-on-its-home-field-advantage-report-says.

59. Jean Eaglesham, *SEC Steers More Trials to Judges It Appoints*, Wall St. J. (Oct. 21, 2014).

60. *See, e.g.*, Gupta v. SEC, 796 F. Supp. 503 (S.D.N.Y. 2003); SEC v. Bebo, 799 F.3d 765 (7th Cir. 2015); Blinder, Robinson & Co. v. SEC, 837 F.2d 1099 (D.C. Cir. 1988). Note that as this book is going to print, a divided panel of the Fifth Circuit Court of Appeals ruled that the SEC's use of in-house courts to bring a securities fraud case was an unconstitutional deprivation of the defendant's Seventh Amendment right to a jury trial. Jarkesy, Jr. v. SEC, No. 20-61007 (5th Cir. May 18, 2022). This decision is likely to be reviewed by the full Fifth Circuit en banc if not the Supreme Court.

61. Stephen J. Choi & A. C. Pritchard, *The SEC's Shift to Administrative Proceedings: An Empirical Assessment*, 34 Yale J. on Reg. 1, 3 (2017).

62. Gideon Mark, *SEC and CFTC Administrative Proceedings*, 19 J. Const. L. 45, 66–68 (Oct. 2016).

accepted as final so long as they are supported by "substantial evidence," a fairly low bar.[63] Its legal interpretations are generally also accepted without much substantial appellate scrutiny.[64]

b. The Commodity Futures Trading Commission

The 1974 Commodity Futures Trading Commission Act created the CFTC to assume responsibility for regulating and enforcing the 1936 Commodity Exchange Act (CEA) which, as the name implies, regulates the trading of futures contracts and options whose value is derived from physical commodities (e.g., oil, precious metals, agricultural goods). The CFTC's core responsibility "is to protect the public interest by deterring and preventing disruptions to market integrity."[65]

Like the SEC, the CFTC is headquartered in Washington, D.C., is led by five presidentially appointed commissioners and has its own Division of Enforcement that investigates and prosecutes violations of the CEA and the CFTC's rules and regulations. The Division of Enforcement can pursue civil enforcement actions against individuals and firms that are formally registered with the CFTC, as well as anyone else engaged in trading or marketing futures, options, swaps, and commodity contracts, including various digital currencies.[66]

In another similarity with the SEC, the CFTC's Division of Enforcement can file enforcement actions in federal court or in its own administrative procedures. In cases brought before its own administrative law judges, the CFTC's remedies are limited to injunctions against future violations, civil monetary penalties, and restitution orders. Unlike the SEC, however, the CFTC uses administration proceedings only for uncontested matters.[67] As such, all contested CFTC cases are filed in federal court, where the CFTC is free to pursue a wider range of remedies, including restraining orders to freeze assets while the litigation is pending, preliminary and permanent injunctions, civil monetary penalties, restitution, and disgorgement of funds obtained through illegal activities.

B. Financial Crime Enforcement Agencies in England and Wales

1. The Crown Prosecution Service

Before passage of the Police and Criminal Evidence Act (PACE) in 1984, British police were responsible for both the investigation and prosecution of crime; trials were conducted by either in-house police solicitors or private solicitors hired on behalf of law enforcement.[68] To modernize this system, the Crown Prosecution Service (CPS) was established in 1985 to ensure uniformity of prosecution decision making and separate the fact investigation from the legal

63. 5 U.S.C. § 706.

64. Chevron, U.S.A., Inc. v. Nat Res. Def. Council, Inc., 467 U.S. 837 (1984).

65. 7 U.S.C. § 5(b).

66. 7 U.S.C. § 13a-1.

67. Gideon Mark, *SEC and CFTC Administrative Proceedings*, 19 J. Const. L. 45, 62–63 (Oct. 2016).

68. Jacqueline S. Hodgson, *The Future of Adversarial Criminal Justice in 21st Century Britain,* 35 N.C. J. Int'l Law 319, 323 (2009).

proceedings.[69] Thus, whereas DOJ prosecutors coordinate closely with the FBI and other law enforcement agencies throughout the investigatory phase of criminal proceedings, the CPS generally prosecutes criminal cases that have been investigated independently by one of the United Kingdom's various police forces and only becomes involved when charges are ready to be filed.

With a staff of roughly six thousand, the CPS is headquartered in London and operates fourteen regional teams throughout England and Wales, each headed by a chief Crown prosecutor (whose authority is similar to that of a U.S. Attorney). The head of the CPS is the director of public prosecutions (DPP), who reports to the attorney general.

There are three Central Casework Divisions within the CPS that specialize on the most complex cases the CPS handles: the International Justice and Organised Crime Division, Special Crime and Counter Terrorism Division, and the Specialist Fraud Division. There is also a dedicated Proceeds of Crime Division that deals with asset freezes and enforcement of confiscation orders. Reflecting an increased focus on financial crime, in March 2021, the CPS announced a new "economic crime strategy" setting out detailed five-year enforcement goals, including the creation of a new specialized court in London that will focus on criminal and civil fraud, cybercrime, and other financial offenses.

In contrast to the DOJ, which is headed by a presidential appointee, the CPS is a politically independent body that is responsible for deciding which cases should be prosecuted and on what charges, as well as providing advice to police, victims, and prosecution witnesses. It is overseen by an external board of advisors that is responsible for the delivery of the CPS's objectives and its wider contribution to the criminal justice system.

Like AUSAs in the United States, Crown prosecutors can prepare cases and present them in court. In a significant contrast with U.S. procedures, however, Crown prosecutors regularly instruct external solicitors and barristers in private practice to litigate on their behalf. When this occurs, the privately retained legal counsel assumes powers equivalent to that of Crown prosecutors.

a. Private Prosecutions

The CPS's role as the chief public prosecutor is not exclusive. Rather, one of the fundamental differences between U.S. and British prosecutions is that in the United Kingdom, criminal cases can be initiated and pursued by private parties. These so-called "private prosecutions" are allowed pursuant to the Prosecution of Offences Act (POA) 1985, section 6, which provides: "nothing in [the POA] shall preclude any person from instituting any criminal proceedings or conducting any criminal proceedings to which the [DPP's] duty to take over the conduct of proceedings does not apply." Because the DPP tends to focus prosecutorial resources on the highest value and readily provable cases, private prosecutions can help fill the gap by targeting financial crimes that might otherwise go unaddressed.

Private prosecutions proceed in the same way as cases brought by the Crown and in many instances will be more expeditious and efficient than ones brought by a government enforcement agency. Private prosecutions can therefore be a logical alternative for financial crime victims in situations where law enforcement may not have sufficient resources or interest to devote to the case.

69. *Id.* at 323–24.

To prevent abuse of the private prosecution system, the POA gives the CPS an advisory role and allows it to take over a private prosecution at any time, either at the request of the defendant or because of its own assessment of the case. If the CPS decides that there are insufficient grounds to provide a reasonable prospect of conviction, it can take over the private prosecution and discontinue the proceedings. This authority was challenged unsuccessfully in *R (Gujra) v. CPS* [2012] UKSC 52, where a private prosecution against three individuals for assault was ordered discontinued by the DPP. The plaintiff appealed, claiming a breach of the POA. The Supreme Court held that the CPS's discretion to terminate a private prosecution did not breach citizens' right to bring private prosecutions under the POA.

The DPP can also take over and discontinue proceedings even where the Full Code Test (see chapter 3) is met if they believe the prosecution is likely to damage the interests of justice—for example, when the private prosecution interferes with the investigation of another criminal offense, where it is motivated by maliciousness, is vexatious, or where the defendant has been promised immunity from prosecution by the CPS or police.

As with all criminal proceedings, a private prosecution begins with information about the alleged offense and the relevant legislation being put before a magistrates' court. The court will then decide whether to issue a summons or arrest warrant (which will be executed by the police). During the investigatory stage, the POA does not permit private prosecutors to access law enforcement resources or employ evidence-gathering powers that are given exclusively to government agents (e.g., search warrants). Rather, private prosecutors are limited to using whatever investigatory means are legally available to private citizens and private investigators (e.g., noninvasive surveillance and interviewing potential witnesses). Obtaining certain types of material, such as that held by banks or corporate entities, may therefore prove difficult. However, mechanisms such as *Norwich Pharmacal* orders (NPOs) can be used by private prosecutors in certain situations to legally compel an innocent third party to disclose certain types of financial information, such as bank account numbers and transaction records, that relate to potential criminal activity.[70]

Similar orders can be applied for with respect to evidence held abroad. Witness summonses can also be used once criminal proceedings have commenced to compel potential witnesses to produce documents or give testimony in court. However private prosecutors secure evidence, they have the same retention and disclosure obligations as the CPS and the Serious Fraud Office (SFO—see chapter 5). Note too that private prosecutors can hire law enforcement to assist with evidence gathering.[71]

---

70. NPOs are compulsory disclosure orders available in England and Wales that allow information to be obtained from third parties who are in some way involved in criminal activity. NPOs are frequently used in civil fraud cases to get bank records, property records, and other financial documents. Parties seeking an NPO from the High Court must establish a likelihood of success on the merits, the necessity of the requested documents, a basis for believing the documents are held by the third party, and that the burden of responding to the request is proportionate. *See Norwich Pharmacal Co v. Customs and Excise Commissioners* [1974] AC 133.

71. *See* R (Virgin Media Ltd.) v. Zinga [2014] EWCA Crim 52 at [41]-[54] (approving private prosecutors' "donation" to the Metropolitan Police Authority in exchange for investigatory assistance).

2. *The Serious Fraud Office*

The SFO was created as part of the Criminal Justice Act 1987 in response to a sharp increase in the number of financial crimes targeting London's financial industry.[72] The SFO's regulatory function is roughly equivalent to the DOJ's Fraud Section; it is a specialized agency responsible for investigating and prosecuting serious or complex fraud and corruption cases involving conduct in England, Wales, Northern Ireland, and internationally.[73] Like the DOJ's MLARS, the SFO also has a proceeds of crime division that focuses on intercepting and seizing illegally obtained funds and assisting foreign law enforcement agencies obtain evidence in cross-border cases involving the United Kingdom. Fraud and corruption offenses that take place in Scotland are investigated by the Scottish national police through their Specialist Crime Division.

The SFO is based in London and is headed by a director who reports to the attorney general for England and Wales. Just as the DOJ is made up of prosecutors and FBI special agents, the SFO includes investigators, solicitors, and barristers, and its legally qualified personnel have a much greater role in the investigation process than Crown prosecutors at the CPS. With just under five hundred total staff, the SFO is a relatively small agency that takes on a selective number of new investigations and prosecutions each year. Compared with the DOJ, which brings tens of thousands of cases (including several thousand white-collar crime prosecutions) annually, the SFO typically has around sixty open investigations at any one time.[74]

While the SFO employs legally qualified personnel in-house, it does not handle criminal trials or most other contentious court proceedings. Instead, the SFO engages solicitors and barristers in private practice to act on its behalf once criminal proceedings have been initiated. Thus, unlike the DOJ, which oversees investigations and conducts all its own court proceedings, the SFO's main function is to investigate potential financial crimes, not to conduct actual litigation in court. Nevertheless, the SFO remains heavily involved in its cases throughout trial and retains ultimate control over strategic decisions (since it is in effect the client on whose behalf its privately contracted barristers and solicitors act).

Each case pursued by the SFO must be individually authorized by the SFO director, who must base his or her decision on the degree of actual or intended harm inflicted by the alleged crime on the public, the reputation and integrity of the United Kingdom as an international financial center, or the country's "economy and prosperity." The SFO director must also consider whether the complexity and nature of the suspected offense warrants the application of the SFO's specialist skills, powers, and capabilities to investigate and prosecute.

In keeping with the British government's Serious and Organised Crime Strategy, the SFO works closely with other law enforcement agencies, including the National Crime Agency, the City of London Police and other regional police forces, Her Majesty's Revenue and Customs (HMRC—the U.K.'s main tax office), and the Financial Conduct Authority (FCA).

---

72. Karen Harrison & Nicholas Ryder, The Law Relating to Financial Crime in the United Kingdom 97 (2d ed. 2017).

73. Criminal Justice Act 1987, s. 1.

74. Serious Fraud Office, Annual Report and Accounts 2020–2021 at 10.

3. Financial Conduct Authority

The FCA is the primary regulator of the U.K.'s financial services industry and financial markets, with a specific mandate to reduce financial crime. It was created in 2012 following intense criticism of its predecessor agency, the Financial Services Authority, in the wake of the 2008/2009 financial crisis. The FCA works alongside the Bank of England's Prudential Regulation Authority (PRA), a quasi-public regulator with supervisory authority over most financial services firms that operate within the United Kingdom. Like the FCA, the PRA has its own investigatory and enforcement powers, but it cannot bring criminal cases.[75]

The FCA's jurisdiction extends to all firms and individuals who are registered, or who should be registered, to conduct regulated services in the financial services sector (essentially making it the equivalent to a combined SEC and CFTC). Its statutory objectives are to ensure that the U.K.'s financial markets function properly, protect consumers, maintain the integrity of the British financial system, and promote effective competition.

The FCA has statutory duties to supervise, monitor, and enforce upon regulated firms to ensure firms and authorized persons comply with their requirements and obligations. The FCA supervises approximately 58,000 financial services firms pursuant to the approach set out in "FCA Mission: Approach to Supervision" (published in April 2019).[76]

It has a range of powers to investigate breaches of the Financial Services and Markets Act 2000 and the Financial Services Act 2012. While the FCA has the authority to pursue criminal prosecutions as well as civil enforcement actions and regulatory proceedings, it rarely utilizes its criminal powers and leaves most serious white-collar crimes to be prosecuted by either the CPS or the SFO.[77]

4. National Crime Agency

The National Crime Agency (NCA) was created by the Crime and Courts Act 2013 as a unified agency designed to combine and replace two predecessor organizations (the Serious Organised Crime Agency and National Fraud Authority). While the NCA is involved in investigating white-collar crimes, it has an expansive jurisdiction that also covers organized crime, weapon and drug trafficking, and cybercrime. With such an expansive remit and limited resources, most major financial crime investigations are led by investigators at the CPS, SFO, and FCA.

And unlike these agencies, the NCA cannot initiate prosecutions on its own. Rather, its function is limited to gathering evidence to support cases brought by prosecutors at the SFO or CPS (just as the FBI does for the DOJ). The NCA is headed by a director general who reports to the home secretary, a cabinet-level officer somewhat equivalent to the secretary of Homeland Security in the United States.

---

75. Bank of England, *The PRA's Statutory Powers and Enforcement*, *available at* https://www.bankofengland.co.uk/prudential-regulation/pra-statutory-powers.

76. Financial Conduct Authority, *FCA Mission: Approach to Supervision* (April 2019), *available at* https://www.fca.org.uk/publication/corporate/our-approach-supervision-final-report-feedback-statement.pdf.

77. Financial Conduct Authority, *Enforcement Annual Performance Report 2018/2019*, *available at* https://www.fca.org.uk/publication/corporate/annual-report-2018-19-enforcement-performance.pdf.

5. *The City of London Police*

While the jurisdiction of the City of London Police is technically limited to London's square-mile central business and financial district, often referred to as "the City," its Economic Crime directorate is the preeminent police force for investigating financial crimes committed throughout England and Wales. Together with the National Fraud Intelligence Bureau (NFIB), the City of London Police run *Action Fraud*, the United Kingdom's national reporting center for fraud and cybercrime.

CHAPTER 1: KEY DISTINCTIONS

United States	United Kingdom
Written Constitution that functions as the "Supreme Law of the Land"	Government power and functions are defined by numerous historic documents and conventions
Criminal laws defined by federal criminal code and fifty state criminal codes	Single criminal code
Parallel federal court system and state court system	Single court system in England and Wales
Twelve circuit courts of appeals with specific geographic boundaries along with one circuit court with national jurisdiction over specific types of cases	Single intermediate appellate court with national jurisdiction
Most court filings publicly available through Public Access to Court Electronic Records (PACER)	Court filings in criminal cases generally only available to the parties
All lawyers are similarly trained and qualified, members of one or more state bars, and must generally be admitted to practice in the specific district court in which they seek to litigate	Legal profession split between barristers and solicitors who are all authorized to practice throughout England and Wales
All federal criminal trials held in district court	Criminal trials held in either magistrates' court or Crown Court; civil cases held in separate court system
Nine Supreme Court justices make up an independent and coequal branch of the federal government	Twelve Supreme Court justices operate independently from the central government
Criminal cases prosecuted by full-time government employees	Criminal court proceedings generally led by barristers and solicitors in private practice hired by law enforcement or private citizens
Automatic right to first-level appellate review in criminal cases	First-level appellate review in criminal cases requires leave to appeal
Criminal violations of federal law only prosecuted by the Department of Justice	Criminal violations of Acts of Parliament can be prosecuted by the Crown Prosecution Service, Serious Fraud Office, Financial Conduct Authority, and other agencies

2 | Law Enforcement's Evidence-Gathering Tools

Government agents investigating complex white-collar crimes need to identify, locate, and obtain voluminous financial information, transaction data, audio recordings, witness statements, and documents. As a result, criminal charges in such cases are typically filed after a lengthy investigation period that can last several years or more. To identify and pursue wrongdoing, U.S. and British law enforcement agencies have extensive powers to obtain evidence within their respective home countries and abroad. This chapter examines the specifics of the investigatory tools each government has at its disposal during the investigatory phase of financial crime matters.

Law enforcement agencies do not, of course, rely exclusively on their ability to force individuals and entities to speak with investigators or to turn over relevant materials. In addition to information and evidence provided to prosecutors by financial crime victims, individuals and entities that in some way participated in the misconduct at issue often will voluntarily turn over relevant materials as well. In many financial crime cases, a significant amount of evidence is voluntarily turned over to prosecutors, and both the U.K. and U.S. governments offer a variety of incentives for individuals and entities to do so (see chapters 6 and 11).

Since corporations can be held criminally liable for crimes committed by their employees, businesses have an inherent incentive to turn over all relevant evidence to the government and assist prosecutors in their pursuit of individual wrongdoers. As explored further in chapter 11, if a firm does this "with sufficient zeal, it generally will be spared prosecution and offered a quasi-civil settlement in the form of a deferred prosecution agreement or non-prosecution agreement."[1] Defendants charged with a financial crime in the context of their employment can thus face the power of law enforcement "leveraged tenfold by [their] own employer's ability and motivation to clear the government's path to [their] door," which reduces their ability to mount an effective defense.[2] It is therefore general practice for prosecutors in the United States and United Kingdom to use "the threat of firm-level criminal liability to persuade corporations to gather evidence of their own employees' wrongdoing and provide it to the government."[3]

1. Samuel W. Buell, *Is the White Collar Offender Privileged?*, 63 Duke L.J. 869 (January 2014).

2. *Id.* at 869-70.

3. *Id.* at 884.

I. LAW ENFORCEMENT'S POWERS TO OBTAIN DOCUMENTS AND TESTIMONY

One of the primary ways DOJ prosecutors build and develop their case is by obtaining evidence via subpoenas issued through a federal grand jury. Although a British innovation, grand juries were abandoned in the U.K. during the early 1930s after they came to be perceived as little more than a rubber stamp for Crown prosecutors.[4] Thus, rather than issue subpoenas for documents and testimony on behalf of the grand jury as American prosecutors do, British law enforcement agencies have statutory powers to independently demand production of documents and testimony on their own.

A. Federal Grand Jury Subpoenas in the United States

A grand jury is a group of sixteen to twenty-three randomly selected people summoned to a district court by a prosecutor investigating a potential federal crime or "whenever the public interest so requires."[5] Federal grand juries typically sit for a term of eighteen months and meet one or more days a week at regular intervals. A grand jury has significant autonomy and is "free to pursue its investigations unhindered by external influence or supervision so long as it does not trench upon the legitimate rights of any witness called before it."[6] The mere possibility that a violation of federal law has occurred is a sufficient basis for a grand jury to act and it may investigate conduct occurring both inside and outside the district in which it sits.[7]

As opposed to the twelve-person "petit" juries used at trial, grand juries do not decide guilt or innocence. Rather, they act "as a kind of buffer or referee between the Government and the people" by independently evaluating "whether there is adequate basis for bringing a criminal charge."[8] Standing between the government and the targets of an investigation, grand juries are designed to protect citizens against unfounded prosecutions.[9] The Fifth

---

4. According to a prominent legal commentator of the time, "For many years the grand jury has done little but ratify the committals for trial by examining justices. Here and there a bill was thrown out, but on no discoverable principle. It is a fact that the court usher, the only official allowed to be with the grand jury, frequently guided their deliberations." Albert Lieck, *Abolition of the Grand Jury in England*, 25 AM. INST. CRIM. L. & CRIMINOLOGY 623 (1934–35).

5. Fed. R. Crim. P. 6(a)(1); United States v. Dionisio, 410 U.S. 1, 17–18 (1973).

6. Dionisio, 410 U.S. at 17–18.

7. United States v. Sisack, 527 F.2d 917, 920 (9th Cir. 1976); Matter of Marc Rich Co., A.G., 707 F.2d 663, 666 (2d Cir. 1983).

8. United States v. Williams, 504 U.S. 36, 47 (1992); *see also* Stirone v. United States, 361 U.S. 212, 218 (1960); *Justice Manual* § 9-11.101 ("While grand juries are sometimes described as performing accusatory and investigatory functions, the grand jury's principal role is to determine whether or not there is probably cause to believe that one or more persons committed a certain federal offense within the venue of the district court.").

9. In re Walsh, 623 F.2d 489, 492 (7th Cir. 1980); *see also* Wood v. Georgia, 370 U.S. 375, 390 (1962) ("[T]his body has been regarded as a primary security to the innocent against hasty, malicious, and oppressive persecution; it serves the invaluable function . . . of standing between the accuser and accused.").

Amendment to the Constitution prohibits prosecutors from charging a felony—defined as any crime carrying a possible prison sentence of at least one year—except through the grand jury process (unless this right is waived by the defendant).[10]

Grand juries meet in closed courtrooms and deliberate in total secrecy.[11] There is no judge, no defendant, and no lawyers present except for one or more DOJ prosecutors (either an AUSA from the local USAO or a Trial Attorney from Main Justice—or both).[12] Grand jurors, prosecutors, and all other participants in grand jury proceedings are strictly prohibited from disclosing any information about what occurs within the grand jury except in certain narrowly defined circumstances.[13]

The only evidence presented to a grand jury is selected by the DOJ, and prosecutors are not required to disclose evidence that may conflict with their theory of the case.[14] Prosecutors have broad discretion to decide what evidence is shown to the grand jury, and courts will defer to their judgment except in situations where grand jurors are intentionally misled or knowingly given false evidence.[15]

The evidentiary rules that govern criminal trials do not apply in the grand jury room; prosecutors are not, for example, prevented from presenting evidence obtained through illegal searches or from relying on hearsay.[16] The allowance for hearsay is a major advantage for the government since it allows prosecutors to make a case before the grand jury using only the testimony of FBI special agents about what others have told them outside of the grand jury room.[17] In this way, prosecutors can secure an indictment without live testimony from any first-hand witnesses and without any form of cross-examination.

If at least twelve grand jurors find probable cause to believe that a person or entity has committed the crime at issue, they will approve a written statement of the charges in the form of an indictment drafted by prosecutors, a so-called "true bill." Once a true bill is returned and the prosecutor approves the probable cause determination, arrest warrants will usually issue soon after.[18] Statistics show that federal grand juries return indictments in more than

---

10. Fed. R. Crim. P. 7(a)(1), (b); United States v. Leichtnam, 948 F.2d 370, 375 (7th Cir. 1991).

11. United States v. Sells Engineering, Inc., 463 U.S. 418, 424-425 (1983).

12. Fed. R. Crim. P. 6(d)(1).

13. Fed. R. Crim. P. 6(e).

14. Williams, 504 U.S. at 51–52. While not a legal requirement, if "a prosecutor is personally aware of substantial evidence that directly negates" a party's guilt, DOJ policy requires it be disclosed to the grand jury. *Justice Manual* § 9-11.33.

15. *See, e.g.*, United States v. Samango, 607 F.2d 877 (9th Cir. 1979) (intentional suppression of favorable testimony); United States v. Gold, 470 F. Supp. 1336 (N.D. Ill. 1979) (failure to divulge exculpatory evidence and other misconduct); United States v. Ciambrone, 601 F.2d 616, 622–23 (2d Cir. 1979) (knowingly obtaining indictment based on false evidence).

16. United States v. Calandra, 414 U.S. 338, 349 (1974); Costello v. United States, 380 U.S. 359, 364 (1956).

17. United States v. Allen, 864 F.3d 63, 78 (2d Cir. 2017) (discussing how witness testimony was relayed to the grand jury through an FBI special agent).

18. United States v. Cox, 34 F.2d 167, 189 (5th Cir. 1965); Fields v. Soloff, 920 F.2d 1114, 1117 (2d Cir. 1990).

ninety-nine percent of the cases presented to them.[19] On the relatively rare occasions when probable cause is not found and a "no bill" is returned, the government has the option of resubmitting the case to a different grand jury.[20] Thus, while the grand jury is a necessary step in the charging process, it is not usually a meaningful impediment for the DOJ to pursue the cases it deems worthy of criminal prosecution.

1. Grand Jury Subpoena Powers

To effectively protect citizens against unfounded criminal prosecutions, grand juries are given broad investigatory powers to identify all facts that may be relevant to a DOJ investigation.[21] They have the authority to subpoena testimony and documents[22] that relate to the investigation in any way, even tangentially: according to the Supreme Court, a grand jury's discretion allows it to compel the production of any "evidence or the testimony of witnesses it considers appropriate."[23]

Although this subpoena power is formally given to the grand jury, in reality it is wielded by the DOJ because it is generally only the prosecutors who determine which witnesses should appear and what documents should be requested.[24] When subjects of an investigation are aware of grand jury proceedings and wish to appear before it to provide an alternative version of events, they may seek permission from prosecutors to do so.[25] The DOJ will usually grant such requests if the individual is willing to waive the Fifth Amendment privilege against self-incrimination (meaning that they cannot selectively choose which questions to answer).[26] There are obvious risks for the target of a criminal investigation to voluntarily subject themselves to questioning under oath from federal prosecutors, and so this option is rarely pursued. Not only can electing to testify inadvertently provide more incriminating evidence, it may also open up the witness to additional charges if their testimony is found to be intentionally untrue.[27]

Grand jury subpoenas may be served anywhere within the United States.[28] When the subpoena target is a U.S. national or resident, grand jury subpoenas can also be served

19. Zachary A. Goldfarb, *Grand Juries Usually Indict at Federal Level,* Wash. Post, Nov. 24, 2014.

20. United States v. Thompson, 251 U.S. 407, 413–15 (1920); *Justice Manual* § 9-11.120.

21. Branzburg v. Hayes, 408 U.S. 665, 686–87 (1972); Williams, 504 U.S. at 47; United States v. R. Enterprises, Inc., 498 U.S. 292, 296 (1991).

22. Subpoenas seeking documents are formally called subpoena *duces tecum* and subpoenas for testimony are called subpoena *ad testficandum.*

23. Calandra, 414 U.S. at 343; Dionisio, 410 U.S. at 17–18; Kastigar v. United States, 406 U.S. 441, 443 (1972).

24. In re Grand Jury Proceedings, 219 F.3d 175, 189 (2d Cir. 2000); United States v. Udziela, 671 F.2d 995, 998 (7th Cir. 1982); In re Grand Jury Proceedings, 486 F.2d 85, 90 (3d Cir. 1973).

25. United States v. Leverage Funding System, Inc., 637 F.2d 645 (9th Cir. 1980).

26. *Justice Manual* § 9-11.152.

27. *See, e.g.*, 18 U.S.C. § 1621 (perjury); 18 U.S.C. § 1001 (giving false statements to government agents).

28. Fed. R. Crim. P. 17(e); *Justice Manual* § 9-11.140.

internationally if a district court judge or magistrate concludes that "particular testimony or the production of the document or other thing by [the subpoena target] is necessary in the interest of justice."[29]

Technically speaking, a grand jury's investigatory powers can only be used to identify and secure evidence in relation to the possible return of an indictment, not to obtain additional evidence against a defendant who has already been charged.[30] The practical importance of this rule is minimal, however, because prosecutors can use the grand jury to secure evidence after an indictment so long as their "dominant purpose" relates to a *possible* "superseding indictment" (which adds additional defendants or crimes to an existing case).[31] Courts afford the DOJ a presumption that its grand jury subpoenas serve a proper purpose, and the burden is on the defendant to establish otherwise.[32] This is a difficult hurdle to overcome and challenges to a prosecution made on this basis rarely succeed.

The grand jury's power to subpoena documents and testimony applies the same irrespective of whether the subpoena recipient is a "target," "subject," or merely a "witness" in the investigation.[33] A "target" is a person as to whom the prosecutor or grand jury already has evidence linking them to the commission of a crime and who is likely to become a defendant in a criminal case. A "subject" is a person whose conduct is within the scope of the grand jury's investigation but who is not considered a possible defendant. A "witness" is merely an individual who may have information relevant to the government's investigation, but who has not necessarily directly observed or participated in potential wrongdoing. If the recipient of a grand jury subpoena is a target or subject of the investigation, DOJ policy is to notify them of their status upon request.[34] When representing a grand jury subpoena recipient, ascertaining their status is thus a critical first step in determining how to respond.

2. *Challenging a Grand Jury Subpoena*

Grand jury subpoenas must be served in accordance with Federal Rule of Criminal Procedure 17 which, as noted above, permits service both within the United States and abroad. A party who has been properly served with a grand jury subpoena but who does not wish to comply can attempt to limit the scope of prosecutors' requests or seek court authorization to avoid

29. 28 U.S.C. § 1783(a).

30. Costello, 350 U.S. at 362; In re Grand Jury Subpoena Duces Tecum Dated Jan. 2, 1985, 767 F.2d 26, 29 (2d Cir. 1985); United States v. Star, 470 F.2d 1214 (9th Cir. 1972); *Justice Manual* § 9-11.120.

31. United States v. Salameh, 152 F.3d 88, 109 (2d Cir. 1998); In re Grand Jury Proceedings, 586 F.2d 724 (9th Cir. 1978).

32. United States v. Leung, 40 F.3d 577, 581 (2d Cir. 1994); United States v. Nguyen, 267 F. App'x 699, 703 (9th Cir. 2008).

33. United States v. Wong, 431 U.S. 174, 179 n. 8 (1977); United States v. Washington, 431 U.S. 181, 190 n. 6 (1977); United States v. Mandujano, 425 U.S. 564, 573–75 and 584 n. 9 (1976); Dionisio, 410 U.S. at 10 n. 8 (1973) ("The obligation to appear is no different for a person who may himself by the subject of the grand jury inquiry.").

34. *Justice Manual* § 9-11.151.

them entirely. Simply failing to respond can result in the subpoena recipient being held in contempt of court and imprisoned until they comply.[35]

a. Motions to Quash

"Grand juries are not licensed to engage in arbitrary fishing expeditions, nor may they select targets of investigation out of malice or an intent to harass."[36] To protect against abusive uses of a grand jury's subpoena powers, Federal Rule of Criminal Procedure 17(c) "empowers the district court[s], on motion, to quash or modify a subpoena 'if compliance would be unreasonable or oppressive.'"[37] What is reasonable depends on the context of the case and the circumstances of the recipient.[38]

Because "the law presumes, absent a strong showing to the contrary, that a grand jury acts within the legitimate scope of its authority," challenges to a grand jury subpoena based on irrelevance, improper purpose, or unreasonableness are very difficult to win.[39] As the Supreme Court put it, a party seeking to challenge a grand jury subpoena "faces a difficult situation" because grand juries do not, as a rule, divulge the possible crime they are investigating. The challenging party may thus "have no conception of the Government's purpose in seeking production of the requested information." "Absent even minimal information, the subpoena recipient is likely to find it exceedingly difficult to persuade a court that 'compliance would be unreasonable.' . . . [Their] unenviable task is to seek to persuade the court that the subpoena that has been served on [him or her] could not possibly serve any investigative purpose that the grand jury could legitimately be pursuing."[40]

Accordingly, motions to quash based on the purported unreasonableness of a grand jury subpoena will generally be denied "unless the district court determines that there is no reasonable possibility that the category of materials the Government seeks will produce information relevant to the general subject of the grand jury's investigation."

As an alternative to arguing unreasonableness, a party can seek to quash a subpoena by claiming that complying with it would be "oppressive." To be sufficiently "non-oppressive" a subpoena must make requests that are specific and targeted at obtaining admissible evidence.[41] This is a relatively low bar that will be satisfied if the government can explain to a court "[what] it expected to find and why it expected to find it" through the requests contained in the relevant subpoena.[42]

---

35. Fed. R. Crim. P. 17(g); Dionisio, 410 U.S. at 4; In re Grand Jury Witness, 835 F.2d 437 (2d Cir. 1987).

36. United States v. R. Enterprises, Inc., 498 U.S. 292, 299 (1991).

37. In re Grand Jury Subpoena Served Upon Doe, 759 F.2d 968, 971 (2d Cir. 1985); *see also* In Re Grand Jury Matters, 751 F.2d 13, 16 (1st Cir. 1984).

38. New Jersey v. T.L.O., 469 U.S. 325, 337 (1985).

39. United States v. Mechanik, 475 U.S. 66, 75 (1986).

40. R. Enterprises, Inc., 498 U.S. at 300.

41. United States v. Nixon, 418 U.S. 683, 700 (1974).

42. United States v. Bing Tang Vo, 78 F. Supp. 3d 171, 181 (D.D.C. 2015) (Rule 17's specificity requirement satisfied if "there is a 'substantial likelihood,' demonstrated through rational inferences, that the

Instead of contesting the underlying legality of a grand jury subpoena, subpoena recipients can seek to limit the breadth of their response by asserting their rights under the Constitution's Fifth Amendment or one of several other possibly applicable privileges discussed below.[43]

b. The Fifth Amendment

The Fifth Amendment to the Constitution states that no person "shall be compelled to be a witness against himself."[44] This privilege "extends to answers that would in themselves support a conviction under a federal criminal statute but likewise embraces those which would furnish a link in the chain of evidence needed to prosecute [an individual] for a federal crime."[45] The Fifth Amendment applies only to communications that are "testimonial."[46] "In order to be testimonial, an accused's communication must itself, explicitly or implicitly, relate a factual assertion or disclose information."[47]

A witness is not, however, "exonerated from answering merely because he declares that in so doing he would incriminate himself—his say-so does not of itself establish the hazard of incrimination. It is for the court to say whether his silence is justified."[48] Thus, when a witness refuses to respond to a question on the basis of self-incrimination, prosecutors can seek a "judicial determination as to the bona fides of the witness' Fifth Amendment claim."[49]

Even when a grand jury witness has a legitimate basis not to testify, prosecutors can compel their testimony by granting the witness immunity from prosecution.[50] As such, if prosecutors determine that a certain individual's testimony is critical to their case, they will usually be able to obtain it: in the words of the Supreme Court, "immunity is the Government's ultimate tool for securing testimony that otherwise would be protected."[51] Unlike the

---

documents being sought contain relevant and admissible evidence"); see also United States v. Alewelt, 532 F.2d 1165, 1168 (7th Cir. 1976) (grand jury's subpoena power "is generally limited only by the requirement that the evidence to be produced cover a reasonable period of time, is relevant to the investigation, and is identified with reasonable particularity").

43. United States v. Mandujano, 425 U.S. 564, 575 (1976).

44. Note that the Fifth Amendment's protections against self-incrimination do not apply to corporations or other entities. *See* Braswell v. United States, 487 U.S. 99, 102 (1988); Bellis v. United States, 417 U.S. 85, 90 (1974). "This is true (1) whether the subpoena is directed to the corporation itself or to [a corporate] custodian in his representative capacity, and (2) regardless of how small the corporation may be." In re Grand Jury Subpoena, 593 F.3d 155, 157 (2d Cir. 2010); *see also* In re Twelve Grand Jury Subpoenas, 908 F.3d 525, 527 (9th Cir. 2018); In re Two Grand Jury Subpoenae Duces Tecum, 769 F.2d 52, 54 (2d Cir. 1985).

45. Hoffman v. United States, 341 U.S. 479, 486–487 (1951).

46. United States v. Hubbell, 530 U.S. 27, 34 (2000); Fisher v. United States, 425 U.S. 391, 409 (1976).

47. Doe v. United States, 487 U.S. 201, 210 (1988).

48. Hoffman, 341 U.S. at 487.

49. Mandujano, 425 U.S. at 575.

50. *Id.*

51. *Id.*; *see also* Ullmann v. United States, 350 U.S. 422, 439 (1956); Piemonte v. United States, 367 U.S. 556, 560 (1961).

more limited "use immunity" afforded by proffer agreements (see below), testimony that is compelled over a Fifth Amendment invocation must be given more comprehensive "use and derivative-use immunity."[52] The procedures and rules governing these issues are codified in the "use immunity" statute (18 U.S.C. §§ 6002-05).

The difference between direct use and derivative use immunity is substantial. When the government grants use and derivative use immunity to a witness, if the witness is subsequently prosecuted, prosecutors bear the burden of demonstrating that all their information and evidence was derived "from a source wholly independent" of the witness's earlier immunized statements. If the government grants only direct use immunity, on the other hand, prosecutors are just prevented from using the immunized statements directly against the witness, but can still use information and investigatory leads derived from those statements.[53]

Where a Fifth Amendment claim is not overridden by immunity, the privilege can be used to resist providing verbal or written responses to prosecutors' questions. It can also be used as a basis to not produce documents requested in a grand jury subpoena in circumstances when the mere act of producing documents is "both incriminating and testimonial."[54] This privilege—called the "act of production" privilege—does not, however, mean that compliance with a grand jury subpoena may be avoided simply "because the demanded documents contain incriminating evidence."[55] Rather, it applies only when the act of producing documents itself has a "compelled testimonial aspect"—that is, where it implicitly communicates "statements of fact" such as that the documents exist, are in the individual's possession or control, and are authentic.[56]

i. The Fifth Amendment in Cross-Border Investigations

Cross-border financial crime prosecutions in the United States will often involve defendants and witnesses who have been interrogated by foreign law enforcement agencies. In such circumstances, the circuit courts have consistently held that, for statements obtained through overseas interrogation to be admissible against the declarant in a U.S. court, they must have been obtained voluntarily and otherwise in compliance with the Constitution.[57]

Confessions procured by foreign law enforcement are evaluated under the Fifth Amendment and *Bram v. United States*, in which the Supreme Court reversed a conviction based on a confession made to a Canadian official: "In criminal trials in the courts of the United States," the Court wrote, "wherever a question arises whether a confession is incompetent

---

52. Kastigar, 406 U.S. at 442.

53. United States v. Plummer, 941 F.2d 799, 803 (9th Cir. 1991).

54. In re Grand Jury Subpoena, 593 F.3d 155, 157 (2d Cir. 2010) (citing United States v. Doe, 465 U.S. 605, 612–13 (1984)); *see also* Fisher v. United States, 425 U.S. 391 (1976).

55. United States v. Hubbell, 530 U.S. 27, 35 (2000).

56. *Id.* at 36–37.

57. Dickerson v. United States, 530 U.S. 428, 433 (2000); In re Terrorist Bombings of U.S. Embassies in E. Africa, 552 F.3d 177, 200 (2d Cir. 2008); United States v. Yousef, 327 F.3d 56, 124, 145 (2d Cir. 2003) ("[T]he law is settled that statements taken by foreign police in the absence of Miranda warnings are admissible if voluntary.").

because not voluntary, the issue is controlled by" the Fifth Amendment's command "that no person shall be compelled in any criminal case to be a witness against himself."[58]

The right against self-incrimination is a personal trial right of any defendant—regardless of citizenship—in an American criminal case. Therefore, the Fifth Amendment can only be violated when a compelled statement is offered *at trial* against the declarant, even if "conduct by law enforcement officials prior to trial may ultimately impair that right."[59] Thus, regardless of the origin of an incriminating statement—that is, foreign or domestic—it cannot be admitted at trial in the United States if it was "compelled." "This is so even when the testimony was compelled by a foreign government in full accordance with its own law."[60]

Practice Note

The Bill of Rights

The Fifth Amendment is contained within the Bill of Rights, the name given to the first ten amendments to the Constitution that were added soon after the Constitution was ratified. Several of these amendments contain important protections and rights for criminal defendants that will be explored throughout this book.

4th Amendment	"The right of the people to be secure in their persons, houses, papers, and effects, against unreasonable searches and seizures, shall not be violated, and no Warrants shall issue, but upon probable cause, supported by Oath or affirmation, and particularly describing the place to be searched, and the persons or things to be seized."
5th Amendment	"No person shall be held to answer for a capital, or otherwise infamous crime, unless on presentment or indictment of a Grand Jury . . .; nor shall any person be subject for the same offence to be twice put in jeopardy of life or limb; nor shall be compelled in any criminal case to be a witness against himself, nor be deprived of life, liberty, or property, without due process of law. . . ."
6th Amendment	"In all criminal prosecutions, the accused shall enjoy the right to a speedy and public trial, by an impartial jury of the State and district wherein the crime shall have been committed . . . and to be informed of the nature and cause of the accusation; to be confronted with the witnesses against him; to have compulsory process for obtaining witnesses in his favor, and to have the Assistance of Counsel for his defense."
8th Amendment	"Excessive bail shall not be required, nor excessive fines imposed, nor cruel and unusual punishments inflicted."

58. 168 U.S. 532, 542 (1897).

59. United States v. Patane, 542 U.S. 630, 637 (2004); Chavez v. Martinez, 538 U.S. 760, 767 (2003).

60. Allen, 864 F.3d at 82.

c. Other Privileges

Depending on the situation, a grand jury subpoena may be subject to a variety of privileges aside from the Fifth Amendment right against self-incrimination. The privileges most likely to be invoked in a grand jury investigation of a financial crime are the attorney-client privilege and the work product privilege (codified within Federal Rule of Evidence 502 and Rule 26(b)(3) of the Federal Rules of Civil Procedure, respectively).[61]

The attorney-client privilege is an evidentiary rule designed to prevent the forced disclosure in a judicial proceeding of confidential communications between an individual or entity and a lawyer made for the purpose of obtaining or receiving legal advice.[62] The policy rationale behind the privilege is to encourage "full and frank communication between attorneys and their clients and thereby promote broader public interests in the observance of law and administration of justice." The holder of the privilege is the client, and lawyers are obliged to protect it to the maximum extent possible on their client's behalf.[63]

In criminal cases especially, the Constitution protects confidential attorney-client communications from the eyes and ears of the government: "if a party demonstrates that the attorney-client privilege applies, the privilege affords all communications between attorney and client absolute and complete protection from disclosure."[64] An intrusion by the government into an attorney-client relationship to obtain confidential information may be deemed a violation of a defendant's Sixth Amendment right to effective assistance of counsel or Fifth Amendment due process rights.[65] In such a situation, a court may suppress evidence gathered as a result of the communication or, in egregious cases where the prejudice cannot otherwise be cured, dismiss the indictment.

A party asserting the privilege must demonstrate that: (i) at the time of the communication the asserted privilege holder was, or was seeking to become, an attorney's client; (ii) the communication was with a member of the bar of a court, or a subordinate; (iii) the communication was made in confidence, and without the presence of third parties, for the purpose of securing legal advice or legal services; and (iv) the privilege has not been waived.[66]

---

61. Note that these are not the only privileges that could possibly apply. *See, e.g.*, Gravel v. United States, 408 U.S. 606 (1972) (grand jury subpoena subject to limitation by "Speech or Debate" clause immunity); Branzburg v. Hayes, 408 U.S. 665 (1972) (finding journalists have qualified privilege to refuse to testify before a grand jury on First Amendment grounds); In re Grand Jury Investigation of Hugle, 754 F.2d 863 (9th Cir. 1985) (holding that grand jury subpoenas can be limited by the privilege for confidential marital communications).

62. *See, e.g.*, Upjohn Co. v. United States, 449 U.S. 383, 389 (1981); United States v. BDO Seidman, LLP, 492 F.3d 806, 815 (7th Cir. 2007); United States v. Mejia, 655 F.3d 126, 132 (2d Cir. 2011); Rehling v. City of Chicago, 207 F.3d 1009, 1019 (7th Cir. 2000).

63. Republic Gear Co. v. Borg-Warner Corp., 381 F.2d 551, 556 (2d Cir. 1967).

64. In re Allen v. McGraw, 106 F.3d 582, 600 (4th Cir. 1997).

65. *See, e.g.*, United States v. Haynes, 216 F.3d 789, 796 (9th Cir. 2000); United States v. Aulicino, 44 F.3d 1102, 1117 (2d Cir. 1995) (unintentional interference with attorney-client relationship may violate defendant's Sixth Amendment rights where government gains confidential information and prejudice results).

66. United States v. Tedder, 801 F.2d 1437, 1442 (4th Cir. 1986).

These protections may also extend to communications made to certain agents of an attorney, including accountants and other experts hired to assist in the provision of legal services.[67] The attorney-client privilege will apply to such agents when the communication in question is "made in confidence for the purpose of obtaining legal advice from the lawyer."[68] Information provided to an expert by a client at the behest of his or her attorney for the purpose of interpretation and analysis is privileged to the extent that it is imparted in connection with the legal representation.

The attorney-client privilege protects the substance of communications, whereas the work product privilege "provides qualified protection for materials prepared by or at the behest of counsel in anticipation of litigation or for trial."[69] There are two types of attorney work product that fall within the doctrine: (i) fact work product, which is "a translation of the factual events involved," and (ii) opinion work product, which "represents the actual thoughts and impressions of the attorney."[70]

The purpose of this privilege is to protect from disclosure an attorney's opinion and impressions of facts learned while representing their client. "At its core, the work-product doctrine shelters the mental processes of the attorney, providing a privileged area within which he can analyze and prepare his client's case."[71]

Unlike the attorney-client privilege, the protection of the work product privilege is "qualified" in that disclosure of work product may be ordered if the party seeking it can demonstrate substantial need for the information and an inability to obtain it by other means without undue hardship.[72]

Both privileges may be waived if a party voluntarily discloses privileged materials or allows their attorney to discuss privileged matters with a third party.[73] However, in certain circumstances a party may share privileged communications with a third party without waiver under the "common interest rule." As discussed further in the next section, this rule "serves to protect the confidentiality of communications passing from one party to the attorney for another party where a joint defense effort or strategy has been decided upon and undertaken by the parties and their respective counsel."[74] It is "unnecessary that there be actual litigation in progress for the common interest rule" to apply. It will also apply even if

---

67. United States v. Schwimmer, 892 F.2d 237, 243 (2d Cir. 1989).

68. United States v. Kovel, 296 F.2d 918 (2d Cir. 1961).

69. In re Grand Jury Subpoena Dated July 6, 2005, 510 F.3d 180, 183 (2d Cir. 2007); *see also* Hickman v. Taylor, 329 U.S. 495 (1947).

70. In re Grand Jury Subpoena, 870 F.3d 312, 316 (4th Cir. 2017).

71. United States v. Fort, 472 F.3d 1106, 1116 (9th Cir. 2007); *see also,* United States v. Nobles, 422 U.S. 225, 238–39 (1975) (because "attorneys often must rely on the assistance of investigators and other agents in the compilation of materials in preparation for trial," "[i]t is . . . necessary that the [work product] doctrine protect material prepared by agents for the attorney as well as those prepared by the attorney himself").

72. *See* In re Grand Jury Proceedings, 219 F.3d 175, 190-91 (2d Cir. 2000); United States v. Adlman, 134 F.3d 1194 (2d Cir. 1998).

73. United States v. White, 887 F.2d 267, 270-71 (D.C. Cir. 1989).

74. Schwimmer, 892 F.2d at 243.

the attorney representing the communicating party is not present when the communication is made.[75]

Under the "crime-fraud exception," the attorney-client and work product privileges will not apply when the underlying communications or work product are used in furtherance of a crime. "The crime-fraud exception has a precise focus: It applies only when the communications between the client and his lawyer further a crime, fraud or other misconduct. It does not suffice that the communications may be related to [an already completed] crime. To subject the attorney-client communications to disclosure, they must actually have been made with an intent to further an unlawful act."[76]

As with a claim under the Fifth Amendment, a party asserting the attorney-client or work product privilege bears the burden of establishing that it applies.[77] Where allegedly privileged communications take place in a foreign country or involve foreign attorneys or proceedings, it is sometimes unclear which country's privilege laws should apply. In such situations, most U.S. courts will defer to the law of the country that has the "predominant" or "the most direct and compelling interest" in whether those communications should remain confidential, unless that foreign law is contrary to American public policy.[78] The jurisdiction with the "predominant interest" is either "the place where the allegedly privileged relationship was entered into" or "the place in which that relationship was centered at the time the communication was sent."[79]

i. Joint Defense Agreements

Individuals who have been subpoenaed to provide testimony or documents as part of a government investigation will often benefit from gathering as much intelligence as possible before deciding how to respond—they will usually want to know, for example, the identities of the other targets and witnesses, what other parties told investigators, the key documentary evidence, and details of the government's theory of liability. To obtain this information while preserving the attorney-client privilege, the various parties involved in a criminal investigation—such as a company and its employees or several potential codefendants—will often enter into a "joint defense agreement" (JDA), which relies on the "common interest" privilege.

While the attorney-client privilege will ordinarily be considered waived where a represented party discloses the contents of a privileged communication to a third party, the common interest privilege creates an exception to this waiver rule. It allows for communications between a client and his own lawyer to remain protected by the attorney-client privilege even when the substance of these communications is disclosed to codefendants or

75. Matter of Grand Jury Subpoena, 406 F. Supp. 381 (S.D.N.Y. 1975).

76. In re Sealed Case, 754 F.2d 395, 399 (D.C. Cir. 1985); In re Antitrust Grand Jury, 805 F.2d 155, 168 (6th Cir. 1986); In re Grand Jury Subpoenas Duces Tecum, 798 F.2d 32, 34 (2d Cir. 1986)).

77. Schwimmer, 892 F.2d at 244; *see also* United States v. Keplinger, 776 F.2d 678, 701 (7th Cir. 1985).

78. Golden Trade, S.r.L. v. Lee Apparel Co., 143 F.R.D. 514, 522 (S.D.N.Y. 1992).

79. *Id.*; *see also* McCook Metals L.L.C. v. Alcoa Inc., 192 F.R.D. 242, 256 (N.D. Ill. 2000).

their counsel for purposes of a common defense.[80] The common interest privilege is thus an exception to the normal waiver rules that "serves to protect the confidentiality of communications passing from one party to the attorney for another party where a joint defense effort or strategy has been decided upon and undertaken by the parties and their respective counsel."[81]

To be eligible for protection, a joint defense communication must be shared between the attorneys of a joint defense group; sharing privileged information directly between represented parties may destroy the privilege.[82] Further, most courts require that for the doctrine to apply, the person with whom the privileged information is shared must have an *identical*—not merely similar—*legal* interest in the subject matter of the communication, which must be made in the course of furthering the ongoing, common defense.[83]

To successfully fend off a challenge to the common interest privilege from the government, the joint defense group will generally need to have entered into a JDA, either formally or informally, so that the party invoking the privilege can demonstrate a meeting of the minds on its key elements.[84] A written contract is not a prerequisite; whether joint defense materials are protected from disclosure depends on the particular facts and circumstances of the relationship between the parties.

Once a joint defense arrangement is established, the common interest privilege prevents one party from disclosing joint defense materials without the other party's consent. Because the privilege is held jointly, each individual party has the power to veto a proposed disclosure.[85] Even if a party exits the JDA group, they will remain under an obligation not to share joint defense materials they received while still within the arrangement. Various complications can arise if a member of the JDA group withdraws and becomes a cooperating witness for the prosecution (see chapter 6). In such situations, it may be difficult for the remaining defendants to cross-examine the defector about information obtained while the defector was still a JDA member.[86] JDA defectors can also be problematic for prosecutors, who must be careful not to receive information that is still covered by privilege under the terms of the JDA agreement.[87]

Because JDAs are specifically designed to facilitate coordination between defendants and limit the amount of information that is discoverable to the government during a criminal

---

80. Hunydee v. United States, 355 F.2d 183, 185 (9th Cir. 1965); United States v. BDO Seidman, LLP, 492 F.3d 806, 815 (7th Cir. 2007).

81. United States v. Bay State Ambulance and Hosp. Rental Serv., 874 F.2d 20, 28 (1st Cir. 1989); *see also* Keplinger, 776 F.2d at 701; Schwimmer, 892 F.2d at 243–44.

82. In re Teleglobe Communications Corp., 493 F.3d at 364.

83. BDO Seidman, 492 F.3d at 816.

84. United States v. Weissman, 195 F.3d 96, 100 (2d Cir. 1999); Denney v. Jenkens & Gilchrist, 362 F. Supp. 2d 407, 415–16 (S.D.N.Y. 2004).

85. In re Grand Jury Subpoena Duces Tecum, 406 F. Supp. 381, 392 (S.D.N.Y. 1975).

86. United States v. Henke, 222 F.3d 633, 637 (9th Cir. 2000).

87. John M. Hillebrecht & Jessica Masella, Understanding Joint Defense Agreements: The Implications for White-Collar Defendants in the Second Circuit, Law.com (Jan. 25, 2019).

investigation, the DOJ has generally treated them with hostility.[88] Courts too have recognized a threat that JDAs can have on the overall integrity of criminal proceedings and, accordingly, have generally found that the existence of a JDA itself is not protected from disclosure.[89]

ii. Attorney-Client Privilege in the Corporate Context

For corporations involved in a regulatory or internal investigation, one of the key initial goals is identifying the full details of the conduct at issue. To do so, outside corporate counsel will almost always request interviews with the employees who may have relevant knowledge. These interviews, and other types of communications between employees and a company's lawyers, can complicate attorney-client privilege issues.

In *Upjohn Co. v. United States*, 449 U.S. 383 (1981), the Supreme Court considered whether communications between a company's in-house counsel and employees during an internal investigation into possible foreign bribery were privileged. During the investigation, company counsel asked certain employees to complete a questionnaire about the payments at issue and to sit for factual debriefing interviews. In response to a subsequent IRS subpoena, Upjohn Co. refused to disclose the questionnaires or notes of the interviews taken by the company's lawyers on the basis of privilege. The IRS challenged this claim in district court, which ruled in favor of the government. After this decision was upheld by the Sixth Circuit Court of Appeals, the company appealed to the Supreme Court, which reversed.

Explaining that the attorney-client privilege "exists to protect not only the giving of professional advice to those who can act on it but also the giving of information to the lawyer to enable him to give sound and informed advice," the Supreme Court held that the privilege protected the questionnaires and the attorneys' notes of their interviews with Upjohn employees.[90]

This decision replaced the previously used "control group" test, which afforded privilege only to communications between a company's lawyers and high-ranking employees who effectively controlled the business, and established that "fact finding which pertains to legal advice counts as professional legal services."[91] Under *Upjohn*, the key question is whether a corporate investigation is related to the rendering of legal services and advice—if it is, all confidential communications between the company's lawyers and employees will generally be protected from disclosure.

---

88. *See, e.g.*, Deborah Stavile Bartel, *Reconceptualizing the Joint Defense Doctrine*, 65 FORDHAM L. REV. 871, 879 (1996) ("Prosecutors oppose confidentiality for joint defense communications because it shields relevant and probative evidence from the fact finder thereby hindering the determination of criminal responsibility of those accused of a crime. Prosecutors also fear that joint defense arrangements may include unlawful efforts to impede justice, provide a group of co-defendants with the opportunity to influence improperly the memories of witnesses, or otherwise permit a concerted attempt to obstruct grand jury investigations.").

89. United States v. Bauer, 132 F.3d 504, 508–09 (9th Cir. 1997) (attorney-client privilege does not cover the identity of an attorney's client); *see also* Hsia, 81 F. Supp. 2d at 11 n.3 (expressing doubt that "either the existence or the terms of a [joint defense agreement] are privileged").

90. 449 U.S. at 390.

91. United States v. Rowe, 96 F.3d 1294, 1296 (9th Cir. 1996); In re Grand Jury Subpoena, 599 F.2d 504, 509 (2d Cir. 1979).

To ensure that this privilege is preserved, corporate counsel will often begin a communication with lower-level employees with an "*Upjohn* warning." A standard *Upjohn* warning informs the employee that the attorney represents the corporation and not the employee personally; specifies that the corporation holds the attorney-client privilege and may waive it in its sole discretion; states that the interview is being conducted so that legal advice can be given to the company; and instructs the employee not to share the substance of any communication with counsel to other employees or anyone else.

d. Proffers

Rather than challenge a grand jury subpoena directly, a subpoena recipient—or anyone else subject to a criminal investigation—may elect to contact prosecutors and request to meet with them for an informal debriefing session outside of the grand jury room, called a "proffer."[92] For the party providing the proffer, the objective is usually to obtain a cooperation agreement or to convince prosecutors not to bring charges.[93] As opposed to when testimony is compelled to be provided before the grand jury, the scope of the subject matter discussed in a proffer is usually agreed upon in advance and a proffer session can be ended by a defendant at any time. Further, a defendant can be, and usually always is, accompanied by counsel during a proffer, whereas they must testify before a grand jury without counsel present.[94]

Most proffers are given pursuant to a written proffer agreement—commonly called *Mezzanetto* or "Queen for a Day" agreements—that provide a prospective (or actual) defendant some limited protections.[95] A standard proffer agreement provides that the government may not use the defendant's statement in its case in chief, but it is free to use leads obtained from it and may use the statement on cross-examination of the defendant and in a variety of other circumstances (see figure 2.1).[96] Such provisions are said to provide "use, but not derivative use, immunity."[97] Although "use immunity" precludes statements made during a proffer session from simply being introduced into evidence at trial, it still allows prosecutors to use these statements against the person making them except in very limited circumstances.[98]

---

92. United States v. Mezzanatto, 513 U.S. 196, 198 (1995); United States v. Stein, 440 F. Supp. 2d 315, 322 n.20 (S.D.N.Y. 2006).

93. United States v. Oluwanisola, 605 F.3d 124, 127 (2d Cir. 2010); *see also* Richard B. Zabel & James J. Benjamin, Jr., *"Queen for a Day" or "Courtesan for a Day": The Sixth Amendment Limits to Proffer Agreements*, 15 No. 9 White Collar Crime Rep. 1 (2001).

94. A grand jury witness can, however, ask to pause their testimony and leave the grand jury room to consult with their counsel elsewhere in the courthouse or outside. *See* Schwimmer, 882 F.2d at 27.

95. Statements made during a proffer session may also be protected under Rule 408 (Compromise Offers and Negotiations) and Rule 410 (Pleas, Plea Discussions, and Related Statements) of the Federal Rules of Evidence. However, the terms of most proffer agreements will require the witness to waive these protections.

96. United States v. Velez, 354 F.3d 190, 195 (2d Cir. 2010); United States v. Krilich, 159 F.3d 1020, 1025 (7th Cir. 1998).

97. United States v. Christian, 111 F. Supp. 3d 287, 305 (E.D.N.Y. 2015).

98. For an extended discussion of the terms of typical proffer agreements and the limited protections they afford potential defendants, *see* Robert I. Smith, III, *Fair Play and Criminal Justice: Drafting Proffer Agreements in Light of Total Waiver of Rule 410*, 66 Ann. Surv. S. Car. L. 809 (Summer 2015).

In other words, a defendant remains free to present evidence at trial inconsistent with his proffer statements, but the consequence for doing so is that the government is then permitted to present the defendant's own words in rebuttal.[99] As such, a person giving a proffer can seriously compromise their ability to defend themselves in the event that their proffer is unsuccessful and they are criminally charged.[100] Further, statements made during a proffer can be used by the government as investigative leads to develop additional information that could be used against the defendant at trial.

Because of these various potential downsides, a proffer between prosecutors and an investigation target will generally be preceded by an "attorney proffer" between prosecutors and the target's lawyer. In a typical attorney proffer, defense counsel will tell prosecutors what their client would "hypothetically" say if he or she were to have a proffer with them. By framing the discussion as hypothetical, the target is protected from prosecutors trying to use the attorney's statements against him; at the same time, the substance of hypothetical discussions need not be memorialized by prosecutors or disclosed to other defendants whose cases may be implicated (even if they include information that could be exculpatory).

The goal of an attorney proffer is to give the government a preview of the target's likely testimony and feel out whether prosecutors consider it credible *before* the target sits down for an interview. In the event prosecutors react positively to the attorney proffer, preliminary discussions can be had about possibly resolving the case against the target through a cooperation agreement, nonprosecution agreement (NPA), or deferred prosecution agreement (DPA) (see chapter 6). If, after an attorney proffer, none of these resolutions appear to be on the table, engaging in further proffers will generally not be in the target's interest (as the government will just learn additional information about the defense strategy or the alleged crime). Conversely, if prosecutors signal a willingness to allow for some sort of favorable resolution, an attorney proffer will usually be followed by one or more proffers with the target himself.

i. Proffers and the Importance of Candor

It is critical for individuals participating in the proffer process to understand the importance of providing fully truthful answers to government investigators. A failure to do so will not only destroy any chance for a favorable plea or cooperation agreement, it can also subject them to additional charges, usually under 18 U.S.C. § 1001 or § 1503.

Section 1001 makes it a crime, punishable by up to five years in prison, to "knowingly and willfully" engage in deception or misrepresent any material fact "in any matter within the jurisdiction of the executive, legislative, or judicial branch of the" federal government. The "knowingly and willfully" standard requires the act in question to "have been made with an intent to deceive, a design to induce belief in the falsity or to mislead," but it does not require an intent to defraud (i.e., an intent to obtain something by way of the deceit).[101] To make out a

99. Velez, 354 F.3d at 196.

100. Oluwanisola, 605 F.3d at 127–28 (noting proffer agreements prohibit the government from using a party's statements except "as substantive evidence to rebut, directly or indirectly, any evidence offered or elicited, or factual assertions made, by or on behalf of [the party] at any stage of a criminal prosecution").

101. United States v. Hopkins, 916 F.2d 207, 214 (1980).

With respect to the meeting of [redacted] ("Client") and his attorney, [redacted] with Assistant United States Attorneys [redacted] to be held at the Office of the United States Attorney for the Southern District of New York on May 16, 2005 ("the meeting"), the following understandings exist:

(1) **THIS IS NOT A COOPERATION AGREEMENT.** The Client has agreed to provide the Government with information, and to respond to questions, so that the Government may evaluate Client's information and responses in making prosecutive decisions. By receiving Client's proffer, the Government does not agree to make a motion on the Client's behalf or to enter into a cooperation agreement, plea agreement, immunity or non-prosecution agreement. The Government makes no representation about the likelihood that any such agreement will be reached in connection with this proffer.

(2) In any prosecution brought against Client by this Office, except as provided below the Government will not offer in evidence on its case-in-chief, or in connection with any sentencing proceeding for the purpose of determining an appropriate sentence, any statements made by Client at the meeting, except in a prosecution for false statements, obstruction of justice or perjury with respect to any acts committed or statements made during or after the meeting or testimony given after the meeting.

(3) Notwithstanding item (2) above: (a) the Government may use information derived directly or indirectly from the meeting for the purpose of obtaining leads to other evidence, which evidence may be used in any prosecution of Client by the Government; (b) in any prosecution brought against Client, the Government may use statements made by Client at the meeting and all evidence obtained directly or indirectly therefrom for the purpose of cross-examination should Client testify; and (c) the Government may also use statements made by Client at the meeting to rebut any evidence or arguments offered by or on behalf of Client (including arguments made or issues raised sua sponte by the District Court) at any stage of the criminal prosecution (including bail, all phases of trial, and sentencing) in any prosecution brought against Client.

(4) The Client understands and agrees that in the event the Client seeks to qualify for a reduction in sentence under Title 18, United States Code, Section 3553(f) or United States Sentencing Guidelines, Sections 2D1.1(b) (6) or 5C1.2, the Office may offer in evidence, in connection with the sentencing, statements made by the Client at the meeting and all evidence obtained directly or indirectly therefrom.

(5) To the extent that the Government is entitled under this Agreement to offer in evidence any statements made by Client or leads obtained therefrom, Client shall assert no claim under the United States Constitution, any statute, Rule 410 of the Federal Rules of Evidence, or any other federal rule that such statements or any leads therefrom should be suppressed. It is the intent of this Agreement to waive all rights in the foregoing respects.

(6) If this Office receives a request from another prosecutor's office for access to information obtained pursuant to this Proffer Agreement, this Office may furnish such information but will do so only on the condition that the requesting office honor the provisions of this Agreement.

(7) It is further understood that this Agreement is limited to the statements made by Client at the meeting and does not apply to any oral, written or recorded statements made by Client at any other time. No understandings, promises, agreements and/or conditions have been entered into with respect to the meeting other than those set forth in this Agreement and none will be entered into unless in writing and signed by all parties.

(8) The understandings set forth in paragraphs 1 through 7 above extend to the continuation of this meeting on the dates that appear below.

(9) Client and Attorney acknowledge that they have fully discussed and understand every paragraph and clause in this Agreement and the consequences thereof.

Figure 2.1 Sample proffer agreement of the Southern District of New York.

Section 1001 violation, prosecutors need not prove that the false statement was made directly to a federal government agency, that the government believed or relied upon it, or that the false statement was written, signed, or sworn.[102] DOJ policy is to not charge a Section 1001 violation in situations in which a suspect merely denies guilt in response to questioning by the government (as opposed to making an affirmative false statement of fact).[103]

Section 1503 prohibits "obstruction of justice," defined as an act that "corruptly or by threats or force, or by any threatening letter or communication, influences, obstructs, or impedes, or endeavors to influence, obstruct, or impede, the due administration of justice."

102. United States v. Uni Oil Co., 646 F.2d 946, 954–55 (5th Cir. 1981); United States v. Lichenstein, 610 F.2d 1272, 1278 (5th Cir. 1980); United States v. Beacon Brass Co., 344 U.S. 43, 46 (1952).

103. *Justice Manual* § 9-42.160.

This provision is violated when a person has a specific intent to obstruct or interfere with a judicial proceeding. To be found guilty, such a person must not only have the specific intent to obstruct, but also must act while knowing that a judicial proceeding was pending at the time and that the act would likely affect such proceeding.

Practice Note

Reverse Proffers

Whereas a proffer is a means for the defendant to provide information to prosecutors, "reverse proffers" are informal meetings held prior to, or after, indictment in which prosecutors walk through their key evidence and explain the legal theory supporting their case. Prosecutors may also indicate the penalties they will likely seek if the individual proceeds to trial and loses. The DOJ's purpose in giving a reverse proffer is generally to convince a defendant of the strength of the case against him or her, agree to plead guilty, and cooperate against others on behalf of the government. Since reverse proffers usually occur prior to indictment, none of the discovery obligations that are imposed on the government post-indictment (see chapter 5) are triggered. This means that there is no obligation to provide the investigation target with a full picture of the evidence or to disclose potentially exculpatory documents or witness statements.

B. The Serious Fraud Office's Section 2 Powers

As noted at the beginning of this chapter, an important difference between British and U.S. financial crime investigations is that grand juries are not used in the United Kingdom. So instead of a prosecutor conducting an investigation using the powers granted to the grand jury, the investigatory powers of British prosecutors are granted directly to them by statute.

For example, the Criminal Justice Act (CJA) 1987 authorizes the director of the SFO to "investigate any suspected offence which appears to him on reasonable grounds to involve serious or complex fraud."[104] Once a matter has been formally opened, the SFO has various powers to obtain relevant evidence that are set forth in CJA 1987 Section 2.[105] A "Section 2 Notice" requesting documents and/or testimony from the recipient is the British equivalent of a U.S. grand jury subpoena. The main differences between the two is that Section 2 may be used to obtain evidence after charges have been filed[106] and permits the SFO to compel testimony, even if it is incriminating as to the person testifying.

While they apply to all individuals and entities under the SFO's jurisdiction, Section 2 powers are usually used to obtain testimony or documents from witnesses to potential wrongdoing, not from the party under investigation. As in the United States, failing to respond to a Section 2 Notice or intentionally providing false testimony or evidence to SFO investigators is a criminal offense.[107]

104. Criminal Justice Act (1987), s. 1(3).

105. For matters involving foreign bribery, the SFO can use its Section 2 powers in the "pre-investigation" phase (i.e., before it has decided to launch a formal investigation). CJA 1987, s. 2A1.

106. R v. Director of Serious Fraud Office, ex p Smith [1993] AC 1.

107. CJA 1987, ss. 2(13)–(15).

1. Serious Fraud Office Powers to Compel Testimony

The SFO director "may by notice in writing require the person whose affairs are to be investigated . . . or any other person whom he has reasons to believe has relevant information to answer questions or otherwise furnish information with respect to any matter relevant to the investigation at a specified place and either at a specified time or forthwith."[108] Section 2 interviews generally take place in the SFO's offices in London or at the interviewee's place of business.[109]

SFO policy is to allow the party being questioned to be accompanied by a solicitor if the SFO "case controller believes it likely they will assist the purpose of the interview and/or investigation, or that they will provide essential assistance to the interviewee by way of legal advice."[110] There is no legal right to have a solicitor present, however, and the SFO places strict limits on their role during a Section 2 interview.[111] For example, an interviewee's solicitor is not permitted to record or transcribe the interview, and the solicitor's role is generally limited to clarifying questions posed by the SFO and advising the interviewee on questions that may implicate a legal privilege. Otherwise, "they must not do anything to undermine the free flow of information which the interviewee, by law, is required to give." If a party's solicitor obstructs the interview process, the SFO can exclude them.

While the United Kingdom recognizes a common law right against self-incrimination, it is less absolute than the U.S. Constitution's Fifth Amendment.[112] For example, a party receiving a Section 2 notice cannot refuse to answer the SFO's questions simply because a truthful answer might reveal their involvement in a crime—rather, a Section 2 interviewee is legally compelled to respond subject to a few limited exceptions. But importantly, just as "Queen for a Day Agreements" provide "use immunity" for statements made during proffer sessions with DOJ prosecutors, a person's statements to the SFO during a Section 2 interview cannot be used against them in a prosecution for the offense being investigated.[113] In other words, all recipients of a Section 2 notice are automatically granted the type of "use immunity" that is negotiated for on a case by case basis in the United States.

---

108. CJA 1987, s. 2(2).

109. *See* The Law Society, *Representing Clients at Section 2 CJA Interviews, available at* https://www.lawsociety.org.uk/en/topics/criminal-justice/representing-clients-at-section-2-cja-interviews.

110. Serious Fraud Office, *Presence of Interviewee's Legal Adviser at a Section 2 Interview: Guidance for Lawyers, available at* https://www.sfo.gov.uk/download/sfo-operational-guidance-presence-interviewees-legal-adviser-section-2-interview-internal-guidance/. This guidance also requires a solicitor attending a Section 2 interview to agree to a number of undertakings. Among other things, these undertakings require the solicitor to agree that (i) all predisclosure documents and documents provided during the interview will be kept confidential, (ii) no such documents will be discussed with anyone other than the interviewee without express SFO authorization, and (iii) the solicitor will not disclose the content of the interview or discuss it with anyone other than the interviewee.

111. R v. Director of the SFO [2015] EWHC 865 (Admin).

112. Saunders v. UK [1996] ECHR 65.

113. CJA 1987, s. 2(8).

Because the protection afforded by use immunity is limited, statements given during a Section 2 interview can be used against the witness in a prosecution for knowingly providing false information or if they provide inconsistent testimony in any subsequent proceeding.[114]

While a Section 2 interviewee has a limited ability to lawfully refuse to answer questions that are irrelevant to the investigation or which call for an opinion, the primary basis on which such a person may not answer the SFO's questions is the legal professional privilege.[115]

a. Legal Professional Privilege in the United Kingdom

Mirroring the attorney-client and work product privileges recognized by U.S. law, legal professional privilege (LPP) in the United Kingdom is comprised of (i) the legal advice privilege (LAP) and (ii) the litigation privilege. These privileges, derived from the common law, are codified in Section 10(1) of the Police and Criminal Evidence Act (PACE) 1984.

The LAP protects confidential communications between a client and the client's lawyer that relate to seeking or receiving legal advice. As long as these elements are satisfied, the LAP will apply whether or not litigation is pending or contemplated.[116] A key distinction between the LAP and its analogue under U.S. law is that it only applies to communications between a lawyer and a client (or an immediate agent of each, such as a paralegal or translator); it does not apply to any communications involving a nonlawyer expert (e.g., accountants and private investigators), even if the expert is assisting the lawyer provide legal advice.[117] For purposes of the LAP, a "lawyer" is defined to include all members of the legal profession (including accredited foreign lawyers), paralegals, and trainee solicitors.

When a lawyer is acting on behalf of a corporate entity, English courts apply a narrow interpretation of who within the corporation constitutes the "client." In *The RBS Rights Issue Litigation* [2016] EWHC 3161 (Ch), the High Court ruled that the "client" in a corporate context is limited to those employees who are authorized to seek and receive legal advice on behalf of the company. This decision has important implications for internal investigations since interviews between the company's lawyers and employees outside the core "client" group will generally not be privileged. A lawyer's notes of such interviews will also not be privileged.[118] As discussed above, the opposite is true in the United States.[119]

---

114. CJA 1987, s. 2(8)–2(8AA).

115. Note that a Section 2 interviewee is not required to disclose information that might violate a duty of banking confidence unless consent is given by the person to whom the obligation of confidence is owed or the SFO director (or a designate) specifically authorizes it. CJA 1987, s. 2(10).

116. Three Rivers District Council and others v. Governor and Company of the Bank of England (No. 6) [2005] 1 AC 610, para. 50.

117. R (Prudential Plc) v. Special Commissioner of Income Tax and Pandolfo [2013] 2 AC 185, para. 29; *see also* Andrew Smith, et al., *The Basics: Does Legal Professional Privilege Apply to All Communications with or Through a Solicitor?* Mondaq, July 29, 2019.

118. Director of the SFO v. ENRC [2017] EWHC 1017 (QB).

119. *See* Upjohn, 449 U.S. at 394–95 (ruling that confidential communications between employees and company counsel made at the direction of corporate superiors are protected by the attorney-client privilege); In re Kellogg Brown & Root, Inc., 756 F.3d 754, 759 (D.C. Cir. 2014) ("In the context of an organization's internal investigation, if one of the significant purposes of the internal investigation was

The scope of the litigation privilege is broader than the LAP in that it protects communications involving a lawyer, his or her client, and third-party agents where adversarial proceedings exist or are reasonably contemplated. In such a situation, the litigation privilege will protect all confidential documents prepared for the "dominant purpose" of giving or obtaining of legal advice.[120] Importantly, regulatory investigations in the United Kingdom, such as those initiated by the FCA, are not presumptively considered to be "adversarial proceedings" and consequently litigation privilege may not apply (although the LAP might).[121] Whether litigation or prosecution is reasonably foreseeable is a factual issue determined on a case by case basis.[122]

Just as in the United States, the party claiming legal professional privilege bears the burden of establishing it. And as with the DOJ, the SFO is generally not reluctant to challenge such claims where they appear to be weakly supported. In *SFO v. ENRC Limited*, for instance, the defendant, an international energy company, claimed that certain documents generated by solicitors and forensic accountants in connection with an SFO investigation of its activities were protected by LPP.[123] In the SFO's view, these documents—including solicitors' notes of interviews with current and former ENRC employees—were not privileged and had to be turned over. When ENRC refused, the SFO applied for, and received, a declaration from the High Court that the materials were not protected because, at the time the materials were created, a criminal prosecution was not "reasonably in prospect" in light of ongoing settlement discussions. While the High Court was reversed on appeal, the *ENRC* case shows a willingness by the SFO to aggressively challenge LPP claims in court.

The protections of the legal professional privilege may be lost where privileged material is intentionally referenced or disclosed in court proceedings, or if it is otherwise not maintained in confidence.[124] While waiver is interpreted relatively strictly against the party asserting privilege under U.S. law, in the United Kingdom, waiver is a more flexible concept. According to the High Court, the mere provision of a privileged document to a third party does not necessarily amount to a waiver of privilege. Instead, the "extent to which there is any such waiver depends on to what extent there is an express or implied restriction on subsequent use of the document." The central issue "is one of fact as to what were the express or implied terms" on which an otherwise privileged document was provided to a party outside of the attorney-client relationship.[125]

---

to obtain or provide legal advice, the privilege will apply [to communications between employees and company counsel].").

120. Rawlinson & Hunter Trustees SA v. Akers [2014] EWCA Civ. 136.

121. Tesco v. Oft [2017] CAT 6.

122. USA v. Philip Morris Inc. [2004] EWCA Civ. 330; Guinness Peat Properties v. Fitzroy Robinson Partnership [1987] 1 WLR 1027, 1035-36.

123. *See, e.g.*, SFO v. Eurasian Natural Resources Corporation Ltd (ENRC) [2018] EWCA Civ. 2006.

124. Great Atlantic Insurance Co. v. Home Insurance Co. [1981] 1 WLR 25; Attorney-General v. Guardian Newspapers Ltd. (No. 2) [1990] 1 AC 109.

125. FM Capital Partners v. Marino [2017] EWHC 3700 (Comm).

Further, U.K. courts recognize the principle of "selective waiver" with respect to privileged information disclosed to law enforcement. In some circumstances, a party may selectively disclose certain privileged documents to investigators while not waiving privilege over all documents pertaining to the same topic. Courts generally will not, however, permit selective disclosure of just a portion of a document or cherry-picking documents for disclosure in a way that can be misleading. Whether or not a selective waiver will be recognized as grounds to resist disclosure to a nongovernmental third party is determined objectively: "where it can be inferred that the person entitled to the benefit of the privilege has given up his right to resist the disclosure of the information in question, either generally or in a particular context," the person's conduct will be considered "inconsistent with his retention of that right."[126]

As in the United States, the legal professional privilege is subject to a "crime-fraud exception." This exception will override the privilege when the authorities can show that privileged materials were made (i) with a specific dishonest criminal purpose and (ii) in furtherance of or in preparation for that purpose. "What has to be shown prima facie is not merely that there is a bona fide and reasonably tenable charge of crime or fraud but a prima facie case that the communications in question were made in preparation for or in furtherance or as part of it."[127]

2. *Serious Fraud Office Powers to Compel Disclosure of Documents*

CJA 1987 Section 2(3) permits the SFO to issue written notices requiring individuals and entities to produce "any specified documents which appear to the Director to relate to any matter relevant to the investigation or any documents of a specified description which appear to him so to relate." Like grand jury subpoena *duces tecum* in the United States, the Section 2 notice may call for production of information or material at a specified place and time or may call for an immediate response. This section also permits the SFO to require the party producing documents to "provide an explanation of any of them" and, if any requested documents are not produced, to require the requested party to disclose, "to the best of his knowledge and belief, where they are." Failure to comply with a Section 2 request for documents without "reasonable excuse" is a criminal offense.

In an important recent decision, the U.K. Supreme Court determined that the SFO's powers under Section 2(3) do not apply extraterritorially, and therefore cannot be used to obtain documents from a non-U.K. company that does not carry on business in the United Kingdom or have a registered office there.[128] That case involved a Section 2(3) notice served on an executive of KBR, Inc. ("KBR"), a U.S. company, while in London. KBR's parent company did not itself have operations in the United Kingdom, but it did have U.K. subsidiaries, including KBR UK, which at the relevant time was under SFO investigation. Pursuant to this notice, the SFO demanded that KBR collect material held in the United States and produce it to the SFO.

KBR applied to quash the notice on the basis that it exceeded the scope of the SFO's powers and contravened the presumption that U.K. legislation does not have extraterritorial effect. Specifically, KBR argued that the SFO could not use its Section 2 powers to require a company incorporated abroad to produce documents held outside of the United Kingdom, even if the

126. Belhaj v. DPP [2018] EWHC 513 (Admin); *see also* AL v. XYZ Ltd [2018] EWHC 856.

127. Butler v. Board of Trade [1971] 1 Ch 680, 689C.

128. R (KBR Inc) v. Director of SFO [2021] UKSC 2.

targeted documents are within a corporate group that includes a British subsidiary. Overruling an earlier decision by the High Court, the Supreme Court agreed with KBR and determined that Section 2 does not apply extraterritorially. As a result of this decision, to the extent the SFO wishes to obtain materials located abroad, it must pursue them through one of the United Kingdom's mutual legal assistance arrangements (MLAs) (discussed in section V.B.).

The *KBR* decision stands in contrast to opinions addressing similar issues by U.S. courts. Under U.S. federal law, a foreign-based corporation may be compelled to disclose documents held abroad to U.S. law enforcement agencies via a subpoena served on a U.S. branch or subsidiary.[129]

3. Challenging the Serious Fraud Office's Use of Its Section 2 Powers

Just as defense counsel for a party receiving a grand jury subpoena can often negotiate its scope and terms with the DOJ, a solicitor representing the recipient of a Section 2 notice can seek to modify its terms in direct discussions with the SFO. If these discussions are unsuccessful, a Section 2 notice recipient can apply for judicial review of the SFO's actions (as KBR did in the case discussed above).

Judicial review—often referred to simply as "JR"—permits a party who has been affected by a decision of a government authority to ask a court to determine whether the government has acted lawfully and fairly.[130] There is no prescribed set of grounds on which judicial review may be sought, but in general they include:

- **Illegality**
  - A government agency will be considered to have acted illegally when it exercises one of its powers improperly or acts beyond the scope of its statutory authority.
- **Irrationality**
  - A government decision or action will be considered irrational if it is so unreasonable that no reasonable person acting reasonably could have made it.[131] This so-called "Wednesbury standard" presents a high hurdle for judicial review claimants and is rarely satisfied.
  - Alternatively, irrationality will be found when a judicial review claimant can show that the government decision was based on irrelevant facts or failed to take account of material facts or issues.
- **Procedural unfairness**
  - A government agency's procedures will be considered unfair if they are unreasonable or if they violate applicable procedures established by statute or by the agency itself.

---

129. *See, e.g.*, Matter of Marc Rich Co. A.G., 707 F.2d 663, 666–67 (2d Cir. 1983) (compelling compliance by a Swiss corporation with a grand jury document subpoena served on a U.S. subsidiary and noting that the test for production is "control, not location"); In re Grand Jury Proceedings, 691 F.2d 1384 (11th Cir. 1982).

130. CPR, Rule 54.1(2).

131. Associated Provincial Picture Houses Ltd v. Wednesbury Corporation [1948] 1 KB 223.

A threshold JR issue is whether the party challenging a government action has "sufficient interest" in the matter to do so. Similar to the concept of standing in the United States, whether a party has sufficient interest is determined by reference to a range of factors, including (i) the public importance of the issue, (ii) the nature of the government's action, (iii) the identity and role of the party, (iv) whether there is a more suitable party to make the judicial review application, and (v) the nature of the remedy sought.[132] Under this standard, British courts can, and often do, permit third parties with no direct interest in the government action at issue to seek judicial review if it is of significant public importance.

Assuming the sufficient interest standard is met, a party wishing to file a judicial review claim in court must then follow the Pre-Action Protocol for Judicial Review.[133] The protocol is designed to encourage parties to reach a negotiated resolution before resorting to the courts. In general, the protocol requires that a party injured by government action first send a letter to the offending government agency specifying the purportedly improper conduct within three months of its occurrence. The government agency must respond within a certain time frame (generally fourteen days). If the issue remains unresolved, the claimant can then proceed to petition the court for various forms of relief (e.g., a quashing order to set aside the government action, a mandatory order enjoining the government to fulfil its legal obligations, or a prohibiting order restraining the government from acting beyond its powers).

Unlike motions to quash a grand jury subpoena in the United States (which must be heard by the relevant district court), judicial review in the United Kingdom is discretionary. For a judicial review claim to move forward, the claimant must convince the court that there is a colorable chance for success on the merits (either through a written application to the court or during a court hearing).

C. The Financial Conduct Authority's Investigatory Powers

The FCA derives its investigatory powers from its governing statute, the Financial Services and Markets Act (FSMA) 2000, as amended by the Financial Services Act (FSA) 2012. The FCA is concerned primarily with regulating "authorised persons"—that is, individuals and entities that are specifically authorized to engage in regulated financial services activities (see FSMA, s.31). But, like the SEC and CFTC, it also has the authority to investigate nonauthorized persons and entities for breaches of FCA rules and for certain specific offenses, such as insider dealing, market abuse, and violations of British anti-money laundering laws.

Just as the SEC sends "Wells notices," the FCA's policy is to give written notice to a person or entity once a formal investigation has been launched, unless there are reasonable grounds not to or one of the statutory exceptions applies.[134] When a notification is made, "if

132. R v. Secretary of State for Foreign and Commonwealth Affairs, ex parte World Development Movement Ltd [1995] 1 All ER 611.

133. U.K. Ministry of Justice, *Pre-Action Protocol for Judicial Review*, *available at* http://www.justice.gov.uk/courts/procedure-rules/civil/protocol/prot_jrv.

134. Financial Services and Markets Act (FSMA), s. 170. A Wells notice—named for John Wells, head of the SEC committee that proposed the idea—is a letter that the SEC may send to individuals or firms to alert them of a pending enforcement action. The purpose of a Wells notice is to give the enforcement

there is a subsequent change in the scope or conduct of the investigation and, in the FCA's opinion, the [individual or entity] is likely to be significantly prejudiced if not made aware of this, [the individual or entity] shall be given written notice of the change. . . . [T]his may include situations where there may be unnecessary costs from dealing with an aspect of an investigation which the FCA no longer intends to pursue."[135] This means that once an investigation is launched, if a target does not receive formal notice that it has ended, it is safe to assume that it remains ongoing.

The FCA's powers to compel disclosure of documents and information relevant to an investigation are set forth in FSMA Sections 165 to 169. Like the SFO, the FCA also has the power to conduct compulsory interviews pursuant to FSMA Sections 171 to 173. "In any particular case, the FCA will decide which powers, or combination of powers, are most appropriate to use having regard to all the circumstances."[136] The FCA's exercise of its powers in any matter is subject to the same judicial review process described above.

1. *Information Requests (FSMA, s. 165)*

Section 165 authorizes the FCA to serve written notice on an authorized person—for example, an exchange or financial services firm—requiring disclosure of specific categories of documents and information related to the FCA's regulatory function.[137] This power can also be exercised against any person "connected with" an authorized person (e.g., officers, managers, and directors) along with investment exchanges and operators of collective investment (i.e., pension) schemes even if not registered with the FCA.[138] If a document subject to the FCA's Section 165 powers is in the possession of a third party, the FCA can require the third party to disclose it (subject to certain exceptions).[139]

In practice, the FCA generally uses Section 165 information requests while deciding whether to open a formal investigation. Once an investigation has begun, the FCA will typically rely on its more robust powers under Sections 171 and 172.

2. *Skilled Persons Report (FSMA, s. 166)*

The FCA can require any authorized person (or any person connected with such an authorized person) to provide "a report on the matter concerned" prepared by the target firm itself or a third-party "skilled person" (usually a law or accounting firm) paid for at the target firm's expense.[140] In effect, this provision allows the FCA to force businesses under its juris-

---

target an opportunity to explain why the enforcement action should not be brought. The SEC is not legally required to issue a Wells notice, so the absence of one does not necessarily mean that an enforcement action is not underway.

135. *FCA Enforcement Guide*, s. 4.1.

136. *Id.*, s. 3.1.

137. FSMA, ss. 165(1), (4).

138. *Id.*, ss. 165(7), (11).

139. *Id.*, ss. 175(1), (5), (5A).

140. *Id.*, s. 166(3).

diction to undergo an investigation conducted by an independent third party. The target company will be on the hook for the "skilled person's" fees, regardless of who the FCA selects.

The FCA will generally not use its powers under Section 166 to gather historic information or evidence for determining whether enforcement action may be appropriate. Rather, skilled persons reports are typically reserved for situations where the FCA's objective is to obtain expert analysis or recommendations for the purposes of seeking remedial action. Where it exercises this power, the FCA will inform both the target firm and the skilled person of the specific concerns that led the FCA to issue a Section 166 notice and the possible uses of the resulting report.[141]

3. Investigations into General and Specific Concerns (FSMA, ss. 167–68)

When the FCA is interested in obtaining evidence for the purpose of deciding whether enforcement action may be appropriate, it will typically appoint an investigator under Section 167. Section 167 investigators have the power to require the subject of the investigation (or any party connected to the subject) to "(a) attend before the investigator at a specified time and place and answer questions; or (b) otherwise to provide such information as the investigator may require."[142] In addition, the investigator "may also require any person [subject to the investigation or otherwise] to produce at a specified time and place any specified documents or documents of a specified description."

Investigators appointed under Section 168 have essentially the same powers as those appointed under Section 167, except that Section 168 investigators have the additional power to interview and demand documents from any party (regardless of whether they are connected to the subject of the investigation) so long as doing so is "necessary or expedient" to the investigation.[143]

4. Investigations to Assist Overseas Authorities (FSMA, s. 169)

At the request of an overseas regulator—such as the DOJ, SEC, or CFTC—the FCA may use its powers under Section 165 to require the production of documents or information, or to appoint a person to investigate a matter on behalf of a foreign government.[144] The FCA has discretion when responding to a foreign regulator's request. When considering whether to use its investigative power under Section 169, the FCA will first consider whether it can obtain the information voluntarily and without using its formal powers. Where that is not possible, the FCA will take into account the factors listed in Section 169(4), giving "particular weight to the seriousness of the case and its importance to persons in the United Kingdom, and to the public interest."[145]

141. *FCA Enforcement Guide*, s. 3.6.

142. FSMA, s. 171(1).

143. *Id.*, s. 172.

144. *Id.*, s. 169.

145. *FCA Enforcement Guide*, s. 3.15.

5. Compulsory Financial Conduct Authority Interviews

As noted above, FCA investigators can require the target of an investigation or any person "connected with" the target to attend a compulsory interview.[146] Like SFO Section 2 interviews, an individual subject to a compulsory FCA interview cannot refuse to answer questions except to the extent that the answer implicates the legal professional privilege. A statement made to an FCA investigator during a compulsory interview is "admissible in evidence in any [noncriminal] proceedings, so long as it also complies with any requirements governing the admissibility of evidence in the circumstances in question."[147] In subsequent criminal proceedings against the interviewee, however, statements made during a compulsory interview cannot be used by prosecutors against them: "(a) no evidence relating to the statement may be adduced, and (b) no question relating to it may be asked, by or on behalf of the prosecution . . . unless evidence relating to it is adduced, or a question related to it is asked, in the proceedings by or on behalf of that person."[148]

This is a stark difference with U.S. practice. In light of the Fifth Amendment privilege, individuals subjected to a deposition or interview by a civil regulatory body in the United States can refuse to answer on the basis of self-incrimination (even if there is no criminal case pending).[149]

An individual subject to a compulsory interview with the FCA, therefore, risks that their statements may be used against them in any subsequent civil proceedings. It may thus be preferable for such an individual to submit to a voluntary interview where answering questions would not be compulsory. However, a person may not choose to attend a voluntary interview in lieu of a compulsory one, nor may they demand a compulsory interview instead of submitting to questioning voluntarily; permission to sit for a voluntary interview in lieu of a compulsory one is granted at the FCA's discretion.[150] An individual who is suspected of a criminal offense will typically be asked to attend an interview voluntarily and be interviewed under caution (discussed below).

D. Investigatory Powers of the Crown Prosecution Service

The investigatory powers of the CPS and Crown prosecutors are specified in the Serious Organised Crime and Police Act (SOCPA) 2005. These powers only apply to investigations of certain offenses, including offenses under the Bribery Act 2010 and offenses under the

---

146. FSMA, ss. 171–72.

147. *Id.*, s. 174(1).

148. *Id.*, s. 174(2). Note that this prohibition does not apply to criminal proceedings against the interviewee for knowingly providing false or misleading information to investigators.

149. Lefkowitz v. Turley, 414 U.S. 70, 76 (1973) ("The [Fifth] Amendment not only protects the individual against being involuntarily called as a witness against himself in a criminal prosecution but also privileges him not to answer official questions put to him in any other proceeding, civil or criminal, formal or informal, where the answers might incriminate him in future criminal proceedings.")

150. *FCA Enforcement Guide*, ss. 4.18–19.

Sanctions and Anti-Money Laundering Act 2018.[151] Otherwise, they are equivalent to the SFO's Section 2 powers.

II. VOLUNTARY INTERVIEWS WITH THE GOVERNMENT

A. Voluntary Interviews with the Federal Bureau of Investigation

During the initial phases of a white-collar crime investigation, FBI agents often seek out potential witnesses to the conduct at issue for informal, voluntary interviews. As a matter of DOJ policy, such interviews are almost never recorded or transcribed (except when the interviewee is in custody).[152] Rather, they are memorialized by the interviewing agents using FBI form FD-302, commonly referred to simply as a "302." During the interview itself, the FBI will typically summarize what was said by the interviewee in a handwritten note. At some point afterwards, one of the FBI special agents who conducted the interview will formalize the handwritten summary into a typed 302; if notes were not taken during the interview, the 302 will be generated based simply on the agents' recollection of what transpired.

There is no requirement that the 302 indicate the questions posed to the interviewee or detail everything that was discussed. Nor is there any requirement that the interviewee be allowed to review the 302 to correct mistakes or inaccuracies before it is finalized. As a result, there is an obvious risk that 302s may lack context or can create an inaccurate or incomplete record of what the interviewee said.

Nevertheless, 302s are often one of the most important pieces of evidence in a criminal case since they are usually the only contemporaneous document capturing what a witness told to investigators.[153] Consequently, whatever is recorded in the 302 will essentially lock the interviewee into the version of events as summarized by the FBI. This can make it difficult for the interviewee to subsequently deviate from what is recorded in the 302 during later interviews or while on the witness stand.[154] And, if the 302 implicates the interviewee in a crime, the 302 can be used by prosecutors to pressure the interviewee into become a cooperating witness for the government in a prosecution against a third party.

For a defendant preparing to defend a criminal case at trial, knowing what the government's witnesses have already told investigators will obviously be a critical part of crafting a defense strategy. But while the government must generally disclose 302s to the defense, it need not do so until shortly before, or even during, trial under the Jencks Act (18 U.S.C.

---

151. Serious Organised Crime and Police Act (SOCPA), s. 61(1).

152. *See* Memorandum from DOJ FBI Office of the General Counsel to All Field Offices and HQ Divisions (Mar. 23, 2006), *available at* https://www.nytimes.com/packages/pdf/national/20070402_FBI_Memo.pdf.

153. *See, e.g.*, Sara Kropf, *What Is an FBI 302? The Problematic Nature of FBI Agents' Interview Memos*, (May 18, 2017), *available at* https://grandjurytarget.com/2017/05/18/what-is-an-fbi-302-the-problematic-nature-of-fbi-agents-interview-memos/.

154. For example, an interviewee whose later testimony contradicts what is recorded in an earlier 302 can subject themself to criminal charges of obstruction of justice (18 U.S.C. § 1503), perjury (18 U.S.C. § 1621), or making false statements (18 U.S.C. § 1001).

§ 3500—discussed in further detail in chapter 5). This usually means that for much of the pretrial phase of a federal criminal case, the prosecution enjoys a significant informational advantage over the defense.

B. Voluntary Interviews with the Serious Fraud Office, Financial Conduct Authority, and Crown Prosecution Service

When an individual agrees to conduct an interview with U.K. law enforcement voluntarily (that is, without being subject to one of the government's statutory powers to compel testimony discussed earlier), the interviews are subject to the Police and Criminal Evidence Act (PACE) 1984.[155] Individuals suspected of committing a criminal offense are generally always interviewed "under caution" to ensure that their statements will be admissible in subsequent proceedings.

As opposed to the FBI's policy of not recording voluntary witness interviews, interviews with the SFO, FCA, CPS and other British law enforcement agencies must generally always be recorded.[156] Further, at the conclusion of the interview the interviewee must be given the opportunity to clarify anything they have said and asked if there is anything they wish to add.[157]

Similar to a "Miranda warning" in the United States,[158] the standard caution used in the United Kingdom when the individual has been offered or has received legal advice is:

> *You do not have to say anything. But it may harm your defence if you do not mention when questioned something which you later rely on in Court. Anything you do say may be given in evidence.*[159]

Pursuant to the terms of this caution, individuals have a right to silence during noncompulsory interviews with law enforcement. A caution must be given if there are "reasonable, objective grounds for suspicion, based on known facts or information which are relevant to the likelihood the offence has been committed and the person questioned committed it."[160] An investigator's failure to give a caution can render the suspect's statements inadmissible in court.

Importantly, however, when an individual elects to remain silent in response to voluntary questioning under caution and is subsequently charged, an adverse inference can be made

155. Police and Criminal Evidence Act (PACE), s. 67(9).

156. PACE Code E, ss. 2–3.

157. *Id.*, ss. 3.19–3.20.

158. The so-called "Miranda warning" derives its name from a 1966 Supreme Court decision, *Miranda v. Arizona,* 384 U.S. 436 (1966), which concluded that "if a person in custody is to be subjected to interrogation, he must be first informed in clear and unequivocal terms that he has the right to remain silent. . . . The warning of the right to remain silent must be accompanied by the explanation that anything said can and will be used against the individual in court."

159. PACE Code C, s. 10.5.

160. *Id.*, Note 10A.

against them in support of proving their guilt during a criminal trial under Section 34 of the Criminal Justice and Public Order Act (CJPOA) 1994. This statute provides:

> (1) **Where, in any proceedings against a person for an offence, evidence is given that the accused—**
>
> (a) at any time before he was charged with an offence, on being questioned under caution by a constable trying to discover whether or by whom the offence had been committed, failed to mention any fact relied on in his defence in those proceedings; or
>
> (b) on being charged with the offence or officially informed that he might be prosecuted for it, failed to mention any such fact . . . being a fact which in the circumstances existing at the time the accused could reasonably have been expected to mention when so questioned, charged or informed, as the case may be . . .
>
> (2) . . .
>
> (c) the court, in determining whether there is a case to answer; and
>
> (d) the court or jury, in determining whether the accused is guilty of the offence charged, may draw such inferences from the failure as appear proper."

The inference is intended to discourage defendants from fabricating a defense during trial and to encourage early disclosure of facts that may be relevant to a genuine defense. As Lord Justice Rose explained in *R v. Roble* [1997] EWCA Crim 118, "The purpose of the [CJPOA] provisions is to permit adverse inferences to be drawn where there has been late fabrication, to this extent, to encourage speedy disclosure of a genuine defence or of facts which may go towards establishing a genuine defence." Lord Justice Rose reasoned further that, if a defendant disclosed information to his solicitor in advance of a police interview or being charged that is "capable of giving rise to a defence," the defendant can admit evidence of such disclosure at trial "to rebut any inference of subsequent fabrication. But if such evidence was not disclosed, or was disclosed at a late stage in the sequence of interview, charge and trial, adverse inferences can be drawn by the jury."

This is a significant difference with U.S. law, which strictly prohibits such an inference being drawn from an individual's silence except in civil proceedings.[161] Note, however, that the adverse inference will only be applied if the accused failed to mention something that he or she "could reasonably have been expected to mention."[162] Whether a person's silence was "reasonable" will depend on the circumstances and courts will consider various subjective factors in making this determination.[163]

161. *See, e.g.*, Baxter v. Palmigiano, 425 U.S. 308, 312 (1976); Griffin v. California, 380 U.S. 609, 612-615 (1965); LaSalle Bank Lake View v. Seguban, 54 F.3d 387, 389-90 (7th Cir. 1995); *see also* Robert Heidt, *The Conjurer's Circle: The Fifth Amendment Privilege in Civil Cases*, 91 YALE L.J. 1062 (1982) (discussing differing implications of invoking the Fifth Amendment privilege in criminal and civil cases).

162. Criminal Justice and Public Order Act (CJPOA), s. 34(1)(b).

163. R v. Condron [1997] 1 WLR 827; R v. Argent [1997] 2 Cr App R 27.

While an adverse inference can seriously diminish a defendant's chance for acquittal, a conviction cannot rest on the inference alone.[164] Moreover, if a defendant remains silent during questioning on the advice of their lawyer, they may avoid an adverse inference if a two-part test is satisfied. Specifically, when a defendant claims his or her silence was based on legal advice, the factfinder must consider (i) whether the defendant genuinely relied on legal advice and (ii) whether it was reasonable for the defendant to do so in the circumstances. As the Court of Appeals stated in *R v. Beckles* [2004] EWCA Crim 2766:

> In our judgment, in a case where a solicitor's advice is relied upon by the defendant, the ultimate question for the jury remains under [CJPOA] section 34 whether the facts relied on at the trial were facts which the defendant could reasonably have been expected to mention at interview. If they were not, that is the end of the matter. If the jury consider that the defendant genuinely relied on the advice, that is not necessarily the end of the matter. It may still have been reasonable for him to rely on the advice, or the advice may not have been the true explanation of his silence. . . . His reasonableness in not mentioning the facts remains to be determined by the jury. If they conclude he was acting unreasonably they can draw an adverse inference from the failure to mention the facts.

Thus, simply claiming that one's solicitor instructed silence will generally not suffice to avoid an adverse inference. For this reason, it is generally good practice for solicitors advising on interviews with government investigators to document their instructions along with the underlying rationale.

1. Pre-Charge Engagement

"Pre-charge engagement" refers to voluntary engagement between investigators and a potential defendant after a formal PACE interview has taken place but before charges are issued. As with the proffer process in the United States, pre-charge engagement is a voluntary process that may be terminated by either party at any time. Pre-charge engagement typically involves the suspect providing assistance to law enforcement in the hope of avoiding charges altogether or, if charges are inevitable, being charged with a less serious offense. To this end, during pre-charge engagement a suspect is usually given the opportunity to identify lines of inquiry that investigators should pursue, identify and grant access to relevant materials, and provide contact details for potential witnesses.[165]

Pre-charge engagement is encouraged by the Code for Crown Prosecutors: with respect to making a charging decision under the Full Code or Threshold Test (discussed in chapter 3), suspects and defense counsel are permitted to submit information to the prosecutor to help inform the prosecutor's decision, and "in appropriate cases, the prosecutor may invite the suspect or their representative to do so."[166] The process is seen as aiding suspects through early identification of lines of inquiry that may lead to evidence or material that points away from them and by narrowing the key issues. At the same time, it can help inform

---

164. R v. Cowan [1996] QB 373.

165. Attorney General's Guidelines on Disclosure (2020), Annex B.

166. Code for Crown Prosecutors, s. 3.4.

a prosecutor's charging decision to avoid a case being charged that would otherwise be stopped later in proceedings when further information becomes available.[167]

Unlike PACE interviews under caution, a suspect participating in pre-charge engagement does not risk an adverse inference for anything he or she might fail to disclose. Accordingly, the attorney general's guidance states that "investigators and prosecutors should not seek to initiate, or agree to, pre-charge engagement in respect of matters where they are likely to seek to rely on the contents of the suspect's answers as evidence at trial. Pre-charge engagement should not therefore be used for putting new summaries of the case to the defense, and where deemed necessary such accounts should be put to the suspect in a further [PACE] interview."[168]

Since, by definition, pre-charge engagement occurs prior to the institution of criminal proceedings, the statutory disclosure rules discussed in chapter 5 are not implicated. Prosecutors must nevertheless consider disclosing potentially exculpatory evidence to a suspect during the pre-charge process "to ensure that the discussions are fair and that the suspect is not mislead as to the strength of the prosecution case."[169] Prosecutors are additionally required to create a full written record, signed and approved by the suspect, of all pre-charge engagement discussions. They must also "record every key action involved in the process, such as the provision of written information on pre-charge engagement to the suspect, any informal discussions with the suspect's representative about entering the process, or any formal letter of invitation sent or received."[170]

III. SEARCH WARRANTS

A. Search Warrants in the United States

Federal law enforcement officers wanting to seize potential evidence from physical premises, computer databases, or electronic devices must generally first obtain a search warrant from a magistrate or district court judge.[171] The scope of items that may be seized pursuant to a search warrant is extremely broad, extending to anything connected to criminal behavior (whether it be "mere evidence" or something used in a crime's commission, the fruits of crime, or contraband).[172] Search warrants are regularly used by the FBI and DOJ in relation to white-collar crimes because, unlike grand jury subpoenas, they allow for potentially relevant evidence to be immediately seized and preserved without first tipping off a prospective defendant that an investigation is underway (thereby minimizing the risk that evidence may be hidden or destroyed).

---

167. Attorney General's Guidelines on Disclosure (2020), Annex B, s. 10.

168. *Id.*, s. 7.

169. *Id.*, s. 22.

170. *Id.*, ss. 25–26.

171. *See* Fed. R. Crim. P. 41.

172. Warden v. Hayden, 387 U.S. 294, 307 (1967); Fed. R. Crim. P. 41(c).

Search warrants are subject to the Fourth Amendment, which "safeguard[s] individual privacy against arbitrary governmental intrusions."[173] "The chief evil that prompted the framing and adoption of the Fourth Amendment was the 'indiscriminate searches and seizures' conducted by the British under the authority of general warrants [during the colonial era]."[174] Accordingly, a "search must be confined to the terms and limitations of the warrant authorizing it" and "must be conducted in a manner that minimizes unwarranted intrusions upon privacy."[175]

The Fourth Amendment applies to any items or premises in which an individual or entity has a "reasonable expectation of privacy," which includes personal computers and other electronic devices, and temporary dwellings such as hotel rooms.[176] Courts have ruled that individuals have a limited expectation of privacy on a computer or other device owned or monitored by their employer.[177] Law enforcement agents can therefore usually obtain a suspect's work emails and documents stored on a work computer or server by simply requesting them from the company (which will typically comply in order to maintain a constructive, cooperative posture with the DOJ). To preserve privilege, therefore, defense counsel should always ensure that communications with a client take place exclusively through personal devices and personal email accounts.

Federal Rule of Criminal Procedure 41 requires the government to execute search warrants "during the daytime, unless the judge for good cause expressly authorizes execution at another time."[178] "Daytime" is defined as the hours between "6:00 am and 10:00 pm according to local time."[179] In white-collar crime cases, FBI agents executing a search warrant against a business will often arrive either very early in the morning (in a so-called "dawn raid") or at the end of the business day.

Under the "plain view" exception, law enforcement is authorized to seize "illegal or evidentiary items visible to a police officer whose access to the object has some prior Fourth Amendment justification and who has probable cause to suspect that the item is connected with criminal activity."[180] Put differently, while executing a valid search warrant, officers can seize other items in plain view that they may come across (even if such other items do not fall within the warrant).[181]

---

173. Phaneuf v. Fraikin, 448 F.3d 591, 595 (2d Cir. 2006); *see also* Byrd v. United States, 138 S. Ct. 1518, 1526 (2018).

174. Payton v. New York, 445 U.S. 573, 583 (1980).

175. United States v. Matias, 836 F.2d 744, 747 (2d Cir. 1988).

176. To mount a successful Fourth Amendment challenge, "a defendant must demonstrate that he personally has an expectation of privacy in the place searched." United States v. Haqq, 278 F.3d 44, 47 (2d Cir. 2002). Thus, a "Fourth Amendment 'search' . . . does not occur unless the search invades an object or area [in which] one has a subjective expectation of privacy that society is prepared to accept as objectively reasonable." United States v. Hayes, 551 F.3d 138, 143 (2d Cir. 2008).

177. *See, e.g.*, United States v. Simons, 206 F.2d 392, 398 (4th Cir. 2000).

178. Fed. R. Crim. P. 41(e)(2)(A)(ii).

179. Fed. R. Crim. P. 41(a)(2)(B).

180. United States v. Gamble, 388 F.3d 74, 76 (2d Cir. 2004).

181. Texas v. Brown, 460 U.S. 730, 742 (1983).

1. Obtaining a Search Warrant

To satisfy the Fourth Amendment, the government must submit an affidavit to a magistrate or district court judge that describes "sufficient facts to induce a reasonably prudent person to believe that a search will uncover contraband or evidence of a crime."[182] This is a relatively low bar: probable cause requires "only a probability or a substantial chance of criminal activity, not an actual showing of such activity."[183] Further, a reviewing court will generally afford substantial deference to law enforcement's determination that probable cause exists, and will limit its "inquiry to whether [the DOJ or FBI] had a 'substantial basis'" for reaching this conclusion.[184]

Once probable cause is established, the warrant must specify the premises or devices to be searched with "particularity." The particularity requirement prohibits warrants from specifying only a generalized offense, leaving it "to the discretion of the executing officials the decision as to which persons should be arrested and which places should be searched."[185] To be sufficiently particular, a warrant must satisfy three requirements: it must (i) identify the specific offense for which law enforcement have established probable cause, (ii) describe the place to be searched, and (iii) specify the items to be seized by their relation to designated crimes.[186] As applied to warrants for business records, the particularity requirement will not be satisfied where the warrant "imposed too wide a time or failed to include one altogether."[187]

Finally, a search warrant must comply with the doctrine of "overbreadth," which is "an intersection point for probable cause and particularity principles." This doctrine recognizes that a warrant's unparticularized description of the items subject to seizure may cause it to exceed the scope of otherwise duly established probable cause. Thus, "a warrant is overbroad if its 'description of the objects to be seized' . . . is broader than can be justified by the probable cause upon which the warrant is based."[188]

If a search warrant is issued without probable cause or fails the particularity or overbreadth requirements, any evidence the government seizes pursuant to the deficient warrant can be precluded from use as evidence under the "exclusionary rule."[189] The exclusionary

182. United States v. Sidwell, 440 F.3d 865, 868 (7th Cir. 2006); *see also* Ornelas v. United States, 517 U.S. 690, 696 (1996); United States v. Walker, 237 F.3d 845, 850 (7th Cir. 2001).

183. Illinois v. Gates, 462 U.S. 213, 243 n.13 (1983).

184. United States v. Raymonda, 780 F.3d 105, 113 (2d Cir. 2015).

185. Steagald v. United States, 451 U.S. 204, 220 (1981); Andreson v. Maryland, 427 U.S. 463, 480 (1976) (warrants cannot permit a "general, exploratory rummaging in a person's belongings"); Kentucky v. King, 563 U.S. 452, 459 (2011).

186. Ulbricht, 858 F.3d at 99 (citing United States v. Galpin, 720 F.3d 436, 445 (2d Cir. 2013)).

187. United States v. Zemlyansky, 945 F. Supp. 2d 438, 454 (S.D.N.Y. 2013); United States v. Levy, 11-cr-62, 2013 WL 664712, at *11 n.7 (S.D.N.Y. Feb. 25, 2013).

188. United States v. Lustyik, 57 F. Supp. 3d 213, 228 (S.D.N.Y. 2014).

189. Weeks v. United States, 232 U.S. 383, 391–93 (1914); Elkins v. United States, 364 U.S. 206, 209 (1960) (exclusionary rule "excludes in a federal criminal prosecution evidence obtained by federal agents in violation of the defendant's Fourth Amendment rights").

rule is a "prudential doctrine" created by the Supreme Court to "compel respect" for the Fourth Amendment and deter violations of the constitutional right against "unreasonable searches and seizures."[190] Under the "fruit of the poisonous tree" doctrine, the exclusionary rule will also apply to any evidence obtained as a direct or indirect result of an unlawful search.[191] While the exclusionary rule provides defendants with a basis to argue that incriminating evidence should be precluded from trial, it is subject to various exceptions (see chapter 6).[192]

a. Special Considerations for Searches of Electronically Stored Information

Search warrants targeting hard drives and other forms of electronically stored information are subject to stricter particularity requirements. This is because the "seizure of a computer hard drive, and its subsequent retention by the government, can give the government possession of a vast trove of personal information about the person to whom the drive belongs, much of which may be entirely irrelevant to the criminal investigation that led to the seizure."[193]

Courts have recognized that once the government obtains authorization to search a hard drive, it could "claim that the contents of every file it chose to open were in plain view and, therefore, admissible even if they implicate the defendant in a crime not contemplated by the warrant." This presents a "serious risk that every warrant for electronic information will become, in effect, a general warrant, rendering the Fourth Amendment irrelevant." Accordingly, "heightened sensitivity to the particularity requirement in the context of digital searches" is necessary.[194]

b. The "All-Records Exception"

White collar crime cases often implicate the "all-records exception," which provides that "when there is probable cause to believe that an entire business is 'pervaded' or 'permeated' with fraud, seizure of all records of the business is appropriate, and broad language used in a search warrant will not offend the particularity requirement." For the all-records exception to apply, the affidavit in support of the search warrant need not necessarily lay out "specific factual evidence demonstrating that every part of the enterprise in question is engaged in fraud"; rather, it must only reference "sufficient factual evidence of fraudulent activity from

190. Davis v. United States, 564 U.S. 229, 236 (2011).

191. Wong Sun v. United States, 371 U.S. 471, 484–85 (1963); Segura v. United States, 468 U.S. 796, 815 (1984) (fruit of the poisonous tree doctrine will only apply if the underlying "illegality is at least the 'but for' cause of the discovery of the evidence").

192. *See, e.g.*, United States v. Leon, 468 U.S. 897 (1984) (establishing the "good faith exception" which permits evidence obtained through an invalid search warrant to be admitted if law enforcement relied on it in good faith); Walder v. United States, 347 U.S. 62, 65–66 (1954) permitting evidence seized in violation of the Fourth Amendment to be used to impeach a defendant's testimony); United States v. Janis, 428 U.S. 433, 455 n.31 (1976) (exclusionary rule does not apply to evidence obtained by searches abroad conducted by foreign officials).

193. United States v. Ganias, 824 F.3d 199, 217 (2d Cir. 2016).

194. United States v. Galpin, 720 F.3d 436, 447 (2d Cir. 2013).

which a magistrate could infer that those activities are 'just the tip of the iceberg.'"[195] Courts assessing the applicability of this exception must be satisfied that the government has provided "sufficient probable cause to believe that the *entire* business operation is a scam."[196]

Practice Note

"Taint" Teams

When a search warrant is executed on a lawyer's home or office, or the offices of an in-house lawyer at a business, there is an inherent risk that investigators may encounter materials protected by a legitimate claim of privilege. Accordingly, the DOJ conducts such searches with caution, and before one can move forward, the AUSA in charge of the investigation must receive authorization from the U.S. Attorney for their district and consult with the Criminal Division's Office of Enforcement Operations, Policy and Statutory Enforcement Unit (PSEU).

To limit the risk that seized materials are ruled inadmissible, DOJ policy sets forth procedures designed to ensure that privileged materials are not improperly viewed, seized, or retained during the course of a search. In keeping with this policy (Justice Manual § 9-13.420), the search warrant must be drawn as specifically as possible to minimize the need to search and review privileged material to which no exception applies. It may nevertheless be necessary for investigators to conduct a limited review of arguably privileged material to ascertain whether the material is covered by the warrant. To protect the attorney-client privilege and to ensure that the investigation is not compromised by exposure to privileged material relating to the investigation or to defense strategy, a special privilege team—called a "taint team"—comprised of agents and lawyers not involved in the underlying investigation is usually created.

Taint teams will review potentially privileged material, isolate it, and send anything that is not privileged to the AUSAs overseeing the case. Since taint teams are DOJ employees and therefore not truly independent, their use has drawn considerable scrutiny from defense lawyers and the courts.[197] To address independence concerns, in particularly sensitive cases, a court may order that a DOJ taint team be replaced by a district court judge or a "special master" (the name given to an external lawyer appointed by the court).

In two recent high-profile cases, taint teams and special masters were used to review materials seized during FBI raids on the homes and offices of former President Trump's two personal attorneys: Michael Cohen and Rudy Giuliani.[198]

In May 2020, the DOJ's Fraud Section announced the creation of a Special Matters Unit, a dedicated, walled-off team of government attorneys focused on overseeing the review of seized documents to ensure that privileged materials are not disclosed to the prosecutors handling the related case. This innovation followed criticism by the Fourth Circuit Court of Appeals of the well-established taint team procedure in *In re Search Warrant Issued June 13, 2019*, 942 F.3d 159, 165 (4th Cir. 2019). There, a law firm whose files were seized by the FBI executing a

195. United States v. Burke, 718 F. Supp. 1130, 1139–40 (S.D.N.Y. 1989).

196. Zemlyansky, 945 F. Supp. 2d at 461.

197. *See, e.g.*, In re Grand Jury Subpoenas, 454 F.3d 511, 523 (6th Cir. 2006); United States v. Esformes, No. 16-20549-CR, 2018 WL 5919517 (S.D. Fla. Nov. 13, 2018); United States v. Elbaz, 396 F. Supp. 3d 583 (D. Md. 2019); In re Search Warrant Issued June 13, 2019, 942 F. 3d 159 (4th Cir. 2019).

198. *See* Eileen H. Rumfelt, *Taint Team or Special Master: One Recent Analysis*, Am. B. Assoc. (Sept. 27, 2018); Jack Queen, *Feds Tread Lightly on Giuliani Devices After "Taint Team" Flak*, Law360, May 7, 2021.

warrant argued that the use of a taint team to filter for privilege is "incompatible with courts' historical protection of the attorney-client privilege and the work-product doctrine." The firm pointed specifically to the inherent risk of "improprieties when government agents are authorized to rummage through attorney-client communications" and the likelihood that this practice "will chill the free flow of information between clients and lawyers." The Fourth Circuit agreed, stating that the use of taint teams has "the Government's fox in charge of guarding the Law Firm's henhouse."

B. Search Warrants in the United Kingdom

1. *Serious Fraud Office Search Warrants*

If SFO prosecutors are unable to obtain evidence through their Section 2 powers, or if they believe that issuing a Section 2 demand would compromise the investigation or be ineffective, they can obtain a search warrant under the Police and Criminal Evidence Act (PACE) 1984 or the Proceeds of Crime Act (POCA) 2002.[199] To do so, a member of the SFO must provide, ex parte, a sworn statement to a magistrate or district judge detailing their grounds for believing that a search warrant is necessary and that the desired documents are on the premises to be searched.[200] Unlike in the United States, the SFO is obligated to disclose anything that might militate against approving the warrant: as it was put by Lord Justice Hughes in *Re Stanford* [2010] 1 WLR 941, the advocate for the SFO must "put on his defence hat and ask himself, what, if he was representing the defendant or a party with a relevant interest, he would be saying to the judge."

If the judicial officer agrees with the SFO's determination, a warrant will be issued authorizing a police officer, generally accompanied by a member of the SFO,

> (a) to enter (using such force as is reasonably necessary for the purpose) and search the premises, and (b) to take possession of any documents appearing to be documents of the description specified in the information or to take in relation to any documents so appearing any other steps which may appear to be necessary for preserving them and preventing interference with them.[201]

In short, while executing a search warrant, the SFO is permitted to seize any documents they reasonably believe to be relevant to their investigation.[202] The warrant must be executed within three months from when it was issued and it must specify, among other things, the statute under which it was issued, the specific location(s) to be searched, and a description of the categories of documents sought.

Search warrants can be challenged by way of a judicial review application lodged in the High Court against the SFO and/or the court that approved the order. In general, High Court judges are more inclined to focus on the extent to which a search has infringed upon

199. CJA, s. 2.

200. *Id.*

201. CJA, s. 5.

202. CJPA, s. 50.

the target's private life—a right codified in Article 8 of the Human Rights Act 1998—and subject those making an ex parte search warrant application to a demanding standard. As an alternative to judicial review, the target of a search warrant can file an appeal against the grant of the warrant under Section 59 of the Criminal Justice and Police Act (CJPA) 2001.

If law enforcement fails to follow the procedural rules in obtaining or executing a search warrant, the warrant may be quashed and any seized property returned. Like the "exclusionary rule" in the United States, British courts can prevent the prosecution from using illegally seized items in any subsequent court proceedings. For example, if an investigating agency has carried out the search and has seized items but failed to leave schedules to the warrant at the searched premises, the search can be ruled unlawful. In *Tchenguiz v. Serious Fraud Office & Others*,[203] arguably the most high-profile example of an authority having a search ruled unlawful, the SFO was shown to have failed to check the credibility of information it presented to the court when applying for the search warrants. As such, the High Court determined the SFO had failed to fulfill its duty of ensuring that "what is put before the judge is clear and comprehensive so that the judge can rely on it and form his judgment on the basis of a presentation in which he has complete trust and confidence as to its accuracy and completeness."[204] The case ended with the SFO publicly apologizing to the two brothers whose homes were raided, paying them £4.5 million in compensation, and being heavily criticized by the court for both a lack of understanding and at least one serious factual omission in its application for the search warrant.[205]

If the High Court quashes a search warrant, it will usually require the seized material to be returned. But under CJPA Section 59, the SFO and other law enforcement agencies can apply to the High Court for permission to retain the material while it reapplies to the Crown Court for, in effect, a new order justifying the old seizure. In these situations, the Crown Court has discretion to authorize the retention of the material seized, despite the unlawfulness of the original search. This discretion can be exercised in circumstances where, if the seized material were to be returned, the court would have grounds to immediately issue another warrant to seize it. As a result, the authorities effectively get a second chance to get a warrant application right.

Practice Note

The SFO's Win in *R (McKenzie) v. SFO*

On June 19, 2015, Colin McKenzie was arrested at Heathrow Airport on suspicion of committing an offense under the Bribery Act 2010 in connection with a $54 million contract awarded to his company. Upon his arrest, police officers seized a USB stick, an iPhone and another mobile device, and a laptop computer pursuant to section 54 of PACE (which authorizes seizure of the personal effects of a person taken into custody). Six days later, the SFO served a notice under section 2(3) of the CJA that required McKenzie to produce further items relevant

203. [2012] EWHC 2254 (Admin).

204. *Id.* at para. 88.

205. Kirstin Ridley, "SFO Settles $500 Million Tchenguiz Damages Claim," Reuters (July 31, 2014), *available at* https://www.reuters.com/article/uk-britain-settlement-tchenguiz-idUKKBN0G00SD20140731.

to its investigation. In response, McKenzie produced an additional mobile device and various other pieces of computer equipment.

Soon thereafter, the SFO notified McKenzie's solicitors that one of the mobile devices appeared to contain materials protected by the LPP. The solicitors were asked to provide a list of search terms so that such material could be identified and isolated for review by independent counsel. In response, the solicitors stated that all of the seized items held LPP materials and refused to provide search terms on the basis that the SFO's procedure for handling potentially privileged documents was unlawful.

Similar to the use of "taint teams" by the DOJ, the policy of the SFO at issue required that all material potentially protected by LPP must be treated with great care to (i) "minimise the risk that LPP material is seen or seized by an SFO investigator or a lawyer involved in the investigation," (ii) "ensure that any LLP material which is seized is properly isolated and promptly returned to the owner without having been seen by an SFO investigator or a lawyer involved in the investigation," (iii) "ensure that any dispute relating to LPP is resolved in advance of the material being seen by an SFO investigator or a lawyer involved in the investigation," and (iv) "ensure that where an SFO investigator or a lawyer involved in the investigation inadvertently sees LPP material, measures are in place to ensure that the investigation and any subsequent prosecution is not adversely affected as a result."[206]

McKenzie argued that this procedure is only lawful where the SFO can establish "that there is no real risk that LPP material will be disclosed to an investigator, and must do so with convincing evidence."[207] Rejecting this argument, Lord Justice Burnett concluded: "The essential aim of the SFO's policy is to ensure that LPP material relevant to an inquiry is not read by anyone involved in the investigation. That aim is uncontroversial, laudable and correct. But it would be too onerous a legal obligation on an investigating authority, in the context of the exercise of statutory powers of seize and production, to require it to demonstrate that there could be no real risk of that happening. . . . [A] seizing authority has a duty to devise and operate a system to isolate potential LPP material from bulk material lawfully in its possession, which can reasonably be expected to ensure that such material will not be read by members of the investigative team before it has been reviewed by an independent lawyer to establish whether privilege exists. That approach to LPP material imports the necessary rigour required by the law for its protection in this context."[208]

2. *Financial Conduct Authority and Crown Prosecution Service Search Warrants*

Like the SFO, the FCA and CPS have statutory authorization to seek search warrants to enter premises where documents or information are held if the holder of the documents or information has failed to comply with a disclosure request or there are grounds for believing that a disclosure request would not be complied with.[209] The application process and requirements for FCA and CPS warrants are the same as for search warrants sought by the SFO.

---

206. [2016] EWHC 102 Admin, para. 8.

207. *Id.* at para. 25.

208. *Id.* at para. 32-34.

209. FSMA, s. 176 (authorizing FCA warrants); SOCPA, s. 66 (authorizing CPS warrants).

IV. WIRE TAPS AND ELECTRONIC SURVEILLANCE

A. Wire Taps and Electronic Surveillance in the United States

1. *Title III Wire Taps*

In two landmark decisions in 1967, the U.S. Supreme Court determined that the Fourth Amendment extends to surreptitious interceptions of communications in situations where the individuals involved have a reasonable expectation of privacy.[210] The following year Congress passed the Omnibus Crime Control and Safe Streets Act of 1968 which contained the Wiretap Act, commonly referred to as "Title III."

Title III imposes strict rules on how private communications can be intercepted, recorded, and used as evidence. "To safeguard the privacy of innocent persons," Title III permits the nonconsensual interception of communications in transit only when "authorized by a court of competent jurisdiction."[211] It also prohibits the use or disclosure of the contents of any communications obtained in violation of the statute. Originally, Title III only covered oral communications over "hard" telephone lines, but was amended by the Electronic Communications Privacy Act (ECPA) of 1986 (18 U.S.C. §§2510-2523) to also include real-time electronic communications (e.g., texts and emails).[212]

In its present form, Title III prohibits the (i) unauthorized, nonconsensual interception of any form of private communication by government agents and private parties, (ii) establishes procedures for government officials to obtain wiretap warrants, and (iii) regulates the disclosure and use of authorized intercepted communications by law enforcement. Specifically, the statute:

- Prohibits the use of the contents and fruits of illegally obtained or intercepted communications as evidence (18 U.S.C. § 2515) and provides procedures for moving to suppress such evidence in court or other official proceedings (18 U.S.C. § 2518(9)–(10)).
- Requires wiretap applications to be authorized by the attorney general or certain other senior DOJ officials prior to being submitted to a judge (18 U.S.C. § 2516(1)).
- Authorizes the interception of private communications but only when law enforcement officials are investigating specified serious crimes and receive prior judicial approval (18 U.S.C. § 2516, 2518(1)-(8)).
- Requires the government to take steps to minimize the interception of irrelevant conversations (18 U.S.C. § 2518(5)).

---

210. *See* Katz v. United States, 389 U.S. 347, 353 (1967); Berger v. New York, 388 U.S. 41, 60 (1967).

211. Gelbard v. United States, 408 U.S. 41, 47 (1972). In certain very limited circumstances (i.e., where there is an immediate risk of death or personal injury, a national security risk, or some other emergency), the government is permitted to intercept private communications without a warrant. 18 U.S.C. § 2518(7); *see also Justice Manual* § 9-7.112 (setting forth procedures for "Emergency Interceptions").

212. Hall v. Earthlink Network, Inc., 396 F.3d 500, 503 (2d Cir. 2005); Konop v. Hawaiian Airlines, Inc., 302 F.3d 868, 874 (9th Cir. 2001).

- Allows the contents of lawfully intercepted communications to be disclosed and used by law enforcement during investigations and as evidence in court proceedings (18 U.S.C. § 2517).
- Prohibits nonconsensual interceptions of communications except as provided for in Title III and subjects nonauthorized interceptions to criminal penalties (18 U.S.C. § 2511).

a. Obtaining Court Authorization for Wiretaps

Obtaining a wiretap is a more difficult and cumbersome process than getting a search warrant. A law enforcement official seeking wiretap authorization must submit an affidavit to a judge setting forth "a full and complete statement of the facts and circumstances" that justify the official's belief that such authorization should be issued.[213] The applicant must also explain "whether or not other investigative procedures have been tried and failed or why they reasonably appear to be unlikely to succeed if tried or to be too dangerous."[214]

Importantly, this "necessity" provision does not require the government to show that it is impossible to pursue a particular investigation without a Title III wiretap; rather, it merely requires the government to "inform the authorizing judicial official of the nature and progress of the investigation and of the difficulties inherent in the use of normal law enforcement methods."[215] The DOJ's insider trading case against prominent hedge fund owner Raj Rajaratnam was one of the first instances where this issue was raised in a white-collar crime context. During its investigation, the DOJ sought, and received, a Title III wiretap on Rajaratnam's personal cell phone for nearly a year (after a number of court-authorized extensions). Following his arrest, Rajaratnam moved to suppress all evidence obtained through the wiretap because, among other reasons, the government's affidavit failed to give "a full and complete statement as to whether or not other investigative procedures have been tried and failed or why they reasonably appeared to be unlikely to succeed if tried or to be too dangerous," as Title III requires.[216] Rejecting this argument, Judge Howell of the Southern District of New York followed earlier case law holding that the "government is not 'required to exhaust all conceivable investigative techniques before resorting to electronic surveillance.'"[217] Instead, an affidavit offered in support of a wiretap warrant need only "provide some basis for concluding that less intrusive investigative procedures are not feasible."

If this initial hurdle is cleared, the judge must then be persuaded that there is probable cause that the requested interception will reveal evidence of one of the long list of offenses in 18 U.S.C. § 2516. If this requirement is met also, the judge may authorize a wiretap for up to

213. 18 U.S.C. § 2518(1)(b).

214. 18 U.S.C. § 2518(1)(c).

215. United States v. Vazquez, 605 F.2d 1269, 1282 (2d Cir. 1979); *see also* United States v. McGuire, 307 F. 3d 1192, 1197 (9th Cir. 2002) ("[Though] the wiretap should not ordinarily be the initial step in the investigation, . . . law enforcement officials need not exhaust every conceivable alternative before obtaining a wiretap.").

216. 18 U.S.C. § 2518(1)(c).

217. United States v. Rajaratnam, 09 Cr. 1184 (RJH), at *34 (S.D.N.Y. Nov. 29, 2010).

thirty days.[218] The thirty-day period may be extended for one or more additional periods of up to thirty days each, but only upon submission of an entirely new application at the end of each period.[219] But in no event may the wiretap be authorized for a period "longer than the authorizing judge deems necessary to achieve the purposes for which it was granted."

b. The Crimes Covered by Title III

As noted, wiretap requests must relate to an investigation pertaining to one of the federal crimes listed in 18 U.S.C. § 2516(1)(a)–(s). Even though this list does not include several traditional white-collar offenses—for example, securities fraud and foreign bribery under the Foreign Corrupt Practices Act (FCPA)—an interception will still be in accordance with Title III so long as prosecutors had an open investigation into one of the listed offenses when the application was made.[220] So, for instance, if a securities fraud investigation is also exploring potential wire fraud—as they often do—a wiretap could be obtained (assuming Title III's other requirements are met). This exact scenario was addressed in Rajaratnam, with the court concluding: "The government must obtain wiretap warrants in good faith—that is, in connection with an offense for which Title III permits wiretapping—not as a subterfuge for gathering evidence of other offenses. If the government does so, any other evidence it happens to intercept will have been intercepted incidentally [and lawfully]."[221]

The bar is even lower when law enforcement seeks to intercept emails and other forms of electronic communication. In such cases, the interception request can relate to an investigation of any federal felony, not just those listed in Section 2516.[222]

c. Consensual Recordings

Title III provides that it "shall not be unlawful" for "a person acting under color of law to intercept a wire, oral, or electronic communication, where such person is a party to the communication or one of the parties to the communication has given prior consent to such interception."[223] This means that, when government agents have obtained the consent of at least one party to a communication, they are permitted to engage in warrantless interceptions of telephone communications, as well as oral and electronic communications.[224]

---

218. 18 U.S.C. § 2518(3); *see* Illinois v. Gates, 462 U.S. 213, 230–32 (1983) (establishing a "totality of circumstances" test for probable cause); United States v. Tortorello, 480 F.2d 764, 775 (2d Cir. 1973) (when probable cause is established as to one party in a conversation, "incriminating statements made by another party to the conversation can be intercepted and used even though probable cause is not established as to him").

219. 18 U.S.C. § 2158(5).

220. *See, e.g.*, United States v. Masciarelli, 558 F.2d 1064, 1067 (2d Cir. 1977).

221. Rajaratnam, 09 Cr. 1184 (RJH), at *7 (S.D.N.Y. Nov. 29, 2010); *see also id.* ("Because Title III authorizes the government to use wiretaps to investigate wire fraud, the government was authorized to use wiretaps to investigate a fraudulent insider trading scheme using interstate wires even though Title III does not specifically authorize wiretaps to investigate insider trading alone.").

222. 18 U.S.C. § 2516(3).

223. 18 U.S.C. § 2511(2)(c).

224. *See* United States v. White, 401 U.S. 745 (1971); United States v. Caceres, 440 U.S. 741 (1979); *Justice Manual* § 9-7.302. Consent may be implied or express. *See, e.g.*, United States v. Corona-Chavez,

The exclusion of consensual recordings from the scope of Title III is highly significant in practice. It allows, for example, the government to secretly record the target of an investigation without a warrant by persuading a cooperating witness to wear a recording device while speaking with the target or having such a device fitted to the cooperating witness's telephone.

The DOJ relied heavily on this technique during a major initiative—led by the USAO for the Southern District of New York—against insider trading in the early 2010s. The key evidence gathered in many of these cases were recordings made by Karl Motey, an investment analyst in the semiconductor industry who pleaded guilty to securities fraud and conspiracy as part of a cooperation agreement with prosecutors. Under the FBI's direction, Motey secretly recorded more than sixty phone calls and in-person conversations with other analysts and investment professionals to elicit incriminating statements about the unlawful use of inside information in securities trading. These recordings were then routed to the FBI field office in New York and used to obtain indictments against a number of other defendants.[225] In light of his extensive assistance to the DOJ, Motey avoided jail and was sentenced only to probation and forfeiture of $40,000.

d. Foreign Wire Taps

Title III does not apply outside of the United States, even if the intercepted communications traverse U.S. territory before or after being intercepted.[226] Courts recognize two exceptions to this general rule. "First, where the conduct of foreign officials in acquiring the evidence is so extreme that [it] shock[s] the judicial conscience . . . [and] [s]econd, where cooperation with foreign law enforcement officials may implicate constitutional restrictions."[227] Within the second category,

> . . . constitutional requirements may attach in two situations: (1) where the conduct of foreign law enforcement officials rendered them agents, or virtual agents, of United States law enforcement officials; or (2) where the cooperation between the United States and foreign law enforcement agencies is designed to evade constitutional requirements applicable to American officials.[228]

2. *The Stored Communications Act*

Title II of the ECPA contains the Stored Communications Act (SCA) (18 U.S.C. §§ 2701–2712), a statute that addresses voluntary and compelled disclosure of "stored wire and electronic communications and transactional records" held by third-party internet service providers (ISPs). The statute "was enacted because the advent of the Internet presented

---

328 F.3d 974, 978 (8th Cir. 2003); United States v. Footman, 215 F.3d 145, 154 (1st Cir. 2000); United States v. Workman, 80 F.3d 688, 693 (2d Cir. 1996).

225. Shira Ovide, *Karl Motey: The Government's Secret Weapon in Insider-Trading Arrests,* Wall Street Journal, Dec. 20, 2010.

226. United States v. Maturo, 982 F.2d 57, 60 (2d Cir. 1992); United States v. Cotroni, 527 F.2d 708, 711–712 (2d Cir. 1975).

227. United States v. Lee, 723 F.3d 134, 140 (2d Cir. 2013).

228. Maturo, 982 F.2d at 61.

a host of potential privacy breaches that the Fourth Amendment [and existing laws] did not address."[229] The fundamental Fourth Amendment concern regarding use of the internet or any other computer network is that a user has a network account consisting of a block of computer storage that is owned by an ISP—for example, personal emails held in a Gmail or Outlook account are stored on servers owned by Google and Microsoft, respectively. Thus, because "providers of electronic communications act as third parties that store and process their user's private files," the user has no "reasonable expectation of privacy" in them, and these files consequently fall outside Fourth Amendment protection.[230] Since ISPs are private businesses, under traditional Fourth Amendment principles, they would be permitted to "search files held under their control and disclose their users' information to the government without violating the Fourth Amendment."[231]

To address this vulnerability, the SCA "'creates a set of Fourth Amendment-like privacy protections by statute regulating the relationship between government investigators and service providers in possession of users' private information.'"[232] The SCA accomplishes this by specifying the procedures law enforcement must follow to compel service providers to disclose stored communications (18 U.S.C. § 2703) and regulating when service providers may voluntarily disclose customer communications and records (18 U.S.C. § 2702).

The SCA also contains provisions prohibiting the intentional, unauthorized accessing of any email accounts stored on a third-party electronic communication service provider's server.[233] Violators of these prohibitions can be subject to both criminal penalties (18 U.S.C. § 2701) and civil liability (18 U.S.C. § 2707).

In March 2018, Congress passed the Clarifying Lawful Overseas Use of Data Act (the CLOUD Act). The CLOUD Act amended the SCA to authorize U.S. law enforcement to demand disclosure of electronic data stored outside of the United States, even where such disclosure might violate the laws of another country. The statute also permits federal officials to enter into executive agreements with foreign governments to obtain access to data stored in the United States that would otherwise be protected by the SCA or ECPA.[234]

The CLOUD Act was designed as a specific response to Microsoft's refusal to comply with a search warrant calling for disclosure of a customer's emails held on a server at a Microsoft datacenter in Dublin, Ireland. Microsoft's motion to quash the warrant was denied

229. Quon v. Arch Wireless Operation Co., 529 F.3d 892, 900 (9th Cir. 2008).

230. Walker v. Coffey, 956 F.3d 163, 166 (3d Cir. 2020); United States v. Miller, 425 U.S. 435, 443 (1976) ("The Fourth Amendment does not prohibit the obtaining of information revealed to a third party . . . even if the information is revealed on the assumption that it will be used only for a limited purpose and the confidence placed in the third party will not be betrayed.").

231. Walker, 956 F.3d at 166–67.

232. *Id.* at 167 (quoting Orin S. Kerr, *A User's Guide to the Stored Communications Act, and a Legislator's Guide to Amending It*, 72 Geo. Wash. L. Rev. 1208, 1210–11 (2004)).

233. Pure Power Boot Camp v. Warrior Fitness Boot Camp, 587 F. Supp. 2d 548, 555–56 (S.D.N.Y. 2008); *see also* Matter of Warrant to Search a Certain E-Mail Account Controlled and Maintained by Microsoft Corp., 829 F.3d 197, 207 (2d Cir. 2016).

234. *See generally*, *The Cloud Act*, Electronic Privacy Information Center, *available at* https://epic.org/privacy/cloud-act/ (last visited June 3, 2021).

at the district court level and the company was subsequently held in civil contempt. On appeal, the Second Circuit reversed the district court and held that requiring Microsoft to disclose the electronic communications in question would be an unauthorized extraterritorial application of the SCA (18 U.S.C. § 2703). The case was then appealed to the Supreme Court. While still pending, Congress passed the CLOUD Act; soon thereafter, the DOJ obtained, pursuant to the new law, a new § 2703 warrant covering the information requested in the original warrant. The case was thereby rendered moot, and Microsoft eventually turned over the requested emails.[235]

3. *Pen Registers and Trap and Trace Devices*

Pen registers are devices that capture the numbers dialed on outgoing telephone calls; trap and trace devices capture the numbers associated with incoming telephone calls. Because these devices do not intercept or record the contents of the communications themselves, Title III does not apply.[236] Rather, their use is governed by the Pen Register and Trap and Trace Statute.[237]

Individuals are not considered to have a reasonable privacy interest protected by the Fourth Amendment in the numbers they dial or the numbers from which they receive phone calls,[238] making it far easier for law enforcement to obtain authorization for pen registers and trap and trace devices than for Title III wiretaps. Under 18 U.S.C. § 3123(a)(1), an attorney for the government may obtain a court order to install one of these devices anywhere in the United States based solely on an affidavit certifying that "the information likely to be obtained by such installation and use is relevant to an ongoing criminal investigation." This is an extremely low bar that law enforcement rarely, if ever, fails to satisfy.

In 2001, the USA PATRIOT Act amended the Pen Register and Trap and Trace Statute to include the collection of noncontent information associated with internet communications (e.g., the URLs of website addresses visited by a particular person or from a particular computer).[239] In light of the heightened privacy concerns surrounding the use of pen registers and trap and trace devices in this context, there are specific DOJ policies and procedures prosecutors must follow to obtain authorization to do so.[240]

---

235. United States v. Microsoft Corp., 138 S. Ct. 1186 (2018).

236. 18 U.S.C. § 2511(h)(i).

237. 18 U.S.C. §§ 3121–27.

238. Smith v. Maryland, 442 U.S. 735, 742 (1979); United States v. New York Tel. Co., 434 U.S. 159, 167 (1977).

239. *See* United States v. Ulbricht, 858 F.3d 71, 96 (2d Cir. 2017) ("[E]-mail and Internet users . . . rely on third-party equipment in order to engaged in communication" and thus "should know that this information is provided to and used by Internet service providers for the specific purpose of directing the routing of information") (quoting United States v. Forrester, 512 F.3d 500, 510 (9th Cir. 2008)); United States v. Wheelock, 772 F.3d 825, 828 (8th Cir. 2014) (holding that individuals "cannot claim a reasonable expectation of privacy in [the] government's acquisition of his subscriber information, including his IP address and name," because it had been "revealed to a third party"); United States v. Graham, 824 F.3d 421, 432 (4th Cir. 2016); United States v. Carpenter, 819 F.3d 880, 887 (6th Cir. 2016).

240. *See Justice Manual* § 9-7.500.

B. Covert Surveillance in the United Kingdom

1. *Investigatory Powers Act 2016*

Covert interception of private communications by U.K. law enforcement is governed by the Investigatory Powers Act (IPA) 2016—nicknamed the "Snooper's Charter" by critics who view the law as creating an intrusive mass surveillance regime. Similar to the function of Title III in the United States, the IPA provides a detailed framework specifying the procedures law enforcement must follow when engaging in interception activities carried out within the United Kingdom that target telecommunication systems, postal services, or electronic data.[241]

But whereas evidence obtained through Title III wiretaps is routinely admitted as evidence in U.S. criminal trials, in the United Kingdom even lawfully intercepted communications cannot be used by either the prosecution or defense in court. Specifically, IPA Section 56(1) states:

> (1) **No evidence may be adduced, questions asked, assertion made or other thing done in, for the purposes of or in connection with any legal proceedings . . . which (in any manner)—**
>
> (a) discloses, in circumstances from which its origin in interception-related conduct may be inferred—
>
> (i) any content of an intercepted communication, or
>
> (ii) any secondary data obtained from a communication, or
>
> (b) tends to suggest that any interception-related conduct has or may have occurred or may be going to occur."

In light of this provision, evidence obtained through wiretaps and other forms of interception is not used in criminal prosecutions in the United Kingdom, subject to certain limited exceptions listed in IPA Schedule 3. Importantly, however, this prohibition does not apply to wiretap evidence lawfully obtained by a foreign authority and given to U.K. law enforcement.[242]

2. *Regulation of Investigatory Powers Act 2000*

Part II of the Regulation of Investigatory Powers Act (RIPA) 2000 sets forth the requirements law enforcement agencies must follow when engaging in any covert surveillance likely to result in the obtaining of private information about a person. Unlike evidence obtained through IPA, evidence secured through the RIPA procedures can be used as evidence in criminal proceedings. But where law enforcement employs covert surveillance methods without proper authorization, any evidence thereby obtained will be subject to being ruled

---

241. An interception will be considered to occur within the United Kingdom if: "(a) the relevant act or, in the case of a postal item, the interception is carried out by conduct within the U.K., and (b) the communication is intercepted (i) in the course of its transmission by means of a public telecommunication system or a public postal service, or (ii) in the course of its transmission by means of a private telecommunication system in a case where the sender or intended recipient of the communication is in the United Kingdom." IPA, s. 4(8).

242. Virdee v. NCA [2018] EWHC 1119; R v. Knaggs [2018] EWCA 1863.

inadmissible at trial (in the same way as the "exclusionary rule" bar functions in the United States).[243]

As the term is used in RIPA, "surveillance" includes monitoring, observing, or listening to individuals, their movements, conversations, or other activities and communications—essentially, surveillance means any type of observation that does not involve a secret interception of private communications (e.g., wiretaps).[244] Surveillance may be conducted with or without the assistance of a surveillance device—defined as "any apparatus designed or adapted for use in surveillance"—and includes the recording of any information obtained.[245] In practice, this means that investigators can plant "bugs" in a suspect's home, office, or car in the hopes that incriminating statements will be overheard and captured. These methods, and any other discrete observation tactics, will be considered "covert" under RIPA because there is an intention to observe a suspect without putting them on notice.[246]

a. Directed and Intrusive Surveillance

RIPA defines two types of surveillance: directed surveillance and intrusive surveillance. Directed surveillance is "covert but not intrusive," conducted "for the purposes of a specific investigation or a specific operation," "in such a manner as is likely to result in the obtaining of private information about a person," and not in "immediate response to events or circumstances."[247] Subject to certain exceptions, intrusive surveillance is covert surveillance that "is carried out in relation to anything taking place on any residential premises or in any private vehicle" and "involves the presence of an individual on the premises or in the vehicle or is carried out by means of a surveillance device."[248]

Authorization for surveillance measures governed by RIPA can be granted by senior government officials at certain agencies without the involvement of the courts.[249] For directed surveillance, these agencies include, among others, any police force, the National Crime Agency (NCA), the Serious Fraud Office (SFO), and Her Majesty's Revenue and Customs (HMRC).[250] Officials at these agencies may grant authorization for directed surveillance only if there are reasonable grounds to believe that the authorization is "necessary" and "proportionate to what is sought to be achieved by carrying it out."[251] As relevant here, authorization will be deemed "necessary" if the surveillance measures at issue need to be used "for purposes

---

243. PACE, s. 78(1); *but see* R v. Khan and others [2013] EWCA Crim 223 (holding evidence obtained through breach of RIPA admissible if law enforcement acted in good faith).

244. Regulation of Investigatory Powers Act (RIPA), s. 48(2).

245. https://www.gov.uk/government/publications/regulation-of-investigatory-powers-act-2000-ripa/regulation-of-investigatory-powers-act-2000-ripa.

246. R v. Secretary of State for the Home Department [2019] EWCA (Civ) 256 ("The word 'covert' in the context of surveillance and RIPA denotes a state of mind that is reflected in the words 'is calculated to ensure' in section 26(9) of RIPA. There must be an intention to conduct the surveillance secretly, in the sense of an intention that it should not become known to the subject.").

247. RIPA, s. 26(2).

248. RIPA, ss. 26(3)–(6).

249. RIPA, s. 30.

250. RIPA, Schedule 1.

251. RIPA, s. 28(2).

of preventing or detecting crime or of preventing disorder" or if their use is "in the interests of the economic well-being of the United Kingdom."[252]

Authorization for intrusive surveillance is similarly only permitted if done "in the interests of national security," "for the purpose of preventing or detecting serious crime," or "in the interests of the economic well-being of the United Kingdom."[253] While intrusive surveillance can be authorized by the commissioner of Police for the City of London, it cannot be authorized by the SFO, FCA, or any of the other agencies typically involved in financial crime prosecutions.[254]

b. Covert Human Intelligence Sources

In addition to addressing surveillance, RIPA governs the use of "covert human intelligence sources" (CHIS). Under the statute, a person will be considered a CHIS if "he establishes or maintains a personal or other relationship with a person for the covert purpose" of using such relationship to "obtain information or to provide access to any information to another person" or disclosing "information obtained by the use of such a relationship, or as a consequence of the existence of such a relationship."[255] A CHIS can be either an undercover police officer or a private citizen (e.g., a business colleague of a person under investigation who has agreed to cooperate with law enforcement).

The use of CHIS may be authorized by senior officials at the SFO, FCA, and various other law enforcement agencies. The authorization requirements for CHIS are the same as those for directed surveillance.[256]

V. CROSS-BORDER EVIDENCE GATHERING

A. Mutual Legal Assistance Treaties in the United States

Investigating cross-border criminal conduct will predictably often involve gathering evidence located in foreign countries. "However, national sovereignty, international treaties, and international law preclude U.S. law enforcement officials from simply flying to a foreign country to conduct searches, question suspects, obtain documents, and proceed with arresting individuals for trial in the United States."[257] The same is true for British law enforcement. Without the agreement of a foreign country, therefore, prosecutors' ability to obtain evidence overseas would be extremely limited.

To facilitate transnational cooperation in criminal investigations and proceedings, the U.S. government uses mutual legal assistance treaties (MLATs). MLATs are agreements between two countries that require their respective law enforcement agencies to assist each other to collect information and evidence. The United States has MLATs in place with dozens

252. RIPA, s. 28(3).

253. RIPA, s. 32(3).

254. RIPA, s. 32(6).

255. RIPA, s. 26(8).

256. RIPA, ss. 29(2), (3).

257. T. Markus Funk, *Mutual Legal Assistance Treaties and Letters Rogatory: A Guide for Judges*, FED. J. CENTER INT'L LIT. GUIDE 1 (2014).

of countries, including the United Kingdom and each of the member states of the European Union.[258] Each individual treaty contains distinct definitions of the party countries' obligations to provide assistance, the scope of that assistance, and the contents that a request for assistance must include.

Importantly, the benefits of MLATs are generally available only to prosecutors and other government officials, not to defendants or their counsel.[259] Therefore, defendants are generally required to seek foreign evidence through the more cumbersome and time-consuming letters rogatory process (codified in 28 U.S.C. §§ 1781–2).

The possible exceptions to this general rule are the MLATs between the United States and Switzerland, the Netherlands, and Turkey, which contain provisions granting defendants permission to access evidence pursuant to an MLAT in the same way as prosecutors.[260] All other MLATs entered into by the United States include language explicitly restricting defense access.[261] The MLAT between the United States and the United Kingdom, for example, "expressly disclaims the existence of any private rights."[262] The relevant provision of this treaty states: "This treaty is intended solely for the mutual legal assistance between the Parties. The provisions of this Treaty shall not give rise to a right on the part of any private person to obtain, suppress, or exclude any evidence, or to impede the execution of a request."[263]

While the terms of each MLAT are negotiated separately, they usually provide for assistance in (i) locating or identifying persons or things, (ii) taking testimony, (iii) requesting searches and seizures, (iv) obtaining documents or electronic evidence, and (v) freezing assets.[264] Both outgoing and incoming requests under MLATs are handled by the DOJ's Office of International Affairs (OIA) without any involvement or oversight from a district court or magistrate judge. Thus, once the OIA approves an American prosecutor's outgoing MLAT request and files it with their counterparts in the relevant country, the foreign country becomes bound to assist the DOJ's investigation under the terms of the applicable MLAT (and the same is true for incoming requests from abroad).

MLATs are powerful investigatory mechanisms that are often critical to the viability of cross-border financial crime prosecutions. Since they are, by design, only available to the DOJ, defendants facing allegations that implicate evidence or witnesses located overseas are at an inherent disadvantage in terms of their ability to identify and collect materials relevant to their defense.[265]

---

258. *Id.*

259. *See* United Kingdom v. United States, 238 F.3d 1312, 1314 (11th Cir. 2012) (explaining that the U.S./U.K. MLAT does not permit criminal defendants to request the production of information); United States v. Sedaghaty, 728 F.3d 885, 916–17 (9th Cir. 2013).

260. *See, e.g.*, United States v. Sindona, 636 F.2d 792 (2d Cir. 1980) (ordering DOJ to provide defense counsel secure evidence under the MLAT with Switzerland).

261. Funk, *supra* note 248, at 17–18; *see also* United States v. Mejia, 448 F.3d 436 (D.C. Cir. 2006); United States v. Jefferson, 594 F. Supp. 2d 655, 674 (E.D. Va. 2009).

262. McLellan, 959 F.3d at 471.

263. *Id.* (quoting U.S.-U.K. MLAT, art. 1, ¶ 3).

264. *Id.* at 5–6 (citing Hon. Virginia M. Kendall & T. Markus Funk, *The Role of Mutual Legal Assistance Treaties in Obtaining Foreign Evidence*, 40 A.B.A. Litig. J. 1, 1–3 (2014)).

265. *See, e.g.*, United States v. McLellan, 959 F.3d 442, 471–76 (1st Cir. 2020) (holding that district courts do not have the authority to compel the government to issue MLAT requests and rejecting defendant's

MLATs are not the only mechanism by which prosecutors can obtain evidence located overseas. In addition to the powers afforded under the CLOUD Act (discussed earlier), the government has information-sharing agreements and memoranda of understanding (MOU) in place with numerous foreign governments that allow for the expedited exchange of information and evidence in situations where an MLAT does not apply. Prosecutors, like defendants, can also seek foreign evidence through the relatively slow letters rogatory process.[266]

1. *MLATs and Statutes of Limitations*

When prosecutors initiate an MLAT request to obtain evidence overseas, they will often file an ex parte application in the relevant district court to toll (i.e., suspend) the statute of limitations under 18 U.S.C. § 3292. Section 3292 "requires a district court to suspend the running of a statute of limitations upon an appropriate application showing: (1) that evidence of an offense being investigated by a grand jury is in a foreign country; and (2) that such evidence has been officially requested."[267] When deciding whether the evidence at issue is actually in a foreign country, a court must find by a preponderance of the evidence "that it reasonably appears, or reasonably appeared at the time the request was made, that such evidence is, or was, in a foreign country."[268]

If the requisite showing is made, the applicable statute of limitations may be tolled for up to three years (beginning on the date the MLAT request was made and ending when the foreign government completes its production of the requested evidence).[269] Courts permit prosecutors to employ MLATs and toll statutes of limitations even when the evidence at issue could have been obtained through a subpoena served within the United States.[270] Tolling orders may not, however, be used merely as a pretext to extend the statute of limitations to gain a tactical advantage over the defendant or to save an otherwise untimely prosecution.[271]

B. Mutual Legal Assistance in the United Kingdom

1. *Mutual Legal Assistance Agreements*

Like their counterparts at the DOJ, prosecutors in Britain can obtain evidence located overseas through various bilateral mutual legal assistance agreements (MLAs).[272] MLAs are generally used for obtaining material that cannot be obtained on a law enforcement to law enforcement

---

argument that the Constitution requires the government to help a defendant obtain evidence through an MLAT request); United States v. Mejia, 448 F.3d 436, 444 (D.C. Cir. 2006) (ruling that government had no obligation to use MLATs to obtain evidence in the possession of a foreign government).

266. *See* DOJ Criminal Resources Manual § 275.

267. United States v. Lyttle, 667 F.3d 220, 224 (2d Cir. 2012).

268. *Id.*

269. 18 U.S.C. § 329(b).

270. Lyttle, 667 F.3d at 225.

271. *See, e.g.*, Jody Godoy, *Ex-Deutsche, Merrill Traders Claim DOJ Misconduct,* Law360, Feb. 26, 2020.

272. For a list of the countries with which the United Kingdom has MLAs, *see* U.K. Home Office, *International MLA & Extradition Agreements the U.K. Is Party to, available at* https://assets.publishing.service.gov.uk/government/uploads/system/uploads/attachment_data/file/516418/Treaty_List.pdf.

basis, particularly that which require coercive measures (e.g., search warrants and court orders) to obtain. MLAs can also be used to obtain foreign assistance in relation to the freezing and confiscation of criminal proceeds located abroad. The process by which MLA requests must be made is set out in the Crime (International Co-operation) (CICA) Act 2003. MLAs can be requested by various "prosecuting authorities" (CICA, s. 7(3)(a)) including the SFO, FSA, and CPS.[273] Because the Crown Dependencies and British Overseas Territories operate their own independent legal systems, the same MLA process must be used for U.K. authorities to obtain evidence from these jurisdictions as with any other foreign nation. Prior to Brexit, the United Kingdom could employ European Investigation Orders (EIOs)—designed to facilitate the MLA process among members of the European Union—but, as of December 31, 2021, EIOs are no longer available to British authorities.[274]

The types of investigatory enquiries that are likely to require MLA requests include:

- Obtaining testimony from an involuntary witness via remote hearings conducted via video-conferencing or transfer of the witness to the United Kingdom.
- Obtaining account information and documentary evidence from overseas banks and financial institutions.
- Requests for search and seizure related to evidence of a crime or to tracing and recovery of criminal proceeds.
- Internet records and the contents of emails, cross-border surveillance, and telecommunications intercepts.
- Service of documents issued by a court or authority in relation to criminal proceedings.[275]

Compared to the thousands of incoming MLA requests the United Kingdom receives and accepts each year, British authorities utilize outgoing requests relatively infrequently. Between 2020 and 2021, for example, the United Kingdom received a total of 13,262 MLA requests (9,134 of which were accepted [69%]) but issued just 605 of its own. The countries most often targeted by outgoing U.K. MLAs in the last five years were the United States and United Arab Emirates.[276]

In a major difference with the MLATs used in the United States, criminal defendants in the United Kingdom can, with court approval, seek foreign evidence using MLAs to the same

273. *See* The Crime (International Co-operation) Act 2003 (Designation of Prosecuting Authorities) Order 2004.

274. U.K. Home Office, *Request for Mutual Legal Assistance in Criminal Matters* (March 2022), *available at* https://assets.publishing.service.gov.uk/government/uploads/system/uploads/attachment_data/file/1069752/Request_for_MLA_in_criminal_matters_guidelines_2022.pdf.

275. J. Beqiraj and R. Mackenzie-Gray Scott, "Mutual Legal Assistance (MLA) in Criminal Matters in the UK and in Developing Countries: A Scoping Study," Bingham Centre for the Rule of Law Report (March 2022), *available at* https://www.law.ox.ac.uk/sites/files/oxlaw/139_mla_report_final.pdf.

276. *Id.*

extent as government investigators.[277] Importantly, however, defense requests can only be made after an individual has been charged, whereas prosecuting authorities can, of course, use MLAs during the investigatory phase as well as after a formal charge has issued.

In another key difference with MLATs, MLAs have no effect on the statute of limitations because there are no statute of limitations for criminal offenses in the United Kingdom (except for misdemeanors). Although British authorities have a theoretically indefinite time to gather evidence located overseas, practical realities make charging very old conduct infeasible and subject to abuse of process claims.

2. *The Crime (Overseas Production Orders) Act 2019*

Once an MLA request is issued, it can take between six months and two years before the requested evidence is transmitted to the United Kingdom. To expedite the process for law enforcement agencies to obtain emails and other forms of electronic data stored abroad, Parliament passed the Crime (Overseas Production Orders) Act (OPO) 2019. OPOs function similarly to MLAs but are designed to be processed more expeditiously. In contrast to an MLA request, which can be made to countries who have not entered into formal assistance agreements with the United Kingdom, OPOs can only be issued to the countries with which the United Kingdom has such agreements in place.[278]

In February 2020, the U.S.-U.K. Agreement on "Access to Electronic Data for the Purpose of Countering Serious Crime" came into force. In the same way as the U.S. CLOUD Act, this agreement allows British authorities to obtain OPOs in U.K. courts that require internet service providers in the United States to turn over (or at least provide access to) emails and other electronic data regardless of where it is stored. While overseas data was accessible under previous law through the MLA process, that process can often take several months, if not years, to bear fruit. Under the new agreement, once an OPO is served on the service provider, the material generally must be produced within seven days.

All the major investigating agencies involved in financial crime matters, including the SFO and FCA, can apply for an OPO. To obtain one, the requesting prosecutor must convince a Crown Court judge that there are reasonable grounds for believing, among other things, each of the following:

- An indictable offense has been committed in the United Kingdom and is the subject of an investigation or formal enforcement proceedings.
- The person against whom the OPO is sought has possession or control of the data at issue.
- The data is likely to be of substantial value to the investigation or proceedings.
- It is in the public interest for all or part of the data to be produced.[279]

277. CICA, s. 7(3)(c); *R v. Forsyth* [1997] 2 Cr App R 299 (holding that a court receiving an MLA request from a defendant should generally grant the request unless grounds exist not to).

278. Overseas Production Order (OPO), s. 1(5).

279. OPO, s. 4.

CHAPTER 2: KEY DISTINCTIONS

United States	United Kingdom
Prosecutor's powers to subpoena testimony and documents largely flow from the grand jury	Law enforcement's investigatory powers to compel disclosures created by statute
Grand jury subpoenas can be quashed on motion if "unreasonable or oppressive"	Compulsory disclosure notices can be resisted through the judicial review process if they are illegal, irrational, or procedurally unfair
Constitutional right against self-incrimination applies to all individuals and can only be overridden by a grant of "use and derivative use" immunity	Absolute right against self-incrimination not recognized but compelled testimony is automatically given "use immunity"
Attorney-client privilege can extend to third-party agents of an attorney (e.g., experts)	Legal advice privilege does not apply to any communications involving a nonlawyer expert
Communications between a company's lawyers and its employees will generally be privileged	A company's counsel can have privileged communications only with "core" employees
Privileged communications will generally lose protection if disclosed to a third party, including the government	Privilege will not be waived by disclosure to third parties if privileged materials are not intended to be subsequently used or sent elsewhere; selective waiver recognized for privileged materials disclosed to law enforcement
Foreign corporations may be compelled to disclose documents held abroad via a grand jury subpoena served on a U.S. branch or subsidiary	To obtain documents held abroad, U.K. law enforcement agencies must make a request pursuant to a mutual legal assistance agreement
Recipients of a grand jury subpoena may file a motion to quash it in the applicable district court	Recipients of a disclosure request from the government may seek "judicial review" of the request after following the Pre-Action Protocol for Judicial Review
Voluntary interviews with the FBI will generally not be recorded; the only contemporaneous record will be made on FBI form FD-302	Voluntary interviews with U.K. law enforcement must generally always be recorded
An individual's silence during an interview with law enforcement cannot be used against them in criminal proceedings	An adverse inference may be drawn in criminal proceedings against an individual who fails to respond to questioning during a voluntary interview with law enforcement
Evidence obtained through an authorized wiretap may be used during criminal proceedings	Evidence obtained through lawful wiretaps may not be used by either the prosecution or defense in criminal proceedings
Benefits of MLATs are usually only available to the government	MLAs can be used by both the prosecution and defense to obtain evidence from overseas jurisdictions
An MLAT request can toll the otherwise applicable statute of limitations for up to three years	MLA requests will not affect when a prosecution may commence since there are no statutes of limitations for either-way or indictable-only offenses in the United Kingdom

3 | Charging Decisions, Charging Instruments, and Bail

Once law enforcement gathers sufficient evidence to prove a crime has been committed by an identifiable individual or entity, prosecutors must determine whether the crime is deserving of prosecution and, if so, what charges to bring. In both the United States and the United Kingdom, charging decisions are influenced by how a potential criminal prosecution relates to government enforcement priorities, the interests of the victims, and the perpetrator's level of culpability.

The DOJ's *Justice Manual* acknowledges, for instance, that "[a] determination to prosecute represents a policy judgment that the fundamental interests of society require the application of federal criminal law to a particular set of circumstances—recognizing both that serious violations of federal law must be prosecuted, and that prosecution entails profound consequences for the accused, crime victims, and their families whether or not a conviction ultimately results."[1] Similarly, the U.K. Code for Crown Prosecutors requires prosecutors "to make sure that the right person is prosecuted for the right offence and to bring offenders to justice whenever possible. Casework decisions taken fairly, impartially and with integrity help secure justice for victims, witnesses, suspects, defendants and the public."[2]

This chapter explores the U.S. and British policy guidelines governing charging decisions, the different charging instruments available in each country, related issues such as double jeopardy and statutes of limitations, and the initial procedures used once a defendant has been charged and arrested.

I. CHARGING DECISIONS

A. Charging Decisions by the Department of Justice

DOJ prosecutors are members of the executive branch of the federal government and thus derive their authority from the president's constitutional duty to "take Care that the Laws [of the United States] are faithfully executed."[3] This authority gives prosecutors broad discretion in determining whether and when to initiate criminal prosecutions, what charges are

1. *Justice Manual* § 9-27.001.

2. Code for Crown Prosecutors, s.2.5.

3. U.S. Const. art. II, § 3; United States v. Armstrong, 517 U.S. 456, 464 (1996).

brought, and who is charged.[4] A prosecutor's charging decisions are given a "presumption of regularity,"[5] meaning that courts will assume prosecutors have acted properly "in the absence of clear evidence to the contrary."[6]

If a prosecutor concludes that there is probable cause to believe that a person or entity has committed a federal offense within his or her jurisdiction and that the admissible evidence will likely sustain a conviction, DOJ policy states that a prosecution should generally be pursued unless: (i) it would serve no "substantial federal interest," (ii) the culprit is subject to effective prosecution in another jurisdiction, or (iii) there exists an adequate noncriminal alternative to prosecution.[7]

Whether there is a substantial federal interest in a particular prosecution turns on the DOJ's evaluation of the following factors:

- Federal law enforcement priorities
- The nature and seriousness of the offense
- The deterrent effect of prosecution
- The prospective defendant's culpability, criminal history, willingness to cooperate in the investigation or prosecution of others, and his or her personal circumstances
- The interests of any victims
- The probable sentence or other consequences if the prosecution results in a conviction[8]

When a potential prosecution is not pursued, the prosecutor making the declination decision is required to keep an internal record of the reasons for doing so; prosecutors are not, however, under any obligation to inform a would-be defendant that a case against them will not be initiated.[9] Because of the use of sealed indictments (see section II.A), not receiving a formal declination from the DOJ can create significant uncertainty for foreign defendants about their status in relation to a DOJ investigation. This is particularly problematic for

---

4. United States v. LaBonte, 520 U.S. 751, 762 (1997); United States v. Batchelder, 442 U.S. 114, 124–25 (1979); Bordenkircher v. Hayes, 434 U.S. 357, 364 (1978).

5. Armstrong, 517 U.S. at 464.

6. United States v. Chemical Foundation, Inc., 272 U.S. 1, 14–15 (1926); Wayte v. United States, 470 U.S. 598, 607 (1985) ("[T]he decision to prosecute is particularly ill-suited to judicial review" and for that reason the government "retains broad discretion as to whom to prosecute."). While there is a federal statute (42 U.S.C. § 1983) that creates a civil right of action for individuals subject to malicious prosecution, plaintiffs' burden in such cases is demanding (generally requiring proof that prosecutors had no probable cause). *See, e.g.*, Savino v. City of New York, 331 F.3d 63, 72 (2d Cir. 2003) ("elements of an action for malicious prosecution are (1) the initiation of a proceeding, (2) its termination favorably to plaintiff, (3) lack of probable cause, and (4) malice"); Bernard v. United States, 25 F.3d 98, 104 (2d Cir. 1994).

7. *Justice Manual* § 9-27.200.

8. *Justice Manual* § 9-27.230; *see also Justice Manual* § 9-27.260 (listing factors that are impermissible for a prosecutor to consider when making charging decisions).

9. *Justice Manual* § 9-27.270.

individuals residing in nonextradition countries who may be left to wonder indefinitely whether they have been indicted under seal and, as a result, whether they are able to travel abroad without fear of arrest.

Once the decision to prosecute has been made, DOJ policy directs prosecutors to pursue the most serious readily proven offenses (i.e., those that carry the highest potential sentences).[10] This policy is subject to a prosecutor's judgment concerning the circumstances of each case, and it may be departed from with the consent of his or her supervisor or senior DOJ officials.

B. Charging Decisions in the United Kingdom

When determining whether to criminally prosecute an individual or entity, prosecutors for the SFO, CPS, and FCA all follow the principles enumerated in the Code for Crown Prosecutors (a document issued by the Director of Public Prosecutions [DPP] under Section 10 of the Prosecution of Offenses Act 1985). The code sets forth two tests for charging decisions: the "Full Code Test" and the "Threshold Test."

Charging decisions in Britain must also be in accordance with the European Convention on Human Rights (ECHR).[11] The ECHR is a treaty signed between forty-seven countries that came into effect in 1953.[12] Because the ECHR has been adopted into domestic U.K. legislation through the Human Rights Act 1998, it continues to apply despite the United Kingdom no longer being a part of the European Union. Similar to the Bill of Rights contained in the U.S. Constitution, the ECHR sets forth a number of fundamental rights, including the right to liberty and security, the right to a fair trial, and the right to not be punishment for conduct that did not constitute a criminal offense at the time it was committed. In practice, the ECHR acts as a "safety valve" or catch-all mechanism for defendants to challenge their treatment at the hands of the government and is often implicated in extradition cases in the United Kingdom and Europe.[13]

1. The "Full Code Test"

In most circumstances—including virtually all financial crime cases—prosecutors are prohibited from starting or continuing a prosecution unless the case at issue has passed the Full Code Test. This test is applied either "when all outstanding reasonable lines of inquiry have

---

10. *Justice Manual* § 9-27.300.

11. Code for Crown Prosecutors, s.2.10.

12. Although it is not a signatory to the ECHR, the United States is one of five "observer countries" of the treaty (along with the Vatican, Canada, Japan, and Mexico).

13. Challenges to detention under the ECHR are generally brought under Article 5, s.4, which states: "Everyone who is deprived of his liberty by arrest or detention shall be entitled to take proceedings by which the lawfulness of his detention shall be decided speedily by a court and his release ordered if the detention is not lawful." In an extradition context, U.K. courts will consider whether a defendant's detention (in the United Kingdom or requesting state) is lawful under English law, complies with the ECHR, and is not arbitrary. R (Kashamu) v. Governor of Brixton Prison [2002] QB 887.

been pursued" or if, prior to the investigation being completed, "the prosecutor is satisfied that any further evidence or material is unlikely to affect the application of the Full Code Test, whether in favour of or against a prosecution."[14]

There are two stages to the Full Code Test: the evidential stage and the public interest stage. At the evidential stage, prosecutors must objectively consider whether there is sufficient evidence to provide a realistic prospect of conviction in light of the anticipated defense. This test is satisfied if an objective assessment of the evidence likely to be admissible at trial indicates that a reasonable factfinder "is more likely than not to convict the defendant of the charge alleged."[15] "A case which does not pass the evidential stage must not proceed, no matter how serious or sensitive it may be." Although it is left to the independent determination of the government instead of private citizens, this test is effectively the same as the "probable cause" standard applied by grand juries in the United States.

At the public interest stage, prosecutors must consider a nonexhaustive set of factors, including (i) the seriousness of the offense, (ii) the culpability of the suspect, (c) the circumstances and nature of the harm caused to the victim, (d) the age and characteristics of the offender, (e) the societal impact of the offense, and (f) whether criminal prosecution is a proportionate response.[16] The Full Code Test acknowledges that in certain cases, "one public interest factor alone may outweigh a number of other factors which tend in the opposite direction."

2. *The "Threshold Test"*

In situations where an offender poses an imminent and substantial danger to the community or there is a likely risk of flight, charges may be issued under the "Threshold Test." The Threshold Test thus allows for quick action in circumstances where a criminal investigation has not yet produced enough evidence to satisfy the evidentiary stage of the Full Code Test described above.[17] As stated in the DPP's guidance on charging decisions, the "Threshold Test is intended to apply to a very limited range of cases where the Full Code Test cannot be met but the overall seriousness of the circumstances of the case justify the making of an immediate charging decision, and there are substantial grounds to object to bail."[18]

The Threshold Test can only be applied where five conditions are met:

- There are reasonable grounds to suspect that the person to be charged has committed the offense. In making this determination, prosecutors "must be satisfied that the material to be relied on at this stage is capable" of being "put into an admissible format for presentation in court," "reliable," and "credible."

14. Code for Crown Prosecutors, s.4.3.

15. *Id.*, s.4.7.

16. *Id.*, s.4.14.

17. *Id.*, s.5.1.

18. CPS, *Charging (The Director's Guidance)*, Dec. 2020, s. 6.2, *available at* https://www.cps.gov.uk/legal-guidance/charging-directors-guidance-sixth-edition-december-2020.

- Further evidence can be obtained to provide a realistic prospect of conviction. Such further evidence "must be identifiable and not merely speculative."
- The seriousness or circumstances of the case justifies the making of an immediate charging decision. This "should be assessed in relation to the alleged offending and should be linked to the level of risk created by granting bail."
- There are continuing grounds to object to bail and in all the circumstances of the case it is proper to do so. This condition requires that the suspect is not suitable to be bailed, even with substantial conditions. For example, "a suspect who poses a serious risk of absconding or interfering with witnesses."
- It is in the public interest to charge the suspect. The Threshold Test only affects the evidentiary stage of the Full Code Test, meaning that the public interest stage must still be satisfied.

Where the Threshold Test is used to charge a suspect, the charging decision will be kept under review and "regularly assessed to ensure that the charge is still appropriate and that continued objection to bail is justified. The Full Code Test must be applied as soon as the anticipated further evidence or materials is received."[19]

3. Selecting Charges

If at least one of the charging tests is satisfied, prosecutors are directed to select charges that "reflect the seriousness and extent of the offending," "give the court adequate powers to sentence and impose appropriate postconviction orders," "allow a confiscation order to be made in appropriate cases where a defendant has benefitted from criminal conduct," and "enable the case to be presented in a clear and simple way."[20] The practical effect of these standards is that prosecutors "may not always choose, or continue with, the most serious charge where the interests of justice can be met by selecting a lesser charge."[21] Public policy further prohibits piling on charges simply to exert unwarranted leverage on a defendant: the CPS code states, "Prosecutors should never proceed with more charges than are necessary just to encourage a defendant to plead guilty to a few . . . or to a less serious one."[22] The same is not necessarily true in the United States, where prosecutors are afforded essentially unfettered discretion in charging a person with one offense or many.[23] This broad authority has been regularly criticized for vesting too much power in the hands of individual prosecutors, who may be tempted to use it merely as a way to create more leverage over a defendant.[24]

---

19. Code for Crown Prosecutors, s.5.11.

20. *Id.*, s.6.1.

21. *Id.*, s.6.2.

22. *Id.*, s.6.3.

23. Jeffrey M. Chemerinsky, *Counting Offenses*, 58 Duke L.J. 737 (2009).

24. See, e.g., Susan R. Klein and Jordan M. Steiker, The Search for Equality in Criminal Sentencing, 2002 Sup. Ct. Rev. 234; Abby L. Dennis, *Reining in the Minister of Justice: Prosecutorial Oversight and the Superseder Power*, 57 Duke L.J. 136 (2007) ("This vast discretionary authority is accompanied

II. CHARGING INSTRUMENTS

A. Federal Charging Instruments in the United States

Once a decision to prosecute is made, the government must consider how, where, and when to formally bring charges. With respect to the specific charging instrument selected—that is, the document that sets out the allegations and statutes violated—the Federal Rules of Criminal Procedure give DOJ prosecutors three different options: a complaint, an information, and an indictment. All these instruments serve the same basic function: they initiate a criminal case, ensure the prosecution's evidence establishes probable cause, and informs the defendant of the charges and the basic factual allegations.

1. Complaints

A complaint is a "written statement of the essential facts constituting the offense charged" sworn to by a federal law enforcement official—generally an FBI special agent—and presented by a DOJ prosecutor to a magistrate judge (or to a state or local judicial officer if a federal magistrate is unavailable).[25] Complaints are typically used prior to indictment to quickly secure an individual's arrest, either because the individual is at risk of fleeing or poses some imminent danger to the public.[26] In these situations, federal agents will seek an arrest warrant from a magistrate judge, who will consider whether the evidence recited in the agents' complaint establishes probable cause for the defendant's arrest.[27] "The purpose of the complaint, then, is to enable the appropriate magistrate . . . to determine whether the 'probable cause' required to support [an arrest] warrant exists."[28]

Because they are issued without the involvement of a grand jury, complaints generally need to include greater detail and specifics than an indictment (which is usually just in a basic outline form). In *Giordenello*, for example, the Supreme Court ruled that a complaint did

by little or no transparency. Indeed, prosecutors determine whom to charge, what charges to file, and how to obtain convictions for those charges in secret. This situation breeds potential for impropriety, as it vests in one official the power to invoke society's harshest sanctions on the basis of ad joc personal judgments, which can often be capricious or politically induced."); James Vorenberg, *Decent Restraint of Prosecutorial Power*, 94 HARV. L. REV. 1554 (1981) ("The existence and exercise of prosecutorial discretion are inconsistent with our most fundamental principles of our system of justice and our basic notions of fair play and efficient criminal administration.").

25. Fed. R. Crim. P. 3.

26. *See* Fed. R. Crim. P. 4(a); United States v. Marion, 404 U.S. 307, 320 (1971) ("To legally arrest and detain, the Government must assert probable cause to believe the arrestee has committed a crime. Arrest is a public act that may seriously interfere with the defendant's liberty, whether he is free on bail or not, and that may disrupt his employment, drain his financial resources, curtail his associations, subject him to public obloquy, and create anxiety in him, his family and his friends.").

27. Giordenello v. United States, 357 U.S. 480, 484 (1958); *see also* Johnson v. United States, 333 U.S. 10, 14 (1948) (noting that the protection afforded by these rules is that the inferences from the facts which lead to the complaint must "be drawn by a neutral and detached magistrate instead of being judged by the officer engaged in the often competitive enterprise of ferreting out crime").

28. Giordenello, 357 U.S. at 486.

"not pass muster" because it failed to provide any basis for the magistrate's determination that probable cause existed. "The complaint," Justice Harlan wrote, "contains no affirmative allegation that the affiant spoke with personal knowledge of the matters contained therein; it does not indicate any sources for the complainant's belief; and it does not set forth any other sufficient basis upon which a finding of probable cause could be made. We think these deficiencies could not be cured by the [magistrate's] reliance upon a presumption that the complaint was made on the personal knowledge of the complaining officer."

In response to the DOJ's argument that its complaint was adequate under the standards used to evaluate indictments, the Court concluded:

> It does not avail the Government to argue that because a warrant of arrest may be issued as of course upon an indictment, this complaint was adequate since its allegations would suffice for an indictment under Federal Rule of Criminal Procedure 7(c). A warrant of arrest can be based upon an indictment because the grand jury's determination that probable cause existed for the indictment also establishes that element for the purpose of issuing a warrant for the apprehension of the person so charged. Here, in the absence of an indictment, the issue of probable cause had to be determined by the Commissioner, and an adequate basis for such a finding had to appear on the face of the complaint.[29]

For felony cases to comply with the Fourth Amendment, once the defendant is arrested, the DOJ will need to obtain an indictment through the grand jury process (unless the defendant agrees to proceed by information only and waives the grand jury process).[30] Waiver will typically occur when some sort of plea agreement has been made or is in the works. Where a defendant has not waived, Federal Rule of Criminal Procedure 48(b) provides that: "If there is unnecessary delay in presenting the charge to a grand jury or in filing an information against a defendant who has been held to answer to the district court, or if there is unnecessary delay in bringing a defendant to trial, the court may dismiss the indictment, information or complaint." Similar time limits are contained in the Speedy Trial Act (18 U.S.C. § 3161—see chapter 6).

2. *Informations*

Like an indictment, an information is a written set of accusations for one or more criminal offenses and describes the factual basis for the charges. The primary difference between an information and an indictment is that an information may be filed by a prosecutor without first presenting evidence to a grand jury. Instead, an information is simply presented to a magistrate judge who then determines whether the document sets forth facts that establish probable cause that a crime occurred. Using an information can thus allow prosecutors to issue charges much more quickly than they can with an indictment, and is often done when the defendant has already reached an agreement with the DOJ to plead guilty.[31]

---

29. *Id.*

30. Misdemeanors, which carry prison sentences of up to one year, can proceed to trial on the basis of a complaint only. *See* Fed. R. Crim. P. 58(b)(1).

31. If a defendant intends to plead guilty, waiving indictment can be a sensible strategic move. Not only will waiver generate goodwill with prosecutors by allowing them to forgo the grand jury, it may limit

Felony offenses can only "be prosecuted by information if the defendant—in open court and after being advised of the nature of the charge and of the defendant's rights—waives prosecution by indictment."[32] Further, the court must accept that the waiver was made "knowingly, intelligently, and voluntarily."[33] Such waivers are not unusual, especially in connection with plea agreements.[34]

If an individual is originally charged by information and does not waive the right to indictment, prosecutors must then seek an indictment through the grand jury process. An individual may not, however, force the DOJ to proceed by information if, in the prosecutor's discretion, indictment by grand jury is more appropriate in the circumstances—for example, if prosecutors wish to obtain more evidence through grand jury subpoenas or if there is particular witness testimony prosecutors want to compel before the grand jury.[35] In other words, a defendant's waiver does not guarantee the case will not proceed by indictment.

Corporations usually are charged by information, regardless of whether they waive indictment, since they are not subject to imprisonment.[36]

3. *Indictments*

As discussed in chapter 2, an indictment is a written statement issued by a grand jury that charges a defendant with one or more federal offenses. The Fifth Amendment states that: "[n]o person shall be held to answer for a capital or otherwise infamous crime, unless on a presentment or indictment of a grand jury." Similarly, Federal Rule of Criminal Procedure 7(a) provides that "[a]n offense which may be punished by imprisonment for a term exceeding one year . . . shall be presented by indictment." Accordingly, in all felony cases, which, by definition, carry sentences of at least one year, indictment by grand jury is considered an "indispensable jurisdictional ingredient of the court's power to try a defendant."[37]

While the grand jury's sign-off is constitutionally required in cases where the right to an indictment is not waived, grand juries rarely deny the government a true bill—and, even when they do, prosecutors can present the case again before a different grand jury to see if they can procure a different result. Consequently, pressing for an indictment following arrest on an information may allow a defendant to slow down the proceedings, but will almost certainly not terminate the case against him or her.

---

the amount of incriminating material the DOJ gathers against them. This can be beneficial at sentencing, when the court's decision will be guided by the extent of the defendant's conduct and culpability as detailed by prosecutors in a sentencing memorandum (see chapter 9).

32. Fed. R. Crim. P. 7(b).

33. United States v. Hoang Van Tran, 234 F.3d 798, 806 (2d Cir. 2000).

34. Matthews v. United States, 616 F.3d 251, 253 (2d Cir. 2010).

35. Rattley v. Irelan, 197 F.2d 585, 586 (D.C. Cir. 1952).

36. *See, e.g.*, United States v. Yellow Freight Sys., 637 F.2d 1248, 1253–55 (9th Cir. 1980).

37. United States v. Ferguson, 758 F.2d 843, 850 (2d Cir. 1985).

Federal law imposes relatively minimal requirements on what details of the alleged offense an indictment or information must contain.[38] Under the Federal Rules of Criminal Procedure, the "indictment or information must be a plain, concise, and definite written statement of the essential facts constituting the offense charged."[39] "An indictment must sufficiently inform the defendant of the charges against him and provide enough detail so that he may plead double jeopardy in a future prosecution based on the same set of events."[40] Indictments are interpreted heavily in favor of their validity; they are read to include facts that are necessarily implied by the specific allegations; and minor errors or deficiencies will generally not render them invalid.[41] Indeed, because of the involvement of a grand jury as a buffer between prosecutors' decision to charge and the initiation of a criminal case in court, indictments are effectively treated as presumptively valid.

Against this backdrop, the test to determine the sufficiency of an indictment merely looks at whether it (i) "contains the elements of the offense charged," (ii) "sufficiently apprises the defendant of what he must be prepared to meet," and (iii) "in case any other proceedings are taken against him for a similar offence, whether the record shows with accuracy to what extent he may plead a former acquittal or conviction."[42] No greater specificity than the statutory language is required "so long as there is sufficient factual orientation to permit the defendant to prepare his defense and to invoke double jeopardy in the event of a subsequent prosecution."[43] "Common sense and reason are more important than technicalities" and the indictment "need not be perfect."[44] In sum, therefore, a facially valid indictment is generally "enough to call for trial of the charge on the merits."[45] For criminal defendants, the upshot of the lenient pleading standards is that, once charges are issued against them, unless the charging instrument has some serious legal flaw, there are usually only two ways for the case to end: by a verdict after trial or a guilty plea.

Although indictments are difficult to successfully challenge on the basis that they fail to properly allege an offense, they are more readily susceptible to attacks under the double

---

38. United States v. Tramunti, 513 F.2d 1087, 1113 (2d Cir. 1975) ("An indictment need do little more than to track the language of the statute charged and state the time and place . . . of the alleged crime.").

39. Fed. R. Crim. P. 7(c)(1).

40. United States v. De La Pava, 268 F.3d 157, 161 (2d Cir. 2001).

41. United States v. LaSpina, 299 F.3d 165, 177 (2d Cir. 2002); Russell v. United States, 369 U.S. 749, 763–64 (1962); United States v. Goodwin, 141 F.3d 394, 401 (2d Cir. 1997) ("[T]he precision and detail formerly demanded are no longer required, imperfections of form that are not prejudicial are disregarded, and common sense and reason prevail over technicalities.").

42. United States v. Coburn, 439 F. Supp. 3d 361, 368 (D.N.J. 2020) (citing United States v. Kemp, 500 F.3d 257, 280 (3d Cir. 2007)); *see also* United States v. O'Brien, 560 U.S. 218, 224 (2010).

43. United States v. Rankin, 870 F.2d 109, 112 (3d Cir. 1989).

44. United States v. Stringer, 730 F.3d 120, 124 (2d Cir. 2013).

45. Costello v. United States, 350 U.S. 359, 363 (1956); but see United States v. Cruikshank, 92 U.S. 542, 558 (1895) ("It is an elementary principle of criminal pleading, that where the definition of an offense, whether it be at common law or by statute, 'includes generic terms, it is not sufficient that the indictment shall change the offense in the same generic terms as in in the definition; but it must state the species—it must descent to particulars.").

jeopardy doctrine, the Constitution's venue requirements, and the applicable statute of limitations (discussed later in this section). But even then, courts interpret these issues under standards that are favorable to the government and thus are not often implicated in the typical white-collar crime case.

Practice Note

Bills of Particulars

Rule 7(f) of the Federal Rules of Criminal Procedure empowers district courts to direct the government to file a "bill of particulars" either on the court's own initiative or at the defendant's request. A bill of particulars is a document drafted by prosecutors that provides more details about the charges contained in the indictment. "A bill of particulars is appropriate where a defendant requires clarification to prepare a defense."[46] The purpose of a bill of particulars is to "minimize the danger of surprise at trial, to aid in preparation and protect against double jeopardy." Even where a bill of particulars is granted, however, the government is not required to share all the evidence it intends to produce at trial, but only its theory of the case.[47]

The denial or grant of a defendant's request for a bill of particulars lies within the court's discretion.[48] If the indictment adequately sets forth the elements of the offense charged and sufficiently apprises the defendant of the key alleged facts to enable him or her to prepare for trial, a bill of particulars is unnecessary.[49] In exercising its discretion on a defendant's motion for a bill of particulars, district courts can consider the complexity of the charges, the clarity of the indictment, and the degree of discovery available to the defendant without the bill.[50]

a. Double Jeopardy

The double jeopardy clause in the Constitution's Fifth Amendment prohibits any person from being "twice put in jeopardy of life or limb" for the same offense. The underlying purpose of this clause is to bar the government from making "repeated attempts to convict an individual for an alleged offense" and protect them "from being subjected to the hazards of trial and possible conviction more than once."[51] While the double jeopardy clause serves

46. United States v. Long, 706 F.2d 1044, 1054 (9th Cir. 1987).

47. United States v. Ryland, 806 F.2d 941, 942 (9th Cir. 1986).

48. United States v. Giese, 597 F.2d 1170, 1180 (9th Cir. 1979); United States v. Kendall, 665 F.2d 126, 134 (7th Cir. 1981).

49. United States v. Bailey, 689 F. Supp. 1463, 1472 (N.D. Ill. 1987).

50. United States v. Swiatek, 632 F. Supp. 985, 988 (N.D. Ill. 1986).

51. Green v. United States, 355 U.S. 184, 187 (1957); *see also* Brown v. Ohio, 432 U.S. 161, 164 (1977) (under the double jeopardy clause "courts may not impose more than one punishment for the same offense and prosecutors ordinarily may not attempt to secure that punishment in more than one trial"); North Carolina v. Pearce, 395 U.S. 711, 717 (1969) (the double jeopardy clause "protects against a second prosecution for the same offense after acquittal. It protects against a second prosecution for the same offense after conviction. And it protects against multiple punishments for the same offense.").

"a constitutional policy of finality for the defendant's benefit," it is subject to a number of important exceptions.[52]

First, in many cases the same conduct may constitute two separate crimes—for instance, a scheme to bribe a foreign official may violate the Foreign Corrupt Practices Act as well as federal laws prohibiting money laundering. For double jeopardy protections to apply, the elements of different crimes charged in successive prosecutions must be the same. Put differently, if two offenses are sufficiently distinguishable (as in the example cited above), a prosecution related to the second offense is permitted after an acquittal on the first. "The applicable rule is that where the same act or transaction constitutes a violation of two distinct statutory provisions, the test to be applied to determine whether there are two offenses or only one, is whether each provision requires proof of a fact which the other does not."[53] This so-called "*Blockburger* test" emphasizes the elements of crimes at issue and is satisfied "notwithstanding a substantial overlap in the proof offered to establish the crimes."[54]

Second, the double jeopardy clause does not prohibit a successive prosecution where a defendant's conviction is reversed on appeal for a procedural error occurring in the prosecution or trial.[55] Rather, the clause only applies where a conviction is reversed on the basis that the evidence presented at trial was legally or factually insufficient to prove the prosecution's case. Thus, a win on appeal for a defendant claiming a procedural error may merely return them to the district court to be tried again.

Third, if a defendant successfully moves for a mistrial, the double jeopardy clause generally does not prohibit a second prosecution.[56] But when a mistrial is ordered by the court without a defendant's consent (i.e., *sua sponte* or at the request of prosecutors), the defendant cannot be retried for the same offense unless there was a "manifest necessity" for the mistrial declaration or "the ends of public justice would otherwise be defeated."[57]

Fourth, because the state and federal governments are considered separate sovereign entities, "state prosecution does not bar a subsequent federal prosecution of the same person for the same act."[58] As recently stated by the Supreme Court, "a crime under one sovereign's laws is not 'the same offense' as a crime under the laws of another sovereign. Under this 'dual-sovereignty' doctrine, a State may prosecute a defendant under state law even if the

52. United States v. Jorn, 400 U.S. 470, 479 (1971).

53. Blockburger v. United States, 284 U.S. 299, 304 (1932).

54. Iannelli v. United States, 420 U.S. 770, 785 n.17 (1975); *but see* Brown, 432 U.S. at 169 (holding that the Fifth Amendment "forbids successive prosecution and cumulative punishment for a greater and lesser included offense"); In re Nielsen, 131 U.S. 176, 187 (1889) ("[W]here . . . a person has been tried and convicted for a crime which has various incidents included in it, he cannot be tried for one of those incidents without being twice put in jeopardy for the same offense.").

55. Burks v. United States, 437 U.S. 1, 14 (1978); United States v. Tateo, 377 U.S. 463, 465 (1964).

56. United States v. Sanford, 429 U.S. 14, 16 (1976); Downum v. United States, 372 U.S. 734, 735–36 (1963).

57. Sanford, 429 U.S. at 15–16.

58. United States v. Coonan, 938 F.2d 1553, 1562 (2d Cir. 1991) (citing United States v. Wheeler, 435 U.S. 313, 316–17 (1978) and Abbate v. United States, 359 U.S. 187, 194–95 (1959)).

Federal Government has prosecuted him for the same conduct."[59] In situations where the same conduct violates state and federal law, it is therefore possible for state and federal authorities to initiate simultaneous or successive prosecutions against a single defendant. The same is true for U.S. prosecutions following a prosecution for the same, or a related offense, in a foreign country.[60] The Supreme Court has been asked to do away with the dual sovereign doctrine in a number of cases but has repeatedly declined to do so.[61]

This unique feature of American law is often implicated in situations where a financial crime has occurred in several different countries. Because the law of most countries—including the United Kingdom—authorize prosecutions of their own nationals for criminal acts committed outside the national territory, parallel investigations in multiple jurisdictions may overlap with each other.[62] "A company or person in this situation faces a critical strategic challenge. One obvious risk is that if a target enters into any agreed-upon outcome such as a guilty plea, a DPA, or NPA, the authorities in [the United States] may learn of it and begin a new investigation seeking further penalties."[63] Norwegian state oil company StatOil learned this the hard way. After the company was successfully prosecuted by Norwegian authorities for bribes paid to Iranian officials, "to its shock—and to the surprise of the Norwegian prosecutors—the DoJ thereupon commenced an independent investigation, which resulted in StatOil agreeing to additional fines for" the same set of facts.[64]

In an exception to the general rule prohibiting interlocutory appeals from nonfinal orders, a defendant who raises a double jeopardy claim in the district court and loses may immediately appeal it.[65]

b. Venue

In addition to the requirements described above, an indictment must be brought in the correct "venue" (i.e., the correct district court). Federal Rule of Criminal Procedure 18 specifies that, unless a statute permits otherwise, "the government must prosecute an offense in a

---

59. Gamble v. United States, 139 S. Ct. 1960, 1964 (2019); *see also* United States v. Dixon, 509 U.S. 688 (1993).

60. United States v. Guzman, 85 F.3d 823, 826 (1st Cir. 1996) ("The black-letter rule is that prosecutions undertaken by separate sovereign governments, no matter how similar they may be in character, do not raise the specter of double jeopardy as that constitutional doctrine is commonly understood."); Chua Han Mow v. United States, 730 F.2d 1308, 1313 (9th Cir. 1984); United States v. Martin, 574 F.2d 1359, 1360 (5th Cir. 1978) ("The Constitution of the United States has not adopted the doctrine of international double jeopardy.").

61. Gamble v. United States, 139 S. Ct. 1960, 1967 (2019) (reviewing double jeopardy decisions and concluding that the law was clear that "a crime against two sovereigns constitutes two offenses because each sovereign has an interest to vindicate"); United States v. Jeong, 624 F.3d 706, 706 (5th Cir. 2010) (rejecting argument that a businessman's corruption conviction in Korea precluded his prosecution in the United States for the same conduct).

62. Frederick T. Davis, International Double Jeopardy: *U.S. Prosecutions and the Developing Law in Europe*, 31 Am. U. Int'l L. Rev. 59 (2016).

63. *Id.* at 59-60.

64. *Id.* at 63.

65. Abney v. United States, 431 U.S. 651 (1977); United States v. Macchia, 41 F.3d 35, 37-39 (2d Cir. 1994).

district where the offense was committed."[66] As to which specific courthouse within such district is appropriate, "due regard" must be given to the "convenience of the defendant, any victim, and the witnesses, and the prompt administration of justice."[67]

The venue requirement stems from the constitutional mandates that trials "shall be held in the State where the . . . Crimes shall have been committed"[68] and "the accused shall enjoy the right to . . . an impartial jury of the State and district wherein the crime shall have been committed."[69] When a defendant is charged with multiple crimes in a single indictment, the government must satisfy venue with respect to each charge.[70] The venue requirement demands "some sense of venue having been freely chosen by the defendant"—in other words, the location where charges are filed must somehow relate to the defendant's conduct or its foreseeable results.[71] The Supreme Court instructs that venue provisions should be "narrowly construed."[72] Nevertheless, a defendant's actual knowledge that an overt act was committed in the district of prosecution is not required: rather, "venue will lie if a reasonable jury could find that it was 'more probable than not' that the defendant 'reasonably could have foreseen' that part of the offense would take place in the district of prosecution."[73]

To determine where a crime has taken place—its so-called *locus delicti*—courts will consider "the nature of the crime alleged and the location of the act or acts constituting it."[74] If the federal statute defining a particular offense does not specify how to determine where the offense was committed, "the locus delicti must be determined from the nature of the crime alleged and the location of the act or acts constituting it."[75] "Where a crime consists of distinct parts which have different localities the whole may be tried where any part can be proved to have been done."[76]

---

66. A number of federal white-collar crime offenses have their own specific venue provisions: for example, money laundering (15 U.S.C. § 1956(i)), securities offenses (15 U.S.C. § 78aa), and investment adviser offenses (15 U.S.C. § 80b-14).

67. Fed. R. Crim. P. 18.

68. U.S. Const. art. III, § 2.

69. U.S. Const. amend. VI; *see also* United States v. Cabrales, 524 U.S. 1, 6 (1998) ("Proper venue in criminal proceedings was a matter of concern to the Nation's founders . . . [and] [t]he Constitution twice safeguards the defendant's venue right."); United States v. Cores, 356 U.S. 405, 407 (1958) ("The provision for trial in the vicinity of the crime is a safeguard against the unfairness and hardship involved when an accused is prosecuted in a remote place.").

70. United States v. Purcell, 967 F.3d 159, 186 (2d Cir. 2020); United States v. Saavedra, 223 F.3d 85, 89(2d Cir. 2001); United States v. Beech-Nut Nutrition Corp., 871 F.2d 1181, 1188 (2d Cir. 1989).

71. United States v. Davis, 689 F.3d 134, 138 (2d Cir. 2005); United States v. Svoboda, 347 F.3d 471, 483 (2d Cir. 2003).

72. Cabrales, 524 U.S. 1, 1.

73. United States v. Kirk Tang Yuk, 885 F.3d 69–70 (2d Cir. 2018)..

74. Cabrales, 524 U.S. at 6–7; United States v. Clark, 728 F.3d 622, 623–24 (7th Cir. 2013).

75. United States v. Tzolov, 642 F.3d 314, 318 (2d Cir. 2011); United States v. Rodriguez-Moreno, 526 U.S. 275, 279 (1999). Some circuit courts, including the Second Circuit, apply a "substantial contacts" analysis to determine when an offense is committed—taking into account "the site of the defendant's acts, the elements and nature of the crime, the locus of the effect of the criminal conduct, and the suitability of each district for accurate fact finding." United States v. Reed, 773 F.2d 477, 481 (2d Cir. 1985).

76. United States v. Lombardo, 241 U.S. 73, 77 (1916); Reed, 773 F.2d at 877.

Many white-collar crimes will involve more than one district—for example, a fraudulent trade may be placed from California on an exchange in New York, or a misleading investment prospectus may be sent to investors in multiple states. In these types of situations, venue will be proper in any district where an "important step in the fraud scheme" occurred, or at least where more than an "immaterial part of the alleged violations" happened.[77] "Venue is proper only where the acts constituting the offense—the crime's 'essential conduct elements'—took place."[78]

Within some circuits, including the Second Circuit, "venue may lie in more than one place if the acts constituting the crime and the nature of the crime charged implicate more than one location."[79] Although not a "formal constitutional test,"[80] the Second Circuit assesses venue in such circumstances through a "substantial contacts" analysis that considers the site of the defendant's acts, the nature of the crime, the locus of the conduct's effects, and the suitability of prosecutors' chosen venue for accurate factfinding.[81] But when an "overt act in furtherance of a criminal conspiracy has been committed in the [chosen] district" the substantial contacts analysis "has no relevance"[82]—that is, the test is reserved for marginal cases.

Certain crimes, such as conspiracy are, by default, considered "continuing offenses." Venue in cases alleging a continuing offense is governed by 18 U.S.C. § 3237, which provides: "any offense against the United States begun in one district and completed in another, or committed in more than one district, may be inquired of and prosecuted in any district in which such offense was begun, continued, or completed." The "traditional rule" in criminal conspiracy cases is that venue is proper in "any district in which an overt act of the conspiracy occurred," even if there is no evidence that the defendant physically entered that district.[83] Instead, courts have routinely held that "[a]ny district in which an overt act in furtherance of the conspiracy was committed is properly designated as the district where the offense was committed, so long as the act was performed (1) by any conspirator, and (2) was undertaken for the purpose of the objectives of the conspiracy."[84] Accordingly, the venue requirement in conspiracy cases is more flexible than those involving noncontinuing offenses and easier for the DOJ to satisfy.

Yet even for noncontinuing offenses, venue can be proper in any district where electronic communications in furtherance of the crime are sent, received, or routed through.[85] Merely

---

77. Como v. Commerce Oil Co., 607 F. Supp. 335, 341 (S.D.N.Y. 1985).

78. Tzolov, 642 F.3d at 318.

79. United States v. Thompson, 896 F.3d 155, 171 (2d Cir. 2018).

80. United States v. Saavedra, 223 F.3d 85, 93 (2d Cir. 2000).

81. Kirk Tang Yuk, 885 F.3d at 57, 70.

82. *Id.*; United States v. Naranjo, 14 F.3d 147 (2d Cir. 1994).

83. United States v. Firtash, 392 F. Supp. 3d 872, 880 (N.D. Ill. 2019) (citing United States v. Ochoa, 229 F.3d 631, 636–37 (7th Cir. 2000)).

84. Kirk Tang Yuk, 885 F.3d at 69; *see also* United States v. Kim, 246 F.3d 186 (2d Cir. 2001) (venue appropriate in New York where defendant knew that "the fraudulent invoices would be paid by a bank in New York"); Naranjo, 14 F.3d at 145, 147 (venue appropriate in New York where defendant's co-conspirator made telephone calls to an undercover agent in Manhattan).

85. United States v. Lange, 834 F.3d 58, 70 (2d Cir. 2016); United States v. Christo, 413 F. App'x 375, 376 (2d Cir. 2011); United States v. Rommy, 506 F.3d 108, 120 (2d Cir. 2007); United States v. Brown, 293 F. App'x 826, 829 (2d Cir. 2008); United States v. Goldberg, 830 F.2d 459, 465 (3d Cir. 1987).

"passing through" a district—by, for example, flying over it or driving through it en route elsewhere—can be sufficient to establish venue.[86]

Where an offense is committed by a defendant acting from overseas, venue will lie in the district "in which the offender, or any one of two or more joint offenders, is arrested or is first brought."[87] "[B]ut if such offender or offenders are not so arrested or brought into any district, an indictment or information may be filed in the district of the last known residence of the offender or of any one of two or more joint offenders, or if no such residence is known the indictment or information may be filed in the District of Columbia."[88] Because where a defendant is arrested or "first brought" before a district court is largely within DOJ's control, the practical effect of this legislation is that a foreign defendant can essentially be tried anywhere the DOJ wants them to be (subject to instances where DOJ abuses its discretion).

If a domestic defendant challenges venue in a pretrial motion to dismiss, the burden is on the government to establish venue by a preponderance of the evidence for each count.[89] Unless the facts alleged in an indictment or information are sufficient to support venue, it is subject to dismissal.[90] However, to satisfy its burden with regard to pleading venue, the government "need only allege that criminal conduct occurred within the venue, 'even if phrased broadly and without a specific address or other information.'"[91] The "government's [pleading] burden is limited to showing that the indictment alleges facts sufficient to support venue."[92] Note that all this requires of the DOJ is to make *allegations* of facts; at the pre-trial stage, the evidence purportedly underlying those facts is generally not scrutinized. The venue pleading standard thus sets a low bar for prosecutors; in practice, this means that courts will generally defer "a ruling on the propriety of the prosecution's choice of venue to trial," where the issue can be assessed in light of the full trial evidence.[93] As a result, pretrial motions to dismiss on the basis of an allegedly improper venue are rarely successful.[94]

In a high profile departure from this general rule, Judge Mayer of the district court in New Haven, Connecticut dismissed without prejudice five substantive counts of market manipulation for failure to plead venue against Andre Flotron, a Swiss national and resident who formerly headed the global precious metals trading desk at UBS. In September 2017, while visiting his girlfriend in the United States, he was arrested upon landing at Newark

86. United States v. Duque, 123 F. App'x 447, 449 (2d Cir. 2005); Kirk Tang Yuk, 885 F.3d at 71–72.

87. 18 U.S.C. § 3238.

88. *Id.*

89. United States v. Rutigliano, 790 F.3d 389, 396 (2d Cir. 2015); United States v. Tingle, 183 F.3d 719, 726–27 (7th Cir. 1999).

90. United States v. Peterson, 357 F. Supp. 2d 748, 751 (S.D.N.Y. 2005).

91. United States v. Ohle, 678 F. Supp. 2d 215, 231 (S.D.N.Y. 2010).

92. United States v. Peterson, 357 F. Supp. 2d 748, 751 (S.D.N.Y. 2005).

93. United States v. Griffith, No. 20-cr-15, 2020 WL 4369650, at *2 (S.D.N.Y. July 29, 2020).

94. United States v. Perez, 575 F.3d 164, 166–67 (2d Cir. 2009); United States v. Stein, 429 F. Supp. 2d 633, 643 (S.D.N.Y. 2006) (concluding that "as long as the indictment alleges venue, a pretrial motion to dismiss based on contrary allegations by the defendant must be denied").

Airport on a federal criminal complaint issued by the District of Connecticut.[95] He was jailed for nearly a month before eventually being released. Because Switzerland does not extradite its citizens, Flotron was deemed a flight risk and given strict bail conditions designed to prevent him from heading home—he was required to post a $4 million bond, wear a GPS ankle monitor, and remain confined to his girlfriend's New Jersey home while awaiting trial.

Because Flotron did not waive his right to indictment, the DOJ subsequently obtained a one-count indictment charging him with single count of conspiracy to commit wire fraud, commodities fraud, and spoofing "in the District of Connecticut and elsewhere." Several months later, prosecutors secured a superseding indictment that added six substantive counts which, unlike the conspiracy count, were all alleged to have occurred in the Northern District of Illinois (the location of the Chicago Mercantile Exchange). Flotron then moved to dismiss those counts for lack of venue. Granting the motion, Judge Mayer noted: "It is highly unusual for a grand jury in Connecticut to return an indictment charging a crime for which there is a no proper trial venue in Connecticut. Federal grand juries in Connecticut don't ordinarily indict bank robberies in Boston, kidnappings in Kansas, or drug dealing in Dallas . . . Because defendant is unwilling to waive his right to venue in the Northern District of Illinois, the parties agree that I must dismiss the substantive counts of the superseding indictment."[96]

Note that if it is apparent from the face of the indictment or information that it has been filed in an improper venue, as it was in *Flotron*, a defendant's failure to object prior to trial will constitute waiver of the issue, meaning that it may not be raised in post-trial motions or an appeal.[97] Thus, even though it may likely be denied, challenging venue through a pretrial motion can be a tactic to merely preserve the issue for later stages of the proceedings.

i. Transferring Venue

The place-of-trial requirements discussed above "do not impede transfer of the proceeding to a different district at the defendant's request if extraordinary local prejudice will prevent a fair trial—a 'basic requirement of due process.'"[98] Venue transfer in federal courts is governed by Federal Rule of Criminal Procedure 21, which gives district courts discretion to transfer criminal proceedings to another district if "so great a prejudice exists in the transferring district that the defendant cannot obtain a fair and impartial trial there." This provision is generally implicated only in emotionally charged, high-profile cases involving crimes like terrorism and kidnapping,[99] but venue transfers have, on occasion, also been raised in major white-collar crime cases.

---

95. As the DOJ described its apprehension strategy: "[Flotron] was arrested on a complaint because we didn't want to lose him," and "[o]nce he's in Switzerland, we have no effective extradition, realistic extradition possibility." United States v. Flotron, No. 17-cr-00220, 2018 WL 1951117 (D. Conn. Feb. 19, 2018).

96. *Id.*

97. United States v. Novak, 443 F.3d 150, 161 (2d Cir. 2006).

98. Skilling v. United States, 561 U.S. 358, 377 (2010).

99. *See, e.g.*, United States v. McVeigh, 918 F. Supp. 1467, 1474 (W.D. Okla. 1996) (transferring trial of suspect in the Oklahoma City bombing).

In the fraud prosecution of former Enron Corporation CEO Jeffrey Skilling, for example, Skilling moved to change the venue of his trial to somewhere aside from Houston, the site of Enron's headquarters before the company's collapse. Skilling contended that hostility toward him in Houston and the widespread pretrial publicity given to his case had "poisoned potential jurors."[100] The motion was denied by the district court upon finding that the media coverage, while extensive, "had been objective and unemotional, and [that] the facts of the case were neither heinous nor sensational."[101] This decision was ultimately upheld by the Supreme Court, which agreed that the "news stories about Enron did not present the kind of vivid, unforgettable information the Court has recognized as particularly likely to produce prejudice, and Houston's size and diversity diluted the media's impact."[102]

Where granted, venue transfers are premised on the theory that trial verdicts should "be induced only by evidence and argument in open court, and not by any outside influence, whether of private talk or public print."[103] The mere fact that jurors may have been exposed to pretrial publicity about the alleged crime or defendant does not, however, presumptively deprive the defendant of due process.[104] Rather, the Supreme Court has emphasized that "[p]rominence does not necessarily produce prejudice, and juror *impartiality* . . . does not require *ignorance*."[105]

In making determinations under Rule 21, courts will weigh factors such as (i) the size and characteristics of the community in which the crime occurred, (ii) the extent to which media coverage included "blatantly prejudicial information of the type readers and viewers could not be reasonably expected to shut from sight," (iii) the time lapsed between media coverage about a crime and the related trial, and (iv) any other indications of possible juror bias.[106]

c. Statutes of Limitations

Statutes of limitations (SOLs) specify the period within which criminal charges must be brought after a crime has been committed, and are the "primary guarantee against bringing overly stale criminal charges."[107] "The purpose of a statute of limitations is to limit exposure to criminal prosecution to a certain fixed period of time following the occurrence of" a criminal act.[108] This limit is designed to protect individuals from having to defend themselves

100. Skilling, 561 U.S. at 358.

101. *Id.*

102. *Id.* at 384; *see also* Nebraska Press Ass'n v. Stuart, 427 U.S. 539, 554 (1976) ("pretrial publicity—even pervasive, adverse publicity—does not inevitably lead to an unfair trial").

103. Patterson v. Colorado ex rel. Attorney General of Colo., 205 U.S. 454, 462 (1907).

104. Murphy v. Florida, 421 U.S. 794, 798–99 (1975); Patton v. Yount, 467 U.S. 1025 (1984).

105. Skilling, 561 U.S. at 381; *see also* Irvin v. Dowd, 366 U.S. 717, 722 (1961) (finding that jurors are not required to be "totally ignorant of the facts and issues involved" because "scarcely any of those best qualified to serve as jurors will not have formed some impression or opinion as to the merits of the case").

106. Skilling, 561 U.S. at 381–84.

107. United States v. Marion, 404 U.S. 307, 322 (1971).

108. Toussie v. United States, 397 U.S. 112, 114 (1970).

against charges when the basic facts have been obscured by the passage of time and to encourage law enforcement "promptly to investigate suspected criminal activity."[109]

Underlying the use of SOLs in the American system is the perception that they provide an appropriate degree of "predictability by specifying a limit beyond which there is an irrebuttable presumption that a defendant's right to a fair trial would be prejudiced."[110] Because SOLs represent fundamental public policy decisions made by Congress, the Supreme Court instructs that "they are to be liberally interpreted in favor of repose," meaning that where there is any doubt, the facts and relevant law in a particular case should be read such that a statute of limitations will bar prosecution.[111]

The general rule is that, if an indictment or other charging instrument is not filed by the last day of the statute of limitations, then the indictment will be time-barred unless the government can establish that it effectively tolled—that is, paused—the statute of limitations.[112] "Statutes of limitations normally begin to run when the crime is complete"[113] and in general run until "the indictment is found or the information is instituted."[114] Complaints are generally not sufficient to toll SOLs.[115] The statute of limitations remains tolled if an information is replaced by an indictment,[116] or if the original indictment is replaced by a superseding indictment, as long as the superseding indictment does not substantially alter the original charge.[117] Further, federal law allows for a defendant to be recharged following dismissal of the original indictment or information regardless of whether the new charging instrument is within the applicable statute of limitations. Specifically, 18 U.S.C. § 3288 provides:

> Whenever an indictment or information charging a felony is dismissed for any reason after the period prescribed by the applicable statute of limitations has expired, a new indictment may be returned in the appropriate jurisdiction within six calendar months of the date of the

---

109. *Id.* at 114–15 ("The purpose of a statute of limitations is to limit exposure to criminal prosecution to a certain fixed period of time following the occurrence of those acts the legislature has decided to punish by criminal sanctions. Such a limitation is designed to protect individuals from having to defend themselves against charges when the basic facts may have become obscured by the passage of time and to minimize the danger of official punishment because of acts in the far-distant past. Such a time limit may also have the salutary effect of encouraging law enforcement officials promptly to investigate suspected criminal activity."); Public Schools v. Walker, 9 Wall. 282, 288 (1870) (statutes of limitations "are made for the repose of society and the protection of those who may [during the limitation] . . . have lost their means of defense").

110. United States v. Marion, 404 U.S. 307, 322 (1971).

111. *Id.* at 323 n.14.

112. United States v. Kozeny, 493 F. Supp. 2d 693, 702 (S.D.N.Y. 2007).

113. Pendergast v. United States, 317 U.S. 412, 418 (1943); *see also* United States v. Guerro, 694 F.2d 898, 901 (2d Cir. 1982) ("The long-established rule is that a statute of limitations begins to run on the day following the day on which the event giving rise to the cause of action occurred.").

114. 18 U.S.C. § 3282(a); *see also* United States v. Pacheco, 912 F.2d 297, 305 (9th Cir. 1990).

115. *See* United States v. Dolan, 113 F. Supp. 757, 762 (D. Conn. 1953).

116. United States v. Burdix-Dana, 149 F.3d 741, 742–43 (7th Cir. 1998).

117. United States v. Liu, 731 F.3d 982, 996–97 (9th Cir. 2013); United States v. McMillan, 600 F.3d 434, 444 (5th Cir. 2010).

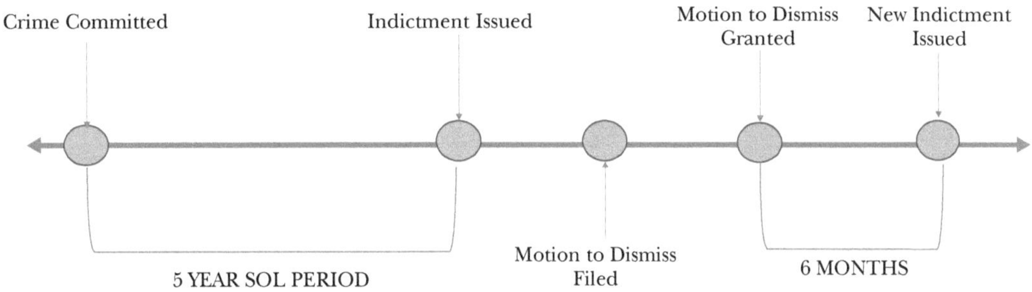

Figure 3.1 Section 3288 Tolling

> dismissal of the indictment or information, or, in the event of an appeal, within 60 days of the date the dismissal of the indictment or information becomes final, or, if no regular grand jury is in session in the appropriate jurisdiction when the indictment or information is dismissed, within six calendar months of the date when the next regular grand jury is convened, which new indictment shall not be barred by any statute of limitations.

Note that this provision does not apply if the original charging instrument was dismissed because it was outside of the statute of limitations "or for some other reason that would bar a new prosecution."[118] A typical timeline in cases implicating Section 3288 is shown in figure 3.1.

While some terrorism-related crimes, murder, and certain other serious violent offenses can be brought at any time, all federal white-collar crimes are subject to a statute of limitations. Most are governed by the general five-year SOL contained in 18 U.S.C. 3282(a): "Except as otherwise provided by law, no person shall be prosecuted, tried, or punished for any offense, not capital, unless the indictment is found or the information is instituted within five years next after such offense shall have been committed."[119]

By statute, Congress has designated certain financial crimes to have a longer statute of limitations (table 3.1).

Although statutes of limitations are intended to protect individuals from having to defend themselves against stale charges, there are various mechanisms that allow the government to effectively extend them for significant periods.

i. Tolling Agreements

Prosecutors may sometimes ask defendants to enter into a tolling agreement that suspends the otherwise applicable statute of limitations for a certain time period. Tolling agreements are typically proposed when the statute of limitations will soon expire but the DOJ has not yet completed its investigation. By entering into a tolling agreement, the target of an

---

118. 18 U.S.C. § 3289 and § 3296 also preserve the government's ability to reindict a defendant in situations where cases are dismissed before a statute of limitations runs, or where charges are dismissed pursuant to a plea agreement (but then the conviction is later vacated).

119. United States v. Kozeny, 493 F. Supp. 2d 693, 701 (S.D.N.Y. 2007) ("Where no statute speaks to the limitations period that applies for a particular offense, 'a "catchall" statute operates' to supply a five-year statute of limitations for noncapital offenses" under [18 U.S.C. §3282].).

Table 3.1 Statute of Limitations for Financial Crimes

Offense	Relevant Statute	Limitation Period
Crimes by or affecting persons engaged in the business of insurance	18 U.S.C. § 1033	10 years
Bank fraud	18 U.S.C. § 1344	10 years
Wire fraud affecting a financial institution	18 U.S.C. § 1343	10 years
Securities and commodities fraud	18 U.S.C. § 1348	6 years
Investment Advisers Act violations	15 U.S.C. § 80b-17	6 years
Tax crimes	26 U.S.C. § 6531	6 years

investigation may hope that prosecutors can be convinced not to file charges during the tolling period through proffers and other forms of informal communication;[120] prosecutors, on the other hand, generally use tolling agreements to preserve their ability to file charges while gathering additional evidence. In any event, refusing a tolling agreement will usually not result in an investigation going away—instead, in most cases, the DOJ will simply respond by accelerating toward charging at least one readily provable count—for example, a conspiracy under 18 U.S.C. § 371—to toll the SOL, and then continue on to gather enough evidence for an indictment or superseding indictment involving additional charges.

Tolling agreements will often include:

> (1) a recitation of the statutory offense(s) at issue in the inquiry; (2) a statement that the parties agree it is in their interests and the interests of justice to enter the agreement to provide time for the government to review information; (3) a specifically defined tolling period (subject to extension); (4) a provision stating that nothing in the agreement shall revive a claim or charge for which the applicable statute of limitations has already run; and (5) an acknowledgement that the act of entering into the agreement does not constitute an admission of wrongdoing.[121]

ii. Statutes of Limitations for Conspiracy and Other "Continuing Offenses"

The most frequently charged federal conspiracy statute—18 U.S.C. § 371—has two elements: (i) an agreement to commit a federal crime, and (ii) at least one "overt act in furtherance" of that agreement (see chapter 4). Even though a Section 371 conspiracy can be charged upon the first overt act, the statute of limitations for such an offense does not begin to run until the last act in furtherance committed by any of the conspirators.[122] This means that, "with

120. *See, e.g.*, United States v. Cote, 544 F.3d 88, 92 (2d Cir. 2000).

121. Evan T. Barr & Christopher H. Bell, *Stopping the Clock: Tolling Agreements in Federal Criminal Cases*, N.Y. L. J. (Jan. 7, 2021).

122. United States v. Stewart, 744 F.3d 17, 21 (1st Cir. 2014) ("Where, as here, a conspiracy charge requires proof of an overt act, the government must show that the conspiracy still existed, and that at least one overt act in furtherance of the conspiracy was committed during the limitations period."); *see also* United States v. Smith, 568 U.S. 106, 107 (2013); Grunewald v. United States, 353 U.S. 391, 396–97 (1957).

respect to conspiracy offenses, the government must 'allege and prove at least one overt act that occurred' within the statute of limitations."[123] Moreover, because the foreseeable acts of one co-conspirator in furtherance of the conspiracy are attributable to all other co-conspirators, the SOL can be extended for the entire conspiracy group based on the act of just one of them.[124]

For instance, if a securities fraud conspiracy began in 2000 and ended with an act occurring in 2018, as long as the final act—committed by any co-conspirator—is within the five-year statute of limitations, the DOJ can charge *all* conspirators for *all* conduct occurring during the entire conspiracy.[125] What constitutes an "overt act" is interpreted extremely broadly and includes, for example, efforts to conceal an otherwise already concluded conspiracy[126] and continued receipt of illegal proceeds from a criminal conspiracy.[127]

Certain conspiracy offenses, such as racketeering conspiracy (18 U.S.C. § 1962(d), do not have an overt act element. The statute of limitations for these crimes begins when the conspiracy's objectives are accomplished, is abandoned, or when a defendant affirmatively withdraws from it (but the SOL for any remaining co-conspirators will not begin until their own withdrawal or the conspiracy is complete).[128] Some federal white-collar crimes like bank fraud (18 U.S.C. § 1344) and health care fraud (18 U.S.C. § 1347(a)) are considered "continuing offenses" and treated the same as conspiracies for SOL purposes.

The favorable statute of limitations in conspiracy cases gives federal prosecutors a powerful tool that they routinely use to prosecute white-collar crimes that mainly occurred many years prior to the filing of charges.

iii. Statutes of Limitations, Foreign Evidence, and Mutual Legal Assistance Treaties

As discussed in chapter 2, the DOJ can seek foreign evidence through MLATs and various other means. Because it may take foreign authorities a significant amount of time to produce the requested materials, prosecutors can make a request to the district court to toll the statute of limitations while their "official request" for foreign evidence—either through an MLAT, letter rogatory, or another arrangement—is pending.[129] The relevant statute, 18 U.S.C. § 3292, states that a period of suspension "shall begin on the date on which the official request is made and end on the date on which the foreign court or authority takes final action on the request." Courts are divided as to what "final action" means—some courts

---

123. United States v. Milstein, 401 F.3d 53, 71 (2d Cir. 2005).

124. United States v. Ben Zvi, 242 F.3d 89, 97 (2d Cir. 2001).

125. United States v. Kozeny, 493 F. Supp. 2d 693, 702 n. 26 (S.D.N.Y. 2007) ("Absent evidence that defendants ceased to be co-conspirators, which is an affirmative defense, any overt act by any of the co-conspirators in furtherance of the conspiracy within the limitations period will make the conspiracy charges timely against all defendants.").

126. Grunewald, 353 U.S. at 406.

127. United States v. Salmonese, 352 F.3d 608, 618 (2d Cir. 2003).

128. United States v. Spero, 331 F.3d 57, 60 (2d Cir. 2003).

129. An "official request" is defined in the statue as "a letter rogatory, a request under a treaty or convention, or any other request for evidence" made by a court or a criminal law enforcement authority of the United States to a court or other authority of a foreign country. 18 U.S.C. § 3292(d).

have determined that "final action" on an MLAT request occurs when the DOJ is satisfied with the foreign government's response, while others have ruled that final action occurs when the foreign government confirms it has exhausted its production of evidence.[130]

Assuming that a Section 3292 suspension request is granted, the applicable statute of limitations can be extended by up to a maximum of three years from the date the request was filed.[131] But this only applies if the request to toll is made prior to the expiration of the statute of limitations.[132] Therefore, simply making an MLAT request will not save an otherwise untimely prosecution.

While Section 3292 can be used to suspend a statute of limitations even if the evidence sought from overseas could have been obtained within the United States,[133] it is not intended to allow prosecutors to make an MLAT request simply as a pretext for tolling the statute of limitations and thereby unfairly prejudice a defendant.[134]

iv. Flights from Justice

Under 18 U.S.C. § 3290, "No statute of limitations shall extend to any person fleeing from justice." The effect of this provision is to toll the statute of limitations starting from when a person begins to evade the authorities until they are apprehended.[135] This prevents a defendant from effectively "running out the clock" by evading arrest. It is the government's burden to show that a defendant fled from justice by a preponderance of the evidence.[136]

As to what constitutes "flight" for statute of limitations purposes, the rule followed in most circuits is that flight occurs when the defendant conceals himself within the jurisdiction, remains outside the jurisdiction after becoming aware of the possibility of prosecution, flees before an investigation begins, departs after an investigation has begun but before charges are filed, absconds to avoid prosecution on another matter, or flees to avoid a civil or administrative case.[137]

4. *Sealed Indictments*

Once an indictment is returned by a grand jury, the DOJ can make a request to have it "sealed" by a magistrate judge, meaning that it will "be kept secret until the defendant is in custody or

---

130. *Compare* United States v. Bischel, 61 F.3d 1429, 1432–34 (9th Cir. 1995) *with* United States v. Meador, 138 F.3d 986, 991–94 (5th Cir. 1998).

131. 18 U.S.C. § 3292(b).

132. *See, e.g.*, United States v. Kozeny, 541 F.3d 166, 174 (2d Cir. 2008).

133. United States v. Lyttle, 667 F.3d 220, 224–25 (2d Cir. 2012).

134. *See* Jack Crowe, *Former Justice Department Attorney Warns that Prosecutorial Abuses Go Beyond FISA Process,* National Review (Feb. 13, 2020).

135. United States v. Rivera-Ventura, 72 F.3d 277, 283–84 (2d Cir. 1995).

136. United States v. Florez, 447 F.3d 145, 149 (2d Cir. 2006).

137. *Statute of Limitation in Federal Criminal Cases: An Overview*, Congressional Research Service at 10 (Nov. 14, 2017), *available at* https://fas.org/sgp/crs/misc/RL31253.pdf.

has been released pending trial."[138] The sealing process is informal, and magistrate judges generally will not require prosecutors to justify their requests to seal in any substantial way.

When an indictment is sealed, "no person may disclose the indictment's existence except as necessary to issue or execute a warrant or summons." After the defendant is arrested, the indictment is unsealed, and the charges become public.

Sealed indictments are often used in situations where the defendant resides or is located outside of the United States, in the hopes that they will unsuspectingly travel to the United States (or a country with which the United States has an extradition treaty) and be more readily subject to arrest.[139] In 2016, for example, Mark Johnson, a British citizen and the global head of foreign exchange trading at HSBC, was arrested on a sealed indictment by the FBI as he attempted to board a plane from JFK Airport in New York back to London.[140] Similarly, in 2015 two South American officials at FIFA—football's world governing body—were arrested, at the DOJ's request, in a predawn raid by Swiss authorities at their hotel in Zurich, Switzerland (where they were attending a high-level FIFA conference). Later that same day, a ninety-two-count indictment was unsealed in federal court in Brooklyn, New York, alleging a decades-long racketeering, wire fraud, and money laundering conspiracy to corrupt international football.[141] By keeping the charges under seal until the defendants traveled to Switzerland, the DOJ was able to orchestrate the defendant's apprehension in a location where extradition was easier to achieve.

In addition to facilitating arrest, sealed indictments give the government the additional benefit of stopping the applicable statute of limitations as of the date the indictment was returned by the grand jury.[142] This gives prosecutors a near-limitless time within which to locate and arrest a subject as long as the underlying indictment was filed within the statute of limitations.[143] "However, when the defendant can demonstrate substantial actual prejudice

---

138. Fed. R. Crim. P. 6(e)(4); *see also* United States v. Srulowitz, 819 F.2d 37, 41 (2d Cir. 1987) ("A simple request for secrecy by the prosecutor . . . is sufficient to invoke the Magistrate's authority to direct sealing."); United States v. DiSalvo, 34 F.3d 1204, 1218 (3d Cir. 1994) (an indictment may be sealed for any legitimate prosecutorial purpose or in the public interest).

139. United States v. Leaver, 358 F. Supp. 2d 255, 266 (S.D.N.Y. 2004) ("Facilitation of arrest, where the accused's whereabouts are unknown, is a proper purpose for sealing, as is the fear that an accused will become a fugitive if he learns of the charges.").

140. Rupert Neate & Jill Treanor, *FBI Arrests Senior HSBC Banker Accused of Rigging Multibillion-Dollar Deal,* The Guardian, July 20, 2016.

141. Press Release, U.S. Department of Justice, Sixteen Additional FIFA Officials Indicted for Racketeering Conspiracy and Corruption (Dec. 3, 2015), *available at* https://www.justice.gov/opa/pr/sixteen-additional-fifa-officials-indicted-racketeering-conspiracy-and-corruption.

142. United States v. Southland Corp., 760 F.2d 1366, 1379–80 (2d Cir. 1985). Note that the 10th Circuit Court of Appeals holds a minority view that the sealing of an indictment does not toll the statute of limitations. *See* United States v. Thompson, 287 F.3d 1244, 1251–52 (10th Cir. 2002).

143. Srulowitz, 819 F.2d at 40 ("[W]hen a sealed indictment is not opened until after the expiration of the time allowed by the statute of limitations for the prosecution of an offense, the statute ordinarily is not a bar to prosecution if the indictment was timely filed); United States v. Muse, 633 F.2d 1041 (2d Cir. 1980).

occurring between the date of sealing and the date of unsealing, the expiration of the limitations period before the latter event warrants dismissal of the indictment."[144]

5. Amending an Indictment

Because the Constitution creates a right to be tried on an indictment returned by a grand jury, "after an indictment has been returned its charges may not be broadened through amendment except by the grand jury itself."[145] This rule prevents a defendant from being tried on charges that are not included in the indictment. In contrast, informations are more flexible in that they may generally be amended "at any time before the verdict or finding" with the consent of the court.[146]

Prosecutors must not only refrain from literally amending an indictment's text without a new vote from the grand jury, they also must not "constructively amend" the indictment through their presentation at trial. "A constructive amendment occurs when the charge upon which the defendant is tried differs significantly from the charge upon which the grand jury voted."[147] Constructive amendment can also occur when the trial evidence alters the essential elements of the charges specified in the indictment. To prevail on a claim that the indictment was impermissibly amended in this way, a defendant "must demonstrate that either the proof at trial or the trial court's jury instructions so altered an essential element of the charge that, upon review, it is uncertain whether the defendant was convicted of conduct that was subject of the grand jury's indictment."[148]

An indictment will not be considered constructively amended where only a superfluous portion of the indictment that is unnecessary for a conviction of the crime charged is removed or altered.[149] Similarly, a constructive amendment will not occur if prosecutors' case at trial is narrower than the charges alleged in the indictment. Rather, a constructive amendment occurs only "where (1) an additional element, sufficient for conviction, is added, or (2) an element essential to the crime charged is altered."[150]

6. Superseding Indictments

DOJ prosecutors will often file one or more "superseding indictments"—informally called "superseders"—throughout the course of a white-collar crime prosecution. Superseding indictments replace all previous indictments in the same case and generally add new charges

144. Srulowitz, 819 F.2d at 40.

145. Stirone v. United States, 361 U.S. 212, 215 (1960).

146. Fed. R. Crim. P. 7(e).

147. United States v. Dove, 884 F.3d 138, 146 (2d Cir. 2018).

148. United States v. Salmonese, 352 F. 608, 620 (2d Cir. 2003).

149. United States v. Miller, 471 U.S. 130, 136–37 (1985).

150. Dove, 884 F.3d at 146; *see also* United States v. Ratliff-White, 493 F.3d 812, 819–20 (7th Cir. 2007) ("A constructive amendment to an indictment is found where a 'complex set of facts' is presented to the jury during the trial which is distinctly different from the set of facts set forth in the charging instrument.").

or additional defendants (and must therefore be obtained through the grand jury process). They are usually filed in response to evidence discovered by prosecutors after the return of an earlier indictment, or upon a reassessment of existing evidence. For the reasons discussed earlier, superseders must be returned by a federal grand jury.

A superseding indictment that does not materially depart from the charges originally brought will "relate back" to the original indictment with respect to the applicable statute of limitations.[151] This means that, as long as the original indictment was timely, a superseding indictment filed outside of the statute of limitations will also be considered timely if it does not significantly alter the original. The reasoning behind the "relate back doctrine" was explained by the Seventh Circuit:

> [O]nce an indictment has been timely filed, the defendant is notified of the charge against him and may begin to prepare his defense. The mere restatement or superficial amendment of the charge in a subsequent indictment does not further prejudice the defendant and thus does not offend the purposes underlying the limitation period. Therefore, a superseding indictment that supplants a still-pending original indictment relates back to the original indictment's filing date so long as it neither materially broadens nor substantially amends the charges initially brought against the defendant.[152]

Superseding indictments may be returned at any time before trial, absent substantial prejudice to the defendant.[153] If a superseder is filed on the eve of trial (or otherwise requires material further preparation by the defense), the court will likely adjourn the trial date if a defendant so requests. Superseding indictments are often sought after a defendant's challenge to the liability theory underpinning the original indictment through a motion to dismiss fails.

B. Charging Instruments in the United Kingdom

Once a decision to charge has been made, the director of the SFO, the DPP, and other senior law enforcement officials are authorized to "institute criminal proceedings against a person by issuing a document (a 'written charge') which charges the person with an offence."[154] The written charge—referred to as an "information"—will include a "requisition" that requires the accused to appear before a magistrates' court at a certain date and time to answer the charges (in the same way as a summons).

Alternatively, prosecutors can seek an arrest warrant under the Magistrates' Courts Act (MCA) 1980. Arrest warrants are only allowed to be issued if "the offence to which the warrant relates is an indictable offence or is punishable with imprisonment" or "the person's

151. United States v. Ross, 77 F.3d 1525, 1536 (7th Cir. 1996).

152. *Id.* at 1537; *see also* United States v. Robilotto, 828 F.2d 940, 949 (2d Cir. 1987); United States v. Pacheco, 912 F.2d 297, 305 (9th Cir. 1990).

153. United States v. Wilks, 629 F.2d 669, 672 (10th Cir. 1980); United States v. Grossman, 843 F.2d 78, 83 (2d Cir. 1988) (finding no error in district court allowing case to proceed where superseding indictment was filed two days prior to trial).

154. Criminal Justice Act (CJA) 2003, s. 29(1).

address is not sufficiently established for a summons to be served on him."[155] To secure an arrest warrant, prosecutors must deliver to the relevant magistrates' court a written warrant application or a copy of the information.[156] The information must include specifics of the offense charged, including "such particulars of the conduct constituting the commission of the offence as to make clear what the prosecutor alleges against the defendant."[157] Informations that do not contain the requisite details are subject to dismissal.[158]

As discussed in further detail in chapter 5, a prosecutor serving an information on a defendant must simultaneously provide substantial preliminary details about the case to inform a defendant's decision on how to plead.[159]

Serious financial crime offenses will generally be "indictable only," meaning that the offender can only be tried based on an indictment (which can be drafted after the information or arrest warrant application). Because there are no grand juries in the United Kingdom, prosecutors can issue an indictment based on their own independent evaluation of the evidence (albeit with some limited judicial oversight).

As in the United States, there are minimal requirements under English law for what details an indictment must contain. In general, indictments need only include, for each count charged, a statement that describes the offense in ordinary language, identifies any legislation that creates it, and sets forth factual allegations about the purported conduct to make clear what the prosecutor believes occurred.[160] In accordance with DPP guidance, "sufficient counts must be included in the indictment to reflect the full criminality alleged and thereby enable the sentencing judge, in the event of conviction, to impose a sentence that properly reflects that criminality."[161]

1. Amending the Indictment

Indictments may be amended at any time before trial, or at any stage during trial, but only with the approval of the Crown Court. Indictments are typically amended to correct a defect or to add new counts or delete existing ones. Courts are given broad leeway in ruling on such amendments and are independently empowered to "order for the amendment of the indictment as the court thinks necessary to meet the circumstances of the case, unless, having regard to the merits of the case, the required amendments cannot be made without injustice."[162]

In light of the relative ease with which prosecutors can amend indictments in the United Kingdom, superseding indictments (discussed earlier) are not a feature of British criminal procedure.

155. Magistrates' Courts Act (MCA), s. 1(4).

156. Criminal Procedure Rules (CrimPR), s. 7.2.

157. *Id.*, s. 7.3(1)(b).

158. Atterton v. Brown [1945] KB 122.

159. CrimPR, s. 8.3.

160. CrimPR, s.10.2(1).

161. CPS, *Drafting the Indictment, available at* https://www.cps.gov.uk/legal-guidance/drafting-indictment.

162. Indictments Act 1915, s. 5(1).

2. *Double Jeopardy in the United Kingdom*

Retrials after an acquittal are permitted in the United Kingdom, but only with respect to certain serious drug offenses and violent crimes,[163] or when "a person has been convicted of an administration or justice offence involving interference with or intimidation of a juror or a witness (or potential witness) in any proceedings which led to the acquittal."[164] In cases involving financial crimes, the common law doctrines of *autrefois acquit* and *autrefois convict* bar retrials of a person who has previously been acquitted or convicted of the same offense.[165] According to the Court of Appeal, "The rationale for this restriction on subsequent prosecution is obvious. It finds reflection in the principle . . . to the effect that no person shall be vexed twice in the same cause. It also finds reflection in the further, and related principle . . . that it is in the public interest that there be finality to litigation."[166]

The rule against double jeopardy applies equally to acquittals by a jury or where a conviction is vacated on appeal. As in the United States, a subsequent prosecution will be considered impermissibly duplicative of an earlier one if it relies on substantially the same facts.[167] This means that the "Crown should not be permitted, save in special or exceptional circumstances, to bring a second set of proceedings arising out of the same incident after the first set of proceedings has been concluded." Instead, the law requires the Crown to "decide at the outset, or at the latest before the conclusion of the first set of proceedings, what charges it wishes to bring arising out of the same incident. Any other approach is unfairly oppressive to a defendant."[168]

Where a defendant has been convicted or acquitted of an offense in an overseas jurisdiction, the double jeopardy rule will generally bar their retrial in the United Kingdom (unless there is a strong countervailing public interest in a domestic prosecution).[169] Thus, in contrast with the "dual sovereign" doctrine followed by U.S. courts, a defendant in the United Kingdom who has been convicted or acquitted in a foreign jurisdiction will generally not be subject to subsequent prosecution by British authorities. In 2010, for example, the SFO declined to prosecute DePuy International Ltd on double jeopardy grounds because the company had already reached a deferred prosecution agreement in the United States for the same conduct.[170]

3. *Statutes of Limitations in the United Kingdom*

Unlike the United States and most other Western nations, the United Kingdom has no statute of limitations for any criminal offense other than minor, summary offenses that must be charged within six months. While there is no strict legal time bar prohibiting prosecutions for very dated conduct, prosecutors usually face a practical limit from the passage of time

163. CJA 2003, s.75; CJA 2003, part 10 and Schedule 5(1).

164. CPIA, s.54.

165. Connelly v. DPP [1964] AC 1254.

166. R v. Wangige [2020] EWCA Crim 1319.

167. *Id.*

168. *Id.*

169. R v. Aughet [1919] 13 Cr App R 101; R v. Thomas [1985] QB 604.

170. See Depuy Pays $7.9 Million to End UK Bribe Case, Fierce Biotech (Apr. 10, 2011).

due to fading memories of witnesses, difficulties in obtaining stale evidence, and public policy considerations. A prosecution based on extremely old conduct may also be susceptible to an abuse of process claim (see chapter 6).

4. Selecting Trial Venues in the United Kingdom

Unlike criminal defendants in the United States, defendants in the United Kingdom do not have a legal right to have their cases heard within the venue where their crimes occurred. Instead, British prosecutors have a large degree of discretion as to the magistrates' court in which they decide to file criminal charges; in turn, the magistrates' court has discretion to determine where trial will be held (which can be another magistrates' court or a Crown Court—for either-way or indictable-only offenses). In making this determination, the magistrates' court must principally consider the "convenience of the defence, the prosecution and the witnesses," and "the expediting of the trial."[171] Because magistrates' courts generally feed into specific Crown Courts, prosecutors can indirectly select the venue in criminal cases by choosing to file charges in a particular magistrates' court. Most major financial crimes are tried in one of two London courts: Southwark Crown Court and the Central Criminal Court—nicknamed the "Old Bailey" after the street where it is located. Sitting just outside the former western wall of the City of London and on the site of a medieval prison, the Old Bailey—which has been destroyed and rebuilt multiple times—has been England's principal criminal justice location for centuries.[172]

Prejudicial concerns regarding a selected trial venue are minimal in the United Kingdom because of the country's far smaller geographic size as compared with the United States. Because England is smaller than New York State, it is essentially impossible for venue to cause significant inconvenience to the defendants, victims, or witnesses involved in a U.K. criminal case.

III. ARREST, PLEAS, BAIL, AND EXTRADITION

Once charges are filed, the defendant must be apprehended or otherwise brought before a court for an initial appearance and bail determination. This process is more complex in cross-border prosecutions involving defendants who reside or are located outside the prosecuting jurisdiction. Because the indicting authority in such cases lacks the power to order an arrest of the foreign defendant on foreign soil, the arrest will be generally made by local

171. MCA, s.7.

172. The Old Bailey's courtrooms are designed to "emphasize the contest between the accused and the rest of the court. The accused stood at 'the bar' (or in 'the dock'), directly facing the witness box (where the prosecution and defence witnesses testified) and the judges seated on the other side of the room. Before the introduction of gas lighting in the early nineteenth century a mirrored reflector was placed above the bar, in order to reflect light from the windows onto the faces of the accused. This allowed the court to examine their facial expressions and assess the validity of their testimony." Clive Emsley, Tim Hitchcock, and Robert Shoemaker, *Historical Background—History of the Old Bailey Courthouse* (May 28, 2022), *available at* https://www.oldbaileyonline.org/static/The-old-bailey.jsp.

authorities at the other country's request. The defendant must then be brought to the charging jurisdiction—either voluntarily or through extradition—for the case to proceed.[173]

A. Initial Pretrial Procedures in the United States

1. Arrest

After a defendant is charged with a crime by indictment, information, or complaint, a magistrate judge will usually issue a warrant for his or her arrest.[174] There is no constitutional right to be arrested at any particular time, however. As the Supreme Court emphasized in *Hoffa*, "[l]aw enforcement officers are under no constitutional duty to call a halt to a criminal investigation the moment they have the minimum evidence to establish probable cause, a quantum of evidence which may fall far short of the amount necessary to support a criminal conviction."[175] This principle allows the DOJ to continue to build their case until at least the expiration of the applicable statute of limitations. Most criminal defendants will have no advance indication they are being investigated until they are arrested, which, in financial crime cases, is often at least several years after the alleged offense occurred.

Under Federal Rule of Criminal Procedure 4(c)(2), an arrest warrant can be executed by the FBI or U.S. Marshall's Service (USMS)[176] anywhere within the United States. If the defendant's whereabouts are unknown or if they are located abroad when the arrest warrant issues, the DOJ can make request for an "International Wanted Notice" (also called a "Red Notice") to be issued (see the following Practice Note). Red Notices are issued by INTERPOL, an international law enforcement organization based in Lyon, France, to all 194 member countries and request that the wanted individual be arrested by law enforcement in whatever country he or she is located as soon as possible. Once an individual is arrested pursuant to a Red Notice, the DOJ will then need to extradite the individual to be prosecuted unless the defendant waives extradition and travels to the United States voluntarily to be prosecuted.

---

173. Although it is possible for a defendant in the United States to be tried in absentia—that is, without his presence in the courtroom—a trial date may not be set before the defendant is brought before the court for arraignment. *See* United States v. Reed, 639 F.2d 896, 903–04 (2d Cir. 1981); United States v. Pastor, 557 F.2d 930, 934 (2d Cir. 1977); United States v. Tortora, 464 F.2d 1202, 1208–09 (2d Cir. 1972). The same is true in England. *See* R v. Jones [2002] UKHL 5 (recognizing that the Crown Court has discretion to proceed with a trial against a defendant who was present at its start, but then absconded). In both jurisdictions, trials in absentia are exceedingly rare.

174. Fed. R. Crim. P. 9(a). At the prosecutors' request, a summons may be issued instead of an arrest warrant. Summonses direct an individual to appear in court at a specified time and date, and can be served on a defendant in the same manner as a civil lawsuit. Fed. R. Crim. P. 4. If the summons is not adhered to, an arrest warrant will then be issued. Summonses are often used when a corporation is indicted.

175. 385 U.S. 293, 310 (1966).

176. The USMS is a bureau within the DOJ that, among other things, protects members of the federal judiciary, apprehends federal fugitives, transports detainees, and manages and sells seized assets acquired by criminals through illegal activities. *See United States Marshals Service FY 2020 Annual Report* (Mar. 2021), *available at* https://www.usmarshals.gov/foia/annual-report-2020.pdf.

When a defendant voluntarily returns to the United States for surrender to the authorities, he or she will usually be immediately detained upon crossing the border (or, when travelling by air, upon landing). Best practice for defense counsel in a voluntary surrender situation is to notify the DOJ of a defendant's travel plans so as to minimize immigration and other logistical issues on arrival. But even in a best-case scenario, being arrested at a border crossing or airport gateway will be an unpleasant and public experience for the defendant.

After arrest, the defendant will typically be taken to a local FBI or USMS office to be fingerprinted and photographed. Depending on when and where arrest occurs, and what, if any, arrangements have been made with the DOJ in advance, the defendant may spend a short time in jail prior to an initial appearance in court. If the arrest occurs on a weekend, it is likely that the defendant will be detained until at least the next working day. Often, foreign defendants will be able to negotiate an agreement with the DOJ in which prosecutors will agree to not seek pretrial detention in exchange for the defendant voluntarily surrendering to U.S. custody. Because the pre-trial process can be lengthy, this exchange is a powerful incentive for defendants to waive extradition (especially from countries like the United Kingdom, where extradition to the United States is rarely refused by local courts).

If the defendant resides or has citizenship in a country that does not extradite to the United States, as in the *Flotron* case discussed earlier, the DOJ will be expected to strongly oppose any bail conditions that might permit the person to leave the United States (as discussed further below).

Practice Note

Arrest and Detention Under the Material Witness Statute

Arrests are not solely reserved for criminal suspects. Rather, the federal material witness statute, 18 U.S.C. § 3144, allows for the arrest and detention of innocent individuals deemed to be critical witness to a pending criminal proceeding who may flee the country.

The statute provides that if there is a showing by affidavit "that the testimony of a person is material in a criminal proceeding, and if it is shown that it may become impracticable to secure the presence of the person by subpoena, a judicial officer may order the arrest of the person." Courts have held that this provision applies equally to trial and grand jury witnesses.[177] Individuals detained under a material witness warrant may not be held if their testimony can be adequately secured by deposition or "if further detention is not necessary to prevent a failure of justice." Where the person can be deposed, the government can detain them "for a reasonable period of time until the deposition can be taken pursuant to the Federal Rules of Criminal Procedure."

2. *Initial Appearance and Bail*

Following arrest on a federal warrant, law enforcement "must take the defendant without necessary delay before a [federal] magistrate judge, or before a state or local judicial officer" for an initial appearance.[178] The district in which the initial appearance must occur depends

177. United States v. Awadallah, 349 F.3d 42, 50 (2d Cir. 2003); In re De Jesus Berrios, 706 F.2d 355, 356–58 (1st Cir. 1983); United States v. Oliver, 683 F.2d 224, 230–31 (7th Cir. 1982).

178. Fed. R. Crim. P. 5(a)(1)(A).

on where the charging instrument is filed and where the defendant is arrested.[179] The judge presiding over the initial appearance must inform the defendant of, among other things, the right to legal counsel, the right not to make a statement and, where the defendant is not a U.S. citizen, the right to request that the government notify a consular officer from the defendant's home country of the arrest.[180]

At the initial hearing, the judge will also make a determination as to whether the defendant should be detained prior to trial or released on bail. In federal criminal proceedings, this determination is governed by the Bail Reform Act (18 U.S.C. §§ 3141–3156). The Bail Reform Act "requires pretrial detention of certain persons charged with federal crimes and directs a judicial officer to detain a person charged, pending trial" if the DOJ can establish, by a preponderance of the evidence, that the defendant is dangerous or a flight risk.[181] The "government carries a dual burden in seeking pretrial detention. First, it must establish by a preponderance of the evidence that the defendant, if released, presents an actual risk of flight."[182] If this burden is satisfied, "the government must then demonstrate by a preponderance of the evidence that no condition or combination of conditions could be imposed on the defendant that would reasonably assure his presence in court."[183]

If the DOJ makes the requisite showing on bail, the court must order the defendant's detention until trial.[184] So that they are able to contest prosecutors' presentation, defendants have the right to counsel during a bail hearing, may testify and present their own witnesses, proffer evidence, and cross-examine witnesses for the government.[185]

The judge presiding over the bail hearing "is not given unbridled discretion in making the detention determination." Rather, certain specific factors must be evaluated. "These factors include the nature and seriousness of the charges, the substantiality of the Government's evidence against the arrestee, the arrestee's background and characteristics, and the nature and seriousness of the danger posed by the suspect's release."[186] The court may also conduct an inquiry into the source of any property to be designated for potential forfeiture or offered as collateral to secure any bond; if the court determines that whatever property is offered will not reasonably assure the appearance of the defendant in court, bail will likely be refused.[187]

In all cases where bail is denied and the defendant is ordered detained before trial, he or she is entitled to expedited appellate review of the detention order.[188]

---

179. Fed. R. Crim. P. 5(c) and 20.

180. Fed. R. Crim. P. 5(d).

181. United States v. Montalvo-Murillo, 495 U.S. 711, 717 (1990); United States v. Ferranti, 66 F.3d 540, 542 (2d Cir 1995); United States v. Gebro, 948 F.2d 1118 (9th Cir. 1991).

182. United States v. Sabhnani, 493 F.3d 63, 75 (2d Cir. 2007).

183. *Id.*

184. 18 U.S.C. § 3142(f).

185. United States v. Salerno, 481 U.S. 739, 742 (1987).

186. *Id.* at 742–43.

187. 18 U.S.C. § 3142(g)(4).

188. 18 U.S.C. §§ 3145(b), (c).

While not directly going to the strength of the prosecutors' case, bail determinations can greatly diminish a defendant's leverage in plea negotiations and chances of a winning at trial. Because the "logistics of jails and prisons make it extremely difficult to prepare an effective trial defense when the defendant is in custody," pretrial detention increases a defendant's incentives to accept a plea bargain. "As a case drags along before trial, each day a defendant spends in jail is one less day of freedom to trade the prosecutor for a sentence reduction or to weigh against taking a run at acquittal. . . . If one is facing, for example, a likely sentence of four or five years in prison in the event of a trial loss and has spent a year in jail awaiting trial, a plea bargain for a sentence of eighteen or twenty-four months becomes nearly irrational to reject, regardless of the merits of the prosecution."[189]

a. Bail Considerations for Well-Resourced Defendants

Defendants charged with white-collar crimes will generally have more financial resources than defendants charged with more "blue-collar" type offenses. This can be a double-edged sword for the defense. Significant assets provide the means to flee the United States and live abroad in a nonextradition country indefinitely, and thereby give prosecutors a basis to argue against bail. At the same time, having a large amount of cash or real estate to pledge as security for a bond is a point in favor of the defendant. Courts weighing these competing claims have expressed reluctance to create a two-tiered bail system that favors the rich, meaning that the ability to post significant assets as collateral may not necessarily translate into bail being granted.

The case against Reza Zarrab is a good example. Zarrab, a dual national of Iran and Turkey, was accused of orchestrating a scheme to allow sanctioned entities, including the government of Iran, to illegally access the U.S. financial system. An extremely wealthy international businessman, Zarrab was arrested on a sealed indictment in Miami on March 21, 2016, while on the way to Disney World with his wife and daughter (and carrying $100,000 in cash).[190] After being brought to the Southern District of New York for a bail hearing, Zarrab argued to be released on the following conditions:

- $50 million personal recognizance bond secured by $10 million in cash
- Travel restricted to the Southern District of New York
- Surrender of all passports with no new applications
- Strict supervision from Pretrial Services (the government agency responsible for monitoring those on bail)
- Home detention with GPS monitoring at a newly leased apartment in Manhattan

---

189. Samuel W. Bell, *Is the White Collar Offender Privileged?*, 63 DUKE L.J. 861 (January 2014).

190. At the time of his arrest, Zarrab's business enterprises included a Turkish gold brokerage and currency exchange, a shipbuilding company in Istanbul named Royal Shipping, a real estate construction company, a furniture manufacturing operation in Istanbul named Royal Mobilya, and a tea brokerage business trading Sri Lankan tea destined for Turkey. According to the DOJ, these businesses generated annual revenues of more than $11 billion.

With respect to the home detention condition, Zarrab proposed that his presence at his apartment would be secured by a private security company that would arrange, at Zarrab's expense, two or more armed (former or off-duty) law enforcement officers to accompany him at all times, one supervisory security professional to oversee the security detail, security at both the apartment and whenever Zarrab left the apartment for medical reasons or to go to court or meet with his lawyers, and a security vehicle with driver whenever such travel was required.[191]

In support of this proposed bail package, Zarrab's lawyers argued to the court: "Because Mr. Zarrab is not charged with a violent crime, is not facing any mandatory minimum prison sentence and is otherwise eligible for bail, we urge this Court not to detain him simply because he is wealthy and lacks ties to the United States. Our bail proposal removes any possible concern of flight." The defense also argued:

> [T]he inequities in the criminal justice system on the state and federal level between people of means and people of not means is not something that is Mr. Zarrab's fault, and it is nothing we are going to remedy in this case. It is sad, but it's true. . . . But that does not mean that you claim someone is very rich and, therefore . . . say [that] you can't use your wealth to create a prison."[192]

In response, the DOJ argued that Zarrab's proposed private security arrangement did not mitigate the risk of flight because, among other reasons, the private security company would be "put in a position where they suffer a conflict of interest because they are jailers being paid by the inmate," and because "a private security firm simply cannot replicate the controlled environment of a federal correctional facility."[193]

After evaluating these arguments along with each of the factors required under the Bail Reform Act, the district court denied bail. As to the proposed home confinement conditions in particular, the court agreed with an earlier Second Circuit case—*United States v. Banki*, 369 F. App'x 152 (2d Cir. 2010)—that "such conditions might be best seen not as specific conditions of release, but simply as a less onerous form of detention available only to the wealthy." Consequently, the court found the privately funded armed guard proposal unreasonable "because it [would] help to foster inequity and unequal treatment in favor of a very small cohort of criminal defendants who are extremely wealthy."

3. Arraignment and Initial Plea

Federal Rule of Criminal Procedure 10 states:

> [An] arraignment must be conducted in open court and must consist of: (1) ensuring that the defendant has a copy of the indictment or information; (2) reading the indictment or information to the defendant or stating to the defendant the substance of the charge; and then (3) asking the defendant to plead to the indictment or information.

---

191. United States v. Zarrab, 15-cr-00867 (RMB) (S.D.N.Y. June 16, 2016).

192. *Id.*

193. *Id.*

As opposed to the initial appearance, which is concerned primarily with the grant or denial of bail, the purpose of an arraignment is to "inform the accused of the charge against him and obtain an answer [i.e., plea] from him."[194] The initial appearance and arraignment will often occur during the same hearing, and in any event must occur within a reasonable time after arrest (unless the defendant agrees to waive it). At the arraignment, the judge will also generally set an initial schedule for pretrial motions and other pretrial hearings.

Once the defendant has been informed of the charges against him, he will be asked to enter one of three possible pleas: not guilty, guilty, or, with the court's and prosecutors' consent, nolo contendere ("no contest"). If a defendant refuses to enter a plea, the court will enter a plea of not guilty by default.

A nolo contendere plea is a conditional plea of guilty whereby the defendant reserves in writing the right to have an appellate court review an adverse determination of a specified pretrial motion (e.g., a motion to dismiss or a motion to suppress key evidence—see chapter 6). For example, a defendant may initially plead not guilty and then move to dismiss the case on the basis that the charges are outside the applicable statute of limitations; if that motion is denied, the defendant may wish to change his or her plea but leave open the possibility of challenging the district court's ruling on appeal. If such a defendant gets the DOJ's consent to plead nolo contendere (which is unlikely) and then prevails on appeal, the guilty plea may then be withdrawn.[195] Nolo contendere pleas are strongly disfavored by the DOJ. Its policy permits AUSAs to consent to such pleas only in the "most unusual circumstances" and only after a recommendation for doing so has been approved by an assistant attorney general, the deputy attorney general, or the attorney general.[196]

Where a plea agreement has been reached by the defendant and prosecutors before arraignment, the existence of the plea agreement must be disclosed to the court. The court will evaluate the plea agreement and decide to accept or reject it based on the specific circumstances of the case.[197] Before doing so, the court will ensure that the "plea is voluntary and did not result from force, threats, or promises (other than promises in a plea agreement) and "that there is a factual basis for the plea."[198]

A defendant can withdraw a guilty or nolo contendere plea (i) "before the court accepts the plea, for any reason or no reason," or (ii) after the plea is accepted but before the court imposes sentence in certain limited circumstances.[199]

4. *Extradition*

Cross-border financial crime cases will, of course, often involve U.S. law enforcement officers charging defendants located overseas. Because their powers to arrest generally end at the U.S. border, unless the defendant voluntarily travels to the United States, prosecutors

---

194. Garland v. State of Washington, 232 U.S. 642, 644 (1914).

195. Fed. R. Crim. P. 11(a)(2).

196. *Justice Manual*, 9-16.010.

197. Fed R. Crim. P. 11(c).

198. Fed. R. Crim. P. 11(b)(2)–(3).

199. Fed. R. Crim. P. 11(d).

must seek the defendant's extradition. Extradition is the formal process "by which a person charged with or convicted of a crime under the law of one state is arrested in another state and returned for trial and punishment."[200] In the United States, "requests for extradition may be granted only pursuant to a treaty."[201] The procedures used in U.S. extradition practice are defined in the relevant treaties and domestic legislation, codified at 18 U.S.C. § 3181 *et seq.*

DOJ policy requires prosecutors to consult with the Criminal Division's Office of International Affairs (OIA) for any matter relating to extradition before taking any action to secure a suspect's return. The OIA is a specialized unit based in Washington, D.C., that provides information and advice to federal and state prosecutors about extradition procedures. The OIA must give its approval before any outgoing or incoming extradition requests may proceed.

a. Extradition to the United States

U.S. prosecutors seeking extradition of a defendant from elsewhere must provide the OIA with an affidavit explaining the facts of the case and the charged offenses, copies of the statutes alleged to have been violated, the applicable statute of limitations, and certified copies of the arrest warrant and complaint or indictment.

If the OIA is satisfied that the case meets the requirements for extradition under the applicable treaty, it will then be forwarded to the Department of State for additional review. While this review is pending, the OIA can ask the foreign government to provisionally arrest the subject while a formal extradition request is being prepared. This is used in situations where the fugitive poses an urgent risk to the public or is a flight risk.

If the State Department also approves of the request, it will then be forwarded to an appropriate overseas embassy, which will then present it to the appropriate foreign ministry. Whether extradition will be granted is a matter of local law in the relevant country. In general, the foreign government's decision on the extradition request is based on the request itself and any evidence presented by the fugitive. In situations where the United States has requested extradition of a defendant in the United Kingdom, the DOJ will be represented in Westminster Magistrates' Court by a Crown prosecutor (see below).

If extradition back to the United States is granted, U.S. Marshals will travel to the country to apprehend the individual and return him or her under a temporary visa—called "Significant Public Benefit Parole"—issued by the Department of Homeland Security to allow the person to travel to the United States.

Because extradition proceedings are generally subject to at least one level of appeal and require final sign off from a high-level official of the foreign government, it may take several years before an extradition request is acted upon.

As of this writing, for example, Wikileaks founder Julian Assange has been fighting extradition from the United Kingdom to the United States on espionage charges for more than two years. The initial ruling from Westminster Magistrates' Court was that Assange could not be extradited because his unstable "mental condition," combined with the prison conditions

200. Austin v. Healey, 5 F.3d 598, 600 (2d Cir. 1993). Note that there is also an extradition process between the different domestic states in the United States pursuant to Art. 4 of the Constitution that is beyond the scope of this book.

201. Restatement (Third) of the Foreign Relations Law of the U.S. § 475 cmt. B. (Am. L. Inst. 1987).

facing him in the United States, were such that extradition would create a severe risk of suicide and be "oppressive" (in violation of his rights under the ECHR and English domestic law). On December 10, 2021, the High Court reversed in light of assurances from the DOJ as to his treatment in U.S. custody: namely, that he would "receive any such clinical and psychological treatment as is recommended by a qualified treating clinician employed or retained by the prison where he is held in custody" and that he would not be held at the highly restrictive "supermax" facility in Florence, Colorado (the location of several other inmates found guilty of similar espionage offenses).[202] As of May 2022, Assange's fate now lies with Priti Patel, the U.K. home secretary, who must give final approval of Assange's removal to the United States.[203]

i. The "Rule of Speciality"

"The rule of specialty is a principle of international law that prohibits extraditing countries from prosecuting a defendant on charges other than those for which he was specifically extradited."[204] In other words, it "requires a country seeking extradition to adhere to any limitations placed on [the] prosecution by the surrendering country."[205] Typically, the rule of specialty is invoked to circumscribe the specific crimes for which a defendant may be tried following extradition. At a basic level, this means that if a defendant is extradited for fraud, he cannot then be tried for murder. The rule of specialty does not otherwise limit how a crime can be prosecuted—it does not, for example, "purport to regulate the scope of proof admissible into evidence in the judicial forum of the requisitioning state" or affect any other criminal procedure rule.[206]

The premise underlying the rule of specialty is the concept of international comity, which generally requires one country to recognize the legal decisions of another, and "is designed to protect the extraditing government against abuse of its discretionary act of extradition."[207] Therefore, "the test of whether trial is for a 'separate offense' should not be some technical refinement of local law, but whether the extraditing country would consider the offense

202. United States v. Assange [2021] EWHC 3313 (Admin), [30]. After Westminster Magistrates' now-vacated ruling denying extradition on the basis of suicide risk in U.S, prisons, this same defence has been raised by a number of high-profile financial crime defendants seeking to avoid extradition to the United States—so far, without success. See Richard Crump, *Briton Can Be Extradited to U.S. on $30M Ponzi Fraud Claims,* LAW360, Jan. 4, 2022 (discussing the case of Anthony Joseph Baker); Murtaza Ali Shah, *U.K. Judge Delays Arif Naqvi's Extradition to the U.S.,* INT'L NEWS, Nov. 13, 2021 (discussing Arif Naqvi and Nirav Modi cases).

203. *See* Ben Quinn, "UK Court Approves Extradition of Julian Assange to US," THE GUARDIAN (Apr. 20, 2022).

204. United States v. Restrepo, 547 F. App'x 34, 45 (2d Cir. 2013).

205. United States v. Baez, 349 F.3d 90, 92 (2d Cir. 2003).

206. United States v. Flores, 538 F.2d 939, 944 (2d Cir. 1976).

207. United States v. Paroutian, 299 F.2d 486, 490–91 (2d Cir. 1962); United States v. Saccoccia, 58 F.3d 754, 766 (1st Cir. 1995); *see also* Hilton v. Guyot, 159 U.S. 113, 163–64 (1895) ("'Comity,' in the legal sense, is neither a matter of absolute obligation, on the one hand, nor of mere courtesy and good will, upon the other. But it is the recognition which one nation allows within its territory to the legislative, executive or judicial acts of another nation, having due regard both to international duty and convenience, and to the rights of its own citizens or of other persons who are under the protection of its laws.").

actually tried 'separate.'"[208] The rule in the majority of circuits is that the "government is not limited strictly to charges described in an extradition warrant but rather may include [in a superseding indictment] additional facts and additional charges as long as the statutory charge is the same."[209] "Put simply, the [g]overnment may present additional facts or amplified allegations [in a superseding indictment] 'so long as [they are] . . . *directed* to the charge contained in the request for extradition.'"[210] "A superseding indictment which charges offenses of the same character as the crime for which the fugitive is extradited does not offend [the rule of specialty] doctrine."[211]

Where a defendant returns to the United States voluntarily by waiving his or her right to extradition, the rule of specialty does not apply.[212] "When a criminal defendant waives extradition, or when the requested country voluntarily transfers a defendant to the requesting country without following the formal procedures of the treaty, the defendant has not been 'extradited' under that treaty."[213] A defendant "waives" extradition when he or she voluntarily consents to return to the requesting jurisdiction outside of the formal extradition process. "Moreover, where a defendant is not transferred pursuant to an extradition treaty, he cannot assert any rights conferred by the treaty. Thus, a criminal defendant's surrender to United States jurisdiction or a requested country's voluntary transfer of a defendant's custody forecloses a rule of specialty defense."[214]

b. Alternatives to Extradition for Returning a Suspect to the United States

Securing a suspect's extradition to the United States may not be possible through normal diplomatic channels for a variety of reasons. For example, if the suspect is located in China, Russia, or some other country with which the United States does not have an extradition treaty or a cooperative law enforcement relationship. Likewise, many countries—including France, Germany, Switzerland, and Lebanon—will not extradite their own citizens, regardless of the existence of an extradition treaty. This citizenship-based extradition protection was famously employed by former Nissan head Carlos Ghosn, who escaped fraud charges in Tokyo by being secreted out of Japan in a box placed onto a private Bombardier jet to Lebanon, his home country.[215]

---

208. Paroutian, 299 F.2d at 490–91.

209. United States v. Masefield, No. 02-cr-441, 2005 WL 236443, at *2 (S.D.N.Y. Feb. 1, 2005).

210. *Id.*

211. United States v. Sturtz, 648 F. Supp. 817, 819 (S.D.N.Y. 1986); see also United States v. Puentes, 50 F.3d 1567, 1576 (11th Cir. 1995); United States v. Andonian, 29 F.3d 1432, 1435–37 (9th Cir. 1994).

212. United States v. Trujillo, 871 F. Supp. 215, 219 (D. Del. 1994).

213. United States v. Herbert, 313 F. Supp. 2d 324, 330 (S.D.N.Y. 2004).

214. United States v. Vega, 07-cr-00707, 2012 WL 1925876, at *8 (E.D.N.Y. May 24, 2012).

215. Leo Lewis, "Extradition in Carlos Ghosn Case Highlights Strength of US-Japan Relations," Financial Times (Mar. 29, 2021). Because citizenship can protect a person from extradition, the purchase of citizenship in extradition adverse countries through "golden visa" programs has become a cottage industry. Golden visas are made generally available by certain countries in the Caribbean, Mediterranean, and elsewhere to anyone willing to make a large domestic "investment" of at least six figures. Because of the possibility of abuse inherent in these programs, they have been routinely

Yet the inability to use formal extradition does not entirely foreclose a suspect's involuntary return to the United States since the DOJ has several alternatives at its disposal. If the fugitive is not a national or lawful resident of the country in which he or she is located, for example, the OIA may ask that country to deport, expel, or otherwise facilitate his or her capture by U.S. authorities. This tactic was successfully used against alleged narco-terrorist, Jamal Yousef. Yousef was indicted by U.S. prosecutors while he was serving a sentence for passport fraud in Honduras. Shortly afterward, he received a conditional release from Honduran custody, was immediately ordered deported, and turned over to the custody of INTERPOL. Accompanied by a U.S. Drug Enforcement Administration (DEA) agent, he was then taken by helicopter to a Honduran air force base and transferred to a private jet bound for New York.[216]

U.S. law enforcement can also pursue suspects even if their host countries are uncooperative. In *United States v. Alvarez-Machain*, 504 U.S. 655 (1992), the Supreme Court ruled that a criminal prosecution may go forward in a U.S. district court even in situations where the defendant was extrajudicially abducted in a foreign country against his or her will. In that case, Humberto Alvarez-Machain, a Mexican medical doctor believed to have participated in the torture and murder of a DEA agent, was forcibly kidnaped by bounty hunters and flown by private plane to El Paso, Texas, where he was arrested by waiting DEA officials. The DEA officials had earlier attempted to engage in informal extradition negotiations with Mexican authorities but were unsuccessful. The DEA then issued a bounty through an unofficial contact in Mexico for the doctor's return to the United States.

The doctor sought to dismiss the indictment on the grounds "that his abduction constituted outrageous governmental conduct" and because he was abducted in violation of the U.S.-Mexico extradition treaty. The Supreme Court rejected these arguments and concluded that, under the so-called "*Ker-Frisbie* doctrine," the trial court's jurisdiction was not affected by the manner in which the accused was brought before it. While a defendant may not be prosecuted in violation of the terms of an extradition treaty, the Court concluded, when a treaty has not been invoked, it is essentially irrelevant how law enforcement gets a foreign suspect back to the United States.[217] In the doctor's case, the Court found that since the U.S.-Mexico treaty did not include an express or implied term prohibiting his abduction,

---

criticized. *See* Francisca Fernando, Jonathan Pampolina, and Robin Sykes, *Citizenship for Sale*, Int'l Monetary Fund (June 2021), *available at* https://www.imf.org/external/pubs/ft/fandd/2021/06/pdf/citizenship-for-sale-fernando-pampolina-sykes.pdf.

216. United States v. Yousef, 08-cr-01213 (S.D.N.Y. June 30, 2011). Yousef later moved to dismiss the DOJ's case on the basis that he had been illegally kidnapped. This argument was rejected by the district court: "A lawful arrest and expulsion, even if performed by armed, masked agents, is simply not a kidnapping. Defendant's suggestion that his abduction was a joint venture between the United States and Honduras, with the United States directing Honduras to expel Yousef, lacks any evidentiary basis. The two countries obviously did cooperate in transferring Yousef to the United States, but there is nothing to indicate that the entire operation was contrived by the United States, nor is it reasonable to assume that the United States forced or directed Honduras to expel Yousef. At best, the United States could request his expulsion, but the decision to expel was that of a sovereign state."

217. Ker v. Illinois, 119 U.S. 436 (1886); *see also* Frisbie v. Collins, 342 U.S. 519, 522 (1952); United States v. Crews, 445 U.S. 463, 474 (1980).

the fact that the extradition treaty was not used to secure his attendance in court was not sufficient reason to dismiss the case. Although acknowledging that the doctor's abduction may have been "shocking" and in "violation of general international law principles," the justices concluded that his "abduction was not in violation of the Extradition Treaty between the United States and Mexico" and therefore did not "prohibit his trial in a court in the United States for violations of the criminal laws of the United States."[218] The opposite is true in the United Kingdom, where courts will typically stay the proceedings for abuse of process if the defendant has been apprehended and brought before the court unlawfully.[219]

Because of their diplomatically sensitive nature, before DOJ prosecutors can take steps towards *Alvarez-Machain*-type abductions and returns, they must seek advanced approval from the OIA and other senior DOJ officials.[220] Another option is to use subterfuge to trick a criminal defendant into leaving a foreign country where they are protected from extradition so as to facilitate their arrest by the United States in international waters or airspace, or in a third country with more favorable extradition rules. In the "Operation Goldenrod" case, for example, the FBI set up an uncover drug sale with Fawaz Younis, a Lebanese national suspected of participating in the hijacking of a Royal Jordanian airliner in 1985. Because Lebanon does not extradite its citizens, the FBI lured Younis aboard a yacht in international waters off Cyprus to finalize what he was led to believe would be a large narcotics transaction. According to an FBI account of this operation, Younis was enticed onboard by two scantily clad women (both of whom were FBI agents). Once on deck, he was arrested and taken aboard a U.S. Navy munitions ship, later transferred to a nearby aircraft carrier, and then flown in a Navy jet to Washington, D.C., for arraignment. He was later convicted of various terrorism offenses and sentenced to thirty years in prison.[221]

In financial crime cases, less-complex lures can be used—such as arranging a business meeting overseas under false pretenses. Lures are obviously more likely to work when the suspect is unaware of the indictment (and thus presumably less cautious about international travel). To avoid tipping a suspect off to pending charges, therefore, the DOJ has the option of filing the charging instrument under seal (as discussed earlier).

If deportation, abduction, or luring is inappropriate or unavailable in a particular case, and the person is a U.S. citizen, the DOJ can ask the State Department to unilaterally revoke the suspect's passport (making expulsion from a foreign country more likely and possibly forcing the person into an extraditable location). On rare occasions, if a fugitive is in a

---

218. Alvarez-Machain, 504 U.S. at 669–70. When Alvarez-Machain went to trial in Los Angeles in 1992, the district court judge granted a motion of acquittal on the ground that the government lacked sufficient evidence to support a guilty verdict. The court concluded that the case against him was based on "suspicion and . . . hunches but . . . no proof," and that the government's theories were "whole cloth, the wildest speculation." Alvarez-Machain v. United States, 331 F.3d 604, 610 (9th Cir. 2001). After returning to Mexico, Alvarez-Machain sued the U.S. government for, among other things, kidnapping, torture, and arbitrary detention. He was later awarded $25,000. *Id.* at 611.

219. Horseferry Road Magistrates' Court, ex p. Bennett [1994] 1 A.C. 42.

220. *Justice Manual*, § 9-15.610.

221. FBI History, *Fawaz Younis/Operation Goldenrod, available at* https://www.fbi.gov/history/famous-cases/fawaz-younis.

country where he or she is a national and consequently not extraditable, the DOJ—through the OIA—can make a request to the foreign authorities to prosecute the person there for a crime committed in the United States.

c. Extradition from the United States

Under the Extradition Act, 18 U.S.C. § 3184 *et seq.*, extradition from the United States may generally only be granted pursuant to an extradition treaty (figure 3.2). "Whenever there is a treaty or convention between the United States and any foreign government," a federal judge receiving a complaint charging any person with a crime in a foreign jurisdiction, may order the individual arrested and conduct a hearing to determine whether there is evidence sufficient to sustain the charge.

Foreign requests for the provisional arrest or extradition of fugitives located in the United States are ordinarily submitted by the embassy of the country making the request to the Department of State, which reviews and forwards them to the OIA. If the OIA determines that the request complies with the relevant treaty requirements, the OIA will forward it to the USAO in the district where the fugitive is believed to be located.[222]

After a request is sent to an appropriate USAO, an AUSA at that office will be assigned to the case and seek a warrant for the fugitive's arrest by presenting to a magistrate or district court judge "competent evidence" that is "sufficient to sustain the charge under the provisions of the proper treaty or convention, or under Section 3181(b)."[223] Simply because a request complies with the threshold requirements, a court must independently authorize the person's removal from the United States. Specifically, the extradition judge must determine whether: (i) there is a treaty in force, (ii) the person arrested is in fact the person sought by

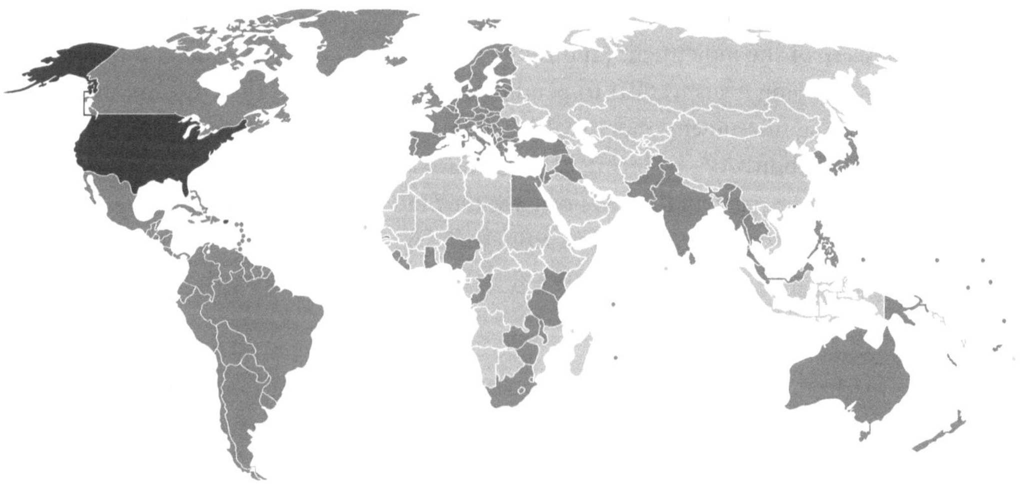

Figure 3.2 Countries with which the United States has extradition treaties (shown in darker gray).

---

222. Mirela v. United States, 416 F. Supp. 3d 98 (D. Conn. 2019).

223. 18 U.S.C. § 3184; *see also* United States v. Fernandez-Morris, 99 F. Supp. 2d 1358, 1360 (S.D. Fla. 1999). Section 3181(b) concerns foreign citizens who have committed crimes of violence against U.S. nationals in foreign countries.

the requesting state, (iii) the crime in question is extraditable under the treaty, (iv) the request sets out probable cause to believe the person committed the charged crime, and (v) there are no treaty grounds that would require denial of extradition.[224] In making this determination, the judge may not defer to bare, conclusory representations in the extradition request itself or in a related Red Notice (discussed in the next Practice Note). Accordingly, the requesting state must submit detailed supporting documents to help establish probable cause.

The 2003 U.S.-U.K. extradition treaty provides, for example, that a request for extradition must include "a copy of the warrant or order of arrest," "a copy of the charging document, if any," and "for requests to the United States, such information as would provide a reasonable basis to believe that the person sought committed the offense for which extradition is requested."[225] Because the United States is exempt from the prima facie requirement that applies to other category 2 countries under the U.K. Extradition Act (see the discussion of "Extradition" in Section III.B), there is a higher standard for incoming extradition requests from Britain than for those coming from the United States to the United Kingdom.

This lopsided feature of the U.S.-U.K. treaty has generated considerable debate in England.[226] It has also led to far more individuals being extradited to the United States from Britain than vice versa—between 2007 and 2020, the U.K. government surrendered 135 British nationals to the United States, 99 of them for nonviolent offenses; during the same period the United States surrendered just 11 people to the United Kingdom. Since 2003, eighty percent of extraditions to the United States from Britain were for nonviolent, financial crimes.

If probable cause is established, the court will issue an arrest warrant. Once in custody, the suspect will appear before a magistrate or district court judge for an initial appearance, bail determination, and a "probable cause" hearing under 18 U.S.C. § 3184 (where the suspect can challenge the evidence used to support the warrant and present any reasons why a statutory bar to extradition applies). This hearing does not consider the merits of the case, and the rules of evidence and criminal procedure do not apply as they would during trial.[227] As the Second Circuit explained, "orders of extradition are *sui generis*. They embody no judgment on the guilt or innocence of the accused but serve only to insure that his culpability will be determined in another and, in this instance, a foreign forum. . . . What is at issue in the proceeding . . . is not punishability but *prosecutability.*"[228]

If the evidence is deemed sufficient, Section 3184 requires the court to certify the individual as extraditable to the secretary of state, who then will make the ultimate decision

---

224. In re Extradition of Atuar, 300 F. Supp. 2d 418, 426 (S.D. W. Va. 2003).

225. Instrument Amending the Treaty of 31 March 2003, U.K.-U.S. Annex. art. 8(3), Dec. 16, 2004, T.I.A.S. No. 10-201.23.

226. *See, e.g.*, Robert J. Dougans, *An Extradition Treaty Unfit for Purpose,* Law Gaz. (March 23, 2020); Rosemary Davidson & Richard Evans, *"This Lopsided Treaty..." Is the US/UK Extradition Treaty Imbalanced?* 6KBW College Hill (April 9, 2020).

227. *See* Charlton v. Kelly, 229 U.S. 447, 456 (1913); Vo v. Benov, 447 F.3d 1235, 1237 (9th Cir. 2006); Mirchandani v. United States, 836 F.2d 1223, 1226 (9th Cir. 1988); 18 U.S.C. § 3184; *Justice Manual* 9-15.700.

228. Skaftouros v. United States, 667 F.3d 144, 155 (2d Cir. 2011).

as to whether the fugitive will be surrendered to the requesting country.[229] The secretary will consider the likely treatment of the suspect in the requesting country and whether the request is motivated by a political or otherwise improper reason. A certification by the office of the secretary of state that a person should be extradited is not directly appealable, meaning that a defendant's only option to continue an extradition challenge following state approval is to seek a writ of habeas corpus.[230]

Once a defendant's routes of challenging extradition are fully exhausted, U.S. authorities will notify the requesting state and the OIA will make arrangements for the person's transfer to that country. The total process can be extremely time consuming, typically lasting at least several years.

i. Defenses to Extradition from the United States

The specific defenses that may be available in any particular case depend on the terms of the relevant treaty or state-to-state arrangement. Most U.S. extradition treaties allow for certain common defenses:

- **Lack of dual criminality.** The alleged act underlying the request must be considered a crime in both the requesting state and the United States.
- **Insufficient evidence.** As discussed above, the target of an extradition request may challenge the evidence supporting it during a "probable cause" hearing.
- **Political offense.** Extradition can be barred because of improper motivations on the part of the requesting state.
- **Procedural flaws.** An otherwise valid request may fail for procedural flaws, such as the lapse of an applicable statute of limitations in the requesting state or treaty provisions preventing extradition of nationals.
- **Human rights.** Extradition will not be ordered if there are significant humanitarian or human rights concerns, and those facing extradition in such circumstances may seek asylum in the United States under 18 U.S.C. § 1158.

ii. Habeas Corpus Challenges to Extradition

As noted above, a finding of extraditability by a court or the State Department is not subject to direct appeal, meaning that higher court review is possible only through a writ of habeas corpus.[231] Habeas corpus is a free-standing right of a defendant to challenge his or her detention in federal court. The scope of inquiry in habeas proceedings is far more limited than in a normal direct appeal. According to the Supreme Court, "[H]abeas corpus is available only

---

229. 18 U.S.C. §§ 3186, 3196.

230. Pena-Bencosme v. Warden, Met. Correctional Ctr., 06-CV-6745 (NGG) (E.D.N.Y. Mar. 25, 2008).

231. Shapiro v. Ferrandina, 478 F.2d 894, 901 (2d Cir. 1973); *see also* Skaftouros v. United States, 667 F.3d 144, 157 (2d Cir. 2011) ("Because extradition orders are regarded as preliminary determinations, and not 'final decisions' appealable as of right under 28 U.S.C. § 1291, they may only be reviewed by a petition for a writ of habeas corpus under 28 U.S.C. § 2241.").

to inquire whether the magistrate had jurisdiction, whether the offense charged is within the treaty and, by a somewhat liberal extension, whether there was any evidence warranting" the probable cause determination.[232]

As for the DOJ's rights of appeal, "if a foreign government's request for extradition has been denied by a judicial officer sitting as extradition magistrate," the only recourse is to file the same request before a different judicial officer and hope for a more favorable outcome.[233]

iii. Extradition Requests Following Initial Denial

Even if a defendant successfully challenges an extradition request at the probable cause hearing, the matter is not necessarily over. This is because U.S. courts have "long recognized that the government is free to pursue extradition notwithstanding initial unsuccessful efforts."[234] It has been "consistently held under the treaties with Great Britain and other countries, that a fugitive from justice may be arrested in extradition proceedings a second time upon a new complaint charging the same crime, where he was discharged by the magistrate on the first complaint or the complaint was withdrawn."[235] Although there are obvious potential abuses that could follow from this authority, the Supreme Court has concluded that there are adequate protections available outside the judicial process: "the protection against unjustifiable vexation and harassment incident to repeated arrest for the same alleged crime must ordinarily be sought, not in constitutional limitations or treaty provisions, but in a sense of responsibility on the part of the public officials charged with duties in this connection."[236]

Accordingly, in the Supreme Court's view, the Constitution does not bar reinstituted extradition proceedings, and relief from the abuse of multiple extradition attempts lies not in courts, "but rather with the fair-mindedness of the government in fulfilling its obligation under treaties of extradition."[237] Put differently, since requests for extradition from the United States are initially reviewed by the State Department and DOJ, courts rely upon these agencies to protect against abuses of the extradition process. The doctrine of res judicata—a judicially created rule that provides that a valid, final judgment on the merits is a bar to further action between the same parties on the same issue—does not apply to findings resulting from extradition proceedings.[238] Considering the constitutional double jeopardy rights, it "is a striking feature of extradition practice that a dissatisfied government is entitled to try again before the authority, which would in no way be bound by the previous decision."[239]

---

232. Fernandez v. Phillips, 268 U.S. 311, 312 (1925); Mirela v. United States, 416 F. Supp. 3d 98, 114 n.10 (D. Conn. 2019); Grin v. Shine, 187 U.S. 181, 192 (1902); Bisram v. United States, 777 Fed. Appx. 563, 565 (2d Cir. 2019).

233. Mirela v. United States, 416 F. Supp. 3d 98 (D. Conn. 2019).

234. Hooker v. Klein, 573 F.2d 1360, 1365 (9th Cir. 1978).

235. Collins v. Loisel, 262 U.S. 426, 429 (1923); United States v. Doherty, 786 F.2d 491, 496 (2d Cir. 1986).

236. Collins, 262 U.S. at 429–30.

237. Hooker, 573 F.2d at 1365.

238. *Id.* at 1368.

239. Mirela, 416 F. Supp. 3d at 104.

Practice Note

INTERPOL Red Notices and Diffusions

Defendants facing extradition will often encounter issues related to the International Criminal Police Organization, better known as INTERPOL, and its Red Notices, which function as global, electronic wanted posters. A "Diffusion" functions in the same way as a Red Notice but is less formal and is sent directly to a selected country or countries.

INTERPOL, based in Lyon, France, is not a global police force: it has no power to arrest anyone, and it does not investigate or prosecute crimes. Rather, it is an intergovernmental organization founded to simply serve as an information-sharing platform between the national police forces of its 194 member countries.

Each INTERPOL member has a designated point of contact—a National Central Bureau (NCB)—within its national police force that is responsible for international law enforcement cooperation. NCBs can access INTERPOL's databases and communicate with each other through INTERPOL's secure communications network, "I-24/7." INTERPOL members can quickly share certain kinds of alerts and requests for information through a system of color-coded notices. Red Notices and Diffusions seek the location of wanted persons and serve as a request to INTERPOL member states to provisionally arrest them pending their extradition or surrender to the requesting country.

Red Notices are not arrest warrants: they are merely a request to locate and provisionally arrest a person, and each INTERPOL member state has discretion on how they will respond. Every Red Notice must reference a national arrest warrant or judicial decision, but INTERPOL will generally not assess the merits of the underlying case or the judicial process that produced it.

Most Red Notices are not publicly available, and they are used when a fugitive's location or travel plans are unknown. Often, the first time a suspect learns a Red Notice has been issued is when they are arrested while traveling across an international border.

In the United States, national law prohibits the arrest of the subject of an INTERPOL Red Notice based upon the notice alone. Instead, DOJ prosecutors who wish to make an arrest based on a red Notice issued by another INTERPOL member country must first submit "reasonably trustworthy information" to a magistrate judge to establish probable cause that the person committed the crime at issue.

In the United Kingdom, the police can, and often do, make arrests on the basis of a Red Notice alone.

The vast majority of Red Notices are not publicly disclosed—of the more than 60,000 Red Notices currently sitting in INTERPOL's databases, roughly ten percent are listed on INTERPOL's website. For defendants, this is problematic because, if they are unaware a Red Notice request has been issued, they are more likely to cross an international border and be arrested—given the routine use of sealed indictments, this risk is particularly pronounced in cases involving the DOJ. There is a process to try to learn of an undisclosed Red Notice, but because all information submitted by an NCB—including the request for a Red Notice itself—is ultimately controlled by the NCB, INTERPOL will generally not disclose the existence of a Red Notice unless the NCB consents. While INTERPOL will typically acknowledge a disclosure request within a month, it may take up to two years to receive a substantive response.

There are also procedures by which a suspect can request INTERPOL to retract or delete Red Notices. To be successful, such requests need to establish a breach of INTERPOL's Constitution, internal rules (particularly its Rules on the Processing of Data, which governs how information submitted by NCBs is treated), or the Universal Declaration on Human Rights.

INTERPOL's internal procedures allow it up to nine months to make a decision on a deletion request; if it is denied, there is no means by which the suspect can make an appeal within INTERPOL, nor is there any recourse available in any national court.

Certain countries with dubious adherence to the rule of law are responsible for a disproportionately large percentage of Red Notice requests—studies suggest that Russian authorities, for example, account for 38% of all Red Notices. This has led to criticism that INTERPOL is often misused to persecute political enemies.[240]

B. Initial Pretrial Procedures in the United Kingdom

1. Initial Hearing

All criminal defendants, including those charged with an indictable-only offense, will make a first appearance after arrest before a magistrates' court. Prior to the initial appearance, prosecutors will generally provide the defendant with certain evidentiary disclosures relating to the charged offense, including "any prosecution material which has not previously been disclosed to the accused and which might reasonably be considered capable of undermining the case for the prosecution against the accused or of assisting the case for the accused" along with anything that might assist the defendant in applying for bail.[241] This is in contrast to the practice in the United States, where the DOJ will generally disclose its evidence only after arraignment.

At the initial hearing, the defendant will be asked to indicate whether he or she intends to plead guilty. If the defendant signals an intention to plead guilty to an indictable-only offense, the magistrates' court will order that a presentence report is prepared and refer the case to the Crown Court for sentencing. Conversely, if the defendant discloses an intention to plead not guilty, the magistrate will set a date for a plea and trial preparation hearing (PTPH) in Crown Court. If the defendant makes no plea, a plea of not guilty will be entered.

Where prosecutors charge one or more either-way offenses, the initial hearing will also consider whether the case should be sent to the Crown Court (a decision that turns on how the accused is likely to plead and the seriousness of the case). When at least one indictable-only offense is charged, the entire case (including any lesser offenses) will be automatically designated for transfer to the Crown Court for further proceedings "forthwith."[242] In determining whether a case should be sent to Crown Court, the magistrates' court will only consider whether the defendant faces an indictable-only or related offense; the court will not consider the legal merits of the prosecutions' case or the strength of their evidence.

240. *See, e.g.*, Sam Meacham, *Weaponizing the Police: Authoritarian Abuse of Interpol*, HARV. INT'L REV. (Apr. 11, 2022); Josh Jacobs, "Has Interpol Become the Long Arm of Oppressive Regimes," THE GUARDIAN (Oct. 17, 2021).

241. CPIA, s. 3(1)(a); CrimPR 8.2; R v. DPP ex parte Lee [1999] 2 Cr. App. R. 304.

242. CDA, s. 51(3); R v. Woolwich Crown Court [2004] EWHC 2172 (Admin). Note, however, that prosecutors and the defendant have a right to seek an adjournment of the transfer where appropriate. CDA, s. 52(2).

a. Notices in Serious or Complex Fraud Cases

Under CDA Section 51B, the DPP, director of the SFO, and certain other "designated authorities" are permitted to serve notice to the magistrates' court that they are "of the opinion that the evidence of the offense charged (a) is sufficient for the person charged to be put on trial for the offense; and (b) reveals a case of fraud of such seriousness or complexity that it is appropriate that the management of the case should without delay be taken over by the Crown Court." Once such a notice is made, the functions of the magistrates' court ceases except for effectuating the transfer to the Crown Court and making a bail determination. A decision by a "designated authority" to issue a Section 51B notice is not "subject to appeal or liable to be questioned in any court."[243] The effect of this provision is to fast-track either-way fraud offenses to the Crown Court when deemed particularly serious or complex.

2. *Bail*

Bail decisions in the United Kingdom are governed by the Bail Act 1976 (BA). As in the United States, there is a statutory presumption in favor of granting bail regardless of the seriousness of the alleged offense.[244] In Crown Court cases, prosecutors and the defendant's solicitor will generally try to negotiate a pre-agreed bail proposal prior to the bail hearing. If such an agreement is not reached, a contested bail hearing will be held at a magistrates' court, which retains the authority to make bail determinations at its discretion. If bail issues arise after a case has already been transferred to the Crown Court, the Crown Court judge will rule on them pursuant to the Criminal Procedure Rules (CrimPR 14).

When the underlying crime at issue is an indictable-only offense, the Bail Act provides a number of possible grounds on which bail may be denied—namely, if there are "substantial grounds" for believing that, if released on bail, the accused would fail to surrender to custody, commit an offense while on bail, or interfere with witnesses or otherwise obstruct the course of justice.[245]

To determine whether bail should be granted and on what terms, courts must consider the following factors:

- The nature and seriousness of the offense and the strength of the prosecution's evidence
- The defendant's character, record, associates, and community ties
- The defendant's bail record
- Any other relevant factor[246]

When bail is granted, the court has the option of granting "unconditional bail" (BA, s. 3(1)) or "bail with conditions" (BA, s. 4). Unconditional bail is the default and will be granted unless one of the statutory exceptions to bail applies. Bail with conditions will be ordered to

243. CDA, s.51B(8).

244. Bail Act (BA), s.4(1).

245. BA, Sch. 1. Part 1 para. 2.

246. *Id.*, para. 9.

the extent considered necessary by the judge to ensure that the defendant will surrender to custody or for any other relevant purpose.

- In contrast to U.S. bail procedures, which require defendants to specifically move for bail relief, courts in England are statutorily required to reconsider earlier bail decisions at every hearing where the defendant is present in court, regardless of whether a bail application is made. Even so, a court "need not hear arguments as to fact or which it has heard previously." Whatever its ultimate decision on bail, the court must provide a statement of its reasoning.[247]
- Defendants have a right to challenge a bail decision by the Crown Court through an appeal to the High Court. The High Court's standard of review is extremely deferential to the Crown Court in bail matters, and the challenging defendant must show that the trial court's decision was "*Wednesbury* unreasonable," or "so outrageous in its defiance of logic or of accepted moral standards that no sensible person who had applied his mind to the question to be decided could have arrived at it."[248] In light of this demanding standard, such challenges are rarely successful.

a. Custody Time Limits

Functioning like the Speedy Trial Act in the United States, custody time limits (CTLs) cap the time a defendant can be held before trial. The maximum period a defendant can be detained is 182 days between the allocation hearing and trial (minus any time spent in custody prior to allocation).[249] Unless extended by the court upon application by the prosecutor under Criminal Procedure Rule 14.18, once this period lapses the defendant must be released on bail (subject to whatever conditions the court sees fit to impose). The prosecutor and the defendant can each appeal an adverse ruling related to an application for an extension to the default custody time limits.[250]

3. The Plea and Trial Preparation Hearing

A plea and trial preparation hearing (PTPH) is the British equivalent of an arraignment in the U.S. system and will take place shortly after a criminal case is transferred to the Crown Court. At this hearing the court clerk will read out the list of offenses the defendant has been charged with from the indictment and ask the defendant to plead guilty or not guilty. If the defendant pleads guilty, the judge can immediately impose a sentence or adjourn sentencing until after a presentencing report can be provided by the probation service (see chapter 9).

Where the defendant pleads not guilty, the purpose of a PTPH is to ensure that all necessary steps have been taken in preparation for trial and to set forth a schedule for the trial itself. Prosecutors and the defense are expected to confer prior to the PTPH and submit a

247. BA, ss. 5(2A) and (3); CrimPR 14.2(5).

248. Council of Civil Service Unions v. Minister for the Civil Service [1985] AC 374, [1984] 3 All ER 935.

249. Reg. 6B, Prosecution of Offences (Custody Time Limits) Regulations 1987.

250. CrimPR 14.19.

joint PTPH form with a proposed case schedule, agreed-upon procedures to gather further necessary evidence, and a list of proposed witnesses.

- PTPHs always occur after the prosecution has made an initial disclosure of the evidence supporting its case (referred to as "used" material—see chapter 5). As noted earlier, this is a significant difference with the procedures in the United States, where initial disclosures are made only after arraignment and after the defendant has entered a plea.

a. *Goodyear* Indications

During the PTPH (or at any other time before trial), the defense can ask the Crown Court judge to give an indication, known as a "*Goodyear* indication," of the likely maximum sentence that would be imposed in the event the defendant pleads guilty. There is no obligation on the court to grant such a request. Rather, *Goodyear* indications will generally only be given where the parties have agreed on a factual basis of the proposed guilty plea and the court has been provided with all relevant evidence. Aside from highlighting any issues along these lines, the prosecutor's role with respect to a *Goodyear* request is limited:

> If the process has been properly followed, it should not normally be necessary for counsel for the prosecution, before the judge gives any indication, to do more than, first, draw the judge's attention to any minimum or mandatory statutory sentencing requirements, and where [they] would be expected to offer the judge assistance with relevant guideline cases . . . to invite the judge to allow him to do so.[251]

These procedures are codified in Criminal Procedure Rule 3.23.

While providing a *Goodyear* indication is within the court's discretion, once given the court is bound not to exceed the sentence indicated.[252] The defendant is then given a "reasonable opportunity" to decide whether to plead guilty or plead not guilty and continue with the proceedings, in which case the indication will cease to have effect.

4. Extradition

Extradition in the United Kingdom is governed by the Extradition Act (EA) 2003, and all extradition matters are heard before the Westminster Magistrates' Court in London. The EA calls for different extradition procedures depending on whether the country requesting extradition of a defendant from the United Kingdom falls within category 1 or category 2.

Category 1 countries are the member countries of the European Union (E.U.) who participate in the European Arrest Warrant (EAW) scheme. The EAW, in force since 2002, provides that an arrest warrant issued by an EAW member country shall be presumptively valid and enforceable in all other member countries. This system was intended to replace the cumbersome system of bilateral extradition agreements between E.U. countries to make extradition within the bloc easier and more efficient. Following the end of the Brexit Transition Period on December 31, 2020, the United Kingdom no longer participates in the EAW.

---

251. R v. Goodyear [2005] EWCA Crim 888.

252. R v. Mustafa Nour Kulah [2007] EWCA Crim 1701.

In one of the first post-Brexit extradition cases to consider the effect of Brexit on EAWs issued before the United Kingdom's final break from the E.U., London hedge fund trader Vijay Sankar argued to the High Court that the end of the Brexit transition period automatically terminated any EAWs pending at that date. Sankar was accused by German prosecutors of criminal involvement in the ongoing "cum-ex scandal," a multibillion-euro fraud scheme that took advantage of certain loopholes in tax laws pertaining to share dividends. The Germans sought Sankar's extradition under an EAW issued in 2020, but as of January 1, 2021, when the United Kingdom's divorce with the E.U. became final, Sankar remained in England. The High Court rejected Sankar's invitation to nullify the still-pending EAW.[253]

Extradition between the United Kingdom and E.U. now follows a system that is similar to that which exists between the E.U. and Norway/Iceland. Like the EAW framework, this system expedites the extradition process. Category 2 countries are non-E.U. countries with which the United Kingdom has an extradition treaty, such as the United States.

The extradition process in Britain is managed primarily by the NCA, CPS's International Justice and Organised Crime Division (IJOCD) and Extradition Unit, and the Home Office (an agency equivalent to the U.S. Department of State). Unlike many European countries, the U.K. government will extradite its own citizens in the same manner as those of any other nationality. This fact contributes to the close cooperation between U.S. and British law enforcement and the significant number of British citizens charged with financial crimes in U.S. courts.

Category 1 Countries			
Austria	Estonia	Ireland	Poland
Belgium	Finland	Italy	Portugal
Bulgaria	France	Latvia	Romania
Croatia	Germany	Lithuania	Slovakia
Cyprus	Gibraltar	Luxembourg	Slovenia
Czech Republic	Greece	Malta	Spain
Denmark	Hungary	Netherlands	Sweden

a. Extradition from the United Kingdom to a Category 1 Country

Part 1 of the EA gives constables, customs officers, and police officers the authority to arrest a person without a warrant if they have reasonable grounds for believing that a Part 1 warrant has been or will be issued in respect of the person by an authority of a category 1 territory.[254] Acting on this authority, defendants subject to Red Notices who travel from or into the United Kingdom are often arrested and detained by border guards after the Red Notice causes their passports to be flagged. Once the wanted person is apprehended, he or she must be brought before the magistrates' court—in person or via video link—within 48 hours for a first appearance and bail hearing. At this hearing, the presiding magistrate will make an

253. *See* Polakowski & Ors v. Westminster Magistrates' Court [2021] EWHC 53 (Admin).

254. Extradition Act (EA), s.5(1).

initial determination on the validity of the arrest and underlying warrant, either remand the person into custody or grant bail, and set a date for the extradition hearing (generally within twenty-one days of arrest).[255] Defendants who are denied bail pending the extradition hearing will often be held at Her Majesty's Prison (HMP) Wandsworth, a crowded, aging Victorian-era facility in southwest London.

At the extradition hearing at Westminster Magistrates' Court, the interests of the requesting government are represented by the CPS Extradition Unit. If the requested person does not consent to extradition, the court will first consider whether the alleged conduct amounts to an "extradition offense," that is, an offense that is subject to serious criminal punishment in both the requesting state and the United Kingdom. If it is, extradition may still be denied based on one of the statutory extradition bars, including:

- **Double jeopardy.** A person's extradition to a category 1 territory is barred by double jeopardy if "it appears that he would be entitled to be discharged under any rule of law relating to previous acquittal or conviction."[256] This requires the court to consider whether U.K. double jeopardy principles would permit trial of the defendant if he or she were theoretically facing charges in England or Wales.
- **Improper motivation by prosecutors** (e.g., prejudice, political persecution).
- **A significant lapse of time.** EA Section 14 states that a "person's extradition to a category 1 territory is barred by reason of the passage of time if it appears that it would be unjust or oppressive to extradite him." This is an obviously fact-intensive inquiry, but, in general, Westminster Magistrates' is receptive to denying extradition on this basis when there has been at least a multiyear delay in initiating proceedings and the requesting state has no valid reason for waiting so long.
- **The Rule of Specialty.** Specialty is treated the same in the United Kingdom and the United States. The only way an accused person can prevent extradition on this basis is if the relevant treaty lacks specialty protections.
- **Forum.** EA Section 19 precludes extradition if the requested extradition would be contrary to the "interest of justice." The forum bar turns on the court's consideration of where the alleged conduct took place, where the loss was incurred, where the key evidence and witnesses are located, and any other issue that may be relevant.

If none of the statutory bars apply, extradition will be ordered unless it would be disproportionate to the crime, incompatible with the person's human rights under recognized international conventions (such as the ECHR), or an abuse of process by the prosecuting state.[257] An individual facing extradition may also challenge detention based on a procedural flaw through a habeas corpus application.[258]

---

255. EA, s.6.

256. EA, s.12.

257. EA, s.10.

258. Jane v. Westminster Magistrates' Court [2019] EWHC 394 (Admin); Gronostajski v. Government of Poland [2007] EWHC 3314 (Admin).

Extradition can also be denied if the requested person is facing prosecution for an unrelated offense in the United Kingdom, is an important witness in U.K. criminal proceedings, is subject to confiscation proceedings, or is already serving a sentence in a British prison. In these circumstances, the extradition hearing will generally be stayed until the domestic matter is resolved.

If the Westminster Magistrates' Court grants extradition to a category 1 country and there is no appeal, the requested person must be extradited within ten days of the expiration of the seven-day notice period for applying for leave to appeal. Where the requested person appeals to the High Court and loses, he or she must be extradited within ten days of the High Court's final decision (unless a further appeal to the Supreme Court is lodged). As in the United States, the appeals process can take several years to run its course.

b. Extradition from the United Kingdom to a Category 2 Country

The procedures for an extradition from the United Kingdom to a category 2 country are more complex than those to category 1 countries, and category 2 requests must be approved by the U.K. Central Authority (UKCA) at the Home Office as well as the courts.

In addition, at extradition hearings involving requests from category 2 countries, the requesting country—acting through the CPS—must establish that there is enough admissible evidence to make out a prima facie case against the defendant, meaning that there is sufficient evidence to warrant a trial if the offense had taken place in England or Wales. In making this determination, the judge must consider whether the prosecution's case, viewed in the most favorable light, is such that no jury could reasonably be expected to convict.

Although they are in category 2, a number of counties—including Australia, Canada, New Zealand, and the United States—are exempt from the prima facie requirement and must only provide "information" regarding the accusation or conviction, which is often presented in the form of a summary affidavit from prosecutors in these countries.[259] These countries are classified as category 2 "Type A" jurisdictions.

Category 2 Type A Countries			
Albania	Curaçao	Moldova	Serbia
Andorra	Faroe Islands	Monaco	Saint Eustatius
Armenia	Georgia	Montenegro	Saint Maarten
Aruba	Greenland	New Zealand	South Africa
Australia	Iceland	Norway	Switzerland
Azerbaijan	Hong Kong	South Korea	Turkey
Bonaire	Israel	Russia	Ukraine
Bosnia/Herzegovina	Liechtenstein	Saba	United States
Canada	Macedonia	San Marino	

259. UK Home Office, "Extradition: process and review," *available at* https://www.gov.uk/guidance/extradition-processes-and-review.

Countries that are not in the E.U. and do not have extradition treaties with the United Kingdom are unclassified under the EA, but it may still be possible for incoming extradition requests from these territories to be granted. Incoming requests from unclassified countries are received by the UKCA and passed to the Home Office, which then decides whether to enter into "special extradition arrangements" in the particular case at issue.

Practice Note

Mike Lynch Extradition Case

In 2011, Mike Lynch, a British tech entrepreneur, engineered the sale of his software company, Autonomy Corp., to California-based Hewlett-Packard for $11.7 billion. Soon after the sale, HP wrote down its investment by approximately $8.8 billion and alleged that Lynch and other Autonomy executives gave misleading accounting statements and valuations during the sales process. The SFO launched an investigation into these allegations but, in 2015, announced that it was closing the file with no action due to a lack of evidence. The SFO's press release stated: "In respect of some aspects of the allegations, the SFO has concluded that . . . there is insufficient evidence for a realistic prospect of conviction. In respect of other aspects . . . jurisdiction over the investigation has been ceded to the U.S. authorities whose investigation is ongoing."

Three years later, Lynch was indicted by a federal grand jury in San Francisco on charges of conspiracy and thirteen counts of wire fraud in connection with the HP transaction. Lynch challenged extradition to the United States on four grounds: (i) dual criminality, (ii) passage of time, (iii) forum, (iv) violation of his rights under the ECHR, and (v) abuse of process.

While these arguments were under court review, Lynch's case generated heated parliamentary debate about the U.S.-U.K. extradition treaty and the DOJ's conduct in general. At a January 23, 2020, hearing in the House of Commons, for example, Member of Parliament (MP) David Davis remarked: "Since we agreed with the U.K.-U.S. extradition treaty in 2003, it has been abundantly clear that the British Government of the day struck a truly dreadful deal—asymmetric, sometimes ineffective and often unfair on British citizens. . . . We now risk yet another serious miscarriage of justice with the U.S. extradition request of Dr. Mike Lynch, a successful and entrepreneurial British businessman." Davis went on to characterize the case as "yet another aggressive attempt by American authorities to exercise extraterritorial jurisdiction. Despite the SFO deciding that there is no basis for a prosecution in the United Kingdom, the United States authorities are doggedly pursuing his extradition."

MP Greg Hands, shadow home secretary when the extradition treaty was proposed, echoed Davis and noted that the British Conservative Party agreed to support the treaty "on the grounds that it was about pedophilia and terrorism and violent crime. That was the sole basis upon which we accepted what we thought at the time was a treaty that made it too easy for the U.S. to extradite. And of course what we are seeing now is that that is not what is happening: the United States is going after white-collar businessmen and seeking to be the judge, jury and executioner for global commercial deals. Since 2003, some 80% of the extraditions were for non-violent crimes. This seems like very strange behaviour when we consider that this is a country that did not convict any American chief executives in the 2008 crisis, which clearly had some frauds behind it."

Despite these protestations, each of Lynch's challenges to extradition were rejected by the Westminster Magistrates' Court in a July 2021 ruling. On January 28, 2022, the British home secretary, Priti Patel, gave final approval for Lynch's extradition. In an accompanying press release, a Home Office spokesperson noted the limited discretion afforded the secretary under the treaty: "Under the Extradition Act 2003, the secretary of state must sign an extradition order if there are no grounds to prohibit the order being made. Extradition requests are only sent to the home secretary once a judge decides it can proceed after considering various aspects of the case.[260]

c. Extradition to the United Kingdom

Outgoing extradition requests to countries other than those in category 1 fall outside of the EA and are made under "royal prerogative"—that is, the powers traditionally held by the monarch or by government ministers that may be used without the consent of Parliament. In non-category 1 cases, the CPS prepares either a "full-order" extradition request—a request that complies with all the relevant treaty or arrangement—or a provisional arrest request—which seeks an arrest while a full-order request can be prepared—and submits it to the UKCA. The UKCA then sends it via diplomatic channels to the relevant country and extradition proceeds under local law.

If extradition is granted in the requested country, the UKCA will be notified by the local British embassy or INTERPOL. British police will then travel to the requested country to collect the person and return them under guard to the United Kingdom.

CHAPTER 3: KEY DISTINCTIONS

United States	United Kingdom
Legality of charging decisions determined by federal law and the Constitution, and must comply with the DOJ's Justice Manual	Charging decisions must comply with Code for Crown Prosecutors as well as the European Convention on Human Rights
Consent of grand jury must be obtained before an indictment may be issued	Prosecutors can issue an indictment without any public oversight
Defendants may plead guilty, not guilty, or nolo contendere	Defendants may only plead guilty or not guilty
Defendants are unable to request an indication of likely sentence prior to entering a plea	To inform their plea, defendants can request a *Goodyear* indication of the maximum sentence the judge will impose
Double jeopardy will not apply to prosecutions initiated by different sovereigns (including foreign governments and the governments of the fifty states)	Double jeopardy will apply to prosecutions brought by foreign governments

(*Continued*)

260. Mike Lynch: Priti Patel Approves Extradition of Autonomy Founder (BBC NEWS, Jan. 28, 2022).

United States	United Kingdom
Defendants have a constitutional right to be tried in the venue within which a substantial portion of their offense took place	Defendants do not have a legal right to a particular venue and trial locations are set at the discretion of the prosecution and the courts
Statutes of limitations apply to all federal white-collar crimes	There is no statute of limitations for any financial crime
Tolling agreements are routinely entered into between the DOJ and white-collar crime defendants to extend the statute of limitations	Tolling agreements are not used because there are no statutes of limitations in financial crime cases
Changes can be secretly filed under seal to facilitate the capture of a defendant who might otherwise flee	Sealed indictments are not used
For prosecutors to substantially amend an indictment or proceed to trial on a superseding indictment, they must present their case to a grand jury	Prosecutors have limited discretion to amend or replace an indictment up until verdict or a guilty plea
Disclosure of the government's evidence occurs only after the defendant has been arraigned	Prosecutors must disclose the evidence supporting its case prior to the defendant's initial appearance in court
Lists of proposed trial witnesses generally only disclosed by the parties shortly before trial	The identities of proposed trial witnesses disclosed by both sides during the plea and trial preparation hearing
Law enforcement cannot make an arrest on the basis of an INTERPOL Red Notice alone	Arrests can be made on the basis of an INTERPOL Red Notice alone

4 | The Main Financial Crimes

The number of distinctly defined crimes in the U.S. federal criminal code is estimated to exceed 4,500, a good percentage of which pertain to some sort of financial misconduct or corporate wrongdoing. On top of that, there are an estimated 300,000 regulatory offenses that carry criminal penalties and many tens of thousands more crimes defined by state law.[1] The volume of offenses is regularly criticized as needlessly complex, overinclusive, and difficult for the average citizen to keep track of and avoid violating. In the words of Professor Julie R. O'Sullivan, "Any discussion of federal penal law must begin with an important caveat: There actually *is* no federal criminal 'code' worthy of the name." According to Professor O'Sullivan, "What the federal government has is a haphazard grab-bag of statutes accumulated over 200 years, rather than a comprehensive, thoughtful, and internally consistent system of criminal law." In her view, Congress's creation of Title 18 in 1948 "accomplished little more than sweeping a host of internally-disorganized statues containing fragmentary coverage into a series of chapters laid out in . . . alphabetical order."[2]

In comparison to the sprawling list of crimes in the United States, parliamentarians in Westminster have put together an arguably more concise and well-organized definitional framework for the different crimes recognized in England and Wales. The U.K. criminal code is also simpler in the sense that there is only one national code, not a national code overlaid on top of fifty separate state codes as there is in the United States. As a result of an effort by British lawmakers over the past two decades to consolidate common law and statutory crimes into unified legislation, the main financial crimes in the United Kingdom are contained within just four acts: the Fraud Act 2006, the Proceeds of Crime Act 2002, the Financial Services and Markets Act 2000, and the U.K. Bribery Act 2010.

This chapter examines the financial crimes in each jurisdiction that are most often implicated in cross-border prosecutions brought the DOJ, SFO, or FCA: fraud, insider trading, bribery, conspiracy, market manipulation, and money laundering. After a general overview of the relevant statutes and each crime's elements under U.S. and English law, there is an examination of the extent to which they reach extraterritorial conduct, the availability of statutory defenses, and their statutory maximum penalties. With respect to the statutory maximums,

1. Brett Tolman, "Curing America's Addiction to Overcriminalization," BLOOMBERG (Oct. 19, 2020).

2. Julie R. O'Sullivan, *The Federal Criminal "Code" Is a Disgrace: Obstruction Statutes as Case Study*, 96 J. CRIM. L. & CRIMINOLOGY 643 (2006).

bear in mind that the actual sentence a defendant will receive is determined in accordance with the sentencing guidelines and procedures discussed in chapter 9; in white-collar crime cases, sentences are generally far below the theoretical maximum.

I. FRAUD

The essence of a fraud offense in the United States and Britain is the same: conduct intended to obtain money or property based on an intentionally false statement of fact or a deliberate omission, or some other type of deception. Since 2006, criminal fraud offenses in the United Kingdom have been consolidated into a single law, the Fraud Act 2006. The U.S. code contains many different fraud statutes that each target specific types of schemes—for example, securities and commodities fraud (18 U.S.C. § 1348), health care fraud (18 U.S.C. § 1347), and bank fraud (18 U.S.C. § 1344). This chapter explores only mail and wire fraud, which are the foundational statutes on which all other U.S. fraud statutes were built.

A. Mail and Wire Fraud in the United States

The mail and wire fraud statutes—18 U.S.C. § 1341 and 18 U.S.C. § 1343, respectively—are some of the most frequently charged federal crimes. As Jed Rakoff, a former AUSA and now a prominent district court judge in Manhattan, put it, "[t]o federal prosecutors of white-collar crime, [these statutes are] our Stradivarius, our Colt 45, our Louisville Slugger, our Cuisinart—and our true love."[3] "First enacted in 1872, the mail fraud statute, together with its lineal descendant, the wire fraud statute, has been characterized as the 'first line of defense' against virtually every new area of fraud to develop in the United States."[4]

The DOJ's affinity for mail and wire fraud charges stems from the fact that they are simple, relatively easy to prove, and adaptable to a wide variety of dishonest activities. The application of these statutes, "too numerous to catalogue, cover not only the full range of consumer frauds, stock frauds, land frauds, bank frauds, insurance frauds, and commodity frauds, but have extended even to such areas as blackmail, counterfeiting, election fraud and bribery." In Judge Rakoff's view, in areas "where legislatures have sometimes been slow to enact specific prohibitory legislation," Sections 1341 and 1343 have "frequently represented the sole instrument of justice that could be wielded against the ever-innovative practitioners of deceit."[5]

At the same time, the statutes' expansive reach has been criticized as occasionally being stretched too far by prosecutors. According to the Seventh Circuit, for instance,

> [m]ail and wire fraud statutes "have long provided prosecutors with a means by which to salvage a modest, but dubious, victory from investigations that essentially proved unfruitful." The mail and wire fraud statutes have "been invoked to impose criminal penalties upon a

---

3. Jed S. Rakoff, *The Federal Mail Fraud Statute (Part I)*, 18 Duq. L. Rev. 771 (1980).

4. *Id.* at 772.

5. *Id.*

staggeringly broad swath of behavior," creating uncertainty in business negotiations and challenges to due process and federalism.[6]

To prevent overreach, the mail and wire fraud statutes are interpreted to target only practices that "deviate far from behavioral norms for business transactions in a market economy governed by the rule of law;" in other words, judges approach novel fraud theories from the premise that "not all conduct that strikes a court as sharp dealing or unethical conduct is a 'scheme to defraud'"[7] and the fraud statutes "do not cover all behavior which strays from the ideal."[8]

The elements of mail and wire fraud are essentially the same except for the means by which the fraudulent communication is transmitted: Section 1341 requires use of the mails, whereas Section 1343 requires use of interstate wire facilities (i.e., telephonic or electronic communications between states or internationally).[9] Using very similar language to the mail fraud statute, wire fraud is defined in Section 1343 as follows:

> Whoever, having devised or intending to devise any scheme or artifice to defraud, or for obtaining money or property by means of false or fraudulent pretenses, representations, or promises, transmits or causes to be transmitted by means of wire, radio, or television communication in interstate or foreign commerce, any writings, signs, signals, pictures, or sounds for the purpose of executing such scheme or artifice, shall be fined under this title or imprisoned not more than 20 years, or both.

Although the mail fraud and wire fraud statutes contain different jurisdictional elements, they both prohibit "'any scheme or artifice to defraud,' or to obtain money or property 'by means of false or fraudulent pretenses, representations, or promises.'"[10] As used in both statutes, "the word 'property' is construed in accordance with its ordinary meaning: 'something of value' in the possession of the property holder."[11] This can include confidential business information belonging to a business or the government,[12] as well as the "interest of a victim in controlling his or her own assets."[13]

---

6. United States v. Weimert, 819 F.3d 351, 356 (7th Cir. 2016) (quoting John C. Coffee, Jr. & Charles K. Whitehead, *The Federalization of Fraud: Mail and Wire Fraud Statutes, in* White Collar Crime: Business and Regulatory Offenses § 9.05, 9–73 (Otto G. Obermaier et al. eds. 1990)).

7. *Id.* at 357.

8. United States v. Colton, 231 F.3d 890, 901 (4th Cir.2000); United States v. Coffman, 94 F.3d 330, 334 (7th Cir. 1996) ("it would not do to criminalize business conduct that is customary rather than exceptional and is relatively harmless"); *see also* G. Richard Shell, *When Is It Legal to Lie in Negotiations?,* 32 Sloan Management Rev. 93, 96 (1991) ("There are thus no legal problems with lying about how much you might be willing to pay or which of several issues in a negotiation you value more highly. Demands and reservation prices are not, as a matter of law, material to a deal.").

9. Pasquantino v. United States, 544 U.S. 349, 355 n.2 (2005); Neder v. United States, 527 U.S. 1, 20 (1999); United States v. Greenberg, 835 F.3d 295, 305 (2d Cir. 2016).

10. Neder, 527 U.S. at 20 (1999); Weimert, 819 F.3d at 354.

11. United States v. Blaszczak, 947 F.3d 19, 31 (2d Cir. 2019).

12. Carpenter v. United States, 484 U.S. 19, 26 (1987); Blaszczak, 947 F.3d at 34.

13. United States v. Binday, 804 F.3d 558, 569 (2d Cir. 2015); United States v. Starr, 816 F.2d 94, 98 (2d Cir. 1987) (in right-to-control cases fraudulent turns on whether the defendant's deception "affect[ed] the very nature of the bargain" between the defendant and the victim).

To prove the existence of a scheme to defraud, the government must also prove that the misrepresentations were material and that the defendant acted with fraudulent intent.[14] To secure a conviction, the government does not need to prove that the fraud was successful or that the intended victims of a fraud scheme were actually injured; only that the perpetrators contemplated some actual harm or injury.[15] As to this element, courts acknowledge that there is a "'fine line between schemes that do no more than cause their victims to enter into transactions they would otherwise avoid'—which do not violate the wire fraud statute—and those schemes that 'depend for their completion on a misrepresentation of an essential element of the bargain.'"[16]

1. *Element 1: Use of Mail or Wire Communications*

Sections 1341 and 1343 apply to anyone who uses the mail or a "wire, radio, or television communication in interstate or foreign commerce" for the purpose of executing a "scheme or artifice to defraud." To be part of the execution of the fraud, the mailing or wire communication must be "incident to an essential part of the scheme," or a "step in the plot."[17] It is irrelevant whether the mailing or wire communication is itself legal or failed to actually further the scheme's purpose.[18] Rather, the "relevant question at all times is whether the [communication] is part of the execution of the scheme as conceived by the perpetrator at the time, regardless of whether the [communication] later, through hindsight, may prove to have been counterproductive and return to haunt the perpetrator of the fraud." In white-collar crime cases, this element is often satisfied with evidence of bank transfers, emails, or telephone calls using U.S. wires.[19]

2. *Element 2: Scheme to Defraud*

To prove a scheme to defraud, the government must establish two things: (i) a material false statement, misrepresentation, or promise, or concealment of a material fact, and (ii) fraudulent intent.[20] A scheme to defraud is a course of conduct that is "reasonably calculated to deceive persons of ordinary prudence and comprehension."[21] This standard is meant "to assure that the defendant's conduct was calculated to deceive, not to grant permission to take advantage of the stupid or careless."[22] In other words, the ordinary prudence standard focuses on the subjective intent of the violator, not the objective capabilities of the victim.

---

14. United States v. Weaver, 860 F.3d 90, 94 (2d Cir. 2017).

15. *Id.* at 95.

16. United States v. Johnson, 945 F.3d 606, 612 (2d Cir. 2019).

17. Badders v. United States, 240 U.S. 391, 394 (1916).

18. Schmuck v. United States, 489 U.S. 705, 714 (1989).

19. *See, e.g.*, United States v. Napout, 963 F.3d 163, 179 (2d Cir. 2020).

20. United States v. Thomas, 377 F.3d 232, 242 n. 7 (2d Cir. 2004); Weimert, 819 F.3d at 354; United States v. Powell, 576 F.3d 482, 490 (7th Cir. 2009).

21. United States v. Drake, 932 F.2d 861, 863 (10th Cir. 1991).

22. Thomas, 377 F.2d at 242.

Accordingly, the "negligence of the victim in failing to discover a fraudulent scheme is not a defense to criminal conduct."[23] Likewise, it is no defense that the victim was too smart or sophisticated to be taken in by the deception.[24]

And while proof of a breach of fiduciary duty is often relevant to a fraud scheme, it is not a necessary element.[25] Fraud can also occur even if the contract governing the underlying transaction is not breached. In *United States v. Binday*, for example, the Second Circuit upheld the fraud convictions of three insurance brokers who induced life insurers to issue policies that were sold to third-party investors (while representing to the insurance companies that the policies were for the applicants' personal estate planning). On appeal, the defendants argued that there was insufficient evidence to show that they contemplated any harm to the insurers since the reason the applicants sought the policy was irrelevant under the contracts.

Rejecting this argument, the court noted that "since a defining feature of most property is the right to control the asset in question, we have recognized that the property interests protected by the [mail and wire fraud] statutes include the interest of a victim in controlling his or her own assets." Accordingly, a "cognizable harm" occurs under these statutes where a scheme "denies the victim the right to control its assets by depriving it of information necessary to make discretionary economic decisions."[26] Yet this right does not render every transaction induced by deceit actionable—the deceit must deprive the victim of "potentially valuable economic information."[27]

Prosecutions brought under a "right to control" wire fraud theory are controversial because they seek to impose criminal punishments on conduct that did not, and was not intended to, cause direct financial injury to the purported victim. The government's typical allegation in such cases is that a defendant withheld or misstated "information that could impact on economic decisions [of another]."[28] The outlines of this theory are defined in a line of cases decided by the Second Circuit.[29] The "common thread" in these cases is "that

23. United States v. Coyle, 63 F.3d 1239, 1243–44 (3d Cir. 1995); *see also* Thomas, 377 F.3d at 243 (collecting cases); United States v. Allen, 201 F.3d 163, 167 (2d Cir. 2000) ("victim's negligence in permitting a crime to take place does not excuse the defendant from culpability for her substantive offense").

24. United States v. Coffman, 94 F.3d 330, 333 (7th Cir. 1996); United States v. Colton, 231 F.3d 890, 903 (4th Cir. 2000).

25. Weimert, 819 F.3d at 367 ("Concealment is often accompanied by a violation of a fiduciary duty, but it need not be."); United States v. Kwiat, 817 F.2d 440, 444 (7th Cir. 1987) (reversing mail fraud conviction of corporate officer through scheme for self-dealing: "Neither the language nor the legislative history of § 1341 hints that it is an all-purpose remedy for corporate mismanagement.").

26. Binday, 804 F.3d at 570.

27. *Id.*

28. United States v. Wallach, 935 F.2d 445, 463 (2d Cir. 1991); *see also* United States v. *Finazzo*, 850 F.3d 94, 97 (2d Cir. 2017) (the DOJ charging wire fraud where the defendant engaged in a kickback scheme with one of his employer's suppliers based on a theory that the defendant had deprived his company "of the opportunity to make informed decisions, . . . seek lower prices for merchandise it purchased from [the supplier], and the opportunity to select other vendors.").

29. *See, e.g.,* United States v. Mittelstaedt, 31 F.3d 1208 (2d Cir. 1994); United States v. Dinome, 86 F.3d 277 (2d Cir. 1996); United States v. Viloski, 557 Fed. App'x 28 (2d Cir. 2014); United States v. Binday, 804 F.3d 558 (2d Cir. 2015).

misrepresentations or non-disclosure of information cannot support a conviction under the 'right to control' theory unless those misrepresentations or non-disclosures can or do result in tangible economic harm."[30] In other words, while the Second Circuit considers the intangible right to control one's assets a cognizable "property" right, to be convicted of wire fraud on a right to control theory a defendant must intend to do two things: deprive another party of this right through a material deception and cause actual pecuniary injury as a result.[31]

Thus, "[i]t is not sufficient . . . [for the government] to show merely that the victim would not have entered into a discretionary economic transaction but for the defendant's misrepresentations" because the "'right to control one's assets' does not render every transaction induced by deceit actionable" as wire fraud.[32] Instead, the defendant's deception must "affect the very nature" of the transaction at issue.[33]

3. Element 3: A Material Misrepresentation or Omission

The "purpose of the element of materiality is to ensure that a defendant actually intended to create a scheme to defraud."[34] "Courts have taken an expansive approach to what counts as a material misrepresentation or concealment in a scheme to defraud."[35] In general, a false statement or omission will be considered material if "it would naturally tend to lead or is capable of leading a reasonable [person] to change [his] conduct."[36] It follows, therefore, that a "false statement is material if it has a natural tendency to influence, or is capable of influencing, the decision of the person to which it was addressed."[37] As explained by the Supreme Court, "under any understanding of the concept, materiality looks to the effect on the likely or actual behavior of the recipient of the alleged misrepresentation," viewed objectively.[38]

30. Finazzo, 850 F.3d at 111.

31. United States v. Johnson, 945 F.3d 606, 614 (2d Cir. 2019) ("The requirement of materiality thus differs from the requirement of fraudulent intent, which is that the misrepresentation must be 'capable of resulting in tangible harm.'"); United States v. Sadler, 750 F.3d 585, 591 (6th Cir. 2014) (more is required than intentional misrepresentations or omissions, and simply "equating deceptions with property deprivation" is insufficient to support a wire fraud charge).

32. Binday, 804 F.3d at 570.

33. Johnson, 945 F.3d at 612; *see also* Binday, 804 F.3d at 568–70, 75 (finding defendant's deception goes to "an essential element of the bargain" if defendant "contemplated harm" to the victim).

34. United States v. Svete, 556 F.3d 1157, 1165 (11th Cir. 2009).

35. Weimert, 819 F.3d at 355.

36. United States v. Rybicki, 354 F.3d 124, 145 (2d Cir. 2003); Neder, 527 U.S. at 16 ("The term 'material' means having a natural tendency to influence, or be capable of influencing, the payment or receipt of money or property.").

37. United States v. Corsey, 723 F.3d 366, 373 (2d Cir. 2013); United States v. Lindsey, 850 F.3d 1009 (9th Cir. 2017).

38. United Health Servs., Inc. v. United States, 136 S. Ct. 1989, 2002 (2016); *see also* Autuori, 212 F.3d at 118 (the materiality element is satisfied if the false pretense or representation has "some independent value" or "bear[s] on the ultimate value of the transaction").

The misrepresentation need not, however, actually have influenced its recipient—the sole issue is its likely effect at the time it was made.[39]

Materiality is assessed in the context in which the relevant communications occurred, meaning that industry practices, prior agreements between the parties, and other information known to the parties at the time of the allegedly false statements are critical to assessing those statements' materiality.[40] Statements between investment professionals, for example, will be held to a higher materiality standard than statements from a stockbroker to an unsophisticated retail investor.[41]

The concept of misrepresentation is broad and reaches false statements of fact as well as misleading half-truths and knowingly false promises. "It can also include the omission or concealment of material information, even absent an affirmative duty to disclose, if the omission was intended to induce a false belief and action to the advantage of the schemer and the disadvantage of the victim."[42] As confirmed by the Second Circuit, "it is just as unlawful to speak 'half truths' or to omit to state facts necessary to make the statements made, in light of the circumstances under which they were made, not misleading."[43]

Defendants will be held liable for any communication they deliberately "caused" to occur, even if it is made by a third party.[44] Further, the false statement or omission need not be made directly to the intended or actual victim, it just needs to be intended to effectuate the overall fraud scheme.[45] The extent to which the intended victim "was too trusting and gullible or, on the other hand, was too smart or sophisticated" is irrelevant since a finding of materiality does not require proof of "actual reliance."[46] All that is required is that a reasonable investor would deem the content of a misstatement a substantial factor in making an investment decision. Proof of actual harm is also not required, so long as materiality and intent to defraud are shown.[47]

---

39. Lindsey, 850 F.3d at 1013.

40. United States v. Green, 698 F. App'x 879, 880 (9th Cir. 2017).

41. United States v. Litvak, 889 F.3d 56, 65 (2d Cir. 2018) ("The reasonable investor in a market in which many individual investors trade will be deemed to be somewhat less schooled and sophisticated than a reasonable investor in a market, like the one now before us, in which only institutions trade with the help of complex computer programs and professional traders.").

42. Weimert, 819 F.3d at 355.

43. Autuori, 212 F.3d at 118.

44. Pereira v. United States, 347 U.S. 1, 8 (1954); United States v. Bortnovsky, 879 F.2d 30, 39 (2d Cir. 1989) (noting that "defendant need not actually intend, agree to or even know of a specific mailing to 'cause' mail to be sent as long as he or she 'does an act with knowledge that the use of mails will follow in the ordinary course of business, or where such can reasonably be foreseen'").

45. United States v. Seidling, 737 F.3d 1155, 1160 (7th Cir. 2013).

46. Weimert, 819 F.3d at 355; United States v. Colton, 231 F.3d 890, 903 (4th Cir.2000) ("If a scheme to defraud has been or is intended to be devised, it makes no difference whether the persons the schemers intended to defraud are gullible or skeptical, dull or bright."); United States v. Pierce, 224 F.3d 158, 166 (2d Cir. 2000) ("The wire fraud statute punishes the scheme, not its success.").

47. Litvak, 889 F.3d at 65.

4. *Element 4: Intent to Defraud*

The intent to defraud element "requires a willful act by the defendant with the specific intent to deceive or cheat, usually for the purpose of getting financial gain for one's self or causing financial loss to another."[48] It can also be established by demonstrating a defendant acted with a "reckless indifference to the truth."[49] The requirement of materiality differs from the requirement of fraudulent intent in that the issue of materiality looks to whether the statement or omission is objectively "capable of resulting in 'tangible harm'"; whereas fraudulent intent requires the defendant to have subjectively contemplated "some actual cognizable harm or injury to their victims by deceiving them."[50]

Fraudulent intent may be apparent where a false representation or omission goes to "the quality, adequacy or price of the [object of the fraud], because the victim is made to bargain without facts obviously essential in deciding whether to enter the bargain."[51] As already mentioned, proof that someone was actually defrauded is not required as long as the defendant acted with fraudulent intent. But the purpose of the scheme "must be to injure, which doubtless may be inferred when the scheme has such effect as a necessary result of carrying it out."[52]

Practice Note

"Honest Services" Wire Fraud

Section 1346 of Title 18 states that the term "scheme or artifice" as used in the wire and mail fraud statutes includes a scheme or artifice to deprive another of the "intangible right of honest services." Honest services fraud is "not something different from wire fraud; it is a type of wire fraud that is explicitly prohibited by [the wire fraud] statute."[53]

Unlike frauds in which the victim's loss is directly related to the defendant's gain, the honest-services theory targets corruption and other schemes that lack such symmetry: "While the offender profited, the betrayed party suffered no deprivation of money or property; instead, a third party, who had not been deceived, provided the enrichment."[54] Even if the scheme resulted in a gain for the betrayed party, courts have reasoned that the defendant may have still criminally deprived that party of its right to "honest services."[55]

Most honest services cases involve bribery of public officials, but they can also occur between private parties. For example, employees have been found guilty of defrauding their

48. United States v. Faruki, 803 F.3d 847, 853 (7th Cir. 2015); Autuori, 212 F.3d at 116 (intentional fraud is established by showing "a 'conscious knowing intent to defraud' . . . [and] that the defendant contemplated or intended some harm to the property rights of the victim.").

49. O'Malley v. New York City Transit Auth., 896 F.2d 704, 706 (2d Cir. 1990).

50. Johnson, 945 F.3d at 614.

51. United States v. Regent Office Supply Co., 421 F.2d 1174, 1182 (2d Cir. 1970).

52. Regent Office Supply Co., 421 F.2d at 1181.

53. Napout, 963 F.3d 163 at 179.

54. Skilling v. United States, 561 U.S. 358, 400 (2010).

55. *See, e.g.*, United States v. Dixon, 536 F.2d 1388, 1400 (2d. Cir. 1976).

employers "by accepting bribes or kickbacks in the course of his employment."[56] Such cases have also targeted election fraud and privacy violations.[57]

In response to challenges from defendants arguing that Section 1346 is unconstitutionally vague and overbroad, federal courts have differed in their interpretation of the statute.[58] In *United States v. Skilling*, an honest services prosecution of a former executive at defunct energy firm Enron, the Supreme Court ruled that Section 1346 criminalizes only bribery and kickback schemes and did not reach "undisclosed self-dealing by a public official or private employee."[59]

The upshot of the *Skilling* decision is that, save for bribes or kickbacks, a public official's fraudulent scheme constitutes mail or wire fraud only when they are intended "for obtaining money or property."[60]

5. *Extraterritorial Reach*

By default, federal criminal laws apply only to domestic conduct. So when foreign conduct is involved, questions arise as to whether a U.S. prosecution exceeds its proper bounds.[61] In light of the "presumption against extraterritoriality," the Supreme Court has held that "[a]bsent clearly expressed congressional intent to the contrary, federal laws will be construed to have only domestic application."[62] But if a predominantly foreign crime has as its "focus" conduct that occurs in the United States, the concerns associated with a potentially improper extraterritorial application of federal law do not come into play.

Compared with the United Kingdom and most other countries, the United States government takes an extremely aggressive and more expansive view of its jurisdiction over defendants who have engaged in conduct mostly or completely from outside its territory. This approach has been subject to heavy criticism within England, especially when it has been applied to British citizens. To cite one example, during a Home Affairs Committee meeting on the U.S.-U.K. Extradition Treaty, a member of Parliament commented on the "overzealousness of U.S. prosecutors" and observed that the DOJ "has quite an exorbitant extraterritorial jurisdiction . . . It has the power to reach out around the world and—provided there is a very, very tenuous connection with the U.S.—it generally has the power

56. United States v. McNeive, 536 F.2d 1245, 1249 (8th Cir. 1976); *see also* Napout, 963 F.3d at 183; United States v. Rybicki, 354 F.3d 124, 141–42 (2d Cir. 2003) (holding that the theory of honest services wire fraud applies to "an officer or employee of a private entity" or "a person in a relationship that gives rise to a duty of loyalty comparable to that owed by employees to employers"); United States v. Milovanovic, 678 F.3d 713, 724 (9th Cir. 2012) (Section 1346 "is not limited to a formal 'fiduciary' relationship well-known in the law, but also extends to a trusting relationship in which one party acts for the benefit of another and induces the trusting party to relax the care and vigilance which it would ordinarily exercise").

57. *See, e.g.,* Cleveland v. United States, 531 U.S. 12, 18, n.2 (2000); McNally v. United States, 483 U.S. 350, 362–64, and nn.1–4 (1987) (Stevens, J., dissenting).

58. Skilling, 561 U.S. at 403, n.36 (discussing the different approaches taken by various circuit courts).

59. *Id.* at 409–10.

60. Kelly v. United States, 140 S. Ct. 1565, 1571–72 (2020).

61. United States v. Hussain, 972 F.3d 1138, 1142 (9th Cir. 2020).

62. RJR Nabisco, Inc. v. European Cmty., 136 S. Ct. 2090, 2100 (2016).

to prosecute."[63] Indeed, regardless of the perpetrator's citizenship, DOJ prosecutors regularly base criminal investigations on the mere fact that U.S. dollars were used to effectuate criminal activity that otherwise took place entirely outside of the United States.[64]

This approach is made possible by the generous two-step framework used by federal courts to analyze extraterritoriality issues. In the first step, courts consider "whether the presumption against extraterritoriality has been rebutted—that is, whether the statute gives a clear, affirmative indication that it applies extraterritorially."[65] If it does, the case may be tried in the United States; if it does not, then courts will "determine whether the case involves a domestic application of the statute" by "looking to the statute's focus."[66] A statute's focus is "'the object of its solicitude,' which can include the conduct it 'seeks to regulate' as well as the parties and interests it 'seeks to protect' or vindicate."[67] If a statute is not extraterritorial under step one, the question under step two becomes whether the conduct that is proscribed took place domestically:

> If the conduct relevant to the statute's focus occurred in the United States, then the case involves a permissible domestic application even if other conduct occurred abroad; but if the conduct relevant to the focus occurred in a foreign country, then the case involves an impermissible extraterritorial application regardless of any other conduct that occurred in U.S. territory.[68]

The Supreme Court has instructed that "[b]ecause a finding of extraterritoriality at step one will obviate step two's 'focus' inquiry, it will usually be preferable for courts to proceed" with these two steps sequentially.[69] But courts may also start at step two in appropriate cases.[70]

Applying this test to wire fraud under Section 1343, courts have recognized that it is not a general fraud statute, but instead criminalizes frauds that specifically involve the misuse of the wires (reflecting a policy choice to "free the interstate wires from fraudulent use, irrespective of the object of the fraud").[71] In other words, the wire fraud statute "protect[s] the instrumentalities of communication, making the use of the . . . wires as part of a fraudulent scheme an independent offense quite separate from any other potentially illegal conduct."[72]

---

63. U.K. Parliament, *The US-UK Extradition Treaty—Home Affairs Contents*, *available at* https://publications.parliament.uk/pa/cm201012/cmselect/cmhaff/644/64403.htm#note41.

64. Frederick T. Davis, *International Double Jeopardy: US Prosecutions and the Developing Law in Europe*, 31 Am. U. Int'l L. Rev. 60 (2016).

65. Morrison v. National Australian Bank Ltd., 561 U.S. 247, 262–65 (2010).

66. *Id.*

67. WesternGeco LLC v. ION Geophysical Corp., 138 S. Ct. 2129, 2137 (2018).

68. RJR Nabisco, 136 S. Ct. at 2101.

69. *Id.* at 2101 n.5.

70. *Id.*

71. Pasquantino v. United States, 544 U.S. 349, 358 (2005).

72. United States v. Garlick, 240 F.3d 789,792 (9th Cir. 2001); *see also* United States v. McLellan, 959 F.3d 442, 469 (1st Cir. 2020); Napout, 963 F.3d at 179.

With respect to mail fraud, courts have similarly understood Congress's concern to be the use of the mails itself, "not on the underlying scheme or a particular fraud victim."[73]

As such, the "focus" of the wire and mail fraud statutes is simply the use of the wires or mails in furtherance of a scheme to defraud.[74] Accordingly, so long as the defendant's use of the wires or mails in furtherance of his fraud has a sufficient domestic nexus—for example, an email routed through a U.S. server or a phone call placed to a recipient in the United States—it will be a "permissible domestic application" of the statutes.[75]

The broad extraterritorial reach of the federal fraud statutes was recently tested before the Second Circuit Court of Appeals in *United States v. Napout*.[76] The appellants in that case, Juan Angel Napout and Jose Maria Marin, were two former executives at FIFA, football's world governing body. The pair were convicted of using their positions to obtain millions of dollars in bribes relating to the sale of marketing and broadcasting rights. Napout and Marin had been presidents of the national football federations in Paraguay and Brazil, respectively. They appealed on the basis that their convictions were the result of an impermissible extraterritorial application of the U.S. honest services wire fraud statute. The crux of their argument was that the United States had no authority to prosecute a scheme involving South Americans that took place almost entirely in South America.

The Second Circuit rejected this argument upon finding that prosecutors needed to show only that the defendants used U.S. wires as an "essential" part of the fraud. On that issue, the panel determined that the DOJ had easily satisfied its burden: at least $2.4 million of Marin's payments were sent to his New York bank account and $2.5 million in cash was paid to Napout in U.S. dollars generated by wire transfers originating in the United States. According to the court, "in the relatively straightforward *quid pro quo* transactions underlying [the bribery] schemes, the *quid* was provided through the use of U.S. wires."[77]

The *Napout* case highlights the importance of U.S. correspondent accounts for jurisdictional purposes. Correspondent accounts (also called "interbank accounts") are used by foreign banks to offer services to their customers in jurisdictions where the banks have no physical presence, and otherwise to facilitate transactions involving such jurisdictions. All foreign transactions involving U.S. dollars must generally be routed through a correspondent account at an American bank.[78] Thus, where U.S. dollars are used to make illicit transactions, the DOJ will likely have a strong basis to claim jurisdiction over the underlying crime.[79]

---

73. Garlick, 240 F.3d at 792; *see also* United States v. Alston, 609 F.2d 531, 536 (D.C. Cir. 1979).

74. Hussain, 972 F.3d at 1145; Napout, 963 F.3d at 179; McLellan, 959 F.3d at 469–70.

75. RJR Nabisco, 136 S. Ct. at 210; United States v. Kim, 246 F.3d 186 (2d Cir. 2001).

76. 963 F.3d 163 (2d Cir. 2020).

77. *Id.* at 181; *see also* United States v. Jefferson, 674 F.3d 332 (4th Cir. 2012); United States v. Elbaz, 332 F. Supp. 3d 960, 973-74 (D. Md. 2018).

78. United States v. Union Bank, 487 F.3d 8, 15 (1st Cir. 2007).

79. *See, e.g.*, United States v. Prevezon Holdings Ltd., 251 F. Supp. 3d 684, 691-92 (S.D.N.Y. 2017).

6. *Criminal Penalties*

Criminal violations of the mail and wire fraud statutes are punishable by up to twenty years in prison and a fine of not more than $250,000.[80]

Significant Recent Wire Fraud Cases against British Defendants

United States v. Bogucki, No. 18-cr-00021 (N.D. Cal.)

Former foreign exchange (FX) trader at Barclays accused of defrauding his client through frontrunning a large dollar/pound transaction related to Hewlett-Packard's acquisition of Autonomy, a U.K.-based software company. Trial resulted in a directed verdict in favor of the defendant under Federal Rule of Criminal Procedure 29.

United States v. Johnson, No. 16-cr-00457 (E.D.N.Y.)

British national and former global head of FX spot trading at HSBC accused of defrauding his client on a $3.5 billion currency trade. Convicted at trial and sentenced to twenty-four months.

United States v. Connolly, No. 16-cr-00370 (S.D.N.Y.)

Former Deutsche Bank traders in London charged with a scheme to manipulate the London Interbank Offered Rate (LIBOR), an interest rate used in financial transactions around the world. Both defendants were convicted at trial but given noncustodial sentences. Convictions overturned on appeal by the Second Circuit.

United States v. McLellan, No. 16-cr-10094 (D. Mass.)

A London-based executive at State Street accused of participating with his boss in Boston in a scheme to defraud international pension funds in relation to the transition of multibillion-dollar investment portfolios. Both convicted (one at trial and one via a cooperation plea agreement) and sentenced to eighteen months and six months, respectively.

United States v. Hussain, No. 16-cr-00462 (N.D. Cal.)

U.K. resident and CFO of British software firm Autonomy Corporation charged with fifteen counts of wire fraud in connection with the sale of Autonomy to Hewlett-Packard. Convicted on all but one count following a two-month trial and sentenced to sixty months, a $4 million fine, and forfeiture of $6.1 million.

B. Offences under the Fraud Act 2006

Before enactment of the Fraud Act (FA) 2006, fraud in the United Kingdom was criminalized under various provisions of the Theft Acts of 1968 and 1978 and the common law offense of conspiracy to defraud.[81] According to a 2002 Law Commission report, these provisions were

80. 18 U.S.C. §§ 1341, 1343.

81. Karen Harrison & Nicholas Ryder, The Law Relating to Financial Crime in the United Kingdom 95 (2d ed. 2017).

difficult for juries to comprehend, especially in complex modern fraud cases: "The charges which are currently employed in such trials are numerous, and none of them adequately describe or encapsulate the meaning of 'fraud.' . . . Thus, at present, juries are not given a straightforward definition of fraud. If they were . . . it should enable them to focus more closely on whether the facts of the case fit the crimes as charged."[82]

In the wake of this conclusion, Parliament passed the FA to consolidate the numerous different fraud offenses into a single act that would make it easier for prosecutors to secure convictions and for defendants to prepare their defense.[83] "A general offense of fraud [was seen as] a useful tool in effective prosecutions" and, at the same time, a benefit to defendants, who would "be better able to understand their options when pleading guilty to the charge; and, if pleading not guilty, they will be better able to conduct their defence."[84]

In keeping with this reasoning, the FA creates a "clear, simple law" "aimed at encompassing fraud in all its forms" instead of focusing on the particular means by which a fraud is committed or who it targets (as U.S. fraud statutes do). The FA creates three distinct fraud offenses: fraud is committed where, with intent to make a gain or to cause loss or to expose another to the risk of loss, a person dishonestly does any of the following:

- Makes a false representation
- Wrongfully fails to disclose information
- Secretly abuses a position of trust[85]

1. *Fraud by False Representation (Fraud Act Section 2)*

An individual is guilty of a fraud by false representation offense if he or she (i) dishonestly makes a false representation and (ii) intends, by making the representation, to make a gain for himself or another, or to cause loss to another or to expose another to a risk of loss.[86] A representation will be considered false if it is objectively untrue or misleading, and the person making it knows that it is, or might be, objectively untrue or misleading.[87] Representations may be express or implied, and include any representations as to fact or law, including representations as to the state of mind of the person making the representation or any other persons.[88] This can include representations implied by conduct—for example, where a person dishonestly uses someone else's credit card (and thereby falsely implies his or her right

82. Law Commission, Report No. 276, Fraud 3 (July 2002).

83. Harrison & Ryder, *supra* note 81, at 96–97.

84. Law Commission, *supra* note 82.

85. Fraud Act (FA), s. 1(2). In addition to these three fraud varieties, Section 11 of the Fraud Act prohibits engaging in any dishonest act to obtain services for which payment is required, with intent to avoid payment. To be guilty of this crime, the defendant must know that the services are made available on the basis that they are chargeable, or that they might be. The defendant must also actually obtain the services at issue.

86. FA, s. 2(1).

87. United Arab Emirates v. Allen [2012] EWHC 1712 (Admin), para. 51.

88. FA, s. 2(3)–(4).

to do so).[89] There is no requirement that the misrepresentation be material, nor is there any statutory limitation on the way in which it is communicated.

While "dishonesty" is a critical element of fraud, it is "an unusual element, because it necessitates a moral as well as a factual inquiry."[90] Because of its subjective, "moral" component, reaching a legal definition of dishonesty has been elusive for British courts and juries: "when fact-finders are asked to consider whether the defendant's conduct was or was not dishonest, the law does not provide them with a definition of the word. The fact finders draw the line, so that dishonesty means what they understand it to mean."[91]

Until recently, the issue of whether a defendant acted with the requisite dishonesty was evaluated under the two-stage test created by the Court of Appeal in *R v. Ghosh*.[92] The first question under *Ghosh* was whether the defendant's behavior was dishonest by ordinary standards of reasonable and honest people. If the answer was no, the prosecution failed. If the answer was yes, then the second question was whether the defendant was aware that his or her conduct would be regarded as dishonest by "reasonable, honest people."[93]

In 2017, the U.K. Supreme Court overturned the thirty-five-year-old *Ghosh* test in *Ivey v. Genting Casinos (UK)* [2017] UKSC 67, a case involving professional poker player Phil Ivey's alleged use of an illicit card counting technique to win £7.7 million during a baccarat session in a London casino.[94] The Court redefined the definition of what constitutes dishonest conduct and stated that the second stage of the *Ghosh* test was "no longer good law." Although a civil case, *Ivey* has created a new standard for how to determine whether a civil or criminal defendant has acted dishonestly.

Specifically, the Court selected the civil law test for dishonesty long used in England and Wales and ordered it applied in the criminal context as well. As this new test was described in *Barlow Clowes International v. Eurotrust International* [2005] UKPC 37: "Although a dishonest state of mind is a subjective mental state, the standard by which the law determines whether it is dishonest is objective. If by ordinary standards a defendant's mental state would be characterised as dishonest, it is irrelevant that the defendant judges by different standards."

This test was considered preferable to that established by *Ghosh* because the importance *Ghosh* placed on the defendant's subjective mindset was seen as creating the possibility of the counterintuitive result that "the less the defendant's standards conform to what society in general expects, the less likely he is to be held criminally responsible for his behavior."[95] Lord Justice Hughes framed the issue as follows:

> When dishonesty is in question the fact-finding tribunal must first ascertain (subjectively) the actual state of the individual's knowledge or belief as to the facts. The reasonableness or otherwise of his belief is a matter of evidence (often in practice determinative) going to whether

89. *See* R v. Lambie [1982] AC 449.

90. Law Commission, *supra* note 82, at 39.

91. *Id.* at 39–40.

92. [1982] EWCA Crim 2.

93. Law Commission, *supra* note 82, at 40.

94. See Booth & Anor v. R [2020] EWCA Crim 575 (confirming that the previously used test set forth in *R v. Ghosh* [1982] QB 1053 has been replaced by the test in *Ivey*).

95. *Ivey*, para. 58

> he held the belief, but it is not an additional requirement that his belief must be reasonable; the question is whether it is genuinely held. When once his actual state of mind as to knowledge or belief as to facts is established, the question whether his conduct was honest or dishonest is to be determined by the fact-finder by applying the (objective) standards of ordinary decent people. There is no requirement that the defendant must appreciate that what he has done is, by those standards, dishonest.[96]

The primary practical importance of the *Ivey* decision is that juries are now required to take note of:

> . . . the defendant's knowledge and beliefs as to the normative standards applicable in society, including apparently, legal normative standards, with the presumable exception of those imported by the requirement not to be dishonest itself. In other words, the defendant's mistaken belief about the content of the law (apart from the law on dishonesty) is permitted to work in her favour in deciding whether she was dishonest.[97]

2. *Fraud by Omission (Fraud Act Section 3)*

To commit fraud by omission, a person must (i) dishonestly fail to disclose information to another that he or she is under a legal duty to disclose, and (ii) intend, by failing to disclose the information, to make a gain for him- or herself or another person, or to cause loss to another or to expose another to a risk of loss.[98] As with a fraud by false representation offense, there is no requirement that the information omitted be material or that the conduct actually result in a loss or gain.

The FA does not define "a legal duty to disclose." But according to the Law Commission's Report on Fraud, "such a duty may derive from statute (such as the provisions governing company prospectuses), from the fact that the transaction in question is one of the utmost good faith (such as a contract of insurance), from the express or implied terms of a contract, from the custom of a particular trade or market, or from the existence of a fiduciary relationship between the parties (such as that of agent and principal)."[99]

3. *Fraud by Abuse of Position (Fraud Act Section 4)*

Section 4 makes it an offense to dishonestly abuse one's position for personal gain or to cause loss to another. It applies where the defendant is in a position in which he is expected to safeguard another's financial interests or not act against those interests—a solicitor or trustee of an investment fund, for example. The Law Commission suggested that the "necessary relationship will be present between trustee and beneficiary, director and company, professional person and client, agent and principal, employee and employer, or between partners. It may

96. *Ivey*, para. 74.

97. Mark Dsouza, *Ivey v. Genting Casinos—What It Does (and What It Does Not)* (January 24, 2018), *available at* https://www.ucl.ac.uk/criminal-law/news/2018/jan/ivey-v-genting-casinos-what-it-does-and-what-it-does-not.

98. FA, s. 3.

99. FA, explanatory notes ss. 18–19.

[also] arise otherwise, for example within a family, or in the context of voluntary work, or in any context where the parties are not at arm's length."[100]

What constitutes "abuse" is not detailed in the statute, but it is intended to be interpreted broadly and includes omissions as well as affirmative misrepresentations.[101]

4. *Extraterritorial Reach*

As in the United States, there is a presumption against the extraterritorial reach of criminal laws passed by Parliament except where there is a specific statutory provision that enables a particular statute to be applied to conduct outside of Britain. Yet, in contrast to the DOJ's routine targeting of conduct that mostly occurs outside the United States, British prosecutors rarely initiate criminal cases against suspects who act predominantly abroad (particularly in financial crime cases).

Jurisdiction for fraud offenses under the Fraud Act 2006 is governed by Section 1 of the Criminal Justice Act 1993 (CJA 1993). Section 1(2)(bb) of this law classifies each of the fraud offenses listed above as "Group A offences." In turn, Section 2 provides that "[i]n relation to an offence under section 1 of the Fraud Act (fraud), 'relevant event' includes (a) if the fraud involved an intention to make a gain and the gain occurred, that occurrence; (b) if the fraud involved an intention to cause a loss or to expose another to a risk of loss and the loss occurred, that occurrence." For purposes of this section, the term "relevant event" is defined to mean "any act or omission or other event (including any result of one or more acts or omissions proof of which is required for conviction of the offence."[102]

While a person may only be "guilty of a Group A offence if any of the events which are relevant events in relation to the offence occurred in England and Wales," such a person may be charged in the United Kingdom regardless of whether or not "he was a British citizen at any material time" or "he was in England and Wales at any such time."[103] In other words, the jurisdiction of the Fraud Act 2006 extends to individuals who act entirely from outside the United Kingdom so long as such conduct resulted in either a gain or loss within the territory of England or Wales.

Practice Note

The 2020 Acquittal of Former Barclays Executives on Fraud Act Charges

The SFO's case against three former executives at British bank Barclays Plc was one of the most high-profile prosecutions stemming from the 2008/2009 financial crisis. After a lengthy investigation, the three men—Roger Jenkins, Tom Kalaris, and Richard Boath—were charged in 2017 with committing fraud by false representation in relation to Barclays' efforts to raise capital from various sovereign wealth funds in China, Japan, Singapore, and the Middle East. The "cornerstone investor" in this plan was Qatar, whose Prime Minister, Sheikh Hamad bin

100. Law Commission, *supra* note 82, at 40.

101. FA, explanatory notes ss. 20–23.

102. Criminal Justice Act (CJA) 1993, s. 2(1).

103. CJA 1993, s. 3(1).

Jassim bin Jabr Al-Thani, had business links with Jenkins, Barclays' senior executive in the region.

To entice these investors, Barclays had authorized a payment to each equalling 1.5 percent of their total investment. Qatar, however, demanded double that. To satisfy the Qataris while not upsetting the other investors, Jenkins and the other defendants found a workaround whereby Qatar would receive an extra 1.5 percent pursuant to an "advisory services" agreement totaling £42 million. Without disclosing this extra payment to the other investors, Barclays was able to secure a total of £4.5 billion in new capital by June 2008. After the collapse of Lehman Brothers that September, Barclays again tapped up the Qataris for additional funds—this time in exchange for a fee of £280 million (which, again, was not publicly disclosed).

In the SFO's view, the defendants' failure to disclose these fees was "plainly a lie" designed to present the fees as "related to genuine services agreements, when in truth they were just a means of paying the Qataris the additional fees."[104] During trial at the Old Bailey, the defense highlighted the fact that none of the defendants had actually been involved in making any public statements about the capital raising exercise; rather, all such statements were made by the bank itself. The SFO's theory was that the defendants had prompted the bank to make the statements without informing its top leaders in London of the side payments. The defendants countered that all the agreements with the Qataris were known to, and approved by, Barclays and its lawyers.

Following a five-month long trial that cost the SFO nearly £10 million, the jury roundly rejected the prosecution's case after less than six hours of deliberation and acquitted all three defendants of all charges.[105] The SFO's parallel case against Barclays was dismissed by the High Court in a judgment that has important implications for corporate criminal liability in the United Kingdom (see chapter 11).

5. *Criminal Penalties*

Violations of the Fraud Act are "either-way" offenses. An individual found guilty of a fraud offense on indictment is subject to imprisonment of up to ten years and an unlimited fine.[106]

II. INSIDER TRADING AND INSIDER DEALING

In both the United States and the United Kingdom, it is illegal to buy or sell a public company's stock when the person making the trading decision is in possession of material, non-public information (MNPI) about that stock (subject to certain exceptions).[107] This offense is known as "insider trading" in the United States and "insider dealing" in the United Kingdom.

During the tenure of Preet Bharara as U.S. Attorney in the Southern District of New York (2009–2017), there was a burst of major insider trading cases initiated in response to

---

104. Andy Verity, "The Inside Story of the Barclays Trial," BBC News (Feb. 28, 2020).

105. Kalyeena Makortoff, "Three Former Barclays Executives Found Not Guilty of Fraud," The Guardian (Feb. 28, 2020).

106. FA, s. 1(3).

107. For a discussion of the academic debate about whether trading on inside information is good or bad for the stock market generally, *see* George W. Dent Jr., *Why Legalized Insider Trading Would Be a Disaster*, 38 Del. J. Corp. Law 248 (2013).

the perceived widespread use of MNPI by investment professionals, especially in relation to "expert networks" who promised stock analysts access to well-placed insiders for a fee.[108] The S.D.N.Y. crackdown netted a number of prominent financial figures, including Raj Rajaratnam (founder of hedge fund Galleon Group), Rajat Gupta (former CEO of consultancy firm McKinsey & Co.), and SAC Capital portfolio manager Mathew Martoma. The district court judge overseeing the Rajaratnam case said that insider trading "is an assault on our free markets" and that Rajaratnam's routine use of illegal inside information "reflects a virus in our business culture that needs to be eradicated."[109]

Many of the cases brought during this initiative were the result of a key government cooperator, Karl Motey, who was once one of the most well-respected semiconductor analysts in the Silicon Valley. After getting picked up by the FBI for trading on insider information himself, Motey turned government witness and reportedly made more than sixty phone calls (covertly recorded by the FBI) to other investment professionals to elicit incriminating information about illegal trading by others. For example, in support of the DOJ's investigation of James Fleishman, a sales manager at expert network firm Primary Global, Motey posed as a potential client and was able to get Fleishman to suggest Primary Global provided its clients with inside information.[110] In light of his extensive cooperation, Motey avoided prison time and was sentenced only to forfeit $40,000.

While there have not yet been any comparable initiatives against insider dealing by British regulators, enforcement statistics suggest that it continues to be a key area of focus by prosecutors at the SFO and FCA.[111]

A. Insider Trading in the United States

1. *Section 10(b) and Rule 10b-5*

There is no statute that explicitly prohibits insider trading in the United States. Instead, the practice is usually prosecuted under the general antifraud provisions of § 10(b) of the Securities Exchange Act of 1934, which states that "[i]t shall be unlawful for any person . . . [t]o use or employ, in connection with the purchase or sale of any security . . ., any manipulative or deceptive device or contrivance in contravention of such rules and regulations as the [SEC] may prescribe."[112] Through this loosely worded provision, Congress granted regulators

108. Gregory Zuckerman & Susan Pulliam, *How an SEC Crackdown Led to Rise of "Expert Networks,"* WALL ST. J., Dec. 17, 2010; Evelyn M. Rusli, *Next Up, a Crackdown on Outside-Expert Firms,* N.Y. TIMES, May 11, 2011.

109. Press Release, U.S. Department of Justice, Hedge Fund Founder Raj Rajaratnam Sentenced in Manhattan Federal Court to 11 Years in Prison for Insider Trading Crimes, (Oct. 13, 2011).

110. Shira Ovide, Karl Motey: "The Government's Secret Weapon in Insider-Trading Arrests," WALL S. J., Dec. 20, 2010.

111. Harrison & Ryder, *supra* note 81, at 138–41.

112. 15 U.S.C. §78(j)(b).

broad powers "to combat manipulative abuses in whatever form they might take, including anti-fraud, prophylactic, and general rulemaking authority."[113]

Eight years after the Exchange Act was passed, the SEC adopted Rule 10b-5 (17 C.F.R. § 240.10b-5) to define Section 10(b)'s prohibitions more specifically. Rule 10b-5 makes it unlawful for any person "[t]o employ any device, scheme, or artifice to defraud" or "[t]o engage in any act, practice, or course of business which operates or would operate as a fraud or deceit upon any person," "in connection with the purchase or sale of any security."[114] As interpreted by the Supreme Court, Rule 10b-5 fits within Section 10(b) such that Rule 10b-5 encompasses only conduct already prohibited by Section 10(b).[115]

Section 10(b) and Rule 10b-5 can be enforced through criminal proceedings brought by the DOJ or through civil proceedings brought by the SEC. The core common elements of insider trading under these provisions are (i) trading in any security[116] (ii) on the basis of (iii) material, (iv) nonpublic information. For an insider trading offense to be prosecuted criminally, the DOJ must additionally prove that the defendant acted "willfully."[117]

Insider trading cases generally do not involve affirmative misrepresentation allegations—instead, violations of Section 10(b) and Rule 10b-5 usually occur in situations where a person trading a particular stock has a duty to disclose information to their counterparty (or to the source of that information) but fails to do so. It is therefore a crime of omission as opposed to one of commission.

In one of the earliest cases to discuss this principle, *Cady, Roberts Co.* (an administrative action brought by the SEC in the 1960s), regulators "decided that a corporate insider must abstain from trading in the shares of his corporation unless he has first disclosed all material inside information known to him."[118] According to the SEC, and as later confirmed by the Supreme Court, the obligation to disclose or abstain arises "from (i) the existence of a relationship affording access to inside information intended to be available only for a corporate purpose, and (ii) the unfairness of allowing a corporate insider to take advantage of that information by trading without disclosure."[119] A failure to comply with this obligation constitutes an "act, practice or course of business" that operates "as a fraud or deceit" under Rule 10b-5.

---

113. Melissa W. Palombo, *The Short-Changing of Investors: Why a Short Sale Price Test Rule Is Necessary in Today's Markets*, 75 Brooklyn L. Rev. 1447, 1488 (2010).

114. 17 C.F.R. § 240.10b-5.

115. United States v. O'Hagan, 521 U.S. 642, 651 (1997).

116. The Exchange Act defines the term "security" to include "common and preferred stock, treasury stock, notes, bonds, debentures, certificates of interest, puts, calls, straddles, options, or privileges on any security, and any security-based swap or other derivative instrument." 15 U.S.C. § 78c(10).

117. 15 U.S.C. § 78ff(a).

118. Chiarella v. United States, 445 U.S. 222, 227 (1980) (quoting Cady, Roberts Co., 40 S.E.C. 907 (1961)).

119. *Id.*; *see also id.* at 230 ("Application of a duty to disclose prior to trading guarantees that corporate insiders, who have an obligation to place the shareholder's welfare before their own, will not benefit personally through fraudulent use of material, nonpublic information.").

From this premise, insider trading in the United States cannot be committed by just "anyone who knowingly receives nonpublic material information from an insider." Instead, "[b]ecause the disclose-or-refrain duty is extraordinary, it attaches only when a party has legal obligations other than a mere duty to comply with the general antifraud proscriptions in the federal securities laws."[120] Put differently, the duty to disclose is created by the relationship between parties and "not merely from one's ability to acquire information because of his position in the market."[121]

Partly because of the absence of a specific insider trading statute, the legal framework governing insider trading since *Cady* has been developed and extensively revised by the federal courts "in a somewhat *ad hoc* manner."[122] Starting in the early 1980s, two strains of insider trading have developed in federal law: the "traditional" or "classical theory" and the "misappropriation theory." The two theories function in parallel, with each criminalizing deceptive efforts to capitalize on MNPI through the purchase or sale of securities.[123]

a. The Classical Theory

Under the classical theory (figure 4.1), a corporate insider commits insider trading when he or she "trades in the securities of his [or her] corporation on the basis of material non-public information" when "a relationship of trust and confidence [exists] between the shareholders of a corporation and those insiders who have obtained confidential information by reason of their position with that corporation."[124] The common thread in classical insider trading cases is thus a breach, whether direct or derivative, of duties to shareholders of the insider's company.[125]

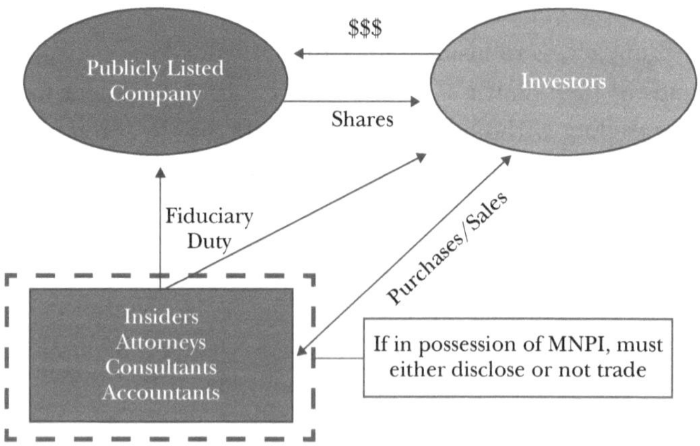

Figure 4.1 The classical theory.

120. Dirks v. SEC, 463 U.S. 646, 657 (1983); *see also* Chiarella, 445 U.S. at 235 n.20.

121. Dirks, 463 U.S. at 658.

122. United States v. Whitman, 904 F. Supp. 2d 363, 367 (S.D.N.Y. 2012) (including an overview of the development of insider trading law in the United States).

123. United States v. O'Hagan, 521 U.S. 642, 652 (1997).

124. *Id.*

125. SEC v. Obus, 693 F.3d 276, 284 (2d Cir. 2012).

The Supreme Court has explained that trading in such circumstances qualifies as a "deceptive device" under Section 10(b) because the corporate insider is using information not known to the trading counterparty (to whom the insider owes a duty of trust). In the Court's view, this relationship gives rise to a duty to disclose or to abstain from trading in order to prevent corporate insiders from taking unfair advantage of uninformed stockholders."[126] Simply put, Section 10(b) prohibits an insider from using MNPI to make "secret profits" at the expense of unwitting shareholders.[127]

The classical theory applies not only to officers, directors, and other permanent insiders of a corporation, but also to attorneys, accountants, consultants, and others who temporarily become fiduciaries of a corporation.[128]

b. The Misappropriation Theory

Whereas the classical theory targets insiders who breach a duty to shareholders, liability under the misappropriation theory is premised on company *outsiders* who deceive those who entrusted them with access to confidential information by using it to trade (figure 4.2). It has also been used to target individuals who tip or trade on the basis of MNPI "purloined from their employers but that pertained to the stock, not of their employer's companies, but of other companies."[129]

According to this theory, "the concept of 'fraud' [under Section 10(b) and Rule 10b-5] includes the act of embezzlement, which is the fraudulent appropriation to one's own use of the money or goods entrusted to one's case by another.'"[130] An outsider thus commits insider trading when he or she "misappropriates confidential information for securities trading purposes, in breach of a duty owed to the source of the information."[131] "The undisclosed

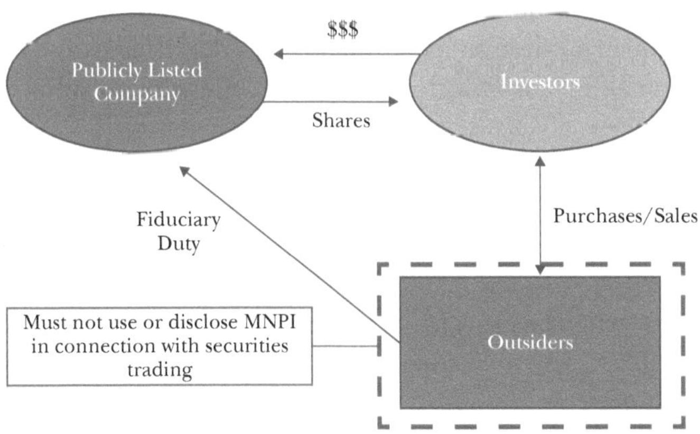

Figure 4.2 The misappropriation theory.

126. Chiarella, 445 U.S. at 228–29.

127. SEC v. Franco, 253 F. Supp. 2d 720, 726 (S.D.N.Y. 2003).

128. Dirks, 463 U.S. at 655 n.14.

129. Whitman, 904 F. Supp. 2d at 367.

130. Carpenter, 484 U.S. at 27.

131. United States v. O'Hagan, 521 U.S. at 652.

misappropriation of [a company's] confidential information, in breach of a fiduciary or similar duty of trust and confidence, 'constitutes fraud akin to embezzlement.'"[132]

Even though the violator does not owe fiduciary duties to his or her trading counterparties, Section 10(b) "does not confine its coverage to deception of a purchaser or seller of securities; rather the statute reaches any deceptive device used 'in connection with the purchase or sale of any security.'" Therefore, "in lieu of premising liability on a fiduciary relationship between a company insider and a purchaser or seller of the company's stock, the misappropriation theory premises liability on a fiduciary-turned-trader's deception of those who entrusted him with access to confidential information."[133]

"The misappropriation theory is thus designed to protect the integrity of the securities markets against abuses by 'outsiders' to a corporation who have access to confidential information that will affect the corporation's security price when revealed, but who owe no fiduciary or other duty to that corporation's shareholders."[134] In the Supreme Court's view, misappropriators of confidential information "deal in deception" and commit an act of fraud: "A fiduciary who '[pretends] loyalty to the principal while secretly converting the principal's information for personal gain 'dupes' or defrauds the principal."[135]

One of the first cases recognizing the misappropriation theory was *Carpenter v. United States*, an insider trading prosecution under Section 10(b) against R. Foster Winans, a *Wall Street Journal* reporter, and two co-conspirators. Winans was an author of a daily column, "Heard on the Street," that discussed the investment case for a selected stock or group of stocks.[136] Because the column was widely read and respected by investors, it had the potential to affect the price of the stocks that it examined. In contravention of the *Journal's* internal policies, Winans sought to capitalize on his advanced knowledge of which stocks would be discussed in each day's column by tipping off his co-conspirators before the *Journal* went to print. The co-conspirators then made prepublication trades on the basis of Winans' information, earning $690,000 in profits over a four-month period.[137] Winans and his co-conspirators were found guilty on all counts (which included insider trading, mail and wire fraud, and conspiracy).

In affirming the convictions on the insider trading counts under Section 10(b), the Supreme Court agreed with the lower courts that "the deliberate breach of Winans' duty of confidentiality and concealment of the scheme was a fraud and deceit on the Journal." Put differently, Winans' implicit undertaking not to reveal his employer's confidential information "became a sham" when he provided the information to his co-conspirators in a scheme to obtain trading profits, thereby infringing the company's exclusive right to use its own confidential information.[138]

---

132. Blaszczak, 947 F.3d at 35 (quoting O'Hagan, 521 U.S. at 654).

133. O'Hagan, 521 U.S. at 652.

134. Id. at 653.

135. *Id.*

136. Carpenter, 484 U.S. at 22.

137. *Id.* at 23–24.

138. *Id.* at 27.

The justices reasoned further that although the victim of the fraud, the *Journal,* "was not a buyer or seller of the stocks traded in or otherwise a market participant, the fraud was nevertheless . . . 'in connection with' a purchase or sale of securities within the meaning of" § 10(b) because the scheme's sole purpose was to buy and sell securities at a profit based on advance information of the column's contents."[139]

Since *Carpenter*, the misappropriation theory has been used to target insider trading involving a violation of a duty of trust or confidence in various situations outside of the employee/employer context. The SEC's Rule 10b5-2 (17 C.F.R. § 240.10b5-2) provides a nonexhaustive list of the circumstances that can give rise to such a duty:

- Whenever a person agrees to maintain information in confidence.
- Whenever the person communicating the MNPI and the person receiving it have a history, pattern, or practice of sharing confidences, such that the recipient knows or reasonably should know that the party transmitting the MNPI expects it to be kept confidential.
- Whenever the person receives or obtains MNPI from his or her spouse, parent, child or sibling, except where the recipient can demonstrate that he or she neither knew nor reasonably should have known that the source of the information expected the information to be kept confidential.

c. Tipper/Tippee Liability

A "tippee"—someone who is not a corporate insider but who nevertheless receives MNPI from a corporate insider (or "tipper")—can also be held liable under Section 10(b) and Rule 10b-5.[140] "'Tippees' of corporate insiders have been held liable under § 10(b) because they have a duty not to profit from the use of insider information that they know is confidential and know or should know came from a corporate insider."[141] As stated by the Supreme Court, "[n]ot only are insiders forbidden by their fiduciary relationship from personally using undisclosed corporate information to their advantage, but they also may not give such information to an outsider for the same improper purpose of exploiting the information for their personal gain."[142] Similarly, the transactions of those who knowingly participate with the fiduciary in such a breach are equally "as forbidden" as transactions by the fiduciary. The tippee's duty to disclose or abstain is thus derivative from the insider's duty.

For a tippee to be guilty of an insider trading violation under the classical theory, the insider "tipper" must breach "his fiduciary duty to the shareholders by disclosing the information to the tippee" in circumstances where "the tippee knows or should know that there has been a breach." Similarly, under the misappropriation theory, a tippee will be liable where the misappropriator of the information violates some duty owed to the source of the information

---

139. *Id.* at 24.

140. Dirks, 463 U.S. at 660.

141. Chiarella, 445 U.S. at 231 n.12; *see also* Shapiro v. Merrill Lynch, Pierce, Fenner Smith, Inc., 495 F.2d 228, 237–38 (2d Cir. 1974).

142. Dirks, 463 U.S. at 659.

and the tippee knows or should know that such breach has occurred.[143] Under both theories, tippees "assume an insider's duty to the shareholders not because they receive inside information, but rather because it has been made available to them improperly."[144]

"In determining whether a tippee is under an obligation to disclose or abstain, it is thus necessary to determine whether the insider's 'tip' constituted a breach of the insider's fiduciary duty."[145] The test for whether the insider/tipper has breached a duty is "whether the [insider/tipper] personally will benefit, directly or indirectly from his disclosure" to the tippee.[146] This so-called "personal benefit test" is a "judge-made doctrine premised on the Exchange Act's statutory purpose" of eliminating the use of insider information for personal advantage.[147]

The personal benefit test can be satisfied by "pecuniary gain or a reputational benefit that will translate into future earnings." A personal benefit will also be inferred where "there may be a relationship between the insider and the recipient that suggests a *quid pro quo* from the latter, or an intention to benefit the particular recipient" or "when an insider makes a gift of confidential information to a trading relative or friend."[148]

Courts in recent years have struggled to define exactly what constitutes a personal benefit within this framework. In *United States v. Newman*, the Second Circuit deviated from existing precedent on this issue and caused a number of insider trading convictions to be overturned.[149] Making it more difficult for prosecutors to prove a personal benefit, *Newman* held that tippees could only be liable under Section 10(b) if (i) the tippee knew that the original source of the information had received a personal benefit in exchange for the disclosure and (ii) the personal benefit was objectively "consequential." In situations where the tipper simply gifted MNPI to a tippee, *Newman* concluded that the personal benefit test would be satisfied only if there was a "meaningfully close personal relationship" between the two.

The DOJ challenged this interpretation in a subsequent prosecution, *United States v. Salman*, brought in the Northern District of California (a court within the Ninth Circuit that was not bound to follow the Second Circuit's *Newman* decision). *Salman* involved an investment banker who shared MNPI with his brother, who then shared it with another relative (Salman) who traded on it. Salman was found guilty on all counts and his conviction was

143. Obus, 693 F.3d at 286–88.

144. Dirks, 463 U.S. at 660; *see also* In re Investors Management Co., 44 S.E.C. 633, 651 (1971) ("[T]ippee responsibility must be related back to insider responsibility by a necessary finding that the tippee knew the information was given to him in breach of a duty by a person having a special relationship to the issuer not to disclose the information.").

145. Dirks, 463 U.S. at 661.

146. *Id.* at 662.

147. Blaszczak, 947 F.3d at 35. Note that the Second Circuit has declined to extend the personal benefit test to insider trading cases brought under the misappropriation theory. *See id.* at 35–36. As of the date of this writing, no other circuit court has followed the Second Circuit's lead.

148. *Id.* at 664; *see also* United States v. Jiau, 734 F.3d 147, 153 (2d Cir. 2013) ("Personal benefit is broadly defined to include not only pecuniary gain but also, *inter alia*, any reputational benefit that will translate into future earnings and the benefit one would obtain from simply making a gift of confidential information to a trading relative or friend.").

149. 773 F.3d 438 (2d Cir. 2014).

affirmed on appeal in a decision that conflicted with *Newman*. The Supreme Court granted certiorari to resolve the circuit split.

Siding with the government and the Ninth Circuit, the Supreme Court ruled that a gift of MNPI to a friend or relative is itself a sufficient personal benefit—that is, the tipper need not receive any financial or other type of reward in return for the disclosure. The justices reasoned:

> [W]hen a tipper gives inside information to a "a trading relative or friend," the jury can infer that the tipper meant to provide the equivalent of a cash gift. In such situations, the tipper benefits personally because giving a gift of trading information is the same thing as trading by the tipper followed by a gift of the proceeds. Here, by disclosing confidential information as a gift to his brother with the expectation that he would trade on it, [the tipper] breached his duty of trust and confidence to [his employer] and its clients—a duty [the defendant] acquired, and breached himself, by trading on the information with full knowledge that it had been improperly disclosed.[150]

After *Salman*, the law appeared settled that it is not necessary for the tipper to receive some form of a "'pecuniary or similarly valuable nature' in exchange for a gift to family or friends."[151] *Salman* left in place, however, the rule that any downstream tippee must have knowledge of fiduciary breach by the original tipper/insider. In other words, for liability to attach to any tippee, they must know that the original tipper received some personal benefit in exchange for his or her tips.

The *Salman* decision prompted Mathew Martoma, a former portfolio manager at Steve Cohen's now-defunct SAC Capital Advisors, to appeal his insider trading conviction—which, he argued, was based on the abrogated *Newman* decision—to the Second Circuit. The Second Circuit rejected the appeal and concluded that *Newman* was not actually in conflict with *Salman*. The panel interpreted *Newman* as holding that the "meaningfully close personal relationship" concept merely requires evidence that suggests either an explicit quid pro quo from tippee to the tipper, or a tippee's intention to benefit the tipper.[152] Despite this clarification, the precise test to be applied to gifts of MNPI between friends or relatives continues to be uncertain within the Second Circuit and other federal jurisdictions.[153]

d. Material Nonpublic Information

As noted, to violate Section 10(b) and Rule 10b-5, a defendant must misappropriate or otherwise improperly use material nonpublic information. Whether the information at issue actually constitutes MNPI is thus a critical threshold issue in any insider trading case. Information is considered material if there is a substantial likelihood that a reasonable investor would find it important in making an investment decision by having significantly altered the

150. Salman v. United States, 137 S. Ct. 420, 428 (2016).

151. *Id.*

152. United States v. Martoma, 894 F.3d 64, 77 (2d Cir. 2017).

153. *See, e.g.*, United States v. Pinto-Thomaz, No. 18-cr-579 (S.D.N.Y. Dec. 6, 2018).

"total mix" of information publicly available.[154] Facts relating to a future event—such as a planned acquisition or divestiture—will be deemed material depending "upon a balancing of both the indicated probability that the event will occur and the anticipated magnitude of the event in light of the totality of the company activity."[155]

Information is nonpublic if it has not been "effectively disclosed in a manner sufficient to insure its availability to the investing public."[156] "What is 'nonpublic' or 'confidential' information is largely a factual issue, turning on such factors as written company policies, employee training, measures the [source of the information] has taken to guard the information's secrecy, the extent to which the information is known outside the [information source's] place of business, and the ways in which [others] may access and use the information."[157] Stated differently, to be nonpublic, "information must be specific and more private than general rumor."[158] Conversely, information becomes public when disclosed "to achieve a broad dissemination to the investing public generally and without favoring any special person or group," or when, although known only to a few persons, their trading on it "has caused the information to be fully impounded into the price of the particular stock."[159]

The Second Circuit recognized in *United States v. Contorinis* that, although the "materiality" and "nonpublic status" are distinct concepts, there is considerable overlap for purposes of an insider trading analysis:

> The content of a piece of information may be of importance in affecting the share price but so well-known that it does not alter the mix of available information and is therefore not deemed to be material. Conversely, the same information, if previously unknown to the public, may alter substantially the mix of information and thus be deemed very material. Information also comes in varying degrees of specificity and reliability, and the extent to which a newly reported item of information alters the total mix may depend on the specificity or reliability of that information.[160]

e. The "Knowing Possession" Standard

To convict a person of insider trading, the government does not need to prove that the person actually used MNPI to inform their trading decisions. Rather, it is sufficient if the government proves that the defendant purchased or sold securities "while knowingly in possession of the material nonpublic information."[161] This "knowing possession" standard is codified in SEC Rule 10b5-1 (17 C.F.R. § 240,10b5-1), which states that a purchase or sale of a security is

---

154. *See* TSC Industries, Inc. v. Northway, Inc., 426 U.S. 438, 449–50 (1976); Affiliated Ute Citizens of Utah v. United States, 406 U.S. 128, 154 (1972); United States v. Contorinis, 692 F.3d 136 (2d Cir. 2012); 17 CFR § 270.8b-2.

155. SEC v. Texas Gulf Sulphur Co., 401 F.2d 833, 849 (2d Cir. 1968).

156. *Id.* at 854.

157. Whitman, 904 F. Supp. 2d at 367.

158. SEC v. Mayhew, 121 F.3d 44, 50 (2d Cir. 1997).

159. *Id.*

160. 692 F.3d 136, 143 (2d Cir. 2012).

161. United States v. Teicher, 987 F.2d 112, 119 (2d Cir. 1993); *see also* United States v. Rajaratnam, 719 F.3d 139, 159 (2d Cir. 2013); United States v. Royer, 549 F.3d 886, 898 (2d Cir. 2008).

presumed to be "'on the basis of' material nonpublic information about that security . . . if the person making the purchase or sale was aware of the material nonpublic information when the person made the purchase or sale." It is not a viable defense, therefore, for someone in possession of MNPI to claim that their trading decision was in fact a result of something other than the MNPI.

2. *Extraterritorial Reach*

As noted above, it is a "longstanding principle of American law 'that legislation of Congress, unless a contrary intent appears, is meant to apply only within the territorial jurisdiction of the United States.'"[162] Thus, "[w]hen a statute gives no clear indication of an extraterritorial application, it has none."[163]

With respect to Section 10(b) and Rule 10b-5, the Supreme Court in *Morrison* determined that the statutes give "no clear indication of extraterritoriality."[164] To the contrary, the Court concluded that the "focus of the Exchange Act is not upon the place where the deception originated, but upon purchases and sales of securities in the United States. Section 10(b) does not punish deceptive conduct, but only deceptive conduct 'in connection with the purchase or sale of any security registered on a national securities exchange or any security not so registered.' . . . [O]nly transactions in securities listed on domestic exchanges, and domestic transactions in other securities, to which § 10(b) applies."[165] Although *Morrison* addressed civil liability, at least two circuit courts have held that it also applies to criminal prosecutions such that criminal liability under Section 10(b) and Rule 10b-5 does not reach conduct "in connection with an extraterritorial purchase or sale of securities."[166]

In the insider trading context, federal courts have read *Morrison* to allow for U.S. jurisdiction over trading activities that largely occur abroad so long as there is some nexus to American markets.[167]

3. Criminal Penalties

Individuals found guilty of willfully violating the insider trading prohibitions are subject to a fine of not more than $5 million and twenty years in prison as to each count.[168] Table 4.1

162. EEOC v. Arabian American Oil Co., 499 U.S. 244, 248 (1991).

163. Morrison, 561 U.S. at 255.

164. *Id.* at 266.

165. *Id.*; *see also id.* at 272 ("Section 10(b) reaches the use of a manipulative or deceptive device or contrivance only in connection with the purchase or sale of a security listed on an American stock exchange, and the purchase or sale of any other security in the United States.").

166. United States v. Vilar, 729 F.3d 62, 67 (2d Cir. 2013); *see also* United States v. Isaacson, 752 F.3d 1291, 1299 (11th Cir. 2014).

167. *See, e.g.*, SEC v. Maillard, 2014 WL 1660024, at *3 (S.D.N.Y. Apr. 23, 2014) (denying motion to dismiss insider trading case, noting that contracts for difference purchased in Luxembourg as a result of insider trading harm the U.S. market); United States v. Martoma, 2013 U.S. Dist. LEXIS 176998, at *14–*17 (S.D.N.Y. Dec. 17, 2013) (insider trading in U.S.-listed ADRs satisfies the *Morrison* test).

168. 15 U.S.C. § 78ff(a).

Table 4.1 Examples of Sentences for Insider Trading

Raj Rajaratnam (13-cr-211 S.D.N.Y.)	Hedge fund owner sentenced to 11 years and fined more than $150 million for a wide-ranging insider trading conspiracy involving a number of high-profile corporate insiders.
Mathew Martoma (12-cr-973 S.D.N.Y.)	Hedge fund portfolio manager at SAC Capital accused of illegally earning more than $276 million in a single insider trading transaction related to a drug to treat Alzheimer's. Sentenced to 9 years and fined $9.38 million.
Perk Hixon (14-cr-227 S.D.N.Y.)	Senior investment banker sentenced to 30 months for trading on MNPI misappropriated from his firm's clients.
John Kinnucan (12-cr-163 S.D.N.Y.)	Technology analyst sentenced to 51 months for bribing company insiders for MNPI and then selling it to investors.
Chip Skowron (11-cr-699 S.D.N.Y.)	Hedge fund portfolio manager sentenced to 5 years for illegal trades related to stocks in the biotechnology sector.
Donald Longuiuel (11-cr-161 S.D.N.Y.)	Hedge fund portfolio manager sentenced to 30 months after trading on MNPI related to various tech stocks and then attempting to destroy the evidence.
Matthew Teeple (13-cr-339 S.D.N.Y.)	Investment analyst sentenced to 5 years for obtaining information about an upcoming tech merger from an insider and then passing it on to his friends and boss, who then traded on it.
David Riley (13-cr-339 S.D.N.Y.)	Corporate insider who passed on MNPI to an investment analyst knowing that it would be used for illegal trading purposes sentenced to 6½ years.
Zvi Goffer (10-cr-56 S.D.N.Y.)	Hedge fund trader who bribed corporate attorneys for inside information sentenced to 10 years.

shows a sample of the sentences imposed during the Southern District of New York's insider trading sweep in the early 2010s.

Practice Note

The STOCK Act

In 2012, Congress passed the Stop Trading on Congressional Knowledge (STOCK) Act, which was designed to prevent lawmakers and congressional aids from trading on confidential government information. Before this law, many assumed that government insiders who traded on MNPI obtained through their positions were exempt from insider trading laws because they had no duty to shareholders or a corporation. The STOCK Act clarified that such employees of Congress do, in fact, have a duty of trust and confidence to the federal government and U.S. citizens, and can be criminally prosecuted under Section 10(b) and Rule 10b-5.

Yet making such a case is complicated for prosecutors because of unique immunities given to members of Congress in the Constitution's Speech and Debate Clause, which provides that "for any Speech or Debate in either House [i.e., the House of Representatives and Senate] . . . [members] shall not be questioned in any other Place." This provision has been interpreted broadly by the courts to essentially bar any form of investigation by the executive branch (including the DOJ) related to congressional business.

Aside from this immunity, insider trading in the congressional context also raises novel materiality issues. This is because the confidential information generally possessed by members of Congress relates to the economy as a whole or a certain industry, not a particular company. No insider trading prosecution has ever been based on this sort of macroeconomic knowledge, and it is unclear how the materiality requirement would be applied in practice.

Hence, as of this writing, no individual has yet been prosecuted under the STOCK Act (despite evidence that members of Congress continue to routinely trade on nonpublic information learned during the course of their official duties).[169]

B. Insider Dealing in the United Kingdom

Unlike U.S. federal law, the United Kingdom has a specific statute that explicitly prohibits securities trading by individuals in possession of material nonpublic information. That statute, Section 52 of the Criminal Justice Act 1993, creates three distinct insider dealing crimes:

- Dealing in securities over a regulated market, directly or through an intermediary, on the basis of inside information.
- Encouraging another person to deal in securities over a regulated market on the basis of inside information.
- Disclosing insider information to another person "otherwise than in the proper performance" of the disclosing party's employment, office, or profession.

These provisions were enacted in response to a directive from the European Union (which Britain was still a part of) to synchronize the rules of each member state related to insider dealing.[170] The United Kingdom has also created a separate set of civil (i.e., noncriminal) insider dealing offenses in the Financial Services and Markets Act (FSMA) 2000, which should be considered in parallel with the criminal provisions detailed below.[171]

1. *Inside Information*

The foundational requirement for any Section 52 offense is inside information which, as in the United States, is generally understood to be nonpublic information that can be expected to have a "significant effect" on a security's price. Parliamentary debates surrounding the drafting of Section 52 reveal that ministers intended for the statute to apply primarily to "dramatic events and major occurrences that would transform a company's prospects"—that is, mergers, acquisitions, product breakthroughs, and major personnel changes.[172]

---

169. *See, e.g.*, Dave Levinthal, *43 Members of Congress Have Violated a Law Designed to Stop Insider Trading and Prevent Conflicts-of-Interest,* Business Insider, Oct. 22, 2021.

170. Council Directive 89/592/EEC (13 November 1989).

171. Financial Services and Markets Act (FSMA) 2000, s. 118.

172. Ken Alexander, *Insider Dealing and Market Abuse: The Financial Services and Markets Act 2000*, ESRC Centre for Business Research, at 14 (Dec. 2001).

Under Section 56(1), information will be deemed "inside information" if it fits each of the following criteria:

- It relates to particular securities or to a particular securities issuer (as opposed to securities or issuers generally).
- It is specific or precise.
- It has not been made public.
- If it were made public it would be likely to have a significant effect on the price of any securities. In other words, the information need not necessarily affect the company from which it was obtained.

It is important to note that this definition of inside information is broad enough to cover nonpublic information relating to a group of companies or to a specific industry, as well as to a specific security.[173]

Since the statute defines inside information in terms of whether it has been "made public," the extent to which information may be publicly known is obviously a key determination when evaluating a possible insider dealing offense. Information will be considered public if it is (i) published in accordance with market rules for the purpose of informing investors and their professional advisors; (ii) contained in records that are available to the public; (iii) can be readily acquired by those likely to deal in any securities; and (iv) is derived from information that has been made public.[174]

To protect legitimate analysis and research in the securities industry, the definition of information that is "made public" also expressly includes quasi-public information that can only be acquired through the exercise of diligence or expertise, is communicated to a section of the public and not to the public at large, can be acquired only by observation or through payment of a fee, or is published only outside the United Kingdom.[175] This means that simply because information is not readily accessible to the vast majority of the investing public, it will only be illegal to trade on when it was obtained unlawfully.

2. *Insiders*

To be liable for an insider dealing offense, an individual must possess information "as an insider." An individual can become an insider by either having direct access to inside information or by obtaining it from another person who has direct access to such information.[176] Section 57 provides:

> (1) ... **a person has information as an insider if and only if—**
>
> (a) it is, and he knows that it is, inside information, and
>
> (b) he has it, and he knows that he has it, from an inside source.

---

173. *Id.* at 15.

174. CJA 1993, s. 58(2).

175. *Id.*, s. 58(3).

176. *Id.*, s.57.

(2) **For the purposes of subsection (1), a person has information from an inside source if and only if—**
   (a) he has it through—
      (i) being a director, employee or shareholder of an issuer of securities; or
      (ii) having access to the information by virtue of his employment, office or profession; or
   (b) the direct or indirect source of his information is a person within paragraph (a).

This provision essentially combines the American concepts of classical insider trading (s. 57(2)) and the misappropriation theory (s. 57(1)). But note that a person does not become "an insider" simply by way of obtaining inside information from an inside source. Rather, the person must subjectively know the information's source and its nature.[177] Unlike in the United States, there is no requirement in the United Kingdom that the person who deals on the basis of inside information or provides such information to others be under a fiduciary obligation not to disclose it. Although this theoretically gives British prosecutors a lower bar to obtain convictions than their American counterparts, as noted earlier, the DOJ has been far more aggressive in going after insider trading.

3. *Applicable Securities*

Like the Exchange Act Section 10(b), the Section 52 offenses apply to a wide range of financial instruments: shares and stock in the share capital of a company, debt instruments issued by a company or public sector body, rights to subscribe for shares or debt instruments (conferred by warrant or otherwise), depositary receipts, options, and futures and other derivatives.[178]

4. *The "Dealing" Offense*

The dealing offense targets those in possession of inside information who use it to engage in securities trading, and contains two elements: (i) possession of information as an insider, and (ii) dealing in securities that are "price-affected" as a result of the information.[179] "Dealing" is broadly defined to include any purchases or sales of securities (either as a principal or agent) directly or through a third party.

If, at the time the agreement to buy or sell is made, the individual entering into the agreement has inside information about the securities at issue he or she will have committed an insider dealing offense.[180] This is similar to the "knowing possession" standard applied in the United States, but in the United Kingdom, there is an affirmative defense available to anyone who can establish that they would have made the same trades even without the information (see below). No such defense is recognized in the United States.

---

177. Harrison & Ryder, *supra* note 81, at 126.

178. CJA 1993, Sch. 2.

179. *Id.*, at s. 52(1).

180. Alexander, *supra* note 172.

5. The "Encouragement" Offense

An "encouragement" insider dealing offense occurs when a person with inside information encourages another person to deal in securities on a regulated market on the basis of this information and the insider knows or has reasonable cause to believe that such dealing will take place. As long as these elements are satisfied, an offense will be committed even if no dealing actually occurs.[181] Note too that it is not necessary for the person with inside information to actually divulge this information—rather, all that is necessary for liability to attach is for the insider to encourage somebody else to trade.[182]

6. The "Disclosure" Offense

Similar to "tippee" liability in the United States, a "disclosure" offense in the United Kingdom occurs when an insider discloses information to another under the reasonable belief that the recipient will use the information to deal, directly or indirectly, in a price-affected security. The disclosure of information must be "otherwise than in the proper performance of the functions of his employment, office or profession."[183]

But in a key difference with tippee liability in the United States, a disclosure offense does not require that the tipper receive a "personal benefit" in exchange for providing the tip of inside information. Again, this theoretically makes insider dealing convictions easier for the SFO and CPS than the DOJ.

7. Affirmative Defenses

In contrast to comparable U.S. law, there are a number of affirmative statutory defenses to the three varieties of insider dealing.[184] With respect to a dealing offense, an individual will not be guilty if that individual can show, by a balance of the probabilities, that he or she (i) did not believe the information was price sensitive, (ii) believed that the information had been publicly disclosed, or (iii) would have executed the same trade even absent the inside information. The same three defenses apply to encouragement offenses. An individual will not be guilty of a disclosure offense if that individual can establish either that he or she did not expect any person to deal in securities as a result of the disclosure or did not expect any such dealing to result in a profit because he or she did not believe the information was price sensitive.

---

181. Harrison & Ryder, *supra* note 81, at 127.

182. While the U.S. Code does not have an aider and abettor statute specifically relating to insider trading, the British "encouragement" theory is available to DOJ prosecutors under 18 U.S.C. § 2: "(a) whoever commits an offense against the United States or aids, abets, counsels, commands, induces or procures its commission, is punishable as a principal. (b) Whoever willfully causes an act to be done which if directly performed by him or another would be an offense against the United States, is punishable as a principal." *See, e.g.*, Superseding Indictment, United States v. Riley, No. 2013-cr-00339 (S.D.N.Y. Feb. 20, 2014) (charging insider trading "caused" by the defendants under 18 U.S.C. § 2).

183. CJA 1993, s. 52(2)(b).

184. *See* CJA 1993, s. 53; *Id.* at Sch. 1, para. 1.

8. Extraterritoriality

The CJA 1993 specifically limits the extraterritorial reach of the insider dealing offenses. Under Section 62, an individual cannot be found guilty of a "dealing" offense (CJA 1993, s. 52(1)) unless "(a) he was within the United Kingdom at the time when he is alleged to have done any act constituting or forming part of the alleged dealing; (b) the regulated market on which the dealing is alleged to have occurred is one which . . . is regulated in the United Kingdom; or (c) [if the offense] involved a professional intermediary [i.e., a broker] and the professional intermediary was within the United Kingdom at the time when he is alleged to have done anything by means of which the offence is alleged to have been committed."[185]

Similarly, an individual cannot be found guilty of an "encouragement" or "disclosure" offense unless "(a) he was within the United Kingdom at the time when he is alleged to have disclosed the information or encouraged the dealing; or (b) the alleged recipient of the information or encouragement was within the United Kingdom at the time when he is alleged to have received the information or encouragement."[186]

9. Criminal Penalties

Depending on its severity, insider trading can be prosecuted as a summary or indictable offense. If brought by indictment in the Crown Court, insider dealing is punishable with a fine, imprisonment for up to ten years, or both.[187] In part because of the lower maximum sentence for insider dealing in the United Kingdom compared with the United States, the insider dealing sentences meted out by British courts have been generally lower than those in the United States. Recent examples of insider dealing sentences are shown in table 4.2.

Table 4.2 Examples of Sentences for Insider Dealing

Martyn Dodgson (2016)	Deutsche Bank managing director sentenced to 4½ years
Andrew Hind (2016)	Businessman "tippee" sentenced to 3½ years
Julian Rifat (2015)	Senior hedge fund trader at Moore Capital sentenced to 19 months
Paul Gerard Coyle (2015)	Tax official at WM Morrison Supermarkets Plc sentenced to 1 year
Richard Anthony Joseph (2015)	Futures trader sentenced to 4 years
Paul Milsom (2013)	Legal & General Investment Management equities trader sentenced to 2 years
Thomas Ammann (2012)	Investment banker sentenced to 34 months
James Sanders (2012)	Investment bander sentenced to 4 years

185. *Id.* at s. 62(1).

186. *Id.* at s. 62(2).

187. *Id.* at s. 61.

III. FOREIGN BRIBERY

Clamping down on foreign bribery and corruption involving domestic transactions or individuals has long been a priority for law enforcement agencies in both the United States and the United Kingdom, but the statutory regimes under which they do so have a number of significant differences.

The cornerstone of the DOJ's anticorruption efforts is the Foreign Corrupt Practices Act (FCPA) (15 U.S.C. §§ 78dd-1, *et seq.*). The FCPA targets corrupt benefits provided to foreign government officials by U.S.-listed companies, U.S. citizens, and entities and individuals who act in furtherance of a bribery scheme while physically present in the United States. While the DOJ has successfully used the FCPA to target a diverse range of corruption schemes, the statute's utility is limited in the sense that it only applies to bribery involving someone working in some sort of foreign government function.

In other words, it does not reach commercial bribery (i.e., bribes paid to private parties), provide for criminal penalties against foreign officials who receive bribes, or prohibit bribes paid to government officials in the United States. To prosecute bribery occurring outside of the FCPA context, therefore, the DOJ will generally employ one of the following: the Travel Act (18 U.S.C. § 1952) (for commercial bribery),[188] 18 U.S.C. § 201 or the "honest services wire fraud statute"—18 U.S.C. § 1346—(for domestic corruption), and the money laundering statutes (for foreign recipients of bribes).

In contrast, the U.K. Bribery Act 2010 applies to commercial bribery as well as that involving government officials in both Britain and abroad. The Bribery Act also criminalizes receiving a bribe, so-called "passive bribery." While the Bribery Act is more expansive than the FCPA in these respects, it is far more restricted in terms of its extraterritorial reach: whereas the FCPA is regularly applied against foreign companies and individuals acting entirely from outside the United States, the Bribery Act's jurisdiction extends only to U.K. nationals and residents, and businesses that operate or are incorporated in the United Kingdom. In an important difference with the FCPA, therefore, the Bribery Act does not apply to non-British businesses whose only connection with the United Kingdom is a securities listing on the London Stock Exchange.

A. The Foreign Corrupt Practices Act

The FCPA was passed by Congress in the late 1970s as a result of the Watergate scandal and wide-ranging investigations into allegations that American companies were regularly

188. The Travel Act applies to any person or business who travels or uses the mail or any facility in interstate or foreign commerce with the intent to (i) distribute the proceeds of any unlawful activity, or (ii) commit any crime of violence to further any unlawful activity, or (iii) otherwise promote, manage, establish, carry on, or facilitate any unlawful activity. United States v. Salameh, 152 F.3d 88, 152 (2d Cir. 1998). "Unlawful activity" is defined to include, among other things, "bribery . . . in violation of the laws . . . of the United States." 18 U.S.C. § 1952(b). The Travel Act therefore covers violations of the FCPA as well as state commercial bribery laws. United States v. Kozeny, 493 F. Supp. 2d 693, 706 (S.D.N.Y. 2007). The Travel Act has been used by the DOJ to target bribery schemes that do not involve payments to a foreign official.

bribing foreign officials to secure contracts from foreign governments.[189] During Congressional debate on the proposed law in 1977, a member of the House noted that:

> 400 corporations have admitted making questionable or illegal payments . . . well in excess of $300 million in corporate funds to foreign government officials, politicians, and political parties. . . . The payment of bribes to influence [foreign officials] is unethical . . . [and] counter to the moral expectations and values of the American public.[190]

This sentiment was echoed by a senator from this time period who described payments to foreign government officials or their intermediaries as:

> [a] serious problem and one which is not taken lightly by responsible governments. It is also a problem more akin to a disease which deeply trouble proponents of our free enterprise system. . . . Bribery poisons this system by destroying the organisms of mutual trust and voluntary cooperation so essential to the free flow of commerce. This ethical decay must be stopped.[191]

Since making payments to foreign officials was not illegal under the federal laws in place at the time, the FCPA was created to fill this gap by explicitly prohibiting participation in overseas corruption by U.S. companies and citizens. When first passed, it was hailed as "a pioneering statute and the first law in the world governing domestic business conduct with *foreign* government officials in *foreign* markets."[192]

Broadly speaking, the FCPA creates two categories of corruption-related crimes: (i) direct or indirect bribery of foreign officials and (ii) failing to keep accurate books and records, or failing to implement internal account controls under the "accounting provisions" (also called the "books and records provisions"). Both types carry criminal and civil penalties (with the former enforced by the DOJ and the latter enforced by the SEC). The DOJ's Fraud Section, part of "Main Justice" in Washington, D.C., has a dedicated FCPA Unit that works with USAOs across the country to prosecute FCPA cases. For an individual to be criminally liable under the FCPA, he or she must have violated the statute "willfully," meaning that the individual's conduct had an intentionally bad purpose.[193]

---

189. Mike Koehler, *The Façade of FCPA Enforcement*, 41 Geo. J. Int'l L. 907, 911–12 (2010). The FCPA was substantially amended in 1998 to bring it in line with the requirements set forth in the Organisation for Economic Co-operation and Development (OECD) Convention on Combating Bribery of Foreign Public Officials in International Business Transactions. Among other changes, the 1998 amendments extended FCPA jurisdiction to foreign persons who commit acts within the United States and to U.S. businesses and nationals who engage in bribery schemes entirely outside of U.S. territory. The amendments also created criminal, rather than just civil, penalties for foreign nationals who are employees or agents of U.S. companies. United States v. Hoskins, 902 F.3d 69, 90–93 (2d Cir. 2018).

190. H. R. Rep. No. 95-640, at 1–2 (1977).

191. Mike Koehler, *The Story of the Foreign Corrupt Practices Act*, 73 Ohio St. L.J. 947 (2012).

192. *Id.* at 930.

193. *See* U.S. Department of Justice & Securities and Exchange Commission, A Resource Guide to the U.S. Foreign Corrupt Practices Act 13 (2d ed.) *available at* https://www.justice.gov/criminal-fraud/file/1292051/download; *see also United* States v. Cassese, 428 F.3d 92, 98 (2d Cir.

1. The Antibribery Provisions of the Foreign Corrupt Practices Act

The bribery provisions only apply to individuals and entities that fall within certain specific categories:

- "U.S. issuers" and their officers, directors, employees, and agents.[194] A U.S. issuer is any company that lists securities—including American Depositary Receipts—on an American exchange or that otherwise is required to file annual reports with the SEC. Also included are companies with a class of securities quoted in the over-the-counter market in the United States.
- "Domestic concerns" and their officers, directors, employees, and agents.[195] A domestic concern is defined as any U.S. citizen or permanent resident (wherever located) and any corporate entity incorporated in the United States or that has its principal place of business there.
- Any person or entity—including foreign nationals and companies—who engages in an act in furtherance of a foreign bribery scheme while physically within U.S. territory.[196]
- Foreign nationals who conspire with or aid and abet a foreign bribery scheme committed by an entity or individual falling within one of the categories above.
    - Note that this category is controversial and not accepted by all U.S. courts (including most notably the Second Circuit Court of Appeals).[197] Until further clarity on this issue is provided by the Supreme Court, the position of U.S. law enforcement is that foreign nationals can commit an FCPA violation as long as they act in concert with a person or entity that is subject to FCPA jurisdiction under one of the above categories.[198]

Assuming that the relevant conduct is committed by a person or entity within one of these three (or four) categories, to prove an FCPA bribery offense the government must show: (i) a direct or indirect payment or promise of payment of any money or gift of "anything of value" (ii) to a "foreign official," (iii) with "corrupt intent," (iv) to obtain or retain business or to secure any improper advantage.[199] Except in cases where FCPA jurisdiction is based

---

2005); United States v. Kozeny, 667 F.3d 122, 132 (2d Cir. 2011) ("The FCPA provides that a person's state of mind is 'knowing' with respect to conduct, a circumstance, or a result, if . . . 'such person is aware that such person is engaging in such conduct; that such circumstance exists or that such result substantially is certain to occur, or such person has a firm belief that such circumstances exist or that such result is substantially certain to occur.'").

194. 15 U.S.C. § 78dd-1.

195. 15 U.S.C. § 78dd-2.

196. 15 U.S.C. § 78dd-3.

197. *Compare* United States v. Hoskins, 902 F.3d 69 (2d Cir. 2018) *with* United States v. Firtash, 392 F. Supp. 3d 872 (N.D. Ill. 2019).

198. *See* U.S. Department of Justice, *supra* note 193, at 36.

199. *See* Chevron Corp. v. Donziger, 974 F. Supp. 2d 362, 596 (S.D.N.Y. 2014).

on an act committed from within the United States, the government must also establish that the bribe scheme made "use of the mails or any means or instrumentality of interstate commerce."[200]

a. "Use of Instrumentalities of Interstate Commerce"

As noted, in FCPA cases brought against U.S. issuers, domestic concerns, and their agents, the government must prove that the defendant made "use of the mails or any means or instrumentality of interstate commerce" in furtherance of the corrupt payments. This element can be satisfied through, among other things, evidence that emails, phone calls, or bank transfers were sent to or from the United States.[201]

b. "Anything of Value"

An FCPA violation need not involve a cash payment. Rather, the term "anything of value" is construed broadly to include money as well as employment offers,[202] travel expenses,[203] and charitable contributions.[204] The FCPA prohibits the giving of anything of value (e.g., gifts, travel expenses, business favors, charitable donations) as long as it is intended to improperly influence a foreign official. There is no materiality threshold, so even relatively small payments or gifts can suffice to establish an FCPA offense.

c. "To a Foreign Official"

The FCPA prohibits providing or promising to provide anything of value "to any person, while knowing that all or a portion of such [thing of value] . . . will be offered, given, or promised, directly or indirectly, to any foreign official."[205] The term "foreign official" is defined to mean "any officer or employee of a foreign government or any department, agency, or instrumentality thereof, or of a public international organization, or any person acting in an official capacity for or on behalf of any such government or department, agency, or instrumentality, or for or on behalf of any such public international organization."[206] This language has been interpreted broadly to essentially cover any officer or employee of a foreign government—regardless of rank or title—and to those acting on a foreign government's behalf.

With respect to individuals working for companies that are owned or controlled by a foreign government, FCPA jurisdiction will turn on whether such companies are "instrumentalities" of the state. In *United States v. Esquenazi*, for example, owners of a U.S.

---

200. 15 U.S.C. §§ 78dd-1(a), 78dd-2(a).

201. *See* Donziger, 974 F. Supp. 2d at 596 ("use of the Internet to send emails in furtherance of bribery scheme sufficient to satisfy the interstate commerce requirement of the FCPA" as was defendant's transfer of funds to a U.S. bank account).

202. Rotec Indus. Inc. v. Mitsubishi Corp., 163 F. Supp. 2d 1268, 1278–79 (D. Or. 2001).

203. United States v. Liebo, 923 F.2d 1308, 1310–11 (8th Cir. 1991).

204. Complaint, SEC v. Schering-Plough Corp., No. 04-cv-00945 (D.D.C. June 9, 2004).

205. 15 U.S.C. § 78dd-2(a)(3).

206. 15 U.S.C. § 78dd-3(f)(2).

telecommunications company were charged with bribing a senior official at Telecommunications D'Haiti, S.A.M. (Teleco).[207] On appeal, the defendants sought to reverse their convictions on the grounds that Teleco was not an "instrumentality" of the Haitian government, and thus outside of the FCPA's scope. Rejecting the defendants' arguments on this point, the Eleventh Circuit Court of Appeals concluded that Teleco was an instrumentality because it was controlled by the Haitian government and performed a function that the government treated as its own.[208]

To decide if a foreign government "controls" an entity, the Eleventh Circuit directed courts and juries to "look to the foreign government's formal designation of that entity; whether the government has a majority interest in the entity; the government's ability to hire and fire the entity's principals; the extent to which the entity's profits, if any, go directly into the governmental fisc, and, by the same token, the extent to which the government funds the entity if it fails to break even; and the length of time these indicia have existed."[209]

As to the second prong of the Eleventh Circuit's test, to determine whether an entity performs a function that the government treats as its own, the relevant factors are "whether the entity has a monopoly over the function it exists to carry out; whether the government subsidizes the costs associated with the entity providing services; whether the entity provides services to the public at large in the foreign country; and whether the public and that foreign country generally perceive the entity to be performing a government function."[210]

d. With "Corrupt Intent"

The term "corruptly" is not defined in the FCPA. However, the Congressional Reports from when the statute was in development indicate it means an intent or desire to wrongfully influence the recipient:

> The word "corruptly" is used in order to make clear that the offer, payment, promise, or gift, must be intended to induce the recipient to misuse his official position; for example, wrongfully to direct business to the payor or his client, to obtain preferential legislation or regulations, or to induce a foreign official to fail to perform an official function. The word "corruptly" connotes an evil motive or purpose.[211]

Similarly, the Fifth Circuit has stated that "corruptly" means to act "knowingly and dishonestly, with the specific intent to achieve an unlawful result by influencing a foreign public official's action in one's own favor."[212] Nevertheless, "there is nothing in that word or

---

207. 752 F.3d 912, 917 (11th Cir. 2014).

208. *Id.* at 928–29.

209. *Id.* at 925.

210. *Id.* at 926.

211. S. Rep. No. 95-114, at 10 (1977); *see also* Donziger, 974 F. Supp. 2d at 597 ("'Corruptly' [under the FCPA] means to act 'knowingly and dishonestly, with the specific intent to achieve an unlawful result by influencing a foreign public official's action in one's own favor.'").

212. United States v. Kay, 513 F.3d 432, 449 (5th Cir. 2007); *see also* Stichting v. Schreiber, 327 F.3d 173, 183 (2d Cir. 2003) ("The word 'corruptly' in the FCPA signifies, in addition to the general element

anything else in the FCPA that indicates [a requirement] that the defendant in fact knew that his or her conduct violated the FCPA to be guilty of such a violation."[213]

When a payment is extracted by way of "true extortion" or duress—that is, on threat of serious injury or death—the bribe payer will not have the requisite "corrupt intent."[214] So, for example, if an overseas-based executive for a U.S. company is forced to pay bribes by a totalitarian leader who physically threatens the executive's family, there will be no FCPA liability. This is because federal criminal law provides that actions taken in such circumstances do not ordinarily constitute crimes. While coercion is a complete defense, a high hurdle must be cleared to establish it. A defendant raising a coercion or duress defense must satisfy three discrete elements: (i) a threat of force directed at the time of the defendant's conduct, (ii) a threat sufficient to induce a well-founded fear of impending death or serious bodily injury, and (iii) a lack of reasonable opportunity to escape harm other than by engaging in the illegal activity.[215]

e. "To Obtain or Retain Business"

The FCPA requires that the corrupt payment or promise be made to assist "in obtaining or retaining business for or with, or directing business to, any person."[216] As with the FCPA's other elements, this so-called "business purpose test" has been interpreted broadly by the courts. It includes bribes paid to secure government contracts, favorable tax treatment, government action against competitors, and essentially anything else that could inure to the bribe payer's commercial advantage.[217]

As explained by the Fifth Circuit Court of Appeals, in enacting the FCPA, "Congress meant to prohibit a range of payments wider than only those that directly influence the acquisition or retention of government contracts or similar commercial or industrial arrangements."[218] This broad reading was also supported by "Congress's intention to implement the [OECD Convention on Combating Bribery of Foreign Public Officials in International Business Transactions], a treaty that indisputably prohibits any bribes that give an advantage to which a business entity is not fully entitled."[219]

Accordingly, the FCPA is interpreted to generally target bribes "paid to engender assistance in improving the business opportunities of the payor or his beneficiary, irrespective of whether that assistance be direct or indirect, and irrespective of whether it be related to

---

of 'general intent' present in most criminal statutes, a bad or wrongful purpose and an intent to influence a foreign official to misuse his official position.").

213. Stichting, 327 F.3d at 183; *see also* United States v. Jennings, 160 F.3d 1006 (4th Cir. 1998) (noting that under 18 U.S.C. § 201 "corrupt intent" is the intent to receive a specific benefit in return for the payment).

214. Kozeny, 582 F. Supp. 2d 535, 540 (S.D.N.Y. 2008).

215. United States v. Gonzalez, 407 F.3d 118, 122 (2d Cir. 2005).

216. 15 U.S.C. § 78dd-1, 78dd-2, 78dd-3.

217. Kozeny, 493 F. Supp. 2d at 705.

218. United States v. Kay, 359 F.3d 738, 749 (5th Cir. 2004).

219. *Id.* at 756.

administering the law, awarding, extending, or renewing a contract, or executing or preserving an agreement."[220] This is a fact-intensive requirement that is assessed on a case by case basis.

2. *Affirmative Defenses to an FCPA Bribery Offense*

In 1988, the FCPA was amended to create two affirmative defenses: the "local law" defense and the "reasonable and bona fide expenditures" defense. The amendments also created a "facilitating payments" exception.

a. The Local Law Defense

A defendant charged with committing an FCPA bribery offense can escape liability if he or she can establish that the payment or offer at issue was permitted under the written laws of the foreign country in which it occurred.[221] In creating this defense, Congress sought "to make clear that the absence of written laws in a foreign officials' country would not by itself be sufficient."[222] Because few—if any—countries explicitly permit bribery of government officials, this defense is thus rarely raised (and is usually unsuccessful when it is).

In *United States v. Kozeny*, for example, the DOJ alleged a bribery scheme involving a program to privatize the State Oil Company of the Azerbaijan Republic (SOCAR). This program gave the president of Azerbaijan discretionary authority as to whether and when to initiate the privatization.[223] The defendants were charged with "making payments to Azeri officials to encourage the privatization of SOCAR and to permit them to participate in that privatization."[224] One defendant—David Bourke—argued that the local law defense applied because the alleged payments were legal under Azeri law for two reasons: (i) they were the result of extortion and were therefore not illegal as to the bribe payer, and (ii) the payments were reported to the Azeri president (which, under Azeri law purportedly rendered the payments legal). Both the DOJ and defense counsel submitted expert reports and testimony on the proper interpretation of Azeri law on these points.[225]

The thrust of Bourke's defense was his claim that, "if an individual is relieved of criminal responsibility [under a foreign legal system], his action was 'lawful' and he may thus avail himself of the FCPA's affirmative defense." The court disagreed, stating:

> For purposes of the FCPA's affirmative defense, the focus is on the *payment*, not the payer. A person cannot be guilty of violating the FCPA if the payment was *lawful* under foreign

---

220. *Id.* at 750.

221. 15 U.S.C. §§ 78dd-1(c)(1), 78dd-2(c)(1), 78dd-3(c)(1).

222. *See* U.S. Department of Justice, *supra* note 193, at 24.

223. 582 F. Supp. 2d 535, 536–37 (S.D.N.Y. 2008).

224. *Id.* at 537.

225. Under Federal Rule of Criminal Procedure 26.1, "[a] party intending to raise an issue of foreign law must provide the court and all parties with reasonable notice. Issues of foreign law are questions of law, but in deciding such issues a court may consider any relevant material or source—including testimony—without regard to the Federal Rules of Evidence."

> law. But there is no immunity from prosecution under the FCPA if a person could not have been prosecuted in the foreign country due to a technicality (e.g., time-barred) or because a provision in the foreign law 'relieves' a person of criminal responsibility. An individual may be prosecuted under the FCPA for a payment that violates foreign law even if the individual is relieved of criminal responsibility for his actions by a provision of the foreign law.[226]

Thus, because the court determined that Bourke's payments were "clearly not 'lawful under the written laws' of Azerbaijan" at the time they were made, the fact that he could not be prosecuted in Azerbaijan for it was irrelevant. In the court's view it was inaccurate "to suggest that the payment itself suddenly became 'lawful'—on the contrary, the *payment* was unlawful, though the *payer* is relieved of responsibility for it."[227]

b. The Reasonable and Bona Fide Expenditure Defense

Pursuant to the reasonable and bona fide expenditure defense, the FCPA will not be violated if the defendant can establish that the purported bribe was "a reasonable and bona fide expenditure, such as travel and lodging expenses," that was "directly related to (A) the promotion, demonstration, or explanation of products or services, or (B) the execution or performance of a contract with a foreign government or agency thereof."[228]

In publicly released guidance on the scope of this defense, the DOJ has expressed the view that certain categories of expenditures on behalf of foreign officials do not warrant FCPA enforcement action—such as travel and expenses to visit company facilities or operations; travel and expenses for training; and product demonstration or promotional activities, including travel and expenses for meetings.[229]

c. The Facilitating Payments Exception

The facilitating payments, or "grease payment," exception states that the FCPA's bribery provisions "shall not apply to any facilitating or expediting payment to a foreign official, political party, or party official the purpose of which is to expedite or to secure the performance of a routine governmental action by a foreign official, political party, or party official."[230] The term "routine governmental action" is defined to mean "only an action which is ordinarily and commonly performed by a foreign official in [the relevant country]."[231] For example, "obtaining permits, licenses, or other official documents to qualify a person to do business in a foreign country," "processing governmental papers, such as visas and work orders," and providing police and fire protection, mail services, utilities, and loading and

226. Kozeny, 582 F. Supp. 2d at 539 (emphasis in original).

227. *Id.* (emphasis in original); *see also id.* 540 ("A payment to an Azeri official that is made under threat to the payer's legal interests is still an illegal payment, though the payer cannot be prosecuted for it.").

228. 15 U.S.C. §§ 78dd-1(c)(2), 78dd-21(c)(2), 78dd-3 (c)(2).

229. *See* U.S. Department of Justice, *supra* note 193, at 24.

230. 15 U.S.C. §§ 78dd-1(b), 78dd-2(b), 78dd-3(b).

231. 15 U.S.C. § 78dd-1(f)(3).

unloading cargo. It expressly does not include "any decision by a foreign official whether, or on what terms, to award new business or to continue business with a particular party, or any action taken by a foreign official involved in the decisionmaking process to encourage" such a decision.[232]

3. Accounting Provisions (15 U.S.C. §§ 78m(b)(2)(A), (B))

The FCPA's accounting provisions—also known as the "books and records" provisions—only apply to "U.S. issuers," their subsidiaries (including foreign ones), and their employees or agents.[233] Their overarching purpose is to "deter bribery of foreign officials by American corporations. Congress believed that almost all such bribery was covered up in the corporation's books, and that to require proper accounting methods and internal accounting controls would discourage corporations from engaging in illegal payments."[234]

Thus, while intended to serve the same anticorruption purposes as the bribery provisions, the accounting provisions do not explicitly prohibit foreign bribery: instead, they require U.S. issuers to make and keep books and records that accurately and fairly reflect their corporate transactions and to maintain an adequate system of internal controls to provide reasonable assurance that all transactions are authorized and properly accounted for.[235] This internal control requirement is "primarily designed to give statutory content to an aspect of management stewardship responsibility [to shareholders]."[236] The focus of the accounting provisions "is not on actual entries into the books and records" of a company but on "management control."

These provisions are often used by U.S. authorities to punish a company suspected of committing foreign bribery but where there is not enough evidence to prove a bribery offense. For example, if a U.S. company has an off-the-books slush fund, it will violate the books and records provisions even if the DOJ or SEC cannot actually prove the slush fund was used to bribe foreign officials.[237] As stated in the DOJ's FCPA guidance manual, "In instances where

232. *Id.*

233. 15 U.S.C. § 78m(b)(2).

234. Lewis on Behalf of Nat'l Semiconductor Corp. v. Sporck, 612 F. Supp. 1316, 1332–33 (N.D. Cal. 1985).

235. 15 U.S.C. §§ 78m(b)(2)(A) and (B); *see also* McConville v. SEC, 465 F.3d 780, 790 (7th Cir. 2006) ("Examples of internal controls include manual or automated review of records to check for completeness, accuracy and authenticity; a method to record transactions complete and accurately; and reconciliation of accounting entries to detect errors."); SEC v. E-Smart Techs., Inc., 82 F. Supp. 3d 97, 109–10 (D.D.C. Feb. 12, 2015).

236. SEC v. World-Wide Coin Invs. Ltd., 567 F. Supp. 724, 749–50 (N.D. Ga. 2013); *see also* In re Ikon Office Sols., Inc., 277 F.3d 658, 672 n.14 (3d Cir. 2002).

237. *See, e.g.*, Press Release, Securities and Exchange Commission, SEC Charges Novartis AG with FCPA Violations (June 25, 2020) (SEC imposing $112 million fine for books and records violation on pharmaceutical company alleged to have made improper payments to healthcare providers in South Korea, Vietnam, and Greece in exchange for prescribing Novartis drugs); Press Release, Department of Justice, Ericsson Agrees to Pay More Than $1 Billion to Resolve Foreign Corrupt Practices Act Case (Dec. 6, 2019) (imposing penalties based on similar allegations).

all the elements of a violation of the anti-bribery provisions are not met—where, for example, there was no use of interstate commerce—companies nonetheless may be liable if the improper payments are inaccurately recorded."[238]

To establish a books and records violation, the government must show that a U.S. issuer or an agent of a U.S. issuer either failed to make and keep account records that fairly reflect the issuer's transactions or failed to employ a system of internal accounting that provides "reasonable assurances" that company transactions are executed in accordance with management's general or specific authorization. "Reasonable assurances" means a degree of assurance that "would satisfy prudent officials in the conduct of their own affairs."[239]

As with the bribery provisions, there is no materiality threshold. Criminal penalties can be imposed against individuals and entities who "knowingly and willfully" violate the FCPA's accounting provisions.[240]

4. *Extraterritorial Reach*

The FCPA is regularly used to target alleged bribery schemes that take place almost entirely overseas.[241] On its face, the statute applies extraterritorially in three ways.

> First, U.S. persons (citizens and permanent residents) and U.S.-organized businesses are prohibited from engaging in corrupt conduct anywhere in the world. U.S. persons and businesses can also be held criminally liable for the corrupt activities of their officers, directors, employees, and third-party agents (regardless of where the conduct occurs). Second, all companies that issue securities in the United States, and all such companies' officers, directors, employees, and third-party agents are subject to FCPA jurisdiction (irrespective of where the company or individuals may be physically located). Third, the FCPA prohibits non-U.S. persons from using the U.S. mails or any instrumentality of interstate commerce to commit bribery (even if such use is from overseas), or doing any other act in furtherance of an FCPA scheme, while physically in the [United States].

The extent to which the FCPA applies to conduct outside the United States by non-U.S. persons is an open legal question that has been answered differently by courts within the Second and Seventh Circuits.

In *United States v. Hoskins*, the Second Circuit considered "whether the government may employ theories of conspiracy or complicity to charge a defendant with violating the [FCPA],

238. U.S. Department of Justice, *supra* note 193, at 39.

239. 15 U.S.C. § 78m(b)(7).

240. 15 U.S.C. § 78ff(a); United States v. Wittig, 568 F. Supp. 1284, 1293 (D. Kan. 2008) ("In order to prove conspiracy to circumvent internal controls, the government must show that the conspirators agreed to commit an offense that requires knowing and willful circumvention of internal controls instituted to satisfy SEC requirements.").

241. *See* Joshua Ray, *The Continuing Façade of FCPA Enforcement; A Critical Look at the Telia DPA*, NYU J. L. & Bus (Summer 2021) (discussing FCPA charges related to a Swedish company's investment in Uzbekistan).

even if he is not in the category of persons directly covered by the statute."[242] In the DOJ's view, a defendant—who is not otherwise expressly subject to the FCPA—can be guilty of an FCPA violation by either conspiring with[243] or aiding and abetting[244] an individual or entity that falls within one of the three categories discussed above. The Second Circuit rejected this argument by turning to the FCPA's legislative history. According to the court, this history reveals "a desire [by Congress] to leave foreign nationals outside the FCPA when they do not act as agents, employees, directors, officers, or shareholders of an American issuer or domestic concern, and when they operate outside United States territory."[245] In other words, if the FCPA does not apply to a defendant as a principal, then it cannot apply to that defendant as a co-conspirator or accomplice.[246]

The opposite conclusion was reached by a Chicago district court judge in *United States v. Firtash*, 392 F. Supp. 3d 872 (N.D. Ill. 2019) after concluding that "controlling Seventh Circuit case law declines to impose the requirement recognized [by the Second Circuit] in *Hoskins*."[247] Disregarding the FCPA's legislative history, the court in *Firtash* focused solely on the statute's text and determined that the defendants—who never acted from within the United States and were not agents of a U.S. person—could be held liable for an FCPA violation under the conspiracy and aiding and abetting statutes.[248]

At present, the correct interpretation of the FCPA's reach to conspirators and abettors remains unaddressed by the Supreme Court.

5. *Criminal Penalties*

For each violation of the FCPA's antibribery provisions, individuals are subject to a fine of up to $250,000 and five years in prison. For each violation of the accounting provisions, individuals are subject to a fine of up to $5 million and imprisonment of up to 20 years (table 4.3).[249]

---

242. 902 F.3d 69, 71 (2d Cir. 2018).

243. Federal law punishes anyone who conspires with another to commit a federal criminal offense. *See, e.g.*, 18 U.S.C. § 371.

244. Under 18 U.S.C. § 2(a), a person who does not personally commit the acts constituting an offense is liable as a principal if he or she "aids, abets, counsels, commands, induces or produces" the commission of those acts by another.

245. Hoskins, 902 F.3d at 93–94.

246. As alternative grounds to reject the DOJ's position, the court stated that under the Supreme Court's two-step framework for analyzing extraterritoriality issues, the government failed to establish "a clearly expressed congressional intent to" allow conspiracy and complicity liability to broaden the extraterritorial reach of the FCPA. *Id.* at 95.

247. Because Chicago is in the Seventh Circuit, the Second Circuit's decision in *Hoskins* was not binding on the court in *Firtash*.

248. Firtash, 392 F. Supp. 3d at 888–92.

249. 15 U.S.C. §§ 78dd-2(g)(2)(A), 78dd-3(e)(2)(A), 78ff(c)(2)(A); 15 U.S.C. § 78ff(a).

Table 4.3 Sample Sentences for Violation of the Foreign Corrupt Practices Act

Joel Esquenazi (09-cr-21010 S.D. Fla.)	Miami-based telecom executive convicted of bribing Haitian officials to secure contracts with a state-owned communications company sentenced to 15 years and more than $3 million in criminal forfeiture
William Jefferson (07-cr-209 E.D. Va.)	Former U.S. congressman convicted of using his position to seek hundreds of thousands of dollars of bribes in exchange for promoting business ventures in Africa sentenced to 13 years and $470,000 in criminal forfeiture
Charles Jumet (09-cr-397 E.D. Va.)	American vice president of Panamanian engineering company convicted of paying a $200,000 bribe to a port administrator and high-ranking official in Panama sentenced to 5 years
Carlos Rodriguez (09-cr-21010 S.D. Fla.)	Convicted co-conspirator with Joel Esquenazi in Haitian bribery scheme sentenced to 7 years and more than $3 million in criminal forfeiture
Benito Chinea (14-cr-240 S.D.N.Y.)	Former CEO of New York broker-dealer Direct Access Partners (DAP) convicted of paying bribes through Swiss bank accounts to officials at Venezuela's state-owned development bank to secure DAP's involvement in bond issuances sentenced to 4 years and forfeiture of $3.6 million

B. The U.K. Bribery Act 2010

Like the United States, Britain is a party to the 1997 OECD Convention on Combatting Bribery, which directs signatory nations to reduce corruption in developing countries by imposing criminal sanctions against bribery in international business transactions.[250] In response to this commitment, Parliament consolidated the various existing laws against bribery and corruption into the Bribery Act (BA) 2010, which came into force on July 1, 2011.

According to accompanying guidance issued by the Ministry of Justice,

> Bribery undermines democracy and the rule of law and poses very serious threats to sustained economic progress in developing and emerging economies and to the proper operation of free markets more generally. The Bribery Act 2010 is intended to respond to these threats and to the extremely broad range of ways that bribery can be committed.[251]

Its criminal provisions are primarily enforced by the SFO, with the FCA focusing on bringing civil regulatory actions (mirroring the DOJ/SEC dynamic in FCPA cases). The DPP or the

250. The OECD, headquartered in France, is an intergovernmental organization founded in the 1960s to promote progressive economic policies. The Convention on Bribery was signed by thirty-eight nations and was made in response to the signatories' recognition "that bribery is a widespread phenomenon in international business transactions, including trade and investment, which raises serious moral and political concerns, undermines good governance and economic development, and distorts international competitive conditions." *See* Organisation for Economic Co-operation and Development, Convention on Combating Bribery of Foreign Public Officials in International Business Transactions, *available at* https://www.oecd.org/corruption/OECDantibriberyconvention.htm?msclkid=e460d4b9c7ca11ecb780101b00d27dcb.

251. Ministry of Justice, *The Bribery Act 2010 – Guidance* (2011), p. 9. (hereinafter *MOJ Bribery Act Guidance*).

director of the SFO must give personal consent to a criminal prosecution of Bribery Act violations before one may commence.

The Bribery Act creates four distinct offenses: (i) promising or giving a bribe (active bribery); (ii) requesting, agreeing to receive, or accepting of a bribe (passive bribery); (iii) bribery of a foreign official; and (iv) failing to prevent bribery on behalf of a commercial organization. With respect to the first three offenses, the jurisdiction of U.K. courts extends to offenses committed within and outside of the United Kingdom if the party committing them has a "close connection" with the United Kingdom by virtue of being a British national or resident or U.K. corporation.[252]

As discussed earlier, the scope of the Bribery Act is considerably broader than the FCPA in that it applies to bribery of officials in the United Kingdom (i.e., not just foreign ones), as well as bribes paid in the private sector. Even though these activities are not prohibited by the FCPA, however, U.S. prosecutors can rely on various other federal statutes to target such conduct (e.g., 18 U.S.C. § 201 (bribery of domestic officials) and the Travel Act (18 U.S.C. § 1952) (commercial bribery)).

1. Active Bribery

Under the Bribery Act Section 1, it is an offense for a person to offer, promise, or give "a financial or other advantage" to another person in one of two "cases":

- **Case 1**: Where the bribe payer intends the advantage to bring about the improper performance by another person of a relevant function or activity or to reward such improper performance.
- **Case 2**: Where the bribe payer knows or believes that the acceptance of the advantage offered, promised, or given in itself constitutes the improper performance of a relevant function or activity.

While this obviously covers the archetypal bribery offense of passing off envelopes of cash to a government official, it is broad enough to reach less explicit "advantages" like gifts, travel expenses, providing employment to an official's relative, and making political or charitable donations.

The term "improper performance" is defined to mean conduct that breaches an expectation that a person acting in a public function will do so in good faith, impartially, or in accordance with a position of trust.[253] Section 1 offenses apply to bribery relating to any function of a public nature, connected with a business, performed in the course of a person's employment or performed on behalf of an entity (both public and private).[254] Where the function takes place—whether in the United Kingdom or elsewhere—is irrelevant as long as there is a "close connection" with Britain.[255]

---

252. Bribery Act (BA), s. 12.

253. *Id.*, s. 3(3)-(5).

254. *Id.*, s. 3(2).

255. *Id.*, s. 3(6).

To determine whether a function has been performed improperly, U.K. courts use an "expectation test" which considers what a reasonable British person would expect in the circumstances. Only the average sensibilities of the British public are relevant. So where the relevant function or activity takes place outside the United Kingdom, "any local custom or practice must be disregarded—unless [the activity at issue] is permitted or required by the written law applicable to that particular country."[256] For example, to prove that hospitality was intended as a bribe, the SFO would need to show that it was intended to induce conduct that breaches the expectations placed on the bribe recipient (as judged by what a reasonable person in the United Kingdom would think).

2. *Passive Bribery*

A person is guilty of a "passive bribery" offense if he or she requests, agrees to receive, or accepts a financial or other advantage in exchange for performing a function improperly or causing another person to do so, or as a reward for such an improper performance.[257] "The mere request, agreement or acceptance of a benefit constitutes improper performance and it neither matter[s] whether the advantage is received directly or through a third party nor whether the benefit is to those same parties or another."[258] In contrast with the FCPA, therefore, the Bribery Act explicitly criminalizes receiving as well as giving bribes. But, as noted above, the U.S. code contains various other statutes federal prosecutors can use to go after bribe recipients, which renders this difference of little practical significance.

3. *Bribery of a Foreign Official*

The Bribery Act Section 6 creates a standalone offense for bribery of a foreign official. Section 6 has substantial overlap with Section 1 but has a different underlying policy focus—namely, "the need to prohibit the influencing of decision making in the context of publicly funded business opportunities by the inducement of personal enrichment of foreign public officials or to others at the official's request, assent or acquiescence."[259]

The primary difference between the elements of a Section 1 and Section 6 offense is that Section 6 does not require proof of conduct that amounts to "improper performance" or an intention to induce such conduct. The omission of this element in Section 6 is in part a recognition of the evidentiary difficulties it would pose for prosecutors in foreign bribery cases. As stated in the Ministry of Justice's Guidance,

> [T]he exact nature of the functions of persons regarded as foreign officials is often very difficult to ascertain with any accuracy, and the securing of evidence will often be reliant on the co-operation of the state any such officials serve. To require the prosecution to rely entirely on section 1 would amount to a very significant deficiency in the ability of the legislation to address this particular mischief.[260]

---

256. *MOJ Bribery Act Guidance*, *supra* note 251, at 10.

257. BA, s.2(2)–(5).

258. Harrison & Ryder, *supra* note 81, at 176.

259. *MOJ Bribery Act Guidance*, *supra* note 251, at 11.

260. *Id.*

Accordingly, a Section 6 offense occurs where a person (i) offers, promises, or gives a financial or other advantage to a foreign public official (or to another party at the official's request or with their assent), (ii) with the intention of influencing the official in the performance of his or her official functions, and (iii) for the purpose of obtaining or retaining business.[261] The influence sought need not relate to the official's specific governmental role. Rather, the statute explicitly notes that it applies to any official function, including those not within the official's specific authority.[262]

The definition of "foreign public official" in Section 6 is essentially identical to that applied by U.S. courts in FCPA cases. It states that a "foreign public official" means an individual who holds "a legislative, administrative or judicial position of any kind, whether appointed or elected of a country outside the United Kingdom," exercises a public function for or on behalf of a foreign country or public agency, or "is an official or agent of a public international organisation."[263] In turn, a "public international organisation" is defined to include organizations whose members are "countries or territories," "governments of countries or territories," "other public international organisations," or a mixture of these.[264]

Section 6 requires prosecutors to show not only that an "advantage" was offered or promised to an official, but also that the official was not permitted to receive the advantage as determined by the written laws of the official's home country or, in the case of an official at a public international organization, the organization's rules.[265] Unlike the FCPA's "local law defense," this is not an affirmative defense—in other words, establishing a violation of a foreign law or an organization's rules is a burden placed on British prosecutors instead of the defendant.

a. Bona Fide Expenditures

According to the SFO's Guidance, bona fide hospitality and promotional expenditures are "an established and important part of doing business and it is not the intention of the Act to criminalise such behavior." Although such expenditures can still be the basis of a Bribery Act offense, the law is not meant to capture "reasonable and proportionate" expenditures intended to improve a business's image, better present its products and services, or "establish cordial relations."[266] Rather, to amount to a bribe under Section 6 there must be an "intention for a financial or other advantage to [improperly] influence the official in his or her official role and thereby secure business or a business advantage."

In addition to proving this intent, prosecutors must also show that there is a direct connection between the advantage and the intention to secure a business benefit. With

261. BA, ss. 6(1)–(3).

262. *Id.*, s. 6(4).

263. *Id.*, s. 6(5).

264. *Id.*, s. 6(6).

265. *Id.*, ss. 6(3), 6(7).

266. *MOJ Bribery Act Guidance*, *supra* note 251, at 12.

respect to this element, the totality of the circumstances will be evaluated for factors such as the type of advantage offered, and the level of influence the official has over awarding a business benefit to the briber payer. The more lavish the advantage given, "the greater the inference that it is intended to influence the official to grant business or a business advantage in return." While the norms of a particular sector are relevant to this analysis, they are not determinative.[267]

b. Facilitation Payments

Unlike the FCPA, the Bribery Act does not explicitly exempt small payments to facilitate routine government action. From the perspective of British lawmakers, "exemptions in this context create artificial distinctions that are difficult to enforce, undermine corporate anti-bribery communication with employees and other associated persons, perpetuate an existing 'culture' of bribery and have potential to be abused."[268]

Nevertheless, the SFO takes account of the difficult business environments in certain regions and sectors that may require (at least unofficially) "grease payments" to expedite minor bureaucratic processes. As such, SFO guidance states that the eradication of facilitation payments is a "long term objective that will require economic and social progress and sustained commitment to the rule of law in those parts of the world where the problem is most prevalent." While the SFO expects business to counteract facilitation payments through its bribery prevention procedures as much as reasonably possible, the practice is not generally subject to criminal prosecution.

4. *Failure to Prevent Bribery*

The Bribery Act Section 7 imposes vicarious liability on companies when an "associated individual" commits a Section 1 or Section 6 bribery offense on their behalf. Individuals will be considered "associated" with a corporate entity if they perform services for the entity (including subsidiaries) as an employee or agent (as determined by reference to all the relevant circumstances and "not merely by reference to the nature of the relationship"). What matters, therefore, is the substance of the purported principal/agent relationship, not titles or its nominal form. If the individual violator is an employee of the entity in question, he or she will be presumed to be "associated" for Section 7 purposes.[269]

> This broad scope means that contractors can be "associated" persons to the extent they are performing services for or on behalf of a commercial organisation. Also, where a supplier can properly be said to be performing services for a commercial organisation rather than simply acting as the seller of goods, it may also be an "associated person."[270]

---

267. *Id.*, at 13.

268. *Id.*, at 18.

269. BA, ss. 8(1)–(5).

270. *MOJ Bribery Act Guidance*, *supra* note 251, at 16.

In light of these liabilities, British companies must ensure all appropriate due diligence is done when dealing with agents and supply chains in foreign countries.

To commit a Section 7 offense, a company must qualify as a "relevant commercial organisation," defined as either: (i) an entity incorporated in the United Kingdom, (ii) an entity that carries on all or part of its business in the United Kingdom, (iii) a partnership formed under U.K. law, or (iv) a partnership (wherever formed) that carries on all or part of its business in the United Kingdom.[271] The Ministry of Justice's Guidance states that prosecutors and courts should be guided by a "common sense approach" in making this fact-specific determination:

> Where there is a particular dispute as to whether a business presence in the United Kingdom satisfies the test in the Act, the final arbiter, in any particular case, will be the courts . . . However, the Government anticipates that applying a common sense approach would mean that organizations that do not have a demonstrable business presence in the United Kingdom would not be caught. The Government would not expect, for example, the mere fact that a company's securities have been admitted to the UK Listing Authority's Official List and therefore admitted to trading on the London Stock Exchange, in itself, to qualify that company as carrying on a business or part of a business in the UK and therefore falling within the definition of a 'relevant commercial organisation' for the purposes of section 7. Likewise, having a UK subsidiary will not, in itself, mean that a parent company is carrying on a business in the UK, since a subsidiary may act independently of its parent or other group companies.[272]

Mirroring the FCPA's accounting provisions, there is no requirement that an individual be first convicted of a Bribery Act offense for Section 7 to apply. Moreover, the Section 7 offense is in addition to, and does not displace, liability under Sections 1 or 6 for a business that itself commits an offense by virtue of the common law "identification principle" (discussed in chapter 11).[273] Section 7 is criminally enforced by the SFO and civilly enforced by the FCA.

As opposed to the other bribery offenses, there is no requirement of a "close connection" with the United Kingdom under Section 7.[274] "So, provided the organisation is incorporated or formed in the U.K., or that the organization carries on a business or part of a business in the U.K. (wherever in the world it may be incorporated or formed) then U.K. courts will have jurisdiction" for a Section 7 offense.[275]

The British government directs commercial organizations to prevent bribery by following six core principles: proportionality to the nature of their activities, top-level commitment of a

---

271. BA, s. 7(5).

272. *MOJ Bribery Act Guidance*, *supra* note 251, at 15–16.

273. In Tesco Supermarkets v. Nattrass [1972] AC 153, the House of Lords (the predecessor to the U.K. Supreme Court) established the so-called "identification principle" that corporate liability arises only where the offense is committed by a natural person who is the "directing mind or will" of the organization. This means that a company will generally not be criminally liable—vicariously or directly—under U.K. law unless a senior officer or board member was personally involved in, or approved of, the wrongdoing (see chapter 11). The failure to prevent offense under Section 7 of the Bribery Act is an exception to this principle.

274. BA, ss. 7(3) and 12(5).

275. *MOJ Bribery Act Guidance*, *supra* note 251, at 9.

business's management, periodic and documented risk assessments, proportionate and risk-based due diligence procedures, effective communication of antibribery policies to employees and agents, and comprehensive monitoring and review of internal procedures. These principles are not one-size-fits-all: "They are intended to be flexible and outcome focused, allowing for the huge variety of circumstances that commercial organisations find themselves in." "Accordingly, the detail of how organisations might apply these principals, taken as a whole, will vary, but the outcome should always be robust and effective anti-bribery provisions" in corporate compliance programs.[276]

5. *Statutory Defenses under the Bribery Act*

The SFO's Bribery Act Guidance makes clear that the law is not intended to "bring the full force of criminal law to bear upon well run commercial organisations that experience an isolated incident of bribery on their behalf."[277] Accordingly, Section 7 provides that companies that would otherwise be liable for a Section 7 offense can raise an affirmative defense that it had in place "adequate procedures designed to prevent persons associated [with them] from undertaking such conduct."[278]

To be successful, this defense must be established by a balance of probabilities. What constitutes "adequate procedures" will depend on the specifics of each case, including "matters such as the level of control over the activities of the associated person and the degree of risk that requires mitigation."[279]

6. *Extraterritorial Reach*

As discussed earlier, the Bribery Act Sections 1, 2, and 6 apply to conduct occurring entirely outside of Britain if the defendant had a "close connection with the United Kingdom" at the relevant time.[280] This includes British citizens and companies organized under U.K. law.

The foreign reach of Section 7 is broader in that it applies to any company or partnership (wherever incorporated) that engages in any business activities within the United Kingdom. It is irrelevant where the underlying bribery took place. The SFO has indicated that it will take a "common sense" approach to the level of business activity required and will look for a "demonstrable business presence," meaning that listing shares on the London Stock Exchange or having a U.K. subsidiary will not necessarily suffice. The opposite is true under the FCPA, and the DOJ routinely imposes FCPA penalties on foreign companies with a bare minimum of relevant U.S. ties.[281]

---

276. *Id.* at 20.

277. *Id.* at 8.

278. BA, s. 7(2).

279. *MOJ Bribery Act Guidance*, *supra* note 251, at 18.

280. BA, s. 12(3).

281. 15 U.S.C. §§ 78dd-1 and 78dd-2 (applying FCPA antibribery provisions to any U.S. issuer or domestic concern).

7. *Criminal Penalties*

Bribery Act prosecutions—other than those brought by the FCA under Section 7—can only be instituted with the personal consent of the DPP or the director of the SFO.[282] Violations of the Bribery Act are "either-way" offenses. An individual found guilty on summary conviction of an offense under Section 1, 2, or 6 is liable to imprisonment of up to twelve months and a fine; individuals convicted on indictment are subject to imprisonment of up to ten years and an unlimited fine. Corporate entities found guilty of a Section 7 offense are subject to an unlimited fine.[283]

From the law's creation in 2010 to date, British prosecutors have secured more than ninety Bribery Act convictions against individuals (forty-six of which were handled by the SFO). The longest sentence meted out to date has been fifteen years in the case against David Mills, a British businessman who, along with his wife and other conspirators, bribed bank officials at Lloyds Bank with escorts and paid vacations into encouraging clients to take out loans they could not afford. Mills then profited by offering to help the clients out of financial difficulty, earning millions of pounds in referral fees and charges for his services, which he used to buy two luxury yachts and a property portfolio that included a villa in Majorca, Spain, and a mansion in the English countryside.[284]

Practice Note

The Coordinated Foreign Bribery Conviction of Glencore

Because of their inherently international aspects, foreign bribery cases often involve coordinated efforts between law enforcement in various different countries. The recent case against Swiss commodity trading and mining company Glencore International A.G. is a good example. On May 24, 2022, Glencore agreed to plead guilty to bribery offenses in the United States, United Kingdom, and Brazil and pay a total of $1.1 billion in fines to the authorities in these countries.

In its plea agreement with the DOJ, Glencore admitted that its employees and agents had engaged in a decade-long scheme to pay more than $100 million to third-party intermediaries with the intent that a significant portion of the cash would be used to pay bribes to officials in Nigeria, Cameroon, Ivory Coast, Equatorial Guinea, Brazil, Venezuela, and the Democratic Republic of Congo. Glencore concealed these bribes by entering into sham consulting agreements, paying inflated invoices, and using intermediary companies to funnel corrupt officials with influence over awarding Glencore contracts.[285]

In the United States, Glencore pleaded guilty to one count of conspiracy to violate the FCPA and was hit with a criminal fine of $428.5 million plus forfeiture and disgorgement of $272 million. In parallel, Glencore's U.K. subsidiary pleaded guilty in Westminster's Magistrates' Court to seven counts of bribery brought by the SFO. The company's sentencing

282. BA, s. 10.

283. BA, s. 11.

284. "Couple Ordered to Pay £10m over Reading HBOS Fraud," BBC News, Sept. 13, 2019).

285. Press Release, U.S. Department of Justice, "Glencore Entered Guilty Pleas to Foreign Bribery and Market Manipulation Scheme" (May 24, 2022).

in the United Kingdom is scheduled for June 21, 2022 and is expected to result in financial penalties of at least $167 million. A separate resolution was reached in Brazil, where the company agreed to pay a fine of $40 million.[286]

IV. CONSPIRACY

The mere agreement between two or more persons to commit a criminal offense is viewed as a "distinct evil" subject to criminal penalties in the United States and Britain. As explained by the U.S. Supreme Court, these laws rest on the assumption that criminal conspiracies pose "'a threat to the public' over and above the threat of the commission of the relevant substantive crime—both because the 'combination in crime makes more likely the commission of [other] crimes' and because it 'decreases the probability that the individuals involved will depart from their path of criminality.'"[287] Moreover, in the Court's view the "combination in crime makes more likely the commission of crimes unrelated to the original purpose for which the group was formed."[288]

Similarly, criminal conspiracy law in the United Kingdom is "based on the [perceived] seriousness of the choice the conspirator makes when he or she exchanges one obligation (to obey the law) for another (the criminal enterprise that he or she agrees to)." For, according to the Law Commission of England and Wales,

> [it] is one thing for a lone actor to discontinue on a criminal path, it's quite another matter where an actor is part of a criminal group. Add to this the observations about how criminal gangs, as opposed to individuals, can achieve economies of scale in criminal enterprise and there emerges a picture of a conspiracy as a particularly dangerous threat of criminal harm of significant magnitude.[289]

Whether or not these assumptions are supported by empirical evidence, conspiracy laws are an important part of a prosecutor's arsenal, especially in the United States.

A. Criminal Conspiracy Offenses in the United States

Federal white-collar crime indictments will almost always charge conspiracy in addition to one or more "substantive offenses"—that is, the crimes that are the alleged ultimate objective of the conspirators. As observed by the Seventh Circuit, "prosecutors seem to have conspiracy on

286. Alex Hamer, "Glencore to Pay $1.2bn in Bribery and Corruption Fines," INVESTORS' CHRONICLE (May 24, 2022).

287. United States v. Recio, 123 S. Ct. 819, 822 (2003) (quoting Callanan v. United States, 364 U.S. 587, 593–94 (1961)).

288. Iannelli v. United States, 420 U.S. 770, 778 (1975).

289. Law Reform Commission, *Inchoate Offenses* 10 (Consultation Paper No. 48, 2008), *available at* https://www.lawreform.ie/_fileupload/consultation%20papers/InchoateCP%20online.pdf.

their word processors as Count I; rare is the case omitting such a charge."[290] Even if the substantive offense is achieved by the conspirators, it does not merge with the conspiracy offense. In most cases, therefore, "separate sentences can be imposed for conspiracy to do an act and for the subsequent accomplishment of that end."[291] Because the decision to stack conspiracy charges on top of one or more substantive offenses is at the sole discretion of prosecutors, conspiracy allows law enforcement to magnify the risks for a defendant to take their case to trial.

The practice of charging conspiracy alongside a substantive offense is a double-edged sword for defendants. On the downside, conspiracies generally have fewer elements than substantive offenses, which can make them easier for prosecutors to prove. Alleging a conspiracy also opens the door for the DOJ to use out of court co-conspirator statements as evidence during trial (through an exception to the normal rules against hearsay contained in Federal Rule of Evidence 801(d)(2)I (see chapter 7). As the DOJ's *Justice Manual* § 9-27.320 specifically recognizes, "in a case in which a substantive offense was committed pursuant to an unlawful agreement, inclusion of a conspiracy count is permissible and may be desirable to ensure the introduction of all relevant evidence at trial." This dynamic makes conspiracy a "power weapon" that the DOJ can use to increase pressure on defendants to plead guilty.[292]

On the flipside, however, certain conspiracy offenses carry lower maximum sentences than the underlying substantive offense. As such, defendants will often take plea agreements requiring them to plead guilty only to the conspiracy charge in exchange for prosecutors dropping the substantive ones (allowing defendants to effectively cap their sentencing exposure at the lower maximum). Without a conspiracy charge in the indictment, the availability of such a bargain would be less likely.

While there are dozens of conspiracy statutes in the U.S. Code, the sections below focus on the two provisions most often implicated in white-collar crime cases: 18 U.S.C. § 371, a general conspiracy provision, and 18 U.S.C. § 1349, which is directed at mail and wire fraud conspiracies. The various other conspiracy crimes follow more or less the structure of one of these two statutes in all material respects.

1. *Section 371 Conspiracy*

Section 371 criminalizes conspiracies to commit any federal offense or to defraud the United States:

290. United States v. Reynolds, 919 F.2d 435, 439 (7th Cir. 1990); Harrison v. United States, 7 F.2d 259, 263 (2d Cir. 1925) ("[C]onspiracy, that darling of the modern prosecutor's nursery."); United States v. Flotron, No. 17-cr-00220, 2018 WL 195117, at *12 (D. Conn. Apr. 25, 2018) ("I don't doubt for a moment the Government's right to charge substantive charges in conjunction with an overarching conspiracy. That's the Government's usual playbook.").

291. Iannelli v. United State, 420 U.S. 770, 777 (1975); *see also* Griffin v. United States, 502 U.S. 46 (1991) (holding that where the evidence in a conspiracy aimed at multiple substantive crimes is determined lacking as to one such crime, a guilty verdict will be allowed to stand if the evidence supports conviction as to any one of them).

292. Jeffrey M. Chemerinsky, *Counting Offenses*, 58 DUKE L.J. 709, 737 (2009).

> If two or more persons conspire either to commit any offense against the United States, or to defraud the United States, or any agency thereof in any manner or for any purpose, and one or more of such persons do any act to effect the object of the conspiracy, each shall be fined under this title or imprisoned not more than five years, or both.

The two prongs of Section 371 are not mutually exclusive and overlap considerably. The primary difference between the two is that, under the "defraud" prong, prosecutors need not point to an underlying federal offense. Rather, they must only establish that the conspirators sought to defraud the federal government by cheating it out of money or property, or by interfering with "one of its lawful functions by deceit, craft, or trickery, or at least by means that are dishonest."[293]

To establish a Section 371 violation under the first prong, the government must prove three elements: (i) the existence of an agreement between two or more persons to commit a specified federal offense, (ii) the defendant's knowing and willful joinder in that common agreement, and (iii) some conspirator's commission of an overt act.[294] Where the object of a conspiracy is a specific-intent crime—that is, one where the defendant is required to intend a specific harm—prosecutors must also establish beyond a reasonable doubt that an alleged conspirator had the specific intent to violate the relevant substantive statute by participating in the alleged conspiracy.[295]

a. Element 1: An Agreement Between One or More People

The agreement element necessarily implies that "at least two persons are required to constitute a conspiracy."[296] This does not mean, however, that criminal liability for one conspirator requires the conviction—or even the identification—of another conspirator.[297] Rather, to sustain a conspiracy conviction it is sufficient if the government proves that the charged conspirator entered into an unlawful agreement with *someone*: "where the existence of a conspiracy has been proved, evidence sufficient to link another defendant with it need not be overwhelming and it may be circumstantial in nature."[298] As a result, charging instruments

---

293. Hammerschmidt v. United States, 265 U.S. 182, 188 (1924); *see also* United States v. Conti, 804 F.3d 977, 979–90 (9th Cir. 2015); United States v. Arch Trading Co., 987 F.2d 1087, 1091 (4th Cir. 1993).

294. United States v. Snype, 441 F.3d 119, 142 (2d Cir. 2006); Ceballos, 340 F.3d at 123-24 ("In order to convict a given defendant of conspiracy, the government must prove that he knew of the conspiracy and joined it with the intent to commit the offenses that were its objectives, that is, with the affirmative intent to make the conspiracy succeed.").

295. United States v. Samaria, 239 F.3d 228, 234 (2d Cir. 2001).

296. Rogers v. United States, 340 U.S. 367, 375 (1951); *see also* United States v. Dumeisi, 424 F.3d 566, 580 (7th Cir. 2005) ("The elements of the crime of conspiracy are not satisfied unless one conspires with at least one true co-conspirator."); United States v. Vallee, 807 F.3d 508, 522 (2d Cir. 2015); United States v. Stevens, 909 F.2d 431 (11th Cir. 1990) (holding that an individual who completely controlled a corporation could not be guilty of a conspiracy with the corporation in the absence of another human actor).

297. *See e.g.*, United States v. Meléndez-González, 892 F.3d 9, 17-18 (1st Cir. 2018); United States v. Contreras, 249 F.3d 595, 598 (7th Cir. 2001). But note that a conviction will not stand if all but one conspirator are acquitted. United States v. Lo, 447 F.3d 1212, 1226 (9th Cir. 2006).

298. Ceballos, 340 F.3d at 124; *see also* United States v. Feldman, 936 F.3d 1288, 1305 (11th Cir. 2019).

UNITED STATES DISTRICT COURT
SOUTHERN DISTRICT OF NEW YORK

UNITED STATES OF AMERICA

- v. -

MICHAEL COHEN,

Defendant.

INFORMATION

18 Cr. __ (WHP)

18 CRIM 602

USDC SDNY
DOCUMENT
ELECTRONICALLY FIL
DOC #:
DATE FILED: AUG 2 1 201

The United States Attorney charges:

Background

The Defendant

1. From in or about 2007 through in or about January 2017, MICHAEL COHEN, the defendant, was an attorney and employee of a Manhattan-based real estate company (the "Company"). COHEN held the title of "Executive Vice President" and "Special Counsel" to the owner of the Company ("Individual-1").

2. In or about January 2017, COHEN left the Company and began holding himself out as the "personal attorney" to Individual-1, who at that point had become the President of the United States.

3. In addition to working for and earning income from the Company, at all times relevant to this Information, MICHAEL COHEN, the defendant, owned taxi medallions in New York City and Chicago worth millions of dollars. COHEN owned these taxi

Figure 4.3 Portion of the charging document in *United States v. Cohen.*

will often refer to unnamed and unindicted alleged co-conspirators (who are both known and unknown to the DOJ). It is DOJ policy not to disclose the names of unindicted co-conspirators. In the information charging President Trump's former attorney, Michael Cohen, with various fraud and campaign finance offenses for example, the DOJ referred to President Trump as "Individual-1" and the Trump Corporation as "the Company" (figure 4.3).[299]

The agreement to commit a federal offense is the core of a conspiracy crime. This agreement need only be tacit rather than explicit, and may be proved through direct or circumstantial evidence from which it can be inferred.[300] Relevant circumstantial evidence may include "the joint appearance of defendants at transactions and negotiations in furtherance of the conspiracy; the relationship among codefendants; mutual representation of defendants to third parties; and other evidence suggesting unity of purpose or common

299. United States v. Cohen, 18-cr-00602 (S.D.N.Y. Aug. 21, 2018).

300. Feldman, 936 F.3d at 1305; United States v. Tull-Abreau, 921 F.3d 294, 305 (1st Cir. 2019); United States v. Samaria, 239 F.3d 228, 234 (2d Cir. 2001).

design and understanding among conspirators to accomplish the objects of the conspiracy."[301] Where an indictment lists more than one object of an alleged conspiracy (e.g., a conspiracy to commit an FCPA and money laundering offense), the evidence "need only be sufficient for any one of the charged objects to sustain a conviction."[302]

Lowering the evidentiary bar for prosecutors even further, to be found guilty of conspiracy, conspirators need not even agree on every detail of the venture as long as there is "proof beyond a reasonable doubt that they agreed on the 'essential nature of the plan.' It is not required that they agree on the ancillary aspects of a scheme not running to the heart of the agreement."[303]

Federal conspiracy law therefore deals with the crime pragmatically by focusing on the conspirators' overall operations or objectives rather than the individual acts of agreement.[304] This so-called "bilateral" perspective was summarized by the Supreme Court in *Blumenthal v. United States*:

> For it is most often true, especially in broad schemes calling for the aid of many persons, that after discovery of enough to show clearly the essence of the scheme and the identity of a number participating, the identity and the fact of participation of others remain undiscovered and undiscoverable. Secrecy and concealment are essential features of a successful conspiracy. . . . Hence the law rightly gives room for allowing the conviction of those discovered upon showing sufficiently the essential nature of the plan and their connections with it, without requiring evidence of knowledge of all its details or the participation of others.[305]

b. Element 2: Defendant's Knowing and Willful Joinder in the Agreement

"Knowledge of the existence and goals of a conspiracy does not of itself make one a coconspirator."[306] Rather, there must be "something more than mere knowledge, approval of or acquiescence in the object or the purpose of the conspiracy."[307] As to what constitutes "something more," courts have held that a defendant must show a "[positive] attitude towards the forbidden undertaking" by promoting the venture, making it his or her own, having a stake in its outcome, or making "an affirmative attempt to further its purposes."[308] Put differently, the evidence must show "informed and interested cooperation."[309]

---

301. United States v. Wardell, 591 F.3d 1279, 1278–88 (10th Cir. 2009).

302. United States v. Moran, 778 F.3d 942, 963 (11th Cir. 2015).

303. United States v. Stavroulakis, 952 F.2d 686 (2d Cir. 1992).

304. *See* Jerome S. Campane, *Chains, Wheels, and the Single Conspiracy*, FBI ENFORCEMENT BULLETIN (Sept. 1981).

305. 332 U.S. 539, 556–67 (1947).

306. United States v. Cianchetti, 315 F.2d 584, 587 (2d Cir. 1963); *see also* Direct Sales Co. v. United States, 319 U.S. 703, 711 (1943).

307. Cianchetti, 315 F.2d at 588.

308. *Id.*

309. Direct Sales Co., 319 U.S. at 713; *see also* United States v. Svoboda, 347 F.3d 471, 477 (2d Cir. 2003) (government required to prove defendant entered agreement "with knowledge of the criminal purpose of the scheme" and "the specific intent to aid in the accomplishment of those unlawful ends").

While a defendant's *knowledge* of a criminal conspiracy can be proven through a showing of "wilful blindness" or "conscious avoidance," evidence supporting these concepts cannot, on their own, establish criminal intent.[310] Under the "wilful blindness" doctrine, courts will consider a defendant to have had actual knowledge of a particular fact (e.g., the existence of a criminal conspiracy) where the evidence shows he "suspected the fact; he realized its probability; but he refrained from obtaining the final confirmation because he wanted in the event to be able to deny knowledge."[311] Similarly, the conscious avoidance doctrine applies to situations where a defendant's knowledge of a conspiracy can be inferred through evidence showing he "[was] aware of a high probability of its existence, unless he actually believe[ed] that it [did] not exist."[312] The justification for these rules is that "deliberate ignorance and positive knowledge are equally culpable. . . . To act 'knowingly,' therefore, is not necessarily to act with positive knowledge, but also to act with an awareness of the high probability of the existence of the fact in question. When such awareness is present, 'positive' knowledge is not required."[313]

c. Element 3: The Overt Act Requirement

Section 371 requires the government to prove that one of the conspirators committed an overt act in furtherance of the conspiracy. "An overt act is any act performed by any conspirator for the purpose of accomplishing the objectives of the conspiracy."[314] The individual being prosecuted does not need to participate in such act to be guilty—rather, "[o]nce a conspiracy is established, and an individual is linked to that conspiracy, an overt act committed by any conspirator is sufficient for all conspirators to be guilty.[315] The overt act need not itself be unlawful, nor does it even need to be part of the underlying substantive offense.[316] Instead, the function of the overt act requirement is simply to ensure "that the conspiracy is at work, and is neither a project still resting solely in the minds of the conspirators nor a fully completed operation no longer in existence."[317]

3. Section 1349 Conspiracy (18 U.S.C. § 1349)

Section 1349, enacted in 2002, provides that "[a]ny person who attempts or conspires to commit any offense [involving mail fraud or one of various other fraud offenses] shall be subject to the same penalties as those prescribed for the offense, the commission of which was the object of the attempt or conspiracy." The effect of this statute is to increase the maximum

310. United States v. Reyes, 302 F.3d 48, 54 (2d Cir. 2002).

311. *Id.*

312. Leary v. United States, 395 U.S. 6, 46 n.93 (1969).

313. United States v. Jewell, 532 F.2d 697, 700 (9th Cir. 1976).

314. United States v. Tzolov, 642 F.3d 314, 319 (2d Cir. 2011).

315. United States v. Thomas, 8 F.3d 1552, 1560 n.21 (11th Cir. 1993).

316. Braverman v. United States, 317 U.S. 49, 52 (1942).

317. Yates v. United States, 354 U.S. 298, 333 (1957).

penalty for conspiracy to commit fraud from the five-year maximum of 18 U.S.C. § 371 to the twenty-year maximum for a substantive fraud offense under 18 U.S.C. § 1343.

Ironically, despite the substantially higher penalties, a Section 1349 offense has fewer elements than Section 371 for prosecutors to prove. Section 1349 omits Section 371's overt act requirements, meaning that a Section 1349 conspiracy can be proven through only two elements: the existence of an agreement between two or more persons to commit a specified federal offense, and the defendant's knowing and willful joinder in that common agreement.[318] Otherwise, the two statutes apply in the same way.

4. *Procedural Implications of Conspiracy Crimes*

Federal conspiracy laws not only contain relatively simple elements, they also provide prosecutors with various ancillary procedural benefits. Specifically, by charging a conspiracy under Section 371, 1349, or any of the numerous other federal conspiracy statutes, prosecutors are able to make use of various legal doctrines that allow conspiracy charges to be brought and proven more easily than substantive crimes.

a. *Pinkerton* Liability

Under the Supreme Court's decision in *Pinkerton v. United States*, members of a conspiracy can be found guilty of any substantive offense committed by a co-conspirator in furtherance of the conspiracy so long as such offense was a "reasonably foreseeable consequence" of the conspiratorial agreement.[319] *Pinkerton* therefore establishes a theory of "conspiratorial vicarious liability."[320]

To find a defendant guilty under a *Pinkerton* theory, prosecutors must first establish beyond a reasonable doubt that (i) both the defendant and the person who actually committed the substantive offense were members of the charged conspiracy at the time the substantive offense was committed, (ii) the substantive offense was committed pursuant to the common plan of the co-conspirators, and (iii) that the commission of the substantive offense was reasonably foreseeable to the defendant.[321] There is no requirement that any particular conspirator participate in, or even know of, the substantive crime for *Pinkerton* liability to attach.[322]

For defendants, *Pinkerton* is obviously problematic because it creates the possibility that prosecutors may erroneously group them together with purported co-conspirators with whom they did not actually conspire. To counteract this risk, the law permits the government to charge a "master conspiracy" with multiple subsidiary schemes, but prevents prosecutors

318. United States v. Roy, 783 F.3d 418, 421 (2d Cir. 2015); United States v. Rogers, 769 F.3d 372, 380 (6th Cir. 2014). Nearly one hundred other federal conspiracy statutes similarly do not contain an overt act requirement. United States v. Pascacio-Rodriguez, 749 F.3d 353, 361–62 (5th Cir. 2014).

319. 328 U.S. 640, 647 (1946); *see also* United States v. McCoy, 995 F.3d 32, 63 (2d Cir. 2021).

320. McCoy, 995 F.3d at 63.

321. *Id.* at 63–64.

322. *See, e.g.*, United States v. Tilton, 610 F.2d 302 (5th Cir. 1980).

from bringing a unified charge against what were actually "multiple unrelated conspiracies.[323] Thus, defendants will often challenge cases alleging a single broad conspiracy rather than a series of discrete conspiracies (which may more accurately fit the alleged facts). To determine whether the evidence supports a finding of a single conspiracy, courts will consider "whether the defendants shared a common goal, any interdependence between the alleged participants, and any overlap among alleged participants, such as the presence of core participants linked to all defendants."[324]

Changes in the conspiracy's membership and differences in the time when different conspirators participated, or shifting emphases in the location of operations do not necessarily require a finding of more than one conspiracy.[325] However, "the participation of a single common actor in what are allegedly two sets of conspiratorial activities does not establish the existence of a single conspiracy."[326]

To illustrate these points, courts employ a "wheel" analogy. When a conspiracy displays a pattern of "separate spokes meeting in the middle" but "without the rim of the wheel to enclose the spokes," it will be improper to charge it as a single conspiracy.[327] Thus, when individuals (the spokes) are engaged in a criminal conspiracy with the same individual or group (the hub), a successful single conspiracy prosecution will depend on whether the spokes can be drawn together (rim around the wheel) into a single agreement.[328] In other words, while the hub will usually always consider his or her dealing with the spokes to be part of a single enterprise, the same is not necessarily true of the spokes: some may be concerned merely with his or her own actions, while others may be in cooperation with, or have knowledge of, the other spokes. Without proof of the latter, courts will hold that the spokes are individual members of multiple conspiracies.[329]

Yet forcing the DOJ to prove multiple conspiracies instead of one is not necessarily to a defendant's advantage since the DOJ can simply charge them with participating in each

---

323. United States v. Kemp, 500 F.3d 257, 288 (3rd Cir. 2007); United States v. Chandler, 388 F.3d 796, 811(11th Cir. 2004).

324. United States v. Gatling, 96 F.3d 1511, 1520 (D.C. Cir. 1996); *see also* Kotteakos v. United States, 328 U.S. 750 (1946); United States v. Geibel, 369 F.3d 682, 689 (2d Cir. 2004) ("[A] single conspiracy is not transformed into multiple conspiracies merely by virtue of the fact that it may involve two or more phases or spheres of operation, so long as there is sufficient proof of mutual dependence and assistance.").

325. United States v. Vila, 599 F.2d 21, 24 (2d Cir. 1979); United States v. Tramunti, 513 F.2d 1087, 1106 (2d Cir. 1975).

326. United States v. Korfant, 771 F.2d 660, 663 (2d Cir.1985); *see, e.g.,* United States v. Macchia, 35 F.3d 662, 668 (2d Cir.1994) (the fact that there was "overlap with respect to a number of characteristics, including time frame, geographic locale, participants, and criminal objective" does not necessarily mean that there was but a single conspiracy); United States v. Papadakis, 510 F.2d 287, 296 (2d Cir.) ("there is no reason why people cannot enter into two separate criminal agreements more or less at the same time").

327. Kotteakos, 328 U.S. at 755.

328. United States v. Levine, 546 F.2d 658, 663 (5th Cir. 1977).

329. Murphy v. United States, 409 U.S. 914 (1973); United States v. Netterville, 553 F.2d 903 (5th Cir. 1977).

separate one—and if just one of the alleged conspiracies is proven, the defendant's total sentencing exposure may not be materially different (see chapter 9).[330]

So-called "chain" conspiracy theories, which focus on the interdependence between multiple conspirators to achieve an ultimate goal, have also been approved by courts:

> The essential element of a chain conspiracy—allowing persons unknown to each other and never before in contact to be jointly prosecuted as co-conspirators—is interdependence. The scheme which is the object of the conspiracy must depend on the successful operation of each link in the chain. An individual associating himself with a "chain" conspiracy knows that it has a "scope" and that for its success it requires an organization wider than may be disclosed by his personal participation. Thus, in a "chain" conspiracy prosecution, the requisite element—knowledge of the existence of remote links—may be inferred solely from the nature of the enterprise.[331]

To prove the existence of a chain conspiracy, the evidence must show that "the success or failure of one conspiracy is independent of a corresponding success or failure by the other."[332] Put differently, no one in the chain profits unless each does his part (figure 4.4). The requisite interdependence is therefore present when each alleged co-conspirator depends on "the operation of each link in the chain to achieve the common goal," which is usually illicit profits in the white-collar context.[333]

Certain interconnected conspiracies do not fit neatly within the chain or wheel categories and are often a combination of both. This type of "chain-wheel" conspiracy was recognized by the Fifth Circuit in *United States v. Perez*, an appeal of the convictions of twelve individual conspirators in a get-rich-quick scam involving staging fraudulent automobile accidents for the purpose of creating false personal injury claims.[334] Each of the phony accidents was set up in the same way: "recruiters" located willing "hitters," who would be responsible for creating

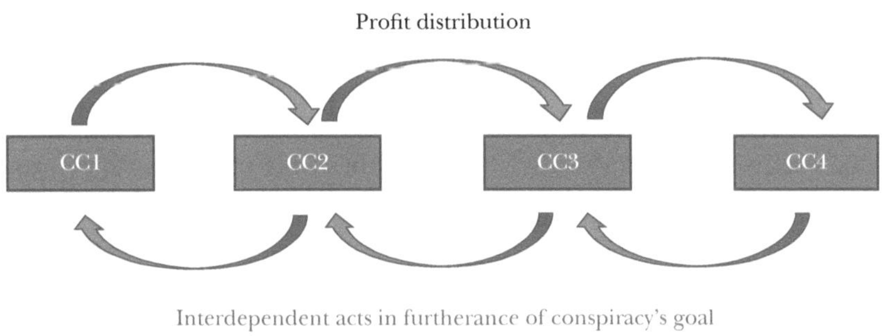

Figure 4.4 Chain conspiracies.

---

330. United States v. Payne, 591 F.3d 46, 62 (2d Cir. 2010).

331. United States v. Elliott, 571 F.2d 880, 901 (5th Cir. 1978); *see also* United States v. Agueci, 310 F.2d 817, 827 (2d Cir. 1962).

332. United States v. Macchia, 35 F.3d 662, 671 (2d Cir. 1994).

333. United States v. Evans, 970 F.2d 663, 670 (10th Cir. 1992); United States v. Smith, 82 F.3d 1261, 1271 (3d Cir. 1996) (finding government failed to prove a chain conspiracy).

334. 489 F.2d 51 (5th Cir. 1974).

a contrived accident with a "target" vehicle occupied by "drivers" and "riders" who were also in a scheme. After the "accident," the members of the target vehicle feigned injury, paid visits to cooperative doctors and lawyers, and then filed personal injury claims with the hitters' insurance company. Insurance proceeds would then be divided among all participants.

Following their convictions in the district court under a chain theory, the defendants asserted "that a variance existed between the indictment charging a single conspiracy involving multiple defendants and the proof which, at best, revealed plural conspiracies involving multiple parties which . . . overlapped upon one another in personnel."[335] In response to this argument, the Fifth Circuit panel stressed the importance of distinguishing between evidence showing a single overall conspiracy and several separate conspiracies: "The necessity for drawing this distinction derives from our interest, clearly our duty, in jealously protecting those accused from the possible transference of guilt of others accused, at least in the eyes and minds of a jury, which so often is claimed to be encountered where en masse prosecutions are undertaken for a conglomeration of separate offenses."[336]

Upon a close examination of the alleged conspiracy, the court concluded that the nature of the agreement between the co-conspirators contemplated an ongoing scheme that would not be able to exist without the continued cooperation of numerous conspirators to maintain it. As such, all defendants were found to be participants in a single common scheme to use the mails to defraud insurance companies. The panel wrote:

> From an operational sense this was not a series of little concoctions to set up a particular collision. It was rather a grand scheme for all to obtain some reward for his/her participation each according to the part played and the risk undertaken. . . . It was one big, and hopefully profitable enterprise, which looked toward successful frequent but none-the-less discreet repetitions, and in which each participant was neither innocent nor unrewarded.[337]

b. Statutes of Limitations in Conspiracy Cases

Federal conspiracy law affects the normal statute of limitations rules in two ways. First, conspiracy is considered a "continuing offense" by default since it typically involves a prolonged course of conduct that is not complete until it has fully run its course.[338] As such, conspiracies are considered to end only when their objectives are achieved, defeated, or affirmatively abandoned by the co-conspirators—that is, not when each of the crime's elements has occurred.[339]

For example, if a conspiratorial agreement is formed on January 1, 2020, the first overt act occurs on March 1, 2020, and the conspiracy is abandoned on January 1, 2022, the SOL will begin on January 1, 2022 (even though the crime could have been charged as of March 1,

---

335. *Id.*, at 57.

336. *Id.*

337. *Id.*, at 64.

338. Payne, 591 F.3d at 69.

339. Grunewald v. United States, 353 U.S. 391, 401–02 (1957); United States v. Wilbur, 674 F.3d 1160, 1176 (9th Cir. 2012).

2020, since, as of that date, all the elements of the offense had been committed). This means that a conspiracy will be deemed to continue until the final overt act occurs, which includes distribution of the conspiracy's proceeds (even if over an extended period).[340]

"The crucial question in determining whether the statute of limitations has run is the scope of the conspiratorial agreement, for it is that which determines both the duration of the conspiracy, and whether the act relied on as an overt act may properly be regarded as in furtherance of the conspiracy."[341] Because what constitutes an "overt act" is interpreted extremely broadly, prosecutors can point to conduct that is significantly attenuated from the underlying conspiracy—in terms of time, geography, participants, and substance—to extend limitation periods in conspiracy cases to reach criminal activity that is much older than would otherwise be possible if only a noncontinuing offense were charged.[342]

For example, if the core conduct in a wire fraud conspiracy began in 2005 and ended in 2010, as long as one of the conspirators continued to receive a benefit from it within the last five years—for example, by receiving payments from a fraudulently obtained contract—all conspirators can be held liable for all conduct going back to 2005. If only a substantive wire fraud charge was brought, however, the case would have been time barred by 2015 under the five-year SOL applicable to most federal crimes.[343]

Despite this, individual conspirators can escape liability for overt acts occurring late in a conspiracy's lifespan if they can establish that they affirmatively withdrew from the conspiracy at an earlier point. To establish withdrawal, a defendant must prove one of two things: either that he or she gave authorities information with "sufficient particularity" to enable them to take some action to end the conspiracy, or communicated withdrawal to the co-conspirators in a manner that "reasonably and effectively" gave notice that he or she would no longer be included in the conspiracy.[344] Merely because co-conspirators had a disagreement or falling out is insufficient on its own to establish withdrawal.[345] "[A]bsent withdrawal, a conspirator's participation in a conspiracy is presumed to continue until the last overt act by any of the conspirators."[346]

---

340. United States v. Davis, 766 F.2d 1452, 1458 (10th Cir. 1985); *see also* United States v. Ben Zvi, 242 F.3d 89, 97 (2d Cir. 2001); United States v. Knowles, 66 F.3d 1146, 1156–57 (11th Cir.1995); United States v. Knuckles, 581 F.2d 305, 313 (2d Cir.1978) ("[I]t is fair to say that where a general objective of the conspirators is money, the conspiracy does not end, of necessity, before the spoils are divided among the miscreants.").

341. Grunewald v. United States, 353 U.S. 391, 396–97 (1957).

342. *See* United States v. Morgan, 748 F.3d 1024, 1036–37 (10th Cir. 2014); United States v. Upton, 559 F.3d 3, 10 (1st Cir. 2009); United States v. Weaver, 507 F.3d 178, 185–86 (3d Cir. 2007). Note that affirmative efforts to conceal a conspiracy—for example, by lying to investigators—will not be "overt acts" for statute of limitations purposes unless concealment was itself a part of the conspiracy. *See* United States v. Bornman, 559 F.3d 150, 153 (3d Cir. 2009); United States v. Turner, 548 F.3d 1094, 1097 (D.C. Cir. 2008); Upton, 559 F.3d at 10.

343. 18 U.S.C. § 3282.

344. United States v. Randall, 661 F.3d 1291, 1294–95 (2011).

345. United States v. James, 712 F.3d 79, 106 (2d Cir. 2013).

346. United States v. Salmonese, 352 F.3d 608, 615 (2d Cir. 2003).

Withdrawal does not equate with innocence or act as a bar to criminal liability. A withdrawing conspirator can still be found responsible for all relevant conduct prior to his or her withdrawal. The legal significance of withdrawal in most cases is thus limited to when the SOL will start.[347]

Practice Note

The FCPA Conspiracy Case Against Charles Jumet

The DOJ's case against Charles Jumet provides a good example of how the conspiracy statutes allow prosecutors to target conduct that occurred long before charges are filed.[348]

Jumet, a U.S. citizen, was an executive at two engineering firms: Ports Engineering Consultants Corporation (PECC), a Panamanian company with offices in Virginia, and Overman de Panama, a Panamanian company that had a management interest in PECC. In late 2009, DOJ charged Jumet with engaging in a conspiracy to violate the FCPA "from at least 1997 through at least in and around July 2003" that involved bribes paid to Panamanian officials in return for awarding PECC contracts to maintain lighthouses and buoys along Panama's coast and waterways.

Even though the last bribe payment took place in September 1999 (more than ten years before charges were filed and thus well beyond the applicable five-year SOL), prosecutors were able to extend the duration of the conspiracy by pointing to relatively attenuated activities in 2000 and 2003. Specifically, a lawsuit filed in Virginia by a co-conspirator against Overman de Panama seeking damages of $84,536 in relation to allegedly deficient engineering services rendered by PECC. Overman de Panama settled the lawsuit in July 2003 by making a $50,000 wire transfer to the plaintiff, who then divvied it up among other co-conspirators to the original bribe scheme.

Following this payment, the Panamanian government resumed making payments to PECC under the earlier lighthouse and buoy contracts. These later payments allowed the DOJ to charge Jumet in 2009 for conduct accruing throughout the entire conspiracy (1997–2003), even though the core activities ceased in 1999.

5. Double Jeopardy in Conspiracy Cases

As discussed in chapter 3, the Constitution's double jeopardy clause forbids the duplicative prosecution of a defendant for the "same offense."[349] Even though the conduct underlying a conspiracy prosecution and a subsequent one charging only a substantive offense may be identical, the Supreme Court has ruled that the elements of these crimes are sufficiently different to render the double jeopardy protections inapplicable.[350] Accordingly, it will not violate double jeopardy if prosecutors charge a conspiracy offense after a prior conviction or acquittal for the substantive offense at which the conspiracy was aimed.[351]

---

347. United States v. Faulkner, 895 F.3d 488, 494 (7th Cir. 2018); United States v. Salazar, 751 F.3d 326, 330–31 (5th Cir. 2015).

348. United States v. Jumet, 09-cr-00397 (E.D. Va. Nov. 10, 2009).

349. Blockburger v. United States, 284 U.S. 299 (1932).

350. United States v. Felix, 503 U.S. 378, 389–90 (1992).

351. *Id.*; *see also* Garrett v. United States, 471 U.S. 773, 793 (1985).

a. Co-Conspirator Statements

The general rule in federal courts against hearsay is that statements made out of court by a declarant who is available to testify at trial may not be introduced as evidence "to prove the truth of the matter asserted in the statement" (see chapter 7).[352] Under Federal Rule of Evidence 801(d)(2)I, however, such a statement is not considered hearsay if it "is offered against a party and is . . . a statement by a coconspirator of a party during the course and in furtherance of the conspiracy." Thus, an audio recording or written statement made by a conspirator out of court can be introduced at trial against another conspirator without the declarant being made subject to cross-examination.[353] Statements made after a defendant's withdrawal from a conspiracy do not fall within this exception.[354]

For this exception to apply, prosecutors must first prove by a preponderance of the evidence that there was a conspiracy involving the declarant and the defendant on trial, and that the statement was made during the course, and in furtherance, of the conspiracy.[355] The statement at issue may not itself be the sole evidence of the conspiracy; rather, there must be some other "extrinsic evidence sufficient to delineate the conspiracy and corroborate the declarant's and the defendant's roles in it."[356]

6. *Extraterritorial Reach*

The extraterritorial reach of an ancillary offense such as conspiracy is "coterminous with that of the underlying criminal statute."[357] This is because, under the two-step test set out in *Morrison*, the "focus" of a conspiracy offense is the substantive object of the conspiracy. A conspiracy will thus qualify as domestic so long as the substantive offense, if executed, would constitute a domestic violation of the relevant statute.[358] By the same token, if the substantive offense applies extraterritorially under *Morrison*, whichever statute is used to charge a conspiracy to commit such crime will apply extraterritorially as well.[359]

7. *Criminal Penalties*

Conspiracies charged under 18 U.S.C. § 371 carry a maximum sentence of five years. For other types of conspiracies, such as those under 18 U.S.C. § 1349, the maximum sentence is the same as for the underlying substantive offense. The idiosyncrasies of how conspiracy offenses are analyzed under the U.S. Sentencing Guidelines is addressed in chapter 9.

---

352. Fed. R. Evid. 801(c).

353. Bourjaily v. United States, 483 U.S. 171, 183 (1987).

354. United States v. Nerlinger, 862 F.2d 967, 974 (2d Cir. 1988).

355. Bourjaily, 483 U.S. at 175; United States v. Mathis, 932 F.3d 242, 254 (4th Cir. 2019).

356. United States v. Mitchell, 596 F.3d 18, 23 (1st Cir. 2010).

357. United States v. Hoskins, 902 F.3d 69, 96 (2d Cir. 2018); United States v. Ballestas, 795 F.3d 138, 144 (D.C. Cir. 2015).

358. United States v. Chao Fan Xu, 706 F.3d 965, 978–79 (9th Cir. 2013).

359. Morrison, 561 U.S. at 262–65.

B. Criminal Conspiracy Offences in the United Kingdom

Although criminal conspiracy charges are an important part of many financial crime cases brought by British prosecutors, conspiracy is not routinely added alongside substantive charges in the United Kingdom like it is in the United States (where federal charging instruments *not* charging conspiracy are relatively rare). This is largely because conspiracy charges have historically been viewed as inherently suspect in the United Kingdom. As a former lord chief justice observed in *R v. Greenfield*: "Conspiracy charges have long been regarded with suspicion by English lawyers. The reasons lie partly in history and partly on procedural difficulties. There have been times in our history . . . when prosecutions for conspiracy were used by the Crown to stifle criticism and prevent agitation for religious, social and economic changes."[360]

Reflecting this perspective, the Criminal Practice Directions require prosecutors to affirmatively justify combining a conspiracy charge with a substantive offense, or else choose between the two.[361] Accordingly, where substantive counts adequately convey the overall criminality of the defendant's alleged actions, a conspiracy count will rarely be added. The rationale for this approach was stated by Lord Cockburn in the 1871 *Boulton* case: "I am clearly of the opinion that where the proof intended to be submitted to a jury is proof of the actual commission of crime, it is not the proper course to charge the parties with conspiring to commit it; for that course operates, it is manifest, unfairly and unjustly against the parties accused."[362] More recently, Mr. Justice Toulson of the Court of Appeal emphasized that "the prosecution should always think carefully, before making use of the law of conspiracy, how to formulate the conspiracy charge or charges and whether a substantive offence or offences would be more appropriate."[363] Considering the function of conspiracy law in the United States outlined earlier, U.S. lawmakers and prosecutors clearly see things much differently.

There are two types of criminal conspiracy offenses in the United Kingdom: statutory conspiracy under the Criminal Law Act (CLA) 1977 and common law conspiracy. The fundamental principle of both is the same: a person is guilty of conspiracy when the prosecution proves the existence of an agreement to commit a crime between two individuals who shared a common purpose or design.

1. *Statutory Conspiracy*

Before 1977, conspiracies were defined by the common law only. According to a report by the Law Commission in 1976, this approach was criticized as casting too wide a net because it broadly criminalized agreements to effect any "unlawful" objective (as opposed to a criminal one). "The exact extent of these 'unlawful' objects (other than crimes) is far from clear," the

---

360. [1973] 1 WLR 1151.

361. Criminal Practice Directions 2015, 10A.4.

362. Boulton [1871] 12 Cox C.C. 87; *see also* R. v. Saik [2006] UKHL 18 ("[I]t is plain that the mere fact that the substantive offence has been committed does not necessarily mean that the individuals guilty of it are also guilty of conspiracy.").

363. R v. Shillam [2013] EWCA Crim 160.

report stated. "A person remains liable to be prosecuted for conspiracy even if the object of the agreement has been achieved. The extended meaning of 'unlawful' thus leads to the result that, so long as two or more combine, they can, in certain circumstances, be punished for doing something which would not be criminal if one of them alone had done it."[364]

Section 1 of the CLA was designed to correct this issue by creating more clarity on the types of agreements that can be subject to criminal sanction. This provision defines the offense of conspiracy as an agreement between two or more persons to engage in a course of conduct that, if carried out in accordance with their intentions, either (i) will "necessarily amount" to or involve the commission of any offense or offenses (defined by the codified or common law of England and Wales) by one or more of the parties to the agreement, or (ii) would do so but for the existence of facts that render the commission of the offense or any of the offenses impossible. As in the United States, therefore, the agreement is the criminal act itself. Yet unlike the U.S. general conspiracy statute—18 U.S.C. § 371—CJA Section 1 does not require any overt act to be done in furtherance of the conspiracy's object.

As in the United States, statutory conspiracy is an "inchoate offence" in that it can be committed regardless of whether the underlying intended offense is or is not committed: "[A conspiracy offense] lies in making an agreement. Implicitly, [Section 1] requires also that the parties intend to carry out their agreement. The offence is complete at that stage."[365] The offense is triable only on indictment, even if the conspirators agreed to commit a crime that is triable only summarily.

The mental state required under Section 1 is an intent to engage in conduct that the conspirators know constitutes an offense.[366] "The conspirators' state of mind must also satisfy the mental ingredients of the substantive offence. If one of the ingredients of the substantive offence is that the act is done with a specific intent, the conspirators must intend to do the prohibited act with the prescribed intent."[367] Accordingly, the *mens rea* required for conspiracy may be stricter than for the underlying substantive offense. For example, certain money laundering offenses can be proven through evidence that a person merely "suspected" that the money or property at issue was illicitly obtained. A *conspiracy* to launder money, on the other hand, requires an intention to launder criminal proceeds or *knowledge* that the specific money involved was in fact derived from a crime.

a. The Agreement Requirement

Conspiracy requires an agreement to commit a criminal offense, but the motives of the conspirators in doing so are irrelevant.[368] While the agreement between co-conspirators can be made implicitly and explicitly, it cannot be a "mere mental operation: it must involve spoken

364. LAW COMMISSION, REPORT NO. 76, CONSPIRACY AND CRIMINAL LAW REFORM 5–6 (1976).

365. Saik [2006] UKHL 18, [3].

366. *Id.*, [5] ("The question always is whether the agreed course of conduct, if carried out in accordance with the parties' intentions, would necessarily involve an offence.").

367. *Id.*, [4].

368. Unlike in the United States, in the United Kingdom, a conspirator can be held liable for an illegal agreement made with an undercover police officer. Yip Chiu-Cheung v. R [1994] 2 All E.R. 924.

or written words or other overt acts. If the defendant repents and withdraws immediately after the agreement has been concluded, they are still guilty of the offense."[369] Because there are generally no statutes of limitations in the United Kingdom, when and whether a conspirator withdraws is less relevant in Britain than in the United States.

An agreement may amount to a conspiracy even if it is conditional or contains some reservation (express or implied). Nonetheless, if there are material matters left outstanding, the arrangement may only amount to negotiations (and thus be insufficient to support a conspiracy charge).[370] This analysis therefore borrows from civil law principles regarding whether a contract has been formed.

In England, as in the United States, conspiracy cases often raise the issue of whether a single conspiracy existed or whether there were actually multiple separate conspiracies. On this point, British courts recognize the validity of "wheel conspiracies," which exist "where one or more defendants huddle at the centre (the hub) and have a number of arrangements with other defendants who appear at the end of spokes that emanate outwards from the hub."[371] In such a situation, conspiracy liability does not turn on whether each individual defendant knows the full extent of the enterprise of the identities of all those involved. Rather, if each defendant, "although ignorant of the details of the others concerned, knows that there are others and that the activity in which he takes part extends beyond his own dealings with the person or persons at the centre, then the evidence discloses one conspiracy."[372]

Despite this, for the defendants on each spoke to have entered into a single agreement, they must have shared a common purpose over and above a mere willingness to engage in similar criminal activity.[373] This concept was explained by the Court of Appeal in *Griffiths*:

> In law all must join in one agreement, each with the others, in order to constitute one conspiracy. They may join in at various times . . . and may not know all the other parties . . . or the full extent of the scheme to which he attaches himself. But what each must know is that there is coming into existence, or is in existence, a scheme which goes beyond the illegal act or acts which he agrees to do."[374]

---

369. Crown Prosecution Service, *Inchoate Offences, available at* https://www.cps.gov.uk/legal-guidance/inchoate-offences.

370. R v. Mills [1963] 1 Q.B. 522, 47 Cr. App. R. 49; R v. O'Brien [1974] 59 Cr. App. R. 222.

371. Paul Jarvis & Michael Bisgrove, *The Use and Abuse of Conspiracy* Crim. L. Rev. 265 (2014).

372. Archbold Criminal Pleading, Evidence and Practice 2014 para. 33–53 (62nd ed., London: Sweet & Maxwell 2013),; *see also* Meyrick [1930] 21 Cr. App. R. 94 at [22].

373. Jarvis & Bisgrove, *supra* note 371, at 265; *see also* R v. Shillam [2013] EWCA Crim 160 (concluding that each conspirator need not know the identity or even existence of other conspirators as long as they joined in a single common criminal purpose); R v. Johnson (Ryan) [2020] EWCA Crim 482 (in both the chain and wheel contexts, an accused must be proved to have shared a common purpose and design with his co-conspirators as opposed to engaging in merely similar or parallel purposes).

374. [1966] 1 Q.B. 589; *see also* Blackstone's Criminal Practice 2014 para.A5.46 (24th ed., Oxford: Oxford University Press 2013) ("Where a series of offences is committed by a group of persons over a long period of time, the prosecution may be tempted to proceed on the basis of a single conspiracy count, in preference to several substantive counts, but this tactic may be misconceived, because such offenses are more likely to be the product of a series of agreements and single conspiracy may be impossible to prove.").

There is no requirement that a person remain a conspirator for the entire duration of a conspiracy.

In addition to wheel and chain conspiracies, English courts recognize "umbrella conspiracies," an idea explored by the Court of Appeal in *Mehta v. R* [2012] EWCA Crim 284. The Mehta case involved seventeen fraudulent loan applications made by various conspirators to the same bank employee (who was in on the scheme). Each of the loans followed the same pattern: a person would open an account and take out a loan supported by three bogus pay slips from "Pemberton Properties," an offshore shell company controlled by Mehta, as proof of income. Because the loans complied with the bank's standard requirements, usually the applications were followed almost immediately by cash transfers of £20,000 or more. The money was then quickly taken out in cash and the loans eventually went into default. Mehta was convicted and sentenced to three years' imprisonment.

On appeal, he argued that his conviction and sentence improperly lumped together a number of distinct conspiracies—most of which were not examined in detail at trial—into a single overarching scheme. Specifically, Mehta's barrister submitted to the Court of Appeal that the case's disposition "was unsafe" because the judges' sentencing remarks revealed that Mehta had been improperly convicted of a conspiracy embracing all the loan applications where there was an insufficient "evidential foundation" for such a theory.[375]

Rejecting this contention, the court identified three relevant propositions in conspiracy case law: first, "a conspiracy requires that the parties to it have a common unlawful purpose or design"; second, "a common design means a shared design," which "is not the same as similar but separate designs"; and third,

> in criminal law (as in civil law) there may be an umbrella agreement pursuant to which the parties enter into further agreements which may include parties who are not parties to the umbrella agreement. So, A and B may enter into an umbrella agreement pursuant to which they enter into a further agreement between A, B and C, and a further agreement between A, B, and D, and so on. In that example, C and D will not be conspirators with each other.[376]

In light of this precedent, the court concluded that a conspiracy is not rendered unsafe simply because the evidence at trial proved the existence of a scheme that was narrower in scope and involved fewer people than the prosecution originally alleged in the indictment.[377]

b. Exemptions from Liability for Statutory Conspiracy

A person cannot be guilty of a Section 1 conspiracy if he or she is the intended victim of the scheme, nor can a person be guilty if he or she conspires only with a spouse, a juvenile, or the

375. *Mehta v. R* [2012] EWCA Crim 284 [28].

376. *Id.* [36].

377. *Id.* [57]. While Mehta's conviction was left to stand, the court remanded the case for resentencing because the sentence imposed by the Crown Court failed to "reflect the scope of the conspiracy which was properly proved." *Id.* [60]. In other words, the Crown Court took account of the as-charged instead of the as-proven conspiracy when determining sentence; an error which, in the Court of Appeal's view, warranted resentencing.

intended victim.[378] So, for instance, a would-be conspirator who intends to enter a criminal conspiracy and believes he is in fact doing so, but who in reality is an unwitting sucker being duped by his compatriots, will not be guilty of conspiracy under the CJA.

c. Co-Conspirator Statements

Like U.S. federal law, the law of England and Wales permits the acts and statements of one party to a common purpose to be used as evidence against any other party if (i) the act or statement was made in the course and furtherance of the common purpose, and (ii) other extrinsic evidence shows the existence of a conspiracy between the declarant and the party against whom the statement is being used.[379]

In other words, simply because a conspiracy has been charged does not mean that the statements of each alleged conspirator may automatically be used against all others unless these additional factors are present. Similarly, a confession after arrest of one conspirator in which they implicate others is only evidence against the declarant (because any common purpose that may have existed is deemed to terminate at the point of arrest). The section in chapter 6 on *Bruton* motions addresses how this issue is treated in the United States.

2. *Common Law Conspiracy to Defraud*

The Criminal Law Act 1977 abolished several common law conspiracy crimes except for common law conspiracy to defraud and common law conspiracy to engage in conduct that "tends to corrupt public morals or outrages public decency" (only the first of which is relevant here).[380] Common law conspiracy to defraud is an indictable-only offense and has only one element: an agreement between one or more persons to defraud, whether or not the intended fraud amounts to a substantive crime or even a tort.

While charging common law conspiracy is still an option for prosecutors, guidance issued by the attorney general specifies an expectation that the common law should be relied on far less frequency than the statutory offenses. In selecting the most appropriate charging theory, prosecutors are directed to consider first whether the available statutory charges "adequately reflect the gravity of the offence," and only if they do not, to proceed under the common law.[381] Common law conspiracy cases are thus becoming increasingly rare.

3. *Criminal Penalties*

Section 1 and common law conspiracies are both punishable by a prison term only if the substantive object of the conspiracy is also punishable with imprisonment—in all other cases, the punishment is limited to a fine only. Unlike with a conspiracy under 18 U.S.C. § 371, the maximum prison term for conspiracies in the United Kingdom is always the same as

378. CLA, s. 2.

379. R v. A Ltd, X, Y [2017] 1 Cr App R 1.

380. CLA, ss. 5(1)–(2).

381. Attorney General's Office, Use of the Common Law Offence of Conspiracy to Defraud (Nov. 29, 2012).

the relevant substantive offense.[382] Where a conspiracy is directed at multiple substantive offenses, the maximum prison term is fixed at whichever carries the longest one.

British courts generally do not recognize *Pinkerton* liability, an American concept which makes each conspirator equally liable for the foreseeable acts of all other conspirators (see the discussion earlier in the chapter). Rather, the Court of Appeal has instructed that when a conspiracy is alleged, "it will be important for a court to analyse carefully the position of an individual offender [when sentencing for conspiracy]. Those involved in a conspiracy can play different roles or be involved in different ways and the court must be astute to avoid a one-size-fits all approach to the [sentencing] guideline."[383]

V. MARKET MANIPULATION

A key function of financial markets is to allow participants to communicate information to one another about their subjective view of a particular instrument's price. An offer to buy a share of stock X for ten dollars, for example, is an implicit signal to the market that, in the prospective buyer's view, the stock's value is approximately that amount (at least insofar as buying it at that price relates to his or her overall position and trading strategy).

By centrally aggregating the pricing opinions of many individual traders and investors, financial markets allow buyers and sellers to reach a rough consensus on an asset's current market value (i.e., the approximate midpoint between supply and demand at any given moment). In this way, markets allow an asset's price to be "discovered" through the transmission of the prices at which various buyers and sellers are willing to transact which, in turn, reflect the independent analyses of those buyers and sellers about an asset's value.[384]

Within this framework, the term "market manipulation" broadly refers to any act that "obstructs the operation of the markets as indices of real value."[385] As characterized by the U.S. Supreme Court in the 1940s, "[M]arket manipulation in its various manifestations is implicitly an artificial stimulus applied to (or at times a brake on) market prices, a force which distorts those prices, a factor which prevents the determination of those prices by free competition alone."[386] Because of its potential for significant market disruption and financial loss to third-party investors, market manipulation is subject to serious criminal sanctions in both the United States and the United Kingdom.

---

382. CLA, s. 3.

383. Cooke [2017] EWCA Crim 1272.

384. Amgen Inc. v. Conn. Ret. Plans & Tr. Funds, 568 U.S. 455, 461 (2013) ("[W]ell developed markets are efficient processors of public information. In such markets, the 'market price of shares' will 'reflect all publicly available information.'"); Basic Inc. v. Levinson, 485 U.S. 224, 246 (1988) ("The idea of a free and open public market is built upon the theory that competing judgments of buyers and sellers as to the fair price of a security brings about a situation where the market price reflects as nearly as possible a just price.").

385. Basic, 485 U.S. at 246.

386. United States v. Socony-Vacuum Oil Co., 310 U.S. 150, 222–23 (1940); *see also* Gurary v. Winehouse, 190 F.3d 37, 45 (2d Cir. 1999).

A. Market Manipulation in the United States

The market manipulation regulations usually implicated in federal criminal prosecutions are contained in the 1934 Exchange Act and the 1936 Commodity Exchange Act.

1. *Exchange Act § 9(a) (15 U.S.C. § 78i(a))*

Like the Exchange Act Section 10(b) (discussed in section A.2), Section 9(a) was designed by Congress to "prevent rigging of the market and to permit operation of the natural law of supply and demand."[387] Yet unlike the more generalized proscriptions of Section 10(b), Section 9(a) describes certain specific market activities to which it applies:

- Creating "a false or misleading appearance of active trading in any security other than a government security, or a false or misleading appearance with respect to the market for any such security" through wash sales or matched orders.
- Engaging in a series of transactions that creates "actual or apparent active trading" or raises or depresses prices "for the purpose of inducing the purchase or sale" of a security by others.
- Knowingly spreading false information about a security to raise or depress its price and thereby induce the purchase or sale of a security by another (in a so-called "pump and dump" scheme).

a. "Matched Orders" and "Wash Sales"

Matched orders and wash sales are two of the most basic ways to manipulate the market and they are explicitly prohibited by the Exchange Act Section 9(a)(1). In these transactions, a manipulator acts as both the buyer and seller, to give the false appearance of arms-length trades without assuming any actual risk.[388] Alternatively, the manipulator can act in concert with other conspirators to give the false appearance that trades are disinterested transactions between independent actors.[389]

To establish a criminal Section 9(a)(1) violation, regulators must prove a wash sale or matched order of a security was made, with the purpose of creating a false or misleading appearance of active trading in that security.[390] Certain courts have held that when wash sales or matched orders are shown to have been done intentionally (i.e., not by mistake), manipulative intent can be inferred.[391]

387. United States v. Stein, 456 F.2d 844, 850 (2d Cir. 1972); *see also* Trane Co. v. O'Connor Secs., 561 F. Supp. 301, 304 (S.D.N.Y. 1983).

388. *See, e.g.*, SEC v. U.S. Envt'l Inc., 155 F.3d 107, 109 (2d Cir. 1988).

389. *See, e.g.*, United States v. Scop, 846 F.2d 135,137 (2d Cir.1988).

390. SEC v. Malenfant, 784 F. Supp. 141, 145 (S.D.N.Y. 1992).

391. *See, e.g.*, SEC v. Masri, 523 F. Supp. 2d 361, 365–75 (S.D.N.Y. 2007).

b. "Marking the Close" and "Painting the Tape"

The price of most publicly traded financial instruments fluctuate throughout each trading day. The two prices that are generally given most attention by investors are the opening price and the closing price. The closing price is particularly significant because it is the primary reference point for determining an asset's performance over a given period.

Because of this, the securities laws include specific prohibitions on activity—variously referred to as "marking the close," "banging the close," or "painting the tape"—meant to artificially affect prices or trading activity just before market close:

> [M]arking the close . . . is a form of market manipulation that involves attempting to influence the closing price of a publicly-traded share by executing the purchase or sale orders at or near the close of normal trading hours. Such activity can artificially inflate or depress the closing price for that security and can affect the price of the market on close orders, which are orders submitted to purchase shares at or near as possible to the closing price.[392]

The purpose of marking the close is to influence the trading decisions of other market participants by creating "actual or apparent active trading in such security."[393] Although Section 9(a)(2) refers only to "transactions," courts have held that this term includes not only completed purchases or sales but also unfilled bids and offers to purchase or sell securities.[394] This expansive interpretation theoretically allows prosecutors to target traders for manipulation even when they have not actually consummated a transaction. The criteria used to differentiate legal bids and offers and those that "paint the tape" is unclear, but U.S. regulators will often focus on situations involving rapidly placed orders near the top of the order book (or at staggered price levels) that serve no apparent legitimate purpose.[395]

c. Pump and Dump Schemes

Pump and dump schemes are a relatively unsophisticated form of market manipulation in which the schemers first artificially inflate the price of a stock (often by bribing stock promoters to sell it or spreading false information) and then dumping it when the stock becomes sufficiently high.[396] Such schemes can be prosecuted under Section 9(a)(3) or SEC Rule 10b-5 (17 C.F.R. § 240.10b-5).[397]

In *SEC v. Diversified Corp.*, 378 F.3d 1219, 1222–23 (Eleventh Cir. 2004), for example, a major holder of a thinly traded, over-the-counter stock sought to inflate the price of his

392. United States v. Georgiou, 742 F. Supp. 2d 613, 624 (E.D. Pa. 2010); *see also* Markowski v. SEC, 274 F.3d 525, 529 (D.C. Cir. 2001); Hunter v. FERC, 711 F.3d 155, 156 (D.C. Cir. 2013).

393. Masri, 523 F. Supp. 2d at 366.

394. *See, e.g.*, SEC v. Lek Sec. Corp., 276 F. Supp. 3d 49, 62 (S.D.N.Y. 2017); SEC v. Malenfant, 784 F. Supp. 141, 145 (S.D.N.Y. 1992).

395. SEC v. Fiore, 416 F. Supp. 3d 306, 316 (S.D.N.Y. 2019).

396. United States v. Downing, 297 F.3d 52, 55 (2d Cir. 2002).

397. United States v. Ware, 577 F.3d 442, 451 (2d Cir. 2009).

shares. In a twist on the typical pump and dump playbook, the stockholder conspired with the company's board to first authorize the issuance of millions of facially unrestricted shares. He then instructed that these shares be issued to several other individuals, who were in on the scheme. Next, he "pumped up" the share price by raising his bid price for shares to indicate that there was a demand for the stock at higher prices—"even when it was higher than the bid price announced by other market makers and there was no demand for the stock." According to the SEC, this practice "distorted the market" because he was essentially bidding against himself and was thereby sending a false signal to investors—"false in the sense that he was not raising his bid to meet a genuine demand for [the company's] shares." To further inflate the stock price, the defendant and his co-conspirators also issued press releases that falsely portrayed the stock as a good investment. After the stock had increased by more than 2,000 percent within a few months, the shares were dumped on the market.

This method of manipulation has often been employed at boiler room–type operations involving high-pressure sales calls placed to vulnerable victims. It can also be done electronically via "cyber" boiler rooms:

> The new "cyber" boiler rooms allow scam artists to conduct sophisticated market manipulations at almost no cost over the Internet from the comfort of their own homes. In four easy steps, a manipulator can consummate the entire fraud. The first step is to set up a site or home page where potential investors can find out about the issuer. In step two, the manipulator, using bulk e-mail or a spamming program, personally contacts potential investors regarding an investment opportunity. In step three, the manipulator begins a "buzz" about the issuer and its shares by posting false information to bulletin boards, newsgroups, and discussion forums. Finally, in step four, the manipulator strengthens the buzz by employing an Internet investment newsletter. It is that easy to hype the stock, and easier still to sell the stock back into the exchanges or over-the-counter markets at a profit and reap the financial rewards of having inflated the stock price.[398]

2. *Exchange Act § 10(b) (15 U.S.C. § 78j)*

Section 4.II.A above discussed how Section 10(b) is used to prosecute insider trading, but this is not the statute's only function. Since Section 10(b) broadly proscribes the use of any "manipulative or deceptive device or contrivance," conduct that violates the more specific prohibitions of Section 9 may also violate Section 10(b) if done with an "intent to deceive, manipulate, or defraud."[399] Section 10(b) therefore covers material misstatements and omissions as well as manipulative acts.

"Manipulation" when used in the context of securities markets is a "term of art" that refers generally to practices such as wash sales, matched orders, or rigged prices, that are intended to mislead investors by artificially affecting market activity.[400] In the majority of circuits, whether conduct artificially affects the market turns on whether the alleged

398. Nancy Toross, *Double-Click on This: Keeping Pace with On-Line Market Manipulation*, 32 Loy. L.A. L. Rev. 1399, 1420–21 (1999).

399. Ernst & Ernst v. Hochfelder, 425 U.S. 185, 193 n.12 (1976); 15 U.S.C. § 78ff.

400. Sante Fe Indus. v. Green, 430 U.S. 462, 476–77 (1977).

manipulator acted to deceive investors as to how other market participants have valued a security. In these circuits, the crucial question is whether the manipulator intended to mislead others into believing that "prices at which they purchase and sell securities are determined by the natural interplay of supply and demand, not rigged by manipulators."[401] The fundamental issue is therefore the manipulator's intent: whether the market is actually manipulated is largely irrelevant, as are the means by which the manipulation is designed to occur.[402] As the Supreme Court has made clear, "conduct itself can be deceptive," and so liability under Section 10(b) does not necessarily require "a specific [deceptive] oral or written statement."[403]

In identifying activity that is outside the "natural interplay of supply and demand," courts will generally consider whether a transaction was intended to send a false pricing signal to the market.[404] This idea is premised on the assumption that in an efficient market, "trading engineered to stimulate [or depress] demand can mislead investors into believing that the market has discovered some positive [or negative] news and seeks to exploit it; the duped investors then transact accordingly."[405] To clearly distinguish between legal and illegal market conduct, courts ask whether the manipulator intended to inject inaccurate information into the marketplace or create a false impression of supply and demand for the security with the intent to artificially inflate or depress the security's price.[406]

Market manipulation is illegal regardless of whether there is a fiduciary relationship between the alleged manipulator and his actual or potential counterparties, but a market manipulation claim cannot be based solely upon misrepresentations or omissions.[407] There must be some sort of actual market activity.[408]

a. Short Selling

By "short selling" a stock or other financial instrument, traders are able to make a bet that its price will decline. A short sale transaction typically takes place in four stages (figure 4.5): first, the short seller borrows the security from a third party and promises to return it at an

---

401. *See, e.g.*, Gurary v. Winehouse, 190 F.3d 37, 45 (2d Cir. 1999); Mobil Corp. v. Marathon Oil Co., 669 F.2d 366, 374 (6th Cir.1981) (stating that the Supreme Court has indicated that manipulation under § 10(b) refers to "means unrelated to the natural forces of supply and demand").

402. Koch v. SEC, 793 F.3d 147, 153–55 (D.C. Cir. 2015); SEC v. Lek Sec. Corp., 276 F. Supp. 3d 49, 60 (S.D.N.Y. 2017).

403. Stoneridge Inv. Partners, LLC v. Scientific-Atlanta, 128 S.Ct. 761, 769 (2008); *see also* United States v. Finnerty, 533 F.3d 143, 151 (2d Cir. 2008) (§ 10(b) requires proof of "manipulation or a false statement, breach of a duty to disclose, or deceptive communicative conduct").

404. ATSI Commn's, Inc. v. Shaar Fund, Ltd., 493 F.3d 87, 100 (2d Cir. 2007); Sullivan Long, Inc. v. Scattered Corp., 47 F.3d 857, 861 (7th Cir. 1995).

405. ATSI, 493 F.3d at 101. The efficient capital market hypothesis, as adopted by the Supreme Court, posits that "the market price of shares traded on well-developed markets reflects all publicly available information." Basic Inc. v. Levinson, 485 U.S. 224, 246 n.24 (1988).

406. GFL Advantage Fund, Ltd. v. Colkitt, 272 F.3d 189, 207 (3d Cir. 2001).

407. United States v. Russo, 74 F.3d 1383, 1391–92 (2d Cir.1996); United States v. Regan, 937 F.2d 823, 829 (2d Cir.1991); Lentell v. Merrill Lynch Co., 396 F.3d 161, 177 (2d Cir. 2005).

408. Santc Fc, 430 U.S. at 476.

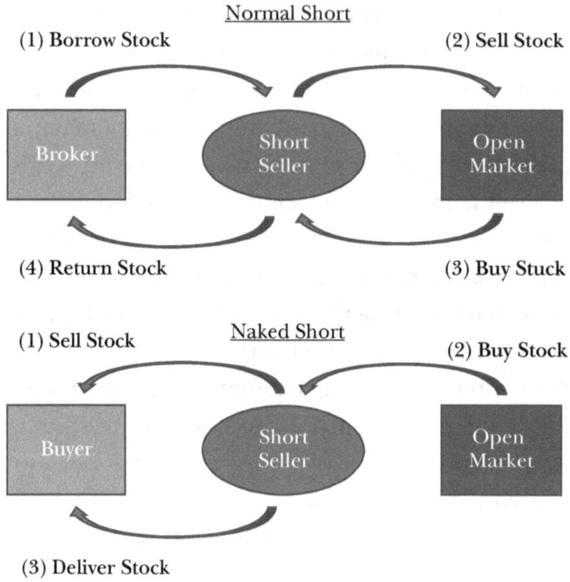

Figure 4.5 Short selling.

agreed-upon date; second, the short seller sells the borrowed security in the market; third, at or around the date the short seller needs to return the security to the lender, he or she buys it back from the market; and last, it is returned to the lender. In a successful short sale, the price at which the short seller buys the security back in step three is less than the price it was sold for in step two (with the short seller pocketing the difference).[409] So-called "naked" short selling occurs when a security is sold without the seller first borrowing it (in the hopes that it can be bought for less than the sale price before delivery must be made to the buyer). Naked short selling is therefore susceptible to misuse because it theoretically allows more shares to be sold short than are actually available, creating potentially artificial downward price pressure.

Short selling—naked and otherwise—is generally allowed by market regulators because, in theory, it increases market liquidity and enhances pricing efficiency by helping to move prices of overvalued securities toward their intrinsic values.[410] In the market manipulation context, taking a short position is conceptually no different than taking a long position.

Thus, short selling, even in high volumes, is not inherently manipulative. To be actionable as a manipulative act, short selling must be willfully combined with "something more" to create a false impression of how market participants value a security.[411] There is no exact definition of what the "something more" must be, but case law suggests that, to be manipulative, short selling must be combined with some sort of misinformation transmitted to the market.[412]

409. 17 C.F.R. § 240.3b-3.

410. GFL, 272 F.3d at 208; Sullivan Long, 47 F.3d at 861–62; In re Scattered Corp. Sec. Litig., 844 F. Supp. 416, 420 (N.D. Ill. 1994).

411. GFL, 272 F.3d at 209; ATSI, 493 F.3d at 99–105.

412. *See, e.g.*, GFL, 272 F.3d at 205; Cohen v. Stevanovic, 722 F. Supp. 2d 416, 424–25 (S.D.N.Y. 2010).

b. A Safe Harbor for "Open-Market" Transactions?

Manipulative conduct is generally characterized as either "traditional manipulation" or "open-market manipulation." Traditional manipulation involves one of the specifically prohibited trading practices listed in the Exchange Act Section 9(a)(1) or some type of explicitly fraudulent conduct under Section 10(b). In open-market manipulation, by contrast, the trading activity is not objectively fraudulent, but may nevertheless constitute illegal manipulation when taken in context.

In other words, open-market transactions are ones that are facially legitimate in all respects—"the transaction is real, . . . beneficial ownership is changing, and the volume of trading is reflective of market activity."[413] From the perspective of law enforcement, what makes such transactions subject to criminal penalties is the subjective intent of the person entering the trade. "The difficulty in such cases, where the activity in question is not expressly prohibited, is to 'distinguish between legitimate trading strategies intended to anticipate and respond to prevailing market forces and those designed to manipulate prices and deceive purchasers and sellers.'"[414] Indeed, some circuits have essentially ruled out open-market manipulation as a viable prosecution theory.

In *GFL Advantage*, for example, the Third Circuit was reluctant to find that otherwise legal conduct could violate securities laws based only on manipulative intent. In its view, the law required evidence of certain types of activity in addition to malintent—for example, unauthorized placements and parking of stock, secret sales without disclosing the real party in interest, guaranteeing profits to encourage short selling by others, fraudulently low appraisals, painting the tape, etc.[415] The court's rationale was guided "by the fact that it is unusual in American law to impose liability based solely on the intent of the actor. There may also be a concern that because of the ambiguity and difficult in establishing intent, prohibition of otherwise legal conduct based only on an actor's intent might chill and deter socially desirable conduct."[416]

In contrast, the D.C. Circuit accepted that open-market transactions can constitute market manipulation if made with criminal intent. In *Markowski v. SEC*, for example, "defendants argued that they could not be convicted of market manipulation based on otherwise legal transactions involving '(1) maintaining high bid prices . . . and (2) absorbing all unwanted securities into inventory' because their bids and trades were 'real.'"[417] Rejecting this argument, the D.C. Circuit found that the antimanipulation statutes reflected "Congress's determination that 'manipulation' can be illegal solely because of the actor's purpose."[418]

---

413. Masri, 523 F. Supp. 2d at 365.

414. *Id.* (quoting GFL Advantage, 272 F.3d at 205).

415. GFL Advantage, 272 F.3d at 205.

416. Masri, 523 F. Supp. 2d at 365.

417. *Id.*, 523 F. Supp. 2d at 366 (quoting Markowski, 274 F.3d 525, 527–28 (D.C. Cir. 2001)).

418. Markowski, 274 F.3d at 529; *cf.* Chris-Craft Indus., Inc. v. Piper Aircraft Corp., 480 F.2d 341, 383 (S.D.N.Y. 1973) ("The securities laws do not proscribe all buying or selling which tends to raise or lower the price of a security. . . . So long as the investor's motive in buying or selling a security is not to create an artificial demand for, or supply of, the security, illegal market manipulation is not

In New York's Second Circuit, the law on open-market manipulation is not yet settled.[419] But in *United States v. Mulheren*, the Second Circuit suggested in nonbinding dicta that a trader could hypothetically be convicted of open-market manipulation where the sole purpose behind the transaction at issue is to artificially affect the price of a security.[420] Lower courts in the Second Circuit have generally followed the reasoning in *Markowski* and rejected the approach in *GFL Advantage*. In *SEC v. Masri*, for example, SDNY District Judge Holwell stated: "[I]f an investor conducts an open-market transaction with the intent of artificially affecting the price of the security, and not for any legitimate economic reason, it can constitute market manipulation." In his view, "Allegations of other deceptive conduct or features of the transaction are only required to the extent that they render plausible allegations of manipulative intent."[421]

The extent to which open-market manipulation is a viable liability theory appears set to be tested in the DOJ's market manipulation case against Bill Hwang. Hwang was the founder of Archegos Capital Management, a multibillion-dollar hedge fund which suffered a spectacular collapse in March 2021 that rippled through the global financial system and caused huge losses for Archegos' counterparties at UBS, Morgan Stanley, and elsewhere.[422] During a pre-trial hearing in Manhattan federal court on June 1, 2022, Hwang's lawyers suggested they intended to base their defense around the holding in *Mulheren*. Unless a plea agreement is reached, whether or not Hwang can be held liable for what his lawyers claim was open-market trading will likely be a key part of his motion to dismiss the charges.[423]

c. Spoofing or Layering under Section10(b) and Rule 10b-5

While spoofing in the commodities markets was explicitly made illegal in the CEA following the enactment of the Dodd-Frank Act (see section V.A.4), the same conduct in other markets

---

established."). *See also* United States v. Radley, 632 F.3d 177 (5th Cir. 2011) (holding that traders could mislead other market participants about their trading intentions with respect to open market orders).

419. *Masri*, 523 F. Supp. 2d at 366.

420. 938 F.2d 364, 366–68 (2d Cir. 1991); *see also* Onel v. Top Ships, Inc., 19-cv-02693, at *3–5 (2d Cir. Apr. 2, 2020) ("In sum, then, a claim of market manipulation [under § 10(b)] requires a showing that the defendants took some action that was intended to mislead the investing public concerning the price of the relevant security, which in turn requires an allegation that the defendants' conduct included a misrepresentation or nondisclosure.")

421. 523 F. Supp. 2d at 366; *see also* In re Initial Public Offering Securities Litigation, 241 F. Supp. 2d 281, 391 (S.D.N.Y. 2003) (finding no authority supporting any additional requirements beyond bad intent in open market cases); SEC v. Kwak, 04-cv-1331, at *2–*4 (D. Conn. Feb. 12, 2008) (rejecting the idea that open-market purchases created a safe harbor for defendants or that Section 10(b) or 9(a) claims) could only be brought in traditional manipulation cases); United States v. Finnerty, 05-cr-00397, at *1 (S.D.N.Y. Oct. 2, 2006) (rejecting the argument that the term "deceptive" is limited to sham transactions and ruling that a "deceptive" act is anything which "tends to deceive" or "has the power to mislead").

422. United States v. Hwang, No. 22-cr-00240 (S.D.N.Y.).

423. Stewart Bishop, "Archegos Boss Assails Feds' Market Manipulation Theory," LAW360 (June 1, 2022).

is prohibited by Section 10(b) and Rule 10b-5.[424] In general, spoofing refers to placing and quickly cancelling orders that are never intended to be executed. Such orders can induce trading by other market participants (e.g., high-speed algorithmic traders) who seek to take advantage of changes to supply and demand in the order book. "Layering" is a type of spoofing that establishes a series of spoof orders placed at different price levels increasingly far from the prevailing best price.

In *SEC v. Lek Sec. Corp.*, for example, the defendants were civilly charged with Section 10(b) violations for engaging in a layering scheme involving the placing of allegedly "non-bona fide orders"—that is, ones they did not "intend to execute and had no legitimate economic reason"—with the "intent of injecting false information into the market about supply or demand" for certain stocks.[425] The alleged purpose of this scheme was to "trick and induce other market participants to execute against orders that [defendants] did intend to execute for the same stock on the opposite side of the market, which the complaint describes as its bona fide orders. Through this scheme, [defendants allegedly sought] more favorable prices on the executions of its bona fide orders than otherwise would have been available."[426]

Lek Securities and the other defendants moved to dismiss the SEC's complaint in its entirety on various grounds. In an opinion addressing the applicability of Section 10(b) to spoofing or layering, the Southern District of New York accepted the SEC's theory and denied the defendants' motion:

> [Market manipulation] broadly includes those practices "that are intended to mislead investors by artificially affecting market activity." In considering whether an act injects false pricing signals into the market, courts recognize that one of the fundamental goals of the federal securities laws is . . . "to prevent practices that impair the function of stock markets in enabling people to buy and sell securities at prices that reflect undistorted (though not necessarily accurate) estimates of the underlying economic value of the securities traded. . . . Market manipulation can be accomplished through otherwise legal means. As the Second Circuit has noted, "in some cases scienter is the only factor that distinguishes legitimate trading from improper manipulation."[427]

Several other courts have also concluded that this type of conduct can violate Section 10(b) and Rule 10b-5.[428] Following the denial of their motion to dismiss, Sam Lek and his company settled the SEC's claims in exchange for a $1.42 million penalty, disgorgement

---

424. *See* John Sanders & Andrew Verstein, *Legal Confusion as to Spoofing*, HUFF. POST, May 12, 2015 (noting that by maintaining separate manipulation laws for securities and commodities futures, U.S. law "prohibits spoofing a half a dozen times, each time with different elements, and only one time by name.").

425. 276 F. Supp. 3d 49, 54 (S.D.N.Y. 2017).

426. *Id.*

427. *Id.* at 59–60 (citing ATSI, 493 F.3d at 102).

428. *See, e.g.*, CP Stone Fort Holdings, LLC v. Does, 2017 WL 1093166, at *4 (N.D. Ill. Mar. 22, 2017); United States v. Milrud, 15-cr-00455 (D.N.J. Sept. 10, 2015); *see also* In the Matter of Terrance Yoshikawa, 87 S.E.C. Docket 2580, 2006 WL 1113518, at *7 n.36 (Apr. 26, 2006) (describing the SEC's history since 1998 of finding spoofing/layering to violate § 10(b) and Rule 10b-5).

of $525,892, and a compliance monitor for three years. The remaining defendants were found liable after trial in November 2019. In March 2020, a final judgment was issued that imposed a nearly $20 million combined penalty (that is currently being appealed).[429]

3. The Commodity Exchange Act's Antispoofing Provision

In addition to combatting manipulation and fraud on stock exchanges, during the Great Depression the U.S. government was concerned with perceived wrongdoing in the commodities markets.[430] To address this issue, Congress passed the Commodity Exchange Act (CEA) in 1936. According to the Second Circuit, the law is a "remedial statute that serves the crucial purpose of protecting the innocent individual investor—who may know little about the intricacies and complexities of the commodities market—from being misled or deceived."[431] In 1974, the CEA was substantially amended by the Commodity Futures Trading Commission Act which, among other things, created the CFTC to assume responsibility for the CEA's regulation and enforcement through civil and administrative actions.[432] The DOJ can criminally prosecute knowing and willful violations of the CEA.

Following the 2008/2009 financial crisis, Congress amended the CEA to add prohibitions on "disruptive practices" in a new section, 7 U.S.C. § 6c(a)(5), which makes it "unlawful for any person to engage in any trading, practice, or conduct on or subject to the rules of a registered entity that—(A) violates bids or offers; (B) demonstrates intentional or reckless disregard for the orderly execution of transactions during the closing period; (C) is, is of the character of, or is commonly known to the trade as, 'spoofing' (bidding or offering with the intent to cancel the bid or offer before execution)."

Of these, the antispoofing provision (ASP) has generated by far the most criminal enforcement activity to date. Yet from its creation, the ASP has been attacked as vague and overbroad by lawyers, academics, and financial industry professionals. Critics have noted in particular that, unlike most legislation, the ASP has no drafting or legislative history—it "simply materialized with no public discussion, [and so] there is literally nothing in the legislative record to illuminate the provision's meaning or reach."[433] Market professionals were also dismayed at the inclusion of the word "spoofing" in the statute since "spoofing" had no accepted meaning in the futures and derivatives markets. During a December 2010 roundtable discussion hosted by the CFTC, for example, the agency's former general counsel noted, "It is hard to imagine how [spoofing] even applies to the futures world or how it should be

---

429. SEC v. Lek Sec. Corp., et al., 17-cv-01789 (S.D.N.Y. 2017).

430. *See generally* Jerry W. Markham, *Law Enforcement and the History of Financial Market Manipulation* 76–87 (Routledge 2015). A commodity futures contract is an agreement to buy or sell a particular commodity at a future date. The price and the amount of the commodity are fixed at the time of the agreement, and in general the contract specifies that it may be fulfilled by either physical delivery of the commodity or cash settlement.

431. Loginovskaya v. Batratchenko, 764 F.3d 266, 270 (2d Cir. 2014).

432. Merrill Lynch, Pierce, Fenner Smith v. Curran, 456 U.S. 353, 388 (1982).

433. Motion to Dismiss, United States v. Coscia, 14-cr-00551, Dkt. #28 (N.D. Ill. Dec. 15, 2014), at 5.

applied."[434] The CEO of the CME Group—one of the world's largest exchange operators—similarly stated that the "statute's definition of 'spoofing' . . . is too broad and does not differentiate legitimate market conduct from manipulative conduct that should be prohibited."[435]

Following these criticisms, the CFTC issued interpretative guidance in May 2013, "to provide market participants and the public with guidance on the manner in which it intends to apply the statutory prohibitions set forth in section 4c(a)(5)." With respect to the ASP, the guidance stated that spoofing

> includes, but is not limited to: (i) submitting or cancelling bids or offers to overload the quotation system of a registered entity; (ii) submitting or cancelling bids or offers to delay another person's execution of trades; (iii) submitting or cancelling multiple bids or offers to create an appearance of false market depth; and (iv) submitting or cancelling bids or offers with intent to create artificial price movements upwards or downwards.[436]

It further stated that the CFTC "does not interpret reckless trading, practices, or conduct as constituting a 'spoofing' violation," nor does it interpret the ASP as "reaching accidental or negligent trading, practices, or conduct." "When distinguishing between legitimate trading (such as trading involving partial executions) and 'spoofing,'" the CFTC explained that it would "evaluate the market context, the person's pattern of trading activity (including fill characteristics), and other relevant facts and circumstances."[437]

Even with this guidance, the ASP continues to be attacked as inherently vague. So far, courts have been largely unreceptive to these arguments.[438]

a. What Is Spoofing?

In the view of prosecutors, spoofing generally consists of placing "trick" orders—orders intended to be cancelled—on one side of the market to deceptively induce other market participants into filling "real" orders lying in wait on the other side. In a typical spoofing scheme, a trader will place one or more relatively small, genuine orders on the opposite side of the market from larger, non–bona fide orders to take advantage of how other traders react to material changes in supply and demand.

To visualize how this looks in the order book, figure 4.6 shows a reproduction of an exhibit introduced by the DOJ in the criminal trial of Michael Coscia, a Chicago-based trader who allegedly designed a high-speed trading algorithm to rapidly place and cancel spoof orders.

The DOJ used this data as circumstantial evidence that the buy orders were "trick" orders that Coscia's trading algorithm entered in order to push the market towards his "real"

---

434. *Id.* at 8.

435. *Id.* at 9; *see also* Motion to Dismiss, CFTC v. Banoczay, et al., 20-cv-05777, Dkt. #22 (Mar. 1, 2021 N.D. Ill.), at 26–30 (arguing that the ASP is unconstitutionally vague).

436. CFTC, *Antidisruptive Practices Authority,* 78 Fed. Reg. 31890–96 (May 28, 2013).

437. *Id.*

438. *See, e.g.,* Joshua Ray, *CFTC Continues to Target Small Overseas "Spoofers,"* TRADERS MAGAZINE (October 12, 2020).

"Trick" Orders

"Real" Orders

Time	Transaction Type	Buy	Sell	Quantity	Price
8:33:19.614	Entered	Buy		18	15427
8:33:19.629	Entered		Sell	176	15430
8:33:19.737	Entered		Sell	145	15429
8:33:19.855	Entered		Sell	74	15428
8:33:19.923	Filled	Buy		10	15427
8:33:19.923	Filled	Buy		8	15427
8:33:19.936	Cancelled		Sell	74	15428
8:33:19.942	Cancelled		Sell	145	15429
8:33:19.945	Cancelled		Sell	176	15430
8:33:19.952	Entered		Sell	18	15428
8:33:19.991	Entered	Buy		176	15424
8:33:20.093	Entered	Buy		183	15425
8:33:20.202	Entered	Buy		171	15426
8:33:20.312	Entered	Buy		165	15427
8:33:20.316	Filled		Sell	1	15428
8:33:20.316	Filled		Sell	3	15428
8:33:20.317	Filled		Sell	1	15428
8:33:20.320	Filled		Sell	5	15428
8:33:20.320	Filled		Sell	5	15428
8:33:20.321	Filled		Sell	3	15428
8:33:20.345	Cancelled	Buy		165	15427
8:33:20.354	Cancelled	Buy		171	15426
8:33:20.355	Cancelled	Buy		183	15425
8:33:20.359	Cancelled	Buy		176	15424

Figure 4.6 Transactions in an alleged spoofing scheme.

sell orders. To show that the buy orders were not intended to trade, DOJ pointed to the fact that they were immediately cancelled after the sell orders were filled (after being left open for just a fraction of a second).

Coscia was eventually convicted and sentenced to three years in prison. In upholding his conviction and sentence on appeal, the Seventh Circuit described the conduct prohibited by the ASP:

> In practice, spoofing, like legitimate high-frequency trading, utilizes extremely fast trading strategies. It differs from legitimate trading, however, in that it can be employed to *artificially move* the market price of a stock or commodity up and down, instead of taking advantage of natural market events . . . This artificial movement is accomplished in a number of ways, although it is most simply realized by placing large and small orders on opposite sides of the market. The small order is placed at a desired price, which is either above or below the current market price, depending on whether the trader wants to buy or sell. If the trader wants to buy, the price on the small batch will be lower than the market price; if the trader wants to sell, the price on the small batch will be higher. Large orders are then placed on the opposite side of the market at prices designed to shift the market toward the price at which the small order was listed.[439]

While the trading sequence described by the Seventh Circuit has come to typify the conduct that law enforcement generally focuses on in spoofing actions, it made clear that all the

439. United States v. Coscia, 866 F.3d 782, 787 (7th Cir. 2017).

ASP requires the government to prove in such cases is an intent to cancel an order at the time it is placed.[440]

b. Evolving Theories of Spoofing Liability

The *Coscia* case was the first criminal prosecution alleging violations of the ASP. Perhaps to hedge against constitutional vagueness challenges to the then-untested law, the DOJ also charged him with commodities fraud under 18 U.S.C. § 1348(1). Section 1348(1) makes it a crime to "defraud any person in connection with any commodity for future delivery." The elements of this crime are (i) fraudulent intent, (ii) a scheme or artifice to defraud, and (iii) a nexus with a security. "False representations or material omissions are not required" for conviction under this provision.[441]

In his appeal, Coscia argued that because all of "his orders were fully executable and subject to legitimate market risk"—that is, open-market transactions—they could not, as a matter of law, be fraudulent or otherwise violate Section 1348(1). But the Seventh Circuit disagreed, finding that his argument "confused illusory orders with an illusion of market movement." The court noted that the evidence supported the conclusion that Coscia "designed a scheme to pump and deflate the market through the placement of large orders. His scheme was deceitful because, at the time he placed the large orders, he intended to cancel the large orders . . . and thus sought to manipulate the market for his own financial gain."[442]

Following Coscia's conviction and the Seventh Circuit's favorable interpretation of the ASP and Section 1348(1), the DOJ and CFTC have brought dozens of additional spoofing cases in the last five years (most often in the Northern District of Illinois, a court bound by decisions of the Seventh Circuit Court of Appeals). While the fundamental conduct at issue in these cases is largely the same as that in *Coscia*, prosecutors' theories of liability have evolved beyond the ASP and Section 1348(1).[443]

In *United States v. Vorley*, for example, the DOJ did not allege violations of the ASP at all (even though spoofing was clearly prosecutors' underlying theory). Instead, prosecutors opted to charge the defendants, both former precious metals traders, with wire fraud in violation of 18 U.S.C. § 1343. In a motion to dismiss the indictment, the defendants argued that the wire fraud statute requires allegations of an affirmative "false statement" and that the case against them failed to do so, since all that was alleged was that they put certain orders into the order book. The district court judge disagreed, however:

> The wire fraud statute proscribes not only false statements and affirmative representations but also "the omission or concealment of material information, even absent an affirmative duty to disclose, if the omission was intended to induce a false belief and action to the advantage

---

440. *Id.* at 795 ("[A] conviction for spoofing requires that the prosecution prove beyond a reasonable doubt that Mr. Coscia knowingly entered bids or offers with the present intent to cancel the bid or offer prior to execution.").

441. United States v. Mahaffy, 693 F.3d 113, 125 (2d Cir. 2012).

442. Coscia, 866 F.3d at 797.

443. *See* Joshua Ray, "Parsing the DOJ's Flawed Spoofing Theory," Law360 (Sept. 10, 2020).

of the scheme and the disadvantage of the victim." And that is precisely what the indictment alleges here.[444]

In *United States v. Smith*, the DOJ used an even more aggressive charging theory. There, prosecutors alleged that four former JP Morgan employees violated the ASP in addition to four alternate substantive offenses: attempted price manipulation, bank fraud (18 U.S.C. § 1344(1), wire fraud affecting a financial institution (18 U.S.C. § 1343), and commodities fraud (18 U.S.C. § 1348(1)). In addition, prosecutors alleged that the defendants had participated in a racketeering conspiracy in violation of the RICO statute (18 U.S.C. §§ 1961–1968),[445] a law drafted in the 1970s to specifically target organized crime leaders. The trial in this case is scheduled to commence before Judge Chang of the Southern District of New York in June 2022.

The different theories used to target spoofing and the dispositions of all DOJ's criminal spoofing cases brought as of January 2022 are summarized in table 4.4.

Table 4.4 Spoofing Cases Brought by the Department of Justice

Defendant	Alleged Statute Violated	Disposition
Michael Coscia 14-cr-00551 (N.D. Ill.)	Spoofing (7 U.S.C. § 6c(a)(5)(C)) Commodities Fraud (18 U.S.C. § 1348)	Guilty after trial Sentence: 36 months
Navinder Sarao 15-cr-00075 (N.D. Ill.)	Spoofing (7 U.S.C. § 6c(a)(5)(C)) Wire Fraud (18 U.S.C. § 1343) Commodities Fraud (18 U.S.C. § 1348)	Guilty plea with cooperation Sentence: 12 months home confinement
David Liew 17-cr-00001 (N.D. Ill.)	Conspiracy (18 U.S.C. § 371)	Guilty plea with cooperation Sentence: 1 day
Andre Flotron 17-cr-00220 (D. Conn.)	Conspiracy (18 U.S.C. § 1349) Commodities Fraud (18 U.S.C. § 1348) Spoofing (7 U.S.C. § 6c(a)(5)(C)) Manipulation (7 U.S.C. § 13(a)(2)) Aiding and Abetting (18 U.S.C. § 2)[a]	Not guilty after trial
Jiongsheng Zhao 18-cr-00024 (N.D. Ill.)	Spoofing (7 U.S.C. § 6c(a)(5)(C)) Manipulation (7 U.S.C. § 13(a)(2))	Guilty plea with cooperation Sentence: time served
John Edmonds 18-cr-00239 (D. Conn.)	Conspiracy (18 U.S.C. § 371) Commodities Fraud (18 U.S.C. § 1348)	Guilty plea with cooperation Sentence: pending
Kamaldeep Gandhi 18-cr-00609 (S.D. Tex.)	Conspiracy (18 U.S.C. § 371)	Guilty plea with cooperation Sentence: pending
Krishna Mohan 18-cr-00610 (S.D. Tex.)	Conspiracy (18 U.S.C. § 371)	Guilty plea with cooperation Sentence: pending

444. United States v. Vorley, 18-cr-00035 (N.D. Ill. Oct. 21, 2019), Dkt. #119 at 6–7.

445. United States v. Smith, 19-cr-00669 (N.D. Ill.).

Defendant	Alleged Statute Violated	Disposition
Edward Bases 18-cr-00048 (N.D. Ill.)	Wire Fraud (18 U.S.C. § 1343) Commodities Fraud (18 U.S.C. § 1348) Conspiracy (18 U.S.C. § 1349)	Guilty after trial Sentence: pending
John Pacilio 18-cr-00048 (N.D. Ill.)	Wire Fraud (18 U.S.C. § 1343) Commodities Fraud (18 U.S.C. § 1348) Conspiracy (18 U.S.C. § 1349) Spoofing (7 U.S.C. § 6c(a)(5)(C)) Manipulation (7 U.S.C. § 13(a)(2))	Guilty after trial Sentence: pending
Jitesh Thakkar 18-cr-00036 (N.D. Ill.)	Spoofing (7 U.S.C. § 6c(a)(5)(C)) Manipulation (7 U.S.C. § 13(a)(2)) Conspiracy (18 U.S.C. § 371) Aiding and Abetting (18 U.S.C. § 2)	Charges dismissed after mistrial
James Vorley 18-cr-00035 (N.D. Ill.)	Wire Fraud (18 U.S.C. § 1343) Conspiracy (18 U.S.C. § 1349)	Guilty after trial (appeal pending) Sentence: 366 days
Cedric Chanu 18-cr-00035 (N.D. Ill.)	Wire Fraud (18 U.S.C. § 1343) Conspiracy (18 U.S.C. § 1349)	Guilty after trial (appeal pending) Sentence: 366 days
Corey Flaum 19-cr-00338 (E.D.N.Y.)	Manipulation (7 U.S.C. § 13(a)(2))	Guilty plea with cooperation Sentence: pending
Christian Trunz 19-cr-00375 (E.D.N.Y.)	Manipulation (7 U.S.C. § 13(a)(2))	Guilty plea with cooperation Sentence: pending
Xiasong Wang 19-mj-06485 (D. Mass.)	Conspiracy (18 U.S.C. § 371)	Pending (no trial date set)
Jiali Wang 19-mj-06485 (D. Mass.)	Conspiracy (18 U.S.C. § 371)	Pending (no trial date set)
Gregg Smith 19-cr-00669 (N.D. Ill.)	Spoofing (7 U.S.C. § 6c(a)(5)(C)) Manipulation (7 U.S.C. § 13(a)(2)) Conspiracy (18 U.S.C. § 371) Wire Fraud (18 U.S.C. § 1343) Commodities Fraud (18 U.S.C. § 1348) Racketeering Conspiracy (18 U.S.C. § 1962(d))	Trial scheduled for 2022
Michael Nowak 19-cr-00669 (N.D. Ill.)	Spoofing (7 U.S.C. § 6c(a)(5)(C)) Manipulation (7 U.S.C. § 13(a)(2)) Conspiracy (18 U.S.C. § 371) Wire Fraud (18 U.S.C. § 1343) Commodities Fraud (18 U.S.C. § 1348) Racketeering Conspiracy (18 U.S.C. § 1962(d))	Trial scheduled for 2022

(*Continued*)

Defendant	Alleged Statute Violated	Disposition
Christopher Jordan 19-cr-00669 (N.D. Ill.)	Spoofing (7 U.S.C. § 6c(a)(5)(C)) Manipulation (7 U.S.C. § 13(a)(2)) Conspiracy (18 U.S.C. § 371) Wire Fraud (18 U.S.C. § 1343) Commodities Fraud (18 U.S.C. § 1348) Racketeering Conspiracy (18 U.S.C. § 1962(d))	Trial scheduled for 2022
Jeffrey Ruffo 19-cr-00669 (N.D. Ill.)	Racketeering Conspiracy (18 U.S.C. § 1962(d))	Trial scheduled for 2022

[a] All counts except for the conspiracy count against Flotron were dismissed on defendant's pretrial motion.

4. *Extraterritorial Reach*

Because none of the antimanipulation statutes discussed above explicitly apply to conduct occurring overseas, under the default position explained in *Morrison*, the extent of their extraterritorial reach turns on the location of their "focus"—that is, the conduct that they are primarily designed to prohibit.[446] The DOJ has brought several manipulation cases against individuals who traded on U.S. exchanges exclusively from overseas.

a. The Exchange Act

In *Morrison*, the Supreme Court concluded that the Exchange Act § 10(b) and SEC Rule 10b-5 only apply to two types of transactions: (i) "transactions in securities listed on domestic exchanges," and (ii) "domestic transactions in other securities."[447] Days after this ruling, however, Congress inserted a provision, Section 929P(b) (15 U.S.C. § 78aa(b)), into the Dodd-Frank Act that appeared to nullify *Morrison* in the context of SEC and DOJ actions under the Exchange Act. Section 929P(b) states:

> The district courts of the United States . . . shall have jurisdiction of an action or proceeding brought or instituted by the [SEC or DOJ] alleging a violation of the antifraud provisions of [the Exchange Act] involving—
>
> (1) Conduct within the United States that constitutes significant steps in furtherance of the violation, even if the securities transaction occurs outside the United States and involves only foreign investors; or
>
> (2) Conduct occurring outside the United States that has a foreseeable substantial effect within the United States.

While the intended effect of Section 929P(b) seems clear, it has generated confusion in the lower courts because it addresses extraterritoriality as a jurisdictional issue, whereas *Morrison* clearly held it be a merits question.[448] The importance of the distinction is that

446. WesternGeco LLC, 138 S. Ct. at 2137 (2018) (quoting Morrison, 561 U.S. at 267)).

447. Morrison, 561 U.S. at 267.

448. *Id.* at 254.

jurisdictional issues concern whether a court can hear a case at all whereas a merits question turns on a court's assessment of the evidence and allegations; the former is susceptible to a pre-trial attack through a motion to dismiss while the latter is much less so.

The uncertainty over this provision was summed up by the Northern District of Illinois: "The plain language of Section 929P(b) and its placement in the jurisdictional section of the Exchange Act indicate that it may be jurisdictional. It is unclear, however, whether the Court's analysis should stop there because it is possible that this interpretation would create superfluity or contradict the legislative intent."[449] In 2019, the Tenth Circuit became the first court of appeals to hold that Section 929P(b) did in fact abrogate *Morrison* in part, and that the Exchange Act's substantive antifraud provisions should apply outside the United States as long as the conduct had either a foreseeable effect in the United States or on U.S. citizens, or occurred in the United States.[450]

Outside of the Tenth Circuit, courts continue to apply the test in *Morrison* in both civil and criminal fraud cases.[451] For example, in 2014, the Second Circuit considered whether this test's first prong allowed suits involving foreign investors, foreign defendants, and shares purchased on a foreign exchange.[452] Even though the shares at issue were cross-listed on the New York Stock Exchange, the court held that *Morrison* precluded application of U.S. law unless the shares involved in the fraud were actually purchased on a U.S. exchange. As to the second prong, another Second Circuit decision concluded a transaction will be considered "domestic" if "irrevocable liability is incurred or title passes within the United States."[453] "Irrevocable liability" attaches "when the parties to the transaction are committed to one another," or, "in the classic contractual sense, there was a meeting of the minds of the parties." How this formula applies to complex cross-border transactions involving quasi-domestic instruments like American depositary receipts remains an open question.[454]

b. The Commodity Exchange Act

The *Morrison* decision and Section 929P(b) apply only to the federal securities laws contained in the 1933 Securities Act and 1934 Exchange Act. The extraterritorial reach of enforcement actions brought under the CEA continue to be assessed under the pre-*Morrison* "conduct and effects" test, which considers (i) "whether the wrongful conduct had a substantial effect in the [United States] or upon U.S. citizens," and (ii) "whether the wrongful conduct occurred in the [United States]."[455] Because of this, the CFTC asserts it has the power to target overseas

---

449. SEC v. Chicago Convention Ctr. LLC, 961 F. Supp. 2d 905, 911 (N.D. Ill. 2013).

450. SEC v. Scoville, 913 F.3d 1204, 1218 (10th Cir. 2019); *see also* SEC v. Traffic Monsoon, LLC, 245 F. Supp. 3d 1275 (D. Utah 2017) (also concluding that Section 929P(b) overruled *Morrison*).

451. United States v. Vilar, 729 F.3d 62, 72 (2d Cir. 2013) (finding *Morrison* applies equally to the civil and criminal contexts).

452. City of Potiac Policemen's & Firemen's Ret. Sys. v. UBS AG, 752, F.3d 173, 179–90 (2d Cir. 2014).

453. Absolute Activist Value Master Fund Ltd. v. Ficeto, 677 F.3d 60, 67 (2d Cir. 2012).

454. *Compare* Parkcentral Global Hut Ltd. v. Porsche Auto Holdings SE, 763 F.3d 198 (2d Cir. 2014) *with* Stoyas v. Toshiba Corp., 763 F.3d 933 (9th Cir. 2018).

455. SEC v. Berger, 322 F.3d 187, 192–93 (2d Cir. 2003).

manipulation so long as it has some effect on U.S. commodities markets and prices (even if the defendant did not actually transact through a U.S. exchange).[456]

The Second Circuit, however, has pushed back on this expansive interpretation. In its 2019 *Prime International Trading* decision, the court concluded that the CEA's antifraud and antimanipulation provisions have no extraterritorial application.[457] The plaintiffs in that case were traders of crude oil futures and derivatives contracts on the New York Mercantile Exchange (NYMEX) who sued companies that produce crude oil in the North Sea. The plaintiffs claimed that the defendants had traded physical crude in Europe to manipulate related benchmark and futures prices in the United States. In affirming the district court's dismissal of the complaint, the Second Circuit concluded that the CEA requires not only domestic transactions, "but also domestic—not extraterritorial—*conduct* by defendants that is violative of a substantive provision of the CEA."[458]

While *Prime Int'l Trading* involved private plaintiffs, it is likely that, at least in the Second Circuit, the same analysis would be applied to DOJ and CFTC enforcement actions. This could make it more difficult for regulators to pursue CEA violations involving manipulative conduct occurring entirely overseas or predominantly affecting futures and derivatives traded abroad.

5. *Criminal Penalties*

Individuals found guilty of a criminal market manipulation offense under the Exchange Act are subject to a maximum of twenty years in prison and fines of up to $5 million.[459] A knowing violation of the CEA's antimanipulation provisions is a felony punishable by up to ten years in prison and a fine of not more than $1,000,000.[460]

B. Market Manipulation in the United Kingdom

Market manipulation under the law of England and Wales is comprised of three elements: "financial dealings that provide fictitious indicators to obtain the price of a monetary tool at a synthetic level," "a series of contracts or orders to establish fabricated devices or products," and "sharing and dispersal of information that provides false or misleading signals."[461]

The U.K.'s antimanipulation regulations are derived from the European Union's Market Abuse Regulation (MAR) No. 596/2014, which came into effect in 2016 (while the United Kingdom was still an E.U. member). The MAR was incorporated into U.K. domestic law through amendments made to the Financial Services and Markets Act 2000 (FSMA) and the

456. Br. For Amicus Curiae CFTC, Prime Int'l Trading, 17-2233 (2d Cir.), Dkt. # 148 at 22–23.

457. Prime Int'l Trading, Ltd. v. BP p.l.c., 937 F.3d 94 (2d Cir. 2019).

458. *Id.* at 107.

459. 15 U.S.S. § 78ff(a).

460. 7 U.S.C. § 13(a).

461. Ester Herlin-Karnell & Nicholas Ryder, Market Manipulation and Insider Trading 2 (Hart Publishing 2019).

Financial Services Act 2012 (FSA), and was therefore unaffected by Brexit in December 2020. Market manipulation can also be targeted under the Fraud Act 2006.

1. The Market Abuse Regulation

The MAR broadly applies to all financial instruments traded on regulated markets. It also applies to financial derivative instruments not traded on a formal trading facility whose "price or value depends on or has an effect on the price or value of a financial instrument [traded on a facility], including, but not limited to, credit default swaps and contracts for difference."[462]

The MAR Article 15 makes it an offense to engage or attempt to engage in prohibited market manipulation activities. Article 12 defines market manipulation to include:

- "Entering into a transaction which gives, or is likely to give, false or misleading signals as to the supply of, demand for, or price of, a financial instrument, a related spot commodity contract or an auctions product based on emission allowance;"
- "Entering into a transaction placing an order to trade or any other activity or behaviour which affects or is likely to affect the price of one or several financial instruments, a related spot commodity contract or an auctioned product based on emission allowances, which employs a fictitious device or any other form of deception or contrivance;"
- "Transmitting false or misleading information or providing false or misleading inputs in relation to a benchmark where the person who made the transmission or provided the input knew or ought to have known that it was false or misleading, or any other behaviour which manipulates the calculation of a benchmark;"
- "The placing of orders to a trading venue, including any cancellation or modification thereof, by any available means of trading, including by electronic means, such as algorithmic and high-frequency trading strategies, and which has [a manipulative effect], by:
    - Disrupting or delaying the functioning of the trading system of the trading venue or being likely to do so;
    - Making it more difficult for other persons to identify genuine orders on the trading system of the trading venue or being likely to do so, including by entering orders which result in the overloading or destabilization of the order book; or
    - Creating or being likely to create a false or misleading signal about the supply of, or demand for, or price of, a financial instrument, in particular by entering orders to initiate or exacerbate a trend."

---

462. Financial Conduct Authority, Market Abuse Regulation (Updated April 25, 2022), *available at* https://www.fca.org.uk/markets/market-abuse/regulation. A "contract for difference" (CFD) is "an agreement between a customer and a financial institution where the difference in the value of a specified asset at the beginning and end of the contract is exchanged." CFDs are roughly equivalent to a futures contract in the United States.

In keeping with the FSMA Section 123, the FCA may impose a civil penalty on any individual found to have engaged in any of the conduct specified in the MAR Article 15. Because the United Kingdom declined to adopt a follow-on E.U. regulation specifying criminal penalties for market manipulation, MAR violations are currently subject to civil penalties only in Britain.

Unlike its equivalent in U.S. law, the MAR gives market participants certain affirmative defenses to market manipulation charges. Under Article 13, a person or entity will not be liable for market manipulation if they can establish that the "transaction, order or behaviour" at issue was "carried out for legitimate reasons, and conform[s] with an accepted market practice."

2. *The Financial Services Act 2012*

Whereas the FSMA includes only civil penalties for market manipulation, the Financial Services Act 2012 (FSA) allows such cases to be charged criminally.[463] The FSA has two provisions pertaining to market manipulation, Sections 89 and 90. Section 89 ("Making misleading statements") makes it "an offence for a person to make a statement or to conceal facts with the intention of inducing another person either to enter into or to refrain from entering into a relevant agreement or to exercise, or refrain from exercising, any rights conferred by a relevant instrument." The offense is committed if a person (i) knowingly makes a false or misleading statement, (ii) is reckless as to whether his conduct may fraudulently induce another to transact, or (iii) dishonestly conceals material facts. Section 90 ("Misleading impressions") makes it "an offence for a person to act or engage in a course of conduct which creates a false or misleading impression as to the market in, or the price or value of, any relevant instruments." Section 90 is violated if a person intends to make the false impression and intends either to (i) induce another person to acquire, dispose of, or subscribe for the investments, or (ii) to make a gain for himself or cause loss to another or to be aware that it is likely to have that result.

3. *Financial Conduct Authority Handbook Guidance*

The FCA has published a handbook providing guidance on the types of behavior likely to be flagged as illegally manipulative.[464] In comparison with similar guidance published by the CFTC, the FCA's is much more comprehensive and specific.

The handbook notes, for example, that the following conduct involves "false or misleading impressions" to other market participants:

- Buying or selling at the close of market with the effect of misleading investors who act on the basis of closing prices, "other than for legitimate reasons."
- "Wash trades"—that is, sales or purchases where there is no change in beneficial interest or market risk, or where the transfer of beneficial interest or market risk is only between parties acting in concert or collusion, "other than for legitimate reasons."

---

463. Financial Services Act (FSA), s. 92.

464. FCA Handbook, *available at* https://www.handbook.fca.org.uk/.

- "Painting the tape"—that is, entering into a series of transactions for the purpose of giving the impression of activity or price movement.
- Entering orders at prices that are higher than the previous bid or lower than the previous offer, and withdrawing them before they are executed, to give a misleading impression that there is demand or supply at that price.

a. What's a "Legitimate Reason"?

As discussed earlier, certain market activity that may be facially manipulative can be permissible as long as it is done for a "legitimate reason." While the handbook does not expressly define this term, it does list the factors that indicate conduct is not for a legitimate reason:

- If the trader "has an actuating purpose behind the transaction to induce others to trade in, bid for or to position or move" prices.
- If the trader "has another, illegitimate, reason behind the transactions, bid or order to trade."
- "If the transaction was executed in a particular way with the purpose of creating a false or misleading impression."

The handbook also lists the factors the FCA considers indicative of legitimately entered orders:

- "If the transaction is pursuant to a prior legal or regulatory obligation owed to a third party."
- "If the transaction is executed in a way which takes into account the need for the market or action platform as a whole to operate fairly and efficiently."
- "The extent to which the transaction generally opens a new position, so creating an exposure to market risk, rather than closes out a position and so removes market risk."
- If the transaction complied with the rules of the relevant market about how transactions are to be executed.

b. What's a "False or Misleading Impression"?

Like their U.S. counterparts, U.K. market manipulation regulations are concerned with market activities that are likely to mislead other traders. In the FCA's view, the following factors are relevant to determine whether market activity will create a false or misleading impression:

- "The extent to which orders . . . or transactions represent a significant proportion of the daily volume of transactions in the relevant [asset or instrument], in particular when these activities lead to a significant change in the price."
- "The extent to which orders . . . or transactions undertaken by persons with a significant buying or selling position . . . lead to significant changes in the price of [a security] or related derivative or underlying asset."
- "Whether transactions undertaken lead to no change in beneficial ownership."

- "The extent to which orders . . . or transactions include position reversals in a short period and represent a significant proportion of the daily volume of transactions" "and might be associated with significant changes in the price."
- "The extent to which orders . . . or transactions are concentrated within a short time span in the trading session and lead to a price change which is subsequently reversed."
- "The extent to which orders . . . change the representation of the best bid or offer prices . . ., or more generally the representation of the order book available to market participants, and are removed before they are executed."
- "The extent to which orders . . . or transactions are undertaken at or around a specific time when reference prices, settlement prices and valuations are calculated and lead to price changes which have an effect on such prices and valuations."

4. The Fraud Act 2006

Section 2 of the Fraud Act makes it an offense for a person to "dishonestly" make a "false representation," if they intend, by making the representation, to make a gain for themselves or another, or cause loss to another or expose another to a risk of loss. Under the Supreme Court's ruling in *Ivey v. Genting Casinos* (discussed earlier in this chapter),[465] whether a defendant acts "dishonestly" is determined through an objective test that assesses whether a defendant has been dishonest by the standards of an ordinary, reasonable individual with the same knowledge or belief as to the relevant facts. A "representation" is false if it is untrue or misleading and the person making it knows that it is, or might be, untrue or misleading. A "representation" may be express or implied and may be regarded as made if it is submitted in any form to any system or device designed to receive, convey, or respond to communications (with or without human intervention).

5. Spoofing Prohibitions in the United Kingdom

Following the lead of the DOJ, CFTC, and SEC, British regulators have deemed spoofing to be a form of market manipulation whereby a trader places non–bona fide orders with the intention to deceive and affect the market price without an intention to execute them. However, there is no specific antispoofing statute in the United Kingdom. Instead, spoofing can be targeted for either civil or criminal prosecution under the MAR, FSA, or FA.

For cases alleging civil violations of these laws, regulators must prove that the trader's behavior created a false or misleading impression in the market (regardless of the trader's intent). In a criminal case, it must be proved that the trader acted with criminal intent and that his or her behavior had an actual false or misleading effect on the market. These standards are similar to those applicable to pre-Dodd-Frank manipulation actions brought by the CFTC and are therefore more stringent than regulators in the United States must prove.[466]

---

465. [2017] UKSC 67.

466. The 2010 Dodd-Frank Wall Street Reform and Consumer Protection Act gave the CFTC enhanced enforcement powers, including through the addition of the antispoofing provision (7 U.S.C. § 6c(a)(5)). Before this law, CFTC manipulation cases were usually brought under CEA § 9(a)(2) (7 U.S.C. § 13(a)(2)).

To date, there have been no criminal prosecutions in the United Kingdom for spoofing, but there have been a number of civil actions targeting the practice brought by the FCA and the Office of Gas and Electricity Markets (Ofgem), which regulates energy markets.[467]

6. *Extraterritorial Reach*

As already noted, the law of England and Wales requires offenses to be tried only in the jurisdiction in which they take place unless there is a specific provision in the relevant statute specifying otherwise. For offenses that may involve domestic and foreign conduct, the common law position is that the offense must have a "substantial connection" to England or Wales for British courts to have jurisdiction. Therefore, when a substantial portion of a cross-border market manipulation offense occurs in England or Wales, courts in these countries will have jurisdiction unless there is a reasonable basis to argue that the conduct ought to be dealt with by a foreign court.[468]

While this rule is similar to the *Morrison* "conduct and effects" test used in the United States, in practice, the extraterritorial reach of U.K. domestic law is much more limited than in the United States, and U.K. regulators have shown far greater reluctance to target overseas defendants for market manipulation offenses.

7. *Criminal Penalties*

A criminal offense under the FSA carries a maximum punishment of seven years' imprisonment and/or an unlimited fine. A fraud offense under the FA Section 2 is punishable by a maximum punishment of seven years' imprisonment and/or an unlimited fine.

VI. MONEY LAUNDERING

At a basic level, money laundering is simply the process of making dirty money—that is, the proceeds from illegal activity—appear to be derived from a legitimate source. It typically involves three steps. First, proceeds from illegal activity are transferred into the financial system. Second, the money is transferred between multiple different parties and accounts to create a paper trail that is difficult to follow back to its origin. Finally, it is further integrated into the financial system through facially legitimate transactions—such as purchases

---

Such claims required the CFTC to establish four elements: (i) the defendant possessed an ability to influence market prices, (ii) an artificial price existed, (iii) the defendant caused the artificial price, and (iv) the defendant specifically intended to cause the artificial price. *See* In re Amaranth Natural Gas Commodities Litigation, 587 F. Supp. 2d 513, 530–31 (S.D.N.Y. 2008); DiPlacido v. CFTC, 364 Fed. Appx. 657, 661 (2d Cir. 2009). This is a high burden that the CFTC has found exceedingly difficult to satisfy: the CFTC has only ever succeeded in one contested action under Section 9(a)(2). *See* 156 Cong. Rec. S3333 (May 6, 2010).

467. See Joshua Ray, et al., *A Primer on Market Manipulation Regulations in the U.S. and U.K.*, (Rahman Ravelli Solicitors Ltd. January 2021).

468. See R v. Smith (Wallace Duncan) (No. 4) [2004] 3 WLR 229.

of real property or other assets—until its provenance is completely obscured.[469] Yet not all of these steps are necessary for a money laundering crime to be committed—all that is required under both U.S. and British law is for illegal proceeds to be used in some type of financial transaction.

Money laundering is subject to severe criminal punishment on both sides of the Atlantic, sometimes even more severe than the underlying crimes with which it is associated.

A. The United States Money Laundering Control Act

The Money Laundering Control Act (MLCA), passed in 1986, has two sections: 18 U.S.C. § 1956 and § 1957. Both sections fall under the generic rubric of "money laundering," but there are significant differences between the two.

Section 1956 prohibits financial transactions that knowingly involve the proceeds of specified unlawful activity for the purpose of disguising the proceeds' nature, location, source, or ownership. Section 1957, in contrast, prohibits engaging in monetary transactions in property from specified unlawful activity, and contains no requirement that the transaction be designed to conceal anything. A defendant must know only that he or she is engaging in a transaction and that the subject of the transaction is criminally derived property to be guilty of a Section 1957 offense.[470] Yet unlike Section 1956, which has no value threshold, Section 1957(a) requires that the property involved have a value greater than $10,000.

By incorporating both sections, Congress designed the MLCA to broadly criminalize the use of U.S. financial institutions as clearinghouses for criminal money laundering and conversion into U.S. currency.[471] In summary, the law "criminalizes behavior that masks the relationship between an individual and his illegally obtained proceeds."[472]

The MLCA complements and functions in parallel with the Bank Secrecy Act (BSA) (31 U.S.C. §§ 5311–5325), which requires U.S. financial institutions to assist American regulators to detect and prevent money laundering through their internal controls and file "suspicious activity reports" (SARs) for any suspect transactions. Compliance with the BSA is overseen by the Financial Crimes Enforcement Network (FinCEN), a division of the U.S. Treasury Department. While the BSA is an important component of U.S. anti-money laundering regulations, it does not impose criminal penalties like the MLCA does, and so will not be covered here in any depth.

---

469. Financial Crime Enforcement Network, *History of Anti-Money Laundering Laws*, *available at* https://www.fincen.gov/history-anti-money-laundering-laws.

470. United States v. Allen, 129 F.3d 1159, 1164–65 (10th Cir. 1997); United States v. Brown, 186 F.3d 661, 670 (5th Cir. 1999) (§ 1957 criminalizes the "mere spending of dirty money"); United States v. Rutgard, 116 F.3d 1270, 1291 (9th Cir. 1997) (§ 1957 "applies to the most open, above-board transaction. The intent to commit a crime or the design of concealing criminal fruits is eliminated"); United States v. Wynn, 61 F.3d 921, 927 (D.C. Cir.) ("Due to the omission of a 'design to conceal' element, section 1957 prohibits a wider range of activity than money 'laundering,' as traditionally understood").

471. United States v. All Assets Held at Bank Julius, 251 F. Supp. 3d 82, 93 (D.D.C. 2017).

472. United States v. Adefehinti, 510 F.3d 319, 322 (D.C. Cir. 2007); *see also* United States v. Wynn, 61 F.3d 921, 926 (D.C. Cir. 1995).

1. 18 U.S.C. Section 1956

Section 1956(a) defines three types of money laundering offenses: domestic money laundering (§ 1956(a)(1)); international money laundering (§ 1956(a)(2)); and undercover "sting" money laundering (§ 1956(a)(3)). It covers actual violations as well as attempted violations. Like conspiracies, attempt requires proof of an intent to commit the underlying offense and the commission of a substantial step in furtherance. But unlike conspiracy, attempt does not require an agreement between two or more individuals, and so can be committed by a person acting alone.[473]

a. Domestic Money Laundering

Section 1956(a)(1) prohibits domestic transactions involving funds that are in fact derived from a "specified unlawful activity" (SUA) and that are engaged in with (i) the intent to promote additional SUA or evade tax ("promotional money laundering"), (ii) knowledge that the transaction is intended to conceal illegal proceeds ("concealment money laundering"), or (iii) knowledge that the transaction is designed to evade anti-money laundering requirements ("evasion money laundering").[474] There is therefore both an objective component—funds were in fact obtained through an SUA—and a subjective one.

The fundamental requirement of a Section 1956(a)(1) violation is the presence of funds that are derived from an SUA. There are more than 250 SUA, including foreign bribery and numerous different fraud offenses.[475] The list of SUA includes certain offenses against a foreign nation, meaning that the MLCA can apply to transactions involving proceeds of crimes that occur entirely overseas. At the same time, the SUA that created the criminally derived proceeds "must be distinct from the money-laundering transaction." Put differently, the MLCA only "criminalizes a transaction in [illicit] proceeds, not the transaction that creates the proceeds."[476] This does not mean, however, that Section 1956 liability requires a conviction for the underlying crime or proof beyond a reasonable doubt that the underlying crime did in fact occur.

To the contrary, while money laundering indictments must include reference to the relevant SUA, they "need not provide elements and other details of the [SUA]"[477] or, when a

---

473. United States v. Resendez-Ponce, 549 U.S. 102, 107 (2007).

474. United States v. Kozeny, 493 F. Supp. 2d 693, 706 n.53 (S.D.N.Y. 2007) ("For the government to prove a violation of section 1956(a)(1)(A)(i), the evidence must establish (1) that the defendant conducted a financial transaction which involved the proceeds of unlawful activity; (2) that he knew that the property involved in the transaction was proceeds of some form of specified unlawful activity; and (3) that he intended to promote the . . . unlawful activity."); *see also* United States v. Tarkoff, 242 F.3d 991, 994 (11th Cir. 2011).

475. 18 U.S.C. § 1956(c)(7).

476. United States v. Mankarious, 151 F.3d 694, 705 (7th Cir. 1998).

477. United States v. Lazarenko, 564 F.3d 1026, 1033 (9th Cir. 2009); United States v. Mankarious, 151 F.3d 694, 703 (7th Cir. 1998); United States v. Raniere, 384 F. Supp. 3d 282, 307 (E.D.N.Y. 2019).

foreign crime is alleged, even specify which foreign law may have been violated.[478] The elements of a money laundering offense do not include, or even implicate, the capacity to actually commit the underlying unlawful activity. Nor is there any threshold amount requirement.

Rather, prosecutors must prove only that the defendant knew that the money or property involved in a transaction was the proceeds of any felony under state, federal, or foreign law. The defendant need not know the exact details of the underlying crime so long as he or she knew that the money or property came from some sort of criminal activity and that the property in fact was derived from an SUA.[479] Further, the defendant's knowledge can be proved through circumstantial evidence.[480]

Defendants will only be liable under Section 1956(a)(1) if they have initiated, received, or otherwise participated in a "financial transaction." A "financial transaction" for purposes of the MLCA is defined to include transfers[481] of money or property—whether it by via a purchase, sale, loan, or gift—that affects interstate or foreign commerce in any way or that involves interstate wires or a financial institution.[482] In complex routing transactions, "each transfer of funds, if it affects interstate or foreign commerce, can be separate" violations.[483] So, for instance, a defendant who receives $100,000 from criminal conduct, withdraws $50,000, and then buys a car with it commits potentially three separate money laundering offenses.[484]

What constitutes a financial transaction has been interpreted extremely broadly by the courts.[485] In *Tarkoff*, for example, the Eleventh Circuit upheld a conviction based on a theory that telephone calls between the United States and Israel to effectuate bank transactions that occurred entirely abroad were "financial transactions" and thus subject to the MLCA.[486]

The term "proceeds" generally means "gross receipts" from criminal activity—as opposed to the crime's profits (receipts minus costs)—except where the money transfers are "inherent in the scheme."[487] As the Supreme Court stated in *United States v. Santos*, "a criminal who enters into a transaction paying the expenses of his illegal activity cannot possibly violate

---

478. Lazarenko, 564 F.3d at 1033–34.

479. 18 U.S.C. § 1956(c)(1); United States v. George, 761 F.3d 42, 48 n.7 (1st Cir. 2014).

480. United States v. Reiss, 186 F.3d 149, 152–53 (2d Cir. 1999).

481. Because "money is inherently fungible, a person is sensibly considered to have engaged in a transfer of money whenever he accepts money in one location and, pursuant to an overall course of conduct, causes the delivery of related money to another location." United States v. Dinero Express, Inc., 313 F.3d 803, 806 (2d Cir. 2002).

482. 18 U.S.C. § 1956(c); United States v. Blair, 661 F.3d 755, 764 (4th Cir. 2011); United States v. Roy, 375 F.3d 21, 23–24 (1st Cir. 2004).

483. BCCI Holdings (Luxembourg) Societé Anon. v. Khalil, 56 F. Supp. 2d 14, 54 (D.D.C. 1999); United States v. Kramer, 73 F.3d 1067, 1072 (11th Cir. 1996).

484. United States v. Prescott, 42 F.3d 1165 (8th Cir. 1994).

485. *See, e.g.*, United States v. Leslie, 103 F.3d 1093, 1101–02 (2d Cir. 1997); United States v. Reed, 77 F.3d 139, 142–43 (6th Cir. 1996).

486. 242 F.3d at 994–95; Leslie, 103 F.3d at 1100 ("The requirement that the transaction or financial institution affect interstate commerce means that proof of a minimal effect on interstate commerce is needed to support federal jurisdiction.").

487. United States v. Ferguson, 412 Fed. Appx. 974, 975–77 (9th Cir. 2011).

the money-laundering statute, because by definition profits consist of what remains after expenses are paid. Defraying an activity's costs with its receipts simply will not be covered by [Section 1956]."[488]

i. Promotional Money Laundering

Promotional money laundering under Section 1956(a)(1)(A)(i) is "different from traditional money laundering because the criminalized act is the reinvestment of illegal proceeds, rather than the concealment of those proceeds."[489] This provision is violated if a person (i) "knowing that the property involved in a financial transaction represents the proceeds of some form of unlawful activity," (ii) "conducts or attempts to conduct such a financial transaction which in fact involves the proceeds of [an SUA], (iii) "with the intent to promote the carrying on of specified unlawful activity."[490]

To prove promotional money laundering under this section prosecutors must prove more than an intent to simply "conceal or disguise" the proceeds of the SUA. Instead, there must be "evidence that the receipt and deposit of laundered funds was made with the intent to promote the specified underlying unlawful activity, be it, for example, by promoting continued illegal activity or by being essential to the completion of the scheme."[491]

ii. Concealment Money Laundering

To prove a concealment offense under Section 1956(a)(1)(B)(i), the government must prove that the defendant participated in a transaction designed in whole or in part "to conceal or disguise the nature, the location, the source, the ownership, or the control of the proceeds of [an SUA]." The key issue is thus the intent of the alleged concealing transaction, not its effect. To establish this intent, prosecutors are required to show efforts "to disguise or conceal the transaction, whether from direct evidence, like the defendant's own statements, or from circumstantial evidence like the use of a third party to disguise the true owner, or unusual secrecy."[492]

But the Supreme Court has rejected arguments that Section 1956(a)(1)(B)(i) applies "whenever a person transported funds in a secretive manner."[493] It is thus insufficient to show merely that secretive aspects facilitated the transportation—"secrecy [must be] the *purpose* of the transportation." In other words, "how one moves the money is distinct from why one moves the money. Evidence of the former, standing alone, is not sufficient to prove the latter."[494] To prove an illegal purpose, prosecutors will often point to the use of shell

---

488. 553 U.S. 507, 517 (2008); *see also* United States v. Quinones, 635 F.3d 590, 599 (2d Cir. 2011) (discussing Santos).

489. United States v. Jolivet, 224 F.3d 902, 909 (8th Cir. 2000).

490. United States v. Cedeno-Perez, 579 F.3d 54, 57 (1st Cir. 2009).

491. United States v. Thorn, 317 F.3d 107, 133 (2d Cir. 2003).

492. United States v. Cruzado-Laureano, 404 F.3d 470, 483 (1st Cir. 2005); *see also* United States v. Magluta, 418 F.3d 1166, 1176 (11th Cir. 2005).

493. Cuellar v. United States, 553 U.S. 564–66 (2008).

494. *Id.* at 566; *see also id.* at 568 ("Although [§ 1956(a)(2)(B)(i)] does not require proof that the defendant attempted to create the appearance of legitimate wealth, neither can it be satisfied solely by

companies, coded language, and complicated transaction structures as affirmative acts reflecting a desire to "quell the suspicions of third parties regarding the nature, location, source, ownership or control of the proceeds" of illicit conduct.[495]

iii. Evasion Money Laundering

The BSA requires financial institutions to file reports of cash transactions exceeding $10,000 and any other suspicious conduct by a customer or client that might signal criminal activity.[496] To get around these requirements, those handling criminal proceeds often try to engage in multiple, relatively small transactions, that are each below the $10,000 threshold. This practice—referred to as "layering" or "structuring"—is prohibited under Section 1956(a)(1)(B)(ii).[497] Yet courts recognize that "currency structuring is not inevitably nefarious" and that "a person who structures a currency transaction [is not] invariably motivated by a desire to keep the Government in the dark."[498]

As such, to establish a criminal structuring offense prosecutors must show that the defendant knew that the transactions at issue were specifically designed to evade a reporting requirement.[499]

b. International Money Laundering

Section 1956(a)(2) is closely similar to Section 1956(a)(1) except that it applies to international "monetary instruments"[500] that are transferred from, into, or through the United States with the intent to engage in promotion, concealing, or evasion money laundering. Thus, whereas Section 1956(a)(1) makes it unlawful to engage in certain types of financial *transactions*, subsection (a)(2) criminalizes the *transportation* of tainted funds across the U.S. border.[501]

When the alleged illicit transportation is conducted to conceal or evade, prosecutors must show that the defendant knew the monetary instrument represented the proceeds of some form of unlawful activity (which need not necessarily be an SUA). In contrast, when the transportation is intended to promote an SUA, prosecutors need not show that the monetary instruments at issue were in fact derived from any criminal activity—all that matters is the transporter's intent.

---

evidence that a defendant concealed the funds during their transport. In this case, the only evidence introduced to prove this element showed that petitioner engaged in extensive efforts to conceal the funds en route to Mexico, and thus his conviction cannot stand."); United States v. Singh, 995 F.3d 1069 (9th Cir. 2021); United States v. Faulkenberry, 614 F.3d 573 (6th Cir. 2010).

495. Prevezon Holdings, Ltd., 251 F. Supp. 3d at696.

496. 31 U.S.C. § 5313(a); 31 C.F.R. § 103.22.

497. Structuring is also made illegal by 31 U.S.C. § 5324.

498. Ratzlaf v. United States, 510 U.S. 135, 144–45 (1994).

499. United States v. Iriele, 977 F.3d 1155, 1173–74 (11th Cir. 2020).

500. "Monetary instruments" include cash, checks, securities, money orders, and negotiable instruments. 18 U.S.C. § 1956(c).

501. Cuellar, 553 U.S. at 550, 556.

c. Money Laundering in "Sting" Operations

A sting operation involves undercover law enforcement activity designed to catch a person in the act of committing a crime. Sting operations are justified on the premise that "money laundering is a crime of subterfuge and concealment" that can be hidden within innocuous-looking bank records.

Section 1956(a)(3)(A) covers situations where the defendant is duped into believing he or she is engaging in money laundering with an undercover officer (when in fact he or she is being set up by law enforcement). This provision replaces the requirement that the money or property at issue is in fact derived from an SUA with a requirement that the defendant must merely believe it to be. The statute is violated when a person (i) with the intent to promote the carrying on of an SUA, (ii) conducts or attempts to conduct a financial transaction, (iii) involving property represented to be proceeds of an SUA or used in the promotion of an SUA.[502]

Stings are controversial because they raise the possibility that a defendant will be entrapped—that is, induced into committing a crime by law enforcement that he otherwise would have never committed. Entrapment is a valid defense to criminal liability and when it is raised requires the government to "prove beyond a reasonable doubt that the defendant was predisposed to commit the criminal act prior to first being approached by government agents."[503] To establish a predisposition, prosecutors may point to evidence such as the defendant's character or reputation, who first made the initial suggestion of criminal activity, profits earned by the defendant, a lack of reluctance by the defendant, and the nature of the government's purported inducement.[504]

2. *18 U.S.C. Section 1957*

Whereas Section 1956 requires there to be some element of promotion, concealment, or evasion, Section 1957 criminalizes all monetary transactions exceeding $10,000 that in fact involve the proceeds of an SUA and where the participants know that the funds are criminally derived (although not necessarily from an SUA).[505] Accordingly, Section 1957 makes otherwise innocent transactions illegal when they are contaminated with illegal proceeds.[506]

Section 1957 creates potential problems for criminal defense attorneys who may often know—or at least strongly suspect—that their fees are being paid with funds that are likely criminal proceeds. To minimize these issues, Section 1957 excludes from the definition of "monetary transactions" any transaction "necessary to preserve a person's right to representation as guaranteed by the sixth amendment to the Constitution."[507] This exception is

---

502. United States v. Davis, 706 F.3d 1081, 1082–83 (9th Cir. 2013); United States v. Ghali, 699 F.3d 845, 845–46 (5th Cir. 2012).

503. Jacobson v. United States, 503 U.S. 540, 548–49 (1992).

504. *See, e.g.*, Mathews v. United States, 485 U.S. 58, 63 (1988); United States v. Mohamud, 843 F.3d 420, 432 (9th Cir. 2016); United States v. Rutgerson, 822 F.3d 1223, 1235 (11th Cir. 2016).

505. United States v. Flores, 454 F.3d 149, 155 (3d Cir. 2006).

506. United States v. Rutgard, 116 F.3d 1270, 1291 (9th Cir. 1997); United States v. Gabriele, 63 F.3d 61, 65 (1st Cir. 1995).

507. 18 U.S.C. § 1957(f)(1).

interpreted narrowly—it only applies to "fees paid for representation guaranteed by the Sixth Amendment in a criminal proceeding and does not extend to attorneys' fees paid for other purposes."[508] Because Sixth Amendment rights attach only after indictment, attorneys representing unindicted individuals during the investigatory phase of a DOJ proceedings will need to tread cautiously with respect to accepting client funds. In certain circumstances, it may be necessary for legal fees to be paid by a third party whose source of legitimate funds is not in doubt.

3. Conspiracy to Commit Money Laundering

Section 1956(h) states that "[a]ny person who conspires to commit any [money laundering offense] shall be subject to the same penalties as those prescribed for the offense the commission of which was the object of the conspiracy." "Conspiring to launder money requires that two or more people agree to violate the federal money laundering statute, and that the defendant 'knowingly engaged in the conspiracy with the specific intent to commit the offenses that [are] the objects of the conspiracy.'"[509]

Unlike conspiracy under 18 U.S.C. Section 371, proof of an overt act in furtherance of the conspiracy is not required under Section 1956(h).[510] In addition, "[c]harges relating to money laundering need not be pled with 'great particularity,' but they must contain 'all essential elements of the offenses."[511] When an indictment lists more than one object of a money laundering conspiracy—for example, some combination of promotion, concealment, and evasion—the evidence "need only be sufficient for any one of the charged objects to sustain a conviction."[512]

4. Extraterritorial Reach

U.S. courts will have extraterritorial jurisdiction for violations of Section 1956 if the laundering is committed by a U.S. citizen, or, if by a foreign national, the conduct occurs in part in the United States.[513] Courts have generally held that "transfer[s] from a foreign account to an account in a U.S. financial institution" as well as "transfer[s] from a U.S. account to a foreign financial institution" occur in part in the United States.[514] Because banking laws require the use of a U.S.-based correspondent account for any international wire transfers of U.S. dollars, virtually any U.S. dollar transaction—regardless of where it is initiated or

---

508. United States v. Velez, 586 F.3d 875, 877 (11th Cir. 2009); *see also* United States v. Blair, 661 F.3d 755, 771 (4th Cir. 2011); United States v. Hoogenboom, 209 F.3d 665, 669 (7th Cir. 2000).

509. United States v. Garcia, 587 F.3d 509, 515 (2d Cir. 2009); United States v. Feldman, 936 F.3d 1288, 1307 (11th Cir. 2019).

510. Whitfield v. United States, 543 U.S. 209, 219 (2005).

511. United States v. Walters, 963 F. Supp. 2d 125, 132–33 (E.D.N.Y. 2013).

512. Moran, 778 F.3d at 963.

513. 18 U.S.C. § 1956(f).

514. Bank Julius, 251 F. Supp. 3d at 93 (collecting cases).

ultimately received—will be routed through the United States and therefore subject to DOJ jurisdiction.[515]

There is extraterritorial jurisdiction for violations of Section 1957 if the defendant is a U.S. citizen or is physically located in the United States while engaging in the illegal conduct.[516]

5. *Criminal Penalties*

Substantive violations of Section 1956 (as well as conspiracies to violate the same) are punishable by a maximum term of twenty years. A maximum prison term of ten years applies to violations of Section 1957 (including conspiracies).[517]

Federal law also permits the DOJ to confiscate the proceeds of any SUA (including any property traceable to such proceeds), as well as any property involved in a money laundering offense.[518] Prosecutors can initiate forfeiture proceedings against a defendant following a criminal conviction or in separate in rem civil proceedings against the property itself. The in rem procedure allows for prosecutors to seize tainted property without having to prove that a money laundering offense actually occurred (see chapter 10).[519]

B. The United Kingdom Proceeds of Crimes Act 2002

The Proceeds of Crimes Act (POCA) 2002 criminalizes money laundering and creates procedures for the authorities to confiscate criminally obtained money and property. The statue also grants law enforcement a number of investigative powers, powers to apply for production and disclosure orders, and powers to restrain or freeze assets to prevent their dissipation while confiscation proceedings are pending.

1. *Money Laundering Offenses*

POCA defines money laundering as "the process by which the proceeds of crime are converted into assets which appear to have a legitimate origin, so that they can be retained permanently or recycled into further criminal enterprise." Like 18 U.S.C. Section 1956, POCA Part 7 makes it an offense to conceal, disguise, convert, transfer, or remove criminal property.[520] Property will qualify as "criminal property" if "(a) it constitutes a person's benefit from criminal conduct or it represents such a benefit (in whole or part and whether directly or

---

515. *See, e.g.*, United States v. Karimova, No. 19-cr-00165 (S.D.N.Y.) (basing jurisdiction for money laundering charges related to alleged bribe payments made to a public official in Uzbekistan on the fact that transactions flowed through correspondent accounts in the United States).

516. 18 U.S.C. § 1957(d).

517. 18 U.S.C. §§ 1956(a) and 1957(b).

518. 18 U.S.C. § 981(a)(1)(C); United States v. Seher, 562 F.3d 1344, 1368 (11th Cir. 2009).

519. United States v. Newman, 659 F.3d 1235, 1239–40 (9th Cir. 2011); United States v. Bodouva, 853 F.3d 76, 77–78 (2d Cir. 2017).

520. POCA ss. 327–29.

indirectly), and (b) the alleged offender knows or suspects that it constitutes or represents such a benefit."[521]

Section 328 targets those who launder on behalf of others. It states that a person will commit an offense "if he enters into or becomes concerned in an arrangement which he knows or suspects facilitates (by whatever means) the acquisition, retention, use or control of criminal property by or on behalf of another person." For POCA purposes, "suspicion" is interpreted to mean that "the defendant must think there is a possibility, which is more than fanciful, that the relevant facts exist. A vague feeling of unease would not suffice. But the statute does not require the suspicion to be 'clear' or 'firmly grounded and targeted on specific facts,' or based upon 'reasonable grounds.'"[522] Although prosecutors are not required to prove the underlying substantive offense from which the proceeds are derived, they must have evidence showing why the source of the money or property at issue is some sort of illegal conduct.[523] Just as the MLCA has an exemption for legal fees, Section 328 has been interpreted as not reaching payments made in the ordinary course of litigation.[524]

Section 329 states that a person will commit an offense if that person acquires, uses, or has in his or her possession criminal property, and knows or suspects that the property is derived from criminal activity. This section does not apply where a person has acquired, used, or had possession of criminal property through the provision of "adequate consideration."[525] Adequate consideration means payment of a proper market price or a similar exchange of equivalent value (including the provision of legal services). However, this exception will not apply if the person knows or suspects that the consideration may help another carry out further criminal conduct.[526]

Part 7 provides certain additional exemptions from liability that mirror the subjective intent element required in U.S. money laundering laws. These exemptions state that a person will not commit an offense if (i) he or she knows, or believes on reasonable grounds, that the relevant criminal conduct occurred outside the United Kingdom, and (ii) the relevant criminal conduct was not, at the time it occurred, unlawful under the criminal law of the foreign country at issue, and is "not of a description prescribed by an order made by the Secretary of State."[527] POCA also exempts a person from money laundering liability if he or she makes an "authorised disclosure"[528] of the illegal transaction or intended to make such a disclosure but had reasonable grounds for not doing so.

---

521. POCA s. 340(3); see also POCA s. 340(5); R v. Rowbotton [2006] EWCA Crim 747.

522. R v. DA Silva [2006] EWCA Crim 1654.

523. R v. Anwoir [2008] EWCA Crim 1354. Unlike 18 U.S.C. § 1956, there are no specific SUAs to which laundering must be connected under POCA.

524. Bowman & Fels [2005] EWCA Civ.226.

525. POCA s. 329(2)(C).

526. POCA s. 329(3)(C).

527. POCA s. 327(2A).

528. The conditions required for a disclosure to be "authorised" are defined in POCA Section 338.

Unlike the MLCA, POCA creates a criminal offense for failing to make a disclosure to the authorities or to an employer (i) while he or she knows or suspects, or has reasonable grounds for knowing or suspecting that another person is engaged in money laundering, (ii) if such knowledge was obtained during a course of business in the regulated sector, and (iii) if he or she can identify the person engaging in money laundering or the location of laundered property, or believes, or should believe, that he or she has information that could be helpful to law enforcement.[529] Individuals who have a reasonable excuse for not making a required disclosure or who are professional legal advisers are exempted from these disclosure requirements. Sections 331 and 332 define a similar failure to disclose an offense but specifically target senior officers of business entities. Even where an individual makes a required disclosure, he or she can face liability for "tipping off" the subject of the disclosure under Section 333A.

Practice Note

Unexplained Wealth Orders (UWOs)

Parliament has long recognized that the United Kingdom is "a hub for dirty money—especially London's prime property market."[530] To combat the issue, the Criminal Finances Act (CFA) 2017 introduced Unexplained Wealth Orders (UWOs). Targeted at organized crime figures and foreign public officials outside of Europe, UWOs place an affirmative burden on the recipients to substantiate their wealth and explain how it was obtained. UWOs can be obtained by the NCA, HMRC, the FCA, the director of the SFO, and the DPP via ex parte application made to the High Court. The court must be satisfied that there are "reasonable grounds for suspecting" that the person's known sources of lawfully obtained income are not sufficient to enable them to obtain the relevant property.

Once the court approves, the order requires the target to produce documents or other evidence relating to the property within a fixed time period. If the target fails to do so or does so insufficiently, the property is presumed subject to forfeiture through a civil recovery order under POCA. UWOs are therefore an investigative tool to make it easier to obtain a CRO by reversing the burden of proof.[531] Law enforcement can couple a UWO with an application for an interim freezing order to prevent the property from being dissipated.

The first UWO was obtained by the NCA against Zamira Hajiyeva, the wife of the imprisoned former chairman of the International Bank of Azerbaijan and the owner of a £12 million Knightsbridge townhouse and a £10 million golf course in the English countryside. In addition to these properties, Hajiyeva reportedly had a $42 million Gulfstream and spent £16 million at Harrods—the London department store—over a ten-year period.[532] The UWO compelled her to explain how she and her husband afforded this lifestyle on his relatively modest government

529. POCA s. 330.

530. Ali Shalchi, *Unexplained Wealth Orders*, House of Commons Library (Oct. 1, 2021) at 3.

531. *Id.* at 10.

532. Dominic Casciani, Harrods Mega-Spender Loses Supreme Court Challenge, BBC News, Dec. 21, 2020.

salary. In December 2020, the Supreme Court rejected Hajiyeva's application for permission to appeal the lower court's refusal to quash the order.

On March 15, 2022, the Economic Crime (Transparency and Enforcement) Act (ECA) 2022 received Royal Assent and became law. In addition to important changes to legislation pertaining to financial sanctions, this statute was designed to reduce the prevalence of "illicit finance" in the United Kingdom property market in two ways. First, it created a Register of Overseas Entities that requires any overseas entity purchasing land in the United Kingdom to identify and register its beneficial owners (defined as anyone holding more than 25 percent of the entity's shares or voting rights). Failure to do so or the submission of false information is a criminal offense.[533] Second, the ECA amended the law relating to UWOs to make it easier for law enforcement to use them. Specifically, the ECA created a new test that allows courts to grant UWOs where "there are reasonable grounds for suspecting that the property has been obtained through unlawful conduct." The ECA also allows law enforcement to apply for an interim freezing order simultaneously with the application for a UWO in order to prohibit the person receiving the UWO from selling the underlying property while the UWO application is pending.[534]

While UWOs are not available to law enforcement in the United States, similar results can be achieved through civil in rem forfeiture (see chapter 10).

2. *Extraterritorial Reach*

Where the underlying criminal conduct occurred is irrelevant with regard to jurisdiction under POCA. All that is required is that the conduct would be illegal under U.K. law if it had in fact occurred there.[535] Therefore, POCA has extraterritorial effect and applies to British citizens based overseas. There is a limited exception to this general rule that provides that a person will not be guilty of a money laundering offense if he or she knew or reasonably believed that the relevant criminal conduct occurred abroad, and that the relevant criminal conduct was not, when it took place, unlawful under the criminal law of that other country.[536] This exception does not apply if the conduct would constitute an offense punishable in the United Kingdom by a sentence of more than twelve months.

3. *Criminal Penalties*

The maximum penalty for violations of POCA section 327 to 329 is fourteen year's imprisonment and/or an unlimited fine.

---

533. ECA s. 32.

534. *Id.* ss. 45-53.

535. R v. Rogers [2014] EWCA Crim 1680; Jedinak v. Czech Republic [2016] EWHC 3525 (Admin).

536. POCA ss. 327(2A), 328(3), 329(2A).

CHAPTER 4: KEY DISTINCTIONS

United States	United Kingdom
Fraud	
Criminal code contains many different fraud statutes targeting specific types of conduct and victims	Fraud offenses consolidated into the Fraud Act 2006
Conviction requires proof of fraudulent intent	Conviction requires "dishonesty" as judged against the ordinary standards of society
Maximum sentence of 20 years and $250,000 fine	Maximum sentence of 10 years and unlimited fine
Insider Trading/Insider Dealing	
Insider trading not specifically defined by statute; prosecuted under § 10(b) of the Securities Exchange Act and Securities and Exchange Commission (SEC) Rule 10b-5	Insider dealing offense defined by Section 52 of the Criminal Justice Act 2003
Insider trading requires proof that the defendant had a duty to disclose arising from a relationship of trust and confidence between parties to a transaction	Any person in possession of information that they know is material and nonpublic violates the law by trading on it
Tipper/tippee liability requires proof that the tipper received a personal benefit in exchange for the tip	No "personal benefit" requirement for tipper/tippee liability
No statutory affirmative defenses	Various affirmative defenses created by statute that can be established by a balance of the probabilities
Maximum sentence of 20 years and $5 million fine	Maximum sentence of 10 years and unlimited fine
Foreign Bribery	
Foreign Corrupt Practices Act (FCPA) does not reach commercial bribery or bribe recipients	Bribery Act 2006 covers commercial bribery and bribe recipients, as well as bribery of domestic officials
FCPA applies to companies who list shares on a U.S. exchange or file reports with the SEC	Listing on the London Stock Exchange insufficient to confer jurisdiction
Liability focuses on corrupt intent of bribe payor	Liability focuses on intended interference with the recipients' government function
Exception for facilitation payments	No statutory facilitation payments exception
Maximum sentence of 5 years and $250,000 fine for bribery violations; 20 years and $5 million for books and records violations	Maximum sentence of 10 years and unlimited fine

(*Continued*)

United States	United Kingdom
Conspiracy	
Conspiracy charges routinely included in indictments alongside one or more substantive offenses	Conspiracy charged infrequently; prosecutors must affirmatively justify the inclusion of a conspiracy charge in an indictment
U.S. Code includes dozens of conspiracy statutes that carry a range of penalties; no federal common law conspiracy	Single statutory conspiracy offense; common law conspiracy recognized
Pinkerton liability applies to any offense that is a reasonably foreseeable consequence of the conspiratorial agreement	*Pinkerton* liability not generally recognized
Maximum sentence of 5 years or the same as the underlying substantive offense	Maximum sentence always the same as the underlying offense
Market Manipulation	
DOJ prosecutors have brought a multitude of criminal "spoofing" cases under the Commodity Exchange Act's (CEA's) antispoofing provision and various other theories	As yet no criminal spoofing prosecutions
Maximum penalty of 20 years and $5 million fine; 10 years and $1 million fine for CEA violations	Maximum penalty of 7 years and unlimited fine
Money Laundering	
Money Laundering Control Act does not impose criminal liability on individuals who fail to report potential money laundering	Proceeds of Crimes Act creates a criminal "failure to disclose" offense
Illicit property targeted through in rem civil forfeiture procedures	Law enforcement can use Unexplained Wealth Orders to compel individuals to substantiate the source of funds used to purchase property in the United Kingdom
Maximum penalty of 10 or 20 years depending on the charging theory	Maximum penalty of 14 years and unlimited fine

5 | Pretrial Discovery and Disclosure

Just as in civil litigation, in criminal cases both parties, the prosecution and defense, formally exchange information and evidence pertaining to the allegations—in the United States this process is called "discovery" and, in the United Kingdom, "disclosure." The overall purpose of the rules governing discovery or disclosure is the same in both countries: to allow the parties a means to adequately investigate the underlying facts, inform the defendant on how to plead, and prepare for trial. The common belief underlying these rules in the United States and Britain is that the disclosure process safeguards the integrity of the criminal justice system and the overall fairness of the trial process.

Nevertheless, especially in the United States, there is a general reluctance on the part of lawmakers and the courts to expand a defendant's ability to access the government's evidence prior to trial except in certain narrowly defined circumstances.[1] Thus, where the discovery rules in U.S. civil litigation "give parties agency by affording them formal power to investigate facts, criminal procedure deems a defendant a passive participant who makes choices based on information managed by the prosecutor."[2] While the disclosure rules in the United Kingdom are in some respects more favorable to defendants, they also impose more substantial obligations on the defense to produce evidence to prosecutors.

---

1. This reluctance has been traced to an underlying belief that too much discovery will frustrate the prosecution of crime. *See* Jerry E. Norton, *Discovery in the Criminal Process*, 61 J. Crim. L. Criminology & Police Sci. 11 (1970) (quoting Judge Learned Hand: "Under our criminal procedure the accused has every advantage. While the prosecution is held rigidly to the charge, he need not disclose the barest outline of his defense. He is immune from question or comment on his silence; he cannot be convicted where there is the least fair doubt in the minds of [the jury]. Why in addition he should in advance have the whole evidence against him to pick over at his leisure, and make his defense, fairly or foully, I have never been able to see. . . . Our dangers do not lie in too little tenderness to the accused. . . . What we need to fear is the archaic formalism and the watery sentiment that obstructs, delays, and defeats the prosecution of crime.").

2. Ion Meyn, *Why Civil and Criminal Procedure are So Different: A Forgotten History*, 86 Fordham L. Rev. 699 (2017).

I. PRETRIAL DISCOVERY IN THE UNITED STATES

District court judges have an overriding obligation to effectuate the "speedy and orderly administration of justice."[3] To carry out this mandate, they have the inherent power to "enter pretrial case management and discovery orders designed to ensure that the relevant issues to be tried are identified, that the parties have an opportunity to engage in appropriate discovery and that the parties are adequately and timely prepared so that the trial can proceed efficiently and intelligibly."[4] This authority is not entirely within a judge's discretion, however.

In criminal cases, there are specific laws and procedural rules pertaining to what and when federal prosecutors must disclose to defendants, and what defendants must disclose to prosecutors. The most important of these are contained in Federal Rules of Criminal Procedure 16 and 26.2, the Jencks Act (18 U.S.C. § 3500), and two Supreme Court decisions (*Brady v. Maryland*, 373 U.S. 83 (1963) and *Giglio v. United States*, 405 U.S. 150 (1972)). In addition to the exchange of evidence between the parties, prosecutors and defense counsel can also seek documents and testimony from third parties via subpoenas (Rule 17) and depositions (Rule 15). Note that the subpoenas discussed in this chapter are different than the grand jury subpoenas discussed in chapter 2.

A. Rule 16 Disclosures

While there is "no general constitutional right to discovery in a criminal case,"[5] Rule 16 allows criminal defendants some limited access to information regarding the government's case. Unlike discovery in civil cases, where some materials are automatically produced as a matter of right, in criminal cases, a defendant must invoke the right to discovery by specifically requesting it.[6] This is typically done through a "Rule 16 letter" to prosecutors early in the case (usually right after arraignment). Rule 16 enumerates categories of information subject to pretrial discovery (Fed R. Crim. P. 16(a)(1)(A)–(B), (E)) and also specifically lists items that are not subject to disclosure, except as otherwise permitted (Fed. R. Crim. P. 16(a)(2)).[7]

The underlying purpose of this rule is to enable the defense to prepare for trial, encourage guilty pleas, and to allow the court to address potential constitutional defects in the prosecution—such as coerced confessions and illegal wiretaps—before trial.[8] It does not, however, entitle a defendant "to discovery of the entirety of the government's case against him."[9]

---

3. United States v. W.R. Grace, 526 F.3d 499, 508–09 (9th Cir. 2008).

4. *Id.*

5. Weatherford v. Bursey, 429 U.S. 545, 559 (1977); United States v. Agurs, 427 U.S. 97, 111 (1976) (the government has no "constitutional duty routinely to deliver his entire file to defense counsel").

6. *See* Ward and Smith, P.A., *Parallel Universe: Navigating Discovery in Concurrent Civil and Criminal Proceedings*, Nat. L. Rev. (Mar. 9, 2017) (examining the various differences in civil and criminal discovery rules).

7. United States v. De La Rosa, 196 F.3d 712, 715 (7th Cir. 1999); United States v. Crass, 50 F.3d 81, 83 (1st Cir. 1995); United States v. Matthews, 20 F.3d 538, 549–50 (2d Cir. 1994).

8. United States v. Percevault, 490 F.2d 129-30 (2d Cir. 1974).

9. *Id.*

Before the adoption of the original iteration of Rule 16 in the 1940s, what evidence prosecutors were required to turn over to defendants was determined on an ad hoc, case by case basis. Rule 16 was designed to provide uniformity to the criminal discovery process and broaden the scope of materials held by the government that defendants are entitled to.[10] It is intended to "protect against trial by surprise."[11] At the same time, Rule 16 requires defendants to provide certain materials to the prosecution (as discussed in Section I(B)). It is a therefore a "rule of checks and balances."[12]

Within fourteen days of arraignment, DOJ prosecutors must meet with defense counsel to agree on a timetable and procedures for pretrial disclosure under this rule.[13] The practical effect of tying Rule 16 disclosures to arraignment is that criminal defendants are not entitled to see any of the government's evidence until after they have submitted to the court's jurisdiction (whether by being arrested and brought to the district or otherwise). For defendants located abroad, this usually means that they will receive no discovery until they are extradited or voluntarily travel to the United States to be arraigned (see section I.B later in the chapter discussing the "fugitive disentitlement doctrine" in this context).

If either side fails to comply with Rule 16, the trial court may "order such party to permit the discovery or inspection, grant a continuance, or prohibit the party from introducing evidence not disclosed, or it may enter such other order as it deems just under the circumstances."[14] The aggrieved party bears the burden of bringing a discovery failure to the court's attention, and whether this burden is satisfied is left to the discretion of the district court.[15]

1. Defendant's Statements (Rule 16(a)(1)(A) and (B))

"Rule 16(a)(1)(A) authorizes broad pretrial discovery of the defendant's statements, whether made during or after the commission of the crime charged; to a government agent, to a grand jury, or to anyone else; and whether obtained surreptitiously or voluntarily."[16] At the defendant's request, Rule 16(a)(1)(A) requires the government to disclose "the substance of any relevant oral statement made by the defendant, before or after arrest, in response to interrogation by a person the defendant knew was a government agent if the government intends to use the statement at trial."[17]

---

10. For a history of Rule 16's development, see Hon. Christina Reiss, *Closing Fed. R. Crim. P. 16(a)'s Loopholes: Why Criminal Defendants Are Entitled to Discovery of All of Their Statements*, AMER. U. CRIM. L. Brief 7, no. 2 (2012).

11. United States v. Meregildo, 920 F. Supp. 2d 437 (2d Cir. 1974).

12. United States v. Cherry, 876 F. Supp. 547, 549 (S.D.N.Y. 1995).

13. Fed. R. Crim. P. 16.1(a); *see also* Fed. R. Crim. P. 12(b)(4).

14. Fed. R. Crim. P. 16(d)(2).

15. United States v. Paiz, 905 F.2d 104, 1027 (7th Cir. 1990).

16. Percevault, 490 F.2d at 126, 129.

17. Fed. R. Crim. P. 16(a)(1)(A). The statute does not self-define any of its terms. "Government agent" has been defined by courts to include only agents of the federal government, not those acting for a state or local government. *See* United States v. Gatto, 763 F.2d 1040, 1048–49 (9th Cir. 1988); United States v. Brazel, 102 F.3d 1120, 1150 (11th Cir. 1997); *but see* United States v. Burns, 15 F.3d 211,

Rule 16(a)(1)(B) requires the government to permit a defendant to inspect and copy or photograph any relevant written or recorded statement by the defendant if the "statement is within the government's possession, custody, or control" and "the attorney for the government knows—or through reasonable due diligence could know—that the statement exists."[18] Note that there is no requirement that such statements be material, intended for use at trial, or the product of government interrogation. Further, "[b]y its plain terms, this rule encompasses both typewritten summaries and contemporaneous handwritten notes" made by government agents.[19] And under Rule 16(a)(1)(B)(iii), the government must also disclose "the defendant's recorded testimony before a grand jury relating to the charged offense."

2. *Defendant's Criminal Record (Rule 16(a)(1)(D))*

Rule 16(a)(1)(D) requires prosecutors to disclose, upon a defendant's request, "a copy of the defendant's prior criminal record that is within the government's possession, custody, or control if the attorney for the government knows—or through due diligence could know—that the record exists." The term "government" as used in this rule refers to federal prosecutors' offices and related executive law enforcement agencies, not to federal courts or probation offices.[20] This obligation is ordinarily discharged by supplying the defendant with a copy of his FBI "rap sheet" listing all prior convictions.[21] The government is not required to supply any information or evidence relating to the underlying facts of defendant's prior crimes.[22]

3. *Documents and Tangible Items (Rule 16(a)(1)(E))*

At a defendant's request, Rule 16(a)(1)(E) requires prosecutors to disclose documents or other tangible objects that are within the government's possession, custody, or control and (i) material to preparing the defense, (ii) intended to be used by the government in its case in chief at trial, or (iii) obtained from, or belongs to, the defendant.

This rule "requires the production of inculpatory as well as exculpatory evidence, which might assist in preparation of a defense."[23] To satisfy the materiality requirement, "a defendant must demonstrate some indication that pretrial disclosure of the evidence would enable

---

214 (1st Cir. 1994) (setting forth the minority position that "government agent" includes any person with law enforcement responsibilities). The term "interrogation" has been interpreted to mean "express questioning" and "any words or actions on the part of the police (other than those normally attendant to arrest and custody) that the police should know are reasonably likely to elicit an incriminating response from the suspect." Rhode Island v. Innis, 446 U.S. 291, 308 (1980); *see also* United States v. Kusek, 844 F.2d 942, 948–49 (2d Cir. 1988).

18. Fed. R. Crim. P. 16(a)(1)(B).

19. United States v. Certified Envtl. Servs., Inc., 753 F.3d 72, 93 (2d Cir. 2014).

20. United States v. Trevino, 556 F.2d 1265, 1270–73 (5th Cir. 1977).

21. United States v. Trejo-Zambrano, 582 F.2d 460, 465 (9th Cir. 1978).

22. United States v. Hourihan, 66 F.3d 458, 463 (2d Cir. 1995).

23. United States v. Baker, 453 F.3d 419, 424 (7th Cir. 2006); *see also* United States v. Marshall, 132 F.3d 63, 68 (D.C. Cir. 1998).

[him or her] significantly to alter the quantum of proof in his or her favor."[24] This is a lower standard than under *Brady* (discussed later in the chapter).

To trigger discovery under this Rule, the evidence requested by the defendant must be in the actual custody or control of the federal government.[25] Material will be considered within the possession of the government only if it is in the actual possession of the prosecutor or if the prosecutor has knowledge of and access to the material while it is in the possession of another federal agency.[26]

4. *Expert Witnesses (Rule 16(a)(1)(E))*

The Federal Rules of Evidence define an "expert witness" as a person "who is qualified as an expert by knowledge, skill, experience, training, or education."[27] As opposed to lay witnesses, suitably qualified experts are permitted to testify as to their opinion or analysis of the evidence as long as their conclusions are scientifically sound.[28] Rule 16(a)(1)(E) requires the government to give the defendant a written summary of any expert testimony that it intends to use during its case in chief at trial.

Experts are regularly called to testify by prosecutors and the defense in white-collar crime cases, for example, to interpret and explain complex trade data, accounting records, and industry practices.

5. *Exceptions to the Government's Rule 16 Obligations*

In addition to specifying what the government must disclose, it also identifies information that is not subject to disclosure. The exceptions include "reports, memoranda, or other internal documents" made by a government attorney or government agent in connection with investigating or prosecuting the case—that is, the type of material subject to protections under the attorney work product doctrine[29]—and statements made by prospective government witnesses, except as provided in the Jencks Act (discussed in section I.D.).[30]

Aside from these statutory exceptions, district courts are granted an inherent right to expand or restrict discovery rights (for either the prosecution or defense). Specifically, Rule 16(d) provides that a court may, for good cause, "deny, restrict, or defer discovery or inspection, or grant other appropriate relief."[31] A party may "show good cause by a written

24. Baker, 453 F.3d at 425; *see also* United States v. Armstrong, 517 U.S. 456, 462-63 (1996); United States v. Clarke, 979 F.3d 82, 97 (2d Cir. 2020).

25. United States v. Chavez-Vernaza, 844 F.2d 1368, 1375 (9th Cir. 1987).

26. United States v. Santiago, 46 F.3d 885, 893 (9th Cir. 1995).

27. Fed. R. Evid. 702.

28. Daubert v. Merrell Dow Pharm., 509 U.S. 579, 592-593 (1993).

29. United States v. Fort, 472 F.3d 1106, 1116 (9th Cir. 2007) (finding that the work product doctrine extends to materials prepared by law enforcement agents as well as prosecutors).

30. Fed. R. Crim. P. 16(a)(2).

31. Fed. R. Crim. P. 16(d)(1).

statement that the court will inspect *ex parte*," and if relief is granted, the court must seal and preserve the entire text of the party's statement.[32]

Rule 16(d)(1) is often implicated by defendant requests for discovery that are denied by the government based on a need for confidentiality[33] and the advisory committee's notes to Rule 16 direct courts to take into account "the safety of witnesses and others, [and] a particular danger or perjury or witness intimidation" when determining whether to deny restrict or defer discovery.[34] This often means that district courts will deny defense requests for the government to supply them with a list of prospective government witnesses (or at least defer its disclosure until shortly before trial).[35] The rationale behind this general rule is that forcing the government to reveal the names of its witnesses before trial "is not in the interest of the effective administration of criminal justice" because it may discourage witnesses from testifying and invite efforts to improperly influence a witnesses' testimony.[36]

Relatedly, prosecutors can limit their Rule 16 production—through redaction or withholding entirely—by invoking the "informer's privilege." The Supreme Court explained this privilege in *Roviaro v. United States*: "what is usually referred to as the informer's privilege is in reality the Government's privilege to withhold from disclosure the identity of persons who furnish information of violations of law to officers charged with enforcement of that law."[37] The privilege covers not only the names of informants, but "information that would tend to reveal the identity of the informant."[38]

To override the informer's privilege, a defendant bears the burden of proving that the disclosure of an informant's identity is "essential to a fair determination" of his or her case.[39] But a defendant's "mere suspicion" that the informant's evidence is "relevant and helpful" under *Brady* will not defeat the government's privilege.[40] If the privilege applies, and if the defendant makes a "'minimal threshold showing' that disclosure would be relevant to at least one defense," then the district court must hold an *in camera* hearing—that is, solely before the judge, without the presence of the defense—so as to minimize the risk of disclosing the informant's identity.[41]

---

32. Fed. R. Crim. P. 16(d)(1).

33. United States v. Innamorati, 996 F.2d 456, 487 (1st Cir. 1993).

34. Fed. R. Crim. P. 16 advisory committee's notes (1966 Amendments); *see also* Fort, 472 F.3d 1106, 1131 (9th Cir. 2007) (Fletcher, J. dissenting) (noting that "[t]he Rules Advisory Committee specifically designed Rule 16 (d)(1) to provide a mechanism to protect witness safety, and to grant considerable discretion to the district court in drafting orders under that rule.").

35. Weatherford, 429 U.S. at 559 (no requirement that prosecution reveal names of all witnesses unfavorable to defendant); United States v. Sukumolachan, 610 F.2d 685, 688 (9th Cir. 1980); United States v. Dark, 597 F.2d 1097, 1099 (6th Cir. 1979).

36. United States v. Bouye, 688 F.2d 471, 473–74 (7th Cir. 1982).

37. 353 U.S. 53, 59 (1957); *see also* United States v. Sai Keung Wong, 886 F.2d 252, 255 (9th Cir. 1989).

38. United States v. Napier, 436 F.3d 1133, 1136 (9th Cir. 2006).

39. Roviaro, 353 U.S. at 59.

40. *See* United States v. Henderson, 241 F.3d 638, 645 (9th Cir. 2000).

41. *Id.*

There is "no fixed rule" governing the court's decision to order the disclosure of *Roviaro* information. District courts must balance the extent to which disclosure would be relevant and helpful against the government's interest in protecting its informants.[42] Most circuits will employ a three-pronged test to conduct *Roviaro* balancing: "(1) the degree of the informant's involvement in the criminal activity; (2) the relationship between the defendant's asserted defense and the likely testimony of the informant; and (3) the government's interest in nondisclosure."[43]

Rule 16 also exempts disclosure of grand jury recordings that involve the testimony of someone other than the defendant, except in certain limited circumstances.[44] In general, to access such materials—which are normally protected by the grand jury secrecy rules in Federal Rule of Criminal Procedure 6—a defendant must show a "particularized need for them."[45] Even when defendants show a legitimate need, district courts are directed to permit disclosure "discretely and limitedly," meaning that grand jury transcripts of third-party testimony are rarely disclosed.[46]

Nevertheless, the Supreme Court has confirmed a trial court's power under Rule6(e) to require disclosure of grand jury testimony "preliminary to or in connection with a judicial proceeding." In *United States* v. *Socony-Vacuum Oil Co.*, for example, the Court acknowledged that "after the grand jury's functions are ended, disclosure is wholly proper where the ends of justice require it."[47]

Practice Note

The "Fugitive Disentitlement Doctrine"

The "fugitive disentitlement" doctrine prevents defendants who have not physically submitted to a U.S. court's jurisdiction from challenging the charges against them or from receiving Rule 16 discovery from prosecutors. As a result, individuals who are charged while living or working abroad must generally leave their home country and travel to the United States (either through extradition or voluntarily), where they will potentially be subject to pretrial detention, as a condition of participating in the criminal litigation process.[48]

---

42. Roviaro, 353 U.S. at 62.

43. *See, e.g.*, United States v. Gonzalo Beltran, 915 F.2d 487, 489 (9th Cir. 1990); United States v. Tenorio-Angel, 756 F.2d 1505, 1509 (11th Cir. 1985).

44. Fed. R. Crim. P. 16(a)(3).

45. Pittsburgh Plate Glass Co. v. United States, 360 U.S. 395, 400, 405 (1959).

46. United States v. Procter Gamble Co., 356 U.S. 677, 683 (1958).

47. 310 U.S. 150, 234 (1940); *see also* Proctor Gamble, 356 U.S. at 683 (noting that problems concerning the use of the grand jury transcript at the trial to impeach a witness, to refresh his recollection, to test his credibility are "cases of particularized need where the secrecy of the proceedings is lifted discretely and limitedly").

48. Under the Bail Reform Act, most foreign white-collar defendants who are deemed flight risks are allowed to avoid pretrial custody in jail, but many are required to stay within the jurisdiction of the district court (particularly when they are from countries where extradition would be difficult (e.g., Switzerland, China)). Considering that the pretrial stage of most federal cases is at least one year

Courts have advanced four rationales for disentitling fugitives: assuring the enforceability of any decision that may be rendered against the fugitive, imposing a penalty for flouting the judicial process, discouraging flights from justice and promoting the efficient operation of the courts, and avoiding prejudice to the prosecution caused by the defendant's escape.[49]

As its name suggests, the fugitive disentitlement doctrine only applies to fugitives from justice, defined as a "a person who, having committed a crime, flees from the jurisdiction of the court where a crime was committed or departs from his usual place of abode and conceals himself within the district."[50] To disentitle a defendant, therefore, a court must first determine that the person is in fact a fugitive. The court may then exercise discretion to disentitle the fugitive, but only if doing so would serve the doctrine's objectives.[51] A "traditional" fugitive is one who flees or otherwise hides from law enforcement. A so-called "constructive-flight fugitive" is a person "who allegedly committed crimes while in the United States but who was outside the country—for whatever reason—when he learned that his arrest was sought and who then refused to return to the United States in order to avoid prosecution."[52]

The fugitive disentitlement doctrine was recently reexamined by the Second Circuit in *United States v. Bescond,* a prosecution against French banker Muriel Bescond. At all times relevant to her indictment, Bescond was a French citizen living in France who worked as the head of the Paris treasury desk at Société Générale (SocGen). U.S. prosecutors in the Eastern District of New York charged Bescond with participating in a scheme to manipulate "USD LIBOR," a benchmark interest rate used to calculate interest rates on various financial instruments.[53]

As a French citizen, Bescond was immune from extradition while in France (since France has a blanket policy against extraditing its citizens)—thus, as long as she remained there, the case against her in the United States would essentially be put on pause indefinitely. Apparently unwilling to forgo international travel, Bescond's counsel filed two motions to dismiss the indictment that included arguments that the indictment lacked a sufficient nexus with the United States, the statute of limitations had run, and that the DOJ had improperly singled her out because of her gender.[54]

---

from arraignment, being forced to reside in the United States can obviously be a significant hardship for foreign defendants who may have family or business interests abroad. It is for this reason that it is often advantageous for foreign defendants to waive extradition in exchange for prosecutors' consent to their return home to prepare for trial.

49. Bar-Levy v. United States Dep't of Justice, 990 F.2d 33, 35 (2d Cir. 1993).

50. Empire Blue Cross v. Finkelstein, 111 F.3d 278, 281 (2d Cir. 1997).

51. United States v. Bescond, 7 F.4th 127 (2d Cir. 2021).

52. Collazos v. United States, 368 F.3d 190, 199 (2d Cir. 2004).

53. Bescond, 7 F.4th at 132; cf. Gao v. Gonzales, 481 F.3d 173, 176–77 (2d Cir. 2007) ("[T]he 'paradigmatic object of the doctrine is the convicted criminal who flees while his appeal is pending.'"); United States v. Awadalla, 357 F.3d 243, 246 (2d Cir. 2004) ("Because Awadalla absconded after challenging his judgment of conviction in this Court, there is no doubt that we have the authority to dismiss his appeal."); United States v. Morgan, 254 F.3d 424, 426–27 (2d Cir. 2001) (holding that the district court properly disentitled a criminal defendant who fled the United States after pleading guilty and before sentencing); Bar-Levy v. U.S. Dep't of Just., 990 F.2d 33, 35 (2d Cir. 1993) ("[T]he alien who is a fugitive from a deportation order should ordinarily be barred by his fugitive status from calling upon the resources of the court to determine his claims.").

54. Bescond, 7 F.4th at 133.

Because she had not surrendered to the United States before filing her motions, Bescond was disentitled by the district court and her motions were denied without reaching their merits. Bescond then appealed. After first concluding that the district court's order was amenable to appeal under the "final judgment rule," the Second Circuit panel considered whether Bescond was properly considered a fugitive; and, if she was, whether the district court abused its discretion in concluding that disentitlement was justified. The panel found in Bescond's favor on both issues.

As to the first, the panel noted that she was neither a traditional fugitive nor a constructive-flight one: "Bescond has neither fled nor concealed herself. . . . Nor is she refusing to return to the United States to avoid prosecution; she simply remains at home, as her home country permits her to do."[55] Recognizing the inherent unfairness of disentitling a defendant who, like Bescond, has a nonfrivolous extraterritoriality claim, the judges concluded: "Labeling a foreign defendant a fugitive can be enough to coerce submission to U.S. jurisdiction wholly regardless of whether the charged statute reaches individuals outside our territory. . . . And if our law does not reach Bescond or her conduct, can it be said that she is in flight from it?"[56]

With respect to whether the district court abused its discretion in labeling Bescond a fugitive, the panel ruled that disentitlement was a "disproportionately severe response" and did not otherwise promote the purposes of the disentitlement doctrine. The district court's failure to consider the prejudice to Bescond from applying the doctrine was criticized in unusually harsh terms:

> Disentitlement enables the government to coerce Bescond's presence in court by imposing financial, reputational, and family hardship regardless of her guilt or innocence, and regardless of whether the indictment charges violations of a statute that applies extraterritorially. So long as the government surmounts the low threshold of securing an indictment, any soul on the planet may be deemed a fugitive, and disentitlement would then bar a challenge to extraterritoriality from abroad, requiring the foreigner to leave home and face arrest and detention to have any hope of securing dismissal. Such a result contravenes the rationales that underly disentitlement and assigns no weight to the sovereignty of other nations.[57]

The order disentitling Bescond was reversed and the case remanded for further proceedings. As of this writing, the merits of Bescond's now-revived motions to dismiss have not yet been addressed by the district court. And note that other district courts have reached opposing conclusions.

In *United States v. Saab Moran,* for example, a Venezuelan diplomat was charged with one count of conspiracy to commit money laundering and seven counts of laundering monetary instruments. Saab Moran declined to travel to the United States to face the charges and the district court in Miami labelled him with "fugitive status." He was later arrested in Cape Verde, where his plane from Venezuela to Iran had stopped to refuel, and the DOJ subsequently secured his extradition to the United States. Finding that the extradition had clearly made him no longer a fugitive, the district court's earlier determination was rendered a moot issue and not reviewed by the circuit court on appeal.[58]

---

55. *Id.* at 140.
56. *Id.* at 141.
57. *Id.* at 143.
58. United States v. Moran, No. 21-11083 (11th Cir. May 2, 2022).

6. *The Defendant's Discovery Obligations*

If a defendant makes a request for disclosure under Rule 16(a)(1)(E) and the government complies, corresponding disclosure obligations are then imposed on the defendant. These obligations require the defendant to disclose, upon the government's request, any documents, photographs, or tangible objects that are within the defendant's possession, custody, or control, and that the defendant intends to use the item in his or her case in chief at trial.[59] Courts will generally permit a defendant to defer reciprocal discovery of any materials that implicate the Fifth Amendment privilege against self-incrimination until he or she testifies at trial.

As discussed in chapter 2, the "Fifth Amendment grants persons the privilege not to provide the State with [self-incriminatory] evidence of a testimonial or communicative nature."[60] This privilege is qualified in the sense that a defendant "may be required to produce specific documents even though they contain incriminating assertions of fact or belief because the creation of those documents was not 'compelled' within the meaning of the privilege." At the same time, the "act of production" doctrine extends the Fifth Amendment privilege to the act of production itself when it may implicitly communicate statements of fact—for example, where the fact that the defendant produced certain documents implicitly causes him to admit "that the papers existed, were in his possession or control, and were authentic."[61] Accordingly, a defendant may only defer or withhold production of evidence that otherwise falls within the defendant's Rule 16(b) discovery obligations if "the act of production would be testimonial."[62]

B. Rule 17(c) Subpoenas

Rule 17(c) of the Federal Rules of Criminal Procedure governs the issuance of document subpoenas—on behalf of either the prosecution or defense—and provides that: "A subpoena may order the witness to produce any books, papers, documents, data, or other objects the subpoena designates. The court may direct the witness to produce the designated items in court before trial or before they are to be offered in evidence."[63]

While Rule 17(c) furthers the Sixth Amendment guarantee that criminal defendants will have compulsory process for obtaining favorable witnesses, it "was not intended to provide an additional means of discovery."[64] Rather, its "chief innovation was to expedite the trial by providing a time and place before trial for the inspection of the subpoenaed materials" rather than having the items brought into court only after trial had commenced.[65]

---

59. Fed. R. Crim. P. 16(b)(1)(A).

60. United States v. Bright, 596 F.3d 683, 692 (9th Cir. 2010).

61. United States v. Hubbell, 530 U.S. 27, 36 (2000).

62. *See* Bright, 596 F.3d at 691.

63. Fed. R. Crim. P. 17(c).

64. Bowman Dairy Co. v. United States, 341 U.S. 214, 220 (1951).

65. *Id.* & n.5.

Whereas grand jury subpoenas can be issued essentially at prosecutors' discretion with little or no court oversight,[66] Rule 17(c) subpoenas—also called "trial subpoenas"—require court authorization and are subject to relatively strict requirements. Under the "*Nixon* standard"—named for a case involving former president Richard Nixon—before a trial subpoena requesting pretrial production of documents can be issued, the requesting party must "make a reasonably specific request for information that would be both relevant and admissible at trial."[67] Put differently, the requesting party "must clear three hurdles: (1) relevancy; (2) admissibility; (3) specificity."[68] This standard does not apply to subpoenas for documents or testimony that are returnable at trial—as to them, district court clerks will issue blank subpoenas to counsel without the involvement of the court.[69] In practice, however, the delivery of evidence on the eve of trial is of limited value because it must be reviewed, interpreted, and incorporated into the defendant's overall strategy on the fly.

The Supreme Court's decision in *Nixon* addressed the standard for trial subpoenas issued by a defendant to the government; it expressly did not decide whether that same standard applied to trial subpoenas issued to third parties.[70] Despite this, the *Nixon* standard has since become the de facto standard for Rule 17 subpoenas to parties other than the government. Defense lawyers and some federal judges have criticized this approach, but it remains the general rule applied in most criminal cases.[71]

While *Nixon* applies equally to requests for pretrial Rule 17 subpoenas made by the prosecution and defense, it is generally only the defense who needs them to build their case. For prosecutors, it is far easier to issue subpoenas via the grand jury. Indeed, because charges in complex white-collar cases are generally preceded by lengthy investigations, by the time an indictment is returned by the grand jury the government has often substantially completed its investigation. And even if prosecutors later discover additional avenues of inquiry post-indictment, they may continue to use the vast investigatory power of the grand jury as long as it reasonably relates to a possible superseding indictment (see chapter 2).

The defendant, on the other hand, usually lacks any authority to request documents—from the government or anyone else—during the investigatory stage of the case against him or her. When they are indicted and the government makes its Rule 16 document production, defendants are often seeing the government's evidence for the first time (whereas the

---

66. United States v. R. Enterprises, Inc., 498 U.S. 292, 297 (1991); United States v. Calandra, 414 U.S. 338, 343 (1974) (a grand jury "may compel the production of evidence or the testimony of witnesses as it considers appropriate, and its operation generally is unrestrained by the technical procedural and evidentiary rules governing the conduct of criminal trials").

67. R. Enterprises, Inc., 498 U.S.. at 299–300.

68. *Id.*; *see also* United States v. Mendinueta-Ibarro, 956 F. Supp. 2d 511, 513 (S.D.N.Y. 2013) ("[T]he party's Rule 17(c) subpoena must be able to reasonably specify the information contained or believed to be contained in the documents sought rather than merely hope that something useful will turn up.").

69. *See, e.g.*, United States v. Beckford, 964 F. Supp. 1010, 1017 (E.D. Va. 1997).

70. United States v. Nixon, 418 U.S. 683, 699 n.12 (1974).

71. *See* Robert J. Anello & Richard F. Albert, *Escaping 'Nixon's' Legacy: The Proper Standard for Rule 17(c) Subpoenas*, N.Y. L.J. (Apr. 2, 2013).

government may have already had years to analyze it). To obtain additional documentary materials that may help build their defense in the runup to trial, defendants have no other options but Rule 17. But because the *Nixon* standard sets such a high bar, defendants have a much more difficult time obtaining evidence than government attorneys do.[72] As Judge Richard Holwell of the Southern District of New York noted, *Nixon*'s requirement that the defendant "specify precisely the documents he wants without knowing what they are borders on rendering Rule 17 a nullity."[73] In other words, *Nixon* imposes such a high bar that defendants will only rarely be able to secure evidence through a Rule 17(c) subpoena.

Accordingly, in most cases the defense will only be able to obtain evidence possessed by the government through Rule 16—a result that courts have explicitly condoned.[74]

1. *Obtaining Evidence from Overseas Through Rule 17*

Although district courts' power to compel documents or testimony is usually limited to the United States, parties can use Rule 17 to seek out documentary evidence and witnesses located overseas through letters rogatory and the Walsh Act (28 U.S.C. § 1783).

"Letters rogatory are the medium, in effect, whereby one country, speaking through one of its courts, requests another country, acting through its own courts and by methods of court procedure peculiar thereto and entirely within the latter's control, to assist the administration of justice in the former country."[75] In the Rule 17 context, a district court may issue a request to a foreign court to recognize and enforce a Rule 17 subpoena through letters rogatory. Such requests are transmitted through diplomatic channels, which can be an extraordinarily time-consuming process—letters rogatory generally do not produce results until a year or more after they issue. While prosecutors will generally employ MLAT arrangements to obtain such evidence (see chapter 2), they can also use letters rogatory if an MLAT is unavailable.[76]

District court judges have both statutory and inherent authority to issue letters rogatory at their discretion.[77] The standard for issuance of letters rogatory is the same as if the evidence were located in the United States, that is, the *Nixon* standard.[78] But even when a court is persuaded to make a letters rogatory request, there is no guarantee that it will produce the

72. United States v. Nachamie, 91 F. Supp. 2d 552, 562–63 (S.DN.Y. 2000) ("Unlike the government, the defendant has not had an earlier opportunity to obtain material by means of a grand jury subpoena.").

73. United States v. Rajaratnam, 753 F. Supp. 2d 317, 321 n.1 (S.D.N.Y. 2011).

74. *See, e.g.*, United States v. Cuthbertson, 630 F.2d 139, 146 (3d Cir. 1980) ("Courts must be careful that rule 17(c) is not turned into a broad discovery device, thereby undercutting the strict limitation of discovery in criminal cases found in Fed. R. Crim. P. 16."); United States v. Ramos, 27 F.3d 65, 68 (3d Cir. 1994) (discovery in criminal cases is limited to Rule 16 with some "additional material" under the Jencks Act and Brady v. Maryland, 373 U.S. 83 (1963)).

75. DBMS Consultants Ltd. v. Computer Associates Int'l, Inc., 131 F.R.D. 367, 369 (D. Mass. 1990).

76. The DOJ has a lengthy internal review process for letters rogatory that requires signoff from the Office of International Affairs (OIA). *See* Criminal Resource Manual § 275.

77. 28 U.S.C. § 1781.

78. United States v. Korogodsky, 4 F. Supp. 2d 262, 265 (S.D.N.Y. 1998).

desired materials from the foreign party (since enforcement will depend on the local law of the relevant country). In practice, it is much more difficult for defendants to obtain materials located overseas than it is for prosecutors (who have at their disposal the far easier MLAT mechanism). This asymmetry can create unique difficulties for defendants facing charges in the United States related to conduct occurring mostly—or even exclusively—in a foreign jurisdiction.

The Walsh Act authorizes courts to issue a subpoena to "a national or resident of the United States who is in a foreign country."[79] However, the Walsh Act "does not authorize issuance of a subpoena" to a foreign national who resides abroad.[80] Courts have regularly held that their inability to subpoena a foreign witness—even one who may exculpate the defendant—does not implicate the Sixth Amendment right to compulsory process because such right only applies "where it is within the power of the federal government to provide it." The rationale for this is that, otherwise, "any defendant could forestall trial simply by specifying that a certain person living where he could not be forced to come to this country was required as a witness in his favor."[81]

2. *Challenging Rule 17(c) Subpoenas*

As with grand jury subpoenas, district courts may quash or modify Rule 17(c) subpoenas if compliance would be "unreasonable or oppressive."[82] To have standing to make such a challenge, "the objecting party must have a personal right or privilege in the information sought."[83] "The claim of privilege or right must be personal to the movant, not to the non-party witness on whom the subpoenas was served."[84]

To defeat a motion to quash made by a party with the requisite standing, federal law requires the party seeking disclosure to show: (i) that the documents are evidentiary and relevant; (ii) that they are not otherwise procurable reasonably in advance of trial by exercise of due diligence; (iii) that the party cannot properly prepare for trial without such production and inspection in advance of trial, and that the failure to obtain such inspection may tend

79. 28 U.S.C. § 1783; *see also* Blackmer v. United States, 284 U.S. 421, 438 (1932) ("The jurisdiction of the United States over its absent citizen, so far as the binding effect of its legislation is concerned, is a jurisdiction in personam, as he is personally bound to take notice of the laws that are applicable to him and to obey them.").

80. Aristocrat Leisure Ltd. v. Deutsche Bank Tr. Co. Ams., 262 F.R.D. 293, 305 (S.D.N.Y. 2009); United States v. Korolkov, 870 F. Supp. 60, 65 (S.D.N.Y. 1994).

81. United States v. Yousef, 327 F.3d 56, 114 n.48 (2d Cir. 2003)

82. Fed. R. Crim. P. 17(c)(2).

83. Estate of Ungar v. Palestinian Authority, 332 Fed. App'x 643, 645 (2d Cir. 2009); US Bank Nat'l. Ass'n v. PHL Variable Ins. Co., No. 12 CIV. 6811 (CM) (JCF), 2012 WL 5395249, at *2 (S.D.N.Y. Nov. 5, 2012) ("The moving party must assert some right or privilege personal to it, such as an interest in proprietary, confidential information that would be disclosed or an interest in maintaining a privilege that would be breached by disclosure.").

84. United States ex rel. Ortiz v. Mount Sinai Hosp., 169 F. Supp. 3d 538, 545 (S.D.N.Y. 2016).

unreasonably to delay the trial; and (iv) that the subpoena application is made in good faith and is not intended as a general "fishing expedition."[85]

Practice Note

Prosecutorial Intimidation of Witnesses

The Fifth and Sixth Amendments entitle a criminal defendant to a meaningful opportunity to present a complete defense, including the opportunity to aid in that defense. Because of the DOJ's power to issue subpoenas through the grand jury and its ability to offer incentives for witnesses to testify (e.g., immunity, nonprosecution agreements, reduced sentences), prosecutors generally have far more effective means to obtain relevant information from witnesses than the defendant does. For if prosecutors are unable to obtain such information involuntarily, they can simply subpoena the recalcitrant witness to appear before a grand jury—if the Fifth Amendment privilege is raised, prosecutors can override it with a grant of immunity (see chapter 2). Defendants, on the other hand, can only issue subpoenas for a witness to show up on the witness stand, but they cannot compel such a witness to speak with them before trial or disclose the substance of their intended testimony. Because of the inherent risk of calling a witness where defense counsel is blind as to what they might say, if a prospective defense witness declines to meet before trial, in most instances they will avoid being called to testify.

Against this backdrop, defendants sometimes claim that the government has done something to improperly intimidate a potential defense witness into not testifying—by, for example, designating them as a "subject" or "target" in the investigation or characterizing them as an "unindicted co-conspirator." This significantly enhances the personal risk to the witness in testifying under oath at trial and correspondingly decreases the likelihood they will elect to do so.

To establish a claim that prosecutors have inappropriately disincentivized a prospective witness from appearing at trial, a defendant must show "that he [or she] was deprived of material and exculpatory evidence that could not be reasonably obtained by other means," "bad faith on the part of the government," and "the absence of fundamental fairness infected the trial."[86] To satisfy this burden, the defendant must adduce evidence that is more than merely speculative.[87] Because courts presume that the DOJ acts in good faith when exercising its executive branch functions, defense motions based on these types of claim rarely succeed.

C. Rule 15 Depositions

Although depositions are theoretically available in criminal cases, their use in practice is extremely limited. Federal Rule of Criminal Procedure 15 permits a court to order that a witness be deposed but only under "exceptional circumstances," "to preserve testimony for

85. Nixon, 418 U.S. at 700.

86. United States v. Lebedev, 932 F.3d 40, 55 (2d Cir. 2019); United States v. Williams, 205 F.3d 23, 29 (2d Cir. 2000).

87. United States v. Bin Laden, 116 F. Supp. 2d 489, 495 (S.D.N.Y. 2000); United States v. Stein, No. 05-CR-888, 2006 WL 1063295, at *2 (S.D.N.Y. Apr. 5, 2006).

trial," and in the interests of justice.[88] This rule is generally invoked only when a witness may not be available to testify at trial, not simply when it would be burdensome or inconvenient for the witness to appear. The party requesting a Rule 15 deposition "must show that (1) the prospective witness is unavailable for trial, (2) the witness' testimony is material, and (3) the testimony is necessary to prevent a failure of justice."[89]

"Foreign witnesses who are not subject to the government's subpoena power and, despite the moving party's appropriate efforts, refuse to travel to this country to testify are routinely found unavailable,"[90] including where the witness is not a U.S. citizen and resides outside the country.[91]

District courts retain broad discretion in determining whether the "exceptional circumstances" requirement has been satisfied (with the burden on the party making the request).[92] In considering whether to permit Rule 15 depositions, the court considers the totality of the circumstances, including, but not limited to, timeliness, the availability of the deponents for trial, whether the depositions are for purposes of discovery or for use at trial, the materiality and helpfulness of the proposed deposition testimony, and the safety of U.S. officials whose safety might be compromised by traveling to the foreign country.[93] The requesting party must also show that the deposition procedures in the foreign country are compatible with fundamental issues of fairness in terms of reliability and trustworthiness.[94]

D. The Jencks Act (18 U.S.C. § 3500)

In *Jencks v. United States*, 353 U.S. 657 (1957), the Supreme Court decided that the defense in a federal criminal prosecution is entitled, under certain circumstances, to obtain, for impeachment purposes, statements made to government agents by government witnesses.

---

88. Trump v. Vance, 140 S. Ct. 2412, 2451 n.15 (2020).

89. United States v. Spencer, 362 F. App'x 163, 164 (2d Cir. 2010); United States v. Cohen, 260 F.3d 68, 78 (2d Cir. 2001).

90. United States v. Al Fawwaz, No. 98-CR-1023, 2014 WL 627083, at *1 (S.D.N.Y. Feb. 18, 2014)); United States v. Abu Ghayth, No. S14-98- CR-1023, 2014 WL 144653, at *2 (S.D.N.Y. Jan. 15, 2014) (same).

91. United States v. Johnpoll, 739 F.2d 702, 709 (2d Cir. 1984) (concluding that a Rule 15 deposition was appropriate where the witnesses were "Swiss nationals in Switzerland" who refused to come to the United States and their testimony dealt with the defendant's "arrangements for transporting the stolen securities and secreting the proceeds from their sale"); United States v. Little, No. 12-CR-647, 2014 WL 1744824, at *2 (S.D.N.Y. Apr. 23, 2014) (granting Rule 15 motion where the witness "established that she is unavailable as a [United Kingdom] citizen who is unwilling to come to the United States to testify").

92. United States v. Omene, 143 F.3d 1167, 1170 (9th Cir. 1998); United States v. Farfan-Carreon, 935 F.2d 678, 679 (5th Cir. 1991).

93. United States v. Olafson, 213 F.3d 435, 442 (9th Cir. 2000); United States v. Drogoul, 1 F.3d 1546, 1556 (11th Cir. 1993).

94. Societe Nationale Industrielle Aerospoatiale v. United States Dist. Ct. S.D. Iowa, 482 U.S. 522 (1987).

In response to this decision, Congress passed the "Jencks Act," codified at 18 U.S.C. § 3500, to specify when statements of government witnesses—so-called "3500 Materials"—must be disclosed. The Jencks Act controls the timing of witness statement disclosure, even if the statements qualify as *Brady* material.[95]

Specifically, the Jencks Act requires that no prior statement of a government witness made to a government agent shall be turned over to the defense until the witness has testified on direct examination.[96] The Jencks Act therefore prohibits a district court from ordering the pretrial disclosure of witness statements over the government's objections.[97]

"This section manifests the general statutory aim to restrict the use of such statements to impeachment,"[98] and was intended to serve several purposes.

> On the one hand, it protects the rights of a defendant by requiring the court to give the defendant access to relevant prior statements of a witness after the witness has testified at trial (18 U.S.C. § 3500(b)). On the other hand, the prosecution cannot be compelled to disclose statements of the witness before he has testified on direct examination (18 U.S.C. § 3500(a)). This unique but limited discovery device represents a legislative determination that access to a witness' statements could be useful in impeaching a witness but was not intended to be utilized in preparation for trial.[99]

The importance of the Jencks Act in federal criminal practice cannot be overstated—it effectively means that a defendant has no right to know, prior to trial, what the government's witnesses told the government about the offense at issue. Because these statements—recorded on FBI Form 302 (see chapter 2)—are generally always critical pieces of evidence, defendants are left at a significant informational disadvantage compared to the government until the trial itself (or just shortly before).[100] Indeed, courts have found that providing information about a government witness to the defense as little as one day in advance of the witness's testimony is appropriate under the Jencks Act.[101] This forces defense counsel to race to analyze

---

95. Jones, 612 F.2d at 455; United States v. Percevault, 490 F.2d 126, 128–29 (2d Cir. 1974).

96. 18 U.S.C. § 3500(a).

97. In re United States, 834 F.2d 283, 286–87 (2d Cir. 1987).

98. Palermo v. United States, 360 U.S. 343, 349 (1959).

99. Percevault, 490 F.2d at 128.

100. Although the government cannot be compelled to disclose statements of prospective witnesses prior to the time prescribed by the Jencks Act, district courts will often use their case management powers to press for an agreement between the parties on an earlier timetable. As acknowledged by the Second Circuit, "[I]n most criminal cases, pretrial disclosure [of witness statements] will redound to the benefit of all parties, counsel, and the court. Indeed, sound trial management would seem to dictate that Jencks Act material should be transmitted prior to trial, especially in complex cases, so that those abhorrent lengthy pauses at trial to examine documents can be avoided. We suggest that the district judge may find the pretrial conference, Fed. R. Crim. P. 17.1, a useful forum for establishing a timetable for discovery and for reaching agreements on the scope of disclosure." Percevault, 490 F.2d at 132.

101. *See* United States v. Ruiz, 702 F. Supp. 1066, 1069–70 (S.D.N.Y. 1989); United States v. Helbrans, No. 19- CR-49701, 2021 WL 2873800, at *19 (S.D.N.Y. July 8, 2021).

the 302s and build them into their cross-examination and overall defense strategy shortly before, or even during, trial.[102]

Under Federal Rule of Criminal Procedure 26.2, the Jencks Act applies not only to trials, but to evidence suppression hearings, preliminary hearings, sentencing, probation hearings, detention hearings, and hearings on motions to vacate a sentence.[103] Rule 26.2 also imposes a reciprocal obligation on defendants to produce any statement made by a defense witness (other than the defendant) "that is in their possession and that relates to the subject matter of the witness's testimony."[104]

The Jencks Act and Rule 26.2 both apply only to "statements," defined as (i) "a written statement made by a [testifying government or defense] witness and signed or otherwise adopted or approved by him"; (ii) "a substantially verbatim recital of an oral statement made by said witness and recorded contemporaneously with the making of such oral statement"; or (iii) "a statement, however taken or recorded, or a transcription thereof, if any, made by said witness to a grand jury."[105] Whether a particular statement fits within one of these discrete categories is often an intense point of contention between the prosecution and defense.[106]

Certain USAOs have an "open disclosure" policy whereby Jencks Act material is disclosed to the defendant at the same time as the government's Rule 16 disclosures; even in those districts, however, defendants have no legal right to compel prosecutors to make such disclosures other than in accordance with statute if for whatever reason they decide not to in a particular case.[107]

1. *Interview Notes*

As a general rule, notes and memoranda prepared by government agents are not discoverable under Rule 16 so long as the government turns over a written report that contains all the information found in the notes or memoranda.[108] Rule 16(a)(2) expressly exempts

102. The Jencks Act is perceived by many in the criminal defense bar as hindering a defendant's ability to receive a fair trial. As two commentators recently characterized the problem: "[B]ecause federal prosecutors often bring cases based entirely upon the statements of cooperating witnesses, a defendant's inability to gain access to those critical statements until the trial is already underway calls into question the fundamental fairness of the proceedings. The prosecutor crafts his or her opening and witness examinations knowing what all the prior statements contain, while the defense counsel is in the dark." Philip Jobe & Marc Greenwald, *Congress Should Amend the Jencks Act Now*, N.Y. L.J. (Feb. 2, 2022).

103. Fed. R. Crim. P. 26.2(g).

104. Fed. R. Crim. P. 26.2(a).

105. 18 U.S.C. § 3500(e); Fed. R. Crim. P. 26.2(f).

106. *See, e.g.*, Goldberg v. United States, 425 U.S. 94 (1976) (notes or summaries of a witness interview made by government agents will be "statements" under § 3500 if the witness confirms they are accurate); Campbell v. United States, 365 U.S. 85 (1961) (typed interview reports prepared by an FBI agent can qualify as "statements" if adopted by the witness or if it includes verbatim statements).

107. *Justice Manual* § 9-5.002 ("Providing broad and early discovery often promotes the truth-seeking mission of the [DOJ] and fosters a speedy resolution of many cases. It also provides a margin of error in case the prosecutor's good faith determination of the scope of appropriate discovery is in error.").

108. United States v. Muhammad, 120 F.3d 688, 699 (7th Cir. 1997); United States v. Coe, 220 F.3d 573, 582 (7th Cir. 2000).

from disclosure "reports, memoranda, or other internal government documents made by an attorney for the government or other government agent in connection with investigating or prosecuting the case."

Furthermore, Rule 16(a)(2) does not authorize the discovery or inspection of statements made by government witnesses or prospective government witnesses except as provided in the Jencks Act. As noted above, the Jencks Act entitles a defendant only to "a written statement made by [a government] witness and signed or otherwise adopted by him."[109] An FBI agent's interview notes are discoverable under the statute only where they relate to the subject matter of a witness's testimony and were "substantially a verbatim transcript of the [witness's] remarks, or were his own written statement adopted and approved by him."[110]

Notwithstanding the above, courts have determined that the Jencks Act does not require the government to preserve notes made in the course of an investigation after the notes have served their purpose in the preparation of interview reports (i.e., FBI 302s).[111] Where there is no bad faith on the part of the government and no prejudice to the defendant, the Jencks Act permits destruction of interview notes that have been incorporated into a formal report.

E. The Government's Obligations under *Brady* and *Giglio*

In *Brady v. Maryland*, 373 U.S. 87 (1963), the Supreme Court ruled that prosecutors have "a constitutional duty to disclose favorable evidence to the accused where such evidence is material either to guilt or punishment."[112] This rule is "based on the requirement of due process" and is designed to "ensure that a miscarriage of justice does not occur."[113] Thus, to "the extent that [a] prosecutor knows of material evidence favorable to the defendant in a criminal prosecution, the government has a due process obligation [grounded in the 5th and 14th Amendment] to disclose that evidence to the defendant."[114] In *Giglio v. United States*, 405 U.S. 150, 154–55 (1972), the Court expanded the scope of mandatory disclosures under *Brady* to include favorable material evidence relating to the credibility of a government witness.[115] While neither decision requires prosecutors to deliver their entire file to defense

---

109. 18 U.S.C. § 3500(e)(1).

110. United States v. Lopez, 6 F.3d 1281, 1288 (7th Cir. 1993), United States v. Starnes, 644 F.2d 673, 681 (7th Cir. 1981); United States v. Morrison, 946 F.2d 484, (7th Cir. 1991) ("If [rough] notes were substantially verbatim recitals of [the witness's] statements, then the government was obligated to turn them over," pursuant to § 3500).

111. United States v. Harris, 542 F.2d 1283, 1292 (7th Cir. 1976).

112. United States v. Certified Env't Servs., Inc., 753 F.3d 72, 91 (2d Cir. 2014).

113. United States v. Bagley, 473 U.S. 667, 674 (1985); United States v. Nejad, 487 F. Supp. 2d 206, 208 (S.D.N.Y. 2020) ("Government lawyers wield enormous prosecutorial power. They must exercise it in a way that is fully consistent with their constitutional and ethical obligations. And it is the obligation of the courts to ensure that they do and hold them accountable if they do not.").

114. United States v. Gil, 297 F.3d 93, 101 (2d Cir. 2002).

115. Certified Env't Servs., Inc., 753 F.3d at 91; *see also* United States v. Brennerman, 818 F. App'x 25, 29 (2d Cir. 2020).

counsel, they must disclose "evidence favorable to the accused that, if suppressed, would deprive the defendant of a fair trial."

Individual prosecutors have "a duty to learn of any favorable evidence known to others acting on the government's behalf in the case, including the police."[116] Knowledge of all evidence in the possession of the government—which can include the DOJ, FBI, and any other state or federal agency working with the prosecution, is attributed to the prosecutor.

1. Materiality

Due process requires only the disclosure of *material* information, not all evidence that might conceivably be of use to the defense.[117] Since *Brady* and *Giglio* issues generally are raised when key evidence is disclosed or uncovered after trial, materiality is assessed retrospectively. Evidence will be considered material for *Brady* and *Giglio* purposes "only if there is a reasonable probability that, had the evidence been disclosed to the defense, the result of the proceeding would have been different."[118]

The "touchstone of materiality" is "reasonable probability," a relatively low standard.[119] The question is not whether the defendant would more likely than not have received a different verdict had the evidence been disclosed, but rather whether "the suppressed evidence could reasonably be taken to put the whole case in such a different light as to undermine confidence in the verdict." "The materiality of the evidence is measured by the effect it would have had on the result of the trial, the focus being on fairness" in light of the entire record.[120] In other words, even if a piece of evidence appears highly material in isolation, if the other evidence of guilt is overwhelming, it will likely not be considered material in context.

To establish a *Brady* or *Giglio* violation, "a defendant must show that: (1) the government, either willfully or inadvertently, suppressed evidence; (2) the evidence at issue is favorable to the defendant; and (3) the failure to disclose this evidence resulted in prejudice."[121] Although there is no precise deadline for when the government is required to disclose *Brady* and *Giglio* material, the rule in most courts is that prosecutors must make the necessary disclosures in time for their effective use at trial by the defendant (see section I.E.3).[122]

116. Kyles v. Whitley, 514 U.S. 437 (1995); *see also* Carriger v. Stewart, 132 F.3d 463, 480 (9th Cir. 1997) (noting that "[b]ecause the prosecution is in a unique position to obtain information known to other agents of the government, it may not be excused from disclosing what it does not know but could have learned").

117. Ostrer v. United States, 577 F.2d 782, 788 n.4 (2d Cir. 1978).

118. *Id.* at 682.

119. Kyles, 514 U.S. at 419, 434 (1995).

120. United States v. Oruche; United States v. Agurs, 427 U.S. 97, 112 (1976).

121. United States v. Kirk Tang Yuk, 885 F.3d 86 (2d Cir. 2018); *see also* Strickler v. Greene, 527 U.S. 263, 281–82 (1999).

122. United States v. Djibo, 730 F. App'x 52, 55 (2d Cir. 2018); United States v. Campbell, 850 F. App'x 102, 109 n.4 (2d Cir. 2021) ("It is well settled that as long as a defendant possesses Brady evidence in time for its effective use, the government has not [committed a Brady violation] simply because it did not produce the evidence sooner.").

2. *Making* Brady *and* Giglio *Determinations*

Federal prosecutors make the initial determination of whether any of the evidence within their possession contains exculpatory evidence or evidence that impeaches the government's case. In other words, what *Brady* and *Giglio* disclosures are made largely depend on how the government assesses each piece of evidence—"the prosecution does not have a constitutional duty to disclose every bit of information that might affect the jury's decision; it need only disclose information favorable to the defense that meets the appropriate standard of materiality."[123] "If the prosecution is uncertain about the materiality of information within its possession, it may submit the information to the trial court for an *in camera* inspection and evaluation."[124] Otherwise, where there is doubt about the exculpatory value of certain information, disclosure is required.[125]

DOJ policy imposes an obligation on AUSAs to "seek all exculpatory and impeachment information from all members of the prosecution team."[126] While the makeup of the "prosecution team" can be a subject of dispute (see section I.E.4), DOJ policy encourages prosecutors to err on the side of inclusiveness when identifying members of the prosecution team for discovery purposes and to make "considered efforts to locate discoverable information."[127]

To ensure that this obligation is carried out, AUSAs are directed to review the full investigation file, investigatory files related to any potential witnesses, "substantive case-related communications" (e.g., written communications among prosecutors and/or FBI agents, and between prosecutors and/or agents and witnesses), information obtained in witness interviews (including any contemporary notes made by interviewers).

Practice Note

Disclosure of Government Communications with Cooperators

Most federal white-collar crime cases will involve at least one "cooperating witness," that is, an individual who has agreed to plead guilty and cooperate against his or her co-conspirators. Because they may affect the cooperator's credibility, defendants will often seek disclosure of all written communications between the cooperator and government agents.

In *United States v. Suarez*, for example, the FBI used Solomon Dwek as a cooperating witness to investigate public corruption in New Jersey.[128] Dwek was instructed by his FBI handlers to hold himself out to be a real estate developer and to offer local officials bribes in exchange for expediting development projects. During the period Dwek was doing so, he exchanged numerous text messages with two FBI special agents.

---

123. United States v. Cadet, 727 F.2d 1453, 1467 (9th Cir. 1984).

124. *Id.*

125. Whiteley, 514 U.S. at 439.

126. *Justice Manual*, 9-5.001.

127. *Justice Manual*, 9-5.000.

128. No. 09-cr-00932, 2010 WL 4226524 (D.N.H. Oct. 21, 2010).

When certain of the officials were charged with bribery offenses, they requested discovery of the text messages. After initially agreeing to disclose them, prosecutors told defendants that they could not produce any of the texts because neither Dwek's mobile phone carrier nor the FBI retained text messages longer than a few days. In light of the DOJ's failure to produce the messages, the defendants filed a motion requesting the court to either suppress Dwek's evidence or issue an adverse inference instruction.

Addressing these issues, the district court first determined that the missing texts constituted "statements" discoverable under the Jencks Act because it assumed that "the agents and the cooperating witness each adopted and approved each message they sent when they affirmatively chose to transmit it." The court also ruled that the missing texts were potentially "fertile ground for cross examination" and related "to the subject matter of the witness's testimony." Since the messages were at one time within the government's possession, the court concluded that prosecutors had a duty to preserve it so that it could ultimately be disclosed to defendants.

As to the appropriate sanction for this failure, the court pointed to Federal Rule of Criminal Procedure 26.2(e), which provides that "[i]f a party who called a witness disobeys an order to produce or deliver [Jencks material], the court must strike the witness's testimony from the record," and "[i]f an attorney for the government disobeys the order, the court must declare a mistrial if justice so requires." Noting that these sanctions are not mandatory in the context of destruction of Jencks material outside of a court order, and that the DOJ had acted in good faith, the court denied suppression but agreed to give the jury an adverse inference instruction as to Dwek's testimony.[129]

3. *Timing of* Brady *and* Giglio *Disclosures*

The "time required for the effective use of a particular item of evidence will depend on the materiality of that evidence" and "the particular circumstances of the case."[130] "*Brady* information must be disclosed . . . in a manner that gives the defendant a reasonable opportunity either to use the evidence in the trial or to use the information to obtain evidence for use in the trial. Thus, the Government must make disclosures in sufficient time that the defendant will have a reasonable opportunity to act upon the information efficaciously."[131] A failure to timely disclose *Brady* material may require a new trial.[132]

The issue of when *Giglio* material should be disclosed, is "analyzed separately," because, as opposed to *Brady* material, "[*Giglio*] material ripens into evidentiary material for purposes of impeachment only if and when the witness testifies at trial."[133] Accordingly, there is no constitutional right to early disclosure of *Giglio* material.[134] Instead, the government may "defer[] production" of *Giglio* material "until closer to the time of the witnesses' testimony"

129. Similar issues have been raised in several subsequent cases. *See, e.g.*, United States v. Harry, 927 F. Supp. 2d 1185 (D.N.M. 2013); United States v. Durante, No. 11-cr-00277 (D.N.J. Feb. 7, 2012); United States v. Pitts, No. 10-cr-00703 (E.D. Pa. Oct. 31, 2011).

130. United States v. Coppa, 267 F.3d 132, 146 (2d Cir. 2001).

131. United States v. Rodriguez, 496 F.3d 221, 27–28 (2d Cir. 2007).

132. United States v. Lewis, 368 F.3d 1102, 1107 (9th Cir. 2004).

133. United States v. Frank, 11 F. Supp. 2d 322, 325 (S.D.N.Y. 1998); United States v. Earls, No. 03-CR-364, 2004 WL 350725, at *8 (S.D.N.Y. Feb. 25, 2004).

134. United States v. Davis, No. 17-CR-615, 2021 WL 826261, at *4 (E.D.N.Y. Mar. 3, 2021).

as long as the defendant still has time to use it effectively.[135] Nevertheless, a court may "order *Brady/Giglio* disclosure at any time as a matter of 'sound case management,'"[136] even if such disclosure might contravene the Jencks Act.[137] The practice in most courts is not to compel immediate disclosure of *Brady/Giglio* materials where prosecutors represent they are aware of and will comply with their disclosure obligations, and the defense does not provide any reason for suspecting the government will not comply.[138]

4. *Scope of Prosecutors' Disclosure Obligations*

As discussed earlier, the Fifth Amendment's Due Process Clause requires the government to disclose favorable material evidence in its knowledge or possession to a criminal defendant.[139] Even though this obligation extends only to material evidence known or possessed by the DOJ, prosecutors are presumed to have knowledge of all evidence gathered in connection with their investigation and have a duty to learn of any favorable evidence known to others acting on the government's behalf in the case.[140]

Accordingly, a "prosecutor is deemed to have constructive knowledge of information known to persons who are a part of the 'prosecution team.'"[141] The government is "reasonably expected to have possession of evidence in the hands of investigators, who are part of the 'prosecution team,'" as well as anyone else who acts as "an arm of the prosecutor" or are "intimately involved in the prosecution."[142] "Whether someone is part of the prosecution team depends on the level of interaction between the prosecutor and the agency or individual."[143] The majority rule is that where a USAO conducts a "'joint investigation' with another state or federal agency [e.g., the SEC or CFTC] . . . the prosecutor's duty extends to reviewing the materials in the possession of that other agency for *Brady* evidence."

"A prosecution team may have many members with different responsibilities. At its core, members of the team perform investigative duties and make strategic decisions about the prosecution of the case." The prosecution team therefore includes any "police officers and federal agents" who submit to the direction of the prosecutor and participate in the investigation" as well as individuals who are not "strategic decision-makers" such as paralegals, translators, and other assistants to the prosecution.[144] The propriety of imputing knowledge

---

135. Frank, 11 F. Supp. 2d at 325.

136. United States v. Taylor, 17 F. Supp. 3d 162, 177 (E.D.N.Y. 2014).

137. Coppa, 267 F.3d at 145.

138. United States v. Mohamed, 148 F. Supp. 3d 232, 246 (E.D.N.Y. 2015).

139. Brady, 373 U.S. at 86.

140. Kyles, 514 U.S. at 437; United States v. Barcelo, 628 F. App'x 36, 38 (2d Cir. 2015).

141. Barcelo, 628 F. App'x at 38.

142. United States v. Morrell, 524 F.2d 550, 555 (2d Cir. 1975); *see also* Avellino, 136 F.3d at 255.

143. United States v. Meregildo, 920 F. Supp. 2d 434, 441 (S.D.N.Y. 2013).

144. United States v. Gupta, 848 F. Supp. 2d 491, 493 (S.D.N.Y. 2012).

to the prosecution is determined by examining the specific circumstances of the person alleged to be an "arm of the prosecutor."[145]

The "relevant inquiry is what the person *did*, not who the person *is*."[146] But simply "interacting with the prosecution team, without more, does not make someone a team member." "Instead, under the totality of the circumstances, the more individuals are with the prosecutor, the more likely they are team members." Among other things, "these circumstances include whether the individual actively investigates the case, acts under the direction of the prosecutor, or aids the prosecution in crafting trial strategy."[147]

Where a USAO conducts a "joint investigation" with another state or federal agency, courts have held that the prosecutor's duty extends to reviewing the materials in the possession of that other agency for *Brady* evidence."[148] But courts "generally agree that the prosecutor's obligations do not extend to agencies that are not law enforcement agencies, even though they may furnish some information to the prosecution."[149] The same is true of private parties, including cooperating government witnesses and cooperating private entities.[150]

a. *Brady* and Deferred Prosecution Agreements

As explained in further detail in chapter 11, white-collar crime cases against individual defendants are often accompanied by a corporate entity—typically their employer during the time of the relevant conduct—entering into a "deferred prosecution agreement" (DPA). The "essence" of a DPA is a bargain that in exchange for a company's cooperation, the DOJ will refrain from prosecuting it. "Under a typical DPA with a corporate defendant, the defendant admits to a statement of facts, submits to the filing of criminal charges against it on the basis of those facts, and agrees to a forfeiture or fine and to institute remedial measures. In exchange, the government agrees to defer prosecution and to ultimately seek dismissal of all charges if the defendant complies with the DPA."[151]

When a defendant's employer has entered into a DPA, the issue arises as to whether the government's *Brady* and other discovery obligations extend to the corporate entity. Since the standard DPA requires the company to disclose to the government "any document, record, or other tangible evidence about which the [the DOJ] may inquire,"[152] at least one court has found that the company's documents are effectively within the government's possession and control.[153] Most courts have rejected such arguments, however, on the basis that the mere

145. United States v. Alvared-Estevez, 671 F. App'x 834, 835 (2d Cir. 2016).

146. United States v. Stewart, 433 F.3d 273, 298 (2d Cir. 2006).

147. Meregildo, 920 F. Supp. 2d at 441–42.

148. Gupta, 848 F. Supp. 2d at 493.

149. Wayne Lafave et al., Criminal Procedure § 20.3(a) (3d ed. 2011).

150. United States v. Garcia, 509 F. App'x 40, 43 (2d Cir. 2013); United States v. Graham, 484 F.3d 413, 417 (6th Cir. 2007); United States v. Lujan, 530 F. Supp. 2d 1224, 1231 (D.N.M. 2008).

151. United States v. HSBC Bank USA, N.A., 863 F.3d 125, 129–31 (2d Cir. July 12, 2017).

152. *See, e.g.*, United States v. State Street Corporation, 21-cr-10153 (D. Mass. May 13, 2021).

153. Stein, 488 F. Supp. 2d at 363–64.

fact that a company has entered into a DPA does not make them a part of the "prosecution" team for discovery purposes.[154]

F. Defense Motions to Compel Discovery

Defendants who have reason to believe the prosecution has failed to fulfil its obligations under Rule 16, *Brady*, or *Giglio* can file a motion with the court asking for an order compelling the DOJ to disclose the desired evidence. For such a motion to be successful, the defendant must make at least a prima facie showing that the requested items are material to his or her defense.[155]

To meet this standard, a defendant cannot rely on general descriptions or conclusory arguments. The defendant must instead "convincingly explain how specific documents will significantly help him uncover admissible evidence, prepare witnesses, or corroborate, impeach, or rebut testimony."[156] Put differently, the defendant must show that the requested documents have more than an "abstract logical relationship" to the issues in the case by indicating that they will enable him to "alter significantly the quantum of proof in his case."[157]

II. PRETRIAL DISCLOSURE IN CROWN COURT PROCEEDINGS

As discussed in chapter 3, British prosecutors are required to turn over all "used" material—that is, the evidence in its possession that it intends to rely upon in the prosecution—prior to the plea and trial preparation hearing (PTPH) and entry of the defendant's initial plea. Thus, "disclosure" in the United Kingdom is the process by which a criminal defendant is provided with access to any material held by prosecutors that might reasonably be considered capable of undermining the prosecution's case, or of assisting the case for the accused, and that has not already been disclosed.

The rules governing disclosure in the United Kingdom are principally contained in the Criminal Procedure and Investigations Act (CPIA) 1996 and Part 15 of the Criminal Procedure Rules 2015 (CrimPR). Application of these rules is guided by the Ministry of Justice's CPIA Code of Practice. In addition to those defined by statute, there are separate disclosure duties under the common law of England and Wales.

A. CPIA Code of Practice for Law Enforcement

The CPIA Code of Practice sets out the manner in which law enforcement officers in England and Wales are required to record, retain, and reveal to the prosecutor materials obtained in the course of a criminal investigation. To ensure that investigations and disclosure operate

---

154. United States v. Josleyn, 206 F.3d 144, 153–54 (1st Cir. 2000); United States v. Ng, No. 18-cr-00538 (S.D.N.Y. Sept. 10, 2021); United States v. Tomasetta, No. 10-cr-1205 (S.D.N.Y. Mar. 16, 2012).

155. United States v. Maniktala, 934 F.2d 25, 29 (2d Cir. 1991).

156. United States v. Caputo, 373 F. Supp. 2d 789, 793 (N.D. Ill. 2005); *see also* United States v. Mandel, 914 F.2d 1215, 1219 (9th Cir. 1990); United States v. Jordan, 316 F.3d 1215, 1250 (11th Cir. 2003).

157. United States v. Ross, 511 F.2d 757, 762–63 (5th Cir. 1975).

effectively and fairly, the United Kingdom employs a system of checks and balances that explicitly divides decision-making authority among the officer in charge of an investigation, the disclosure officer, and the prosecutor.[158] This is in contrast to the practice in the United States, where the DOJ prosecutors handling a case are also responsible for making discovery decisions, except in the limited circumstances where "taint teams" or special masters are used (see chapter 2).

As the title suggests, the "officer in charge" is responsible for the overall conduct of an investigation and for ensuring that proper procedures are in place for recording and retaining information that may be relevant to the conduct under suspicion. A "disclosure officer" is responsible for examining material obtained by police during an investigation, providing this material to prosecutors, and disclosing it to defendants at the direction of prosecutors. Disclosure officers function independently from the law enforcement officials in charge of criminal investigations, to ensure there are no conflicts of interest. British prosecutors are generally less directly involved in criminal investigations than their counterparts at the DOJ. While prosecutors in England may participate in pre-charge interviews and help guide investigations, their role is mainly to assess the legal significance of evidence obtained by investigators, make charging decisions, and present the Crown's case in court. The attorney general directs investigators and disclosure officers to "be fair and objective" and to "work together with prosecutors to ensure that disclosure obligations are met."[159]

Investigators are required to ensure that all reasonable lines of inquiry are investigated, whether they point toward or away from any particular suspect. Throughout an investigation, investigators are further required to "always have in mind their obligation to retain and record all 'relevant material,' defined as anything that 'has some bearing on any offense under investigation or any person being investigated, or on the surrounding circumstances of the case.'"[160] Material that is presumed to meet the test for disclosure (discussed below) must always be retained and recorded.

Disclosure officers and investigators must inspect, view, listen to, or search for all relevant material. It is then up to the prosecutor to determine which relevant material is used as evidence and which material is classified as "unused"—that is, material that is relevant but does not form part of the prosecution's case against an accused. As stated by the House of Lords at a time when it still functioned as the highest court in the United Kingdom,

> Fairness ordinarily requires that any material held by the prosecution which weakens its case or strengthens that of the defendant, if not relied on as part of its formal case against the defendant, should be disclosed to the defence. Bitter experience has shown that miscarriages of justice may occur where such material is withheld from disclosure. The golden rule is that full disclosure of such material should be made.[161]

How material that forms part of an investigation may be categorized and treated is illustrated in figure 5.1.

---

158. CPIA Code of Practice, s. 2.1.

159. Attorney General's Guidance on Disclosure (2020), s. 8.

160. *Id.*, s. 18.

161. R v. H [2004] UKHL 3.

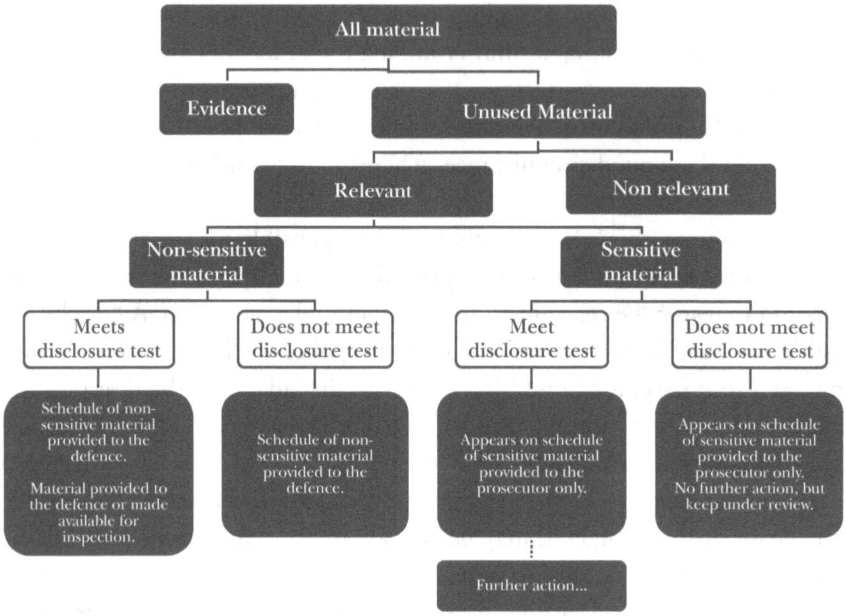

Figure 5.1 Categorization of materials in an investigation to determine relevance for disclosure.

(*Source:* Attorney General's Guidance on Disclosure [2020].)

1. *Material Held by Government Departments*

A government department that is not involved in an investigation will sometimes have relevant material; for example, the FCA may hold information about the target of an SFO investigation. When investigators or prosecutors are aware that this may be the case, they are required to notify the relevant government department, disclose the nature of the investigation, and request that it turn over any relevant material (which it must then do unless there is some privilege or other legal basis not to). This right to request material notwithstanding, investigators and prosecutors "cannot be regarded to be in constructive possession of material held [elsewhere in the government] simply by virtue of their status" as fellow government agents. The steps taken to identify and obtain relevant material held within the government should be recorded by the investigator and the prosecutor.[162]

2. *Material Held by Third Parties*

In financial crime investigations, relevant material is often held by third parties such as securities exchanges, financial institutions, or a suspect's employer. While these parties are generally not directly involved in criminal investigations, investigators have an obligation to take all reasonable steps to identify and obtain relevant material they may possess (either through requests for voluntary disclosure or by using the investigatory powers described in

162. Attorney General's Guidance on Disclosure (2020), ss. 31–37.

chapter 2). Where these measures are unsuccessful, prosecutors may make an application for a production order under Section 2 of the Criminal Procedure (Attendance of Witnesses) Act (CPA) 1965. Under this provision, the Crown Court may issue a witnesses summons requiring a third party to provide testimony in court or produce documentary evidence if satisfied that the "person is likely to be able to give evidence likely to be material" and "it is in the interests of justice" to secure it.

If material is obtained from a third party, it must be treated in accordance with CPIA and be disclosed if it meets the disclosure test, unless the party to whom the materials belong can establish a reason they should not be.[163] Appropriate reasons include that the requested material is not likely to be material evidence or that there are grounds (such as confidentiality) that outweigh the reasons disclosure is requested.[164]

3. Material Located Overseas

The obligation to pursue all reasonable lines of inquiry extends to material located outside of the United Kingdom. Where it appears that potentially relevant material is overseas, the investigator or prosecutor must take all reasonable steps to obtain it, either through informal requests or by using its powers under its the United Kingdom's MLAs (discussed in chapter 2) or the Crime (International Co-operation) Act 2003, which pertains to orders freezing property and the exchange of evidence between the United Kingdom and member countries of the European Union. Because the ability of British law enforcement to acquire such materials is dependent on the law of the relevant foreign country, "there is no duty on the prosecutor to disclose relevant material held overseas by entities not subject to the jurisdiction of the courts in England and Wales."[165]

Rather, the obligation under CPIA is to take all reasonable steps and, where investigators are allowed to examine foreign materials but not allowed to make copies or take notes, "there is no breach by the prosecution in its duty of disclosure by reason of its failure to obtain such material, provided reasonable steps have been take to try and obtain it."[166] In any event, the prosecution's position in relation to overseas material must be clearly set out in writing in a disclosure management document (DMD) so that the court and the defense can assess it.

4. The Disclosure Management Document

The DMD outlines law enforcement's approach to disclosure and is prepared under the assumption that it will be provided to the defense and the court at an early stage in any related criminal proceedings (generally at the same time as initial disclosures are made). DMDs are required in all cases in Crown Court and are prepared by the Crown prosecutor.

---

163. CPIA, s. 16.

164. CrimPR 17.6(3).

165. Attorney General's Guidance on Disclosure (2020), s. 48.

166. *Id.*, s. 49.

DMDs describe how disclosure responsibilities have been managed between investigators and prosecutors. They include a summary of the prosecution's case, along with the prosecutor's preliminary understanding of the likely defense case (including information revealed during any interviews with the defendant). At the prosecutor's option, DMDs may also describe the key issues in dispute, along with the lines of inquiry that have been taken into such issues. Where relevant, DMDs will usually also contain details on how electronic materials were gathered and examined, how video footage was obtained, how materials were sought from third parties and from overseas, and the credibility of potential prosecution witnesses.[167] There is no comparable obligation for AUSAs.

B. Disclosure under the Criminal Procedure and Investigations Act

Similar to the requirements set down by the U.S. Supreme Court in *Brady* and *Giglio*, CPIA Section 3 requires prosecutors to disclose to a defendant any "prosecution material" that "might reasonably be considered capable of undermining" the prosecution's case or assisting the defense. This statutory obligation is triggered only after the defendant has pleaded not guilty and the case has been sent for trial to the Crown Court, and continues through the end of trial.[168] Prior to this stage in the proceedings, what the prosecution is required to disclose is governed by the common law (see section II.C).

"Prosecution material" is defined as any material "which is in the prosecutor's possession" or that the prosecutor has inspected in connection with the defendant's case. Unlike in the United States, a defendant's right to evidence under this section is automatic—that is, there is no requirement that the defendant make a formal request for disclosure like there is under Federal Rule of Criminal Procedure 16.

The CPIA does not require prosecutors to disclose either neutral material or material that is adverse to the defendant.[169] Rather, such material is listed on a schedule that alerts the defense to its existence but does not need to be disclosed. A full log of disclosure decisions and the reasons for those decisions must be kept on file and made available to the prosecution team, which should include a "reviewing lawyer" who engages in an ongoing review of the prosecution's disclosure obligations.

Under the CPIA Code of Practice para. 6.6, there is a rebuttable presumption that certain categories of evidence will meet the test for disclosure. These include any previous accounts made by a witness or complainant, interview records with actual or potential witnesses or suspects, and any material casting doubt on the reliability of a witness.

1. *Initial Disclosures*

The timing of initial disclosures depends on nature of the charges and how the defendant is expected to plead. As discussed in chapter 3, where it is expected that the case will be sent to the Crown Court for trial after a plea of not guilty, initial disclosures are generally

---

167. *Id.*, ss. 86–95.

168. CPIA, s. 7A.

169. R v. H and others [2004] UKHL 3, p. [17] and [35].

served prior to the PTPH, which must occur within twenty-eight days of a defendant's initial appearance in the magistrates' court.[170] In cases prosecuted by the SFO and other large and complex cases, making a full initial disclosure is often not possible prior to the PTPH. In such circumstances, prosecutors are directed to make initial disclosures in phases pursuant to a DMD.

Initial disclosures must provide the defense with copies of, or access to, any materials in the prosecution's possession that might reasonably be considered capable of undermining the case or of otherwise assisting the defendant.[171] In deciding whether materials should be included in initial disclosures, prosecutors must consider: the use that might be made of it in cross-examination and to undermine the reliability or credibility of a prosecution witness; its capacity to support arguments for the exclusion of evidence or a stay of proceedings; its capacity to explain the defendant's conduct; and its relevance to any expert or scientific evidence in the case. Materials should be assessed holistically, since "whilst items taken alone may not be reasonably considered capable of undermining the prosecution case or assisting the case for the accused, several items together can have that effect."[172] If there is no material meeting this disclosure test within the prosecutors' possession, they must provide a written confirmation of that fact to the defendant.[173]

a. Public Interest Immunity from Disclosure

In some financial crime cases, there may be material held by the prosecution that may meet the test for initial disclosure but that cannot be disclosed without the risk of serious prejudice to an important public interest. For example, when an investigation involves the use of informers, under-cover agents, or covert surveillance, which cannot be disclosed without exposing individuals to the risk of personal injury or jeopardizing the success of future law enforcement operations.

In these circumstances, the CPIA allows prosecutors to apply to the court for an order to withhold material in whole or in part from the defendant.[174] In ruling on such an application, the court must consider, among other things, the likelihood of a serious prejudice to an important public interest if the material is disclosed, the relevance of the material to the defendant's case, and whether there are alternative ways to provide disclosure without risking injury to a public interest.[175] In weighing these issues, the judge "should involve the defence to the maximum extent possible without disclosing that which the general interest requires to be protected but taking full account of the specific defence which is relied upon.

170. CrimPR 9.7(5)(a)(ii). The PTPH will include scrutiny of the prosecution's DMD and will involve the defense identifying the likely trial issues and additional lines of inquiry that should be pursued. Where the defense believes that the prosecution has not adequately discharged its obligations, such issues should be raised at the PTPH.

171. CPIA, s. 3.

172. Attorney General's Guidance on Disclosure (2020), ss. 79–86.

173. CPIA, s. 3(b).

174. CrimPR 15.3.

175. R v. H and others [2004] UKHL 3.

There will be very few cases indeed in which some measure of disclosure to the defence will not be possible."[176]

Under the attorney general's guidelines, "if the prosecutor concludes that a fair trial cannot take place because material which satisfies the test for disclosure cannot be disclosed and that this cannot be remedied by an application for non-disclosure in the public interest, through altering the presentation of the case or by any other means, then they should not continue with the case."[177]

2. *Witness Statements*

As discussed in chapter 2, government witnesses in U.S. criminal cases almost always meet with prosecutors—usually multiple times—prior to trial to discuss their anticipated testimony. The only record of these meetings are FBI 302 reports, which are in summary form and generally do not record the questions being asked by prosecutors. The witness will have no chance to review the 302 for accuracy, and a defendant will usually have no opportunity to see the 302s relevant to his or her case until right before trial under 18 U.S.C. § 3500.

The procedures by which a prospective witness's pretrial statements are memorialized in the United Kingdom are substantially different. In Crown Court trials, any witness intending to give oral testimony in court on behalf of the prosecution or the defense must first provide a formal witness statement to all other parties. Unlike FBI 302s, witness statements in the United Kingdom are usually detailed and must always be reviewed by the witness, signed, and declared true to the best of the witness's knowledge and belief.[178]

For individuals who are likely to appear as witnesses on behalf of prosecutors in a financial crime case, the witness statements are usually drafted by SFO investigators after one or more interviews with the witness under the SFO's Section 2 powers (see chapter 2). In another break with U.S. practice, solicitors for the defense can request copies of any witness statements and tape recordings of the relevant interviews to ensure the final statement is consistent. The statements of defense witnesses are generally drafted by the defendant's solicitors, who must take care to include only statements that the witness could reasonably be expected to provide if giving live testimony in court.[179]

Because witness statements in the United Kingdom are always adopted as accurate by the witness, they can be introduced into evidence even if the witness does not give oral testimony at trial so long as all the parties and the court give consent.[180]

---

176. *Id.*

177. Attorney General's Guidance on Disclosure (2020), s. 120.

178. CJA 1967, s. 9(2); CrimPR 16.2.

179. R v. Kellett [1976] 1 QB 372.

180. CrimPR 16.4.

Practice Note

Witness Preparation in the United Kingdom

From the British perspective, witnesses are improperly coached in the United States. There, it is typical for prosecutors and defense counsel to meet with witnesses they intend to call at trial multiple times to go over the questions that will be asked and what the witness's responses will be. There will also usually be extensive preparation for how the witness will respond to questions expected to be asked on cross-examination. While the vast majority of attorneys involved in this process are careful to avoid improperly influencing the witness's testimony, pressure to remember events in a certain way cannot always be avoided—especially for cooperating witnesses whose punishment depends largely on the degree to which their testimony is helpful against another defendant.

The proper scope of witness preparation in the United Kingdom is governed by the Bar Standards Board (BSB) Handbook (a document similar to the state-by-state Rules of Professional Conduct governing attorneys in the United States). Rule C9.4 of the BSB Handbook states that legal counsel "must not rehearse, practise with or coach a witness in respect of their evidence."

In *R v. Momodou,* the Court of Appeal emphasized that while witness coaching is flatly prohibited, it is permissible for witnesses to be familiarized with the layout of the court, the likely sequence of events during their testimony, and an objective description of cross-examination techniques. In the court's view, such arrangements prevent a witness's testimony from being hampered by ignorance of court procedures and are therefore not only permissible but desirable.[181] In terms of how witness familiarization efforts should be conducted, the court gave broad guidance:

(1) Any familiarization should be supervised by a solicitor or barrister who does not have personal knowledge of the matters in issue in the trial or hearing in question.

(2) Records should be kept of all those present during the familiarization sessions, and all materials provided to the witness must be retained.

(3) None of the material provided to the witness should bear any similarity to the issues in the criminal proceedings at issue, and nothing should play on or trigger the witness's recollection of events.

(4) If discussion of the relevant criminal proceedings begin, it must be stopped, and advice must be given as to precisely why it is impermissible, with a warning against the danger of evidence contamination and the risk that the course of justice may be perverted. A note should be made if and when any such warning is given.

Although the Court of Appeal's guidance permits a witness to participate in a mock examination-in-chief and cross-examination, strict protocols must be used to ensure their testimony is not improperly influenced. The sole purpose of such a mock session must be to simply give a witness greater familiarity with and confidence in the process of giving oral evidence. If the solicitor or barrister running the session perceives any risk that it might enable a witness to add a specious quality to his or her evidence, they should refuse to take further part in it.[182]

181. [2005] EWCA Crim 177.

182. The Bar Council Ethics Committee, *Witness Preparation* (November 2019).

3. The Prosecution's Duty to Call Witnesses

Although prosecutors have broad discretion as to which witnesses to call to testify at trial, this discretion is not completely unfettered. Under the Court of Appeal's ruling in *R v. Russell-Jones* [1995] Cr App Rep 538, the prosecution must have present at court all those witnesses whose statements have been served on the defense and on whom the prosecution intend to rely so that they can be subject to cross-examination by the defendant. Moreover, the prosecution must normally call or offer to call all witnesses who have given direct evidence of a primary fact in the case unless, in the prosecutors' judgment, there is good reasons to regard the witness's evidence as unworthy of belief. In making this judgment, prosecutors must act in the interests of justice so as to promote a fair trial—that is, a witness cannot be deemed unreliable simply because their testimony differs from other witnesses or is one that is unfavorable to the prosecution's case.

Where witness statements have been taken but not served on the defense as used material, prosecutors are not under any duty to call those witnesses at trial.[183]

4. The Defense Case Statement

To a far greater extent than under Federal Rule of Criminal Procedure 16(a)(1)(E), criminal defendants in the United Kingdom must make disclosures about their defense to prosecutors. In Crown Court cases, defendants must serve a defense case statement (DCS) in a timely manner—generally twenty-eight days—after the prosecution makes initial disclosures. Under CPIA Section 6A, the DCS must: (i) set out the nature of the accused's defense, including any particular defenses on which he or she intends to rely; (ii) indicate the matters of fact on which the accused takes issue with the prosecution and explain why; and (iii) indicate any point of law (including in relation to the admissibility of evidence or an abuse of process) that the defense wishes to raise. Although generally not relevant in financial crime cases, Section 6A also requires disclosures if the defendant plans to raise an alibi.

DCSs must be specific—they cannot "make general and unspecified allegations in order to seek far reaching disclosure and should not describe the defence in ambiguous or limited terms."[184] However, no defense statement is required if the defendant does not plan to put on an affirmative defense case.[185] If prosecutors deem a defense statement lacking, they may make an application to the court for an order that a more adequate defense statement be made.

The defense statement is intended to help direct law enforcement toward further lines of evidence that should be pursued. Prosecutors are required to send defense statements to investigators along with guidance on further investigation into the key issues. For example, per the Judicial Protocol on the Disclosure of Unused Material in Criminal Cases, the defense must "engage and assist in the early identification of the real issues in the case and, particularly in the larger and more complex cases, to contribute to the search terms to be used for, and the parameters of, the review of any electronically held material." The Attorney General's Guidelines similarly call for the defense "to play their role to ensure that the prosecution are

183. R v. Richardson [1994] 98 Cr. App. R. 174

184. Attorney General's Guidance on Disclosure (2020), s. 123.

185. R v. Malcom [2011] ECA Crim 2069.

directed to material which might reasonably be considered capable of undermining the prosecution case or assisting the case for the accused. This process is key to ensuring prosecutors make informed determinations about disclosure of unused material. The [DCS] is important in identifying the issues in the case and why it is suggested that the material meets the test for disclosure." This framework makes the defendant a much more active participant in the investigation process in the United Kingdom than in the United States.

It is important for the defense statement to be as comprehensive as possible, since defense requests for further disclosure under CPIA Section 8 will generally only be entertained if relevant to an issue already identified in the defense statement.[186] "If it is not, then a further or amended defense statement should be sought and obtained by the prosecutor before considering the request for further disclosure."[187] If a DCS's deficiencies are not corrected (or if it is served late or not at all), CPIA Section 11(5) provides that the "court or any party may make such comment as appears appropriate" and the "court or jury may draw such inferences as appear proper in deciding whether the accused is guilty of the offence concerned."

a. Disclosure of Defense Witnesses

To the extent not already included in a defense statement, defendants are required to give to the court and the prosecutor a notice indicating whether he or she intends to call any other persons as witnesses, and if so, provide their contact details and any information in the defendant's possession that may help law enforcement locate them. If, after providing a list of prospective witnesses, the defendant decides to call a person who is not on the list or discovers any information that should have been included, "he must give an appropriately amended notice to the court and prosecutor."[188] Defendants are similarly required to provide notice of "any expert opinion for possible use as evidence at the trial."[189]

5. *Continuing Disclosure and Applications for Specific Disclosure*

As noted, CPIA Section 7A imposes on prosecutors a continuing duty to disclose any material that might be reasonably capable of undermining the case for the prosecution or assisting the case for the defendant. To satisfy this obligation, prosecutors must consider any issues raised by the defense during the PTPH, as well as during any further hearings and after receipt of a DCS.

While the Attorney General's Guidelines caution that "disclosure must not be an open-ended trawl of unused material," CPIA Section 8(2) provides that "if the accused has at any time reasonable cause to believe that there is prosecution material which is required by [S]ection 7A to be disclosed to him and has not been, he may apply to the court for an order requiring the prosecutor to disclose it." A Section 8 application is only permitted once a DCS has been served and after the defense has taken all reasonable means to obtain the desired materials.[190]

---

186. *See also* CrimPR 15.5.

187. Attorney General's Guidance on Disclosure (2020), s. 126.

188. CPIA, s. 6C.

189. CPIA, s. 6D.

190. CrimPR, 15.5.

6. *Third-Party Disclosure Applications*

Like the prosecution, criminal defendants in the United Kingdom can seek a court order compelling the production of documents held by third parties under CPA Section 2. The application must be made as soon as practicable after the requesting party becomes aware of the grounds for doing so and must include an explanation as to what evidence the third party can provide, why it is likely to be material, and why the interests of justice require that it be produced.[191] "Speculative enquiries without any proper basis in relation to third party material are to be discouraged; in accordance with the CPIA Code of Practice and the Attorney General's Guidelines on Disclosure . . . there must be some reason to believe [the third party] may have relevant material."[192] This is much more lenient than the *Nixon* test used for Rule 17 subpoenas in the United States and, in general, U.K. defendants' have a greater ability to secure evidence held by third parties than defendants in the United States.

Similar to a motion to quash a subpoena in the United States, the third party who is the subject of a disclosure application can lodge an objection with the court to invalidate or limit it.[193]

C. Common Law Disclosure

Aside from their obligations under the CPIA, prosecutors are required to consider whether justice and fairness requires disclosure of evidence earlier than is required by statute under the U.K.'s "common law disclosure" rules.[194] These rules require the disclosure officer, regardless of a defendant's anticipated plea, to certify that, to the best of the officer's knowledge and belief, no information has been withheld that would assist the accused in the preparation of the defense case, including the making of a bail application. Common law disclosure generally requires immediate disclosure of the following:

- Any previous convictions of the victim or a key witness if that information could reasonably be expected to assist the accused when applying for bail.
- Material that might enable an accused to make an early application to stay the proceedings as an abuse of process.
- Material that might enable an accused to make representations about trial venue on a lesser charge.
- Material that would enable an accused to prepare for trial which may be significantly less effective if disclosure is delayed (e.g., names of eyewitnesses whom the prosecution does not intend to use).[195]

---

191. CrimPR, 17.3.

192. CPS & NPCC, Joint Protocol on Third Party Material (2018), para. 3.2.

193. CrimPR, 17.6.

194. R v. DPP ex parte Lee [1999] 2 All Er 737.

195. CPS Disclosure Manual: Chapter 2 (Oct. 21, 2021), *available at* https://www.cps.gov.uk/legal-guidance/disclosure-manual-chapter-2-general-duties-disclosure-outside-cpia-1996.

D. Consequences of Disclosure Failures

As with a failure by the DOJ to make *Brady* and *Giglio* disclosures,[196] a failure by Crown prosecutors to make all required disclosures can have serious ramifications on their case. Most often, the court will make an order under PACE Section 78 limiting or excluding the admissibility of certain prosecution evidence to ensure the defendant receives a fair trial.[197] In situations where the court finds the prosecution's disclosure failure to have resulted in serious prejudice to the defense that cannot be overcome with evidentiary rulings, the case may also be stayed or dismissed as an abuse of process.

If the defense fails to make a required disclosure, sanctions can include (i) denial of the right to make an application for unused material under CPIA Section 8, (ii) the court drawing inferences from any failure in deciding whether the accused is guilty of an offense, and (iii) a wasted costs order (if the failure results in additional expense for the prosecution).

Practice Note

The Serious Fraud Office's Disclosure Failure in the Zaid Akle Case

Zaid Akle was an oil industry executive at Monaco-based Unaoil who was charged by the SFO with bribing officials at an Iraqi state-run oil company. Akle's alleged co-conspirators in this scheme included the members of the Ahsani family (Cyrus and Saman Ahsani) who controlled Unaoil, Basil Al Jarah, Unaoil's local partner in Iraq, and Paul Bond (a Unaoil executive).

In 2016, Akle and Al Jarah were arrested in the United Kingdom and the Ahsanis were arrested in Monaco at the request of British authorities. After being released on bail, Cyrus Ahsani and the family patriarch, Ata, fled for Lebanon and Iran, respectively (neither of which have extradition treaties with the United Kingdom). Saman remained in Monaco.

While the SFO was engaged in extradition proceedings against Saman in the Monegasque courts, he was detained on a U.S. arrest warrant in Italy (a short drive away from his home in Monaco). Italy subsequently extradited Saman to the United States to face FCPA and money laundering allegations; in light of these developments, the SFO abandoned its investigation of the Ahsanis and refocused on Akle and Al Jarah. Meanwhile, Cyrus voluntarily surrendered to U.S. jurisdiction and cut a package deal with the DOJ with his brother and father: Ata would pay a penalty of $2.25 million and face no further action; and Cyrus and Saman would plead guilty to bribery charges and cooperate against others involved. Pursuant to this arrangement, Cyrus and Saman Ahsani entered plea agreements in March 2019.[198]

Meanwhile, back in England, Al Jarah pleaded guilty to making corrupt payments in July 2019 pursuant to a cooperation agreement with the SFO. On October 8, 2020, Al Jarah was sentenced to forty-two months' imprisonment (reduced from ten years as a result of his guilty plea and cooperation).

---

196. The USAO for the Southern District of New York, one of DOJ's most preeminent outposts, has recently come under fire for repeated failures to disclose *Brady* and *Giglio* materials to the defense. *See* Jack Queen, "'Bury It': Inside a Hidden Evidence Scandal that Rocked SDNY," LAW360 (Mar. 15, 2021); Lauren Briggerman, et al., "SDNY Grapples with Judicial Rebukes," BLOOMBERG LAW (Nov. 10, 2020).

197. R v. Boardman [2015] EWCA Crim 175.

198. United States v. Ahsani, 2019-cr-00147 (S.D. Tex.). The Ahsani's had not yet been sentenced as of May 2022, suggesting that they were continuing to cooperate with U.S. authorities.

As the SFO prepared its case against Akle and Bond for trial, it indicated that it would seek to adduce evidence of Al Jarah's conviction under Section 74 of PACE as part of its proof against Akle.[199] The SFO also disclosed, as part of its schedules of unused material under the CPIA, documents referring to contacts between the SFO and David Tinsley, a private investigator in the United States who was working with the Ahsanis' U.S. defense attorney.

Despite repeated requests from Akle, the SFO refused to provide copies of any of these materials. This then forced Akle to submit an application for specific disclosure of the Tinsley materials under CPIA Section 8. The basis for this application was an argument that Tinsley's conduct had been such that Al Jarah's guilty plea was unreliable evidence of the alleged conspiracy and would therefore cause unfair prejudice. In support of this position, Akle's counsel submitted that Al Jarah's plea appeared to have been improperly influence by Tinsley, described as a "fixer seeking to negotiate between the Ahsanis, the U.S. authorities and the U.K. authorities" who placed improper pressure on Al Jarah.

Akle's Section 8 application failed to compel the SFO to disclose its Tinsley-related materials and, shortly before trial, he filed an abuse of process application. Not wanting to disrupt the trial schedule, the Crown Court judge took the application under advisement and reserved decision until a later date.

Akle was subsequently convicted at trial and his abuse of process application was then re-addressed. After reviewing some of the undisclosed materials in camera, in a written ruling the Crown Court noted that "Tinsley, who had no official title or status but had acted as an agent or broker on the instructions of and in the interests of the Ahsanis, had had contact with [Lisa Osofsky], the Director of the SFO." During those conversations, Tinsley told Osofsky and others at the SFO "that he would be able to deliver pleas of guilty from [Al Jarah] and Akle, which he suggested would lead to consequential convictions of others."[200] Despite finding it to be "ill advised," the Crown Court did not consider the Tinsley/SFO engagement to constitute abuse of process; Akle's conviction was left to stand and he was subsequently given a five-year sentence. He then appealed to the Court of Appeal (which listed the case for argument on July 1, 2021).

As oral argument on his appeal approached, the barrister representing the SFO advised the parties that there had been inadequate disclosure of the Tinsley materials, and the court thereafter directed the SFO to turn over all the documents on several of its unused materials schedules (amounting to 650 pages). In summary, the newly disclosed documents revealed numerous communications between Tinsley and the SFO that suggested much closer coordination than the SFO had previously let on.

In the Court of Appeal's view, the SFO's failure to disclose these documents earlier constituted a clear violation of its CPIA obligations:

> When copies were requested by the defence, they should have been provided. The refusal to provide them was a serious failure by the SFO to comply with their duty. It cannot be justified by reference to the precise terms of the [S]ection 8 request when that request specifically raised Tinsley's conduct as the basis on which the admission of the evidence would be challenged. That failure was particularly regrettable given

199. PACE, s. 74(1) states: "In any proceedings the fact that a person other than the accused has been convicted of an offence by or before any court in the United Kingdom . . . shall be admissible in evidence for the purpose of proving that that person committed that offence." See chapter 7 for further details on this provision.

200. R v. Akle and Bond [2021] EWCA Crim 1879, [44]–[45].

that some of the documents had a clear potential to embarrass the SFO in their prosecution of this case. . . .

Tinsley did not act for either [Al Jarah] or Akle, each of whom was legally represented in this country; and there was a clear conflict between their respective interests and the interests of the Ahsanis. The [SFO] case team quite rightly declined, for a considerable time, to have any dealings with Tinsley in relation to the cases against [Al Jarah] and Akle . . .

In summary, we are satisfied that there was a material failure of disclosure which significantly handicapped the defence in arguing that the evidence of [Al Jarah's] convictions should be excluded pursuant to [S]ection 78 of PACE. We think it striking that in resisting the application to exclude such evidence, the SFO relied on the fact that [Al Jarah] was legally represented when he decided to plead guilty to the charges against him, and on the concession by defence counsel that it was not possible to discharge the burden imposed on the defence by [S]ection 74 of PACE. Had the documents been disclosed, neither of those arguments would have been available to the SFO: the documents would have shown, much more clearly than appeared from the summaries in the schedules, that the SFO knew that Tinsley was deliberately operating behind the backs of [Al Jarah's] lawyers, and that Tinsley wanted to control whom BAJ spoke to; and we think it wholly unlikely that the concession, which was made on the basis of the schedule entries alone, would have been made. . . .

For those reasons, we are satisfied that the convictions of Akle are not safe. He was prevented from presenting his case in its best light. We grant leave to appeal on grounds 2 and 3, and allow the appeal on those grounds. His convictions must therefore be quashed."[201]

CHAPTER 5: KEY DISTINCTIONS

United States	United Kingdom
Defendants must affirmatively seek evidentiary disclosures from the government following arraignment	Disclosure of the prosecution's "used material" is automatic once charges are filed
Evidence that could be relevant to a case but that is not required to be disclosed need not be described to the defense	Prosecutors must disclose a schedule of "unused material" to the defendant
Defendants only have a right to summaries of prior statements of witnesses to government investigators; such summaries are generally only made available right before trial	Transcripts of witness interviews and all written witness statements obtained by prosecutors are part of the standard disclosures
Fugitive disentitlement doctrine generally bars fugitives from participating in the discovery process	Fugitive disentitlement doctrine not recognized

(Continued)

201. *Id.*, [96]–[97], [99], [105], [108].

United States	United Kingdom
Defendant need only disclose the evidence he or she intends to rely on at trial	Defendant must serve a defense case statement setting forth the evidence on which he or she intends to rely at trial as well as details about the nature of the defense theory
Depositions can be taken in extraordinary cases where a key witness is unable to testify at trial	Depositions not permitted
Witness statements are virtually never recorded, transcribed, or reviewed by the witness for accuracy	Witness statements are always reviewed by the witness for accuracy and oral statements are generally always recorded or transcribed
Prospective trial witnesses usually engage in extensive preparation for their testimony with the party who intends to call them	Witness preparation is strictly curtailed to avoid the possibility that a witness's testimony is improperly influenced

6 Resolving and Challenging a Case before Trial

Once an individual is formally charged with a criminal offense, there are typically only three ways for the case to end: by a jury verdict following trial (or by a directed verdict after the prosecutor's case in chief); a guilty plea (pursuant to an agreement with prosecutors or otherwise); or dismissal before trial for some significant defect in the underlying investigation or charging instrument. From a defendant's perspective, achieving an optimal outcome while avoiding the severe cost and uncertainty of a criminal trial is obviously the most desirable option.

In cases where outright dismissal or an attractive plea agreement are not realistically on the table, a defendant preparing for trial will want to challenge prosecutors' legal theories and evidence as much as possible through pretrial motions to the court (referred to as "applications" in the United Kingdom). This chapter covers the types of challenges defendants often make in financial crime cases in advance of trial, and the procedures used to negotiate and reach plea and cooperation agreements in both countries.

I. PRETRIAL MOTIONS TO CHALLENGE THE PROSECUTORS' CASE IN THE UNITED STATES

A. Motions to Dismiss an Indictment

Pretrial motions to dismiss an indictment in full or in part are made pursuant to Federal Rule of Criminal Procedure 12(b), which allows a party to raise "any defense, objection, or request that the court can determine without a trial on the merits." This rule allows a defendant to seek dismissal for various legal defects in the prosecution or charging instrument: for example, improper venue, unreasonable delay, failure to state an offense, and improper joinder.[1] "To successfully challenge the sufficiency of an indictment, a defendant must demonstrate that the indictment did not satisfy one or more of the required elements and that he suffered prejudice from the alleged deficiency."[2] The test is "not whether the indictment could have been formed in a more satisfactory manner, but whether it conforms to minimal constitutional standards."[3]

1. Fed. R. Crim. P. 12(b)(3) (listing possible grounds for Rule 12(b) motions).
2. United States v. Vaughn, 722 F.3d 918, 925 (7th Cir. 2013).
3. United States v. Hausmann, 345 F.3d 952, 955 (7th Cir. 2003).

Because a "court's use of its supervisory power to dismiss an indictment directly encroaches upon the fundamental role of the grand jury," dismissal is granted only in "unusual circumstances."[4] It is "an extraordinary remedy reserved only for extremely limited circumstances implicating fundamental rights."[5] As such, the requirements for the government to sustain an indictment are very low: indictments need do "little more than to track the language of the statute charged and state the time and place (in approximate terms) of the alleged crime" and are read "to include facts which are necessarily implied by the specific allegations made."[6]

Moreover, "the facts alleged by the government must be taken as true" and contrary assertions of fact by the defendants will not be considered.[7] It is therefore improper for the court to address the sufficiency of the evidence underlying the indictment, except in the rare circumstances where the DOJ has already made "a full proffer of the evidence it intends to present at trial."[8] This is because indictments are "not meant to serve an evidentiary function," but rather are intended to merely inform defendants of the crimes with which they are charged, allow them to prepare a defense, and protect them from double jeopardy.[9] Simply put, "if a grand jury returns a lawful indictment that provides adequate notice and states a federal crime, a defendant who pleads not guilty ordinarily must proceed to trial in order to be vindicated."[10] Indeed, statistics show that only about eight percent of federal criminal cases are dismissed.[11]

An indictment may be dismissed, however, where it "fails to allege the essential facts constituting the offense charged".[12] In other words, dismissal is required where the conduct alleged in the indictment as a factual basis for the offense is not actually prohibited by the language of the statute.[13] There are no common law crimes in the federal system; therefore, the adequacy of an indictment will often turn on the interpretation of statutory language because federal crimes "are solely creatures of statute."[14]

Courts interpreting a criminal statute will first examine the plain language of the law itself under the "assumption that the ordinary meaning of that language accurately expresses the legislative purpose."[15] When the statutory language is clear, courts will apply it as written

4. United States v. Ballestas, 795 F.3d 138, 148 (D.C. Cir. 2015).

5. United States v. De La Pava, 268 F.3d 162 (2d Cir. 2001).

6. United States v. Rigas, 490 F.3d 208, 229 (2d Cir. 2007); De La Pava, 268 F.3d at 157, 162 (indictments "need not be perfect, and common sense and reason are more important than technicalities").

7. United States v. Velastegui, 199 F.3d 590, 592 n.2 (2d Cir. 1999).

8. United States v. Perez, 575 F.3d 164, 166 (2d Cir. 2009).

9. United States v. Juwa, 508 F.3d 694, 701 (2d Cir. 2007).

10. United States v. Griffith, 20-cr-15 (PKC), at *1 (S.D.N.Y. Jan. 27, 2021).

11. U.S. Courts, Criminal Statistical Tables for the Federal Judiciary (Dec. 31, 2021), *available at* https://www.uscourts.gov/statistics/table/d-4/statistical-tables-federal-judiciary/2021/12/31.

12. Russell v. United States, 369 U.S. 749, 768 (1962) (stating that "an important corollary purpose" of the requirement that an indictment state the elements of an offense "is to inform the court of the facts alleged, so that it may decide whether they are sufficient in law to support a conviction, if one should be had").

13. *See, e.g.*, United States v. Pirro, 212 F.3d 86, 91-93 (2d Cir. 2000); United States v. Pacione, 738 F.2d 567, 572 (2d Cir. 1984); United States v. Mennuti, 639 F.2d 107, 113 (2d Cir. 1981).

14. Dowling v. United States, 473 U.S. 207, 213 (1985).

15. United States v. Albertini, 472 U.S. 675, 680 (1985).

since, in the federal system, the task of creating new laws is reserved to Congress. If it is not, courts will turn to the overall statutory purpose and its legislative history.[16] Finally, courts will employ the "rule of lenity," which requires that any unclear or ambiguous law is interpreted in the manner most favorable to a criminal defendant: as emphasized by the Supreme Court, "when choice has to be made between two readings of what conduct Congress has made a crime, it is appropriate, before [courts] choose the harsher alternative, to require that Congress should have spoken in language that is clear and definite."[17]

1. Motions to Dismiss under the "Void for Vagueness Doctrine"

The Fifth Amendment's guarantee that "[n]o person shall . . . be deprived of life, liberty, or property, without due process of law" forbids vague criminal laws. Consequently, no person can "be held criminally responsible for conduct which he could not reasonably [have] understand to be proscribed."[18] In light of these principles, criminal defendants may seek to dismiss an indictment under the "void for vagueness" doctrine.

This doctrine requires that a penal statute define the criminal offense with sufficient definiteness that ordinary people can understand what conduct is prohibited and in a manner that does not encourage arbitrary and discriminatory enforcement.[19] If a reasonable person would have been on notice that his or her conduct was at risk, and reasonable guidelines for enforcement exist, the due process concerns raised in a vagueness challenge are overcome.[20]

Vagueness inquiries are therefore directed at two concerns: fair notice and arbitrary and discriminatory prosecutions. Under the fair notice prong of this test, a court must determine whether the statute, either standing alone or as construed, made it reasonably clear at the relevant time that the defendant's conduct was criminal.

The arbitrary enforcement prong requires that a statute give "minimal guidelines" to law enforcement authorities, so as not to "permit a standardless sweep that allows policemen, prosecutors, and juries to pursue their personal predilections."[21] In other words, the Constitution does not allow Congress to "set a net large enough to catch all possible offenders, and leave it to the courts to step inside and say who could be rightfully detained, and who should be set at large."[22] Yet a statute will not be considered improperly vague "simply because it requires law enforcement to exercise some degree of judgment."[23]

16. *See* Boyle v. United States, 129 S.Ct. 2237, 2246 (2009); *see also* United States v. Nelson, 277 F.3d 164, 193 (2d Cir. 2002).

17. United States v. Bass, 404 U.S. 336, 347 (1971).

18. United States v. Lanier, 520 U.S. 259, 265 (1997); F.C.C. v. Fox Television Stations, Inc., 132 S. Ct. 2307, 2317 (2012) ("A fundamental principle in our legal system is that laws which regulate persons or entities must give fair notice of conduct that is forbidden or required.").

19. United States v. Coscia, 866 F.3d 782, 791 (7th Cir. 2017); United States v. Napout, 963 F.3d 163, 181 (2d Cir. 2020).

20. United States v. Pitt–Des Moines, Inc., 168 F.3d 976, 987 (7th Cir.1999).

21. Mannix v. Phillips, 619 F.3d 187, 197 (2d Cir. 2010).

22. City of Chicago v. Morales, 527 U.S. 41, 60 (1999).

23. Coscia, 866 F.3d at 794.

Vagueness challenges to statutes not threatening the free speech and freedom of religion rights in the First Amendment are examined in light of the facts of the case at hand and on an "as-applied basis."[24] This means that a defendant must prove that the specific prosecution against him or her arose from arbitrary enforcement. This inquiry "involves determining whether the conduct at issue falls so squarely in the core of what is prohibited by the law that there is no substantial concern about arbitrary enforcement because no reasonable enforcing officer could doubt the law's application in the circumstances."[25]

Before striking a federal statute as impermissibly vague, courts will first try to save it through a more limited interpretation if it is reasonable to do so.[26] If the "general class of offenses to which the statute is directed is plainly within its terms, the statute will not be struck down as vague" so long as the targeted conduct can be made "constitutionally definite by a reasonable construction of the statute."[27]

Vagueness issues often arise in the white-collar crime context because the definitions of such crimes are usually broader than "street crimes" and focus more on the defendant's mental state when engaging in an otherwise legal activity. For "[i]t is much less clear what it means to 'devise a scheme or artifice to defraud' another, or convey something of value to an official that counts as a bribe . . . than what it means to . . . 'possess heroin with the intent to distribute.' A statute that prohibits all false statements in matters of federal government jurisdiction covers a massively larger realm of behavior than one that bans possession of firearms by convicted felons."[28]

Practice Note

Michael Coscia's "Void for Vagueness" Motion to Dismiss

As discussed in chapter 4, Michael Coscia was the first person to be criminally prosecuted for "spoofing," a crime created by an amendment to the Commodities Exchange Act (CEA) in 2010.[29] Coscia was the principal of Panther Energy Trading LLC, a high-frequency futures trading firm in Chicago.[30]

The indictment alleged that Coscia developed a high-frequency trading algorithm that allowed him to enter and cancel large-volume orders in a matter of milliseconds. According to prosecutors, the purpose of this strategy was to create artificial movement in futures markets so as to allow Coscia to buy and sell futures contracts at better prices than would have otherwise

24. United States v. Coppola, 671 F.3d 220, 235 (2d Cir. 2012) (quoting Maynard v. Cartwright, 486 U.S. 356, 361 (1988)).

25. Farrell v. Burke, 449 F.3d 470, 494 (2d Cir. 2006).

26. Skilling v. United States, 561 U.S. 358, 403 (2010) (directing district courts to strive to "construe, not condemn, Congress' enactments" because of their strong presumptive validity).

27. United States v. Harriss, 347 U.S. 612, 618 (1954).

28. Samuel W. Buell, *Is the White Collar Offender Privileged?*, 63 Duke L.J. 842 (January 2014).

29. The statute makes it unlawful to engage in trading that "is, is of the character of, or is commonly known to the trade as, 'spoofing' (bidding or offering with the intent to cancel the bid or offer before execution)." CEA § 4c(a)(5).

30. United States v. Coscia, 100 F. Supp. 3d 653, 655 (N.D. Ill. 2015).

been available. The essence of the prosecution theory was that Coscia's quickly cancelled, large-volume orders created "a false impression regarding the number of contracts available in the market" and "fraudulently induce[d] other market participants to react to the deceptive market information that he created."[31]

Coscia filed a motion to dismiss the indictment in which he argued, among other things, that the CEA's antispoofing provision (ASP) was unconstitutionally vague because it "fails to offer any ascertainable standard that separates spoofing from legitimate trade practices."[32] In support of this argument, Coscia contended that there was no commonly understood meaning of "spoofing" in the world of futures trading; a point confirmed, he alleged, by debates surrounding interpretive guidance on the ASP that was issued by the CFTC in 2013. According to Coscia, the ongoing debate surrounding the meaning of spoofing at the time of his alleged offense illustrated that the legality of his conduct was an "open question from the outset."[33]

In response, the DOJ argued that there was never any serious debate as to whether the conduct alleged in the indictment—intentionally entering bids and offers with the intent to cancel them—falls within the meaning of the statute.

The district court assessed these positions and considered whether the ASP was indeed unconstitutional as applied to Coscia's conduct. Accepting all of the indictment's factual allegations as true, the court noted the significance of the ASP's "intent to cancel" requirement: "When the government must prove intent and knowledge, these requirements do much to destroy any force in the argument that application of the statute would be so unfair that it must be held invalid."[34] From this perspective, the court concluded that the ASP was not void for vagueness because the conduct alleged in the indictment clearly involved "bidding or offering with the intent to cancel" (which was specifically prohibited in the statute).[35] This determination was subsequently upheld on appeal to the Seventh Circuit. Following this favorable ruling, the DOJ has brought the majority of its spoofing cases in the Northern District of Illinois, a court bound by the decisions of the Seventh Circuit.

2. *Motions to Dismiss under the Speedy Trial Act (18 U.S.C. § 3161)*

The Constitution's Sixth Amendment states that in all criminal prosecutions, "the accused shall enjoy the right to a speedy and public trial." This provision creates a "safeguard to prevent undue and oppressive incarceration prior to trial, to minimize anxiety and concern accompanying public accusation and to limit the possibilities that long delay will impair the ability of an accused to defend himself."[36] In contrast to statutes of limitations, this safeguard becomes relevant only when a prosecution has begun and extends only to individuals who have been criminally charged. As the Supreme Court stated in *United States v. Marion*, the Sixth Amendment "afford[s] no protection to those not yet accused" and does not "require the Government to discover, investigate, and accuse any person within any particular period

31. *Id.*

32. *Id.* at 656.

33. *Id.* at 657.

34. *Id.* at 659 (quoting United States v. Cherry, 938 F.2d 748, 754 (7th Cir. 1991)).

35. *Id.*

36. United States v. Ewell, 383 U.S. 116, 120 (1966); *see also* Klopfer v. North Carolina, 386 U.S. 213, 221–226 (1967); Dickey v. Florida, 398 U.S. 30, 37–38 (1970).

of time." Rather, it simply gives a guarantee to a criminal defendant that prosecutors "will move with the dispatch that is appropriate to assure him an early and proper disposition of the charges against him."[37]

The Sixth Amendment's speedy trial assurance is codified in the Speedy Trial Act (18 U.S.C. § 3161). Section 3161(b) sets forth the time limit in which the government must seek an indictment: "Any information or indictment charging an individual with the commission of an offense shall be filed within thirty days from the date on which such individual was arrested or served with a summons in connection with such charges." Importantly, however, the statute excludes any period of delay resulting from, among other things:

- "[O]ther charges against the defendant"
- "[A]ny pretrial motion, from the filing of the motion through the conclusion of the hearing on, or other prompt disposition of, such motion"
- "[A]ny proceeding relating to the transfer of a case or the removal of any defendant from another district"
- "[C]onsideration by the court of a proposed plea agreement to be entered into by the defendant and the attorney for the Government"

Also excluded is any period of delay in prosecution resulting from a written agreement between the DOJ and the defendant, the absence or unavailability of the defendant or an essential witness, the joinder for trial with a codefendant, or a continuance granted by any judge on his or her own motion or at the request of the defendant or the government.[38]

Under Section 3162(a)(1), in any case where an individual is charged via complaint and "no indictment or information is filed within the time limit required by [S]ection 3161(b) as extended" for one of the reasons above, such charges "shall be dismissed or otherwise dropped." Whether a violation of the speedy trial right has occurred is evaluated pursuant to a balancing test in which four factors are weighed: length of delay, the reason for the delay, the defendant's assertion of his or her right, and prejudice to the defendant.[39]

---

37. 404 U.S. 307, 313–15 (1971). But note that Federal Rule of Criminal Procedure 48(b) authorizes dismissal of an indictment, information, or complaint if "there is unnecessary delay in presenting the charge to a grand jury or in filing an information against a defendant who has been held to answer to the district court, or if there is unnecessary delay in bringing a defendant to trial." This rule only applies to post-arrest situations since, "[u]ntil this event occurs, a citizen suffers no restraints on his liberty and is not the subject of public accusation." *Id.* at 19. "Passage of time, whether before or after arrest, may impair memories, cause evidence to be lost, deprive the defendant of witnesses, and otherwise interfere with his ability to defend himself. But this possibility of prejudice at trial is not itself sufficient reason to wrench the Sixth Amendment from its proper context. Possible prejudice is inherent in any delay, however short; it may also weaken the Government's case." *Id.*

38. 18 U.S.C. § 3161(h).

39. United States v. Jackson, 508 F.2d 1001, 1003–04 (7th Cir. 1975).

3. Motions to Dismiss for Prosecutorial Misconduct

While not impossible, defendants arguing that an indictment should be dismissed due to the government's misconduct face an extremely heavy burden.

For a dismissal motion to succeed on this basis, "a defendant must show that the government's conduct is so outrageous that common notions of fairness and decency would be offended were judicial processes invoked to obtain a conviction."[40] Examples of unconstitutionally outrageous conduct include "coercion" or severe violations of the defendant's "person." A court may also dismiss an indictment because of misconduct before the grand jury, but only where the government's misconduct compromised the "integrity of the grand jury's functions."[41] In either case, the defendant must establish that the alleged prosecutorial misconduct in fact occurred and that the defendant was prejudiced as a result.[42]

B. Motions to Suppress Evidence

Federal Rules of Criminal Procedure 12(b)(3)(C) and 41(h) allow a defendant to make a pretrial motion to suppress evidence on the basis of a constitutional or statutory violation by law enforcement. Motions to simply exclude—rather than suppress—evidence are generally made shortly before trial and are called motions in limine (see chapter 7). In white-collar crime prosecutions that are based largely on certain key pieces of evidence, a defendant who successfully suppresses such evidence may have the case against them dismissed or substantially weakened. Yet even when a white-collar defendant succeeds on a suppression motion, the victory "is unlikely to stop a case that is typically based on a mosaic of documents and testimony rather than a pivotal admission or piece of forensic proof."[43] Moreover, evidence in white-collar crime cases is usually subpoenaed or supplied to the government voluntarily or through regulatory channels, meaning that there are fewer items of evidence to attempt to suppress.[44]

Suppression motions are derived from the "exclusionary rule," which has traditionally been used to bar from trial physical, tangible materials (such as documents, tape recordings, and computer hard drives) obtained through an unlawful invasion. The exclusionary rule protects a defendant's Fourth Amendment rights by denying prosecutors the ability to use evidence secured by government agents through unlawful means at trial.[45] Pursuant to the "fruit of the poisonous tree" doctrine, the exclusionary prohibition extends to direct and indirect products of illegal government conduct—including tangible items, words overheard in the course of an unlawful search, or confessions or statements of the accused obtained during an

---

40. United States v. Al Kassar, 660 F.3d 108, 121 (2d Cir. 2011).

41. United States v. Williams, 504 U.S. 36, 46 (1992).

42. Bank of Nova Scotia v. United States, 487 U.S. 250, 263 (1988).

43. Buell, *supra* note 28, at 858.

44. *Id.* At 857-58.

45. Weeks v. United States, 232 U.S. 383 (1914).

illegal arrest and detention.[46] Yet evidence is not "fruit of the poisonous tree" simply because it would not have been obtained but for illegal actions by the police. Instead, the key question is whether the evidence at issue has "been come at by exploitation of [the primary illegality] or instead by means sufficiently distinguishable to be purged of the primary taint."[47]

Further, under the "independent source" doctrine, if law enforcement is able to later obtain through lawful means the same evidence that was initially obtained illegally, the exclusionary rule will not apply.[48] "In the classic independent source situation, information that is received through an illegal source is considered to be cleanly obtained when it arrives through an independent source."[49] This is a considerable loophole that substantially waters down the benefit of the exclusionary rule to defendants.

Fourth Amendment rights are personal rights, meaning that they "may be enforced by exclusion of evidence only at the instance of one whose own protection was infringed by the [unlawful] search and seizure" and not a third party.[50] Thus, a defendant cannot base a motion to suppress on a violation of another's Fourth Amendment rights.

1. Motions to Suppress Fruits of an Unlawful Search Warrant

As discussed in chapter 2, the Fourth Amendment requires law enforcement to submit an affidavit to a magistrate or district court judge explaining why there is probable cause to believe that the requested search will uncover contraband or evidence of a crime. Any affidavits used to obtain evidence relevant to a particular case will generally be made available to criminal defendants during discovery. While courts are required to afford search warrant affidavits a "presumption of validity,"[51] a defendant can move to suppress evidence obtained through execution of the warrant if he or she can show the basis on which the warrant was issued was invalid.[52] These motions are generally based on attacks on the supporting affidavit on three bases: (i) overbreadth or lack of specificity, (ii) intentional material misrepresentations or omissions, and/or (iii) failure to establish probable cause for the subsequent search.

As a threshold matter, a defendant seeking to suppress the fruits of a search on Fourth Amendment grounds must show he or she had a "legitimate expectation of privacy" in the place searched. "Where the premises searched is a business, defendants seeking suppression must establish both that they are associated with the business and that they have a legitimate expectation of privacy in the part of the business that was searched."[53]

---

46. Wong Sun v. United States, 371 U.S. 471, 484 (1963); United States v. Crews, 445 U.S. 463, 470 (1980).

47. Wong Sun, 371 U.S. at 487–88; Nardone v. United States, 308 U.S. 338, 341 (1939).

48. Nix v. Williams, 467 U.S. 431, 443 (1984).

49. United States v. Silvestri, 787 F.2d 736, 739 (1st Cir. 1986).

50. Simmons v. United States, 390 U.S. 377, 389 (1968).

51. United States v. Martin, 426 F.3d 68, 73 (2d Cir. 2005).

52. *See, e.g.*, United States v. Wey, 15-cr-611 (S.D.N.Y. Jun.13, 2017)

53. O'Connor v. Ortega, 480 U.S. 709, 718 (1987).

a. Intentional Misrepresentations or Omissions

A defendant moving to suppress on the basis of intentional misrepresentations or omissions must first make a substantial and detailed preliminary showing that there are in fact intentional or reckless material misrepresentations or omissions in the underlying search warrant affidavit.[54] If the defendant can satisfy this initial two-part test—which requires a showing of subjective intent and objective materiality—he or she must then demonstrate that had the misrepresentation or omission not been included, the affidavit would have been insufficient to establish probable cause. If this hurdle is cleared, an evidentiary hearing—called a "*Franks* hearing"—must be held by the court to determine whether the affidavit was in fact deliberately false or misleading.[55]

Courts evaluate motions for a *Franks* hearing to an exacting standard and they are not often granted (especially where a defendant primarily alleges that there are omissions, as opposed to misrepresentations, in the search warrant affidavit).[56] This standard gives substantial deference to law enforcement: every statement in a warrant affidavit need not be true and, since "all storytelling involves an element of selectivity," it is "not necessarily constitutionally significant that an affidavit omits facts which, in retrospect, seem significant."[57] But when an affidavit is based in part on hearsay information, it must also provide enough of the circumstances from which the affiant drew his or her conclusions to have allowed the magistrate to verify the conclusions and confirm that they are not based merely on rumor or reputation.[58]

To successfully move for suppression, a defendant must demonstrate, by a preponderance of the evidence, both the affiant's *intent* to mislead the issuing judge and the *materiality* of the affiant's falsehoods or omissions.[59] With respect to the intent requirement, a defendant must show that the misrepresentations or omissions in the search warrant affidavits were "the result of the affiant's deliberate falsehood or reckless disregard for the truth."[60] The determination of whether a person acted deliberately or recklessly is a factual question of intent. The standard for an intentional misrepresentation or omission is clearer than the standard for a reckless misrepresentation or omission.[61]

54. Southerland v. City of New York, 681 F.3d 122, 126–27 (2d Cir. 2012).

55. Franks v. Delaware, 438 U.S. 154 (1978).

56. Rivera v. United States, 928 F.2d 592, 604 (2d Cir. 1991); United States v. Dupree, 781 F. Supp. 2d 115, 144 (E.D.N.Y. 2011); United States v. Chesher, 678 F.2d 1353, 1359 (9th Cir. 1982).

57. United States v. Vilar, No. 05–CR–0621, 2007 WL 1075041, at *27 (S.D.N.Y. Apr. 4, 2007).

58. Spinelli v. United States, 393 U.S. 410, 416 (1968); United States v. Perez-Esparza, 609 F.2d 1284, 1287 (9th Cir. 1979).

59. *See* Rajaratnam, 719 F.3d at 145–46 (discussing two-prong *Franks* showing); *see also* Southerland, 681 F.3d at 126–27.

60. Canfield, 212 F.3d at 717–18.

61. *See* Vilar, 2007 WL 1075041, at *26 ("'The meaning of an intentional falsehood is self-evident,' but the definition of 'reckless disregard' in the Franks context is less clear."); United States v. Kunen, 323 F.Supp.2d 390, 395 (E.D.N.Y. 2004).

"The Supreme Court in *Franks* did not define the term 'reckless disregard' other than to state that 'allegations of negligence or innocent mistake are insufficient.'"[62] In *Rajaratnam*—a case involving the billionaire founder of hedge fund Galleon Group—the Second Circuit concluded that a subjective test governs the recklessness inquiry.[63] Accordingly, in the Second Circuit and most other circuits, for allegations of intentional and reckless falsehoods a defendant must show that "the intent" behind the misstatement or omission was "to mislead the judicial officer into approving the requested warrant."[64] An inaccuracy that is the result of negligence or innocent mistake is insufficient.

The "guideposts for determining recklessness are different when evaluating" misrepresentations and omissions.[65] In the context of the former, courts generally ask whether the affiant "made a false statement with knowledge that the statement was false," "had a serious doubt as to the truth of the statement when [he or she] made it," or "had obvious reason to doubt the veracity of the statement."[66] In the context of reckless omissions, courts generally consider "whether the omitted information was clearly critical to assessing the legality of the search."[67]

There is some disagreement among the courts of appeals as to "whether recklessness can be established where a reasonable affiant would know that omitted information would be important to the reviewing court."[68] In the Second Circuit, a showing that omitted information was "clearly critical" is not, by itself, sufficient to establish that a government affiant acted with reckless disregard for the truth.[69] Instead, a court must consider the full record—"especially the *Franks* hearing testimony regarding the states of mind of the government agents"—and find "credible and probative evidence" that the omission of information in an application was "designed to mislead or was made in reckless disregard of whether [it] would mislead."[70]

---

62. United States v. Rajaratnam, No. 09–CR–1184, 2010 WL 4867402, at *8 (S.D.N.Y. Nov. 24, 2010) (quoting *Franks*, 438 U.S. at 171).

63. *See* Rajaratnam, 719 F.3d at 153 ("[The recklessness] inquiry, which looks to the mental states of mind of government officials, is said to be a 'subjective' test rather than an 'objective' one.").

64. Vilar, 2007 WL 1075041, at *25.

65. Rajaratnam, 2010 WL 4867402 at *9

66. *Id.*; *see also* Vilar, 2007 WL 1075041, at *26 ("[M]ost circuits that have considered the question have embraced a subjective test for recklessness . . . that one 'recklessly disregards' the truth when one makes allegations while entertaining serious doubts about the accuracy of those allegations.").

67. Rajaratnam, 2010 WL 4867402, at *9; *see also* Vilar, 2007 WL 1075041, at *27 (explaining that "recklessness may be inferred where the omitted information was 'clearly critical' to the probable cause determination" (citing Rivera v. United States, 928 F.2d 592, 604 (2d Cir.1991))).

68. *See, e.g.*, Wilson v. Russo, 212 F.3d 781, 788 (3d Cir. 2000) (citing United States v. Jacobs, 986 F.2d 1231, 1235 (8th Cir.1993)).

69. Rajaratnam, 719 F.3d at 154 ("A wiretap applicant does not necessarily act with 'reckless disregard for the truth' simply because he or she omits certain evidence that a reviewing court, in its judgment, considers to be 'clearly critical.'"); *see also id.* at 154–55 (finding that the district court erred in finding recklessness, where the court's "view that the [omitted information] was 'clearly critical' [was] the *only basis* for [its] conclusion that the government omitted certain information . . . with 'reckless disregard for the truth'" and instructing courts to consider "*all* of the evidence presented at the *Franks* hearing").

70. *Id.* at 154–56.

In sum, to the extent a defendant believes that law enforcement exercised poor judgment in not including certain information, that would, at best, support a claim of negligence and be insufficient to clear the first *Franks* hurdle.[71] With respect to the materiality requirement, the defendant must demonstrate by a preponderance of the evidence that the misrepresentations or omissions in the search warrant affidavits were necessary to the issuing judge's probable cause finding. To determine if misrepresentations or omissions are material, a court corrects the errors and then resolves de novo whether the hypothetical corrected affidavit still establishes probable cause.[72] Since probable cause "is a fluid concept—turning on the assessment of probabilities in particular factual contexts," the Supreme Court has endorsed a "totality-of-the-circumstances approach" to evaluating it.[73]

2. **Bruton** ***Motions***

In *Bruton v. United States*, 391 U.S. 123, 126 (1968), the Supreme Court ruled that the Sixth Amendment right of confrontation is violated when one defendant's out-of-court confession or other statement that implicates a codefendant is admitted at their joint trial.[74] Under Federal Rule of Evidence 802(d), such a statement is admissible against the declarant, but generally inadmissible against the nondeclarant codefendant. In a joint trial, this creates a situation "where the jury will hear the statement of one defendant pointing the finger at another defendant, but if that defendant (the speaker) does not take the stand, then the other [codefendant] does not have an opportunity to confront and cross-examine the speaker."[75]

Bruton issues will often be raised alongside severance motions (see section I.D), but even when *Bruton* applies, severance is not automatic since there are various "alternative ways" that the DOJ can use a statement to prove the confessor's guilt without infringing the non-confessor's confrontation rights. For example, the Supreme Court has permitted prosecutors

---

71. Vilar, 2007 WL 1075041, at *29; *see also* Rajaratnam, 719 F.3d at 155 (finding that the district court's "inference" of recklessness was "particularly inappropriate where the government [came] forward with evidence indicating that the omission resulted from nothing more than negligence"); *id.* (relying on *Franks* testimony that the affiant omitted information, where she testified that "it never occurred to [her], never crossed [her] mind to" include the omitted information, "[because] [she] didn't think about" that information as relevant to the allegations in the affidavit (alterations in original)).

72. *See* Rajaratnam, 719 F.3d at 146–47 (explaining that courts correct errors in an affidavit to determine if probable cause exists based on a hypothetical corrected affidavit, and further noting that, in the context of omissions, courts "insert the omitted truths" into the hypothetical corrected affidavit (internal quotation marks omitted)); Southerland, 681 F.3d at 127 (explaining that courts correct errors in an affidavit to determine if probable cause still exists); Canfield, 212 F.3d at 718 ("If the corrected affidavit supports probable cause, the inaccuracies were not material to the probable cause determination[,] and suppression is inappropriate.").

73. Illinois v. Gates, 462 U.S. 213, 232, 230 (1983); *see also* United States v. Falso, 544 F.3d 110, 117 (2d Cir.2008).

74. Ryan v. Miller, 303 F.3d 231, 247 (2d Cir. 2002) (the crux of the Sixth Amendment is that "the government cannot introduce at trial statements containing accusations against the defendant unless the accuser takes the stand against the defendant and is available for cross examination").

75. United States v. Garcia, Case No: 11-cr-68-EJL (D. Idaho Dec. 17, 2012).

to solve the *Bruton* problem by simply redacting a codefendant's name or replacing it with neutral pronouns.[76] Not all redactions sufficiently protect a defendant's Sixth Amendment rights, however. Rather, their effectiveness depends on "whether the neutral allusion sufficiently conceals the fact of explicit identification to eliminate the overwhelming probability that a jury hearing the confession at a joint trial will not be able to follow an appropriate limiting instruction [from the judge]."[77] This analysis considers whether the redacted statement gives "any indication to the jury that the original statement contained actual names" and whether the statement, standing alone, otherwise connects codefendants to the crime.[78] The key issue is whether the redacted statement, viewed in isolation from the other evidence, incriminates a nondeclarant codefendant.[79] If it does, the court must either exclude the statement at a joint trial or order a severance.

Redacted statements that simply replace a name with "obvious indications of alteration" fall within *Bruton* because they "refer directly to the existence of the nonconfessing defendant."[80] As such, neutral word substitutions must be done so that the redacted statement resembles something that "might actually have been said by a person admitting his own culpability in the charged conspiracy while shielding the specific identity of his confederate."[81] By contrast, when substitutions or redactions indicate alteration, they are "more likely to emphasize than to conceal the fact that the declarant had specifically inculpated someone."[82] In those circumstances, admission of the statement will violate *Bruton*.[83]

3. Motions for a Kastigar *Hearing*

The Fifth Amendment prevents a person from being compelled to be a witness against himself in any criminal case. Therefore, where an individual is unable to assert the Fifth and is compelled to be a witness against himself, any use, in any manner, of the compelled statements is prohibited. In *United States v. Kastigar*, 406 U.S. 441 (1972), the Supreme Court upheld the constitutionality of the federal use immunity statute, 18 U.S.C. §§ 6002-03, which, as

76. Gray v. Marlyland, 523 U.S. 185, 192 (1998).

77. United States v. Jass, 569 F.3d 47, 61 (2d Cir. 2009).

78. United States v. Tutino, 883 F.2d 1125, 1135 (2d Cir. 1989).

79. United States v. Williams, 936 F.2d 698, 700–01 (2d Cir. 1991); *see also* Crawford v. Washington, 541 U.S. 36 (2004).

80. Jass, 569 F.3d at 58.

81. *Id.* at 62.

82. *Id.* at 59; *see also* Gray, 523 U.S. at 193 (an obvious deletion will call the jurors' attention to the removed name and cause them to speculate about the reference).

83. *See, e.g.,* Taylor, 767 F. Supp. at 431–32 (replacement of codefendants' names "with generic, neutral pronouns is insufficient to cure the prejudice to them because the Government's proposed redactions make it apparent that [declarant] was referring to his co-defendants"); Figueroa v. Portuondo, 96 F. Supp. 2d 256, 261 (S.D.N.Y. 1999) (introduction of statements redacted "by replacing the names of the co-defendant with non-specific phrases" failed to satisfy *Bruton* where "the context of the references, and the manner of use during trial, made it clear that [codefendant's] name was the name that had been redacted; thus, the very purpose of the redaction was compromised").

discussed in chapter 2, provides that "no testimony or other information compelled under the [compulsion] order (or any information directly or indirectly derived from such testimony or other information) may be used against the witness in any criminal case." In the Court's view, "this total prohibition on use provides a comprehensive safeguard, barring the use of compelled testimony as an 'investigatory lead,' and also barring the use of any evidence obtained by focusing investigation on a witness as a result of his compelled disclosures."

To ensure that a witness's prior immunized testimony is not used, directly or indirectly, against him in a subsequent criminal case, *Kasitgar* held that "once a defendant demonstrates that he has testified, under a state [or federal grant] of immunity, to matters related to the federal prosecution, the federal authorities have the burden of showing that their evidence is not tainted by establishing that they had an independent, legitimate source for the disputed evidence." The government's burden is not limited to "negation of taint"; rather, it must affirmatively "prove that the evidence it proposes to use is derived from a legitimate source wholly independent of the compelled testimony." The government must meet this burden by a preponderance of the evidence and cannot meet it by simply asserting that immunized testimony or information was not used, for example, by submission of a conclusory affidavit.[84]

Prosecutors facing a *Kastigar* challenge are thus required to prove that their charging decision was not in any way affected by the compelled testimony or any information derived from it.[85] Prosecutors must also show that the grand jury was not shown any evidence that was derived or influenced by the defendant's compelled statements.[86] The government may also violate the Fifth Amendment when a cooperating witness's exposure to compelled testimony motivates that witness to cooperate and testify against the defendants.[87]

Where the issue of compelled testimony is raised, a defendant can request the court to hold a "*Kastigar* hearing." The defendant's burden on such a motion is minimal: he must only show that in his immunized statements he testified on matters related to the prosecution at issue. In contrast, the burden on the prosecution to establish an independent source for evidence against a defendant is "heavy" but not impossible: most courts adopt the position that a "mere tangential influence that privileged information may have on the prosecutor's thought process in preparing for trial is not an impermissible 'use' of that information."[88]

While the district court has discretion to hold the hearing before, during, or after the trial, it is the general practice in most circuits to defer such a hearing until after trial.[89] The court can then evaluate whether the government's trial evidence was from independent sources (and thereby avoid disclosure of the government's proof before trial).

84. United States v. Nanni, 59 F.3d 1425, 1432 (2d Cir. 1995).

85. United States v. Kristel, 762 F. Supp.1 100, 1109 (S.D.N.Y. 1991).

86. United States v. Tantalo, 680 F.2d 903, 908–09 (2d Cir. 1982); *but see* Slough, 641 F.3d at 554 (noting that the Second Circuit, along with some other circuits, has not banned all nonevidentiary uses of compelled testimony, and stating that "at least as to decisions to indict, we join those circuits refusing to find such decisions vulnerable on the ground of links to immunized statements").

87. United States v. Allen, 160 F. Supp. 3d 684, 690 (S.D.N.Y. 2016).

88. United States v. Velasco, 953 F.2d 1467, 1474 (7th Cir. 1992).

89. United States v. Helmsley, 941 F.2d 71, 80 (2d Cir. 1991).

The remedy for a *Kastigar* violation is ordinarily "the suppression at trial of a defendant's compelled testimony" Rather than dismissal of the indictment.[90] Therefore, if a court reviewing the matter after trial finds a *Kastigar* violation, it must consider whether the failure to suppress any tainted evidence at trial was harmless error. There are exceptions to this rule, however. When "the defendant testifies under immunity before the same grand jury returning the indictment or when the immunized testimony is placed before the indicting grand jury," the indictment must be dismissed. Similarly, "when the government concedes that the indictment rests almost exclusively on tainted evidence," the indictment must also be dismissed.

C. *Daubert* Motions to Exclude Expert Evidence

In *Daubert v. Merrell Dow Pharmaceuticals, Inc.*, the Supreme Court established the standard for admitting scientific expert testimony as evidence in federal court.[91] Concluding that Federal Rule of Evidence 702 superseded a more lenient standard that required only a threshold showing of such testimony's general acceptance in the scientific community, the Court enumerated a new test (now generally known as the "*Daubert* standard"). In keeping with this test and Rule 702, when faced with a proffer of expert scientific testimony "the trial judge must determine at the outset . . . whether the expert is proposing to testify to (1) scientific knowledge that (2) will assist the trier of fact to understand or determine a fact in issue."[92] In other words, the expert's testimony must be both reliable and relevant.

The first prong of this test requires that the expert's proposed testimony has a "reliable basis in the knowledge and experience of the relevant discipline."[93] While the Court noted that many factors bear on this inquiry and refused to set out an exclusive checklist, it identified the following issues as relevant: (i) whether the theory or technique can be and has been tested, (ii) whether it has been subjected to peer review, (iii) whether the technique has a high known or potential rate of error, and (iv) whether the theory has attained general acceptance within the scientific community.[94] In evaluating these factors, the Court emphasized that the inquiry required by Rule 702 is "a flexible one" that "assign[s] to the trial judge the task of ensuring that an expert's testimony both rests on a reliable foundation and is relevant to the task at hand."[95] Nevertheless, the focus of the district court "must be solely on the [expert's] principles and methodology, not on the conclusion that they generate."[96]

---

90. United States v. Rivieccio, 919 F.2d 812, 814 (2d Cir. 1990) ("It is fundamental in our system of criminal justice that 'an indictment returned by a properly constituted grand jury is not subject to challenge on the grounds that it was based on unconstitutionally obtained evidence.'"); United States v. Fuller, 149 F. Supp. 2d 17, 21 (S.D.N.Y. 2001).

91. 509 U.S. 579 (1993).

92. *Id.* at 584–87.

93. Kumho Tire Co., Ltd. v. Carmichael, 526 U.S. 137, 149 (1999); *see also* Estate of Barabin v. Asten-Johnson, Inc., 740 F.3d 457, 463 (9th Cir. 2014) (it is the duty of the district court to "act as a gatekeeper to exclude junk science that does not meet Federal Rule of Evidence 702's reliability standards").

94. Daubert, 509 U.S. at 593–94.

95. *Id.* at 594, 598; *see also* United States v. Cordoba, 104 F.3d 225, 227 (9th Cir. 1997).

96. Daubert, 509 U.S. at 597.

The test's second prong, relevancy, sets a low bar, demanding only that the evidence "logically advances a material aspect of the proposing party's case."[97]

Originally intended to screen out only "junk science," the *Daubert* test has been extended to apply to technical and other specialized knowledge. *Daubert* motions are routinely used by the prosecution and defense in white-collar crime cases to try to exclude the other side's expert.[98]

D. Motions to Sever

Federal Rule of Criminal Procedure 14(a) permits a defendant to make a motion to sever his or her trial from that of codefendants on the basis of unfair prejudice.

This rule is essentially the converse of Rule 8(b), which permits joinder of multiple defendants in a single trial: "The indictment or information may charge two or more defendants if they are alleged to have participated in the same act or transaction, or in the same series of acts or transactions, constituting an offense or offenses. The defendants may be charged in one or more counts together or separately. All defendants need not be charged in each count." In keeping with this rule, "multiple defendants cannot be tried together on two or more 'similar' but unrelated acts or transactions; [rather,] multiple defendants may be tried together only if the charged acts are part of a series of acts or transactions constituting an offense or offenses."[99] In other words, "joinder is proper where two or more persons' criminal acts are 'unified by some substantial identity of facts or participants,' or 'arise out of a common plan or scheme.'"[100] Courts give prosecutors' decision to jointly charge defendants substantial deference. For example, "The mere allegation of a conspiracy presumptively satisfies Rule 8(b), since the allegation implies that the defendants named have engaged in the same series of acts or transactions constituting an offense."[101]

Even when a defendant is properly joined, he may seek to sever his case for trial if joinder is prejudicial under Rule 14(a). "Whether to grant or deny a severance motion is committed to the sound discretion of the trial judge."[102] "There is a preference in the federal system for joint trials of defendants who are indicted together,"[103] especially where the defendants are alleged to have participated in a common plan or scheme.

Given this presumption, a "district court should grant a severance motion only if there is a serious risk that a joint trial would compromise a specific trial right of the moving

97. Daubert v. Merrell Dow Pharm., Inc., 43 F.3d 1311, 1315 (9th Cir. 1995); *see also* Primiano v. Cook, 598 F.3d 558, 563 (9th Cir. 2010) ("Expert opinion testimony is relevant if the knowledge underlying it has a valid connection to the pertinent inquiry.").

98. *See, e.g.*, United States v. Vorley, No. 18-cr-00035 (N.D. Ill. July 27, 2020) (spoofing defendant challenging under *Daubert* the government's proffered expert as to the alleged impact of spoofing on financial markets).

99. United States v. Turoff, 853 F.2d 1037, 1043 (2d Cir. 1988).

100. United States v. Cervone, 907 F.2d 332, 341 (2d Cir. 1990).

101. United States v. Friedman, 854 F.2d 535, 561 (2d Cir. 1988).

102. United States v. Salameh, 152 F.3d 88, 115 (2d Cir. 1998).

103. Zafiro v. United States, 506 U.S. 534, 537 (1993).

defendant or prevent the jury from making a reliable judgment about guilt or innocence."[104] This is a difficult burden to meet and defendants are not entitled to severance merely because they may have a better chance of acquittal in separate trials.[105] Nor does "the fact that evidence may be admissible against one defendant but not another . . . necessarily require a severance."[106]

E. Motions for a Change of Venue

The Fifth and Sixth Amendments to the Constitution guarantee defendants a fair trial by a panel of impartial, indifferent jurors. Where the location of a criminal trial makes fulfillment of these guarantees uncertain, defendants can make a motion to transfer venue, prior to jury selection, under Federal Rule of Criminal Procedure 21(a). To successfully change venue, defendants must make a showing of presumed prejudice, which arises only when "prejudicial publicity so pervades or saturates the community as to render virtually impossible a fair trial by an impartial jury drawn from that community."[107]

A district court has broad discretion when deciding on a motion for transfer of venue and may consider all the relevant circumstances to reach a determination, including the degree and timing of adverse publicity. To succeed on a motion to change venue under Rule 21(a), defendants must show "a reasonable likelihood that prejudicial news prior to trial will prevent a fair trial."[108] The courts have rarely found such prejudice, particularly in white-collar crime cases.[109]

F. Removing Surplusage

Federal Rule of Criminal Procedure 7(d) permits a district court to "strike surplusage from the indictment or information" upon motion by the defendant. Motions to strike surplusage "will be granted only where the challenged allegations are not relevant to the crime charged and are inflammatory and prejudicial."[110] Statements providing background are generally considered relevant and need not be struck. Courts in the Second Circuit and elsewhere usually await the presentation of the government's evidence at trial before ruling on a motion to strike surplusage.[111]

---

104. United States v. Rosa, 11 F.3d 315, 341 (2d Cir. 1993).

105. Zafiro, 506 U.S. at 540.

106. United States v. Rittweger, 524 F.3d 171, 179 (2d Cir. 2008).

107. Mayola v. Alabama, 623 F.2d 992, 997 (5th Cir. 1980).

108. United States v. Maldonado-Rivera, 922 F.2d 934, 966–67 (2d Cir. 1990).

109. Nebraska Press Association v. Stuart, 427 U.S. 539, 554 (1976).

110. United States v. Mulder, 273 F.3d 91, 99 (2d Cir. 2001).

111. United States v. Scarpa, 913 F.2d 993, 1011 (2d Cir. 1990).

G. Duplicity

Defendants may challenge an indictment based on "duplicity," that is, an improper joining of two or more offenses in the same count.[112] "The overall vice of duplicity is that the jury cannot in a general verdict render its finding on each offense, making it difficult to determine whether a conviction rests on only one of the offenses or both."[113] Courts analyze a count's duplicitousness based on "(1) whether defendant's alleged actions may legitimately be regarded as a single course of conduct during a discrete time period; and (2) whether defendant would be prejudiced by his prosecution on a single-count basis."

Duplicitous indictments can prejudice a defendant by allowing him or her to be convicted by a less-than-unanimous verdict and by creating the "possibility as to the basis of the verdict [and therefore] subject the defendant to double jeopardy in the event of a subsequent prosecution."[114] If the count does not adequately reveal the government's case against the defendant, neither the government's revelation of more detailed information "at a comparatively late stage in the proceedings" nor "extensive" pretrial discovery may "cure[] the defects" of a duplicitous count.

The remedy for a duplicitous count when raised before trial is dismissal of that count, with the prosecution then permitted to seek a reformulated superseding indictment.[115] When duplicitousness is raised after or during trial, courts may decide to correct the error through a jury instruction.[116]

A pre-trial duplicitousness challenge was successfully made by former precious metals trader John Pacilio in a market manipulation and spoofing case in Chicago. The count at issue alleged that Pacilio had engaged in a spoofing scheme "on or about at least July 16, 2011, and continuing through in or around at least November 2014." Pacilio argued that the antispoofing statute does not permit the government to prosecute a substantive count of spoofing as a "scheme" and that the indictment's "undifferentiated allegation that [he] engaged in spoofing involving unidentified trading episodes over a multi-year period violates his Fifth Amendment right to have the evidence that the government presents to his trial jury track the evidence presented to his grand jury."[117] District Court Judge John Z. Lee agreed, ruling that because each alleged spoofing episode is a discrete event, federal law does not allow spoofing to be charged as a scheme. Pacilio's victory was short-lived, however: Judge Lee determined that the "proper remedy is dismissal of the duplicitous count, allowing the

112. Fed. R. Crim. P. 12(b)(3)(B).

113. United States v. Buchmeier, 255 F.3d 415, 425 (7th Cir. 2001); Helmsley, 941 F.2d at 91 (duplicity creates the "possibility of a non-unanimous jury verdict" by muddling the specific crime for which the defendant was convicted).

114. United States v. Tanner, 471 F.2d 128, 139 (7th Cir. 1972).

115. Davis, 471 F.3d at 790; United States v. Droms, 566 F.2d 361, 363 n.1 (2d Cir. 1977).

116. United States v. Marshall, 65 F.3d 1097, 1112 (7th Cir. 1996); Helmsley, 941 F.2d at 91.

117. United States v. Bases, No. 18-cr-00048 (N.D. Ill. Mar. 25, 2020).

government to seek a clearer superseding indictment," which it then did.[118] Pacilio and his co-defendant were subsequently convicted at trial.[119]

II. PRETRIAL CHALLENGES TO THE PROSECUTORS' CASE IN THE UNITED KINGDOM

A. Applications to Dismiss an Indictment

As in the United States, criminal defendants in the United Kingdom can seek to dismiss the case against them on a pretrial motion to the Crown Court. But whereas defendants in the United States are strictly limited to seeking dismissal based on *legal* defects on the face of the charging instrument (accepting all its factual allegations as true), motions to dismiss in Britain focus on *evidentiary* weaknesses in the prosecutions' case. As such, a motion to dismiss a criminal case in the United Kingdom is much more akin to a motion for summary judgment under the Federal Rules of Civil Procedure than to U.S.-style motions to dismiss in criminal cases. This is a significant difference that is due, in part, to the deference given a grand jury's determination of probable cause in the United States, the routine use of written witness statements in the United Kingdom, and the much earlier disclosures of evidence that occur in the U.K. system (see chapter 5).

The dismissal procedure for indictable offenses is set forth in CrimPR 3.20. This rule requires a defendant to submit an application to dismiss within twenty-eight days after service of the prosecution's evidence and before the defendant's arraignment. The application must do each of the following:

- Explain why the prosecution's evidence would not be sufficient for the defendant to be properly convicted.
- Ask for a hearing, if the defendant wants one, and explain why it is needed.
- Identify any witness whom the defendant wants to call to give evidence in person, with an indication of what evidence the witness can give.
- Identify any material already served that the defendant thinks the court will need to determine the application.
- Include any material not already served on which the defendant relies.

Prosecutors are then given fourteen days to respond. Like the defendant, prosecutors can request to call their own witnesses to challenge the application and can produce (and rely on) any relevant materials not already disclosed to the defense.

Under Schedule 3 of the Crime and Disorder Act (CDA) 1998, the Crown Court must dismiss an indictment if it appears that "the evidence against the applicant would not be

---

118. Jon Hill, "Ill. Judge Axes Ex-Merrill Lynch Trader's Spoofing Charge," LAW360 (Oct. 19, 2020).

119. Dave Michaels, "Two Ex-Bank of America Traders Accused of Spoofing Found Guilty," WALL S. J. (Aug. 4, 2021).

sufficient for him to be properly convicted." In making this determination, "the judge will decide not only whether there is any evidence to go to a jury, but whether the evidence is sufficient for a jury to properly convict. That exercise requires the judge to assess the weight of the evidence."[120] As is often the case in financial crime prosecutions, "where the evidence is largely documentary, and the case depends on the inferences or conclusions to be drawn from it, the judge must assess the inferences or conclusions that the prosecution proposes to ask the jury to draw from the documents, and decide whether it appears to him that the jury could properly draw those inferences and come to those conclusions."[121]

If the defendant's application to dismiss is successful, the judge will quash all or some of the charges and, as to such charges, no further proceedings may be brought except by way of an application to the High Court for a "voluntary bill of indictment."[122] A voluntary bill is "an exceptional procedure." The High Court's "consent should only be granted where good reason to depart from the normal procedure is clearly shown and only where the interests of justice, rather than considerations of administrative convenience, require it."[123] To succeed, prosecutors must demonstrate that the Crown Court's decision to dismiss was made either (i) without regard to a relevant statutory provision or judicial authority, (ii) without consideration of new evidence that could not be put before the Crown Court at the time of the dismissal hearing, (iii) without a rational foundation, or (iv) on the basis of a technicality.[124]

British prosecutors are unable to appeal a Crown Court's decision on a dismissal application, meaning that seeking a voluntary bill is their only recourse. Likewise, the defense also cannot appeal an adverse ruling on a dismissal application (in the same way that the rules against interlocutory appeals prevent defendants from immediately challenging an unfavorable outcome on a motion to dismiss in the United States).

B. Duplicity

In addition to challenging the evidentiary basis of an indictment, criminal defendants can lodge objections to the charges based on technical defects in the charging instrument, such as improper duplicity. In *R v. Greenfield* [1973] 1 W.L.R. 1151, the Court of Appeal held that duplicity is an error in form that must be apparent in the wording of the count itself and not appear from a consideration of the evidence. As in the United States, duplicity occurs when a single count charges a defendant with two or more separate offenses (that do not amount to the same course of conduct).[125]

If a count is duplicitous, the Crown Court has discretion to either quash it or grant prosecutors' leave to amend the indictment.

120. R v. Galbraith [1981] 73 Cr.App.R. 124.

121. R (Inland Revenue Commissioners) v. Kingston Crown Court [2001] EWHC Admin 581.

122. CDA s. 51.

123. Criminal Practice Direction II (Preliminary proceedings) 10B.

124. R v. Arfan [2012] EWHC 2450 (QB); SFO v. Evans [2014] EWHC 3803 (QB).

125. CrimPR 10.2(2).

C. Severance

All defendants alleged to be involved in a single offense may be joined together in a single count (including principal violators and those who only assisted or encouraged the crime). Where the allegations underpinning the individual offenses of several defendants are so related in time or by other factors that the interests of justice are best served by them being tried together, the Crown Court may try them jointly even if the indictment does not contain a joint count charging them with acting in concert.[126]

If defendants have been improperly joined, they may apply to the Crown Court for severance of the joint counts into separate trials.[127] At the court's discretion, severance may be ordered where the admissibility of the evidence is not the same against each defendant or where the trial would otherwise be unduly long and complicated. Conversely, severance may be denied if a joint trial would conserve judicial resources and where fairness dictates that the defendants should be afforded a common verdict.

D. Applications to Exclude Unfair Evidence

The traditional rule in English courts was that all relevant evidence is admissible, regardless of how it was obtained. As a nineteenth century judge put it, "It matters not how you get it; if you steal it even, it would be admissible in evidence."[128] While this rule has not been completely abandoned, Section 78 of the Police and Criminal Evidence Act (PACE) 1984 now provides an important exception. This rule allows judges to exclude proposed prosecution evidence "if it appears to the court that, having regard to all the circumstances, including the circumstances in which the evidence was obtained, the admission of the evidence would have such an adverse effect on the fairness of the proceedings that the court ought not to admit it." Thus, while there is no exact analogue to the U.S. exclusionary rule, PACE Section 78 gives British judges a roughly comparable power to exclude improperly obtained evidence.[129] But importantly, there is nothing equivalent to the fruit of the poisonous tree doctrine in the United Kingdom—meaning that if evidence is merely derived from illegally obtained evidence but was itself lawfully obtained, it will likely be admissible.

Similarly, PACE Section 76(2) permits exclusion of improperly obtained confessions. Under this rule, once the prosecution indicates that it will admit evidence of a confession by the defendant, if the defense represents to the court that the admission resulted from oppression or is otherwise unreliable, the burden shifts to the prosecution to prove "beyond reasonable doubt that the confession (notwithstanding that it may be true) was not obtained as aforesaid."

---

126. R v. Assim [1966] 2 Q.B. 249; CrimPR 3.29.

127. CrimPR 3.29.

128. R v. Leathem [1861] 8 Cox CC 498.

129. A and Others v. Secretary of State for the Home Department [2005] UKHL 71.

E. Other Technical Defects

In addition to duplicity and improper joinder, an indictment can be challenged for various other technical defects, including that it charges an offense (i) that is not known to the law, (ii) for which any necessary consents to the prosecution have not been obtained, (iii) that would amount to an abuse of process if the prosecution were permitted to pursue it, (iv) for which the defendant has already been convicted, acquitted, or pardoned, (v) against a defendant who is immune from prosecution or whose acts are not subject to the jurisdiction of the Crown, and (vi) against a defendant who has been extradited or repatriated from abroad with an offense that is not permitted by the relevant extradition treaty.[130]

F. Abuse of Process

While it is generally up to the prosecution, not the court, to decide whether a criminal case should be commenced or continued, courts have an overriding duty to promote justice and prevent injustice. To fulfil this duty, judges have an inherent power to stay an indictment if allowing the prosecution to proceed would amount to an abuse of process. As the Court of Appeal described this authority, "abuse of process jurisdiction suggests that, notwithstanding that the prosecution or prosecuting authority may be blameless, as a matter of principal, the judge is vested with jurisdiction to order that proceedings should be stayed."[131]

This power is only exercised in exceptional circumstances since "even great difficulties created for the defence are almost always capable of being addressed by the trial process itself."[132] Its fundamental purpose is to prevent an unfair trial in which the defendant is unduly prejudiced in the presentation of his or her case and to preserve the integrity of the criminal justice system.

> Cases in which it may be unfair to try the accused will include, but are not confined to, those cases where there has been bad faith, unlawfulness or executive misconduct. In such a case, the court is concerned not to create the perception that it is condoning malpractice by law enforcement agencies or to convey the impression that it will adopt the approach that the end justifies the means: the touchstone is the integrity of the criminal justice system.[133]

In deciding whether to stay a case, courts must first consider whether other procedural measures—such as the exclusion of specific evidence or a corrective jury instruction—might adequately prevent trial unfairness such that the prosecution can continue. Courts are prevented from ordering a stay merely to discipline the prosecution or police or because the court believes the prosecution was unwise from a policy perspective.[134]

---

130. R v. Central Criminal Court, *ex p* Director of the SFO [1993] 1 WLR 949.

131. R v. Momodou [2005] EWCA Crim 177.

132. *Id.*; *see also* Attorney General's Reference (No 1 of 1990) [1992] Q.B. 630, CA; Attorney General's Reference (No 2 of 2001) [2004] 2 A.C. 72, HL.

133. R v. Crawley [2014] EWCA Crim 1028.

134. R v. Crown Court at Norwich *ex parte* Belsham [1992] 94 Cr. App. R. 382, QBD.

The burden of establishing that the bringing or continuation of criminal proceedings amounts to an abuse of the court's process is on the defendant. The standard of proof is the balance of probabilities.[135] It will normally be necessary for the defense to prove not only that an abuse has taken place but that the accused has been so prejudiced in the presentation of his or her case as a result that a fair trial is not possible.

1. Unreasonable Delay

Article 6 of the European Convention on Human Rights (ECHR) entitles a person charged with a criminal offense to a "fair and public hearing within a reasonable time by an independent and impartial tribunal." If a defendant raises a challenge on the basis of unreasonable delay, the Crown Court has discretion to order a stay after assessing the following factors: (i) whether the prosecution had reasonable grounds for the delay, (ii) whether there is a risk of serious prejudice to the defense if a trial is held, and (iii) whether the delay has affected the admissibility or availability of critical evidence. If, having considered these factors, the judge concludes that a fair trial will not be possible, he or she must grant a stay.[136] However, a permanent stay should be the exception rather than the rule, meaning that a stay will not be an appropriate remedy if there are other means to protect the defendant's ECHR rights (e.g., expediting the proceedings to the greatest extent possible).

2. Failing to Obtain, Losing, or Destroying Evidence

Where there has been a failure to obtain or retain evidence in violation of the obligations imposed on law enforcement under the CPIA (see chapter 5), it may amount to an abuse of process and a stay in the proceedings. However, even where a CPIA violation has clearly occurred, a stay is not automatic. Rather, there generally must also be a showing of either bad faith or an extremely serious error on the part of the police or the prosecution authorities. It must also be clear that the accused could not be fairly tried, regardless of whatever remedial measures the court might impose. Accordingly, stays based on lost or unobtained evidence are granted only in exceptional cases.[137]

3. Adverse Publicity

An abuse of process may occur by excessive or adverse media reporting. The test used to evaluate such a claim is whether the risk of prejudice from adverse publicity is so grave that, despite whatever measures the court might adopt, a fair trial will be impossible.[138]

---

135. R v. Telford Justices *ex parte* Badhan [1991] 2 Q.B. 78; R v. Great Yarmouth Magistrates *ex parte* Thomas [1992] Crim. L.R. 116.

136. R v. S (S.P.) [2006] 2 Cr. App. R. 23, CA.

137. R (Ebrahim) v. Feltham Magistrates' Court [2001] 1 All ER 831; PP v. Fell [2013] EWHC 562 (Admin).

138. Coulter v. H.M. Advocate [2003] 1 A.C. 641; R v. Abu Hamza [2007] 1 Cr. App. R. 27.

4. *Nondisclosure of Evidence by the Prosecution*

Just as U.S. prosecutors face repercussions for *Brady* and *Giglio* violations, a failure to disclose relevant evidence to a defendant can result in a British judge finding an abuse of process (as discussed earlier in relation to the SFO's case against Zaid Akle). Where it is accepted that a disclosure failure has occurred, whether it amounts to an abuse of process will turn on considerations of the gravity of the charges, risk of injustice, nature and materiality of the failure, effect on the jury, waste of court resources, and availability of alternative sanctions short of completing halting the proceedings.[139]

In *DPP v. Petrie* [2015] EWHC 48 (Admin), the High Court noted that a "wholesale failure on the part of the prosecution to comply with its disclosure obligations may require the prosecution to offer no evidence, in accordance with the professional code for prosecutors and the guidance set out in the CPS/ACPO Disclosure Manual." The possibility of such an outcome, in the court's view, "serves to illuminate that only rarely will recourse to an abuse of process argument be necessary or appropriate."

A "no evidence" order was recently given in a high-profile fraud case brought by the SFO against two former executives of a British logistics and consultancy firm, Serco Group Plc. The executives were charged with falsifying Serco's profit margins on a contract for electronic monitoring of criminal offenders on behalf of the Ministry of Justice. The prosecution came on the heels of a long-running investigation that resulted in Serco entering into a Deferred Prosecution Agreement and paying more than £20 million in penalties. In April 2021, during the executives' trial in Southwark Crown Court, the SFO disclosed serious errors in its disclosure of certain exculpatory materials. According to one of the executive's solicitors, the undisclosed evidence "clearly showed that these charges were, in fact, company policy."[140]

Following this revelation, the SFO asked for an adjournment so that it could seek a retrial, but the presiding judge, Mrs. Justice Tipples, refused on the basis that it was not in the public's interest to do so. Instead, the SFO was directed to offer no evidence against the executives and the jury was instructed to return not guilty verdicts. As opposed to simply dismissing the indictment, a "no evidence" order is preferable in that it gives defendants double jeopardy protection since it results in acquittal (see chapter 2).

III. PLEA AGREEMENTS IN THE UNITED STATES

A. Noncooperation Plea Agreements

Approximately ninety-seven percent of federal convictions are the result of guilty pleas. Hence, the number of cases that are decided by a verdict after trial is a small minority of the total number of prosecutions the DOJ brings. Over the last four decades, the percentage of criminal cases going to trial has steadily declined—from nearly twenty percent in the 1970s, to five percent in 2000, and to less than two percent today. As the late Supreme Court

139. R v. Salt [2015] EWCA Crim 662.

140. Jasper Jolly, "Trial of Former Serco Executives Collapses as SFO Fails to Disclose Evidence," The Guardian, Apr. 26, 2021).

Justice Anthony Kennedy put it, "Horse trading [between prosecutor and defense counsel] determines who goes to jail and for how long. That is what plea bargaining is. It is not some adjunct to the criminal justice system; it is the criminal justice system."[141]

This shift has been attributed to various factors, including Congress's decision to greatly increase the potential sentences for many crimes and prosecutors' routine practice of bringing multiple charges for the same conduct (including ones that are relatively easy to prove, such as conspiracy—see chapter 4).[142]

Another significant factor is that defendants often receive substantially longer sentences at trial than they would have through a plea agreement—the so-called "trial penalty" phenomenon. Defendants who "take their case to trial and lose receive longer sentences than even Congress or the prosecutor might think appropriate, because the longer sentences exist on the books largely for bargaining purposes. This often results in individuals who accept a plea bargain receiving shorter sentences than other individuals who are less morally culpable but take a chance and go to trial."[143] A 2018 study found, for instance, that on average, defendants who insist on a trial receive sentences three times longer than those of defendants who plead guilty.[144]

The trial penalty has been justified on the grounds that longer sentences following trial are necessary to induce defendants to accept responsibility for their alleged misconduct and because, without a high settlement rate, courts would be overloaded with trials.[145] This predicament was described by a legal scholar in the 1930s, when the court system was far less stressed than it is today, as follows: "If all defendants should combine to refuse to plead guilty, and should dare to hold out, they could break down the administration of criminal justice . . . The truth is that a criminal court can operate only by inducing a great mass of actually guilty defendants to plead guilty."[146]

Justified or not, the practical effect of these realities has been a transfer of sentencing power to prosecutors. As district court judge Jed Rakoff argued:

> Under intense pressure to find ways to avoid the immense sentences they will face if they go to trial and are convicted, virtually all defendants—whether innocent or guilty—beg prosecutors to let them plead guilty to reduced charges. The net result is that prosecutors, rather than judges, now effectively determine the sentences to be imposed in most cases. They do this in plea bargains hammered out in the prosecutors' offices in unrecorded conversations with defense counsel—sessions in which, because of the pressure on defendants to reduce their sentencing exposure, the prosecutors effectively hold most of the cards.[147]

---

141. *Missouri v. Frye*, 566 U.S. 134, 144 (2012).

142. *See* Kyle Graham, *Overcharging*, 11 Ohio St. J. Crim. L. 701 (2014).

143. Rachel E. Barkow, *Separation of Powers and the Criminal Law*, 58 Stan. L. Rev. 989, 1034 (2006)

144. Carissa Byrne Hessick, "The Constitutional Right We Have Bargained Away," The Atlantic, (Dec. 24, 2021).

145. *See* David S. Abrams, *Putting the Trial Penalty on Trial*, 51 Duquesne L. Rev. 777 (2013).

146. H. Lummus, The Trial Judge 46 (1937).

147. Judge Jed S. Rakoff, *Why Prosecutors Rule the Criminal Justice System—and What Can Be Done About It*, 111 Nw. U. L. Rev. 1429, 1432 (2017).

The now-ubiquitous plea-bargaining process—whereby the DOJ makes a concession (e.g., a reduced charge or a lower sentencing recommendation) in exchange for a defendant's self-conviction—is a relatively recent innovation, which began to be used ever more frequently starting in the mid-twentieth century.[148]

1. Plea Agreement Procedure

The plea agreement process has been accepted as a means by which the defendant and the government can allocate risk, obtain benefits, achieve finality, and save resources.[149] The successful negotiation of a plea agreement turns on the willingness of the defendant to accept guilt and the disposition of the prosecutor, who has no obligation to offer such an agreement.[150]

By law, plea negotiations occur outside of judicial oversight. Federal Rule of Criminal Procedure 11(c) states that "an attorney for the government and the defendant's attorney, . . . may discuss and reach a plea agreement. The court must not participate in these discussions." In exchange for a guilty or nolo contendere plea from the defendant, prosecutors can agree that the DOJ will either:

- Not bring, or will move to dismiss, other charges (Fed. R. Crim. P. 11(c)(1)(A)).
- Recommend, or agree not to oppose the defendant's request, that a particular sentence or sentencing range is appropriate or that a particular provision of the Sentencing Guidelines (see chapter 9) does or does not apply (Fed. R. Crim. P. 11(c)(1)(B)). Such a recommendation or request is not binding on the district court.
- Agree that a specific sentence or sentencing range is the appropriate disposition of the case (Fed. R. Crim. P. 11(c)(1)(C)).

Regardless of the plea agreement's terms, it must be disclosed in open court when the defendant enters a guilty plea. It is only at that point that the court begins to exercise a degree of oversight. Yet even then, the district court's role is limited to ensuring that pleas—whether the product of an agreement or otherwise—satisfy the constitutional requirement that they be knowing, intelligent, and voluntary.[151] The record must also show that the defendant

---

148. Albert W. Alschuler, *Plea Bargaining and Its History*, 79 COLUM. L. REV. 1, 26–40 (1979); The Troubling Spread of Plea-Bargaining from America to the World, THE ECONOMIST (Nov. 11, 2017) ("Plea-bargaining took off in America around 1920 with Prohibition, which led to a steep increase in the number of criminal offences. By 1930 the number of federal prosecutions under the Prohibition Act alone was eight times the total figure for all federal prosecutions in 1914. Bargaining with defendants to plead guilty in return for lighter punishment seemed like the only way to cope. Prohibition ended in 1933, but plea bargains did not. Since 1970, when the Supreme Court ruled that they were permissible, they have become ubiquitous.").

149. United States v. Quinones, 511 F.3d 289, 323 (2d Cir. 2007).

150. United States v. Hall, 212 F.3d 1016, 1022 (7th Cir. 2000); United States v. Springs, 988 F.2d 746, 749 (7th Cir. 1993) ("Prosecutors need not offer discounts and may withdraw their offers on whim. Defendants have no substantive right to bargain-basement sentences.")

151. Boykin v. Alabama, 395 U.S. 238, 244 (1969).

voluntarily relinquished his or her privilege against self-incrimination, (ii) right to trial by jury and to confront his or her accusers, that he or she understood the nature of the charges, and the consequences of a plea.[152]

Beyond these essentials, the Constitution "does not impose strict requirements on the mechanics of plea proceedings."[153] While Fed. R. Crim. P. 11 requires certain additional safeguards, violations of such rules do not ordinarily render a plea constitutionally infirm and thus vulnerable to collateral attack to a circuit court of appeals.[154]

A guilty plea is equivalent to a conviction: "more is not required; the court has nothing to do but give judgment and sentence."[155] Where the plea agreement falls under either Fed. R. Crim. P. 11(c)(1)(A) or (C), the court may accept it, reject it, or defer a decision until a presentence report has been produced (see chapter 9). If the plea agreement is rejected, the court must give the defendant an opportunity to withdraw the plea and advise him or her that if the plea is not withdrawn, the case may be disposed of less favorably than the plea agreement contemplated.[156] Where the plea agreement is made under Fed. R. Crim. P. 11(c)(1)(B), the court must advise the defendant that he or she has no right to withdraw the plea if the sentencing judge does not follow the recommendation or request.

As noted above, plea agreements made under Rule 11(c)(1)(C) are unique in that they specify a specific sentence or sentencing range as the appropriate sentence. While the sentencing judge retains the discretion to accept or reject the agreement, if it is accepted, the court is then bound to apply a sentence that adheres to its terms (subject to certain limited exceptions).[157] Because they limit the sentencing discretion of the court, plea agreements under 11(c)(1)(C) are usually reserved for situations where the DOJ is unwilling to enter into a plea agreement without reasonable assurance as to what sentence the district court will impose. Not all USAOs offer 11(c)(1)(C) agreements as a matter of policy.

Most plea agreements require the defendant to admit their guilt in open court through an "allocution" statement. The exact language of the allocation is generally agreed upon in advance between the prosecution and defense. The purpose of an allocution is to provide the court with a sufficient factual basis to evaluate the voluntariness or appropriateness of the plea.

a. Interpreting and Enforcing Plea Agreements

Because a plea agreement is essentially a contract between the government and the defendant, it is construed using the ordinary rules of contract interpretation.[158] Most importantly, courts

152. United States v. Escamilla-Rojas, 640 F.3d 1055, 1062 (9th Cir.2011); Tanner v. McDaniel, 493 F.3d 1135, 1146–47 (9th Cir.2007); Little v. Crawford, 449 F.3d 1075, 1080 (9th Cir.2006).

153. Escamilla-Rojas, 640 F.3d at 1062; Higgason v. Clark, 984 F.2d 203, 208 (7th Cir.1993) ("Putting a factual basis for the plea on the record has become familiar as a result of statutes and rules, not as a result of constitutional compulsion.").

154. *See, e.g.*, United States v. Timmreck, 441 U.S. 780, 783–84 (1979).

155. Kercheval v. United States, 274 U.S. 220, 223 (1927).

156. Fed. R. Crim. P. 11(c)(5).

157. United States v. Austin, 676 F.3d 924, 930 (9th Cir. 2012).

158. United States v. Woltmann, 610 F.3d 37, 39 (2d Cir. 2010). Where a straight application of contract principles would lead to an unjust result, courts will look beyond contract law in interpreting plea agreements. United States v. Barron, 172 F.3d 1153, 1157 (9th Cir. 1999) ("A plea bargain is not

employ the principle that any ambiguities in the agreement "are to be construed unfavorably to the drafter." In the context of plea agreements, the DOJ is usually the drafter and so must ordinarily bear the "responsibility for any lack of clarity."[159] Ambiguities are therefore resolved in favor of the defendant.

Following contract law, once a district court has accepted a plea agreement, it has the discretion to compel the government's specific performance of its terms.[160] As stated by the Supreme Court, "when a plea rests in any significant degree on a promise or agreement of the prosecutor, so that it can be said to be part of the inducement or consideration, such promise must be fulfilled."[161]

2. Alford *Pleas*

In *North Carolina v. Alford*, 400 U.S. 25 (1970), the Supreme Court established the principle that an express admission of guilt "is not a constitutional requisite to the imposition of criminal penalty." Rather, the Court determined that an "individual accused of crime may voluntarily, knowingly, and understandingly consent to the imposition of a prison sentence even if he is unwilling or unable to admit his participation in the acts constituting the crime." Closely similar to a plea of nolo contendere, an *Alford* plea effectively asserts innocence, whereas a nolo contendere plea refuses to admit guilt. As with nolo contendere pleas, the DOJ is generally averse to permitting *Alford* pleas and certain USAOs refrain from entertaining them at all. This position is driven by a recognition that "the public might well not understand or accept the fact that a defendant who denied his guilt was nonetheless placed in a position of pleading guilty and going to jail."[162]

In districts where they are permitted, AUSAs may not consent to an *Alford* plea except in the most unusual of circumstances and only after recommendation for doing so has been approved by an assistant attorney general, the associate attorney general, the deputy attorney general, or the attorney general. Further, DOJ policy requires that, in any case in which the defendant tenders a plea of guilty but denies that he or she has in fact committed the offense, the AUSA handling the case should present to the district court all facts known to the government that support the conclusion that the defendant is in fact guilty.[163]

---

a commercial exchange. It is an instrument for the enforcement of the criminal law. What is at stake for the defendant is his liberty. . . . What is at stake for the government is its interest in securing just punishment for violation of the law and its interest that an innocent act not be punished at all. The interests at stake and the judicial context in which they are weighed require that something more than contract law be applied.").

159. United States v. Transfiguracion, 442 F.3d 1222, 1228 (9th Cir. 2006); United States v. De la Fuente, 8 F.3d 1333, 1338 (9th Cir. 1993).

160. United States v. Anthony, 93 F.3d 614, 616 (9th Cir. 1996).

161. Santobello v. New York, 404 U.S. 257, 262 (1971); *see also* United States v. Lezine, 166 F.3d 895, 901 (7th Cir. 1999) ("[Plea] agreements are contracts, and the Government is obliged under the law of contracts to fulfill any promises it makes in exchange for the defendant's guilty plea.").

162. United States v. Bednarski, 445 F.2d 364, 366 (1st Cir. 1971).

163. *Justice Manual* § 16.015.

Even where the DOJ consents, there is no requirement that the district court accept an *Alford* plea. This is because a defendant has no constitutional right to have his or her guilty plea accepted by the court.[164] In the majority of circuits, district courts have discretion to reject a guilty plea because the defendant protests innocence pursuant to Fed. R. Crim. P. 11. The policy reasons behind this discretion are twofold. "The first is that a conviction affects more than the court and the defendant; the public is involved. However legally sound the *Alford* principle, . . . the public might well not understand or accept the fact that a defendant who denied his guilt was nonetheless placed in a position of pleading guilty and going to jail." Second, in the absence of discretion, if the court refused to accept a plea, "the defendant after trial and a conviction and a sentence not to his liking could return and freely litigate the correctness of the court's finding that the requirements of Rule 11 had not been fully met."[165]

B. Cooperation Plea Agreements

The purpose of a traditional, noncooperation plea agreement is simply to obtain the defendant's guilty plea and terminate the proceedings. In contrast, cooperation plea agreements are investigatory tools used by the government to incentivize the cooperator to help investigate or prosecute other individuals or entities, usually co-conspirators. Such agreements are permitted because "although the Fifth Amendment prohibits compelling a person to incriminate himself, the Constitution does not prohibit compelling a person to incriminate another."[166] Cooperators who have pleaded guilty to their involvement in the offense at issue are deemed inherently credible (at least in the United States) under the logic that: "If the person already has been convicted, either after trial or upon a guilty plea, for participating in the events about which he/she testifies, his/her testimony is apt to be far more credible than if it appears to the trier of fact that he/she is getting off 'scot free.'"[167]

In most instances, the co-conspirator with the lowest degree of culpability in an offense is offered the opportunity to plead guilty and cooperate against those who prosecutors believe bear more responsibility—cooperation agreements, in other words, are a way for the government to use "the little fish to catch the big fish."[168] Complex white-collar crime cases will almost always involve at least one cooperator.

The standard cooperation agreement used by most USAOs will state, in pertinent part:

> Defendant agrees to cooperate fully with the United States Attorney's office and such other law enforcement agencies as either of the foregoing may require by: (a) providing truthful information and testimony concerning [the alleged offense] and (b) appearing at such grand jury proceedings, hearings, trials, and other judicial proceedings as may be required by the [relevant USAO]. The United States reserves the right to evaluate the nature and extent of

---

164. Santobello v. New York, 404 U.S. 257, 262 (1971) (holding district courts "may reject a plea in exercise of sound discretion").

165. United States v. Bednarski, 445 F.2d 364, 366 (1st Cir. 1971).

166. Alschuler, *supra* note 148, at 4.

167. *Justice Manual* § 9-27.600.

168. Robert R. Stang, Plea Bargaining, Cooperation Agreements, and Immunity Orders (2018).

> defendant's cooperation and to advise the Court of the nature and extent of any such cooperation at the time of sentencing. The United States agrees that if, in the sole and unfettered discretion of the United States, the circumstances of defendant's cooperation warrant a departure by the Court from the Sentencing Guidelines range determined by the Court to be applicable, the United States will make a motion pursuant to Section 5K1.1 of the Sentencing Guidelines stating that defendant has provided substantial assistance in the investigation or prosecution of another person who has committed an offense. If it is determined by the United States to make such a motion, the amount of the departure requested in such motion will lie in the complete and sole discretion of the United States Attorney.

The "carrot" from the defendant's perspective is the possibility of prosecutors submitting a "5K letter" to the district court in advance of sentencing (which will always occur after his or her cooperation is complete; i.e., after the cases against his or her co-conspirators are concluded). 5K letters detail the extent of and benefits derived from the cooperation and make a recommendation to the court to depart from the sentence suggested by the Sentencing Guidelines (see chapter 9).

Because they often present the best chance for a defendant to receive the lowest possible sentence, cooperation agreements are highly sought after. Yet even where a defendant is desperate to cooperate, there is no obligation on the DOJ to enter into a cooperation agreement. Rather, cooperation agreements are generally only offered after multiple debriefing sessions between the defendant and prosecutors at which the defendant's credibility and culpability will be carefully scrutinized and assessed. Only if prosecutors are convinced that the defendant will be of substantial help in securing another's conviction and is being fully truthful about their criminal activity (including any crimes unrelated to the pending indictment) will a cooperation agreement be a possibility.[169]

Whether or not to submit a 5K letter is solely within prosecutors' discretion. "Because the prosecution often is in the best position to evaluate the quality of a defendant's cooperation and to decide whether to make a substantial-assistance motion [i.e. a 5K letter], this decision, like other prosecutorial determinations, may be subjected to only limited review" by courts.[170] Since almost all cooperation agreements give the government discretion to determine the extent of the defendant's assistance, courts will merely assess whether the prosecutor has made its determination in good faith, which "demands only that the government have honest dissatisfaction with the defendant's efforts."[171] DOJ policy requires all 5K letters to be approved by high-level officials within the relevant USAO or Main Justice.[172]

When a defendant claims that the government has acted in bad faith in refusing to move for a downward departure from the Sentencing Guidelines, the government may rebut this allegation by explaining its reasons for refusing to depart. The defendant must then make

---

169. *Justice Manual* § 9-27.420.

170. United States v. Knights, 968 F.2d 1483, 1487 (2d Cir. 1992).

171. United States v. Tarbell, 728 F.3d 122, 128 (2d Cir. 2013); United States v. Rexach, 896 F.2d 710, 713 (2d Cir. 1990).

172. *Justice Manual* § 9-27.400.

a showing of facts suggesting bad faith "to trigger some form of hearing on that issue."[173] Whether to hold a hearing and whether it will involve oral argument only or presentation of evidence are left to the discretion of the district court judge.[174]

The government cannot, however, unilaterally determine that a defendant has breached a plea agreement. Rather, when the prosecution seeks to escape an obligation under a plea agreement on the grounds that the defendant has failed to meet some precondition, the defendant is entitled to an evidentiary hearing. "[O]ne requisite safeguard of a defendant's [due process] rights is a judicial determination, based on adequate evidence, of a defendant's breach of a plea bargaining agreement."[175] In such an inquiry, the court must determine whether there has been a "substantial breach" of the plea agreement.[176] In the absence of a finding of substantial breach on the part of the defendant, the government must fulfill its obligations under the agreement.[177]

C. Nonprosecution Agreements

Nonprosecution agreements (NPAs) differ from cooperation agreements in that they do not require the cooperator to plead guilty. As such, NPAs are typically reserved for individuals who might have been tangentially involved in wrongdoing or who otherwise have minimal culpability.[178] NPAs obligate the person to cooperate fully with investigators and not to commit any criminal offenses for a certain set period of time. In return, they provide that the DOJ will not initiate a prosecution for one or more specific crimes (provided that the agreement's terms are fully complied with).

DOJ policy states that NPAs are appropriate when the person's "timely cooperation appears to be necessary to the public interest and other means of obtaining the desired cooperation are unavailable or would not be effective."[179] For example, NPAs can be used when the "person may be unwilling to cooperate fully in return for a reduction of charges," "it may be impossible or impractical to rely on the statutory provisions for compulsion of testimony or production of evidence," or "where compliance with the statute of limitations or the Speedy Trial Act" precludes the more lengthy cooperation agreement process.[180]

NPAs need not necessarily be reduced to writing, although unwritten agreements are generally disfavored by DOJ policy and the courts. Where a defendant claims that an implicit NPA has been entered into, whether an agreement in fact existed is evaluated according to

173. United States v. Khan, 920 F.2d 1100, 1106 (2d Cir. 1990).

174. U.S.S.G. § 6A1.3; United States v. Olvera, 954 F.2d 788, 792 (2d Cir. 1992).

175. United States v. Calabrese, 645 F.2d 1379, 1390 (10th Cir. 1981).

176. United States v. Wood, 780 F.2d 929, 931–32 (11th Cir. 1986).

177. United States v. Lezine, 166 F.3d 895, 901 (7th Cir. 1999).

178. *Justice Manual*, § 9-27.600 (relevant factors to be considered for NPAs include the importance of the investigation, the value of the person's cooperation to the investigation, the person's relative culpability and criminal history, and the interests of any victims).

179. *Id.*

180. *Id.*

the principles of contract law.[181] As to this point, a district court "must consider the possibility that immunity discussions . . . never progressed to a meeting of the minds and formation of an enforceable bargain." Nonetheless, "even if no actual agreement is determined to exist, according to principles of promissory estoppel, the government can be held to any clear and unambiguous promise of immunity it makes to a defendant, upon which the defendant reasonably relied to his or her detriment."[182] The defendant bears the burden of proving the existence of any such agreement.

As with all agreements with the DOJ, courts have held that NPAs only bind the particular USAO that entered into it. In *United States v. Annabi*, 771 F.2d 670 672 (2d Cir. 1985), for example, the Second Circuit held: "A plea agreement binds only the office of the United States Attorney for the district in which the plea is entered unless it affirmatively appears that the agreement contemplates a broader restriction." Under this principle, courts cannot infer multidistrict or nationwide application from the mere fact that an agreement uses phrases like "the government" or "the United States."[183] This means that the protection NPAs provide is limited: they usually will not preclude prosecution by another USAO or for any crime not specified in the agreement. Indeed, DOJ policy specifically requires that "no district or division shall make any agreement, including any agreement not to prosecute, which purports to bind any other district(s) or divisions without the approval of the U.S. Attorney(s) in each affected district and/or the appropriate Assistant Attorney General."[184]

D. Sentence Reductions under Rule 35(b)

A defendant's failure or unwillingness to enter into a cooperation agreement prior to sentencing does not completely foreclose the possibility of securing a sentence reduction for assistance provided after the fact. Under Fed. R. Crim. P. 35(b), the government may make a motion, within one year of sentencing, requesting that the court reduce an already-imposed sentence if the defendant provided substantial assistance in investigating or prosecuting another person.

If the assistance occurs later than one year after sentencing, a reduction may also be made but only if the defendant's substantial assistance involved "information not known to the defendant until one year or more after sentencing," "information provided by the defendant to the government within one year of sentencing, but which did not become useful to the government until more than one year after sentencing," or "information the usefulness of which could not reasonably have been anticipated by the defendant until more than one year after sentencing and which was promptly provided to the government after its usefulness was reasonably apparent to the defendant."

181. United States v. Aleman, 286 F.3d 86, 89 (2d Cir. 2002).

182. United States v. Sattar, No. 02-395, 2003 WL 22510398, at *2 (S.D.N.Y. Nov. 5, 2003).

183. United States v. Salameh, 152 F.3d 88, 120 (2d Cir. 1998); United States v. Gonzalez, 93 F. App'x 268, 270 (2d Cir. 2004).

184. *Justice Manual* § 9-27.614.

IV. PLEA AGREEMENTS IN THE UNITED KINGDOM

Plea bargaining is a feature of British criminal procedure, although to a lesser extent than in the United States. Compared with the more than ninety percent plea rate in the United States, in 2020 seventy-nine percent of Crown Court criminal cases ended in guilty pleas (a sharp ten percent increase from 2019 attributed in part to the decreased court capacity caused by the COVID-19 pandemic).[185] A number of factors have been identified as explaining the less frequent use of plea bargaining in the British system: less pressure on the courts, prosecutors' more limited role in making sentencing recommendations, and a more flexible sentencing process.[186] Moreover, unlike the Federal Rules of Criminal Procedure, which specifically contemplate plea bargaining, historically there have been no specific protocols in England for how plea bargaining should occur.

The historic reluctance to formalize plea bargaining began to change in 2009 when the attorney general issued guidance on plea discussions in serious or complex fraud cases. This guidance states that prosecutors must not charge more or more serious charges simply to encourage a defendant to plead guilty to a subset or lesser charge. Where a defendant wishes to plead guilty to some, but not all, of the charges or to a different, less serious charge, prosecutors are permitted to accept such pleas if they believe the court will still pass an adequate sentence. The Code for Crown Prosecutors states that a guilty plea must never be accepted merely because it is convenient.

When deciding whether to accept a plea to a lesser charge, the Code requires prosecutors to ensure the interests of the victims are considered, as well as whether it is in the public interest to accept the plea. In all cases, the court must be informed of the factual basis of any plea and, where a defendant pleads guilty to the charges but on the basis of facts that are different from the prosecution's case, the court may hold an evidentiary hearing.

As in the United States, the purpose of plea bargaining in the United Kingdom is to narrow the issues with a view to reaching a just outcome at the earliest possible time and agreement on a joint submission as to the appropriate sentence. In all cases, plea agreements must be reasonable, fair, and just, and safeguards must be used to ensure defendants are not under improper pressure to make admissions. These safeguards include the recording of all interrogations of suspects and defendants, a requirement that detailed records be kept of all plea negotiations, and a policy preventing prosecutors from initiating plea discussions with someone who lacks a legal representative.

To initiate plea discussions, British prosecutors must send an individual's solicitor a letter asking whether the defense wishes to enter into negotiations and setting a deadline to respond. Where the defense agrees, the prosecution will respond with another letter detailing how the negotiation process will proceed and what use can be made by the prosecution of information provided by the defendant in the course of the negotiations. Similar to the "use immunity" protections given in U.S. proffer agreements and Federal Rule of Evidence 408, prosecutors in the United Kingdom may not use the fact that the defendant has engaged in plea discussions as substantive evidence of guilt, nor may they use any information provided by the defendant

185. Ministry of Justice, Criminal Court Statistics Quarterly (Dec. 17, 2020).

186. Philip A. Thomas, *Plea Bargaining in England*, J. CRIM. LAW & CRIMINOLOGY (1978).

as evidence of the offense under investigation. Prosecutors can, however, use information given by the defendant to develop investigatory leads and to prosecute him or her for any ancillary offense (such as money laundering in connection with an underlying fraud).

Like the provision of a "reverse proffer" by DOJ prosecutors, in the United Kingdom, plea discussions are guided by a "statement of case" provided to the suspect by the prosecution, which will include a summary of the allegations and relevant evidence. The prosecution need not disclose its entire file, but it must ensure that the evidence disclosed is not misleading as to the strength of its case.

Unlike plea negotiations in the United States, which are almost always conducted off the record, the Attorney General's Guidelines state: "It is essential that a full written record is kept including details of every offer or concession made by each party, and the reasons for every decision taken by the prosecutor. Meetings between the parties should be minuted and the minutes agreed and signed."[187] No such requirement exists in the United States; to the contrary, the DOJ's general practice is to avoid documenting plea discussions so as to minimize the creation of new, discoverable evidence that might be useful to the defense.

A. Turning Queen's (or King's) Evidence

Like the DOJ, SFO and Crown prosecutors may engage in plea bargaining where the defendant agrees to testify against a co-conspirator. Cooperators in England are pejoratively referred to by the slang term "supergrasses," a designation first coined in 1973 when Bertie Smalls, the leader of a London gang of bank robbers, struck a deal with the authorities to testify against his erstwhile compatriots.[188]

Today, dealings between prosecutors and prospective supergrasses—officially referred to as "assisting offenders"—are governed by the Serious Organised Crime and Police Act (SOCPA) 2005, the Court of Appeals decision in *R v. Blackburn* [2007] EWCA Crim 2290, and guidance issued by the DPP and the director of the SFO. Compared with the United States, where cooperators are routinely used by the DOJ, supergrass arrangements are employed extremely sparingly in the United Kingdom: between May 2020 and April 2021, the CPS entered into just six such agreements, a figure in line with previous years.[189] These statistics reflect a fundamental skepticism of the practice of incentivizing criminals to help secure convictions. As the Court of Appeal stated in *Blackburn*:

> There never has been, and never will be, much enthusiasm about a process by which criminals receive lower sentences than they otherwise deserve because they have informed on or given evidence against those who participated in the same or linked crimes, or in relation to crimes in which they had no personal involvement, but about which they have provided useful information to the investigating authorities. However, like the process which provides for a reduced

187. U.K. Attorney General, *Guidelines for Plea Discussions in Cases of Serious or Complex Fraud* (Nov. 29, 2012), *available at* https://www.gov.uk/guidance/plea-discussions-in-cases-of-serious-or-complex-fraud–8.

188. Dick Hobbs, "Bertie Smalls: Armed Robber Turned Supergrass," The Independent (Mar. 1, 2008).

189. Letter from the DPP to the Attorney General on SOCPA Agreements (Oct. 2, 2021).

> sentence following a guilty plea, this is a longstanding and entirely pragmatic convention. The stark reality is that without it major criminals who should be convicted and sentenced for offences of the utmost seriousness might, and in many cases, certainly would escape justice. . . .
>
> The solitary incentive to encourage co-operation is provided by a reduced sentence, and the common law, and now statute, have accepted that this is a price worth paying to achieve the overwhelming and recurring public interest that major criminals, in particular, should be caught and prosecuted to conviction.[190]

The SFO has been similarly reluctant to use the testimony of defendants whose cooperation was incentivized through immunity or sentencing leniency. While there are isolated instances of the SFO pursuing this tactic—for example, *R v. Forsyth* [2011] Crim 2437—it remains extremely rare. And while the SFO has indicated an intention to use more cooperators to gather evidence surreptitiously through secret recording devices and other means, there has not yet been any indication that this policy has been implemented.[191]

1. Serious Organised Crime and Police Act Section 71

This provision provides that if a prosecutor "thinks that for the purposes of the investigation or prosecution of an indictable offence or offence triable either way it is appropriate to offer any person immunity from prosecution for any offence he may give the person a written" immunity notice. Once an immunity notice is issued, "no proceedings for an offence of a description specified in the notice may be brought against that person in England and Wales or Northern Ireland except in circumstances specified in the notice." Immunity notices under Section 71 therefore function in the same way as an NPA in the United States. And as with an NPA, an immunity notice can be voided if the recipient fails to fully comply with its conditions.

Immunity under Section 71 is reserved for the "most exceptional cases." The guidelines issued by the attorney general specify that immunity notices are only appropriate where "it is of more value to have a suspected person as a witness for the Crown rather than as a possible defendant," "the obtaining of information about the extent and nature of criminal activities is of greater importance than the possible conviction of the offender," and/or "it is unlikely that any information could be obtained without an offer of immunity."[192] Reflecting their exceptional nature, immunity notices must be preapproved by the attorney general.

2. Serious Organised Crime and Police Act Section 72

Section 72 of SOCPA provides for more limited benefits than Section 71 in that it merely precludes prosecutors from using the defendant's statements against them rather than barring a prosecution altogether. Specifically, Section 72 states that "if a prosecutor thinks that

---

190. Blackburn, EWCA Crim 2290, at [22].

191. Martin Bentham, "Wear a Wire or Face Jail, White-Collar Criminals Are Warned by Top British Law Enforcement Official," EVENING STANDARD, Apr. 26, 2019.

192. CPS, *Queen's Evidence—Immunities, Undertakings and Agreements Under the Serious Organised Crime and Police Act 2005* (Nov. 16, 2020), *available at* https://www.cps.gov.uk/legal-guidance/queens-evidence-immunities-undertakings-and-agreements-under-serious-organised-crime.

for the purposes of the investigation or prosecution of an indictable offence or an offence triable either way, it is appropriate to offer any person an undertaking that information of any description will not be used against the person in any proceedings to which this section applies he may give the person a written notice," called a "restricted use undertaking." Accordingly, a restricted use undertaking does not prevent the assisting offender from being prosecuted where there is evidence aside from the offender's own testimony justifying or supporting a prosecution against him or her.

3. Serious Organised Crime and Police Act Section 73

Section 73 is the British equivalent of U.S.S.G. 5K1.1. It states that if a defendant, "following a plea of guilty is either convicted in the Crown Court or is committed to the Crown Court for sentence, and has, pursuant to a written agreement made with a specified prosecutor, assisted or offered to assist the investigator or prosecutor in relation to that or any other offence," the court may take into account the extent and nature of the assistance given or offered.

"SOCPA does not include any direct provision suggesting the level of discount appropriate to be provided to the defendant who enters into and performs the SOCPA agreement."[193] As such, the level of the sentencing discount is a fact-specific decision for the court (and is not mandatory irrespective of the terms of any agreement struck with prosecutors). There is no equivalent to Fed. R. Crim. P. 11(c)(1)(C) in the British system, meaning that prosecutors cannot enter any form of plea agreement that binds the court to impose a sentence within a specified range.

To assist the court in sentencing, SOCPA calls for law enforcement to supply a report setting out the quantity and quality of the assistance given, the results arising from it (e.g., arrests or prosecutions directly attributable to the assisting offender's information), and an assessment of the risks that the assisting offender and his or her family face as a result of cooperation. The report should also indicate the extent to which the offender has admitted criminality and steps taken to secure "full cleansing" (discussed later in the chapter). Where a judge passes a sentence that is less than it would have been but for the assistance given or offered, this fact may be stated in open court and, in doing so, the judge must state what the greater sentence would have been in the absence of the assistance.[194] If there are reasons to believe that a supergrass or his or her family's safety will be threatened on account of his or her cooperation, the court may give notice in writing of that fact and of the sentencing discount applied.

4. Serious Organised Crime and Police Act Section 74

In the same way as Fed. R. Crim. P. 35(b), SOCPA Section 74 permits prosecutors to enter into an agreement post-sentencing that refers the sentence back to the Crown Court in exchange for the offender's assistance in another prosecution. A Section 74 referral may be made at any time while the person is still serving a sentence and it is in the interests of justice to do so.

---

193. R v. Blackburn [2007] EWCA Crim 2290.

194. SOCPA, s. 73(3).

A referral back to the Crown Court is not an appeal against the original sentence. Rather it starts an entirely new sentencing process based on a change in circumstances. As such, it is not without risks for the assisting offender because the Crown Court can increase the original sentence (particularly if the court finds that the offender has failed to comply with an agreement with prosecutors). Further, the Crown Court may consider whether the defendant has sought to manipulate the system by holding back information known to them at the original sentencing in the hope of passing on false or manufactured information in an attempt to receive an ex post facto discount.

Section 74 permits both the defendant and the prosecution to appeal the Crown Court's renewed sentencing decision to the Court of Appeal (with leave).

5. *Cooperation Agreement Process*

There is no statutorily prescribed process by which SOCPA negotiations must be conducted, and the procedures followed in any given case will depend on whether the offender's assistance is intended for use in court or for investigatory purposes only. Nevertheless, the CPS considers the following progression of steps to be best practice.

a. Obtaining a Provisional View

Because investigators in Britain generally work more independently from prosecutors than they do in the United States, the first step toward a SOCPA agreement is for investigators to obtain a "provisional view" on the matter from a CPS or SFO prosecutor. For proposed section 72 agreements, the prosecutor's provisional view must be in writing. The basis for the provisional view will typically be information disclosed to investigators during a debriefing session with the defendant's solicitor or the defendant.

b. Scoping Interviews

Once a possible SOCPA agreement is greenlighted by a prosecutor, a scoping interview with the potential assisting offender will then be conducted to gather further specifics about what assistance he or she can provide. If the scoping exercise is successful, the prosecutor will proceed to the full debriefing procedure. In stark contrast to the process in the United States—where interviews of prospective cooperators are never recorded or transcribed—scoping interviews in the United Kingdom are audio recorded as a matter of course to avoid allegations that the offender's assistance was improperly induced or influenced.[195]

To further protect the integrity of the process, scoping interviews are carried out by law enforcement officers from the assisting offender team under the direction of a an accredited debrief manager (all of whom are otherwise independent from the investigation at issue). While such interviews will usually be done under caution, if the assisting offender does not wish to speak under caution or it is believed that he or she will be inhibited from providing

195. R v. Clark and Others [2001] EWCA Crim 975.

all relevant information while under caution, the prosecutor may choose to issue a proffer letter and then proceed with the interview not under caution.

Proffer letters explain to the defendant that the purpose of the scoping interview is to help with the decision as to whether to enter into an assistance agreement, not to obtain admissions in relation to offenses under investigation. In particular, proffer letters will usually (i) state that neither the letter itself nor the subsequent scoping interview represents any promise or undertaking on the part of the prosecutor in relation to how the offender will eventually be dealt with, (ii) provide guarantees as to confidentiality, and (iii) undertake not to use the fact that the offender is willing to be interviewed or the content of the scoping interview as evidence against the offender. In the same way as proffer agreements in the United States, proffer letters in the United Kingdom will make clear that the prosecution reserves the right to rely upon the offender's statements in the interview as evidence against him or her in any subsequent prosecution for perjury or perverting the course of justice and to rely upon any evidence derived from the interview.

As an alternative to a proffer letter, prosecutors are permitted to receive information solely from the offender's solicitor instead of directly from the offender, but this is generally disfavored as a matter of CPS policy.

c. Investigator Authorization and Preparation of Draft Agreement

Following the scoping interview, the investigator must seek written authorization, from an officer of assistant chief constable rank or its equivalent, to proceed with a written agreement (and, if required, a cleansing interview). Once authorization is obtained, the prosecutor should draft a written agreement that specifies the range of assistance that is to be provided and any benefit the offender should expect.

d. Cleansing Interview

The purpose of a cleansing interview is for the assisting offender to reveal the totality of his or her criminal history right back to childhood. This purging process is essentially an insurance policy for the Crown so that prosecutors can present the individual to the jury as a criminal who has at least been honest about all of his or her wrongdoing. Cleansing interviews are optional when the offender assistance will be used for information gathering purposes only; they are required whenever the offender will be giving testimony in court.

There is no immunity granted to the offender in relation to offenses described during the cleansing interview. Rather, during this stage the assisting offender may be arrested or reported for each offense for which he or she has not been previously arrested or prosecuted.

e. Final Written Agreement

After the cleansing interview (if one is required), the draft assistance agreement will be signed by a prosecutor and the assisting offender. The decision to enter into the agreement at this point in the process is within the prosecutor's discretion, meaning that the offender has no right to require an agreement to be finalized.

CHAPTER 6: KEY DISTINCTIONS

United States	United Kingdom
Defendants can only seek to dismiss an indictment based on legal defects (assuming all factual allegations are true)	Defendants can make an application to dismiss an indictment based on evidentiary weaknesses in the prosecutions' case
Defendants are not permitted to call fact witnesses or introduce evidence in support of a motion to dismiss	Defendants can call fact witnesses and submit evidence in support of a motion to dismiss
Timeframe for when criminal proceedings must begin after indictment governed by the Speedy Trial Act	Timeframe for when criminal proceedings must begin after indictment governed by Article 6 of the European Convention on Human Rights
District courts can dismiss indictments but cannot order prosecutors to offer no evidence at trial	Crown Court can order prosecutors to offer no evidence at trial if there is a serious disclosure failure or other abuse of process
More than 97% of federal convictions are the result of guilty pleas	Fewer than 80% of criminal cases end in guilty pleas
Fruit of the poisonous tree doctrine can preclude admission of evidence derived from unlawfully obtained evidence	Fruit of the poisonous tree doctrine not recognized
Negotiation of plea agreements is done without any involvement or oversight by the district court	Plea negotiations are subject to court oversight and must proceed in accordance with the Attorney General's Guidance
Nonprosecution agreements used to entice the cooperation of individuals who have not been criminally charged	Prosecutors rely on their powers to compel testimony from witnesses and the Serious Organised Crime and Police Act Section 1
Plea agreements made under Federal Rule of Criminal Procedure 11(c)(1)(C) create a binding sentencing range on the district court judge once accepted	Plea agreements do not limit the Crown Court's sentencing discretion
Plea negotiations are never recorded or transcribed	A full written record of all plea negotiations must be kept and signed by all parties
Cooperating witnesses routinely used to secure convictions of others	The testimony of assisting offenders is used to secure convictions only in rare cases
Sentencing judges need not specify what the sentence would have been without the defendant's cooperation	Sentencing judges must specify the sentencing discount given to a cooperating defendant
Interviews with cooperating witnesses never recorded and are only memorialized in Federal Bureau of Investigation (FBI) 302 reports	Scoping interviews with assisting offenders must always be recorded and transcribed
Interviews with cooperating witnesses conducted by the prosecutors and FBI agents handling the investigation	Interviews with assisting offenders conducted by an independent team of investigators
Testimony of cooperating witnesses viewed as inherently reliable	Credibility of assisting offenders' testimony is viewed with deep skepticism

7 | Trial Procedure and Evidentiary Rules

After pretrial motions and other preliminaries have been addressed, a criminal case will proceed to trial unless a plea or some other resolution has been reached by the parties. Trial procedures in the United Kingdom And the United States are based on a common premise: that the adversarial process—in which advocates for opposing parties make their cases before a neutral factfinder—is the most reliable way to determine the truth of what actually happened.

This is in contrast with the inquisitorial systems used in most European countries, where judges—not prosecutors—conduct investigations, interview witnesses, and render fact determinations. In countries that use an inquisitorial model (e.g., France, Germany, the Netherlands), juries are rarely used, and the parties are not substantively involved in the factfinding process. The defendant in these countries is little more than a passive witness who is not expected to pursue an independent investigation or present evidence to support his or her own version of events.[1]

An adversarial trial is a carefully choreographed presentation of evidence before a factfinder (usually a jury) which will then decide on guilt or innocence. Legal issues are decided by the trial judge, as is the defendant's sentence upon a finding of guilty. Overriding the entire process are the rules governing what evidence may be put before the jury and the manner in which it is introduced.

This chapter provides an overview of trial procedures and evidentiary rules employed by U.S. district courts and Crown Courts of England and Wales in criminal cases.

I. TRIAL PROCEDURE IN THE UNITED STATES

Trials in federal criminal cases are extraordinarily rare. According to a recent report, of the nearly 80,000 criminal cases brought by the DOJ in 2018, just two percent went to trial. For this small minority of defendants, the odds of success are not favorable: the DOJ's nationwide trial conviction rate in 2018 was eighty-three percent, meaning that overall, only 320 of 79,704 total federal defendants (fewer than one percent) that year were acquitted after trial.[2]

---

1. Jacqueline S. Hodgson, *The Future of Adversarial Criminal Justice in 21st Century Britain*, 25 N.C. J. Int'l L. 319 (2009) (comparing adversarial and procedural criminal justice systems).

2. John Gramlich, *Only 2% of Federal Criminal Defendants Go to Trial, and Most Who Do Are Found Guilty*, Pew Research Center (June 11, 2019).

Perhaps because of these grim statistics and the "trial penalty" discussed in chapter 6, the number of defendants proceeding to trial has been steadily decreasing in recent decades—dropping from seven percent in 1998 to two percent in 2018—and is expected to continue to trend downward for the foreseeable future.[3] As the Supreme Court put it, the reality is that "criminal justice today is for the most part a system of pleas, not a system of trials. Ninety-seven percent of federal convictions and ninety-four percent of state convictions are the result of guilty pleas."[4]

In the rare cases that do proceed to trial, trial calendars are set by each individual district court and many district courts and district court judges have local practices and procedures governing how trials should proceed. Yet in general, criminal trials in the federal system will follow these steps: motions in limine → jury selection → opening statements → government's case in chief → the defense case (if any) → rebuttal → closing arguments → verdict. As discussed below, at different points throughout this process, both sides can file motions aimed at ending the case before it reaches the jury.

A. Motions in Limine

Motions in limine, or "motions on the threshold," give district courts the opportunity to rule in advance of trial on "the admissibility and relevance of certain forecasted evidence."[5] Such motions are typically filed in bulk by the parties shortly before trial and will be granted only if the evidence in question is ruled inadmissible for any conceivable purpose. Having at least some evidentiary issues resolved before trial begins allows the DOJ and defense counsel to better prepare their case: "The prudent use of the in limine motion sharpens the focus of later trial proceedings and permits the parties to focus their preparation on those matters that will be considered by the jury. Some evidentiary submissions, however, cannot be evaluated accurately or sufficiently by the trial judge in such a procedural environment. In these instances, it is necessary to defer ruling until during trial, when the trial judge can better estimate its impact on the jury."[6]

B. Juries

A criminal defendant's right to a trial by jury is enshrined in the Constitution's Sixth Amendment, and Federal Rule of Criminal Procedure 23(a) entitles a defendant to a trial by jury unless he or she waives this right in writing (and both the court and prosecutors consent). In a nonjury trial—known as a "bench trial"—the district court judge will act as factfinder and determine the defendant's guilt.

3. *Id.*

4. Lafler v. Cooper, 566 U.S. 156, 169 (2012).

5. United States v. Chan, 184 F. Supp. 2d 337, 340 (S.D.N.Y. 2002).

6. Jonasson v. Lutheran Child and Family Services, 115 F.3d 436 (7th Cir. 1997); *see also* Wilson v. Williams, 182 F.3d 562, 566 (7th Cir. 1999) ("Motions in limine are designed to avoid the delay and occasional prejudice caused by objections and offers of proof at trial; they are more useful if they can serve these purposes, which they do only if objections (and offers of proof) can be foregone safely.").

In jury trials, guilt or innocence will be determined by unanimous vote of the jury, which will generally involve twelve people (with up to six alternates who will substitute for jurors who are for some reason no longer able to participate). At any time before the verdict, the parties may, with the court's approval, stipulate in writing that the jury may consist of less than twelve jurors or that a jury of less than twelve may return a verdict if the court finds it necessary to excuse a juror after the trial begins without an alternate available. After the presentation of evidence has concluded and the jury has retired to deliberate, the court may permit a jury of eleven persons to return a verdict, even without a stipulation by the parties, if the court finds good cause for excusing a juror (e.g., a serious illness).[7]

1. Jury Selection and Voir Dire

The first stage of a jury trial is selection of the jury. Generally, the district court will mail a jury summons to people randomly selected from a list of registered voters and people with drivers licenses who live within the relevant district.[8] The minimum threshold requirements for jury service are to be a U.S. citizen who has lived in the district for at least one year, ability to speak and read English, and to not have a felony criminal record. The number of individuals summoned for jury duty is at the court's discretion but will always exceed twelve; the more high-profile or complex a criminal case is, the more potential jurors will be summoned. For example, in the emotionally charged fraud trial of former Enron executive Jeff Skilling, jury summonses were mailed to four hundred people.[9]

Once at the courthouse, the pool of potential jurors will be questioned and challenged by the judge and lawyers for both sides in a process called voir dire (French for "to speak the truth"). Although the Constitution makes no mention of voir dire, the law recognizes the important role this process plays in ensuring the fair and impartial criminal jury mandated by the Sixth Amendment.[10] Voir dire helps the trial court and the parties to identify and weed out individuals who cannot be expected to evaluate the evidence impartially or follow the court's legal instructions.[11]

There are no hard-and-fast rules governing the depth or breadth of voir dire, meaning that district court judges are afforded "ample discretion" in determining how best to conduct it.[12] This "discretion extends both to the decision whether to propound questions proffered by counsel and whether jurors should be questioned collectively or individually out of the

---

7. Fed. R. Crim. P. 23(b).

8. 28 U.S.C. § 1861 (requiring juries to be "selected at random from a fair cross section of the community in the district or division wherein the court convenes").

9. Skilling v. United States, 561 U.S. 358, 371 (2010).

10. *See* Morgan v. Illinois, 504 U.S. 719, 729 (1992) (observing that "part of the guarantee of a defendant's right to an impartial jury is an adequate voir dire to identify unqualified jurors").

11. *See* Rosales-Lopez v. United States, 451 U.S. 182, 188, (1981); United States v. Stewart, 433 F.3d 273, 303 (2d Cir. 2006).

12. *See* United States v. Wood, 299 U.S. 123, 145–146 (1936) ("Impartiality is not a technical conception. It is a state of mind. For the ascertainment of this mental attitude of appropriate indifference, the Constitution lays down no particular tests and procedure is not chained to any ancient and artificial

presence of other jurors."[13] The practice in most district courts is for voir dire to be conducted by the district court judge. To facilitate voir dire, district courts can also employ written questionnaires (that the parties may or may not be involved in drafting). Questionnaires are often used where a large number of prospective jurors must be screened or where there has been extensive pretrial publicity (under the assumption that many may have to be excused for lack of impartiality).[14]

During voir dire, the jury box is randomly filled with twelve jurors from the total pool—called the "venire"—who may then be challenged "for cause." Jurors may only be removed for cause on certain "narrowly specified, provable, and legally cognizable bas[es] of partiality."[15] While a "defendant is entitled to a fair trial by an impartial jury which will render its verdict based upon the evidence and arguments presented in court without being influenced by outside, irrelevant sources," this does not mean that venire members "must be wholly ignorant of a case's facts." Instead, it is sufficient if potential jurors "can lay aside [their pretrial] impression or opinion" during deliberations.[16] There are no limits to the number of for cause challenges that can be made, and the court retains its own discretion to excuse any number of jurors for cause. As jurors are eliminated for cause, a replacement enters the jury box (a process that is repeated until twelve jurors and up to six alternates remain). The seating of any juror who should have been dismissed for cause requires reversal of the eventual verdict.[17]

Once twelve jurors are in the jury box and there are no further for cause challenges, both sides are given six peremptory challenges—where more than one defendant is being tried jointly, the defendants are given an aggregate total of ten peremptory challenges. The district court has discretion to "allow additional peremptory challenges to multiple defendants, and may allow the defendants to exercise those challenges separately or jointly."[18] Peremptory challenges can be used to strike a potential juror without the need for any reason or justification (so long as they are not used to exclude potential jurors on the basis of their race, ethnicity, or gender).[19]

Peremptory challenges are generally exercised under either of two basic approaches: in the "jury box" system, twelve members of the pool are selected by lot to enter the jury box; counsel for each side then alternatively exercises challenges for cause and their allotted number of peremptory challenges against those seated in the jury box and against those drawn to replace any of the first twelve who have been challenged. When both sides have either used

---

formula."). Rosales-Lopez v. United States, 451 U.S. at 189; United States v. Lawes, 292 F.3d 123, 128 (2d Cir. 2002); Fed. R. Crim. P. 24(a).

13. United States v. Hawkins, 658 F.2d 279, 283 (5th Cir. 1981).

14. In the fraud case against Theranos founder Elizabeth Holmes, for example, defense attorneys asked the trial judge to give potential jurors a questionnaire with more than one hundred questions (which prosecutors challenged as "deeply intrusive"). Sara Randazzo, *Theranos Founder Elizabeth Holmes's 100 Questions for Jurors Are Scrapped*, WALL STREET J., June 15, 2021.

15. Swain v. Alabama, 380 U.S. 202, 220 (1965).

16. United States v. Chagra, 669 F.2d 241, 249 (5th Cir. 1982).

17. United States v. Martinez-Salazar, 528 U.S. 304, 316 (2000).

18. Fed. R. Crim. P. 24.

19. Batson v. Kentucky, 476 U.S. 79 (1986); Gomez v. United States, 490 U.S. 858, 873 (1989).

or waived their allotted challenges, the twelve members of the venire then in the jury box become the petit jury for trial. In the "struck jury" system, an initial panel is drawn by lot from those members of the array who have not been challenged or excused for cause; the size of this initial panel equals the total of the number of petit jurors who will hear the case (twelve in a federal criminal trial), plus the combined number of peremptories allowed to both sides. Each side then exercises their peremptory challenges on an alternating basis against the initial panel until they exhaust their allotted number and are left with a trial jury of twelve (plus alternates). Under either system, procedural details vary according to local practice.[20]

C. Opening Statements

Unlike closing arguments after all evidence has been presented to the jury, opening statements are not one of the "traditions of the adversary factfinding process that has been constitutionalized in the Sixth and Fourteenth Amendments."[21] There are no federal statutes or rules dealing with opening statements and, accordingly, the granting and timing of opening statements are matters within the discretion of the trial judge.[22] Nevertheless, the practice in most district courts is to allow opening statements by both the prosecution and the defense, even where the defense does not intend to call its own witnesses. Where openings are permitted, defense counsel must generally make their opening immediately after the prosecution (i.e., they cannot wait until the close of the prosecutor's evidence to make their opening).

The function of an opening statement is merely to "state what evidence will be presented," and to provide an "outline of proposed proof." It is not "an occasion for argument."[23] As each side's first opportunity to address the jury, opening statements are a critical way to frame the issues and alert the jury to what types of evidence they should be prepared to hear and evaluate.

D. The Government's Case in Chief

Because the prosecution bears the burden of proof in criminal cases, the government's case in chief is presented first. This consists of one or more witnesses being called to testify in open court.[24] Documents, recordings, and other types of evidence are generally introduced into evidence through the testimony of a witness who has first-hand knowledge of it or can otherwise speak to its authenticity. In the limited circumstances when depositions have been taken under Federal Rule of Criminal Procedure 15, the district court can permit a recording of the deposition to be played to the jury as if the deponent were testifying live from the witness box.

Aside from giving the mandatory oath or affirmation to testify truthfully, there are relatively few requirements on who may be called as a witness or how their testimony is elicited. The Federal Rules of Evidence provide that a nonexpert witness may testify to a matter only

20. United States v. Blouin, 666 F.2d 796–97 (2d Cir. 1981).

21. Herring v. New York, 422 U.S. 853, 857 (1975).

22. United States v. Salovitz, 701 F.2d 17 (2d Cir. 1983).

23. United States v. Dinitz, 424 U.S. 600, 612 (1976).

24. Fed. R. Crim. P. 26.

if proper foundation is first laid—that is, evidence, which can consist of the witness's own testimony, must first be introduced that shows the witness has personal knowledge of the topics they are testifying about.[25] The order in which witnesses are called is within the prosecutor's discretion, although the court retains authority to control the mode and order of examining witnesses and presenting evidence so as to facilitate determination of the truth, avoid wasting time, and protect the witness. Leading questions are usually not permitted on direct examination except as necessary to lay a foundation for the witness's testimony. However, when a "hostile" witness or adverse party is called, leading questions can be used on direct with the court's permission.[26]

After a government witness has testified on direct examination, they will be subject to cross-examination from the defense (who are permitted to pose leading questions). Per Federal Rule of Evidence 611, the scope of cross-examination is generally not allowed to extend beyond the subject matter of direct and matters affecting the witness's credibility. If defense counsel wishes to question the witness about matters beyond this scope, they must generally recall them during the defense case and examine them on direct.

On both direct and cross-examination, the questioning attorney can refresh the witness's memory with documents—for example, a 302 from an FBI interrogation session. Initially, such documents can be shown only to the witness, who will review it and then be questioned about it. If the witness confirms that their memory is in fact refreshed by the document, whatever portion of the document that relates to the witness's testimony can be introduced into evidence (i.e., shown to the jury).[27] After cross, prosecutors can then conduct a redirect examination to explain or refute any matters raised during cross. The defendant will then have the option of a re-cross before the witness is excused.

To prevent a witness tainting the testimony of a later witness, the court may exclude potential witnesses—other than the defendant—from the courtroom until called.

E. The Defense Case

The defendant has no obligation to put forth any evidence, and the jury is not permitted to consider the absence of a defense case as an indication that the defendant did in fact commit the alleged crime.[28] If the defense elects to make its own presentation, it will usually focus on either refuting prosecutors' evidence or establishing an affirmative defense. The defense case is presented in the same way as during the government's case in chief. In many white-collar crime trials, the defendant will often call only an expert witness to testify on his or her behalf (as opposed to any fact witnesses).

---

25. Federal Rules of Evidence (FRE) 602.

26. United States v. Brown, 603 F.2d 1022 (1st Cir. 1979).

27. FRE 612; *see also* FRE 613(b) ("Extrinsic evidence of a witness's prior inconsistent statement is admissible only if the witness is given an opportunity to explain or deny the statement and an adverse party is given an opportunity to examine the witness about it, or if justice so requires.").

28. Despite this, research on mock juries has shown that a majority of jurors penalize defendants for not taking the stand under the common intuition that an innocent person would want to explain that

1. Calling the Defendant to Testify

Deciding whether the defendant will testify at trial is a critical strategic decision, and roughly fifty percent of defendants elect to do so.[29] From the defendant's perspective, the key benefit of testifying is to present his or her version of the facts or provide context to any of the prosecutions' evidence; on the flipside, testifying opens the defendant up to cross-examination, attacks on his or her character, and the risk of appearing evasive or untruthful in front of the jury. If the defendant performs poorly on the stand, this impression—instead of the prosecution's evidence—can become the focal point of the entire proceedings and shift the jury's sentiment in favor of the prosecution. Accordingly, many defendants choose to keep the focus on the weaknesses in the prosecutor's presentation of evidence instead of putting forward their own.

Nevertheless, a defendant's testimony can be critical to a successful outcome, especially in white-collar crime cases, where the defendant's intent is often the main issue in dispute. Whether or not a defendant takes the witness stand is one of the four fundamental tactical decisions that he or she must make personally (the other three being whether to plead guilty, waive a jury trial, or make an appeal).[30] In other words, calling the defendant to testify is not a tactical decision that can be made by defense counsel (as opposed to, for example, what motions in limine to file or what questions to pose on cross-examination of a government witness). If a defendant wants to testify and his or her lawyer knows or suspect he or she will be untruthful, ethical rules generally require the lawyer to withdraw from the representation so as to not suborn perjury and deceive the court.[31]

F. Rebuttal

If the defendant puts in evidence, the government can present one or more rebuttal witnesses to refute it. If the defendant calls an expert witness, prosecutors will often call their own rebuttal expert. Unlike experts called during prosecutors' case in chief, there is no obligation that the defense be given advance notice of expert rebuttal testimony.[32]

G. Rule 29 Motions for Acquittal

Either after the close of the prosecution's case in chief or after the close of all evidence, Federal Rule of Criminal Procedure 29 allows a defendant to make a motion for acquittal "of any offense for which the evidence is insufficient to sustain a conviction." The district court can also order an acquittal at these same intervals on its own initiative. When the defendant submits a Rule 29 motion, the court can reserve decision, submit the case to the jury, and then

---

fact. Melissa Chan & Madeleine Carlisle, "From Ghislaine Maxwell to Kim Potter, It's the Risk Every Defendant Weighs," TIME (Dec. 29, 2021).

29. *Id.*

30. Jones v. Barnes, 463 U.S. 745, 751 (1983).

31. Dennis A. Rendleman, *What to Do When Your Client Lies*, AM. B. ASSOC. (September 2019).

32. Fed. R. Crim. P. 16(a)(1)(G); United States v. Silva, 118 F. App'x 133 (9th Cir. 2004).

decide the motion after the jury returns a verdict.[33] Many district courts choose this option since jury verdicts are less susceptible to reversal on appeal than a Rule 29 motion granted in the defendant's favor.

A defendant challenging the sufficiency of the evidence through Rule 29 "bears a heavy burden."[34] The reviewing court is required to "'view the evidence presented in the light most favorable to the government," and "all permissible inferences must be drawn in the government's favor."[35] The evidence must be viewed in its totality and the government need not completely negate every theory of innocence advanced.

Under this demanding standard, a "judgment of acquittal can be entered only if the evidence that the defendant committed the crime alleged is nonexistent or so meager that no rational trier of fact could have found the essential elements of the crime beyond a reasonable doubt."[36] Where a finding of reasonable doubt or no reasonable doubt are both "fairly possible," the district court must submit the case to the jury or defer to the jury's findings (if the Rule 29 motion is decided after a verdict is reached).[37]

Practice Note

The Successful Rule 29 Motion in *United States v. Bogucki*

Robert Bogucki was the U.S. head of currency trading for Barclays, the British bank. In connection with Hewlett Packard's 2011 acquisition of U.K. software company Autonomy plc for $11.1 billion, Bogucki oversaw a multibillion-dollar purchase of options for British pounds on behalf of HP that was designed to hedge currency fluctuations while the acquisition was pending. The transaction was structured in two tranches: in the first tranche, Barclays purchased £2 billion worth of options and in the second tranche bought an additional £4 billion. Bogucki was accused by the DOJ of frontrunning the transaction by using his foreknowledge of HP's foreign exchange purchases to make profitable trades for Barclays at HP's expense. In 2018, he was indicted on charges of conspiracy and wire fraud by the USAO for the Northern District of California, in San Francisco. At trial, the DOJ presented two alternative theories of guilt. In the first, prosecutors contended that Bogucki had committed wire fraud by either misappropriating confidential information in violation of a duty of trust or confidence. The crux of this theory was that Barclays received confidential information about HP's currency hedge and that the provision of this information created an implicit duty on the part of Barclays not to use that information for its own profit. The second theory was that Bogucki had deprived HP of its property through material misrepresentations and half-truths.

After the government rested its case, Bogucki moved for an acquittal on all counts under Rule 29. The basis of his motion was that prosecutors had failed to prove that his statements to HP were material, a critical element of a wire fraud offense under either of prosecutors' theories. After reviewing the evidence adduced during the DOJ's case in chief on this point, the district court stated:

33. Fed. R. Crim. P. 29(b).

34. United States v. Landesman, 17 F.4th 298, 319 (2d Cir. 2021).

35. *Id.; see also* United States v. Merriweather, 777 F.2d 503, 507 (9th Cir. 1985).

36. United States v. Jones, 965 F.3d 190, 193–94 (2d Cir. 2020).

37. United States v. Jabar, 19 F.4th 66, 76 (2d Cir. 2021).

> None of the five pieces of evidence the Government has produced in its case in chief can sustain a finding that a reasonable jury could conclude beyond a reasonable doubt that Defendant made false statements or material omissions that were capable of influencing a person [in] HP's position to part with money or property. None of these facts, thus, can satisfy the materiality requirement for the charges of wire fraud and conspiracy to commit wire fraud. . . . The Court therefore concludes that, pursuant to Federal Rule of Criminal Procedure 29, no jury could reasonably find that Defendant Robert Bogucki made material false or fraudulent pretenses, representations, or promises.[38]

Critical to the court's analysis on this point was evidence showing the nature of the relationship between Barclays and HP and general industry practices surrounding large foreign exchange transactions. Even when viewed in the light most favorable to the government, the court concluded that there was "simply no evidence in the record that, in the context of an arms-length transaction in which the parties bluffed and 'BS-ed' each other, operated as principals, looked out for their own interests, and understood the other party to be 'posturing,' rather than providing strictly true information, someone in HP's position could, objectively, be induced by the statements in this case to part with money or property."[39] Summarizing prosecutors' case, the court found that it was brought on "the basis of conduct that violated no clear rule or regulation, was not prohibited by the agreements between the parties, and indeed was consistent with the parties' understanding of the arms'-length relationship in which they operated. The Court cannot permit this case to go to the jury on such a basis."[40]

H. Motions for a Mistrial

A mistrial occurs when a jury is unable to reach a unanimous verdict or if there is either a serious procedural error, improper admission of evidence, or misconduct that fundamentally undermines the fairness of the proceedings. Mistrials are not equivalent to an acquittal; they merely terminate the existing proceedings and allow for the defendant to be retried. Because of this, mistrials raise issues under the Constitution's Double Jeopardy Clause (see chapter 3).

"The critical double jeopardy inquiry in the mistrial context is whether the defendant sought or consented to the mistrial."[41] Where the court declares a mistrial without the defendant's consent, a new trial is barred unless there was a "manifest necessity" for the mistrial. Conversely, where the defendant consents to the mistrial, he or she may be retried unless the judge or prosecutor intentionally provoked the defendant to consent to the mistrial.[42] Even where a mistrial results in a retrial, the mistrial can benefit defendants by allowing them to rejigger their defense on the basis of the preview of the prosecutions' case in the first trial. Depending on the strength of that original case, defendants can also use a mistrial as leverage to secure a more favorable plea agreement than was initially possible.

38. United States v. Bogucki, No. 18-cr-00021 (N.D. Cal. Mar. 4, 2019).

39. *Id.*

40. *Id.*

41. United States v. Rivera, 802 F.2d 593, 597 (2d Cir. 1986).

42. Oregon v. Kennedy, 456 U.S. 667, 672, 673–80 (1982).

Before a judge orders a mistrial, each defendant and the government must be given "an opportunity to comment on the propriety of the order, to state whether that party consents or objects, and to suggest alternatives."[43]

I. Closing Arguments

"Closing arguments are the chronological and psychological culmination of a jury trial. They are the last opportunity to communicate directly with the jury."[44] During closing arguments (also called summation), both sides give a summary of the key evidence, how it relates to the crime charged, and why the evidence compels a verdict in their favor.

In keeping with Federal Rule of Criminal Procedure 29.1, the government presents its closing argument first, followed by the defense, and then a rebuttal. The purpose of the sequence in this rule "is to give the defendant the chance to respond to the government's case and argument in an informed manner. Rebuttal provides the government with the opportunity to respond to defendant's arguments. It does not allow the government to bring in new matters."[45] Within these confines, district courts have broad discretion to ensure a fair procedure in final arguments.

Nevertheless, the courts of appeals have, on occasion, reversed convictions based on improper comments made by prosecutors during closing arguments if they "were so prejudicial that they rendered the trial in question fundamentally unfair."[46] For example, in *Floyd v. Meachum*, the Second Circuit found that the "cumulative effect of the prosecutor's persistent and clearly improper remarks amounted to such egregious misconduct as to render Floyd's trial fundamentally unfair."[47] Included among the statements the panel took issue with were "repeated references to the Fifth Amendment" which it viewed "as an improper comment on [Floyd's] failure to testify" and "an impermissible attempt to dilute the State's burden of proof and to undermine the presumption of innocence."[48] The court also found fault in the prosecutor's explicit request that the jury consider her own personal integrity and professional ethics before deliberating on the evidence (which, in effect, impermissibly implied that the prosecutor personally vouched for the government's witnesses).[49] Finally, the prosecutor characterized Floyd, who did not testify, "as a liar literally dozens of times" throughout her summation. The court concluded that "[w]hile each instance of prosecutorial misconduct, standing alone, might not justify reversal, the effect of them all requires it."[50]

---

43. Fed. R. Crim. P. 26.3.

44. Thomas A. Mauet, Trial Techniques 387 (8th ed. 2010).

45. United States v. Garcia, 94 F.3d 57, 63 (2d Cir. 1996).

46. Garolfolo v. Coomb, 804 F.2d 201, 206 (2d Cir. 1986); *see also* Donnelly v. DeChristoforo, 416 U.S. 637, 645 (1974).

47. 907 F.2d 347, 353 (2d Cir. 1990).

48. *Id.*

49. *Id.* at 354.

50. *Id.* at 357.

J. Jury Instructions

Either before or after closing arguments, the district court must instruct the jury on the applicable law and how it should evaluate the trial evidence. Both sides are permitted to propose their own preferred jury instructions to the judge, who then has the discretion to accept or reject them. "A party who objects to any portion of the instructions or to a failure to give a requested instruction must inform the court of the specific objection and the grounds for the objection before the jury retires to deliberate."[51] Failure to lodge such an objection will result in a waiver of the issue for purposes of appeal (except if an instruction is so blatantly erroneous as to affect a defendant's "substantial rights").[52]

Some circuit courts issue their own model jury instructions to use as a template. The Seventh Circuit, for example, has published nearly one thousand pages worth of model jury instructions to be used in criminal cases.[53] These instructions cover virtually all issues that a jury may be requested to consider, including the presumption of innocence and burden of proof, the credibility of witnesses, and the definition of key legal terms (e.g., "knowingly," "willfully," and "specific intent").

K. Verdicts

Jury verdicts of guilty or not guilty in federal criminal cases must be returned to the judge in open court and must be unanimous as to all counts. In multiple defendant cases or cases involving multiple charges, if the jury cannot reach a unanimous decision as to any defendant or as to any count, it can return a verdict just on those counts on which it has agreed.[54]

If the jury cannot agree on a verdict on one or more counts, the court may declare a mistrial on those counts and schedule a retrial of the defendant as to those counts (if prosecutors elect to do so). Alternatively, the jury may find the defendant guilty of a lesser included offense, or an attempt to commit the charged offense "if the attempt is an offense in its own right."[55] In light of the Constitution's double jeopardy protections, a not guilty verdict is final and "absolutely shields the defendant from retrial" on whatever charges the verdict was reached.[56]

1. Allen *Charges*

If during deliberations the jury indicates that it cannot reach a unanimous verdict, the district court judge may issue a so-called "*Allen* charge" directing the jurors to continue their deliberations and try to obtain unanimity—it is a "dynamite charge . . . intended to break-up

---

51. Fed. R. Crim. P. 30.

52. Fed. R. Crim. P. 52(b).

53. *The William J. Bauer Pattern Criminal Jury Instructions of the Seventh Circuit* (2020 ed.), *available at* https://www.ca7.uscourts.gov/pattern-jury-instructions/pattern_criminal_jury_instructions_2020edition.pdf.

54. United States v. Cunningham, 145 F.3d 1385, 1388–90 (D.C. Cir. 1998).

55. Fed. R. Crim. P. 31.

56. Tibbs v. Florida, 457 U.S. 31, 41 (1982).

the log-jam" in the jury room."[57] A traditional *Allen* charge reminds the jurors about the importance of obtaining a verdict and encourages them to listen "to each other's arguments" while also emphasizing that "the verdict must be the verdict of each individual juror, and not a mere acquiescence in the conclusion of his fellows."[58]

Whether an *Allen* charge is appropriate in a given case "hinges on whether it tends to coerce undecided jurors into reaching a verdict. Coercion may be found when jurors are encouraged to abandon, without any principled reason, doubts that any juror conscientiously holds as to a defendant's guilt." Accordingly, a necessary component of any *Allen*-type charge requires the trial judge to admonish the jurors not to surrender their own conscientiously held beliefs.[59] Appellate courts have thus approved the use of *Allen* charges so long as they are given by the district court, in "an evenhanded, noncoercive manner," and the court states that it would prefer a unanimous verdict if it can be accomplished "without any juror yielding a conscientious conviction which he or she may have."[60] In other words, a proper *Allen* charge will "caution the jurors never to abandon their conscientiously held beliefs, even if holding firm will result in a deadlock."[61]

2. *Inconsistent Verdicts*

There is no requirement that a jury's verdict be consistent across all the crimes and defendants that may be grouped together in a single indictment. For example, if a defendant has been charged alongside an alleged co-conspirator, there is nothing inherently improper about the jury finding one of the conspirators guilty of conspiracy and the other not guilty (even though there can be no one-man conspiracies).[62] Rather, the federal courts have long maintained that "[c]onsistency in the verdict is not necessary. Each count in an indictment is regarded as if it was a separate indictment."[63] Where the jury reaches an inconsistent verdict, "the most that can be said is that the verdict shows that either in the acquittal or the conviction the jury did not speak their real conclusions, but that does not show that they were not convinced of the defendant's guilt."[64]

Put differently,

> inconsistent verdicts—even verdicts that acquit on a predicate offense while convicting on the compound offense—should not necessarily be interpreted as a windfall to the Government at the defendant's expense. It is equally possible that the jury, convinced of guilt, properly

---

57. United States v. Crispo, 306 F.3d 71, 76 (2d Cir. 2002).

58. Allen v. United States, 164 U.S. 492, 501 (1896).

59. United States v. Strothers, 77 F.3d 1389, 1391 (D.C. Cir. 1996) (reversing conviction due to trial judge's failure to give the required admonition not to surrender honest convictions); United States v. Mason, 658 F.2d 1263, 1268 (9th Cir. 1981) (reversing conviction due to lack of cautionary language and observing that "[i]f cases grappling with Allen have a common thread, it is this: the integrity of individual conscience in the jury deliberation process must not be compromised").

60. United States v. Burke, 700 F.2d 70, 80 (2d Cir. 1983).

61. Smalls v. Batista, 191 F.3d 272, 283 (2d Cir. 1999).

62. United States v. Garcia, 882 F.2d 699, 705 (2d Cir. 1989).

63. Steckler v. United States, 7 F.2d 59, 60 (2d Cir. 1925).

64. Dunn v. United States, 284 U.S. 390, 393 (1932).

> reached its conclusion on the compound offense, and then through mistake, compromise, or lenity, arrived at an inconsistent conclusion on the lesser offense. But in such situations the Government has no recourse if it wishes to correct the jury's error; the Government is precluded from appealing or otherwise upsetting such an acquittal by the Constitution's Double Jeopardy Clause.[65]

Thus, in the Supreme Court's view, inconsistent verdicts

> present a situation where "error," in the sense that the jury has not followed the court's instructions, most certainly has occurred, but it is unclear whose ox has been gored. Given this uncertainty, and the fact that the Government is precluded from challenging the acquittal, it is hardly satisfactory to allow the defendant to receive a new trial on the conviction as a matter of course.[66]

II. THE FEDERAL RULES OF EVIDENCE

The admissibility and use of evidence at a federal criminal trial is governed by the Federal Rules of Evidence (FRE), which were originally drafted by the Supreme Court and then enacted into law by Congress in 1975. Their underlying purpose is to "to administer every proceeding fairly, eliminate unjustifiable expense and delay, and promote the development of evidence law, to the end of ascertaining the truth and securing a just determination." To the extent practicable, therefore, district courts must conduct jury trials "so that inadmissible evidence is not suggested to the jury by any means."[67]

District courts are granted substantial discretion in making evidentiary determinations. A challenge to such a determination can be waived by the party against whom evidence is admitted if they fail to make a timely objection or motion to strike on a specific ground (unless the ground is apparent from the context). Once the court rules definitively on the record—either before trial on a motion in limine or during the trial itself—a party need not renew an objection or offer of proof to preserve a claim of error for appeal.[68]

The FRE provisions that are most often relevant in white-collar crime trials are outlined below.

A. FRE 106—Completeness

Federal common law requires that "when one party has made use of a portion of a document, such that misunderstanding or distortion can be averted only through presentation of another portion, the material required for completeness is ipso facto relevant and therefore

---

65. United States v. Powell, 469 U.S. 57, 65 (1984).

66. *Id.*; *see also* United States v. Romano, 879 F.2d 1056, 1060 (2d Cir. 1989) ("jury is free to exercise its historic power of lenity if it believes that a conviction on one count would provide sufficient punishment").

67. FRE 102.

68. FRE 103.

admissible."[69] This doctrine permits "a party against whom a part of a writing or utterance has be introduced to 'in his turn complement it by putting in the remainder, in order to secure for the tribunal a complete understanding of the total tenor and effect' of the whole."[70]

FRE 106 codifies this rule of completeness. To prevent the introduction of snippets of evidence in a way that may be misleading to the jury, the rule provides that "if a party introduces all or part of a writing or recorded statement, an adverse party may require the introduction, at that time, of any other part—or any other writing or recorded statement—that in fairness ought to be considered at the same time."[71] Courts have interpreted FRE 106 to require that a document be admitted when it is essential to explain an already admitted document, to place the admitted document in context, or to avoid misleading the factfinder.[72]

This rule is subject to two qualifications: the portions sought to be admitted (i) must be relevant to the issues and (ii) only those parts that qualify or explain the subject matter of the portion offered by the opponent need be admitted.[73]

Unlike the broader common law rule, FRE 106 does not cover oral statements—for practical reasons, it is limited to writings and recorded statements only. In most circuits, however, FRE 611(a) is interpreted to fill this gap by requiring "a party offering testimony as to an utterance to present fairly the 'substance or effect' and context of that statement, just as the common law doctrine requires."[74]

B. FRE 401 and 402—Relevance

FRE 402 creates a presumption that all irrelevant evidence is inadmissible and that all relevant evidence should be admitted unless the Constitution, a federal statute, or a specific FRE provides otherwise. Under FRE 401, relevant evidence is defined as that which "has any tendency to make a fact more or less probable than it would be without the evidence" where "the fact is of consequence in determining the action."

As the advisory committee notes accompanying Rule 401 state, "Problems of relevancy call for an answer to the question whether an item of evidence, when tested by the processes of legal reasoning, possesses sufficient probative value to justify receiving it in evidence." The standard of probability under the rule is "more probable than it would be without the evidence."

The fact to which the evidence is directed need not be in dispute for it to be relevant: "even if a district court believes the evidence is insufficient to prove the ultimate point for

69. Beech Aircraft Corp. v. Rainey, 488 U.S. 153, 172 (1988).

70. United States v. Williams, 930 F.3d 44, 58 (2d Cir. 2019); *see also* United States v. Castro, 813 F.2d 571, 575–76 (2d Cir. 1987) (the adverse party can demand that an omitted portion "be placed in evidence if necessary to explain the admitted portion, to place the admitted portion in context, to avoid misleading the jury, or to ensure fair and impartial understanding of the admitted portion").

71. United States v. Soures, 736 F.2d 87, 91 (3d Cir. 1984).

72. United States v. Marin, 669 F.2d 73, 84 (2d Cir. 1982).

73. United States v. Walker, 652 F.2d 708, 710 (7th Cir. 1981).

74. Williams, 930 F.3d at 59.

which it is offered, it may not exclude the evidence if it has the slightest probative worth."[75] While the advisory committee recognized that "situations will arise which call for the exclusion of evidence offered to prove a point conceded by the opponent," it specified that such a ruling should be made on the basis of considerations such as waste of time and undue prejudice (see FRE 403), rather than under any general requirement that evidence is admissible only if directed to matters in dispute.

C. FRE 403—Exclusion of Relevant Evidence

FRE 403 grants a trial judge discretion to exclude plainly relevant evidence "if its probative value is substantially outweighed by the danger of unfair prejudice." "Unfair prejudice" within this context means "an undue tendency to suggest decision on an improper basis, commonly, though not necessarily, an emotional one."[76] In reaching a decision on whether to exclude evidence under this rule, district courts are directed to consider the probable effectiveness or lack of effectiveness of a limiting instruction to the jury and whether alternative means of proof are available.[77]

So long as the district court has "conscientiously balanced the proffered evidence's probative value with the risk for prejudice, its conclusion [to preclude evidence pursuant to FRE 403] will be disturbed only if it is arbitrary or irrational."[78] Thus, even if ultimately deemed erroneous, a judge's decision to preclude evidence under Rule 403 warrants reversal only if it "had a substantial and injurious effect or influence on the jury's verdict."[79]

D. FRE 404(a)—Character Evidence

While FRE 404(a)(1) establishes the general proposition that "evidence of a person's character or character trait is not admissible to prove that on a particular occasion the person acted in accordance with the character or trait," there are important exceptions to this rule as it relates to criminal defendants and witnesses.

First, "a defendant may offer evidence of the defendant's pertinent trait, and if the evidence is admitted, the prosecutor may offer evidence to rebut it."[80] In other words, the defendant may elect to put his or her "character in issue" but only at the cost of allowing prosecutors to offer contrary evidence; whether the benefits of introducing character evidence is worth the risks of the jury seeing damaging evidence that would otherwise be inadmissible must therefore be carefully weighed. As to whether a defendant has in fact put his or her character

75. DXS, Inc. v. Siemens Med. Sys., Inc., 100 F.3d 462, 475 (6th Cir. 1996).

76. Old Chief v. United States, 519 U.S. 172, 180 (1997).

77. A limiting instruction is a direction from the trial judge for the jury to consider a piece of evidence for a specific permissible purpose and ignore it for any other purpose. While it may be difficult for jury members to follow such an instruction in practice, courts assume that they will. Greer v. Miller, 483 U.S. 756, 766 n.8 (1987).

78. United States v. Awadallah, 436 F.3d 125, 131 (2d Cir. 2006).

79. United States v. Spoor, 904 F.3d 141, 153 (2d Cir. 2018).

80. FRE 404(a)(2)(A).

in issue, courts have reasoned that a defendant's mere "denial of guilt is not evidence of good character subject to bad character rebuttal."[81]

Even if character evidence is admissible under this rule, the form of that evidence is limited by FRE 405, which provides that proof of character may only be made in the form of opinion or reputation testimony. But on cross-examination of a character witness, "the court may allow an inquiry into relevant specific instances of the person's conduct."[82] Further, in the limited instances when character itself is "an essential element of a charge, claim, or defense, the character trait may also be proved by relevant specific instances."[83] Accordingly, FRE 404(a) and 405 combine to establish a two-part test: the court will first consider whether the evidence is relevant; if it is, the court will determine whether the evidence should be limited to reputation and opinion testimony.[84]

Second, FRE 404 states that evidence of a witness's character may be admitted pursuant to FRE 607, 608, and 609. Rule 607 permits a witness's credibility to be attacked by any party (including the one who called the witness to testify). Under Rule 608, "A witness's credibility may be attacked or supported by testimony about the witness's reputation for having a character for truthfulness or untruthfulness, or by testimony in the form of an opinion about that character. But evidence of truthful character is admissible only after the witness's character for truthfulness has been attacked."

This exception is often implicated in situations where a witness is testifying pursuant to an agreement with the DOJ to cooperate. The existence of such an agreement is a "double-edged sword" not necessarily favorable to the prosecution or the defense.[85] On the one hand, a cooperation agreement can provide ammunition for the defense to impeach the credibility of a government witness, both by specifying the benefits the cooperator has received or will receive for testifying at the government's behest and also by revealing the witness's criminal background or other prior wrongdoing.[86] At the same time, the government can use cooperation agreements to rehabilitate witnesses whose credibility has been questioned. That is because cooperation agreements generally contain so-called "truth-telling" provisions, which "set out promises to testify truthfully as well as penalties for failure to do so, such as prosecution for perjury and reinstatement of any charges dropped pursuant to the deal."[87] Overall, it is generally the case that a witness's cooperation agreement bolsters more than it impeaches his or her credibility.[88]

---

81. United States v. Grable, 200 F. App'x 670, 672 (9th Cir. 2006).

82. FRE 405(a).

83. FRE 405(b).

84. United States v. Smith, 230 F.3d 300, 307 (7th Cir. 2000). Relevancy under the first prong of this test is assessed using a lower threshold than regular evidence under FRE 401. According to the Second Circuit, the justification for this is "based on notions of fairness rather than logic; the defendant who, with the considerable forces of government arrayed against him and who may have little more than his good name to defend himself, should not be precluded from presenting even such minimally probative evidence. Thus, Rule 404(a) (1) requires only that the proffered evidence of a character trait *relate to some element at issue in the case.*" United States v. Han, 230 F.3d 560, 561 (2d Cir. 2000).

85. United States v. Arroyo-Angulo, 580 F.2d 1137, 1146 (2d Cir.1978).

86. United States v. Cosentino, 844 F.2d 30, 32 (2d Cir. 1988).

87. *Id.* at 32–33.

88. United States v. Edwards, 631 F.2d 1049,1052 (2d Cir.1980).

The government may not, however, introduce the bolstering aspects of a cooperation agreement unless and until the witness's credibility has been questioned in ways that "open the door" to the admission of the agreement. This proposition stems from the evidentiary rules relating to relevance, hearsay, bias, and completeness that, taken together, establish that "absent an attack on the veracity of a witness, no evidence to bolster his credibility is admissible."[89] An attack opening the door to such rehabilitation may take different forms: for instance, a witness's credibility is often tested by a sequence of attack on cross-examination followed by rehabilitation on redirect; an attack also may come in a defendant's opening statement if it "sufficiently implicates the credibility of a government witness."[90] Once such an attack has been launched, the district court has broad discretion to admit rehabilitative evidence of credibility.[91]

And even though the government may not introduce the bolstering aspects of an agreement until after the witness's credibility has been attacked, this restriction does not apply to an agreement's impeaching aspects (i.e., the fact of the guilty plea), which the government is free to introduce even on the witness's direct examination.[92] Prosecutors may not, however, personally vouch for their witness's truthfulness in any circumstances.[93]

Except insofar as it relates to a criminal conviction admitted under Rule 609, "extrinsic evidence is not admissible to prove specific instances of a witness's conduct in order to attack or support the witness's character for truthfulness." But on cross-examination, the court can allow specific instances to be inquired into to the extent they are probative of the truthfulness of the witness or another witness whose character the witness being cross-examined has testified about.[94]

Practice Note

Introduction of a Witness's Guilty Plea to the Crime at Issue

As discussed in chapter 6, the DOJ will often enter into cooperation agreements with one or more codefendants that require the cooperator to plead guilty and testify against others in exchange for leniency at sentencing. The fact that a codefendant has pleaded guilty to a crime may not be used as substantive evidence of guilt against the defendant on trial—in other words, the fact that a co-conspirator pleaded guilty to conspiring with the defendant cannot be used

89. Arroyo-Angulo, 580 F.2d at 1146.

90. Cosentino, 844 F.2d at 33.

91. *Id.*

92. *Id.* ("It may sometimes be useful . . . to develop impeaching matter in direct examination of a 'friendly' witness in order to deprive an adversary of the psychological advantage of revealing it to the jury for the first time during cross-examination."); *see also* United States v. Carr, 424 F.3d 213, 227 (2d Cir. 2005) (even in the absence of a prior attack on credibility, "the elicitation of the fact of the agreement and the witness'[s] understanding of it, as a motivation for the witness to testify for the Government, should be permitted on direct examination in order to anticipate cross-examination by the defendant which might give the jury the unjustified impression that the Government was concealing this relevant fact.").

93. United States v. Modica, 663 F.2d 1173, 1179 (2d Cir.1981).

94. FRE 608(b).

as evidence that the defendant is guilty of conspiracy.[95] Nevertheless, evidence of a cooperator's guilty plea is often introduced by the defendant for the purpose of impeaching the government witness's credibility (usually accompanied by a limiting instruction from the judge).

In recognition of this routine tactic, some circuits, including the Second, permit the introduction of a witness's guilty plea and cooperation agreement by prosecutors during direct examination.[96] This allowance is an exception to the otherwise-prevailing rule that "credibility generally may not be supported until it has first been attacked."[97] Courts justify this exception "on the ground that to defer the introduction of such evidence as to the witness' motivation to favor the government until it is brought out on cross-examination by the defendant might give the jury the unjustified impression that the government was concealing this relevant fact."[98]

E. FRE 404(b)—Prior Bad Acts

FRE 404(b)(1) precludes the use of evidence of "other crimes, wrongs, or acts" committed by the defendant "to prove the character of a person in order to show action in conformity therewith." But 404(b)(2) creates a broad exception that permits such "prior bad acts" evidence to be admitted for any other purpose, "such as proving motive, opportunity, intent, preparation, plan, knowledge, absence of mistake, or lack of accident."

Yet even if the trial court determines that the evidence at issue does indeed tend to prove knowledge or one of the other permitted grounds, a defendant is entitled to have the probative value weighed against the risk of unfair prejudice under Rule 403. In other words, Rule 404(b)(2) functions as an exception to 404(b)(1), but not as an exception to Rule 403.[99]

One issue that often arises in the 404(b) context is whether evidence of a defendant's other crimes is admissible under this rule or some other rule of evidence. Evidence of uncharged criminal conduct is not evidence of "other crimes, wrongs, or acts" within the meaning of Rule 404(b) if that conduct is "inextricably intertwined with the evidence regarding the charged offense."[100] In such circumstances, the uncharged crime evidence is necessary to "complete the story of the crime on trial," and thus, appropriately treated as "part of the very act charged," or, at least, proof of that act, and therefore is admissible under Rule 401.[101] Evidence of an unrelated crime will be considered Rule 404(b) evidence if: (i) the prior act is similar enough and close enough in time to be relevant, (ii) the evidence is clear

---

95. United States v. Ganim, 256 Fed. App'x 399, 402 (2d Cir. 2007); *see also* United States v. Toliver, 541 F.2d 958, 967 (2d Cir. 1976) (co-conspirator's "plea of guilt and testimony for the government should not color [the jury's] view of the evidence against the remaining defendants").

96. *See, e.g.*, United States v. Blackwood, 456 F.2d 526, 529 (2d Cir. 1972).

97. United States v. Singh, 628 F.2d 758, 761 (2d Cir. 1980).

98. Blackwood, 456 F.2d at 529.

99. United States v. McElmurry, 776 F.3d 1061, 1067 (9th Cir. 2015); United States v. Cherer, 513 F.3d 1150, 1157 (9th Cir. 2008) ("If evidence satisfies Rule 404(b), the court must then decide whether the probative value is substantially outweighed by the prejudicial impact under Rule 403.")

100. United States v. Towne, 870 F.2d 880, 886 (2d Cir. 1989).

101. United States v. Concepcion, 983 F.2d 369, 392 (2d Cir. 1992).

and convincing, (iii) the probative value of the evidence outweighs its risk of prejudice, and (iv) the evidence is needed to prove an essential element of the charged offense.[102]

The admission of Rule 404(b) evidence is within the discretion of the district court. In keeping with the four-part test created by the Supreme Court in *Huddleston v. United States*, this discretion should be used to admit prior bad act evidence when it is (i) offered for a proper purpose, (ii) relevant, (iii) substantially more probative than prejudicial, and (iv) at the defendant's request, accompanied by an appropriate limiting instruction to the jury.[103] These are relatively stringent requirements and, to satisfy them, a mere "reliance on an offer of proof is simply not enough;" the district court must "read every word" of what will be put before the jury in order to decide its prejudicial effect.[104]

1. Notice Requirement

Because of its inherent unfairly prejudicial effect and so as to give the defendant a "fair opportunity" to challenge it, admission of Rule 404(b) evidence is subject to a notice requirement in criminal cases: before trial (pursuant to a schedule set by the district court), prosecutors must provide reasonable notice of what evidence they intend to introduce and on what legal basis they expect to do so. Because 404(b) evidence can have a major impact on a trial outcome, obtaining a ruling on the admissibility of the government's proffered 404(b) materials is often a critical stage in the pretrial process.

F. FRE 408—Compromise Offers and Negotiations

To encourage settlement and plea discussions between the parties in a criminal case, FRE 408 makes two categories of evidence inadmissible either to prove or disprove a disputed claim or to impeach by a prior inconsistent statement or contradiction:

1. Furnishing, promising, or offering—or accepting, promising to accept, or offering to accept—a valuable consideration in compromising or attempting to compromise the claim.
2. Conduct or a statement made during compromise negotiations about the claim—except when offered in a criminal case and when the negotiations relate to a claim by a public office in the exercise of its regulatory, investigative, or enforcement authority.

Not all circuits recognize that Rule 408 applies in criminal as well as civil cases.[105] In jurisdictions that take the opposite view, the effect of Rule 408 in criminal cases is to grant statements made during plea negotiations immunity from use against the declarant in the event that such

---

102. United States v. Wormick, 709 F.2d 454 (7th Cir. 1983).

103. 485 U.S. 681 (1988).

104. United States v. McElmurry, 776 F.3d 1061, 1068 (9th Cir. 2015).

105. United States v. Bailey, 327 F.3d 1131, 1144 (10th Cir. 2003) (noting that the Second, Sixth, and Seventh Circuits have held that FRE 408 only applies to civil cases).

negotiations break down and the case goes to trial; such statements may still be admissible against a third party. Further, even when Rule 408 applies, the evidence can be admitted for purposes other than establishing liability, such as proving a witness's bias or prejudice, negating a contention of undue delay, or proving an effort to obstruct a criminal investigation.

G. FRE 410—Pleas, Plea Discussions, and Related Statements

FRE 410 provides that statements made in the course of plea discussions between a criminal defendant and a prosecutor are generally inadmissible against the defendant.[106]

There are two key exceptions to this rule: such statements are:

> admissible (i) in any proceeding wherein another statement made in the course of the same . . . plea discussions has been introduced and the statement ought in fairness to be considered contemporaneously with it, or (ii) in a criminal proceeding for perjury or false statement if the statement was made by the defendant under oath, on the record and in the presence of counsel.[107]

Like other evidentiary privileges, the privilege created by FRE 410 may be varied or waived at the defendant's request, leaving open the possibility that a defendant may offer such statements into evidence for his or her own tactical advantage.[108]

H. FRE 702—Testimony by Expert Witnesses

The general rule is that lay witnesses cannot offer opinion testimony unless the opinion is rationally based on the witness's first-hand perception, helpful to clear understanding of their testimony or determining a fact in issue, and not based on scientific, technical, or other specialized knowledge.[109]

Properly qualified expert witnesses are given far greater leeway. Under Rule 702, experts are allowed to give opinion testimony so long as it relates to the subject of their expertise and is deduced from reliable methods.

1. *The* Daubert *Standard*

FRE 702 permits expert testimony if it "will help the trier of fact to understand the evidence or to determine a fact in issue." As discussed in chapter 6, the Supreme Court's decision in *Daubert v. Merrell Dow Pharms., Inc.*, 509 U.S. 579, 597 (1993) requires trial courts to make a preliminary determination that the expert's proposed testimony is reliable. *Daubert* does not require a court to admit or to exclude evidence based on its persuasiveness; rather it requires a court to admit or exclude evidence based on its scientific reliability and relevance.

---

106. *See also* Fed. R. Crim. P. 11(e)(6).

107. FRE 410(b).

108. United States v. Mezzanatto, 513 U.S. 196, 205 (1995).

109. FRE 701.

Thus, an expert's "inference or assertion must be derived by the scientific method" to be admissible. A trial judge has broad latitude not only in determining whether an expert's testimony is reliable, but also in deciding how to determine the testimony's reliability.[110]

Daubert sets forth a nonexhaustive list of guideposts for district courts to consult in assessing the reliability of expert testimony: (i) whether the scientific theory can be or has been tested; (ii) whether the theory has been subjected to peer review and publication; and (iii) whether the theory has been generally accepted in the relevant scientific, technical, or professional community.[111] In addition, the advisory committee's notes to Rule 702 suggest that district courts gauge expert reliability by looking at whether (i) the testimony relates to "matters growing naturally and directly out of research they have conducted independent of the litigation, or whether they have developed their opinions expressly for purposes of testifying"; (ii) "the expert has adequately accounted for obvious alternative explanations"; and (iii) "the expert is being as careful as he would be in his regular professional work outside his paid litigation consulting."[112]

I. FRE 801—The Definition of Hearsay

The FRE define hearsay to mean a statement—including oral and written assertions or nonverbal conduct (e.g., a head nod)—that (i) the declarant does not make while testifying at the current trial and (ii) that is offered in evidence to prove the truth of the matter asserted.[113] As such, whether a statement qualifies as hearsay turns on where and by whom it was made, and the purpose for which it is offered as evidence.

Explicitly excluded from this definition are two categories of out-of-court statements:

- Prior statements of a testifying witness.
    - A prior inconsistent statement of a witness that was made under penalty of perjury at a trial, deposition, or other proceeding is not hearsay.
    - A prior consistent statement of a witness that is offered to rebut a suggestion that his or her testimony was recently fabricated or to otherwise rehabilitate the witness's credibility is not hearsay.
- An opposing party's statement that is offered against that party.
    - Such a statement is not hearsay if it was made by the party or the party's agent or employee, was adopted or believed to be true by the party, or was made by the party's co-conspirator during and in furtherance of the alleged conspiracy.

As discussed in chapter 4, the hearsay exclusion allowing out-of-court statements made by a defendant's co-conspirators against the defendant is critically important in many prosecutions. But note that it is not necessary for the defendant to actually be on trial for conspiracy

---

110. Kumho Tire Co., Ltd. v. Carmichael, 526 U.S. 152 (1999).

111. Daubert, 509 U.S. at 593–94.

112. FRE 702 Advisory Committee's Notes (2000 Amends.); *see also* Fuesting v. Zimmer, Inc., 421 F.3d 528, 534–35 (7th Cir. 2005).

113. FRE 801(c).

in order for this exclusion to apply. Rather, prosecutors need only provide sufficient evidence to convince the court that it is more likely than not that a conspiracy existed, the defendant and the declarant were members of the same conspiracy, and the proffered statement was made during the course of and in furtherance of the conspiracy.[114] Evidence supporting these elements can be submitted to the court before trial through a motion in limine, and the court can admit the statement subject to a later determination that, based on other evidence admitted at trial, the government has proved by a preponderance of that evidence all three requisite foundational elements.[115] Where necessary, district courts can also hold a "full blown" preliminary hearing to consider all evidence concerning the statement.[116]

J. FRE 802—The Rule against Hearsay

FRE 802 states that hearsay is not admissible unless a federal statute or the Supreme Court explicitly permits otherwise. This general prohibition is premised on the theory that out-of-court statements are inherently unreliable: the declarant might be lying, might have misperceived the events that are being related, might have faulty memory; or the declarant's words might be misunderstood or taken out of context by the listener. And the ways in which these dangers are minimized for in-court statements—for example, the oath given to witnesses, the jury's ability to observe witnesses' demeanor, and the right of the opponent to cross-examine—are generally absent for things said out of court.[117]

Nonetheless, the Federal Rules of Evidence also recognize that some kinds of out-of-court statements are less exposed to these hearsay dangers, and therefore except them from the general rule that hearsay is inadmissible (as discussed below).

K. FRE 803 and 804—Exceptions to the Rule against Hearsay

FRE 803 contains a long list of categorical exceptions to the rule against hearsay. The exceptions that often come into play during white-collar crime trials include:

- Recorded recollections—a record that (i) concerns a matter the witness once knew about but can no longer remember accurately, (ii) was made or adopted by the witness when the matter was fresh in his or her memory, and (iii) accurately reflects his or her knowledge at the time.
- Records of a regularly conducted activity—a record that was made at or near the time by someone with knowledge and was kept in the normal course of a regularly conducted activity of a business or organization, if, and only if, a custodian or other qualified witness can certify these conditions are met, and the opponent fails to show that the source of information or the method or circumstances of preparation indicate a lack of trustworthiness.

---

114. United States v. Santiago, 582 F.2d 1128, 1130 (7th Cir. 1978).

115. *Id.* at 1131.

116. United States v. Andrus, 775 F.2d 825, 836–37 (7th Cir. 1985).

117. Williamson v. United States, 512 U.S. 594, 598–99 (1994).

- Public records—a record or statement of a public office if it concerns a matter observed while under a legal duty to report (e.g., a matter observed by law enforcement) and the opponent fails to demonstrate it lacks trustworthiness.
- A person's reputation among their associates or community.

FRE 804 contains additional exceptions pertaining to situations where the declarant is "unavailable" to testify at trial. To qualify as unavailable under this rule, the party offering the statement into evidence must establish that the declarant: (i) is exempted from testifying about the subject because of a valid privilege (e.g., the Fifth Amendment privilege), (ii) refuses to testify despite a court order to do so, (iii) testifies to not remembering the subject matter, (iv) is precluded from appearing in court because of a physical or mental illness, or (v) cannot be located or otherwise compelled to provide testimony.[118]

If at least one of these conditions apply, the following nonexhaustive types of statements made by an unavailable declarant will be excluded from the rule against hearsay:

- Former testimony given during a court proceeding or deposition that is offered against a party who previously had an opportunity or motive to develop it through direct, cross, or redirect examination.
- Statements made against the declarant's self-interest (under the presumption that a person would only consciously harm his or her interest if the statement is in fact true).

L. FRE 805—Hearsay Within Hearsay

Hearsay within hearsay (or "double hearsay") issues arise when a statement that is itself hearsay contains one or more statements that are also hearsay: for example, a written affidavit that contains a statement, offered for its truth, made to the affiant by another party. Under FRE 805, a statement that constitutes multiple levels of hearsay is only admissible if each individual level independently falls within one of the exceptions to the rule against hearsay: "Hearsay within hearsay is not excluded by the rule against hearsay if each part of the combined statements conforms with an exception to the rule."

M. FRE 806—Attacking and Supporting the Declarant

When a declarant's out-of-court statement is admitted into evidence through a hearsay exception, the declarant becomes in effect a trial witness. As such, the declarant's credibility is subject to impeachment and support as though he or she had actually given live testimony. For these purposes, FRE 806 allows the court to "admit evidence of the declarant's inconsistent statement or conduct, regardless of when it occurred or whether the declarant had an opportunity to explain or deny it." The rule further provides that, if the party against whom the statement is admitted calls the declarant to testify, the party "may examine the declarant on the statement as if on cross-examination" (meaning that the use of leading questions is allowed).

---

118. FRE 804(a).

N. FRE 807—The Residual Hearsay Exception

Simply because a statement is hearsay and does not qualify for any of the above exceptions does not necessarily mean it will be precluded from being introduced into evidence at trial in light of the residual hearsay exception in FRE 807. This catchall exception allows for admission of otherwise inadmissible hearsay if two conditions are satisfied: "(1) the statement is supported by sufficient guarantees of trustworthiness—after considering the totality of circumstances under which it was made and evidence, if any, corroborating the statement; and (2) it is more probative on the point for which it is offered than any other evidence that the proponent can obtain through reasonable efforts."

To prevent this exception from swallowing the rule against hearsay, the residual exception should only be applied in "extraordinary circumstances where the court is satisfied that the evidence offers guarantees of trustworthiness and is material, probative and necessary in the interest of justice."[119]

III. TRIAL PROCEDURE IN THE CROWN COURT

Compared with the United States, criminal trials in the United Kingdom are far more common, and far more commonly decided in a defendant's favor. Statistics show that the CPS prosecuted a total of 69,713 individuals in 2019 (the last year prior to the COVID-19 pandemic).[120] The outcomes of these cases are shown in table 7.1.

Putting the final three data points together reveals that 11,244 defendants (16.3 percent of the total) chose to contest their cases at trial. Of these, 4,776 were acquitted through a verdict either during or after trial; this results in a CPS trial conviction rate of just fifty-eight percent. Counting those cases resulting in a guilty plea, CPS's overall conviction in 2019 was approximately eighty one percent.[121]

Table 7.1 Outcomes of Criminal Cases in the United Kingdom in 2019

Outcome	Number	% of Total
Defendant not apprehended	999	1.43
Acquittal ordered by judge pretrial	8,264	11.85
Guilty plea	49,206	70.58
Acquittal ordered by judge after or during trial	399	0.57
Acquittals by jury after trial	4,377	6.28
Convictions after trial	6,468	9.28

119. United States v. Tome, 61 F.3d 1446, 1452 (10th Cir. 1995).

120. *See* Crown Prosecution Service, *Annual Report Data 2018–2019*, *available at* https://www.cps.gov.uk/publication/annual-report-and-key-measures.

121. The number of cases brought by the SFO is negligible compared to the CPS and does not materially affect these statistics. According to the SFO's Annual Report for 2019–2020, for example, the agency

In comparison, the DOJ charged 87,266 individuals in 2019 (6,544 of whom were accused of a white-collar offense). [122] Of these, a total of 2,025 defendants went to trial in district courts (309 or fifteen percent of whom opted for bench trials).[123] This means that approximately two percent of defendants in the federal system chose to proceed to trial (a percentage eight times lower than in England). Just 276 of the 2,025 defendants tried in 2019 were found not guilty, giving the DOJ a trial conviction rate of more than eighty-six percent. When the more than ninety-three percent of cases that resulted in guilty pleas that year are added to these statistics, the DOJ's overall conviction rate was nearly ninety-five percent. More specifically, of the 79,310 federal criminal cases that reached a resolution in 2019, 75,143 resulted in convictions (94.7%), 276 resulted in acquittals after trial (<1%), and 4,491 (5.6%) cases were dismissed (either on defendant's own motion or voluntarily by prosecutors).

While there are no doubt a wide range of reasons for these starkly different statistics between the two countries, one factor is likely to be the different procedural and evidentiary rules governing criminal trials in the United Kingdom; those pertaining to financial crime prosecutions are outlined in the following sections.

A. Preparatory Hearings

In complex financial crime cases, Crown Court judges may decide to hold a preparatory hearing before the jury is sworn in for the purpose of identifying the material issues that are likely to be raised during the trial, deciding on any request by the prosecution to proceed without a jury, assisting the judge's management of the trial, or considering questions as to the severance or joinder of charges.[124]

At the hearing, the judge may also make determinations on the admissibility of evidence and any outstanding legal issues. To facilitate this process, the Crown Court judge will generally require prosecutors to supply the court and the defendant in advance with a "case statement" detailing the principal facts of the prosecution's case, the witnesses who will speak to those facts, any exhibits relevant to those facts, any proposition of law on which the prosecution proposes to rely, and the potential penalties in the event of a conviction.[125] Prosecutors must also give notice "of documents the truth of the contents of which ought in the prosecution's view to be admitted and of any other matters which in their view ought to be agreed."[126]

---

reported charging just six individuals and trying only thirteen (at least eight of whom were presumably charged in years prior to 2019). Over a four-year period (2015–2019), the SFO recorded a sixty-two percent success rate by defendant. Serious Fraud Office, *Statement from the Director* (July 15, 2020).

122. Considering that the U.S. population is roughly five times larger than that of the United Kingdom, on first blush this figure suggests that British prosecutors charge far more cases relatively. But the DOJ is not the only prosecuting authority: the vast majority of criminal prosecutions in the United States are filed at the state and local levels and, considering that an estimated 100 million civil and criminal cases are filed annually in the state courts, the number of such cases that involve criminal charges is in the many millions.

123. Department of Justice, *United States Attorneys' Annual Statistical Report* (2019), *available at* https://www.justice.gov/usao/page/file/1285951/download.

124. CJA 1987, s. 7(1).

125. *Id.*, s. 9.

126. *Id.*, s. 9(4)(c).

The prosecution's case statement is for trial management purposes only, is not put before the jury, and has no evidential value. Nor does it limit the evidence that prosecutors can admit during their case in chief. However, if prosecutors later depart from the case disclosed in the case statement, the judge or defense counsel may comment on that fact before the jury, which "may draw such inference as appears proper."[127] As Lord Justice Taylor stated in *Mayhew*,

> It would be undesirable for case statements to be put as a matter of course before juries as if they were projections of the indictment or particulars thereof. The object of ordering a case statement is to inform the opposing party of the case that is intended to be put forward so as to facilitate preparation for trial and avoid surprise. If there is a significant departure, then . . . the jury may be apprised of it.[128]

Once prosecutors have produced their case statement, the judge may than direct the defendant to make whatever objections he deems appropriate and "give the court and the prosecution a notice stating the extent to which he agrees with the prosecution as to documents and other matters [raised in the case statement] and the reason for any disagreement."[129] "If a judge orders a preparatory hearing, the trial shall begin with that hearing."[130]

1. *Interlocutory Appeals of Rulings at the Preparatory Hearing*

Under Part 37 of the Criminal Procedure Rules and Sections 35 and 36 of the CPIA, the prosecution and the defense can both seek immediate appellate review of a binding ruling made by the Crown Court during the preparatory hearing. A party seeking such review must first seek permission from the Crown Court (either orally, immediately after the ruling is made, or in writing, within two days).[131] The opposing party may then make their own representations to the court for why the appeal should or should not be granted.[132]

B. Jury Selection

The Juries Act 1974 provides that all individuals aged between 18 and 76 who are registered to vote in local or national elections, who have "been ordinarily resident in the United Kingdom, the Channel Islands or the Isle of Man for any period of at least five years," and who are not mentally or physically incapacitated, shall be qualified to serve as jurors in Crown Court trials.[133] As in the United States, the pool of potential jurors is summoned for service via mail notifications sent at random by the lord chancellor. This group then forms the panel from which the actual trial jury will be selected.[134]

127. *Id.*, s. 10(2).

128. [1992] Crim. L.R. 313, CA.

129. CJA 1987, s. 9(5)(b).

130. *Id.*, s. 8(1).

131. CrimPR 37.4.

132. CrimPR 37.5.

133. Juries Act 1974, s. 1.

134. CrimPR 25.6(2).

Once the panel arrives at the designated Crown Court at the time specified in the lord chancellor's notification, the court will then "select the jury by drawing at random each juror's name from among those so summoned."[135] Crown Court juries must consist of at least twelve people, with up to two additional alternates permitted where the court expects the trial to last more than four weeks.[136]

1. Challenging Jurors

In all cases where a criminal offense is being tried on indictment, the prosecution and the defendant may challenge any of the jurors selected from the panel for cause in what is called a "challenge to the polls."[137] In contrast to the jury selection procedures in the United States, there are no peremptory challenges in the United Kingdom and all for cause challenges are subject to court review and approval.[138] Any such challenge must be lodged before the juror is sworn in and the challenging party must provide prima facie evidence of the reasons why the juror is unqualified to serve at the time the challenge is made. The court will then conduct a hearing (in camera or publicly) at which the challenging party bears the burden of establishing the grounds for the juror's bias or disqualification by a balance of the probabilities.[139] There is no limit to the number of for cause challenges that may be made.

Jurors may also be excluded by the court at its discretion—for example, where a juror is infirm or has difficulties speaking English or hearing.[140]

After the jury has been selected, the court will inform them of "each offence charged in the indictment to which the defendant pleads not guilty" and explain "that it is their duty, after hearing the evidence, to decide whether the defendant is guilty or not guilty."[141]

C. Opening Speeches

As in the United States, U.K. criminal procedure rules do not obligate either side to make an opening speech (the British equivalent of an opening statement). But the Criminal Practice Directions strongly encourage their use by the prosecution: "[P]rosecution opening speeches are invaluable. They set out for the jury the principal issues in the trial, and the evidence which is to be introduced in support of the prosecution case."[142] Hence, generally, the practice of prosecutors in complex financial crime cases is to make an opening statement.

---

135. CrimPR 25.6(4).

136. CrimPR 25.6(6).

137. Juries Act 1974, s.12(1); CrimPR 25.8. While the parties may also object to the entire panel of jurors in a so-called "challenge to the array," this right is reserved for the rare situations where there is a fundamental flaw in the summoning process.

138. Juries Act 1974, s. 12(1)(b). The use of peremptory challenges was abolished by the Criminal Justice Act 1988, s. 118.

139. CrimPR 25.8.

140. Ford [1989] QB 868.

141. CrimPR 25.9(2)(a).

142. Criminal Practice Direction 25A.1.

With respect to the content of a prosecutor's opening, "[a]part perhaps from reminding the jury of the burden and standard of proof, the presumption should be that [it] should not address the law." Rather, it is the prosecution's "duty to simply outline the facts upon which the Crown intends to rely. It is highly undesirable for prosecuting counsel in so doing to use unnecessarily emotive language which on any view can only excite sympathy for the victim or prejudice against the accused in the minds of the jury."[143] The Practice Directions go on to state:

> [I]t is desirable for prosecuting counsel to warn the jury that neither sympathy nor prejudice should be allowed to influence their approach to the evidence or their assessment of the witnesses. The jury's approach to all the evidence should be one of clinical objectivity. Counsel for the prosecution throughout a case ought not to struggle for the verdict against the prisoner, but they out to bear themselves rather in the character of ministers of justice assisting in the administration of justice.[144]

Once the prosecution opens, the court may "invite the defendant concisely to identify what is in issue, in necessary in terms approved by the court."[145] If the defendant declines, the judge may decide to simply give the jurors a copy of any defense statement submitted during pretrial discovery (edited if necessary to exclude any reference to inappropriate matters or inadmissible evidence).

Importantly, however, the defense is not permitted to make an opening speech if no fact witness other than the defendant will be called to testify during trial.[146] If additional fact witnesses will be called during the defense case, defense counsel can give a full opening outlining the defense's evidence and criticizing the prosecutors' evidence.

D. The Prosecution's Presentation of Evidence

Following opening statements, the prosecution will introduce the evidence on which its case relies. As in the United States, evidence in Crown Court can be introduced through the calling of witnesses and the production of documents and other physical objects. During direct examination, prosecutors generally may not ask leading questions as to any contested point. Once prosecutors conclude their direct, the witness will be cross-examined by defense counsel and then re-examined by the Crown.

E. Submission of "No Case to Answer"

At the end of the prosecution's case, the defendant may make a submission of "no case to answer," which asks the court to "acquit on the ground the prosecution evidence is insufficient for any reasonable court properly to convict." Using a similar approach to that applied

143. *Id.*

144. *Id.* (citing Banks [1916] 2 K.B. 621 at 623.

145. Fed. Crim. P. 25.9(2)(c).

146. Criminal Evidence Act 1898, s. 2.

to Rule 29 motions in the United States, Crown Court judges are directed to consider a "no case" submission as follows:

> (1) If there is no evidence that the crime alleged has been committed by the defendant, there is no difficulty. The judge of course will stop the case.
>
> (2) The difficulty arises where there is some evidence but is of a tenuous character because of the inherent weakness or vagueness or because it is inconsistent with other evidence. (a) Where the judge comes to the conclusion that the Crown's evidence, taken at its highest, is such that a jury properly directed could not properly convict on it, it is his duty, on a submission being made, to stop the case. (b) Where however the Crown's evidence is such that its strength or weakness depends on the view to be taken of a witness's reliability, or other matters which are generally speaking within the province of the jury and where on one possible view of the facts there is evidence on which a jury could properly come to the conclusion that the defendant is guilty, then the judge should allow the matter to be tried to the jury.[147]

The court may also order such an acquittal on its own initiative.[148] If the court determines that the prosecution's evidence is sufficient to put the case to the jury, it will then ask whether the defendant intends to give evidence in person. If the defendant declines to do so, the court must explain "the right to give evidence in person, and that if the defendant does not give evidence in person, or refuses to answer a question while giving evidence, the court may draw such inferences as seem proper."[149]

F. Presentation of Evidence by the Defense

At the end of the prosecution's presentation of evidence, the court will ask whether the defendant intends to testify. If the answer is no, the court must explain the defendant's right to testify and that failure to do so allows the court to "draw such inferences as seem proper."[150] If the defendant does elect to testify, he or she must do so before calling any other witness or introducing any other evidence.[151] Regardless of whether the defense offers any evidence, defense counsel can summarize the defense case at this stage—for example, by explaining why a particular prosecution witness is not credible, why the evidence is insufficient, etc.

G. Rebuttal

If the prosecution has evidence that has not already been introduced that can rebut evidence put in by the defense, it can be offered after the defense case. Unlike the procedural rules in the United States, in the United Kingdom, a defendant can also offer rebuttal evidence in

---

147. R v. Galbraith [1981] 2 All ER 1060.

148. CrimPR 25.9(2)(e).

149. CrimPR 25.9(2)(f).

150. *Id.*

151. CrimPR 25.9(2)(h).

response to rebuttal evidence introduced by prosecutors.[152] The extent of such rebuttal and whether multiple rounds will be allowed is left to the discretion of the trial judge.

H. Jury Instructions and Summing Up

While the court has discretion to provide jurors with directions about the relevant law at any stage of the trial where it will assist them to evaluate the evidence, after each side's evidence has been presented, and before summations, the court must: "(a) summarise for the jury, to such extent as is necessary, the evidence relevant to the issues they must decide; (b) give the jury such questions, if any, as the court invites jurors to answer in coming to a verdict; [and] (c) direct the jury to retire to consider its verdict."[153] During the judge's "summing up" of the case, the jurors will be reminded of the core issues, provided with a summary of the nature of the evidence relating to each issue, and given a balanced account of the points raised by the parties.[154] The standard jury instructions Crown Court judges are required to give are contained in the Crown Court Compendium (2021).[155] At the judge's option, its instructions can be memorialized in a Written Directions of Law and given to the jury to assist it during deliberations.

In complex financial crime cases, the general practice is for Crown Court judges to also give the jury a written "route to verdict," which is a sequence of questions on the key legal and fact issues that the jury should answer in turn so as to reach an ultimate outcome.[156]

I. Final Representations

Prosecutors are given the right to make final representations (also known as a "closing speech") under Criminal Procedure Rule 25.9(j). Defendants are given a comparable right in Section 2 of the Criminal Procedure Act 1865.

J. Applications to Stay Proceedings for Abuse of Process

A defendant can submit an application to stay proceedings for an abuse of process at any time before the jury retires to consider its verdict.[157] Whether such an application should be heard is at the discretion of the trial judge.[158] The defendant bears the burden of proving an abuse of process by a balance of probabilities.[159]

---

152. CrimPR 25.9(i).

153. CrimPR 25.14(3).

154. CPD 2020, 26K.21. Note that Crown Courts will often deliver the summing up in two parts: legal instructions before the parties' closing speeches and a factual summary afterward. CrimPR 25.14(2).

155. *Available at*, https://www.judiciary.uk/publications/crown-court-compendium-published/.

156. CrimPR 25.14(4).

157. CrimPR 3.28(2).

158. F (S) [2011] EWCA Crim 1844.

159. Crown Court at Norwich, *ex p.* Belsham [1992] 94 Cr. App. R. 382.

K. Verdicts

Although the jury will be initially instructed to give best efforts toward reaching a unanimous verdict on each count, unanimity is not always required. If, after deliberating for at least two hours, the jury is unable to reach a unanimous verdict on any count, the court can choose "to invite a majority verdict."[160] In which case, the judge will call the jurors back to the court and advise them as follows:

> As you may know, the law permits me, in certain circumstances, to accept a verdict which is not the verdict of you all. Those circumstances have not as yet arisen, so that when you retire [again] I must ask you to reach a verdict upon which each one of you is agreed. Should, however, the time come when it is possible for me to accept a majority verdict, I will give you a further direction.[161]

Until this direction is given, a majority verdict is not permitted.

If the jurors are still unable to reach a unanimous verdict after being given the majority direction, they will be called back to court again and told that the point has been reached when a nonunanimous verdict can be accepted. The number of votes needed to sustain a majority verdict will depend on the number of jurors who remain on the jury: if it is the full twelve or eleven, at least ten votes are needed; if there are only ten jurors left, nine votes are needed. Majority verdicts are not permitted in instances where there are only nine jury members involved in deliberations. If a verdict is then able to be reached by the required majority of jurors, the verdict will have the same force and legal effect as if it were unanimous.

If the jury is unable to reach even a majority verdict after deliberating for a reasonable period, they will be considered unalterably "hung" and the judge will discharge them. The prosecution is then given the option of retrying the defendant on any counts for which the jury was hung.

In a major difference with U.S. practice, judges in the United Kingdom are permitted to express their own opinion of the case implicitly or explicitly to the jury so long as the issues are ultimately left to the jury members to decide on their own.[162] In other words, it is permissible for a judge to strongly hint at the verdict he or she prefers, or frame the issues in such a way as to favor one side, during the summing up.

L. Defendant's Costs Orders

Acquitted defendants in the United States are generally not entitled to any monetary compensation to cover the costs of their legal fees. In the United Kingdom, by contrast, where "any person is not tried for an offence for which he has been indicted or sent for trial," or "is tried on indictment and acquitted on any count in the indictment, the Crown Court may make a defendant's costs order in favor of the accused."[163] Cost orders in favor of a defendant are

160. CrimPR 25.14(5)(c).

161. CPD 2020, 26Q.1.

162. Cohen and Bateman [1909] 2 Cr. App. R. 197, CCA.

163. Prosecution of Offences Act (POA), 16(2).

paid from the British treasury "in such amount as the court considers reasonably sufficient to compensate him for any expenses properly incurred by him in the proceedings." Where the court considers it inappropriate to recover the full amount spent for his defense, the court has discretion to order payment for such lesser amount as it considers "just and reasonable."[164]

Practice Note

Reporting Restrictions on Crown Court Trials

Crown Court trials typically proceed under the "open court" rule, meaning that they are generally open to the public. This rule is subject to a general exception for instances where an open court would create a risk of prejudice to the administration of justice. "When considering the need to depart from the 'open court' principle, a distinction is to be drawn between matters which should never meet the public gaze and matters where the concern ends with the conclusion of the trial, or related proceedings; in the latter situation the risk of prejudice to the administration of justice can often be dealt with by an order under s. 4(2) of the Contempt of Court Act 1981."[165] Section 4(2) allows the court, "where it appears to be necessary for avoiding a substantial risk of prejudice to the administration of justice . . ., [to] order that the publication of any report of the proceedings, or any part of the proceedings, be postponed for such period as the court thinks necessary for that purpose."

This provision has been used in situations where co-conspirators proceed to trial separately and at different times. To avoid prejudicing whoever is tried second, the results of the first trial may be ordered withheld from the public until after the second trial is concluded.

IV. EVIDENTIARY RULES IN THE UNITED KINGDOM

A. Bar on Irrelevant Evidence

Judges have an overriding duty to prevent the admission of irrelevant evidence. Like the Federal Rules of Evidence, the test for relevance is a loose one: a judge must only consider the interests of justice and the respective interests of the prosecution and defense.[166]

B. Hearsay

The common law rule on the admission of hearsay in the United Kingdom is essentially the same as it is in the United States: "an assertion other than one made by a person while giving oral evidence in the proceedings is inadmissible as evidence of any fact or opinion asserted."[167] This rule (combined with Sections 114 and 115 of the Criminal Justice

164. POA, 16(6)-(6A).

165. Archbold, Criminal Pleading: Evidence and Practice § 4-5 (Sweet & Maxwell 2020).

166. Brown (Milton) [1998] 2 Cr. App. R. 364, CA.

167. The Criminal Justice Act 2003 defines hearsay as a "statement not made in oral evidence that is evidence of any matter stated." CJA 2003, s. 114(1) (see figure 7.1). A "statement" is "any representation of fact or opinion made by a person by whatever means" (including representations "made in a

Act 2003) makes hearsay presumptively inadmissible, meaning that it can only be used as evidence at trial and certain other criminal proceedings if it falls within a statutory or common law exception, the parties agree to admit it, or the court determines its admission is in the interests of justice. The main implication of this rule is that witnesses must generally give oral evidence in court from first-hand knowledge and may not repeat what other people have told them.[168] For example, unless it falls within a recognized exception: (i) written records are inadmissible evidence of the matters they contain, (ii) a written witness statement cannot be a substitute for the witness's personal appearance in the witness box, and (iii) previous out-of-court statements made by a testifying witness is inadmissible evidence of the matters they contain.[169]

The Criminal Procedure Rules require any party who wants to introduce certain types of hearsay—that is, hearsay that is admissible in the interests of justice (CJA, s. 114(1)(d)), statements by an unavailable witness (CJA, s. 116) or that are in a prepared statement (CJA, s. 117(1)(c)), or constitutes multiple hearsay (CJA, s. 121)—to first serve notice on the court and the other parties identifying the hearsay and explaining the legal basis for its admission.[170] Advance notice is not necessary for any hearsay type not specified in this rule—for example, business records (CJA, s. 117), prior inconsistent statements (CJA, s. 119). If a party fails to provide notice when notice is required, the court may still admit it, but may draw such inferences as appear proper from the failure to give notice.

1. The Interests of Justice Exception (Section 114(d))

By permitting a court to admit otherwise inadmissible hearsay if it is satisfied that doing so is in the interests of justice, Section 114(d) of the CJA creates a catchall exception similar to the residual exception of Federal Rule of Evidence 807 (see section II.N). In deciding whether to exercise its discretion under this rule, the court must consider the statement's probative value, what alternative evidence exists to prove the same matter, its overall importance to the case, its reliability, and the extent to which admitting it would unfairly prejudice the party against whom it is admitted.[171]

---

sketch, photofit or other pictorial form"). *Id.*, s. 115. The term "matter stated" is defined as "something stated by someone with the apparent purpose of (i) causing another person to believe it, or (ii) causing another person, or a machine, to act or operate on the basis that the matter is as stated." *Id.*

168. Under CJA 2003 Section 134, the hearsay rules apply at trials, Newton hearings, and preparatory hearings. They do not apply for purposes of bail hearings and sentencing.

169. CJA 2003, Explanatory Notes Part 11.

170. CrimPR 20.2. The procedure for objecting to the proposed use of hearsay evidence is addressed in CrimPR 20.3. If no objection is made, the hearsay is treated as if the parties agreed to its use (i.e., it is automatically admissible). CrimPR 20.3(2). As with all other evidentiary rules, the hearsay procedures are variable at the court's discretion. CrimPR 20.5; see also CJA, s. 126 (permitting the court to exclude otherwise admissible evidence if it determines it will result in undue waste of time or results in unfair prejudice that outweighs its utility).

171. CJA 2003, s. 114(2).

The Court of Appeals has made clear that Section 114(d) should not be used simply as a shortcut around the normal hearsay prohibitions; rather, it should only be invoked after all other possible exceptions have been considered.[172]

2. *Unavailable Witnesses (Section 116)*

Where a witness is unavailable to testify in court because of death or illness, his or her location outside the United Kingdom, or some other good reason, the witness's out-of-court hearsay statements may be admissible.[173] For example, if a witness has given a statement to investigators and then dies or leaves the jurisdiction, the statement may be admitted as evidence in court.

The burden of proof for establishing that a witness is in fact unavailable lies on the party seeking to admit the witness's out-of-court statement. For prosecutors, the standard is beyond a reasonable doubt; the defense must establish unavailability by the balance of probabilities.

3. *Business and Other Documents (Section 117)*

Statements contained in business documents are admissible to prove the matter stated if each of the following conditions are met: (i) oral evidence would be admissible as evidence of the matter, (ii) the document was created or received by a person in the course of his or her occupation or as the holder of a government office, (iii) the person who supplied the information contained in the statement had personal knowledge of the matters dealt with, and (iv) in the case of multiple hearsay, each person passing on the statement received it in the course of his or her occupation or office.[174] Section 117 therefore permits the admissibility of a range of corporate documents, including company correspondence, hospital records, and financial records. Admission of Section 117 materials is usually automatic unless the court exercises its discretion to exclude the evidence because its reliability is questionable in light of its source, the way it was prepared or received, or its contents.[175] The test is in favor of admissibility rather than exclusion.

If a document that otherwise falls under Section 117 was prepared in contemplation of criminal proceedings (e.g., an investigator or police officer's notes), the party seeking to admit it must also show that the declarant is either unavailable or could not be expected to remember the matters referred to.

4. *Common Law Exceptions (Section 118)*

In addition to the above statutory exceptions, Section 118 preserves the following common law categories of admissible hearsay:

- Public records such as dictionaries, maps, public registers, court records, and evidence relating to a person's age or date or place of birth.

---

172. EED v. R [2010] EWCA Crim 1213.

173. CJA 2003, s. 116.

174. CJA 2003, s. 117.

175. *Id.*, s. 117(7).

- Evidence of a person's reputation, to prove his or her good or bad character or family traditions.
- Statements that are made by a person "so emotionally overpowered by an event that the possibility of concoction or distortion can be disregarded," that accompany an act that can be "properly evaluated as evidence only if considered in conjunction with the statement, or that relate to a physical sensation or mental state." This exception is known as the "res gestae"—Latin for "things done"—doctrine.
- Confessions and admissions by agents, and statements made "by a party to a common enterprise" with the defendant.[176] This includes admissions made by lawyers acting for a defendant.[177]
- The body of expertise relevant to the field of an expert witness.

5. *Previous Statements by a Witness (Sections 119 and 120)*

A testifying witness's previous *inconsistent* statements are admissible "as evidence of any matter stated of which oral evidence by him would be admissible" as long as he admits making the statement or extrinsic evidence proves that he made it.[178]

Where a party suggests that a testifying witness has recently fabricated testimony, a previous *consistent* out-of-court statement by the witness is admissible as evidence of any matter stated.[179] This includes "a statement made by the witness in a document (a) which is used by him to refresh his memory while giving evidence, (b) on which he is cross-examined, and (c) which as a consequence is received in evidence in the proceedings." In situations where a testifying witness has not been accused of fabrication, a previous consistent statement may still be admissible if the witness adopts the statement as true and if one of three conditions is met:

- Condition 1—the statement identifies or describes a person, object, or place.
- Condition 2—the statement was made by the witness when the matters stated were fresh in his or her memory but he or she does not remember them, and cannot reasonably be expected to remember them, well enough to give oral evidence of them in the proceedings.
- Condition 3—the witness is a victim of the alleged offense and the statement consists of a complaint about the offense (whether made to law enforcement or otherwise).

176. Statements made by one defendant during the course and for the purpose of advancing a common enterprise are admissible against all other codefendants alleged to be involved in the same enterprise. Applicability of this rule is determined through a three-pronged test that determines whether (i) the statement was in fact made by a party to the alleged common enterprise, (ii) the statement is "reasonably open to the interpretation of having been made in furtherance" of the common enterprise, and (iii) there is some other extrinsic evidence of the common enterprise's existence. R v. A Ltd, X, Y [2017] 1 Cr App R 1.

177. R (Firth) v. Epping Justices [2011] 4 All ER 326.

178. CJA 2003, s. 119.

179. CJA 2003, s. 120.

6. *Multiple Hearsay (Section 121)*

Multiple hearsay (or "hearsay within hearsay") refers to situations where the evidence for the hearsay evidence is itself hearsay, that is, where the information being used to prove a matter is related through more than one person before it is recorded. For example, an email from one person that relays a statement made to that person by someone else.

Under Section 121, a hearsay statement is not admissible to prove the fact that an earlier hearsay statement was made unless either of the statements are admissible as business records or prior statements of a testifying witness, all the parties agree, or the court "is satisfied that the value of the evidence in question, taking into account how reliable the statements appear to be, is so high that the interests of justice require the later statement to be admissible for that purpose."

7. *The "Safety Valve" Exception (Section 114(1)(d))*

Just as the FRE contain a residual hearsay exception, the CJA includes a provision allowing for the discretionary admission of hearsay that does not fall within any of the other exceptions but that is deemed reliable and necessary in the interests of justice. In deciding whether to admit hearsay under this "safety valve" exception, the Crown Court must consider: (i) its probative value in relation to a matter in issue in the proceedings and how it relates to other evidence already admitted, (ii) what alternative nonhearsay evidence is available to address the same fact issue, (iii) the circumstances in which the statement was made and how reliable it appears to be, and (iv) and the extent of unfair prejudice to the party against whom the statement is to be admitted.

8. *Use of Written Witness Statements in Criminal Proceedings*

While the primary statute governing hearsay is CJA 2003, Section 9 of the predecessor law (CJA 1967) remains in force. Under this provision, a written statement by any person shall be admissible as evidence to the same extent as if they gave oral testimony in court if each of the following conditions are met: (i) the statement purports to be signed by the person who made it; (ii) the statement contains a declaration that it is true to the best of the person's knowledge and belief and that he made the statement knowing that he is liable to prosecution for perjury if he willfully stated anything which he knew to believe was false or did not believe to be true; (iii) the statement is served on all parties prior to it being tendered in evidence; and (iv) the other parties do not object to it being admitted.[180] Even where a written witness statement is admitted into evidence, the court or the party admitting such evidence may still call the witness to testify.[181]

C. Bad Character Evidence

As the Law Commission noted in an October 2001 report to Parliament, "[q]uestions of admissibility of bad character arise in criminal trials daily, case by case, affecting the vital interests of those involved." In the Commission's view, admission of such evidence should be

180. CJA 1967, s. 9(2).

181. *Id.*, s. 9(4).

R v Twist – 3 stage approach

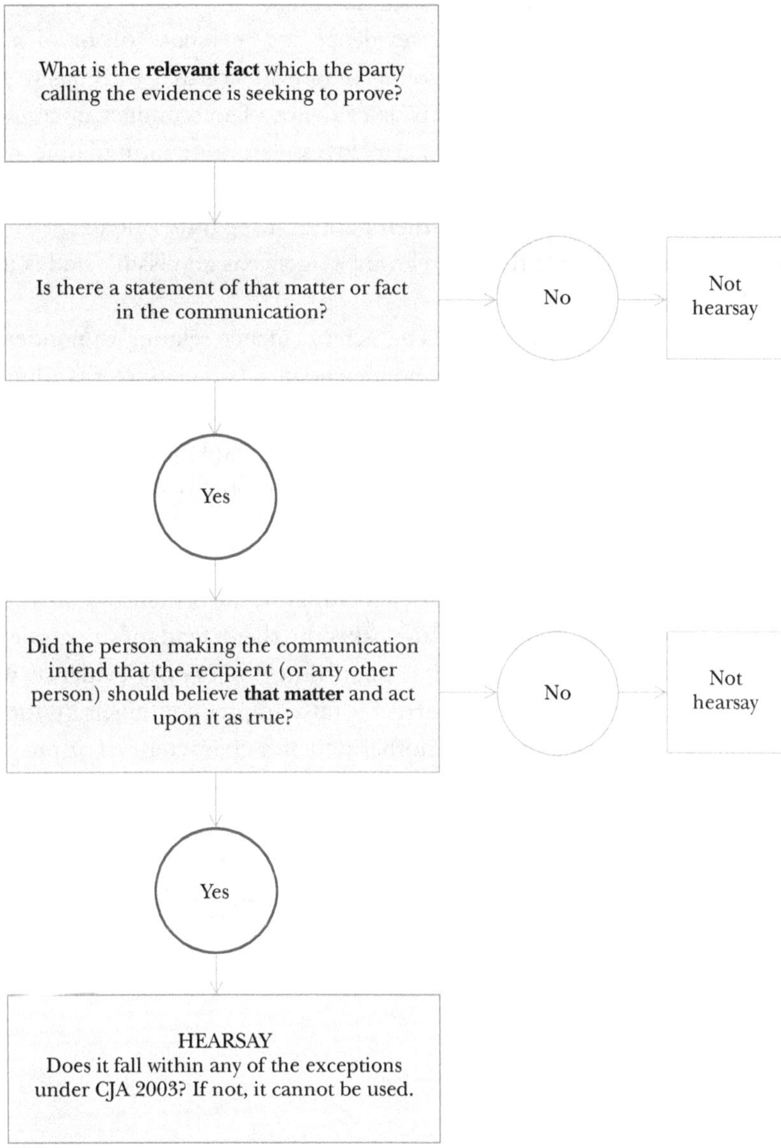

Figure 7.1 U.K. Hearsay Analysis.

(*Source:* Crown Prosecution Service, https://www.cps.gov.uk/sites/default/files/documents/legal_guidance/Hearsay-three-stage-flowchart.pdf.)

guided by structured process "which reflects the fact that often a person's misconduct will have significance for determining the matters in issue, but also recognizes that fact-finders, whether lay or professional, are susceptible, however much they try to avoid it, to having their good judgment either overborne or distorted by prejudice."[182] To correct the "haphazard mixture of statue and common law rules" that governed bad character evidence at the

182. The Law Commission, Evidence of Bad Character in Criminal Proceedings 1.6 (Report No. 273 October 2001).

time of the report, the Law Commission suggested a number of reforms in this area that ultimately were codified in the Criminal Justice Act 2003.[183]

The CJA 2003 defines "bad character evidence" as "evidence of, or of a disposition towards, misconduct on [a] person's part, other than evidence that—(a) has to do with the alleged facts of the offence [at issue]; or (b) is evidence of misconduct in connection with the investigation or prosecution" (e.g., lying to investigators or intimidating witnesses).[184] Such evidence, which includes the fact that a defendant has been previously convicted of an offense, is generally inadmissible to prove their guilt of a separate offense.[185] This rule is an exception to the general principle that all relevant evidence is admissible and is itself subject to a number of exceptions.

There are separate exceptions for bad character evidence relating to nondefendant witnesses and actual defendants. Evidence of a nondefendant's bad character is admissible if it is "important explanatory evidence" or has high probative value in relation to a core matter at issue in the proceedings. Evidence is considered important explanatory evidence if the court or jury would find it impossible or difficult to understand other evidence in the case and its value for understanding the case as a whole is substantial.[186]

Evidence of a defendant's bad character is admissible if it falls within one of the so-called "seven gateways": if all parties agree to admit it, the evidence is introduced by the defendant (or is given in answer to a question asked by the defendant in cross-examination and was intended to elicit that evidence), it is important explanatory evidence, it has significant probative value, it is necessary to correct a false impression given by the defendant, or the defendant has made an attack on another person's character.[187] For purposes of this rule, a defendant will be considered to have given a false impression if he "is responsible for the making of an express or implied assertion which is apt to give the court or jury a false or misleading impression about the defendant"; a defendant will be responsible for his own in-court statements, out-of-court statements made under caution that are then introduced into evidence, assertions made by defense witnesses or elicited by the defense on cross-examination, and any other out-of-court statements that the defendant introduces into evidence.[188]

---

183. CJA 2003 Section 99 explicitly abolished all existing common law rules governing the admissibility of bad character in criminal proceedings except for the common law rule allowing evidence of a person's reputation to be used for proving his or her bad character.

184. CJA 2003, s. 98. Section 98(a) has no temporal qualification and applies "to evidence of incidents whenever they occurred so long as they were to do with the alleged facts of the offence." R v. Lunkulu [2015] EWCA Crim 1350; *see also* R v. McNeill [2007] EWCA Crim 2927 ("The words of the statute 'has to do with' are words of prima facie broad application . . . embracing anything directly relevant to the offence charged, provided at any rate they were reasonably contemporaneous with and closely associated with its alleged facts.").

185. CJA 2003, s. 101.

186. CJA 2003, s. 102.

187. CJA 2003, s. 101.

188. CJA 2003, s. 105.

Once admitted through one of the gateways, bad character evidence can be used for any purpose for which it is relevant, with the weight attached left up to the jury.[189] As an additional safeguard against an unfair trial, the court retains the power to discharge a jury or order an acquittal where bad character evidence is admitted at trial and later determined to be so contaminated or unreliable as to make any conviction unsafe.[190]

1. Procedure for Admitting Bad Character Evidence

The procedure for admitting and objecting to bad character evidence is contained in Part 21 of the Criminal Procedure Rules. As with hearsay evidence, a party wishing to admit bad character evidence must first serve notice on the court and other parties.[191] Any party who objects to the evidence must then submit an application to the court to consider the objection within ten days of receiving the notice. The court must then give its reasons for any decision to allow or refuse the proffered evidence.[192]

D. Confessions

Under the law of England and Wales, a "confession" is "any statement wholly or partly adverse to the person who made it, whether made to a person in authority or not and whether made in words or otherwise."[193] The admissibility of confessions is governed by PACE Section 76, which states that "[i]n any proceedings a confession made by an accused person may be given in evidence against him in so far as it is relevant to any matter in issue in the proceedings and is not excluded by the court." If, however, the defense makes a representation to the court that the confession was obtained by oppression[194] or made in circumstances that render it inherently unreliable, the burden shifts to prosecutors to establish "beyond a reasonable doubt that the confession (notwithstanding that it may be true) was not [so] obtained."[195] Even if the confession itself is ruled inadmissible, its exclusion will not affect the admissibility of any facts discovered as a result of the confession.

Where one codefendant has made a confession, PACE permits another codefendant to use that confession as evidence to support his or her own innocence. Specifically, under PACE Section 76A(1), "In any proceedings a confession made by an accused person may be given in evidence for another person charged in the same proceedings (a co-accused) in so far as it is relevant to any matter in issue in the proceedings and is not excluded by the court" as being unreliable or obtained by oppression.

---

189. R v. Highton [2005] 1 WLR 3472.

190. CJA 2003, s. 107.

191. CrimPR 21.2-4.

192. CrimPR 21.5; CJA 2003, s. 110.

193. PACE, s. 82(1).

194. "Oppression" is defined to include torture, inhuman or degrading treatment, and the use or threat of violence (whether or not amounting to torture). PACE, s. 76(8).

195. PACE, s. 76(2).

E. Exclusion of Unfair Evidence

PACE Section 78 permits the court to "refuse to allow evidence on which the prosecution proposes to rely to be given if it appears to the court that, having regard to all the circumstances, including the circumstances in which the evidence was obtained, the admission of the evidence would have such an adverse effect on the fairness of the proceedings that the court ought not to admit it." As discussed in chapter 6, this provision gives judges in the U.K. a discretionary power to exclude improperly obtained evidence that is much the same as the U.S. exclusionary rule.

F. Expert Evidence

Expert evidence is evidence furnished to the court for the purposes of providing the judge and jury with information that is likely to be outside their experience or knowledge.[196] A suitably qualified expert witness can provide the court with a statement of opinion on any admissible matter calling for his or her relevant expertise.

Under the Criminal Procedure Rules, expert witnesses' overriding duty is to the court (not whichever party engaged them to provide an opinion). As such, they are required to provide objective and unbiased opinions, and to actively assist the court by specifically defining their areas of expertise, drawing the court's attention to any question that would be outside the expert's area of expertise when giving oral evidence, and disclosing whether their opinion has changed over time.[197]

Experts are also obliged to disclose to the party instructing them anything of which the expert is aware that might reasonably be thought capable of undermining their expert opinion or detracting from their credibility or impartiality.[198] This includes (i) any fee arrangement under which the amount or payment of the expert's fees is in any way dependent on the outcome of the case; (ii) any conflict of interest of any kind, other than a potential conflict disclosed in the experts report; (iii) adverse judicial comment; (iv) any case in which an appeal has been allowed by reason of a deficiency in the expert's evidence; (v) any adverse finding, disciplinary proceedings or other criticism by a professional, regulatory, or registration body or authority; (vi) a criminal conviction in circumstances that suggest dishonesty or a lack of integrity; and (vii) lack of an accreditation or other commitment to prescribed standards where that might be expected.

1. Expert Reports in the Crown Court

Where a party wishes another party to admit as fact a summary of a proposed expert's conclusions, the party must first serve the summary on the court and other parties as soon as practicable after the defendant whom it affects pleads not guilty.[199] The opposing party must respond setting out which of the expert's conclusions are admitted and, for any conclusions that are disputed, the basis for the dispute.[200]

---

196. Criminal Practice Direction V, Evidence 19A Expert Evidence.

197. CrimPR 19.2.

198. CrimPR 19.2(3)(d).

199. CrimPR 19.3(1).

200. CrimPR 19.3(2).

In situations where the expert's summary is disputed in whole or in part, the party advocating for the expert's evidence must produce an expert report.[201] Rule 19.4 specifies that the expert report must substantiate the expert's opinions and conclusions by:

- Detailing their qualifications and relevant experience.
- Detailing any documents or other information that the expert relied on in creating his or her report.
- Setting out the substance of all facts given to the expert that are material to the opinions expressed in the report, or upon which those opinions are based.
- Identifying any facts in the report that are derived from the expert's own knowledge.
- Identifying any third party whose opinion the expert is relying on and, where there is a range of opinions among experts on a certain issue, summarizing the range of opinions and giving reasons for the expert's own opinion.
- Providing enough information to allow the court to decide whether the expert's opinion is sufficiently reliable to be admissible as evidence.
- Summarizing the conclusions reached and affirming that the report is true and accurate to the best of the expert's knowledge.[202]

While a party producing an expert report must usually disclose all evidence on which the expert relies, if there is certain sensitive evidence that the party does not wish to disclose, Rule 19.9 allows the party to withhold such evidence but only with leave of the court.

2. *Statutory Rules on the Admission of Expert Evidence*

Section 30 of the Criminal Justice Act 1988 allows an expert report to be admitted as evidence of fact and opinion, whether or not the expert provides oral testimony in court. But if the expert is not testifying, leave of the court is required before the expert's report may be introduced.[203] In considering whether to grant leave, the court must consider the contents of the report, why the expert is not testifying, any unfairness to the defendant, and the extent to which the Criminal Procedure Rules have been complied with.[204]

3. *Common Law Rules on the Admission of Expert Evidence*

The general rule under the common law is that witnesses can only testify as to matters within their personal knowledge, and that testimony regarding a witness's opinion or belief is inadmissible. The common law rule on expert evidence is an exception to this rule and allows for the introduction of expert opinion evidence where: (i) it will assist the court and jury in a specialized topic or field; (ii) the expert has relevant expertise; (iii) the expert is able to provide

201. CrimPR 19.3(3).

202. CrimPR 19.4; *see also* R v. Henderson [2010] EWCA Crim. 1269.

203. CrimPR 19.3(4).

204. CJA 1988, s. 30(3).

impartial, unbiased, and objective evidence; and (iv) the expert's conclusions are based on a reliable process or theory.

In a 2011 report on "Expert Evidence in Criminal Proceedings in England and Wales," the Law Commission recommended the creation of a statutory test for the admissibility of expert evidence. Parliament, however, declined to create new legislation. Accordingly, the admissibility and weight of expert evidence still largely remains governed by the common law and the Criminal Procedure Rules.

4. *Challenging the Admission of Expert Evidence*

Defendants can make an application for the court to exclude expert evidence proffered by the prosecution on the grounds that its probative value is outweighed by its prejudicial effect, or if it is insufficiently helpful to the jury in reaching its conclusions.[205]

Expert evidence can also be challenged on the grounds that it is based on a new or otherwise untrusty technique or theory. If such a challenge is raised, the party seeking to introduce the expert evidence must show that the technique or theory is sufficiently sound to be admissible as evidence by, for example, stating whether it has ever been tested or subject to peer review, its known or potential error rate, and the extent to which it is generally accepted among experts in the field.[206]

Challenges to expert evidence on the grounds of a procedural error are generally more likely to succeed than those based on substantive objections.

CHAPTER 7: KEY DISTINCTIONS

United States	United Kingdom
Less than 2% of federal criminal cases proceed to trial	More than 16% of criminal cases proceed to trial
Department of Justice (DOJ) trial conviction rate of more than 86%	Crown Prosecution Service (CPS) trial conviction rate of 58%
DOJ's overall conviction rate is ~95%	CPS's overall conviction rate is 81%; Serious Fraud Office conviction rate is 62%
Admissibility of certain evidence decided before trial through motions in limine	Admissibility of certain evidence decided during the preparatory hearing
Prosecutors need only disclose a list of prospective witnesses and evidentiary exhibits prior to trial	The prosecution must provide a case statement in advance of trial to the defense; jury can make an adverse inference if trial presentation materially differs

(Continued)

205. PACE, s. 78; R v. H [2014] EWCA Crim. 1555.

206. Lundy v. R [2013] UKPC 28; R v. Clarke [1995] 2 Cr. App. R. 425.

United States	United Kingdom
Jurors can be excluded through for cause and a set number of preemptory challenges	Jurors can be excluded through for cause challenges only
Defense can present its case in whichever order it deems fit	If defendant testifies, he or she must do so before calling any other witnesses or introducing any other evidence
Defendant not ordinarily allowed to reply to introduce evidence in response to prosecutor's rebuttal	Defendant permitted to make a sur-rebuttal to prosecutors' rebuttal
District judges provide the jury with legal instructions only	Judges provide the jury with legal instructions and give a factual summing up of each side's case
Impermissible for district judges to indicate the verdict the jury should reach	Judges may give their opinion on the case to the jurors

8 | Post-Verdict Motions and Appeals

A jury verdict is not the end of a criminal case. In both the United States and the United Kingdom, prosecutors and defendants have a variety of mechanisms available to challenge the jury's factual determination and any legal rulings made by the trial judge. This chapter covers the procedures governing post-verdict challenges that can be brought before the trial court and appellate courts in both jurisdictions. Appeals of a defendant's sentence are covered separately in chapter 9.

I. POST-TRIAL MOTIONS IN THE UNITED STATES

Post-trial motions are made to the district court trial judge, not a circuit court of appeal. There is not an equivalent procedure to make post-trial applications to the Crown Court in the United Kingdom.

A. Motions for an Acquittal

As discussed in chapter 7, criminal defendants may move for an acquittal under Federal Rule of Criminal Procedure 29 at the end of the government's case in chief or before the case goes to the jury. District court judges will often reserve decision on such motions until after the jury has returned its verdict. If the defendant is found guilty, the court may then rule on the earlier motion, set the verdict aside, and enter an acquittal as to all or some counts.[1]

To recap the demanding Rule 29 standard, a defendant challenging the sufficiency of the evidence bears the "heavy burden" of establishing that, even when viewed in the light most favorable to the government and with all permissible inferences drawn in the government's favor, a rational jury could not find the defendant guilty beyond a reasonable doubt.[2] If the jury's guilty verdict is at least "fairly possible," it must be upheld.[3] In other words, the trial

1. Fed. R. Crim. P. 29(c).

2. United States v. Autuori, 212 F.3d 105, 114 (2d Cir. 2000) (the Rule 29 standard is "whether upon the evidence, giving full play to the right of the jury to determine credibility, weigh the evidence, and draw justifiable inferences of fact, a reasonable mind might fairly conclude guilt beyond a reasonable doubt").

3. United States v. Guadagna, 183 F.3d 122, 130 (2d Cir. 1999).

judge must respect the jury's factfinding function and defer to its determinations on the weight of the evidence and the credibility of the witnesses, and to its choice between the competing inferences that can be drawn from the evidence.[4]

Even so, the jury's inferences must be reasonable. "An inference is not a suspicion or a guess. It is a reasoned, logical decision to conclude that a disputed fact exists on the basis of another fact that is known to exist."[5] Where a fact to be proved is also an element of the charged offense, "it is not enough that the inferences in the government's favor are permissible"—rather, the court "must also be satisfied that the inferences are sufficiently supported to permit a rational juror to find that the element, like all elements, is established beyond a reasonable doubt."[6]

As to this point, direct evidence is not necessarily required since the government "is entitled to prove its case solely through circumstantial evidence, provided, of course, that the government still demonstrates each element of the charged offense beyond a reasonable doubt."[7] If the evidence viewed in the light most favorable to the prosecution gives equal or nearly equal circumstantial support to a theory of guilt and a theory of innocence, "then a reasonable jury must necessarily entertain a reasonable doubt."[8]

B. Motions for a New Trial

Federal Rule of Criminal Procedure 33 allows district courts to "vacate any judgement and grant a new trial if the interest of justice so requires." Rule 33 motions are subject to variable time limits: when based on newly discovered evidence, they must be filed within three years after the verdict or finding of guilt; when based on any other ground, they must be filed within fourteen days.

Although a trial court has broader discretion to grant a new trial pursuant to Rule 33 than to grant a motion for a judgment of acquittal under Rule 29, awarding a defendant a new trial is "reserved for only the most extreme cases," and courts "approach such motions with great caution."[9]

"In evaluating a Rule 33 motion, the court must examine the entire case, take into account all facts and circumstances, and make an objective evaluation, keeping in mind that the 'ultimate test' for such a motion is 'whether letting a guilty verdict stand would be a manifest injustice.'"[10] District courts have a duty to assure that competent, satisfactory, and sufficient evidence in the record supports the jury verdict, and a district court

4. United States v. Reifler, 446 F.3d 65, 94 (2d Cir. 2006).

5. United States v. Pauling, 924 F.3d 649, 656–57 (2d Cir. 2019).

6. *Id.*; *see also* United States v. D'Amato, 39 F.3d 1249,1256 (2d Cir. 1994) ("[T]he government must introduce sufficient evidence to allow the jury to reasonably infer that each essential element of the crime charged has been proven beyond a reasonable doubt.").

7. United States v. Lorenzo, 534 F.3d 153, 159 (2d Cir. 2008).

8. United States v. Hawkins, 547 F.3d 66, 71 (2d Cir. 2008).

9. United States v. Hagler, 700 F.3d 1091, 1101 (7th Cir. 2012).

10. United States v. Alston, 899 F.3d 135, 146 (2d Cir. 2011).

may therefore "grant a new trial if the evidence does not support the verdict."[11] While the district court may weigh the evidence and credibility of witnesses, it must take care "not to usurp the role of the jury" as factfinder.[12] Accordingly, courts should defer to the jury's resolution of conflicting evidence and assessment of witness credibility. Only in the exceptional circumstance where there is "a real concern that an innocent person may have been convicted" may a district court "intrude upon the jury function of credibility assessment" and grant a Rule 33 motion.[13]

Although there is no exact definition of what constitutes an "extraordinary circumstance" sufficient to warrant Rule 33 relief, the Second Circuit has recently provided guidance: "a district court may not grant a Rule 33 motion based on the weight of the evidence alone unless the evidence preponderates heavily against the verdict to such an extent that it would be manifest injustice to let the verdict stand."[14] Under the "preponderates heavily" standard, "a district court may not reweigh the evidence and set aside the verdict simply because it feels some other result would be more reasonable." "To the contrary, absent a situation in which" the evidence was "patently incredible or defied physical realities," "where an evidentiary or instructional error compromised the reliability of the verdict," or where the government's case depends upon strained inferences drawn from uncorroborated testimony, "a district court must defer to the jury's resolution of conflicting evidence."[15] In applying the "preponderates heavily" standard, a district court must be careful to consider any reliable trial evidence as a whole, rather than on a piecemeal basis.[16]

In seeking a new trial based on newly discovered evidence, the defendant must demonstrate that the new evidence "(1) was discovered after trial, (2) could not have been discovered sooner through the exercise of due diligence, (3) is material and not merely impeaching or cumulative, and (4) probably would have led to acquittal."[17]

While both the Rule 29 and Rule 33 analyses in this context require an assessment of evidentiary sufficiency, they have different governing legal standards. As explained, the Rule 33 inquiry requires an objective evaluation of the evidence and an assessment of whether the evidence preponderates heavily against the verdict. The Rule 29 standard, in contrast, looks to whether there were sufficient grounds for the jury to find the defendant guilty beyond a reasonable doubt. Accordingly, a Rule 33 motion may properly be granted even where a Rule 29 motion is denied.

11. United States v. Archer, 977 F.3d 181, 187 (2d Cir. 2020).

12. United States v. Canova, 412 F.3d 331, 349 (2d Cir. 2005).

13. United States v. McCourty, 562 F.3d 458, 475–76 (2d Cir. 2009).

14. Archer, 977 F.3d at 188; *see also* United States v. Sanchez, 969 F.2d 1409, 1415 (2d Cir. 1992) ("It surely cannot be said in this case that the evidence 'preponderates heavily against the verdict, such that it would be a miscarriage of justice to let the verdict stand.'").

15. Archer, 977 F.3d at 188.

16. *Id.* at 189.

17. United States v. O'Malley, 833 F.3d 810, 813 (7th Cir. 2016).

C. Motions to Stay Sentence Pending Appeal

Defendants who have been found guilty, sentenced to a term of imprisonment, and filed for an appeal may ask the district court to stay their sentence while their appeal is pending. District courts are required to deny such requests unless the defendants can establish that (i) they are not likely to flee or pose a danger to the community if released and (ii) that the appeal is not for the purpose of delay and raises a substantial question of law or fact likely to result in reversal, a new trial, or a noncustodial sentence.[18] An appeal will be considered to involve a "substantial question" if it is one that could reasonably be expected to be decided in the defendant's favor.[19] This a relatively demanding standard that essentially requires defendants to show there are "exceptional reasons why their detention [pending appeal] would not be appropriate."[20]

A district court's order denying or granting a stay of pending appeal is subject to immediate review by a circuit court.[21]

II. CRIMINAL APPEALS IN THE UNITED STATES

As noted in Chapter 7, less than twenty percent of defendants who proceed to trial in federal cases are acquitted. Odds are, therefore, that criminal defendants will end up challenging their conviction to a circuit court of appeal. In practice, this means that taking care to preserve issues for a potential appeal to a circuit court is a critical component of defendants' strategy before and during trial. Generally, to preserve an issue for appeal a party must make a timely and specific objection to the district court.[22] If no such objection is made, the party may be deemed to have forfeited or waived the issue.[23]

Whereas an issue that has been waived may not be raised on appeal at all, an issue that is merely forfeited may still be considered at the appellate level only under the strict "plain error" standard. On plain error review, a circuit court will have the discretion to reverse a decision in the district court only if it is (i) in fact an error, (ii) plain or obvious, (iii) affects substantial rights of the injured party, and (iv) "seriously affects" the fairness, integrity, or public reputation of judicial proceedings in general.[24]

When the plain error standard is inapplicable, circuit courts will usually assess a matter occurring in the district court under the "harmless error" standard, which calls for convictions to be affirmed if the error at issue did not materially affect the outcome of the

---

18. 18 U.S.C. § 3143(b); *see also* Fed. R. Crim. P. 38(b).

19. United States v. Valera-Elizondo, 761 F.2d 1020, 1024 (5th Cir. 1985).

20. United States v. DiSomma, 951 F.2d 494, 496 (2d Cir. 1991).

21. Fed. R. App. P. 9.

22. Fed. R. Crim. P. 51(b); Fed. R. Crim. P. 30(d); FRE 103(a).

23. United States v. Olano, 507 U.S. 725, 733 (1993); *see also* United States v. Carter, 720 F.2d 941, 945 (7th Cir. 1983) ("It is a well-established general proposition that a litigant cannot present to this court as a ground for reversal an issue which was not presented to the trial court and which it, therefore, had no opportunity to decide.").

24. United States v. Thomas, 274 F.3d 655,667 (2d Cir. 2001).

proceedings.[25] "The main purpose of this rule is to ensure that appeals courts do not become slaves to technical errors—forced to reverse any conviction upon the finding of any, even harmless, error."[26] The burden of establishing that an error was harmless is placed on the prosecution: if the error implicates a right under the Constitution (e.g., the Fifth Amendment right against self-incrimination), prosecutors must show beyond a reasonable doubt that the error did not at all contribute to the verdict; for all other errors, prosecutors need only show that the verdict was not "substantially influenced" by an improper ruling.[27]

In addition to selecting between one of these two standards of review, appellate courts must also decide how much deference to give to the district court: questions of law are reviewed de novo, fact issues are reviewed for clear error, and discretionary matters are reviewed for an abuse of discretion. Of these, the de novo standard is the least deferential, since it gives appellate courts the ability to reach their own independent conclusion regardless of what the district court found. Where an issue involves a mixed question of law and fact, the appropriate standard will be decided based on the appellate court's view of which component predominates.[28]

The majority (more than sixty percent) of appeals against criminal convictions are affirmed. Appeals court data show that between ten percent and fifteen percent of such appeals result in a complete reversal of the conviction, four percent are reversed in part, twelve percent are remanded to the district court for further proceedings, and eight percent are dismissed.[29]

A. The "Final Judgment Rule"

Courts of appeals "have jurisdiction of appeals from all *final decisions* of the district courts of the United States."[30] Known as the "final judgment rule," federal law "requires 'that a party must ordinarily raise all claims of error in a single appeal following final judgment on the merits.'"[31] In a criminal case, the final judgment rule "prohibits appellate review until conviction and imposition of sentence."[32] This means that a defendant may not generally appeal an adverse ruling on a motion to dismiss, admission of evidence, or other preliminary matters until after the proceedings in the district court have concluded.[33]

---

25. Fed. R. Crim. P. 52(a); 28 U.S.C. § 2111.

26. United States v. Tussa, 816 F.2d 58, 66 (2d Cir. 1987).

27. Chapman v. California, 386 U.S. 18, 24 (1967); Kotteakos v. United States, 328 U.S. 750, 765 (1946).

28. United States v. Selioutsky, 409 F.3d 114, 119 (2d Cir. 2005).

29. Michael Heise, *Federal Criminal Appeals: A Brief Empirical Perspective*, 93 Marq. L. Rev. 825, 829 (2009).

30. 28 U.S.C. § 1291.

31. Flanagan v. United States, 465 U.S. 259, 263 (1984); *see also* Will v. United States, 389 U.S. 90, 96–98 (1967) ("All our jurisprudence is strongly colored by the notion that appellate review should be postponed, except in certain narrowly defined circumstances, until after final judgment has been rendered by the trial court.").

32. Flanagan, 465 U.S. at 263.

33. Because grants of a criminal defendant's motion to dismiss effectively terminate the case, such rulings are immediately appealable to the circuit court by the DOJ.

The purpose of this rule is to "minimize appellate-court interference with the numerous decisions [trial judges] must make in the pre-judgment stages of litigation" and reduce "the ability of litigants to harass opponents and to clog the courts through a succession of costly and time-consuming appeals."[34] Because these interests "are 'especially compelling in the administration of criminal justice,'" the policy underlying the final judgment rule "is at its strongest in the field of criminal law."[35]

The final judgment rule is, however, subject to certain exceptions that permit a court of appeals to exercise jurisdiction absent a final judgment on the merits in certain limited circumstances. Specifically, under the "collateral order doctrine," a court of appeals has jurisdiction to review a district court order that "conclusively determine[s] the disputed question," "resolve[s] an important issue completely separate from the merits of the action," and is "effectively unreviewable on appeal from a final judgment."[36] The third prong of this test "is satisfied only where the order at issue involves 'an asserted right the legal and practical value of which would be destroyed if it were not vindicated before trial.'"[37] For example, an order denying a motion to reduce bail is immediately appealable under the collateral order doctrine because bail affects the "traditional right to freedom before conviction" and "serves to prevent the infliction of punishment prior to conviction."[38]

Because it works against the policy justifications of the final judgment rule, circuit courts apply the collateral order doctrine "with the utmost strictness in criminal cases."[39] As relevant to white-collar crime cases, only two types of orders have been recognized by the Supreme Court to fall within the collateral order doctrine: orders regarding bail and motions to dismiss on double jeopardy grounds.[40]

Circuit courts may also exercise "pendent" appellate jurisdiction in certain interlocutory appeals—that is, appeals occurring while district court proceedings are still ongoing. This means that when a circuit court has jurisdiction to review "an interlocutory appeal of one ruling," it may also "exercise jurisdiction over other, otherwise unappealable interlocutory decisions, where such rulings are 'inextricably intertwined' with the order over which [the circuit court] properly ha[s] appellate jurisdiction, or where review of such rulings is 'necessary to ensure meaningful review' of the appealable order."[41] Pendent appellate jurisdiction is available only in "narrowly circumscribed" circumstances, to avoid encouraging "parties to parlay [reviewable] collateral orders into multi-issue interlocutory appeal tickets,

34. Flanagan, 465 U.S. at 263–64.

35. *Id.* at 264.

36. *Id.* at 265.

37. Midland Asphalt Corp. v. United States, 489 U.S. 794, 799 (1989); *see also* Sell v. United States, 539 U.S. 166, 177 (2003).

38. Stack v. Boyle, 342 U.S. 1, 3–4, 6 (1951); *see also* United States v. Gold, 790 F.2d 235, 239 (2d Cir. 1986).

39. Flanagan, 465 U.S. at 265.

40. Stack,342 U.S. at 1; Abney v. United States, 431 U.S. 651 (1977).

41. Atlantica Holdings, Inc. v. Sovereign Wealth Fund Samruk-Kazyna JSC, 813 F.3d 98, 116–17 (2d Cir. 2016).

thereby undermining the general rule that an appeal may not be taken until a final judgment has been entered."[42] Pendant review is discretionary and will only be exercised in "exceptional circumstances."[43]

B. Defendant's Appeal of Conviction

Under 28 U.S.C. Section 1291, criminal defendants are permitted to pursue a first-level appeal of a conviction as of right (meaning that the consent of the relevant circuit court is not required). The first step in doing so is to file a notice of appeal by the applicable deadline (typically) within fourteen days of the judgment or order being appealed, or the filing of the government's notice of appeal (whichever is later).[44] The filing of a notice of appeal "confers jurisdiction on the court of appeals and divests the district court of its control over those aspects of the case involved in the appeal."[45]

After the notice is filed, the circuit court will issue an order establishing a schedule for each side to file briefs. The circuit court panel assigned to the case will then review the briefs and the trial record; the panel can either decide the appeal on the briefs and record alone or it may ask the parties to participate in an oral argument (particularly if the panel is inclined to reversing the conviction based on the briefs).

After oral argument, if any, the panel will then issue a written ruling; at the panel's option, it can issue a per curiam opinion that simply affirms or reverses the district court's decision without discussion. There is no required timeline within which a circuit court panel must issue a decision; while the median time between the notice of appeal and a final decision is approximately nine months, appeals in many cases take substantially longer.[46]

The most common grounds on which defendants in white-collar crime cases appeal their convictions are (i) sufficiency of the evidence, (ii) erroneous evidentiary rulings, and (iii) improper jury instructions.

1. *Appeals Challenging the Sufficiency of the Evidence*

Just as with motions for acquittal under Federal Rule of Criminal Procedure 29, a defendant seeking to challenge the sufficiency of the evidence supporting his or her conviction on appeal bears a heavy burden: "Only where the record contains no evidence, regardless of how it is weighed, from which the jury could find guilt beyond a reasonable doubt, may an appellate court overturn the verdict."[47] Put differently, the standard for determining the sufficiency of the evidence at trial is "whether, after reviewing the evidence in the light most favorable to the government, any rational trier of fact could have found the essential elements of the crime

42. *Id.*

43. *Id.*

44. Fed. R. App. P. 4(b)(1); *see also* Fed. R. App. P. 3.

45. United States v. Ransom, 866 F.2d 574, 575 (2d Cir. 1989).

46. U.S. Courts, *Just the Facts: U.S. Courts of Appeals* (Dec. 20, 2016), *available at* https://www.uscourts.gov/news/2016/12/20/just-facts-us-courts-appeals.

47. United States v. Tipton, 964 F.2d 650, 657 (7th Cir. 1992).

beyond a reasonable doubt."[48] When the trier of fact is a jury (as opposed to a district court judge), circuit courts must defer to reasonable inferences drawn and the weight it gave to the evidence.[49]

If prosecutors pursue two distinct theories of the same offense—for example, insider trading under both the classical and misappropriation theories (see chapter 4)—and both are submitted to the jury and the evidence supports one theory but not the other, the verdict should be affirmed.[50]

Practice Note

Reversal of Convictions on Appeal in *United States v. Connolly*

Matthew Connolly and Gavin Black were two derivative traders at Deutsche Bank. Connolly was based in New York and Black was based in London. As part of a large-scale investigation by U.S. and U.K. authorities into manipulation of LIBOR—a benchmark interest rate set daily by the British Bankers' Association (BBA)—Connolly and Black were indicted in the Southern District of New York on charges of conspiracy to commit wire and bank fraud in violation of 18 U.S.C. Section 1349 and several substantive counts of wire fraud under 18 U.S.C. Section 1343. The crux of the prosecution's theory was that the defendants had induced coworkers into submitting false statements to the BBA in order to illegally influence LIBOR and benefit Deutsche Bank's trading positions. In short, the defendants were alleged to have caused Deutsche Bank to submit misleading interest rates at which it could borrow money (an important number that was then fed into the LIBOR calculation).

The pair were convicted at trial for conspiracy as well as substantive wire fraud: Connolly was sentenced to six months of home confinement plus eighteen months of supervised release; Black was sentenced to nine months of home confinement in the United Kingdom plus a $300,000 fine. On appeal, Connolly and Black argued that the evidence was insufficient to show that the LIBOR-related statements that they induced were in fact false.[51]

The key issue before the Second Circuit panel was whether, drawing all inferences in favor of the government, the conduct proved at trial fell within the scope of the wire fraud statute. After acknowledging that wire fraud does not require proof of an actual false statement so long as defendants are shown to have engaged in some form of deception such as a half-truth, the panel noted that the "federal fraud statutes are not catch-all laws designed to punish all acts of wrongdoing or dishonorable practices."[52] Viewed through this lens, the court concluded that the DOJ's case rested on a fundamentally faulty premise—namely, that there was one objectively true interest rate that, but for the defendant's conduct, would have been submitted to the BBA. In the court's view, the trial evidence showed the opposite: there were many factors that Deutsche Bank was permitted to consider when submitting its rates to the BBA and "there was no one true rate it was required to submit."[53]

48. Jackson v. Virginia, 443 U.S. 307, 319 (1979).

49. United States v. Beverly, 913 F.2d 337, 360 (7th Cir. 1990).

50. United States v. Rutkoske, 506 F.3d 170, 176 (2d Cir. 2007).

51. United States v. Connolly, No. 19-cr-03806, slip op. at 3–5 (2d Cir. Jan. 27, 2022).

52. *Id.* at 31.

53. *Id.* at 38.

Accordingly, the court concluded that the government "failed to produce any evidence that any DB LIBOR submissions that were influenced by the bank's derivatives traders were not rates at which DB could request, receive offers, and accept loans in DB's typical loan amounts; hence the government failed to show that any of the trader-influenced submissions were false, fraudulent, or misleading."[54] This failure was deemed fatal to the entire prosecution, even though it was accepted that the defendants took steps to shift LIBOR in their favor: "While defendants' efforts to take advantage of DB's position as a LIBOR panel contributor may have violated any reasonable notion of fairness, the government's failure to prove that the LIBOR submissions did not comply with the BBA LIBOR Instruction and were false or misleading means it failed to prove conduct that was within the scope of the statute prohibiting wire fraud schemes."[55]

2. *Appeals Challenging Evidentiary Rulings*

A district court is given broad discretion to make decisions regarding the admissibility of evidence, meaning that trial judges are empowered to choose among a range of permissible outcomes. Such decisions are therefore given "special deference" and will lead to reversal only upon a finding of an abuse of discretion, which generally requires establishing that the district court acted arbitrarily or irrationally.[56]

3. *Appeals Alleging Improper Jury Instructions*

Challenges to jury instructions are reviewed de novo by the courts of appeals.[57] Even so, "the district court is afforded substantial discretion with respect to the precise wording of instructions so long as the final result, read as a whole, completely and correctly states the law."[58] As such, a conviction may be reversed on the basis of an erroneous jury instruction only if the instructions given to the jury as a whole did not correctly inform them of the applicable law and were thereby misleading. Even imperfect jury instructions are insufficient to overturn a conviction absent a showing that they actually prejudiced the defendant.[59]

If the defendant made a contemporaneous objection to a district court's instruction that is subsequently determined to be wrong, the appellate court will apply a harmless error analysis to determine whether it constitutes reversible error.[60] If no contemporaneous objection is made, the appellate court will apply the more lenient "plain error" standard.

54. *Id.* at 53.

55. *Id.*

56. United States v. Evans, 27 F.3d 1219, 1232 (7th Cir. 1994); United States v. Pitre, 960 F.2d 1112, 1119 (2d Cir. 1992).

57. United States v. Liew, 856 F.3d 585, 595–96 (9th Cir. 2017) ("We review the formulation of jury instructions for abuse of discretion, but review de novo whether those instructions correctly state the elements of the offense and adequately cover the defendant's theory of the case.").

58. United States v. Marr, 760 F.3d 733, 743 (7th Cir. 2014); *see also* United States v. Kaplan, 836 F.3d 1199, 1215 (9th Cir. 2016).

59. Kaplan, 836 F.3d at 1199.

60. United States v. Munguia, 704 F.3d 596, 598 (9th Cir. 2012).

4. *Appeals and the Fugitive Disentitlement Doctrine*

As discussed in chapter 5, the fugitive disentitlement doctrine generally precludes "fugitives" from participating in the court process. This doctrine is often used to dismiss an appeal filed by a defendant who flees the jurisdiction before the circuit court renders a decision.[61]

In a 1993 decision, the Supreme Court refined the scope of the disentitlement doctrine by expressly requiring a nexus between fugitivity and the course of appellate proceedings.[62] The defendant in that case fled but was then recaptured prior to appealing his sentence. The Eleventh Circuit dismissed his appeal by reason of his prior flight. When the case reached the Supreme Court, the justices determined that continued disentitlement once the defendant was back in custody was improper: "Absent some connection between . . . fugitive status and [the fugitive's] appeal, as provided when a defendant is at large during the ongoing appellate process, the justifications advanced for dismissal of fugitives' pending appeals generally will not apply."[63] The Court thus vacated the Eleventh Circuit's decision because it was based on "the faulty premise that any act of judicial defiance, whether or not it affects the appellate process, is punishable by appellate dismissal," and remanded for consideration of whether such a connection existed.

C. Appeals by the Prosecution

Appeals by the prosecution in criminal cases are "something unusual, exceptional, [and] not favored" at least in part because of the risk they pose to the policies behind the double-jeopardy prohibition.[64]

The DOJ's ability to appeal matters occurring before the district court have has thus been limited by statute (18 U.S.C. § 3731) to narrow categories of orders terminating the prosecution (e.g., a grant of a motion to dismiss with prejudice) and grants of release from detention. This statute is strictly construed against the government's right of appeal.[65] Prosecutors' ability to challenge a defendant's sentence is covered in chapter 9.

D. Rehearing and Rehearing En Banc

Appeals are initially heard before a panel of three circuit court judges (see chapter 1). If an appellant is unhappy with the panel's decisions, they can petition for a rehearing before the same panel on a "point of law or fact that the petitioner believes the court has overlooked or misapprehended."[66] An appellant generally may not raise an issue for the first time in a rehearing petition "unless a manifest injustice would otherwise result."[67]

---

61. Ortega-Rodriguez v. United States, 113 S.Ct. 1199, 1203 (1993); Eisler v. United States, 338 U.S. 189 (1949); United States v. Baccollo, 725 F.2d 170, 171 (2d Cir. 1983); In re Prevot, 59 F.3d 556, 562–65 (6th Cir. 1995).

62. Ortega-Rodriguez, 113 S.Ct. at 1205–07.

63. *Id.* at 1208.

64. Carroll v. United States, 354 U.S. 394, 400 (1957); Fong Foo v. United States, 369 U.S. 141 (1962).

65. Carroll v. United States, 354 U.S. 394, 399–400 (1957).

66. Fed. R. App. P. 40(a)(2).

67. DeWeerth v. Baldinger, 38 F.3d 1266, 1274 (2d Cir. 1994).

Dissatisfied appellants may also seek a rehearing en banc, which are heard before all the judges within the circuit, where the panel's decision conflicts with a decision of the Supreme Court or another panel within the same circuit or where the case "involves one or more questions of exceptional importance."[68] En banc review requires a majority vote of the circuit court judges and is relatively rare.

III. CRIMINAL APPEALS IN THE UNITED KINGDOM

As discussed in chapter 1, the Court of Appeal (Criminal Division) is the immediate appellate court for Crown Court judgments or other decisions relating to trial on indictment.[69] For lesser crimes or matters not proceeding to trial, appeals concerning an order of the Crown Court "on the ground that it is wrong in law or is in excess of jurisdiction, by applying to the Crown Court to have a case stated by that court for the opinion of the High Court."[70] Like appeals courts in the United States, the High Court can review the lower court's decision under a range of standards. The High Court has discretion to grant relief if it determines that the decision below exceeded the court's jurisdiction, was in breach of the "rules of natural justice," was an error of law, or is otherwise "Wednesbury unreasonable" (i.e., "outrageous in its defiance of logic or accepted moral standards").[71]

Unlike in the United States, defendants in the United Kingdom have no automatic right to appeal their conviction to the Court of Appeal. Instead, under the Criminal Appeal Act (CAA) 1968, either the Court of Appeal must give leave or a "certificate that the case is fit for appeal" must be obtained from the Crown Court judge within twenty-eight days of the conviction.[72] Crown Court certificates of appealability are granted only for "exceptional reasons."[73] Relatively few applications for leave to appeal convictions are granted: in 2019 to 2020, out of a total of 510 conviction applications considered, leave was granted for just forty four of them (less than ten percent).[74]

The Court of Appeal may allow an appeal against conviction only "if they think the conviction is unsafe." If the court is instead satisfied "despite any misdirection or any irregularity in the conduct of the trial or any fresh evidence, that the conviction was safe," the appeal will be dismissed.[75]

---

68. Fed. R. App. P. 35(b).

69. Senior Courts Act 1981, s. 28(2).

70. *Id.* s. 28(1).

71. West Sussex Q.S., ex p. Albert and Maud Johnson Trust Ltd [1973] 1 Q.B. 188, DC; Assoc. Provincial Picture Houses Ltd. v. Wednesbury Corp. [1948] 1 KB 223.

72. Criminal Appeal Act (CAA) 1968, s. 1(2).

73. Bansal [1999] Crim. L. R. 484.

74. Courts and Tribunals Judiciariy, *Court of Appeal (Criminal Division) Annual Report 2019-2020*, *available at* https://www.judiciary.uk/wp-content/uploads/2021/05/6.7429_JO_Court_of_Appeal_Criminal_Division_2019_20_WEB-v2-with-tweak.pdf.

75. Graham [1997] 1 Cr. App. R. 302.

The test for an unsafe conviction is subjective, and requires each member of the court to ask themselves, "Have I a reasonable doubt, or even a lurking doubt, that this conviction is unsafe?" If the answer is yes, the appeal should be allowed (i.e., granted in the defendant's favor).[76] In answering these questions, the court will give considerable deference to the factual findings of the Crown Court: as Lord Justice Widgery said in *Cooper*, "It has been said over and over again throughout the years that this Court must recognize the advantage which a jury has in seeing and hearing the witnesses, and if all the material was before the jury and the summing-up was impeccable, this Court should not lightly interfere."[77]

To determine whether a conviction is unsafe, the Court of Appeal will hear legal arguments from each side and, in exceptional cases, hear fresh evidence. In a major difference with the practice in U.S. circuit courts, in fact, the Court of Appeal

> may, if they think it necessary or expedient in the interests of justice—(a) order the production of any document, exhibit or other thing connected with the proceedings, the production of which appears to them necessary for the determination of the case; (b) order any witness to attend for examination and be examined before the Court (whether or not he was called in the proceedings from which the appeal lies); and (c) receive any evidence which was not adduced in the proceedings from which the appeal lies."[78]

Whether exercise of these discovery powers is appropriate in any given appeal turns on the court's evaluation of the whether the evidence (i) appears to be capable of belief, (ii) supports a ground for appeal, (iii) would have been admissible in the underlying proceedings, and (iv) was omitted from the underlying proceedings for a legitimate reason.[79]

In appeals where new evidence is considered, determining whether the conviction was unsafe requires the Court of Appeal to consider the effect the evidence would likely have had on the jurors if it had been admitted during trial; if the court concludes that it "might reasonably" have affected the jurors' decision to convict, the conviction must be regarded as "unsafe."[80]

If the conviction is found to be unsafe, the Court of Appeal has the option of ordering a retrial if it appears "that the interests of justice so require."[81] Alternatively, the Court of Appeal can quash the conviction by directing the Crown Court to replace it with a judgment and verdict of acquittal.[82] The Court of Appeal can also find the defendant guilty of an alternative offense: CAA Section 3 provides that "where the appellant has been convicted of an offence to which he did not plead guilty and the jury could . . . have found him guilty of some other offence, and . . . it appears to the Court of Appeal that the jury must have been satisfied

76. Stafford v. DPP [1974] AC 878.

77. [1969] 1 Q.B. 267.

78. CAA 1968, s. 23(1).

79. *Id.*

80. Pendleton [2002] 1 WLR 72; Stafford [1974] A.C. 878.

81. CAA 1968, s. 7(1).

82. CAA 1968, s. 1.

of facts which make him guilty of the other offence," the court may "substitute for the verdict found by the jury a verdict of guilty of the other offence."

A. Appeals to the Supreme Court

A defendant can appeal a decision of the Court of Appeal to the Supreme Court if granted leave to do so by the Supreme Court or if the Court of Appeal certifies that the case involves an important legal issue.

According to Criminal Procedure Rule 43.2, a prospective Supreme Court appellant must first lodge an application to the Court of Appeal identifying the "point of law of general public importance" for which review is sought and giving reasons why that point of law ought to be considered by the Supreme Court. Upon receiving the application, the Court of Appeal must "decide whether to order the detention of a defendant who would have been liable to be detained but for the decision of the court" and determine any application for bail pending appeal.[83]

If the Court of Appeal refuses to certify the appeal, the defendant may then make an application directly to the Supreme Court.

CHAPTER 8: KEY DISTINCTIONS

United States	United Kingdom
Convictions can be vacated through the grant of a post-trial motion made to the district court	Crown Court convictions can only be vacated upon application to one of the intermediate appellate courts
Direct criminal appeals can only be made to one of the circuit courts of appeal	Direct criminal appeals can be made to either the High Court or the Court of Appeal depending on the issue raised
Criminal defendants have an automatic right of appeal to the circuit courts of appeal	Criminal defendants must be granted leave to appeal by the appellate court or their case must be certified as appealable by the Crown Court
Circuit courts have no power to order discovery or to hear witness testimony	Court of Appeal can order the production of evidence and testimony

83. CrimPR 43.3.

9 | Sentencing and Imprisonment

Former U.S. Supreme Court Justice Anthony Kennedy once remarked, "The hardest thing—as we know in the judicial system, one of the hardest things is sentencing."[1] Sentencing is an unfortunate reality of practicing criminal law and it is a difficult business for judges, prosecutors, defense counsel, and defendants alike. Considering that the vast majority of criminal cases end in conviction—eighty-one percent in the United Kingdom and nearly ninety-five percent in the United States—it is a critical part of criminal litigation. Indeed, since most individuals charged with serious offenses in both jurisdictions resolve their cases through guilty pleas, sentencing hearings are often the only substantive legal proceeding following arrest.

As detailed in this chapter, the legal frameworks governing sentencing in federal district courts and Crown Courts are substantially different in many key respects, as are the U.S. and U.K. government's policies regarding imprisonment. These differences are directly reflected in their respective incarceration statistics.

The United States is notorious for having by far the highest number of prisoners in the world relative to other countries and the second highest in absolute terms. Even after a steady reduction in incarceration levels over the past decade, at the end of 2019, there were still approximately 2.1 million individuals in state and federal custody; in comparison to the country's total population, this number equates with a rate of 358 per 100,000.[2] In comparison, China, with a population nearly four times as large, had the second highest number of inmates in 2019, with 1.7 million (although actual figures may be higher).[3] In relation to China's population size, its incarceration rate was 119. The total prison population in the United Kingdom in 2019 was 79,412 and its incarceration rate was 132.[4]

The durations of sentences in the United States are also much longer than in much of the rest of the world. As of March 2021, the average sentence imposed on federal prisoners was

1. Dorsey v. United States, 132 S. Ct. 2321 (2012) (No. 11-5683).

2. *See* E. Ann Carson, *Prisoners in 2020—Statistical Tables*, DOJ Office of Justice Programs (Dec. 2021). Counting just adult residents, the U.S. incarceration rate is 810 per 100,000. *See* John Gramlich, *America's Incarceration Rate Falls to Lowest Levels Since 1995*, Pew Research Center (Aug. 16, 2021).

3. World Prison Brief, *Highest to Lowest—Prison Population Total, available at* https://www.prisonstudies.org/highest-to-lowest/prison-population-total?field_region_taxonomy_tid=All.

4. *Id.*

147 months (12.25 years).[5] The average custodial sentence length in the United Kingdom is 24.9 months (less than seventeen percent of the average in the United States.).[6]

I. SENTENCING PROCEDURES IN THE UNITED STATES

Once a guilty verdict has been reached, Federal Rule of Criminal Procedure 32(b) requires the district court judge to "impose sentence without unnecessary delay." The practice in most district courts is to set a sentencing date roughly ninety days from the date of the verdict; whether the defendant must be held in custody prior to sentencing depends on the position taken by prosecutors and application of the Bail Reform Act (as discussed in chapter 3).

Between the verdict and sentencing, the U.S. Probation and Pretrial Services Office will examine the circumstances of the offense and may request to interview the defendant to understand any personal characteristics that may be relevant to sentencing.[7] Following this investigation, Probation will prepare a presentence report (PSR). PSRs are confidential documents given only to the parties and the sentencing judge that give details of the offense, the impact to the victims, the defendant's criminal history, and any other relevant circumstances relating to the proper punishment.[8] Aside from providing these details, the main purpose of the PSR is to calculate the applicable sentencing range under the Sentencing Guidelines (discussed in detail later in the chapter) and identify any bases for imposing a sentence outside of that range.[9] Most critically, the PSR will also include a nonbinding recommendation on what sentence the district court should impose (which may or may not be disclosed to anyone aside from the judge).[10]

Once the PSR is prepared, the Probation Office must provide a copy to the defendant and the DOJ at least thirty-five days prior to the sentencing date.[11] Within fourteen days of receiving the PSR, both sides may submit written objections to the probation officer assigned

---

5. U.S.S.C., *Federal Offenders in Prison March 2021*, *available at* https://www.ussc.gov/sites/default/files/pdf/research-and-publications/quick-facts/BOP_March2021.pdf.

6. Ministry of Justice, *Criminal Justice Statistics Quarterly* (May 19, 2022), *available at* https://assets.publishing.service.gov.uk/government/uploads/system/uploads/attachment_data/file/1076569/cjs-bulletin-december-2021.pdf.

7. The Probation and Pretrial Services Office is part of the Administrative Office of the U.S. Courts, and thus independent of the DOJ. Its main function is to draft presentence reports and administer probation and supervised release for defendants charged in federal cases.

8. Office of Prob. & Pretrial Servs. Presentence Investigation Report (Publication 107, 2007); United States v. Pabon-Cruz, 321 F. Supp. 2d 570, 572d (S.D.N.Y. 2003) ("Since the law permits and even requires the Court to seek out a broad range of information for sentencing, the Probation Department plays an invaluable role by collecting and independently verifying information and making it available to the Court.").

9. Fed. R. Crim. P. 32(d).

10. *Id.* at 32(e)(3).

11. *Id.* at 32(e)(2).

to the case, who may then revise it as appropriate.[12] At least seven days before sentencing, Probation will deliver the final PSR to the parties and the court.[13] Pursuant to a schedule set by the district court judge, the defendant and the DOJ will then submit a "sentencing memorandum" setting forth their respective positions as to the correct sentence. Some judges require sentencing memoranda to be submitted simultaneously, while others require them to be submitted sequentially (usually with the DOJ's being submitted second).

At the sentencing hearing, the judge will address any outstanding objections to the PSR and may adopt any undisputed portions as a conclusive finding of fact.[14] Before imposing sentence, the court must allow prosecutors and defense counsel, as well as the defendant, an opportunity to speak.[15] The district court judge will then enter a judgment, setting forth the plea or jury verdict, and the defendant's sentence. While the judge has broad sentencing discretion, the sentence imposed must at least involve consideration of the Sentencing Guidelines and the factors delineated in 18 U.S.C. Section 3553(a) as discussed in the following section.

A. Overview of the Sentencing Guidelines

Before 1984, sentencing in the federal court system was almost entirely unregulated: "judges sentenced without any legal constraints other than broad statutory penalty ranges . . . and there was virtually no appellate review of the sentences imposed."[16] Moreover, once district court judges decided upon a sentence, they were not required to give any reasons for why they arrived at that particular punishment. This led to significant disparities in the sentences imposed on different defendants for similar crimes and a random patchwork of sentencing procedures among the district courts. As one district court judge described the situation, judges' "substantially unbounded discretion," combined with their varying backgrounds and perspectives, produced "arbitrary, random, [and] inconsistent" sentencing decisions.[17]

To create a more uniform system, in 1984 Congress passed the Sentencing Reform Act (SRA) which, among other things, created the U.S. Sentencing Commission as an independent agency of the judicial branch of the federal government.[18] In enacting the SRA, Congress expressed "its general belief that existing federal sentences were often too lenient for certain types of offenders, including violent offenders, drug trafficking offenders, and major white-collar offenders."[19] The SRA directed the Commission to draft guidelines that provided

---

12. *Id.* at 32(f)(3).

13. *Id.* at 32(g).

14. *Id.* at 32(i)(3).

15. *Id.* at 32(i)(4).

16. Brent E. Newton & Dawinder S. Sidhu, *The History of the Original United States Sentencing Commission*, 1985–1987, Hofstra L. Rev. (2017).

17. *Id.* at 1184.

18. The Sentencing Commission is made up of seven individuals, appointed by the president and confirmed by the Senate, who serve staggered six-year terms. At least three Commission members must be federal judges; the other four are typically academics.

19. Newton & Sidhu, *supra* note 16, at 1181.

"certainty and fairness in meeting the purposes of sentencing" and "avoided unwarranted disparities among defendants with similar records who have been found guilty of similar criminal conduct while maintaining sufficient flexibility to permit individualized sentences when warranted by mitigating or aggravating factors."[20] Pursuant to these directives, the Commission created the U.S. Sentencing Guidelines (USSG), which went into effect in 1987.

The Guidelines were originally designed to make sentencing a formulaic procedure that effectively removed most of the discretion district court judges had previously enjoyed. They gave judges a narrow range within which they were required to sentence each particular defendant, unless a specific exception applied. Where a "court found such an exception and exercised its limited discretion to sentence outside the applicable Guidelines range, the court was said to be engaging in a 'departure' from the Guidelines."[21] While judges retained the ability to depart from the calculated sentencing range in extraordinary cases, the Guidelines were in most instances mandatory and strictly enforced by the circuit courts of appeals.

More than a decade after they were created, in 2005, the Supreme Court ruled that the Guidelines' mandatory nature was unconstitutional in *United States v. Booker*.[22] Based on an analysis of defendants' rights under the Sixth Amendment, *Booker* concluded that the statute that made the Guidelines mandatory (18 U.S.C. § 3553(b)(1)) "must be severed and excised."[23] Following this decision, the Guidelines are now merely advisory and function simply as a starting reference point for an individualized assessment of the facts and circumstances of each case and of each individual defendant.[24] Post-*Booker*, courts recognize three types of sentences. "(1) a sentence within a properly calculated Guidelines range; (2) a sentence that includes an upward or downward departure as allowed by the Guidelines; and (3) a non-Guideline[s] sentence or a variance that is outside of the relevant Guidelines range."[25]

The controlling sentencing statute is 18 U.S.C. Section 3553, which requires district courts to impose a sentence that is "sufficient, but not greater than necessary" to accomplish the objectives of punishment in criminal cases.

B. Applying the Sentencing Guidelines

Even though they are now strictly advisory, to determine an appropriate sentence, district courts must begin their sentencing analysis by calculating the applicable range under the Guidelines' Sentencing Table (shown in figure 9.1), which contains a vertical axis for the applicable offense level and a horizontal axis for the defendant's criminal history category.

---

20. *Id.* at 1185.

21. United States v. Mejia-Huerta, 480 F.3d 713, 721 (5th Cir. 2007).

22. 543 U.S. 220 (2005).

23. *Id.* at 245.

24. United States v. Cavera, 550 F.3d 180, 189 (2d Cir. 2008).

25. United States v. Brantley, 537 F.3d 347, 349 (5th Cir. 2008). The term "departure" refers only to sentences imposed under the Guidelines while "variance" is used to refer to decisions made under 18 U.S.C. Section 3553(a). Irizarry v. United States, 553 U.S. 708, 714 (2008); United States v. Jacobs, 635 F.3d 778, 782 (5th Cir. 2011).

SENTENCING TABLE
(in months of imprisonment)

	Offense Level	Criminal History Category (Criminal History Points)					
		I (0 or 1)	II (2 or 3)	III (4, 5, 6)	IV (7, 8, 9)	V (10, 11, 12)	VI (13 or more)
	1	0–6	0–6	0–6	0–6	0–6	0–6
	2	0–6	0–6	0–6	0–6	0–6	1–7
	3	0–6	0–6	0–6	0–6	2–8	3–9
Zone A	4	0–6	0–6	0–6	2–8	4–10	6–12
	5	0–6	0–6	1–7	4–10	6–12	9–15
	6	0–6	1–7	2–8	6–12	9–15	12–18
	7	0–6	2–8	4–10	8–14	12–18	15–21
	8	0–6	4–10	6–12	10–16	15–21	18–24
	9	4–10	6–12	8–14	12–18	18–24	21–27
Zone B	10	6–12	8–14	10–16	15–21	21–27	24–30
	11	8–14	10–16	12–18	18–24	24–30	27–33
Zone C	12	10–16	12–18	15–21	21–27	27–33	30–37
	13	12–18	15–21	18–24	24–30	30–37	33–41
	14	15–21	18–24	21–27	27–33	33–41	37–46
	15	18–24	21–27	24–30	30–37	37–46	41–51
	16	21–27	24–30	27–33	33–41	41–51	46–57
	17	24–30	27–33	30–37	37–46	46–57	51–63
	18	27–33	30–37	33–41	41–51	51–63	57–71
	19	30–37	33–41	37–46	46–57	57–71	63–78
	20	33–41	37–46	41–51	51–63	63–78	70–87
	21	37–46	41–51	46–57	57–71	70–87	77–96
	22	41–51	46–57	51–63	63–78	77–96	84–105
	23	46–57	51–63	57–71	70–87	84–105	92–115
	24	51–63	57–71	63–78	77–96	92–115	100–125
	25	57–71	63–78	70–87	84–105	100–125	110–137
	26	63–78	70–87	78–97	92–115	110–137	120–150
	27	70–87	78–97	87–108	100–125	120–150	130–162
Zone D	28	78–97	87–108	97–121	110–137	130–162	140–175
	29	87–108	97–121	108–135	121–151	140–175	151–188
	30	97–121	108–135	121–151	135–168	151–188	168–210
	31	108–135	121–151	135–168	151–188	168–210	188–235
	32	121–151	135–168	151–188	168–210	188–235	210–262
	33	135–168	151–188	168–210	188–235	210–262	235–293
	34	151–188	168–210	188–235	210–262	235–293	262–327
	35	168–210	188–235	210–262	235–293	262–327	292–365
	36	188–235	210–262	235–293	262–327	292–365	324–405
	37	210–262	235–293	262–327	292–365	324–405	360–life
	38	235–293	262–327	292–365	324–405	360–life	360–life
	39	262–327	292–365	324–405	360–life	360–life	360–life
	40	292–365	324–405	360–life	360–life	360–life	360–life
	41	324–405	360–life	360–life	360–life	360–life	360–life
	42	360–life	360–life	360–life	360–life	360–life	360–life
	43	life	life	life	life	life	life

November 1, 2016

Figure 9.1 Sentencing table.

The district court must calculate the number for each axis; where they meet is then the guidelines range. For example, a defendant with an offense level of fourteen and a criminal history category of I is subject to a sentencing range of fifteen to twenty-one months.

The calculated range cannot be presumed reasonable and judges have wide discretion to vary from the Guidelines on any rational basis, including policy considerations and disagreements with the Guidelines themselves.[26] As such, district courts are free to find that the Guidelines fail to "properly reflect the § 3553(a) considerations" or that the "case warrants a different sentence regardless."[27]

The standard of proof applicable to all factual findings relevant to the Guidelines calculation is preponderance of the evidence.[28] This is so even when one of the facts at issue is whether the defendant committed a crime other than the offense charged or an offense for which the defendant was acquitted at trial.[29] As such, a defendant charged with multiple related counts but only convicted on one count can have a guidelines calculation based on all counts (since the judge need only find that an offense occurred by a preponderance, whereas the jury must decide guilt beyond a reasonable doubt). Under this reasoning and the instructions set forth in USSG Section 1B1.3(a)(2), courts have approved guidelines calculations that included conduct related to counts that were dismissed or not even charged, conduct underlying offenses for which the defendant was acquitted, and conduct that cannot be prosecuted because of a statute of limitations.[30]

1. Step 1: Calculating the Offense Level

The offense level is designed to measure a crime's seriousness using three datapoints: the "base offense level," the "specific offense characteristics," and any relevant "adjustments." Where a defendant has committed multiple different, but related, crimes that involve substantially the same harm, for guidelines purposes the crimes are aggregated into a single group; the crime with the highest base offense level is then used to determine the offense level for the group as a whole.[31]

The base offense level is determined by reference to the Statutory Index, which lists all of the criminal statutes in the federal criminal code and cross-references the relevant provision in Chapter 2 of the Guidelines. For example, an FCPA violation under 15 U.S.C. Section 78dd-1 is cross-referenced to USSG Section 2C1.1 which, in turn, specifies a base offense level of fourteen if the defendant was a public official or twelve if otherwise. Wire fraud (18 U.S.C. § 1343), market manipulation (7 U.S.C. § 6c), and securities fraud (15 U.S.C. § 78j) are all assigned a base level of six or seven under Section 2B1.1.

Each of the Chapter 2 provisions give instructions for adding points to the base offense level depending on the specific offense characteristics (SOCs), which give a rough way of comparing a particular crime's severity against others in the same category. For financial crimes, the SOCs are almost entirely dependent on the amount of loss. For example, Section 2B1.1 sets forth a range of point increases for fraud offenses from zero (for crimes causing loss of

---

26. Kimbrough v. United States, 552 U.S. 85, 101 (2007).

27. Rita v. United States, 551 U.S. 338, 351 (2007).

28. United States v. Garcia, 413 F.3d 201, 220 n.15 (2d Cir. 2005).

29. United States v. Martinez, 525 F.3d 211, 215 (2d Cir. 2008).

30. United States v. Quintero, 937 F.2d 95, 97 (2d Cir. 1991); United States v. Perdomo, 927 F.2d 111, 114 (2d Cir. 1991); United States v. Watts, 519 U.S. 148, 151–57 (1997); United States v. Silkowski, 32 F.3d 682, 688 (2d Cir. 1994).

31. USSG §§ 3D1.2, 3D1.3.

$6,500 or less) to thirty (for crimes causing loss of more than $550,000,000). Converted into the sentencing table, Section 2B1.1 thus calculates sentencing ranges for fraud of between zero and six months to 262 months (nearly twenty-two years).

Because raw loss amounts are not always fungible—a fraud causing a loss of $100,000 to a vulnerable victim is a more harmful offense than a fraud causing the same loss to a bank—the use of loss amounts as the most heavily weighted variable in determining fraud sentences has been criticized for producing irrationally long sentences.[32] In one recent instance, Judge Garaufis of the Eastern District of New York declared:

> As far as this Court can tell, the Sentencing Commission's loss-enhancement numbers do not result from any reasoned determination of how the punishment can fit the crime, nor any approximation of the moral seriousness of the crime. . . . Given the feeble underpinnings of the loss enhancement, it is particularly galling that this factor is often more or less *solely* responsible for a white-collar offender's Guidelines sentence. . . . That this situation continues unabated is a great shame for the many offenders sentenced under this Guideline who do not receive a sentence that makes any sense for the actual crime of conviction.
>
> Many in the legal community have urged the Sentencing Commission to right this grievous wrong, and today I add my name to that lengthy list of judges, practitioners, scholars, and other commentators.[33]

Numerous judges and legal commentators have likewise observed that the outsized impact of Section 2B1.1 is especially pronounced and unjustified in cases involving high loss amounts.[34] The reason why loss amount is such a significant part of the Guidelines calculation can be traced back to amendments made by Congress in the early 2000s following a series of major financial crime scandals such as the multibillion-dollar Worldcom and Enron frauds. These amendments consolidated the guidelines for fraud, embezzlement, and property destruction into a single Section 2B1.1, created a more severe loss table, and

---

32. United States v. Adelson, 441 F. Supp. 2d 506, 509 (S.D.N.Y. 2006).

33. United States v. Johnson, 2018 WL 1997975, at *3–*4 (E.D.N.Y. Apr. 27, 2018) (emphasis in original); *see also* United States v. Watt, 707 F. Supp. 2d 149, 151 (D. Mass. 2010) (undue focus on loss amount renders Guidelines of "no help"); United States v. Gupta, 904 F. Supp. 2d at 351 ("By making a Guidelines sentence turn, for all practical purposes, on [§ 2B1.1], the Sentencing Commission . . . effectively guaranteed that many such sentences would be irrational on their face."); United States v. Faibish, 2015 WL 4637013, at *2 (E.D.N.Y. Aug. 3, 2015) ("The loss table is but one example of the seemingly mindless acceleration of penalties for economic crimes incorporated in the current Sentencing Guidelines regime.").

34. *See, e.g.*, Corsey, 723 F.3d at 378–79; 380 (Underhill, J., concurring) ("the loss guideline is fundamentally flawed, especially as loss amounts climb . . . [and] [t]he widespread perception that [it] is broken leaves district judges without meaningful guidance in high-loss cases. . . . The higher the loss amount, the more distorted is the guideline's advice to sentencing judges."); Faibish, 12-cr-00265 (E.D.N.Y.), Sent'g Tr., Mar. 10, 2016, ECF No. 271 at 23:1-12 ("[T]he guidelines . . . are just mindlessly accelerated once you have numbers of any size added in the loss or gain table."); Frank O. Bowman, III, *Sentencing High-Loss Corporate Frauds After Booker*, 20 FED. SENT'G REP. 167, 168 (2008) (for defendants "convicted of fraud offenses associated with very large guidelines loss calculations, the guidelines are now divorced from both the objectives of Section 3553(a) and, frankly, common sense").

added various nonloss SOCs: for example, if the crime involved a violation of the securities law and the defendant was an officer and director of a public company or associated with a broker dealer (add four levels); if it was committed from outside the United States (add two levels); and if it involved "sophisticated means" (add two levels). The "dizzying array" of SOC add-ons have "accreted over time, as Congress and the U.S. Sentencing Commission (not to mention the public) have responded to waves of market disruption by looking for ways to make punishments more severe for corporate criminals."[35]

Even without applying any of the new SOCs, by 2003 the revised loss table routinely produced sentencing ranges over 250 months (twenty or more years) for fraud offenses—a *seven hundred percent increase* from the maximum possible sentence for fraud under the original version of the Guidelines issued just sixteen years earlier.[36] This massive increase has been criticized as being politically driven and lacking basis in "past practice or a coherent statement of sentencing purposes."[37]

Because the amount of loss is such a massive determinant in the guidelines calculation, it is often a significant point of contention during sentencing proceedings. Application Note 3 to Section 2B1.1 creates a general rule that loss is the greater of actual loss or intended loss. "Actual loss" is defined to mean "the reasonably foreseeable pecuniary harm that resulted from the offense." "Intended loss" is "the pecuniary harm that the defendant purposely sought to inflict" and "includes intended pecuniary harm that would have been impossible or unlikely to occur."

The court need only make a reasonable estimate of the loss since the "sentencing judge is in a unique position to assess the evidence and estimate the loss based upon that evidence."[38] In making this estimation, judges are directed to consider factors such as the fair market value of the property unlawfully taken, the approximate number of victims multiplied by the average loss to each victim, the reduction that resulted from the offense in the value of equity securities or other corporate assets, and general factors like the scope and duration of the offense and revenues generated by similar operations.[39]

---

35. Samuel W. Buell, *Is the White Collar Offender Privileged?*, 63 DUKE L.J. 835 (January 2014).

36. *Compare* 1987 U.S.S.G. § 2F1.1 *with* 2003 U.S.S.G. § 2B1.1. The original 1987 fraud guideline was itself intentionally ratcheted up to far exceed the sentences that judges had historically deemed were appropriate for such crimes. *See Corsey*, 723 F.3d at 380; Mark W. Bennett, *et al.*, *Judging Federal White-Collar Fraud Sentencing*, 102 IOWA L. REV. 939, 948, n.35 (Mar. 2017). Although the Commission reviewed statistics of past white-collar sentences in creating this guideline, it simply "deleted from its calculations the 50% of offenders who received probation." *See* Bennett, *supra*, at 950, n.48. Even so, the maximum possible sentencing range under the original Guidelines was thirty to thirty-seven months. *See* 1987 U.S.S.G. § 2F1.1.

37. *See* Jeffrey Parker & Michael Block, *The Limits of Federal Criminal Sentencing Policy*, 9 GEO. MASON L. REV. 1001, 1052 (2001); *see also Corsey*, 723 F.3d at 380 ("[T]he increases in the recommended Guideline ranges for fraud crimes [were] directed by Congress, without the benefit of empirical study of actual fraud sentences by the Sentencing Commission."); *Gupta*, 904 F. Supp. 2d at 351 ("[T]he numbers assigned by the Sentencing Commission to various sentencing factors appear to be more the product of speculation, whim, or abstract number crunching than of any rigorous methodology—thus maximizing the risk of injustice.").

38. USSG 2021, Section 2B1.1 Application Note 3(C).

39. *Id.*

After the base offense level and SOCs have been determined, the sentencing judge must then make any necessary "adjustments" under USSG Chapter 3. The Chapter 3 provision most often relevant in white-collar crime cases is that relating to the defendant's "aggravating role" in the offense. Under Section 3B1.1, the defendant's offense level is increased by between two and four points depending on whether he or she was an organizer, leader, or mere supervisor of criminal activity and whether he or she oversaw the conduct of five or more other co-conspirators. If the defendant obstructed or attempted to obstruct the investigation (including by destroying evidence or providing knowingly false testimony), two points are added.[40] To encourage guilty pleas, a defendant who "clearly demonstrates acceptance of responsibility for his offense" without putting the government to its burden at trial is able to secure a deduction from his or her offense level of up to three points.[41]

2. *Calculating the Criminal History Category*

The criminal history category "is a rough effort to determine the defendant's disposition to criminality, as reflected in the number and nature of his prior contacts with the law."[42] In the Sentencing Commission's view, a defendant's record of past criminal conduct is directly relevant to his sentence in a subsequent case: "A defendant with a record of prior criminal behavior is more culpable than a first offender and thus deserving of greater punishment. General deterrence of criminal conduct dictates that a clear message be sent to society that repeated criminal behavior will aggravate the need for punishment with each recurrence."[43]

Compared with the offense level calculation, calculating the applicable criminal history category is relatively straightforward. Each defendant starts with a score of zero: three points are then added for each prior sentence exceeding eleven months; two points are added for each prior sentence of at least sixty days not already counted; and one point is added for any other sentence not already counted (up to a total of four). If the defendant committed the offense at issue while already serving another sentence or while on probation, parole, or supervised release, another two points are added.[44]

For purposes of this calculation, any sentence imposed within fifteen years of the defendant's latest offense conduct is generally considered relevant. Sentences resulting from convictions in foreign countries are not counted, but may be considered under USSG Section 4A1.3 (Departures Based on Inadequacy of Criminal History Category).[45]

---

40. USSG 2021 § 3C1.1.

41. USSG § 3E1.1.

42. Frank O. Bowman III, *Departing Is Such Sweet Sorrow: A Year of Judicial Revolt on "Substantial Assistance" Departures Follows a Decade of Prosecutorial Indiscipline*, 29 Stetson L. Rev. 7, 11 (1999).

43. USSG 2021, Chapter 4, Introductory Commentary.

44. USSG §4A1.1.

45. USSG §4A1.2(e), (h).

3. "Substantial Assistance" Departures under Section 5K1.1

The primary enticement for defendants to plead guilty and enter into a cooperation agreement with prosecutors is the possibility that a 5K letter will be submitted on their behalf to the sentencing judge. USSG Section 5K1.1 provides that "[u]pon motion of the government stating the defendant has provided substantial assistance in the investigation or prosecution of another person who has committed an offense, the court may depart from the guidelines." In terms of how significant of a departure is warranted, district courts are instructed to consider the usefulness of defendants' assistance, the reliability of their information or testimony, the degree to which defendants or their families were placed into danger on account of their cooperation, and the timeliness of their decision to cooperate.[46] To allow the court to evaluate these factors on a complete record, cooperators are almost always sentenced after the proceedings against the targets of the cooperation have fully concluded (i.e., after there is no further need for the cooperators' assistance).

The standard format of a 5K letter provides a brief description of the cooperators' offense, the maximum penalties applicable, the terms of the plea agreement, a guidelines range calculation, and, most importantly, an overview of the duration and nature of their cooperation.[47] "Whether such a letter is merited is confided to the sole determination of the government, subject only to constitutional limitations."[48]

5K letters are merely a recommendation from the DOJ for a departure and do not have any binding effect. They do, however, limit the district court's otherwise broad sentencing discretion. In *United States v. Johnson*, for example, the Second Circuit ruled that the district court had erred by giving a cooperator a substantially higher sentence than called for by the plea agreement and guidelines because, in the court's view, the defendant violated the terms of his cooperation agreement (even though the DOJ still submitted a 5K letter). The panel concluded:

> [A]lthough a district court alone may determine what effect to give to a 5K1.1 letter, in so doing may consider the extent of downward departures or variances received by other similarly situated defendants who have cooperated, and may even decline a reduction from the Guidelines altogether, the court here erred in the course of exercising its discretion by (1) "substantially increasing [defendant's] sentence from what it otherwise would have been" and (2) giving as a reason for the increase the government's failure to comply with the purported customary prosecutorial practice of voiding cooperation agreements upon breach by the defendant. The 5K1.1 letter, which the government saw fit not to revoke in [defendant's] case despite his breach of the cooperation agreement, allows a downward departure from the Sentencing Guidelines in cases where a defendant provides substantial assistance to the government. . . .
>
> That the government usually voids cooperation agreements upon a breach by the defendant should not be reason to constrain a district court from giving proper effect to a 5K1.1

46. USSG § 5K1.1(a).

47. *See* DOJ Sample 5K1.1 Letter, United States v. Bjorn, No. 03-cr-652 (E.D. Pa.), *available at* https://www.justice.gov/atr/case-document/governments-sentencing-memorandum-and-motion-guidelines-downward-departure-ussg-1.

48. United States v. Johnson, 567 F.3d 40, 52 (2d Cir. 2009).

letter if the government decides to submit a 5K1.1 letter notwithstanding the defendant's breach of the co-operation agreement.[49]

Because the standard DOJ practice in complex white-collar crimes matters is to try to enter into a cooperation agreement with at least one conspirator, 5K letters are submitted with relative frequency—a study of sentencing data from 2014 found nearly 10,000 5K letters were submitted to district courts that year (roughly 12.5% of all defendants).[50] In terms of how much of a departure will be granted, the same study found that the DOJ's submission of a 5K letter resulted in an average decrease of 52.6% from the bottom of the original guideline range.[51] Unlike in the United Kingdom, there is no requirement that the sentencing judge specify what the sentence would have been without the defendant's cooperation.

C. 18 U.S.C. Section 3553

After calculating the suggested sentence under the Guidelines, sentencing courts must apply the provisions of 18 U.S.C. Section 3553 to reach a sentence that is "sufficient but not greater than necessary" to achieve the four purposes of criminal punishment: retribution, deterrence, incapacitation, and rehabilitation.[52] In making this determination, Section 3553(a) requires consideration of:

(1) the nature and circumstances of the offense and the history and characteristics of the defendant;

(2) the need for the sentence imposed—(A) to reflect the seriousness of the offense, to promote respect for the law, and to provide just punishment for the offense; (b) to afford adequate deterrence to criminal conduct; (C) to protect the public from further crimes of the defendant; and (D) to provide the defendant with needed educational or vocational training, medical care, or other correctional treatment in the most effective manner;

(3) the kinds of sentences available;

(4) the kinds of sentence and the sentencing range established [under the Sentencing Guidelines] . . .;

(5) any pertinent policy statement issued by the Sentencing Commission . . . ;

(6) the need to avoid unwarranted sentencing disparities among defendants with similar records who have been found guilty of similar conduct; and

(7) the need to provide restitution to any victims of the offense.

There is no restriction on the types of information that district court judges may use when weighing these factors; instead, the "sentencing court is entitled to rely on any type of

49. 567 F.3d 40, 52 (2d Cir. 2009).

50. US Sentencing Commission, *The Use of Federal Criminal Procedure 35(b)* (Jan. 2016) at 8, *available at* https://www.ussc.gov/sites/default/files/pdf/research-and-publications/research-publications/2016/Rule35b.pdf.

51. *Id.* at 18.

52. 18 U.S.C. § 3553(a)(2).

information known to it" including anything that sheds light on the defendant's background, history and behavior.[53] Accordingly, the normal evidentiary principles—including those relating to hearsay and illegally seized materials—do not generally apply at the sentencing stage.[54]

This rule is rooted in the statutory directive that "no limitation shall be placed on the information concerning the background, character, and conduct of a person convicted of an offense which a court of the United States may receive and consider for the purpose of imposing an appropriate sentence."[55] In practice, this allows defendants to attach to their sentencing memorandum letters from friends and family describing the defendant's good deeds, family situation, and remorse, even though such letters would normally be barred by the FRE as hearsay (see chapter 7). The sentencing memorandum of Raj Gupta, the former CEO of McKinsey & Co. who was convicted of insider trading, included more than four hundred such letters (including from global luminaries like Bill Gates and former UN secretary-general Kofi Annan).[56] The outpouring of support was not enough to avoid prison, however; Gupta still received a sentence of twenty-four months.

D. The Sentencing Hearing

Sentencing hearings must follow a fairly rigid procedure set forth in Federal Rule of Criminal Procedure 32 and 18 U.S.C. Section 3553(c). The district court must verify that the defendant and the defendant's attorney have read and discussed the PSR, give the defendant and prosecutors a written summary of any information excluded from the PSR but on which the court will rely in sentencing, and allow the parties to comment on the PSR's sentencing determinations "and other matters relating to an appropriate sentence."[57] If there remain any significant fact disputes between the DOJ, Probation, and/or the defendant at the time of the sentencing hearing the court may permit the parties to introduce evidence, including calling witnesses to provide live testimony. After receiving such evidence (if any) and reviewing the written submissions of the parties, the sentencing court will accept any undisputed portion of the PSR as fact and then rule on any live factual disputes that may affect sentencing.

Before imposing sentence, the court must give the defendant and the defendant's attorney an opportunity to speak or present any information to mitigate the sentence. After or before the defendant's presentation, the DOJ must also be given an opportunity to speak for the same duration permitted defense counsel. Any victims of the crime who are present at sentencing must also be permitted a chance to "be reasonably heard."[58]

As to the prosecutor's role in sentencing, the *Justice Manual* suggests a focus on attempting to ensure that the relevant facts and sentencing factors are brought to the court's attention

---

53. United States v. Miller, 116 F.3d 641, 685 (2d Cir. 1997); *see also* United States v. Tucker, 404 U.S. 443, 446 (1972) (sentencing court's discretion is "largely unlimited either as to the kind of information [the court] may consider, or the source from which it may come").

54. United States v. Napolitano, 761 F.2d 135, 139 (2d Cir. 1985); United States v. Tejada, 956 F.2d 1256, 1264 (2d Cir. 1992).

55. 18 U.S.C. § 3661.

56. Anita Raghavan, The Billionaire's Apprentice 402 (2013).

57. Fed. R. Crim. P. 32(i).

58. *Id.*

fully and accurately, and "making sentencing recommendations in appropriate cases." Depending on the nature of the offense and any other relevant circumstance, the DOJ may or may not argue forcefully for the imposition of a particular sentence or sentencing range. As stated in the *Justice Manual*, "the attorney for the government should apply relevant sentencing factors to the facts in a way that most accurately and convincingly supports the government's recommended sentence." Because judges are often presented with voluminous information at sentencing, the DOJ considers justice to be best served "when prosecutors distill that information to its most salient points and provide judges with a persuasive framework through which to understand the significance of the case, the impact on the victims, the importance of general and specific deterrence, and the need for the requested punishment and rehabilitation plan to achieve a just result."[59]

In terms of deciding on an actual recommendation, prosecutors are directed to make an individualized assessments of the facts and circumstances of each case and the characteristics and history of the defendant.[60] Knowing that district court judges often sentence below the Guidelines range, standard DOJ practice is to recommend a sentence within the guidelines to effectively set a high starting point from which the judge will likely then depart.

Once each side's position has been addressed, the district court judge is required to state in open court the reasons behind the particular sentence imposed and any departure or variance taken from the guidelines range. "A court may not modify a term of imprisonment once it has been imposed except pursuant to statute" (for example, under Fed. R. Crim. P. 35(b) (see below)).[61] While a defendant will receive a separate sentence for each individual count of conviction, the default is that all such sentences should run concurrently; meaning that the total effective sentence is set by the highest individual sentence.[62] There is no constitutional right to a concurrent sentence, however, and district courts have the discretion to issue consecutive sentences unless specifically barred by statute.[63]

E. Appealing a Sentence

After a defendant is sentenced, the district court must advise him or her of any right to appeal.[64] Under 18 U.S.C. Section 3742, a defendant as well as the government may file a notice of appeal in the district court if there are grounds to argue that it was substantively or procedurally incorrect. Once such a notice is filed, the district court will send it to the relevant court of appeals for consideration.[65]

---

59. *Justice Manual*, § 9.27-720.

60. *Id.*, § 9.27-730.

61. United States v. Gotti, No. 02-cr-00743, 2020 WL 497987, at *1 (S.D.N.Y. Jan. 15, 2020).

62. USSG § 5G1.2(d); 18 U.S.C. § 3584 (providing that for sentences on multiple counts "the terms may run concurrently or consecutively"); Garrett v. United States, 471 U.S. 773, 793 (1985) ("The presumption when Congress creates . . . distinct offenses is that it intends to permit cumulative sentences.").

63. United States v. White, 240 F.3d 127, 135 (2d Cir. 2001).

64. Fed. R. Crim. P. 32(j).

65. 18 U.S.C. § 3742(d).

Following the Supreme Court's decision in *Booker*, the circuit courts of appeal are constrained to review sentences for reasonableness.[66] Reasonableness review requires an examination of the length of the sentence (substantive reasonableness), as well as the procedure employed in arriving at the sentence (procedural reasonableness), and is conducted under the deferential "abuse of discretion" standard.[67]

This means that as to the substantive component of a sentencing decision, the circuit court "will not substitute its own judgment for the district court's on the question of what is sufficient to meet the § 3553(a) considerations in any particular case."[68] Therefore, a substantive determination of a district court will be set aside only in "those special cases where the range of permissible decisions does not encompass the district court's determination."[69] When conducting substantive review, circuit court panels will take into account the totality of the circumstances, "giving due deference to the sentencing judge's exercise of discretion, and bearing in mind the institutional advantages of district courts."[70]

Procedural reasonableness, on the other hand, requires the circuit court to objectively examine whether the district court failed to calculate the guidelines range or calculated it directly, treated the guidelines as mandatory, did not give proper consideration to the Section 3553(a) factors, made clearly erroneous factual findings, or deviated from the guidelines without sufficient explanation.[71] As judged against these factors, a sentence is procedurally unreasonable if a district court committed an error of law in the course of exercising its sentencing discretion.[72] If a significant procedural error is identified, the case can be remanded to the district court for explanation or correction.

II. IMPRISONMENT IN THE UNITED STATES

The federal prison system is administered by the Bureau of Prisons (BOP), which is part of the DOJ. It currently consists of 122 prisons operated at five different security levels:

- Minimum: also known as federal prison camps (FPCs), minimum security prisons have dormitory-style housing and limited or no perimeter fencing. They typically hold between one hundred and four hundred inmates and have relatively low staff-to-inmate ratios.

66. Booker, 543 U.S. at 260–61, 125 S.Ct. 738; *see also* United States v. Fernandez, 443 F.3d 19, 26–27 (2006).

67. United States v. Canova, 485 F.3d 674, 679 (2d Cir. 2007); *see also* Gall, 128 S.Ct. at 591.

68. United States v. Cavera, 550 F.3d 180, 189 (2d Cir. 2008).

69. *Id.*

70. *Id.* at 190.

71. United States v. Rattoballi, 452 F.3d 127, 131–32 (2d Cir. 2006).

72. Crosby, 397 F.3d at 114; United States v. Selioutsky, 409 F.3d 114, 118 (2d Cir. 2005); United States v. Sanchez, 517 F.3d 651, 661–62 (2d Cir. 2008).

- Low: these prisons have double-fenced perimeters, dormitory- or cubicle-style housing (i.e., no cells), and robust work and educational programs. Low-security prisons usually hold more than one thousand inmates and are often beyond their as-designed maximum capacities.
- Medium: medium security prisons have strengthened perimeter fencing and inmates are mainly held in either single or multiperson cells. Prisoners' degree of freedom within the prison is much lower than in low- or minimum-security facilities.
- High: also known as United States penitentiaries (USPs), these prisons have highly secured perimeters, exclusively cell-type housing, extremely controlled internal environments, and a high staff-to-inmate ratio.
- Administrative: the BOP's administrative facilities each have special remits, such as the detention of pretrial offenders, treatment of inmates with serious medical conditions, or the containment of extremely dangerous or escape-prone inmates. Except for the Administrative-Maximum Security Penitentiary (ADX) in Florence, Colorado,[73] all administrative facilities are capable of holding inmates in all security categories.

While district court judges can make a designation recommendation when handing down a sentence, the specific prison where defendants are assigned to serve their sentences is within the sole discretion of the BOP. In exercising this discretion, the BOP is guided by its Inmate Security and Custody Classification Manual.[74] The Classification Manual's overriding objective is to place inmates in a facility that is commensurate with their security needs and within five hundred miles of their primary residence.

Like the Sentencing Guidelines, BOP designations are made by assigning each inmate a numeric score based on a list of personal characteristics and offense factors. All designations are made by the Designation and Sentence Computation Center (DSCC), located in Grand Prairie, Texas. After a sentence is given by the district court, the DSCC will be sent the PSR, the district court's judgment, and various other documentation from the U.S. Marshal's Service and the DOJ. The DSCC will then input the offender's information into a database—called SENTRY—to calculate the appropriate security level.

If the defendant has been allowed to self-surrender to prison, they will start with a score of –3; if not, they will start with a score of zero. Next, their offense will be given a "severity score" of between zero and seven. The defendant's criminal history will then be assessed and assigned a score of between zero and ten (with ten indicating previous prison terms of at least

73. The ADX Florence "supermax" prison, unofficially known as the "Alcatraz of the Rockies," is the most secure prison in the federal system, designed to hold the most violent, predatory, and escape-prone prisoners. Inmates are confined to their cells twenty-three hours per day, have extremely limited contact with other inmates and staff, and are under constant surveillance. On January 4, 2021, District Judge Baraitser of Westminster's Magistrate Court denied the DOJ's request to extradite Wikileaks founder Julian Assange partly because of humanitarian concerns that Assange would be placed at ADX Florence. This decision was subsequently reversed by the High Court after the DOJ offered assurances that Assange would not be sent to the ADX.

74. BOP, Inmate Security Designation and Custody Classification (Program Statement 5100.08), *available at* https://www.bop.gov/policy/progstat/5100_008cn.pdf.

Security Level	Custody Level	Male	Female
MINIMUM	COMMUNITY and OUT	0–11 points	0–15 points
LOW	OUT and IN	12–15 points	16–30 points
MEDIUM	OUT and IN	16–23 points	*
HIGH	IN and MAXIMUM	24+ points	31+ points
ADMINISTRATIVE	All custody levels	All point totals	All point

Figure 9.2 Designated security levels.

four years); a history of violence and escape attempts will add further points. Points will also be assigned based on the defendant's age (ranging from zero for those fifty-five and older to eight for anyone under twenty-four), educational level, drug and alcohol abuse, and the length of sentence. Once all the relevant data is entered into SENTRY, the defendant will be designated to one of the five security classifications based on their overall score (figure 9.2).

While most white-collar crime defendants will be designated to either a minimum- or low-security facility by SENTRY, BOP designations also turn in part on where space is available and can therefore be unpredictable.[75]

Irrespective of their "security point score," BOP policy requires all foreign nationals to be designated in at least a low-security prison.[76] Current BOP policy also requires most foreign nationals convicted of financial crimes to be held in a privately operated prison facility.[77] As opposed to comparable BOP-run facilities, private prisons are known to house nonviolent offenders together with inmates of more serious security classifications and their security

---

75. *See, e.g.*, United States v. Lally, 2011 WL 5926937, at *1 (D. Mass. Nov. 29, 2011) (cooperating, first-time white-collar defendant eligible for an FPC under BOP policy designated to a "'work cadre' at the maximum security Metropolitan Detention Centre in Brooklyn"); Walter Pavlo, *Maximum Security Federal Prisons Have 'Minimum Security' Inmates*, FORBES (July 14, 2016) (describing the experiences of a "first time white-collar offender" sent to a maximum security prison despite not qualifying for such a high level of security per BOP's own policies).

76. BOP Program Statement 5100.09 at 50 ("A male or female inmate who is not a citizen of the United States . . . shall be housed in at least a Low security level institution.").

77. DOJ Inspector General, "Review of the Federal Bureau of Prisons' Monitoring of Contract Prisons," at i (Aug. 2016) (BOP policy is to "contract[] with privately operated institutions . . . to confine federal inmates who are primarily low security, criminal alien adult males with 90 months or less remaining to serve"); Priscila Mosqueda, *Migrants in Texas's Federal Prisons Subjected to "Shocking Abuse,"* THE GUARDIAN, June 10, 2014 (quoting BOP "policy to contract out bed space for non-US citizen inmates in order to make space available for US citizen inmates in BOP facilities so they can receive required programming"). This policy represents a reversal of the Obama administration's initiative to complete phase-out the use of private prisons in light of findings that "[t]hey simply do not provide the same level of correctional services, programs, or resources . . . [or] the same level of safety and security" as BOP facilities. Sally Q. Yates, Deputy Attorney General, "Reducing our Use of Private Prisons," Aug. 18, 2016, *available at* https://www.justice.gov /archives/opa/file/886311/download.

levels are accordingly much higher.[78] Foreign nationals are also ineligible for prerelease into a halfway house or home confinement towards the end of their sentences, meaning that they generally serve "harsher time" than American citizens.[79]

Moreover, even when foreign nationals complete their prison sentence, Immigration and Customs Enforcement (ICE) is required by statute to immediately transfer them to an ICE detention facility to await deportation back to their home countries.[80] This post-"release" immigration detention generally means a further term of detention of at least one month or more.[81] The time an inmate will spend in ICE custody is difficult to predict or control, and effectively extend whatever sentence imposed by the district court. Due to its reputation for expediting removal proceedings, foreign defendants will often try to secure a designation at the low security prison in Allenwood, Pennsylvania so as to minimize any period of ICE detention.[82]

A. International Custody Transfers

The Transfer of Offenders to and from Foreign Countries Act (18 U.S.C. §§ 4100–4115) creates a framework for transfer of inmates between the United States and foreign countries. The law originated as a response to complaints made to lawmakers about the treatment of U.S. citizens in Mexican jails during the 1970s. Congress subsequently negotiated a treaty between Mexico and the United States that permitted nationals of each country to serve their sentences in their native country. The Transfer Act was then enacted in October 1977 "to provide the implementation procedures for offender transfer treaties with Mexico and Canada as well as for similar future treaties."[83]

---

78. Conti, ECF No. 229 at 23–24. The conditions in private prisons and the private prison industry in general have been the subject of severe criticism. *See, e.g.*, LAUREN-BROOKE EISEN, INSIDE PRIVATE PRISONS: AN AMERICAN DILEMMA IN THE AGE OF MASS INCARCERATION (Columbia Univ. Press 2018).

79. United States v. Navarro-Diaz, 420 F.3d 581, 588 (6th Cir. 2005); United States v. Pacheco-Soto, 386 F. Supp. 2d 1198, 1205 (D. N.M. 2005) ("[S]olely because of Defendant's status as a deportable alien [ ] he faces an unwarranted increase in the severity of his sentence. He likely will not be eligible for any early release [and] he will not be able to serve his sentence in a minimum security prison. . . . These consequences are severe and unfair.").

80. 8 U.S.C. § 1226(c) (requiring detention of criminal alien "when the alien is released [from prison], without regard to whether the alien is released on parole, supervised release, or probation"). The conditions in ICE detention facilities are often worse than actual prisons. *See, e.g.*, Andrew Gumbel, *Immigrants Tell of Cruelty, Illness and Filth in US Detention*, THE GUARDIAN (Sept. 12, 2018), Rory Carroll, *Immigration Detention Centers Marred by "Needless Deaths,"* THE GUARDIAN (May 8, 2017).

81. United States v. Ramirez-Ramirez, 365 F. Supp. 2d 728, 732-33 (E.D. Va. 2005).

82. To help influence their prison designation, defendants can employ prison consultants to liaise with the BOP. *See* Jack Hitt, "Want to Do Less Time? A Prison Consultant Might Be Able to Help," N.Y. Times (June 7, 2022).

83. In re Manuel P., 215 Cal. App. 3d 48, 64 (Cal. Ct. App. 1989); *see* 18 U.S.C. § 4102 (the attorney general may "transfer offenders under a sentence of imprisonment . . . to the foreign countries of which they are citizens or nationals," and "make regulations for the proper implementation of such treaties").

The Transfer Act is "applicable only when a treaty providing for such a transfer is in force, and shall only be applicable to transfers of offenders to and from a foreign country pursuant to such a treaty."[84] It designates the attorney general to "act on behalf of the United States as the authority referred to in a treaty," and authorizes the attorney general to transfer and receive offenders and to issue implementing regulations.[85] It also sets forth the procedures by which offenders shall be received into custody and transferred to the authority of the other party to the treaty. "For example, the Transfer Act addresses transfer of juveniles and offenders on probation and parole; the length of sentence and conditions of confinement; verification of prisoner consent to transfer; and bars transfer while a direct appeal or collateral attack is pending."[86]

The Transfer Act does not, however, "provide substantive guidelines by which the Attorney General should exercise his discretion" in consideration of transfer applications,[87] meaning that the attorney general's discretion is constrained only by the terms of the relevant treaty.[88] The Transfer Act provides that the attorney general is authorized, but not required, "to transfer offenders . . . to the foreign countries of which they are citizens of nations."[89] As such, the attorney general's decision to grant or deny a transfer application is not subject to judicial review.[90]

International prison transfers are governed by the Bureau of Prisons' Treaty Transfer Program.[91] BOP policy requires all potential transferees from or to the United States to satisfy various threshold eligibility requirements, including: (i) a transfer treaty must exist between the United States and the offender's home country; (ii) the offender must be a citizen or national of the country to which he or she is seeking transfer; (iii) the offender, the sentencing country, and the receiving country must all consent to the transfer; and (iv) the offense must be recognized as a crime in both the sentencing and receiving country.[92]

Requests for transfers from the United States are subject to various layers of authorization. First, the warden of the prison where the inmate is held must verify that the inmate is eligible for transfer. Second, the warden's determination will then be reviewed by the BOP's Central Office and the DOJ.[93] If the DOJ approves the transfer request, the relevant nation will be notified and asked if it consents to the transfer. If the requested nation consents, the

---

84. 18 U.S.C. § 4100(a). The word "transfer" is defined to mean "a transfer of an individual for the purpose of the execution in one country of a sentence imposed by the courts of another." 18 U.S.C. § 4101(j).

85. *Id.* §§ 4102(1)–(4).

86. Sluss v. U.S. Dep't of Justice, 898 F.3d 1242, 1250–51 (D.C. Cir. 2018).

87. Scalise v. Thornburgh, 891 F.2d 640, 645 (7th Cir. 1989).

88. 18 U.S.C. § 4100(a).

89. 18 U.S.C. §§ 4102(1), (3).

90. Yosef v. Killian, 646 F. Supp. 2d 499, 508–09 (N.D.N.Y. 2009); *see also* Scalise, 891 F.2d at 648–49; Bagguley v. Bush, 953 F.2d at 660, 662 (D.C. Cir. 1991); Coleman v. Reno, 91 F. Supp. 2d 130, 132 (D.D.C. 2000).

91. 28 CFR § 0.96b. BOP is part of the DOJ and thus under the attorney general's ultimate oversight.

92. BOP Program Statement on Transfer of Offenders To or From Foreign Countries (Apr. 10, 2015), at 4.

93. 28 CFR § 527.45.

DOJ will arrange for a hearing before a U.S. magistrate judge to confirm that the prisoner does in fact consent to the transfer.[94] Once consent is verified, the DOJ and BOP will coordinate to effectuate the transfer. Inmates who are denied transfer to their home countries by a U.S. government official may reapply for transfer no earlier than two years after the denial (subject to certain exceptions). An inmate who was approved for the transfer by the United States but denied treaty transfer by his home country may not reapply through the BOP but must instead address the denial directly with the government of the foreign country.[95]

When an inmate is transferred to the US, their release date and any period of post-incarceration supervised release will be determined by the United States Parole Commission.[96] The inmate will then serve their sentence as if they were convicted in a U.S. district court of a similar offense.[97]

1. The Convention on the Transfer of Sentenced Persons

The 1983 Convention on the Transfer of Sentenced Persons is an international treaty governing the transfer of prisoners between member nations, which include both the United States and the United Kingdom.[98] The Convention provides that an individual incarcerated in one country may "express his interest" in a potential transfer either to the "sentencing State" or the "administering State," that is, the country to which transfer is sought. The actual transfer decision requires the approval of both countries, in addition to the prisoner. After a country receiving a request for transfer is notified of the request, the Convention requires the country to promptly inform the other country of its decision. The Convention does not provide any guidelines or factors that either country must consider in determining whether a transfer is appropriate.[99]

To be eligible for transfer under the Convention, a sentenced person must, among other things, have at least six months of their sentence left to serve.[100] While this requirement can be waived in "exceptional cases," it generally means that a transfer will not be possible for offenders serving sentences of two years or less (due to the lengthy review process that must first occur within the transferring state).

III. SENTENCE REDUCTIONS IN THE UNITED STATES

The Sentencing Reform Act (SRA) of 1984 eliminated parole in the federal criminal justice system. Prior to this change, federal law provided that "any prisoner, serving a sentence of five years or longer, who is not earlier released . . ., shall be released on parole after having

94. *Id.* at § 527.46(c).

95. BOP Program Statement on Transfer of Offenders To or From Foreign Countries (Apr. 10, 2015), at 9.

96. 18 U.S.C. § 4106A(b)(1)(A); Gomez v. U.S. Parole Comm'n, 829 F.3d 398 (5th Cir. 2016).

97. United States v. Sosa-Sauceda, 260 F. App'x 589, 592 (4th Cir. 2008).

98. Council of Europe, Convention on the Transfer of Sentenced Persons (ETS No. 112), *available at* https://www.coe.int/en/web/conventions/full-list?module=signatures-by-treaty&treatynum=112.

99. Qadar v. Mayorkas, 18-cv-06817 (S.D.N.Y. Mar. 24, 2021).

100. Convention on the Transfer of Sentenced Persons (ETS No. 112), Art. 3.

served two-thirds of each consecutive term or terms [of imprisonment]" so long as he has not "seriously or frequently violated [prison] rules and regulations."[101] Prisoners serving terms of more than one but less than five years were eligible for parole after serving one-third of their total term.[102]

Since the SRA became effective in 1987, inmates can generally only secure early release under the "good time credit" provisions of 18 U.S.C. Section 3624. Section 3624(b) provides that "a prisoner who is serving a term of imprisonment of more than 1 year [other than a life sentence], may receive credit toward the service of the prisoner's sentence of up to 54 days for each year of the prisoner's sentence imposed by the court, subject to determination by the [BOP] that, during that year, the prisoner has displayed exemplary compliance with institutional disciplinary regulations." The effect of this provision is to allow the BOP to lop off up to fifteen percent of a prisoner's sentence as an incentive for good behavior while incarcerated.

But importantly, this allowance is only given to inmates serving sentences of more than one year. This means that a defendant sentenced to exactly one year will need to serve the entire term, while a defendant sentenced to 366 days will likely only spend roughly ten and half months behind bars. For this reason, "year and a day" sentences are routinely imposed, especially in white-collar crime cases or in any other case where a full year in prison is deemed too harsh.

A. Sentence Reductions under Rule 35(b)

5K letters are not the only way those who cooperate with the government can receive sentencing credit. Another, though less often used, route to a departure is Federal Rule of Criminal Procedure 35(b), which permits a court, upon the government's motion, to impose a new, reduced sentence on account of a defendant's cooperation *after* he or she has already been sentenced. Instead of presenting courts a general opportunity for leniency, the effect of this rule is to confer an "entitlement on the government" that allows it to obtain "valuable assistance" and then ask a sentencing court to reduce the defendant's sentence as "compensation" for that assistance.[103]

To encourage timely cooperation, Rule 35(b) provides a general rule that a defendant is only eligible for a departure based on the provision of "substantial assistance" to the government in a case against another person within one year of his or her original sentencing. However, the rule also provides that the government can move for a 35(b) departure after this one-year deadline if the defendant's cooperation involved (i) "information not known to the defendant until one year or more after sentencing," (ii) information provided within one year that "did not become useful to the government until more than one year after sentencing," or (iii) if the defendant could not have "reasonably anticipated" that the information would be useful until more than a year after sentencing.

---

101. 18 U.S.C. § 4206(d) (repealed).

102. 18 U.S.C. § 4205(a) (repealed).

103. United States v. Shelby, 584 F.3d 743, 745 (7th Cir. 2009).

Compared with 5K letters, Rule 35(b) motions are far rarer, tend to be concentrated in particular jurisdictions (e.g., the Eastern District of Virginia and Southern District of Florida), and usually involve drug trafficking and firearms offenses.[104]

IV. SENTENCING PROCEDURES IN THE UNITED KINGDOM

Since December 2020, sentencing procedures in the United Kingdom have been governed by the Criminal Procedure Rules and the Sentencing Act (SA) 2020, with Parts 2 to 13 of this law making up the so-called "Sentencing Code."

After a defendant has pleaded guilty or been convicted after trial, the Crown Court has the option of imposing sentence immediately. But especially in complex financial crime cases, sentencing will often be adjourned for up to six months to permit the probation service time to create a presentence report (PSR).[105] In contrast, PSRs are always mandatory in the United States and sentencing always takes place in a stand-alone hearing after a conviction has been obtained. The SA also permits presentence reports to be given orally in open court in certain situations, whereas PSRs in the United States are always provided to the parties and the court confidentially and in writing.[106]

At the sentencing hearing, the prosecutor will summarize the prosecution case (if sentencing takes place after a guilty plea), identify any offense that the prosecutor proposes should be taken into consideration in sentencing, disclose any previous convictions by the defendant, provide statements (if any) from victims, and identify applicable sentencing guidelines and any aggravating and mitigating factors affecting the defendant's culpability.[107] Just as sentencing memoranda are provided to district court judges in the United States, both sides in complex financial crime cases in the United Kingdom will generally provide written submissions to the court in a "Note on Sentence." Before passing sentence, the court must give the defendant an opportunity to make representations and introduce evidence relevant to mitigation.

Where there is a dispute as to the factual basis on which sentencing should proceed, the prosecution can present evidence in support of its position in a so-called "Newton hearing" (named after *R v. Newton* [1982] 77 CA 13). Newton hearings are only held if the defense, in mitigation, departs from the facts as opened by the prosecution in a manner that is material to the central issue and which is capable of belief, that is, it is not so manifestly absurd or implausible that it would be a waste of the court's time to hear evidence and the departure is substantial and, if accepted, is likely to affect sentence.[108]

---

104. U.S. Sentencing Commission, *The Use of Federal Criminal Procedure 35(b)* (Jan. 2016) at 9–12, *available at* https://www.ussc.gov/sites/default/files/pdf/research-and-publications/research-publications/2016/Rule35b.pdf.

105. CrimPR 25.16(2); SA, s. 30(2).

106. SA, ss. 31(4)–(5).

107. CrimPR 25.16(3).

108. R v. Hawkins [1985] 7 Cr. App. R. (S) 351; R v. Underwood [2004] EWCA Crim 2256.

When the court has taken into account all the relevant evidence, information, and PSR (if any), the court must pass sentence at the earliest opportunity and give an explanation of the reasons underlying the specific sentence imposed.[109] Custodial sentences in the United Kingdom generally begin immediately following the sentencing hearing (even if the defendant was previously granted bail); in most financial crime cases in the United States, the defendant is given a date (usually at least ninety days from sentencing) to "self-report" to a BOP-designated prison. After a sentence is imposed by the Crown Court or magistrates' court, the defendant will be handcuffed and transferred to a temporary reception prison before being transferred to a permanent location for the remainder of his or her sentence.

A. Exercise of the Crown Court's Discretion when Imposing Sentence

The Crown Court has the discretion to impose a range of possible sentences, from a custodial sentence, to a fine only, to a conditional or absolute discharge. Just as district courts in the United States must consider the Section 3553(a) factors, a Crown Court's sentencing decision must be made with regard to the overall purposes of sentencing—that is, the punishment of offenders, the reduction of crime and deterrence, rehabilitation of offenders, protection of the public, and the making of reparation by offenders to their victims.[110] The Crown Court must also adhere to the "totality principle," which requires imposition of a sentence that is proportionate to the overall seriousness and circumstances of the offense.

Sentences must also follow any applicable sentencing guideline established by the Sentencing Council for England and Wales (SC) (or its predecessor, the Sentencing Guidelines Council), "unless the court is satisfied that it would be contrary to the interests of justice to do so."[111] Following the same basic model as the U.S. Sentencing Commission, the SC was created in 2010 to promote greater transparency and consistency in sentencing. It is made up of fourteen members drawn from members of the judiciary, academics, and solicitors and barristers in private practice. Judicial appointments to the SC are made by the lord chief justice with the agreement of the lord chancellor; nonjudicial appointments are made by the lord chancellor with the consent of the lord chief justice following an open competition.

1. Applying the Sentencing Guidelines

The SC's sentencing guidelines apply in much the same way as the federal sentencing guidelines in the United States in that they set forth a formula to identify a starting sentencing range and appropriate variances up and down to account for specific features of each individual offense and offender. The SC's "Definitive Guideline on Fraud, Bribery and Money Laundering Offences" (S-22) is the guideline most often implicated in financial crime cases. It specifies offense ranges for different types of offenses along with various categories within each offense range that reflect varying degrees of seriousness. Unlike the single Sentencing Table used in the United States, the U.K. guidelines use different sentencing tables based on the type of offense at issue.

---

109. CrimPR 25.16(7); SA, s. 52.

110. SA, s. 57(2).

111. SA, s. 59.

Harm A - Loss caused or intended		
Category 1	£500,000 or more	Starting point based on £1 million
Category 2	£100,000 – £500,000 or Risk of category 1 harm	Starting point based on £300,000
Category 3	£20,000 – £100,000 or Risk of category 2 harm	Starting point based on £50,000
Category 4	£5,000 – £20,000 or Risk of category 3 harm	Starting point based on £12,500
Category 5	Less than £5,000 or Risk of category 4 harm	Starting point based on £2,500
Risk of category 5 harm, move down the range within the category		

Figure 9.3 Offense categories based on loss.

To see how the U.K. guidelines operate in practice, below is a step-by-step calculation of the sentencing range for fraud under Section 1 of the Fraud Act 2006.

Step 1: Determine the offense category based on the culpability of the offender and the amount of harm caused. Culpability is assessed on a three-step scale—lesser culpability, medium culpability, and high culpability—based on the offender's role, the number of victims, the extent to which the crime was preplanned or extended over a long duration, and its level of sophistication.

Harm is initially assessed by the actual, intended, or risked loss as may arise from the offense and assigned a category in accordance with the table shown in figure 9.3.

The court should then take into account the level of harm caused to the victim(s) or others to determine whether it warrants the sentence being up to the corresponding point in the next category or further up the range of the initial category.

- **High impact: move up a category; if in category 1 move up the range**
  - Applied to crimes causing serious detrimental effect on the victim and where the victim is particularly vulnerable.
- **Medium impact: move upward within the category range**
  - Applied to crimes causing considerable detrimental effect on a victim who is not particularly vulnerable.
- **Lesser impact: no adjustment**
  - Applied to all situations not otherwise covered above.

Step 2: Use the appropriate starting point (as adjusted in step one) to reach a sentence within the category range in the table shown in figure 9.4. Where the value is larger or smaller than the amount on which the starting point is based, upward or downward adjustments may be made as appropriate.

After determining the correct starting point, the court must then identify whether there are additional factual elements that should result in an upward or downward adjustment. Factors that increase the seriousness of the offense include any previous convictions, steps taken to prevent the victim from reporting the crime to the prosecution or otherwise impede an

	Culpability		
Harm	A	B	C
Category 1 £500,000 or more	**Starting point** 7 years' custody	**Starting point** 5 years' custody	**Starting point** 3 years' custody
Starting point based on £1 million	**Category range** 5 – 8 years' custody	**Category range** 3 – 6 years' custody	**Category range** 18 months' – 4 years' custody
Category 2 £100,000 – £500,000	**Starting point** 5 years' custody	**Starting point** 3 years' custody	**Starting point** 18 months' custody
Starting point based on £300,000	**Category range** 3 – 6 years' custody	**Category range** 18 months' – 4 years' custody	**Category range** 26 weeks' – 3 years' custody
Category 3 £20,000 – £100,000	**Starting point** 3 years' custody	**Starting point** 18 months' custody	**Starting point** 26 weeks' custody
Starting point based on £50,000	**Category range** 18 months' – 4 years' custody	**Category range** 26 weeks' – 3 years' custody	**Category range** Medium level community order – 1 years' custody
Category 4 £5,000 – £20,000	**Starting point** 18 months' custody	**Starting point** 26 weeks' custody	**Starting point** Medium level community order
Starting point based on £12,500	**Category range** 26 weeks' – 3 years' custody	**Category range** Medium level community order – 1 year's custody	**Category range** Band B fine – High level community order
Category 5 Less than £5,000	**Starting point** 36 weeks' custody	**Starting point** Medium level community order	**Starting point** Band B fine
Starting point based on £2,500	**Category range** High level community order – 1 year's custody	**Category range** Band B fine – 26 weeks' custody	**Category range** Discharge – Medium level community order

Figure 9.4 Offense categories assessed by harm to the victim.

investigation. Factors that reduce seriousness or reflect personal mitigation include an absence of previous convictions, remorse, evidence of a good character, age and medical condition, status as primary caregiver for a dependent relative, and extent of cooperation with the investigation.

Step 3: apply reductions for a timely guilty plea under SA Section 73. Depending on what stage in the proceedings the defendant pleads guilty, the resulting reduction in sentence can be up to a maximum of one-third. The reduction in sentence for a guilty plea can also be taken into account by imposing one type of sentence instead of another (e.g., a community sentence rather than a custodial sentence).[112]

Step 4: apply appropriate reductions for any assistance given to the prosecution in accordance with a written agreement with prosecutors under SA section 74.

Step 5: if the offender has been convicted of more than one offense or is already serving another sentence, consider whether the total sentence is just and proportionate to the overall offending behavior.

Step 6: where the offense has resulted in loss or damage, the court must consider whether to make a confiscation or compensation order, or any other ancillary order that may be appropriate.

Step 7: consider whether to give credit to any time spent on bail under Section 240A of the Criminal Justice Act 2003 and SA Section 325.

2. *The "Custodial Sentence Threshold"*

Even where the sentencing guidelines suggest a term of imprisonment, a custodial sentence must not be imposed for a financial crime unless it passes the custodial sentence threshold under SA Section 230(2), which states: "The court must not pass a custodial sentence unless it is of the opinion that—(a) the offence, or (b) the combination of the offence and one or more offences associated with it, was so serious that neither a fine alone nor a community sentence can be justified for the offence." In forming its opinion under this provision, the court must take into account all information that is available to it about the circumstances of the offense or offenses, including the PSR and any aggravating or mitigating factors.

3. *Taking Other Offenses into Consideration*

In a unique feature of British criminal procedure, a *defendant* can ask for offenses that have not been the subject of any charge to be taken into consideration ("TIC'd") during sentencing. TIC'd offenses are crimes for which the defendant has not been prosecuted but for which he admits guilt solely for the purposes of sentencing on another, potentially unrelated crime. When a defendant makes a TIC request, the sentencing court may formally take the other admitted-to offense and pass a longer sentence than would be the case if the court were dealing only with the counts in the indictment.[113]

For the defendant, the TIC procedure may result in a higher sentence but provides the corollary benefit of precluding a later prosecution on the crimes admitted to under double

---

112. Sentencing Council, Reduction in Sentence for a Guilty Plea—Definitive Guideline (June 2017).

113. R v. Batchelor 1952 36 C.A.R. 64.

jeopardy principles. For the prosecution, the TIC procedure helps to expedite resolution of past offenses that might otherwise escape prosecution altogether.

Any offenses to be TIC'd must be listed on a schedule, which is then signed by the defendant. In court, the defendant must be asked personally (not through a representative) whether he or she has received the list and, if so, whether he or she admits each of the offenses and wishes them to be taken into consideration. Courts are directed to not allow offenses of a different nature than those in the indictment to be TIC'd.

V. IMPRISONMENT IN THE UNITED KINGDOM

When a defendant is given a custodial sentence, the sentence usually will begin on the day it is imposed; hence, even defendants who are out on bail during the pendency of their case will be taken into custody immediately after the sentencing hearing. Thus, when a custodial sentence is likely, defendants must make all necessary arrangements to prepare for a prison term before the sentencing hearing (whereas in the United States, this can usually be done in the period—usually ninety days—between the sentencing hearing and the surrender date).

The prison system in the United Kingdom is devolved, with separate agencies overseeing the prisons located in England and Wales, Scotland, and Northern Ireland. Prisons in England and Wales are operated by Her Majesty's Prison and Probation Service (HMPPS), an executive agency sponsored by the Ministry of Justice. As noted earlier in this chapter, the United Kingdom holds a far lower number of prisoners per capita (~132/100,000) than the United States does (~358/100,000). But the U.K.'s incarceration rate is much higher than other countries in Western Europe: Germany's rate per 100,000 is 76, the Netherlands' is 76, and France's is 105.[114] "The prison population of England and Wales has quadrupled in size between 1900 and 2018, with around half of this increase taking place since 1990."[115] The upward trend is expected to continue for the near future, with government estimates indicating a prison population in England and Wales of nearly 99,000 by 2026 (up from approximately 78,756 as of June 2021).[116]

There are a total of 117 prisons in England and Wales, with those holding male prisoners divided into four security categories:

- Category A: high-security prisons for prisoners posing a threat to the public or having a propensity for escape. There are currently eight Category A prisons, including the notorious HMP Belmarsh in southeast London that is reserved for high-profile, high-risk inmates. Belmarsh has a forty-eight cell High Security Unit (HSU) that is the most secure detention facility in the United Kingdom (causing it to be referred to as the "British version of Guantanamo Bay").[117]

---

114. Duncan Campbell, "Britain's Prisons are Becoming Ever More Like the Failed US System," The Guardian (Nov. 1, 2021).

115. Georgina Sturge, *UK Prison Population Statistics* at 5 (Oct. 29, 2021), *available at* https://researchbriefings.files.parliament.uk/documents/SN04334/SN04334.pdf.

116. *Id.* at 4.

117. Denise Winterman, "Belmarsh—Britain's Guantanamo Bay?," BBC News (Oct. 6, 2004).

- Category B: medium-security prisons designed for inmates who do not need to be subject to maximum security measures but for whom escape must still be made very difficult.
- Category C: roughly equivalent to low-security prisons in the United States; most prisoners in the United Kingdom are held in Category C prisons.
- Category D: prisons with minimal security that allow eligible prisoners to spend part of their day outside of the prison to work or pursue education.

A prisoner's initial categorization is reassessed every six months during the first four years of their sentence. For sentences longer than four years, a reassessment is made every year until the last two years of their sentence, when they are reassessed every six months. Unlike in the United States, there is no automatic minimum category applied to prisoners who are non-U.K. nationals.

VI. SENTENCE REDUCTIONS IN THE UNITED KINGDOM

Not only are the maximum statutory sentences and guidelines ranges for financial crimes materially lower in the United Kingdom than in the United States, but offenders in the United Kingdom usually only serve half of their prison sentences in custody. For all determinate prison sentences of twelve months or more, the offender will spend the first half in custody and the second half in the community "on license" (i.e., probation). Offenders who break any license conditions—by, for example, committing another crime—could be sent back to prison to serve the remainder of their sentence. For prison sentences of less than twelve months, the offender is normally released automatically halfway through.[118]

A. Alteration of Crown Court Sentence under the "Slip Rule"

Unless an appeal against sentence is pending (see the next section), the Crown Court may vary or rescind a sentence at any time within fifty-six days of the date the sentence was imposed.[119] Sentences are usually altered under this so-call "slip rule" when further information becomes available to the court after sentencing or when the court has made a legal or factual error.

The law governing use of the slip rule was summarized by the Court of Appeal in *R v. Warren* [2017] EWCA Crim 226 as follows:

> (1) Where an error occurs in the factual basis of sentence it should be pointed out to the court as soon as possible and consideration should be given to correcting it at the earliest opportunity, preferably by revisiting sentence on the same day rather than a subsequent day.
>
> (2) A judge should not use the slip rule simply because there is a change of mind about the nature or length of the sentence but the slip rule is available where the judge is persuaded that he had made a material error in the sentencing process whether of fact or law. . . .

---

118. Sentencing Council, *Determinate Prison Sentences* (2022), *available at* https://www.sentencingcouncil.org.uk/sentencing-and-the-council/types-of-sentence/determinate-prison-sentences/.

119. SA, s. 385.

(3) The sooner the slip rule is invoked in such a case the better . . . but there is a 56-day cut off in any event.

(4) A judge should not be unduly influenced by the prospect of a reference being made to change the sentence that he thought was right at the time by the mere threat of a review by the Attorney General. If the judge concludes that the sentence was not wrong in principle and was not unduly lenient, he should not change his mind simply because there is the possibility of a reference. . . .

B. Appealing against Sentence from the Crown Court

A defendant can appeal against a sentence imposed by the Crown Court through the same procedure available to challenge a conviction.[120] To have a sentence reviewed by the Court of Appeal, leave to appeal must be obtained within twenty-eight days of the sentencing hearing. If an appeal is permitted, the Court of Appeal may hear new evidence not presented during the original proceedings if it appears reliable, may afford any basis for allowing the appeal, is admissible under the normal evidentiary rules, and there is a reasonable explanation for why it was not disclosed to the Crown Court.[121]

An appeal against sentence can be made on the basis that the Crown Court made a legal error or imposed a sentence that was unreasonably excessive. If the Court of Appeal agrees that the Crown Court's sentence was in error, it can quash the sentence or substitute a new sentence "or make such order as they think appropriate for the case and as the court below had the power to pass or make when dealing with him for the offence." The Court of Appeal may not, however, impose a more severe sentence than that imposed by the Crown Court.[122]

Practice Note

The U.S. v. U.K. Guidelines

To see how the differences in how the U.S. and U.K. sentencing guidelines operate in practice, consider the respective sentencing ranges that would apply to a hypothetical defendant convicted at trial of one count of fraud causing a loss of $5 million. Assume this defendant acted alone and that his crime involved sophisticated methods and more than ten victims. Assume also that the defendant has no criminal history.

Sentencing Range in the United States

Under USSG Section 2B1.1(a) the base offense level for this offense would be seven (assuming the offense was wire fraud or another fraud offense with a statutory maximum of twenty years).

The $5 million loss then adds eighteen levels and the number of victims adds two; the sophistication of the crime adds another two. The total offense level would therefore be twenty-nine, which translates into a sentencing range of 87 to 108 months.

120. CrimPR, part 39.

121. CAA 1968, s. 23(1)(C).

122. CAA 1968, s. 11(3).

If this defendant received a sentence at the low end of this range, he could expect to serve at least seventy-four months (more than six years) in custody.

Sentencing Range in the United Kingdom

Because of its loss amount and sophistication, this crime would be a "high impact" Category 1 offense, with a starting sentencing range of between sixty and ninety-six months (five to eight years).

If the defendant was sentenced at the bottom of this range, he could expect to serve only thirty months (two and a half years) in custody—less than half of what he would serve if sentenced in the United States.

CHAPTER 9: KEY DISTINCTIONS

United States	United Kingdom
Incarceration rate of 358 per 100,000 people	Incarceration rate of 132 per 100,000 people
Average sentence of 147 months	Average sentence of 24.9 months
Sentencing judge not required to specify the amount of discount given in recognition of defendant's cooperation	Sentencing judge required to specify what sentence would have been without defendant's cooperation
Foreign inmates automatically assigned to a low-level prison	Inmates' nationality has no bearing on their security designation
Five levels of prison security, including administrative maximum (aka "supermax")	Four levels of prison security with no equivalent to the U.S. supermax
Federal prisoners can receive a maximum sentence reduction of 15% for "good time"	Prisoners generally only serve 50% of their sentences in custody
Presentence reports (PSRs) mandatory in all cases; sentencing always occurs in a standalone hearing usually 90 days after the verdict	PSRs not mandatory and sentencing can be determined on the same day as the verdict
White-collar criminals will usually be allowed to self-report to prison on a certain date following their sentencing hearing	Sentences often begin immediately after the sentencing hearing, even in financial crime cases
A defendant's other crimes may be factored into his or her sentence, but doing so will not result in a double jeopardy bar to later prosecution for such crimes	Defendant can request other crimes be taken into consideration by sentencing judge so as to secure double jeopardy protections for such crimes

10 | Pre- and Post-Conviction Asset Seizure and Restraint

Law enforcement aims to not only punish white-collar criminals with prison sentences and fines but also to deny them the ability to enjoy the proceeds of their criminal activity. To further the second component of this goal, U.S. and British authorities use various statutory remedies to force wrongdoers to forfeit illegally obtained assets. In simple terms, asset forfeiture is "something to which the right is lost by the commission of a crime of fault or the losing of something by way of penalty."[1]

The overarching purpose of asset forfeiture is to deprive criminals of the proceeds of their crimes, remove the financial incentives of criminal activity, and recover property that can be used to compensate victims. As a former AUSA put it,

> Asset forfeiture takes the profit out of crime. There is an element of simple justice in ensuring that a wrongdoer is deprived of the fruits of illegal acts, but there is also an element of general deterrence. . . . [C]onvicting the defendant, but not forfeiting the illegally gained benefits, gives others the impression that a life of crime is worth the risk.[2]

Similarly, the CPS has published an Asset Recovery Strategy that stresses the importance of asset recovery and directs CPS prosecutors to consider it in every case in which a defendant has financially benefited from criminal conduct.[3] According to the CPS, "Criminal profits are the life-blood of organised crime and professional fraudsters as these profits are often reinvested in further criminal activities. By taking away the profits that fund crime, we can help to disrupt the cycle that sustains these organisations and fraudsters."

I. ASSET FORFEITURE IN THE UNITED STATES

Asset forfeiture issues related to federal crimes are overseen by the DOJ's Money Laundering and Asset Recovery Section (MLARS). Through the Asset Forfeiture Program (AFP), the MLARS works in conjunction with other federal, state, and local law enforcement agencies

1. Black's Law Dictionary at 332 (Abridged Fifth Edition).

2. Stefan Cassella, *Overview of Asset Forfeiture Law in the United States*, U.S. Attorneys' Bulletin 8 (November 2007).

3. Crown Prosecution Service (CPS), *Proceeds of Crime* (Dec. 19, 2019), *available at* https://www.cps.gov.uk/legal-guidance/proceeds-crime.

throughout the country to promote the use of asset forfeiture as a tool to "deter, disrupt, and dismantle criminal enterprises."[4] There are three types of forfeiture: criminal, civil, and administrative. To ensure that a defendant cannot move potentially forfeitable assets beyond the reach of the government, federal law allows prosecutors to seek court orders restraining assets prior to trial or conviction.

The scope of assets that are subject to forfeiture is extremely broad: for most felonies, forfeiture automatically extends to any property "constituting or derived from" the proceeds of the crime and any property "used, or intended to be used, in any manner or part, to commit, or to facilitate" the crime.[5] For forfeiture purposes, "proceeds" constitute any property the wrongdoer would not have obtained but for the crime, including appreciation in value of property purchased with such proceeds.[6] The term "property" is also defined broadly and includes "real property . . . tangible and intangible personal property, including rights, privileges, interests, claims, and securities."[7]

Moreover, under the Comprehensive Forfeiture Act (CFA) (21 U.S.C. § 853), legal title to forfeitable property is considered to automatically vest in the United States government immediately "upon the commission of the act giving rise to forfeiture."[8] As the Supreme Court explained in *United States v. Stowell*, as soon as the owner of forfeitable assets committed the illegal act, the forfeiture provisions take effect, "and (though needing judicial condemnation to perfect it) operate[] from that time as a statutory conveyance to the United States of all the right, title and interest then remaining in the [owner]; and was as valid and effectual, against all the world, as a recorded deed."[9] In other words, the CFA "reflects the application of the long-recognized and lawful practice of vesting title to any forfeitable assets, in the United States, at the time of the criminal act giving rise to forfeiture."[10]

A. Preconviction Asset Restraints

Under 21 U.S.C. § 853(e)(1), prosecutors can ask district courts to "enter a restraining order or injunction, require the execution of a satisfactory performance bond, or take any other action to preserve the availability of property [subject to forfeiture]." DOJ policy specifies that such measures should be sought at the inception of all cases involving real or personal property that is subject to (i) a mortgage or other installment payment contract, (ii) undue diminution in value if not properly maintained, or (iii) pledged as security or transferred to another person.[11]

---

4. Department of Justice, *About the Asset Forfeiture Program, available* at https://www.justice.gov/afms/about-asset-forfeiture-program-afp.

5. 21 U.S.C. § 853(a); 18 U.S.C. § 981(a)(1)(C); 28 U.S.C. § 2461(c).

6. United States v. Real Property Located at 22 Santa Barbara Dr., 264 F.3d 860, 873 (9th Cir. 2001); United States v. Hawkey, 148 F.3d 920, 928 (8th Cir. 1998).

7. 21 U.S.C. § 853(b).

8. *Id.*, § 853(c).

9. 133 U.S. 1, 19 (1890).

10. Caplin Drysdale, Chartered v. United States, 491 U.S. 617, 627 (1989)

11. Craig Gaumer, *Criminal Forfeiture*, U.S. Attorneys' Bulletin 25 (November 2007).

If a restraining order is deemed insufficient to assure the availability of property for forfeiture, a district court may, upon the ex parte request of the government, issue a warrant authorizing the seizure of any personal property subject to forfeiture.[12]

In *United States v. Monsanto*, the Supreme Court rejected a lower court ruling that Section 853's pretrial restraining order provisions contain an implied exemption for assets that a defendant wishes to use to retain an attorney.[13] The Court wrote: "In enacting §853, Congress decided to give force to the old adage that 'crime does not pay.' We find no evidence that Congress intended to modify that nostrum to read, 'crime does not pay, except for attorney's fees.'"[14] Although a pretrial asset restraint can of course limit defendants' ability to hire the legal counsel of their choice, the Court saw no issue in terms of Fifth Amendment due process rights or the Sixth Amendment right to counsel: "neither the Fifth nor Sixth Amendment to the Constitution requires Congress to permit a defendant to use assets adjudged to be forfeitable to pay that defendant's legal fees."[15]

B. Criminal Forfeiture

As opposed to the in rem procedure used in civil forfeiture (discussed below), criminal forfeiture is an in personam proceeding against a defendant who has been convicted of an offense: criminal "forfeiture serves no remedial purpose, is designed to punish the offender, and cannot be imposed upon innocent owners." There is no single law providing for criminal forfeiture; rather, for each federal crime that authorizes criminal forfeiture, there is a separate forfeiture statute permitting the criminal forfeiture of property.[16] For forfeiture to be included in a criminal sentence, it must be authorized by a relevant statute and the indictment must have included a forfeiture notice.[17]

After a guilty plea or conviction in cases where the DOJ seeks forfeiture, the district court must determine what property is subject to forfeiture under the applicable statute.[18] "If the government seeks forfeiture of specific property, the court must determine whether

12. *Id.* at 26; 21 U.S.C. § 853(f).

13. 491 U.S. 600, 614 (1989).

14. *Id.*

15. *Id.*; *see also* Caplin Drysdale, 491 U.S. at 626 ("A defendant has no Sixth Amendment right to spend another person's money for services rendered by an attorney, even if those funds are the only way that defendant will be able to retain the attorney of his choice."); *id.* at 631 ("It is our view that there is a strong governmental interest in obtaining full recovery of all forfeitable assets, an interest that overrides any Sixth Amendment interest in permitting criminals to use assets adjudged forfeitable to pay for their defense.").

16. Heather J. Garretson, *Federal Criminal Forfeiture: A Royal Pain in the Assets*, 18 Rev. L. Soc. J. 48 (2008).

17. Fed. R. Crim. P. 7(c)(2) and 32.2.

18. Note that under Fed. R. Crim. P. 32.2(b)(4), either side may request that the jury, rather than the trial judge, act as factfinder with respect to forfeiture. In cases where such a request has been made, the jury can make the determination based on evidence already in the record or after a separate evidentiary hearing. Fed. R. Crim. P. 32.2(b)(1); *see also* United States v. Davis, 177 F. Supp. 2d 470, 483 (E.D. Va. 2001).

the government has established the requisite nexus between the property and the offense. If the government seeks a personal money judgment, the court must determine the amount of money that the defendant will be ordered to pay."[19] The court's determination of what, if any, property is subject to forfeiture may be based on evidence already in the record from the trial or as submitted in the sentencing proceeding.[20] The government has the burden of proof to establish the propriety of forfeiture by showing a nexus between the property and the crime by a preponderance of the evidence.[21]

The requisite nexus can be established, and the property forfeited, if the property was: "involved in" the underlying offense; is "traceable to" property that was involved in the offense; constitutes "proceeds" of the offense; or is "derived from" proceeds of the offense.[22] Monies paid to a defendant as a result of the scheme are "proceeds" subject to forfeiture, without regard to whether the victim received anything in return.[23]

Once the government has made such a showing, the district court must enter a preliminary order of forfeiture specifying the specific dollar amount or directing the forfeiture of specific property.[24] This order is a personal judgment against the defendant, meaning that the government may seek to satisfy it through forfeiture of "substitute assets"—legitimate assets owned by a defendant of equal value to the amount to be forfeited—if it can show that the defendant caused directly forfeitable property to be rendered unavailable.[25] The preliminary order authorizes the government to seize specific property subject to forfeiture and to conduct any discovery the court considers appropriate "in identifying, locating, or disposing of the property."[26] The issue of whether any innocent third party may have an interest in the forfeitable property is irrelevant at this stage.

At sentencing, the preliminary order of forfeiture becomes final and is incorporated into the judgment against the defendant. The court may include such conditions in the final forfeiture order that are "reasonably necessary to preserve the property's value pending an appeal."[27] The court also retains jurisdiction to amend forfeiture orders at any time to include property identified later, provided the property was included in the original order or is substitute property.[28]

---

19. Fed. R. Crim. P. 32.2.

20. United States v. Capoccia, 503 F.3d 103, 109–10 (2d Cir. 2007).

21. United States v. Garcia-Guizar, 160 F.3d 511, 518 (9th Cir. 1998); United States v. Schlesinger, 396 F. Supp. 2d 267, 271 (E.D.N.Y. 2005).

22. Capoccia, 503 F.3d at 117.

23. United States v. Webber, 536 F.3d 584, 603 (7th Cir. 2008) (explaining that since "[r]estitution is remedial in nature, and its goal is to restore the victim's loss," whereas forfeiture is punitive and "seeks to disgorge any profits that the offender realized from his illegal activity[,] . . . restitution is calculated based on the victim's loss, while forfeiture is based on the offender's gain")

24. Fed. R. Crim. P. 32.2(b)(2).

25. 21 U.S.C. § 853(p); 18 U.S.C. § 1963(m).

26. Fed. R. Crim. P. 32.2(b)(3).

27. *Id.*

28. *Id.*, 32.2(e)(2)(B).

Where a crime has been engaged in jointly by multiple co-conspirators, a single conspirator can be held liable for disgorgement of all the proceeds from the reasonably foreseeable acts of his or her co-conspirators. As recognized by the Second Circuit, "The extension of forfeiture to proceeds received by actors in concert with a defendant may be deemed to be based on the view that the proceeds of a crime jointly committed are within the possessory rights of each concerted actor, i.e. are 'acquired' jointly by them and distributed according to a joint decision."[29] While "property need not be personally or directly in the possession of the defendant, his assignees, or his co-conspirators in order to be subject to forfeiture," the property must have, at some point, been under the defendant's control or the control of his or her co-conspirators.[30] But, as discussed below, this does not mean that forfeiture may extend to a situation where the proceeds go directly to an innocent third party and are never possessed by the defendant.

1. *Third-Party Rights and Ancillary Proceedings*

If the preliminary forfeiture order consists of anything other than a money judgment against the defendant, prosecutors must address any interests third parties may have in the subject property.[31] To alert such third parties to the pending forfeiture, prosecutors are required to provide written notice in a manner that is reasonably expected to reach them.[32] If a third party files a petition asserting an interest in the forfeitable property, the district court will then conduct an ancillary proceeding.[33]

To succeed in arresting the forfeiture, a third party must submit a petition showing that he is the property's true owner of some or all of the property and that his interest is exempt from forfeiture. To do so, the third party bears the burden of proving by a preponderance of the evidence that he either (i) held a superior interest to the defendant at the time of the crime or (ii) that he was a bona fide purchaser for value of the property at a time when he did not know or have reason to know that it was tainted by illegality.

Before conducting a hearing on the petition, the court may permit the parties to conduct discovery in accordance with the Federal Rules of Civil Procedure.[34] At the close of discovery, either party may move for summary judgment. If multiple third-party petitions are filed in the same case, an order dismissing or granting one petition cannot be appealed until rulings are made on all the petitions, unless the court determines that there is no just reason for delay.[35]

When the ancillary proceeding is over, the court will enter a final order of forfeiture by amending the preliminary order as necessary to resolve any third-party rights. If no third-party petition is filed after reasonable notice, the preliminary forfeiture order simply becomes

29. United States v. Contorinis, 692 F.3d 136, 147 (2d Cir. 2012).

30. *Id.*

31. Fed. R. Crim. P. 32.2(c)(1); 21 U.S.C. § 853(n)(1); 18 U.S.C. § 1963(1)(l).

32. 21 U.S.C. § 853(n)(1).

33. Fed. R. Crim. P. 32.2(c)(1).

34. *Id.*, 32.2(c)(1)(B).

35. *Id.*, 32.2(c)(3).

the final order. A defendant cannot object to the entry of the final order on the ground that the property belongs, in whole or in part, to a codefendant or third party.[36]

2. *Criminal Forfeiture in Money Laundering Cases*

Criminal forfeiture based on money laundering violations differs in some respects from forfeiture based on fraud or some other offense. As noted, 18 U.S.C. Section 982(a)(1) subjects to forfeiture any property "involved in" a money laundering offense, or any property "traceable to such property." Thus, forfeiture based on a defendant's money laundering is permitted not only with respect to the laundered monies themselves, but also with respect to property that is used to commit or facilitate the offense, including money or other property that is commingled with or obtained in exchange for it.[37] "Facilitation occurs when the property makes the prohibited conduct less difficult or more or less free from obstruction or hindrance."[38] "Property 'traceable to' means property . . . the acquisition [of which] is attributable to the money laundering scheme rather than from money obtained from untainted sources."[39]

The broad scope of forfeiture in the money laundering context can be used to seize assets in a variety of situations—such as untainted money that a defendant used to conceal or disguise tainted funds, a legitimate business used as a front for money laundering, and real property, securities, and luxury items in which illicit funds were invested.[40] Money laundering forfeiture is thus able to reach essentially any assets that have a "substantial connection" to the laundering itself: "if the Government's theory of forfeiture is that the property was used to commit or facilitate the commission of a criminal offense, or was involved in the commission of a criminal offense, the Government shall establish that there was a substantial connection between the property and the offense."[41]

C. Civil Forfeiture

"Federal civil forfeiture law is a prosecutor's secret weapon, a valuable tool used to guarantee that wrongdoers do not reap the financial benefits of criminal activity or continue to use

36. Gaumer, *supra* note 11, at 29.

37. Schlesinger, 396 F. Supp. 2d at 271 (S.D.N.Y. 2005) (collecting cases); *see also* United States v. Reiner, 397 F. Supp. 2d 101, 112 (D. Me. 2005) (noting authority that "the standard for determining what funds are 'involved in' a money laundering offense is less demanding than that for establishing 'proceeds'" of a crime under § 981(a)(1)) (citing United States v. McGauley, 279 F.3d 62, 76–77 (1st Cir. 2002)).

38. United States v. Wyly, 193 F.3d 289, 302 (5th Cir. 1999).

39. United States v. Bornfield, 145 F.3d 1123, 1135 (10th Cir. 1998); *see also* United States v. Voigt, 89 F.3d 1050, 1084–87 (3d Cir.) ("We hold that the term 'traceable to' means exactly what it says," i.e., "that the property . . . has some nexus to the property 'involved in' the money laundering offense").

40. United States v. McGauley, 279 F.3d 62, 77 (1st Cir. 2002) (commingling of $55,000 of fraud proceeds with $190,000 of clean funds supported forfeiture of the entire amount); United States v. Baker, 227 F.3d 955 (7th Cir. 2000) (upholding forfeiture of entire business that was used to launder funds); In re Restrain of Bowman Gaskins Financial Group Accounts, 345 F. Supp. 2d 613, 621 (E.D. Va. 2004) (same).

41. 18 U.S.C. § 983(c)(3).

the tools of their illegal trade."[42] The courts have sanctioned civil forfeiture actions initiated in parallel to a related criminal prosecution and DOJ policy directs prosecutors to use civil forfeiture as a way to supplement criminal cases.[43]

In civil forfeiture, the DOJ brings a civil action against the property itself in a so-called in rem proceeding, meaning that it "is the property which is proceeded against, and . . . held guilty and condemned as though it were conscious instead of inanimate and insentient."[44] The civil forfeiture statute, 18 U.S.C. Section 981, calls for the forfeiture of the proceeds traceable to hundreds of felony offenses, including wire fraud and any offense constituting a "specified unlawful activity" under the money laundering statute (18 U.S.C. § 1956(c)(7)). From prosecutors' perspective, the primary advantage of civil versus criminal forfeiture is that there is no need for a criminal conviction; rather, property can be subject to civil forfeiture "even if the owner is acquitted of or never called to defend against criminal charges."[45]

To initiate a civil forfeiture action, the government simply files a verified complaint alleging that the property in question is subject to forfeiture under the applicable forfeiture statute (which is generally 18 U.S.C. § 981 in white-collar crime cases). To survive a motion to dismiss, a forfeiture complaint must state enough factual detail to "support a reasonable belief that the government will be able to meet its burden of proof at trial."[46]

Anyone who wishes to lay claim to some or all of the subject property must file a timely claim and then answer the forfeiture complaint.[47] Once such a claim is filed, the case proceeds to discovery and motion practice under the Federal Rules of Civil Procedure. If the case is not resolved on summary judgment, it will then proceed to a bench trial. At trial, the burden is initially on the government to establish, by a preponderance of the evidence, that there are reasonable grounds to believe there is a nexus between the defendant property and illegal conduct.[48] Once this burden is met, the onus then shifts to the claimant to affirmatively prove both their interest in the property and that they obtained it innocently.[49] Two types of innocent owner defenses are recognized: one applicable to persons who owned the property when the illegal activity was occurring and the other applicable to those who acquired their interest in the property after the illegal conduct occurred.

Individuals making a claim under the first defense must prove by a preponderance either that that they did not know of the illegal conduct or, upon learning of it, did all that reasonably could be expected, under the circumstances, to terminate the illegal use of the property.[50]

---

42. Craig Gaumer, *A Prosecutor's Secret Weapon: Federal Civil Forfeiture Law*, U.S. ATTORNEYS' BULLETIN 59 (November 2007).

43. United States v. Ursery, 518 U.S. 267–68 (1996).

44. Various Items of Personal Property v. United States, 282 U.S. 577, 581 (1931).

45. United States v. Property Identified as 3120 Banneker Dr., N.E., Washington, D.C., 691 F. Supp. 497, 499 (D.D.C. 1988); United States v. Dunn, 802 F.2d 646, 647 (2d Cir. 1986).

46. Fed. R. Civ. P. Supplemental Rule G(2)(f).

47. *Id.*, Supplemental rule G(5)(a); 18 U.S.C. § 983(a)(4)(B).

48. 18 U.S.C. § 983(c); Marine Midland Bank, N.A. v. United States, 11 F.3d 1119, 1126 (2d Cir. 1993).

49. 18 U.S.C. § 983(d)(1); United States v. Parcel of Property, 337 F.3d 225, 229–30 (2d Cir. 2003).

50. 18 U.S.C. § 983(d)(2).

To succeed under the second defense, claimants must show that they qualify as a bona fide purchaser for value of the property and that, at the time they acquired it, did not know and were reasonably without cause to believe that the property was subject to forfeiture.[51]

If no claimant steps forward or the claimants that do fail to establish one of the innocent owner defenses, the court will enter judgment for the government and clear title to the property will pass to the United States government.

Practice Note

The Civil Forfeiture Case against Jho Low

Jho Low is an Asian financier who has been accused by the DOJ of orchestrating a conspiracy among officials in Malaysia and the U.A.E. to embezzle more than $4.5 billion from 1Malaysia Development Berhad (1MDB), an investment development fund controlled by the Malaysian government. DOJ alleged that Low had laundered this money through banks in the United States, Switzerland, Singapore, and Luxembourg and used it to "engage in extravagant spending sprees, acquiring one-of-a-kind artwork and luxury real estate, gambling freely at casinos, and propping up his lavish lifestyle."[52] Low—called the "Asian Great Gatsby"—has been indicted for various bribery and money laundering offenses in the Eastern District of New York. As of June 2022, he has not been apprehended by U.S. authorities and is believed to be living as a fugitive abroad.[53]

Since the criminal case against Low will remain suspended until he is apprehended or otherwise submits to U.S. jurisdiction, the DOJ initiated a parallel civil forfeiture action in the Central District of California that targeted his assets based in the United States and elsewhere.[54] The property at issue included, among other things, a $415 million stake in music publisher EMI, a Bombardier jet, a penthouse apartment at One Columbus Circle (on the edge of New York's Central Park), a mansion in the so-called "Bird Streets" in the Hollywood Hills, several luxury properties in London, the Viceroy Hotel in Beverley Hills, an interest in New York's Park Lane Hotel, and a $120 million superyacht (the *Equanimity*). On October 30, 2019, Low and the DOJ entered into a Consent Judgement of Forfeiture pursuant to which Low and his family members agreed to forfeit all such assets without admitting liability on the underlying indictment.

D. Administrative Forfeiture

With respect to tainted property other than real property or personal property (not including cash) valued at under $500,000, law enforcement can seek its forfeiture through an administrative, rather than the judicial, process.[55] Administrative forfeiture begins when a federal

51. 18 U.S.C. § 983(d)(3).

52. Press Release, Department of Justice, U.S. Reaches Settlement to Recover More than $700 Million in Assets Allegedly Traceable to Corruption Involving Malaysian Sovereign Wealth Fund (Oct. 30, 2019).

53. Carmela Chirinos, "Meet Jho Low," FORTUNE (Mar. 7, 2022).

54. United States v. Any Rights, No. 16-civ-05364 (C.D. Ca.).

55. 19 U.S.C. § 1607 (setting maximum dollar value on administrative forfeiture of personal property); 18 U.S.C. § 985(a) (real property may not be forfeited administratively).

law enforcement agency seizes property discovery during an investigation (usually pursuant to a judicial warrant). Once the property is seized, the agency must give notice of its intent to forfeit it to anyone with a potential interest, as well as by publication in a newspaper.

If no one files a claim within the applicable time period, the agency concludes the matter by entering a declaration of forfeiture that has the same force and effect as a judicial forfeiture order. If someone does file a claim, the government must initiate a civil forfeiture claim in federal court.[56] Administrative forfeiture is therefore only possible when the forfeiture is uncontested.

E. International Forfeiture

The DOJ's ability to mandate forfeiture of illicit proceeds is not limited to assets located in the United States. To the contrary, the U.S. government has a number of MLATs and other types of cooperation agreements with foreign law enforcement that allows it to target overseas assets for civil or criminal forfeiture and for foreign governments to enforce their own forfeiture orders against assets in the United States.

For forfeiture requests emanating from the DOJ, prosecutors must first identify and locate foreign assets that may be subject to in rem or in personam forfeiture. Once forfeit assets are located, the MLARs can initiate a request to the relevant country to freeze or seize such property during or after the forfeiture process proceeds in the United States. Once a final forfeiture order has been issued by a district court, the DOJ can then send it to the foreign government for enforcement or repatriation of the assets.[57]

Foreign forfeiture requests made to the United States will be enforceable so long as they are based on a "violation of foreign law that would constitute a violation of an offense for which property could be forfeited under Federal law if the offense were committed in the United States."[58]

1. *Forfeiture of Correspondent Bank Accounts*

A correspondent bank account is an intermediary account established by one bank at another bank that is used to receive deposits from, make payments on behalf of, or handle other financial transactions. For example, a Swiss bank may have correspondent accounts with a U.S. bank in order to process U.S. dollar transactions. Through a provision of the PATRIOT Act, law enforcement is permitted to seek in rem forfeiture of funds held in correspondent bank accounts held by foreign banks in the United States as substitution for criminal funds held on deposit at banks in foreign countries.[59] For example, if tainted funds are known to be held in an account with a Chinese bank, the DOJ can seek an equivalent amount from the Chinese bank's U.S. correspondent account, even if the tainted funds never transited through such account and even if none of the funds in the correspondent account are traceable to

56. Cassella, *supra* note 2, at 13.

57. 28 U.S.C. § 1355(b).

58. 28 U.S.C. § 2467(a)(2)(A).

59. 18 U.S.C. § 981(k).

the underlying offense.[60] The underlying assumption of this statute is that the correspondent bank will make itself whole by seizing the forfeited amount from the wrongdoer's foreign deposit account.[61]

Neither the correspondent bank nor the foreign bank have standing to contest such an action except in two situations: (i) where the foreign bank is alleged to have been the wrongdoer in the acts giving rise to the forfeiture (§ 981(k)(4)(B)(ii)(I)) or (ii) where the foreign bank establishes by a preponderance of the evidence that, prior to the seizure/restraint of funds, the wrongdoer had fully closed his or her account or withdrawn all tainted funds (§ 981(k)(B)(ii)(II)).

II. ASSET CONFISCATION IN THE UNITED KINGDOM

Asset forfeiture is generally referred to as "confiscation" in the United Kingdom and is principally governed by the Proceeds of Crime Act (POCA) 2002. Like U.S. federal law, POCA creates both civil and criminal confiscation mechanisms.

A. Preconviction Asset Restraints

Prosecutors can make an application to the Crown Court for a preconviction restraint order under POCA section 41. Restraint orders have the effect of freezing property anywhere in the world with the aim of preserving it for any eventual confiscation order; such orders can be made against either a criminal defendant or a person merely under investigation (along with any other person holding property potentially subject to confiscation). Restraint orders can be sought only when at least one of five conditions is satisfied:

1. A criminal investigation has begun in England and Wales and there are reasonable grounds to suspect that the alleged offender has obtained financial benefits from the alleged criminal conduct.
2. Criminal proceedings have begun and there is reasonable cause to believe the defendant has obtained financial benefits from the alleged criminal conduct.
3. The prosecutor has applied or is likely to apply to the Crown Court to make or reconsider a confiscation order or make a confiscation order when the defendant has absconded from the jurisdiction.
4. The prosecutor has applied or is likely to apply to the Crown Court to reconsider a previously ordered benefit amount.
5. The prosecutor has applied or is likely to apply to the Crown Court to reconsider a previously ordered benefit amount.[62]

---

60. *Id.*, § 981(k)(2).

61. United States v. Funds on Deposit in Account No. 890-00571713, 487 F.3d 8 (1st Cir. 2007).

62. Proceeds of Crimes Act (POCA), s. 40.

Regardless of which of these conditions is satisfied, prosecutors must also be able to show there is a real risk that assets may be dissipated if a restraint order is not made.[63] Where the amount the defendant has benefited from as a result of particular criminal conduct exceeds the value of all his or her assets or the lifestyle provisions are triggered, it will often be appropriate to restrain the defendant from dealing with all of his or her assets. Any person who holds assets jointly with the defendant may be specifically restrained from dealing with those jointly held assets. The recipient of a tainted gift may be restrained from dealing with any realizable property they hold up to the current value of the gift.[64]

At the court's discretion, a restraint order may be made subject to exceptions for reasonable legal expenses unrelated to the offense under investigation, reasonable living expenses, or for the purpose of enabling the person to carry on any trade or business.[65]

B. Confiscation Orders under the Proceeds of Crimes Act Section 6

POCA Section 6 provides for confiscation orders after a defendant has been convicted or committed to be sentenced in Crown Court. The court must make a confiscation order if it is asked to do so by the prosecutor or if the court believes "it is appropriate to do so" on its own evaluation of the case.[66] Confiscation issues are handled by a specialist unit within the CPS, CPS Proceeds of Crime (CPSPOC).

A prosecutor seeking a Section 6 order must provide the court a statement of relevant information tying the assets to the defendant or the criminal offense; if the prosecutor believes the defendant has a "criminal lifestyle" the statement must include evidence of such a lifestyle.[67] The court may then order the defendant to indicate the extent to which he or she accepts the prosecutions' statements and provide evidence related to any matters that he or she contests.[68] If the defendant fails to do so without reasonable excuse, the court "may draw such inference as appropriate."[69] Where a third party is believed to have an interest in the defendant's property, the court can also order such third party to provide any relevant information.[70]

After receiving the parties' submissions, the court must hold a hearing to determine whether the defendant has a criminal lifestyle (as defined by POCA Section 75) on a balance of probabilities. If the defendant is found to have a criminal lifestyle, the court must decide the extent to which the defendant has benefited from his or her criminal conduct generally. If the defendant does not have a criminal lifestyle, the court must decide whether

63. Jennings v. CPS [2005] 4 All ER 391.

64. Crown Prosecution Service, *Proceeds of Crime* (Dec. 19, 2019), *available at* https://www.cps.gov.uk/legal-guidance/proceeds-crime.

65. POCA, s. 41(3); Luckhurst and Golding [2020] EWCA Crim 1579.

66. POCA, s. 6(3).

67. *Id.*, s. 16.

68. *Id.*, s. 17.

69. *Id.*, s. 18.

70. *Id.*, s. 18A.

he or she has benefited from the particular crime at issue.[71] If the defendant has benefited from the conduct, the court must include a confiscation order as part of his or her sentence, requiring that the defendant pay the "recoverable amount," to the extent that it would not be disproportionate to do so.[72]

The recoverable amount is the amount of illicit benefit the defendant received, unless he or she can show that the available amount is less, in which case the recoverable amount is the "available amount" or a nominal amount if the available amount is zero.[73] If the defendant has a criminal lifestyle, the court is permitted to make the following assumptions when calculating the recoverable amount: any property transferred to the defendant within six years of the defendant's conviction is considered a result of such lifestyle; any property held by the defendant on the date of his or her conviction is the result of criminal conduct; any expenditure met by the defendant within six years of being criminally charged was met with illegally obtained property.[74]

The available amount is calculated by adding two data points: (i) the total value of all "free property" held by the defendant less all "obligations [to creditors or other third parties] which have priority" at the time of the confiscation order; and (ii) the value of all "tainted gifts"—that is, transfers of tainted property—made by the defendant to third parties.[75] For this purpose, a "gift" is considered to be any property transfer for consideration of significantly less value than the property's actual market value at the time of transfer.[76] "Realizable property" is any "free property" held by the defendant or a recipient of a tainted gift, regardless of whether it is traceable to the offense of conviction and regardless of whether it is located in the United Kingdom or elsewhere.[77]

To calculate the value of property for confiscation purposes, the court will use the market value at the time the property was obtained or the date of the confiscation hearing (whichever is greater).

Where it appears to the court that an innocent third party holds an interest in property that will likely be covered by a confiscation order, confiscation may proceed against the defendant's interest only after the third party has been given a reasonable opportunity to make his or her own representations.[78]

Criminal confiscation under Section 6 is only available with respect to the offenses listed in POCA Schedule 2, which include money laundering but not other financial crimes like fraud and bribery.

71. *Id.*, ss. 6(4)(b), (c), 8.

72. *Id.*, s. 6(5).

73. *Id.*, s. 7(2)(a).

74. A defendant will be considered to have a criminal lifestyle if he has committed certain drug-related offenses or if the offense of conviction constitutes "conduct forming part of a course of criminal activity" or was committed over a period of at least six months. POCA, s. 75.

75. *Id.*, s. 9.

76. *Id.*, s. 78(1).

77. *Id.*, ss. 83, 84.

78. *Id.*, s. 10.

1. Satisfying the Confiscation Order

Unless the defendant can establish an inability to do so, the full amount of a confiscation order must be paid on the day the order is made. If the defendant is not able to satisfy the order immediately, the Crown Court can set forth a payment deadline that is no later than three months from the confiscation hearing; this deadline can then be extended upon the defendant's request at the court's discretion.[79] If any amount is not paid by the relevant deadline, interest will accrue at a rate determined by Section 17 of the Judgments Act 1838.

When making the confiscation order, the court will also determine a default prison sentence that will apply if the defendant fails to pay without good reason.[80] Under Section 129 of the Sentencing Act 2020, the duration of the default term is determined by the confiscation amount: for orders up to £100,000, the default term is two years; orders up to £250,000 are subject to a term of three years; anything over £1 million results in a default sentence of ten years.

Confiscation orders are enforced by the magistrates' court in conjunction with the CPSPOC. Various enforcement tools are available, including payment orders on banks holding tainted funds (POCA, s. 67), seized property orders (POCA, s. 67A), and the appointment of an enforcement receiving. If any of the defendant's realizable property is located abroad, the CPSPOC can make an MLA request to the relevant foreign authorities to have the U.K. restraint or confiscation order registered and enforced in that other jurisdiction. If the assets are sold by the requested country, the money raised from that sale may be returned in whole or in part (subject to either treaty obligations or an asset sharing agreement) but the whole sum raised by the sale of those assets will be applied to the outstanding confiscation order.

C. Civil Recovery

The CPS Asset Recovery Strategy states: "Those committing organised crime and economic crime are careful not only to hide their assets but also their involvement in offences. If a criminal prosecution is not feasible, civil recovery may present an opportunity to deprive criminals of their profits." Like the civil forfeiture process in the United States, civil recovery is a form of conviction-less asset forfeiture that allows for the recovery of illegally obtained property through in rem civil proceedings before the High Court.[81] But whereas federal civil forfeiture is only available to the DOJ, a variety of U.K. law enforcement agencies—the CPS, SFO, NCA, FCA, and HMRC—can initiate civil recovery cases.

Civil recovery proceedings follow the Civil Procedure Rules and are subject to the civil standard of proof (balance of probabilities), meaning that prosecutors must establish that it is more likely than not that the target property represents the proceeds of unlawful conduct in the United Kingdom or abroad.[82] To make this showing, it is not necessary to prove the commission of a particular criminal offense by a particular person on a specific date.

79. *Id.*, s. 11.

80. *Id.*, s. 35.

81. *Id.*, s. 240.

82. *Id.*, s. 241.

Rather, it is sufficient that the property was obtained through offending of a particular type (e.g., fraud, bribery).[83] This cannot be done solely on the basis that the person holding the property has no identifiable lawful income to warrant their lifestyle. However, the absence of any evidence from the person to explain their lifestyle, or the giving of a false explanation, allows the court to infer that the source of the income was unlawful. As the action is against the property and not the person, the person who holds the assets that are the subject of the order might not be the person who carried out the unlawful conduct, and a civil recovery order is not a conviction or a sentence.[84]

Civil recovery actions are begun with law enforcement serving a claim form on the "person who the authority thinks holds recoverable property" and "any other person who the authority thinks holds associated property which the authority wishes to be subject to a recovery order, wherever domiciled, resident, or present."[85] Before or after serving the claim form, law enforcement may elect to apply to the magistrates' court ex parte for a property freezing order.[86] Freezing orders have the effect of prohibiting "any person to whose property the order applies from in any way dealing with the property."[87] The court will grant a freezing order if it is satisfied "that there is a good arguable case (a) that the property to which the application for the order relates, is or includes recoverable property, and (b) that, if any of it is not recoverable property, it is associated property."[88]

Civil recovery is pursued far less frequently in the United Kingdom than in the United States. Studies suggest, for instance, that, since 2000, the DOJ and Treasury Department have collectively recovered at least $45.7 billion in civil forfeiture revenue and, that of all the DOJ's forfeiture cases during this period, eighty-four percent were civil.[89] In comparison, the CPS had no civil recovery cases until 2016, when it recovered a total of £7 million; in the years since then, civil recovery has recovered an additional £39 million.[90] Compared to the United States, this civil recovery amount is a fraction of the amount the U.K. authorities obtained through criminal forfeiture over the same period. One likely reason behind this disparity is the fact that civil recovery, like all other civil litigation in the United Kingdom, follows the English costs rule (i.e., the loser must generally pay the other side's legal costs); in other words, law enforcement bears the risk of having to pay the legal fees incurred by the property owner if a civil recovery action is unsuccessful.

---

83. *Id.*, s. 242.

84. Attorney General's Guidance, Asset Recovery Powers for Prosecutors (Nov. 29, 2012).

85. POCA, s. 243.

86. *Id.*, s. 245A.

87. *Id.*

88. *Id.* "Associated property" is defined in POCA Section 245 to include interests in recoverable property or property held in common with recoverable property (e.g., real property owned as a tenancy in common).

89. Nick Sibilla, Congressman Introduces New Bill to Abolish Civil Forfeiture, FORBES (Dec. 22, 2020).

90. U.K. Home Office, Asset Recovery Statistical Bulletin: Financial Years Ending 2016 to 2021 (Sept. 9, 2021).

CHAPTER 10: KEY DISTINCTIONS

United States	United Kingdom
Legal title to forfeitable property is considered to automatically vest in the U.S. government upon commission of the underlying crime	Legal title will only vest in the U.K. government after confiscation proceedings have concluded
Co-conspirators can be held jointly and severally liable for disgorgement of all the proceeds for all the reasonably foreseeable acts of co-conspirators	Joint and several liability among co-conspirators not recognized
Law enforcement can seek forfeiture of substitute assets held in U.S. correspondent bank accounts	Law enforcement cannot seek confiscation of clean assets held in U.K. correspondent bank accounts
Amount subject to criminal forfeiture determined only by reference to the amount of criminal proceeds obtained	Amount subject to confiscation determined in part by the defendant's "available assets"
Criminal forfeiture available for most felonies	Criminal confiscation not available for fraud and bribery
Failure to satisfy a criminal forfeiture order can subject the defendant to a prison sentence only after contempt of court proceedings have been initiated	Failure to pay a confiscation order by the relevant deadline can automatically subject the defendant to a default prison sentence
Civil forfeiture routinely used by law enforcement	Civil recovery rarely used by law enforcement
Government not liable to pay legal costs of property owner if civil forfeiture action unsuccessful	Government must pay legal costs of property owner if civil recovery action unsuccessful

11 | Corporate Criminal Liability and Deferred Prosecution Agreements

White collar crime prosecutions against individual defendants will often run in parallel with enforcement actions against the corporate entities that employed them. Even though entities cannot, of course, be imprisoned, the mere possibility of charges can have severe monetary and reputational consequences.

The demise of U.S. accounting firm Arthur Andersen in 2002 is a good example of the potential "death sentence" indicted companies may face. Formerly one of the "big five" accountancies, Andersen was indicted by a grand jury in Houston, Texas, for one count of obstruction of justice in connection with a cover up of its work for Enron Corporation, the energy firm that spectacularly imploded in one of the largest-ever financial frauds.[1] Enron was a major Andersen client, generating annual fees in excess of $58 million, and a number of Andersen partners had joined Enron as senior officers and directors. By the fall of 2001, Enron and Andersen were alerted to SEC interest in Enron's accounting records and both firms understood that a regulatory action was highly probable. Even though Andersen was not itself initially under investigation, its partners saw that it would likely be implicated in whatever happened to its marquee client: as one partner wrote in an email on October 26th, "the problems are just beginning and we will be in the cross-hairs. The marketplace is going to keep the pressure on this and it's going to force the SEC to be tough."[2] Andersen received an SEC subpoena two weeks later.

Despite outside counsel's advice to implement a document retention policy, Andersen employees in its Houston office shredded close to two tons of records in the weeks leading up to the subpoena: internal records showed that the quantity of carted paper waste from this location jumped from a daily average of 500 pounds to 2,500 pounds between October 25 and November 8, when the subpoena was served. The next day, the Houston team was advised by email: "No more shredding. . . . We have been officially served for our documents."[3] Enron declared bankruptcy less than a month later.

On March 7, 2002, Andersen was indicted for obstructing an official proceeding of the SEC (18 U.S.C. § 1512(b)(2)) by knowingly, intentionally, and corruptly persuading its employees to shred Enron-related documents "in an effort to protect itself and its largest

---

1. *The Enron Scandal (2001)*, Int'l Banker (Sept. 29, 2021).

2. United States v. Arthur Andersen, LLP, 374 F.3d 281, 286 (5th Cir. 2004).

3. *Id.* at 286–87.

single account."[4] Andersen was convicted at trial just three months later; the firm was subsequently ordered to pay a fine of $500,000, serve five years' probation, and, most importantly, to entirely stop auditing public companies (which in effect shut down its business). Approximately 28,000 people lost their jobs at the company in the United States alone.[5]

After the conviction was upheld by the Fifth Circuit Court of Appeals, Andersen was granted certiorari by the Supreme Court. The main issue on appeal was whether the district court had incorrectly instructed the jury on the meaning of "corruptly persuades" such that jurors did not need to find any consciousness of wrongdoing in order to convict.[6] Reversing the Fifth Circuit, the Supreme Court found that the jury instructions had erroneously "diluted the meaning of 'corruptly' so that it covered innocent conduct."[7] The case was then remanded to the district court; rather than retry the case, the DOJ moved to dismiss the indictment. Despite its legal reversal of fortune, the damage of the earlier conviction was already fatal, and Andersen was never revived as a going concern.

Following widespread criticism that the DOJ's pursuit of Andersen had been misguided, even notwithstanding the faulty jury instruction, and caused disproportionate harm on innocent employees,[8] the policies governing criminal prosecutions of entities in the United States has developed substantially in the past fifteen years. As one commentator put it, "[T]he idea that corporate prosecutions are unjustifiably dangerous [after Andersen] has lived on and dominates academic discussions of corporate wrongdoing. . . . Following this torrid criticism, . . . the DOJ has embraced the use of DPAs [deferred prosecution agreements] as an alternative means of enforcing the criminal law against many large companies."[9] The advantages of this strategic shift are obvious: "[B]y using DPAs, the DOJ avoids the potential collateral consequences of indictment and conviction while obtaining structural reforms and the corporation's aid in prosecuting individual corporate officers."[10]

Today, the vast majority of corporate investigations are resolved before an indictment is filed through DPAs, nonprosecution agreements (NPAs), or plea agreements. Even fewer result in trials: out of 3,485 total corporate criminal prosecutions between 1992 and 2019, only 29 were tried to verdict, with the remainder (more than ninety-nine percent) resolved pretrial.[11]

In recent years, British prosecutors have begun to follow the DOJ's lead in seeking to resolve corporate criminal liability through negotiated settlements rather than indictments

4. *Id.* at 283.

5. Elizabeth K. Ainslie, *Indicting Corporations Revisited: Lessons of the Arthur Andersen Prosecution*, 43 Am. Crim. L. Rev. 107 (2006).

6. Arthur Andersen, LLP v. United States, 544 U.S. 696, 698 (2005).

7. *Id.* at 706.

8. Ainslie, *supra* note 5, at 117–18.

9. Gabriel Markoff, *Arthur Andersen and the Myth of the Corporate Death Penalty: Corporate Criminal Convictions in the Twenty-First Century*, 15 U. Penn. J. Bus. L. 797, 806–07 (2013).

10. *Id.* at 807.

11. Lev L. Dassin, et al., "Representing Corporations in United States Attorney's Office and DOJ Investigations," in Defending Corporations and Individuals in Government Investigations 224 (Fetterman & Goodman, eds., 2020).

(albeit on a much smaller scale since U.K. law makes it far more difficult for law enforcement to take action against entities, for the reasons discussed later in this chapter). Since 2015, the Serious Fraud Office (SFO) has secured a dozen DPAs and seems poised to continue to use and expand this enforcement tool for the foreseeable future.

I. CORPORATE CRIMINAL LIABILITY IN THE UNITED STATES—THE LEGAL FRAMEWORK

In its 1909 *New York Central & Hudson River Railroad* decision, the Supreme Court recognized for the first time that corporate entities can be criminally prosecuted and convicted for the acts of their agents under the respondeat superior principles traditionally applied to civil torts. The Court wrote: "[W]e see no good reason why corporations may not be held responsible for and charged with the knowledge and purposes of their agents, acting within the authority conferred upon them."[12] Acknowledging that "the great majority of business transactions in modern times are conducted" through corporations, the Court reasoned that giving "them immunity from all punishment because of the old and exploded doctrine that a corporation cannot commit a crime would virtually take away the only means of effectually" combating corporate wrongdoing.[13]

The ability of Congress to impose criminal liability on business entities for the acts or omission of its agents within the scope of their employment is now a well-entrenched feature of federal law.[14] While certain criminal statutes expressly create corporate liability (e.g., the Foreign Corrupt Practices Act (15 U.S.C. § 788dd-1)), in most instances, the federal criminal code is made applicable to corporations through a general provision that defines the words "person" and "whoever" to include "corporations, companies, associations, firms, partnerships, societies, and joint stock companies as well as individuals."[15]

A. Respondeat Superior

Although a corporation has no independent state of mind, as a general rule corporate entities can be held liable for the criminal acts of their employees if done on their behalf and within

12. 212 U.S. 481, 495–96 (1909).

13. *Id.*

14. United States v. Hilton Hotels Corporation, 467 F.2d 1000, 1004 (9th Cir. 1973) (collecting cases). Corporate criminal liability remains a controversial topic, however, with many legal commentators arguing that it should be abandoned by the courts altogether. The fundamental objection from this perspective is that corporate entities, as artificial legal creations, "cannot in any meaningful sense have mens rea or be 'guilty' of a criminal offense. Moral responsibility is reserved for persons who possess certain capabilities, which are a prerequisite of moral desert and criminal punishment. Since corporations do not possess these capabilities, they are not proper subjects of criminal liability." Sara Sun Beale, *The Development and Evolution of the U.S. Law of Corporate Criminal Liability* (Dec. 2013) at 11, *available at* https://papers.ssrn.com/sol3/papers.cfm?abstract_id=2375318.

15. 1 U.S.C. § 1.

the scope of the employees' authority.[16] The premise of this concept has been explained as follows:

> A corporation, itself, cannot attend a meeting or make decisions; it must act through agents, such as its officers, directors and employees. In order for a corporation to be responsible for the acts or statements of one of its agents it is not necessary that the corporation specifically authorize the agent to commit the act or make the statement. A corporation is legally bound by the acts and statements of its agents done or made within the scope of their employment or their apparent authority. Acts within the scope of employment are acts done on behalf of a corporation and directly related to the performance of the type of duties the employee has general authority to perform. Apparent authority is the authority which outsiders could reasonably assume that the agent would have, judging from his position with the company, the responsibilities previously entrusted to him, and the circumstances surrounding his past conduct.
>
> When the act of the agent is within the scope of his employment or his apparent authority, the corporation is held legally responsible for it, although what he did may be contrary to his actual instructions and may be unlawful.[17]

In determining whether such liability may attach, it is irrelevant whether the agent's acts advanced the interests of the employer. As the Second Circuit noted, "Presumably no tortious act by an agent redounds to the benefit of the principal where the latter is held responsible for the damage which results. Yet if this reasoning were followed no principal would ever be liable."[18]

The critical issue in the respondeat superior context is instead the bounds of an agent's actual or apparent authority and whether the criminal act fell within such bounds.[19] This relatively low standard provides federal prosecutors with broad discretion in deciding to pursue a criminal case against corporations. And the "ease with which a company can theoretically be held liable for its employees' misconduct means that companies confront at least the possibility of criminal liability in essentially any instance where business-related wrongdoing has occurred within the company's ranks."[20]

---

16. United States v. Ingredient Technology Corp., 698 F.2d 88, 99 (2d Cir. 1983); United States v. Demauro, 581 F.2d 50, 53 (2d Cir. 1978); Std. Oil Co. of Tex. v. United States, 307 F.2d 120, 127–28 (5th Cir. 1962).

17. United States v. American Radiator Standard Sanitary Corp., 433 F.2d 174, 204–05 (3d Cir. 1970); *see also* New York Central, 212 U.S. at 493–94 (holding that corporations can be held criminally responsible for acts an agent "has assumed to perform for the corporation when employing the corporate powers actually authorized").

18. J.C.B. Super Markets, Inc. v. United States, 530 F.2d 1119, 1122 (2d Cir. 1976).

19. *See, e.g.*, United States v. Ionia Management S.A., 555 F.3d 303, 309–11 (2d Cir. 2009); United States v. Potter, 463 F.3d 9, 25 (1st Cir. 2006); United States v. Sun-Diamond Growers of Cal., 138 F.3d 961, 970 (D.C. Cir. 1998).

20. Dassin et al., *supra* note 11, at 232–33.

B. The Collective Knowledge Principle

In *United States v. Bank of New England*, the First Circuit Court of Appeals confronted the defendant bank's conviction on thirty-one violations of the Currency Transaction Reporting Act (31 U.S.C. §§ 5311-22), which requires banks to report cash transactions of more than $10,000 to the Treasury Department.[21] At issue were a series of large check cashing transactions by a bank customer, James McDonough, at various branches in the Boston area. Despite each being above the Bank Secrecy Act's reporting threshold, the Bank of New England failed to notify the Treasury for any of McDonough's transactions; a grand jury subpoena to the bank and a criminal indictment followed soon after.

The jury found the bank liable on all counts. On appeal, it argued that its conviction was due to the district court judge's erroneous jury instruction on the definition of the terms "a pattern of illegal activity" and "willfully" as used in 31 U.S.C. Section 5322(b), which states: "A person willfully violating [a provision to Title 31] as part of a pattern of illegal activity involving transactions of more than $100,000 in a 12-month period shall be fined." The bank objected to the district court's instruction on the ground that it was impermissibly broad and failed to distinguish between a pattern of conduct by McDonough and a pattern of activity by the bank.[22]

The First Circuit rejected this claim, holding that while it was "technically correct" that the instruction failed to make this distinction, the bank's argument ignored "the rest of the charge in which the court repeatedly informed the jury that each defendant must be judged separately." In the panel's view, to "argue that the Bank must be divorced from McDonough is to ignore reality; McDonough made the withdrawals. The question for the jury was whether the Bank knowingly and willfully broke the law by failing to report them."[23]

With respect to the willfulness instruction, the bank argued that the trial judge had improperly conflated knowledge with intent so as to effectively relieve the government of its obligation to prove willfulness. The district court's instruction was: "Knowingly simply means voluntarily and intentionally. It's designed to exclude a failure that is done by mistake or accident, or for some other innocent reason. Willfully means voluntarily, intentionally, and with a specific intent to disregard, to disobey the law."[24] The judge also instructed that knowledge of individual employees acting within the scope of their employment is imputed to the employer: "if any employee knew that multiple checks would require the filing of reports, the bank knew it, provided the employee knew it within the scope of his employment." And further, that the bank's "knowledge is the sum of the knowledge of all of the employees. . . . So, if Employee A knows one facet of the currency reporting requirement, B knows another facet of it, and C a third facet of it, the bank knows them all."[25]

The bank contended that this "collective knowledge" concept was a misapplication of the law that essentially invited the jury to convict "for negligently maintaining a poor

21. 821 F.2d 844 (1st Cir. 1987).

22. *Id.* at 852.

23. *Id.* at 853.

24. *Id.* at 855.

25. *Id.*

communications network that prevented the consolidation of the information held by its various employees."[26] Rejecting this argument, the panel found that a collective knowledge instruction of the sort used here was "entirely appropriate in the context of corporate criminal liability."[27]

> The acts of a corporation are, after all, simply the acts of all of its employees operating within the scope of their employment. The law on corporate criminal liability reflects this. Similarly, the knowledge obtained by corporate employees acting within the scope of their employment is imputed to the corporation. Corporations compartmentalize knowledge, subdividing the elements of specific duties and operations into smaller components. The aggregate of those components constitutes the corporation's knowledge of a particular operation. It is irrelevant whether employees administering one component of an operation know the specific activities of employees administering another aspect of the operation.[28]

From this perspective, the panel found that the district court's instruction "was not only proper but necessary" and that the evidence clearly proved that the bank had collective knowledge of the CTRA requirements and collectively knew McDonough's transactions needed to be reported.[29]

The collective knowledge doctrine first recognized in *Bank of New England* is now widely followed, permitting the imposition of corporate criminal liability even when prosecutors cannot prove that any single employee had the necessary criminal intent.[30]

C. The Department of Justice's Principles of Corporate Prosecution

Although the DOJ has ample legal mechanisms to criminally charge corporations at its discretion, federal prosecutors' primary focus is on targeting the individuals most responsible for corporate misconduct. This focus translates into a general willingness to decline the prosecution of companies that self-disclose misconduct, cooperate with investigators, and implement remedial measures.

The DOJ's corporate prosecution policy is driven by a belief that concentrating "on wrongdoing by individuals from the very beginning of any investigation of corporate misconduct" helps accomplish three goals: (i) making it easier to identify the full extent of corporate

26. *Id.* at 856.

27. *Id.* (collecting cases).

28. *Id.*; *see also* United States v. T.I.M.E.-D.C., Inc., 381 F. Supp. 730, 738 (W.D. W.Va. 1974) ("[A] corporation cannot plead innocence by asserting that the information obtained by several employees was not acquired by any one individual who then would have comprehended its full import. Rather the corporation is considered to have acquired the collective knowledge of its employees and is held responsible for their failure to act accordingly.").

29. Bank of New England, 821 F.2d at 857.

30. *See, e.g.*, Steere Tank Lines, Inc. v. United States, 330 F.2d 719, 724 (5th Cir. 1963); United States v. Science Applications Intern. Corp., 653 F. Supp. 2d 87, 99 (D.D.C. 2009) ("It is both appropriate and equitable to conclude that a company's fraudulent intent may be inferred from all of the circumstantial evidence including the company's collective knowledge.").

misconduct, (ii) increasing the likelihood that those with relevant information will be identified and provide information about other individuals involved; and (iii) maximizing "the likelihood that the final resolution will include charges against culpable individuals and not just the corporation."[31]

Indeed, DOJ policy directs prosecutors to consider corporate and individual liability separately: "Prosecution of a corporation is not a substitute for the prosecution of criminally culpable individuals within or without the corporation. . . . Provable individual criminal culpability should be pursued, particularly if it relates to high-level corporate officers, even in the face of an offer of a corporate guilty plea or some other disposition of charges against the corporation."[32]

In keeping with guidelines originally drafted by then-Deputy Attorney General Eric Holder in 1999 (the so-called "Holder Memo"), in determining whether to bring charges against an entity, prosecutors must evaluate a number of factors including:

- The nature and seriousness of the offense
- The pervasiveness of wrongdoing within the corporation
- The entity's history of similar misconduct
- The entity's "timely and voluntary disclosure of wrongdoing" and its willingness to cooperate, "including as to potential wrongdoing by its agents"
- The effectiveness of its corporate compliance program at the time of the offense and at the time of the charging decision
- Any voluntary remedial actions taken since the wrongdoing
- "Collateral consequences, including whether there is disproportionate harm to shareholders, pension holders, employees, and others not proven personally culpable, as well as impact on the public arising from the prosecution"[33]

1. *Incentives For Entities to Self-Report and Cooperate*

In the same way as 5K Letters incentivize individual cooperators, the Holder Memo and subsequent amendments make clear that cooperation is a potential "mitigating factor" by which a corporation "can gain credit in a case that otherwise is appropriate for indictment and prosecution." In 2017, the DOJ announced its FCPA Corporate Enforcement Policy, which created a presumption that, absent pervasive wrongdoing or the involvement of senior managers, prosecutors will decline to prosecute a company that voluntarily discloses wrongdoing, fully cooperates in the investigation (including by making employees available for interviews), and swiftly remediates a foreign bribery offense.[34] Moreover, companies that self-report but are not eligible for a declination can still receive up to a fifty percent reduction

31. *Justice Manual* § 9-28.010.

32. *Id.* § 98-28.210.

33. *Id.* § 98-28.300.

34. Dassin et al., *supra* note 11, at 236.

from the applicable fine under the Sentencing Guidelines. In March 2018, this policy was extended to all criminal cases involving corporations, not just FCPA offenses.[35]

Although this policy provides that a company's failure to cooperate means only that it will lose mitigation credit, and not that it will be indicted, commentators have noted that in practice, this is a "distinction without a difference." As one law professor put it, "[T]o challenge the DOJ's theories, its interpretation of facts, or to raise valid and legitimate [legal] defenses is not to cooperate with the investigation—a key factor in DOJ's ultimate decision of whether to seek a criminal indictment against a company." Because of this, many corporations may "opt to disclose even ambiguous conduct to the DOJ and agree to whatever settlement terms the DOJ views proper (notwithstanding the salient fact that such conduct may not even [be unlawful]."[36]

Moreover, according to the DOJ's policy on Individual Accountability for Corporate Wrongdoing—better known as the "Yates Memo" after former Deputy Attorney General Sally Q. Yates—companies will be denied cooperation credit unless they "completely disclose to the [DOJ] all relevant facts about individual misconduct."[37] While intended to prevent executives from shielding themselves from liability through a corporate resolution, this policy has been criticized for placing overwhelming pressure on entities not only to decline to challenge law enforcement's allegations, but to gear internal investigations toward identifying evidence of their employees' personal guilt, even where it may not be clear that such guilt exists. As two prominent defense lawyers have observed, the Yates Memo "affect[s] the incentives of company counsel when conducting investigations" because it directs "prosecutors to judge corporate cooperation according to the nature and extent of incriminating information disclosed to the government." Consequently, they argued, "the Yates Memorandum may, in close cases, lead company counsel to overinterpret the facts, or find wrongdoing where the record is more consistent with innocent mistake or uncertainty."[38]

D. Deferred Prosecution Agreements in the United States

In a typical DPA with a corporate defendant, the entity will admit to a statement of facts, submit to the filing of criminal charges against it based on those facts, and agree to a forfeiture or fine and institute remedial measures. In exchange, the DOJ will agree to defer prosecution for

35. *Id.*

36. Mike Koehler, *The Façade of FCPA Enforcement*, 41 Geo. J. Int'l L. 907, 925–26 (2010); *see also* Joshua L. Ray, *The Continuing Façade of FCPA Enforcement*, 17 N.Y.U. J.L. & Bus. 547 (Summer 2021) (examining a corporate settlement of FCPA charges that were not legally or factually supported).

37. Memorandum from Sally Q. Yates, Deputy Att'y Gen., Dep't of Just., On Individual Accountability for Corporate Wrongdoing (Sept. 9, 2015).

38. Elkan Abramowitz & Jonathan Sack, *Deferred Prosecution Agreements in Decline? Enforcement Implications*, N.Y. L.J., Jan. 5, 2016, at 4; see also Aruna Viswanatha & Dave Michaels, "Flaws Emerge in Justice Department Strategy for Prosecuting Wall Street," Wall St. J., July 5, 2021 (quoting a former federal prosecutor as stating, "[t]he system of corporate cooperation creates such strong incentives for companies to assist the government with its investigations that it can lead to corporate counsel acting like deputized members of the Department of Justice rather than private defense lawyers").

a set period. Once the agreement's conditions are fulfilled, prosecutors will move to dismiss the charges with prejudice and enter a nolle prosequi with the court.[39]

If prosecutors determine that the entity has breached the DPA, the government may scrap the agreement and pursue the prosecution or simply seek additional penalties.[40]

In some cases, particularly those involving large multinational organizations, the DOJ will require a subsidiary to plead guilty as a condition of the parent entity's entry into a DPA. As part of the DPA entered into by Goldman Sachs in relation to its involvement in the 1MDB foreign bribery scandal, for example, the company agreed to a monetary penalty of $2.9 billion and to have one of its foreign subsidiaries (Goldman Malaysia) plead guilty in the Eastern District of New York.[41] The same tactic was used against Russian telecom firm Mobile TeleSystems PJSC (MTS) in connection with a foreign bribery offense in Uzbekistan. Like Goldman, MTS agreed to a large monetary penalty ($850 million) and a guilty plea by its Uzbek subsidiary, Kolorit Dizayn Ink LLC.[42]

Compared with the United Kingdom, the practice of using DPAs to resolve corporate criminal liability is far more prevalent in the United States: between 2000 and 2021, the DOJ entered into 608 such agreements; during that same period, U.K. authorities entered into just twelve.[43] While the DOJ's Principles of Corporate Prosecution do not explicitly make reference to the monetary benefits of corporate settlements, DPAs and NPAs have resulted in enormous payments to the Treasury. Since 2010, such agreements have garnered close to $64 billion for the U.S. government,[44] enough to fund the operations of the entire FBI—an agency with more than 35,000 employees—for nearly seven years.[45]

1. Deferred Prosecution Agreement Compliance Monitors

For particularly serious corporate violations, the DOJ can require the imposition of an independent monitor as one of the conditions specified in a DPA or other corporate settlement. According to the DOJ, "[a] monitor's primary responsibility is to assess and monitor a corporation's compliance with the terms of the agreement specifically designed to address and reduce the risk of recurrence of the corporation's misconduct, and not to further punitive goals."[46] DOJ policy states further that a "monitor should only be used where appropriate given the facts and circumstances of a particular matter. For example, it may be appropriate

39. "A nolle prosequi is a unilateral act by a prosecutor, which ends the pending proceedings without an acquittal and without placing the defendant in jeopardy." Roberts v. Babkiewicz, 582 F.3d 418, 420 (2d Cir. 2009). A nolle prosequi can be entered at any time before a jury verdict or guilty plea is entered.

40. United States v. HSBC Bank USA, N.A., 863 F.3d 125, 129 (2d Cir. 2017).

41. United States v. The Goldman Sachs Group, Inc., No. 20-cr-00437 (E.D.N.Y.).

42. United States v. Mobile Telesystems PJSC, No. 19-cr-00167 (S.D.N.Y.).

43. Gibson Dunn & Crutcher LLP, 2021 Year-End Update on Corporate Non-Prosecution Agreements and Deferred Prosecution Agreements (Feb. 3, 2022).

44. *Id.*

45. Federal Bureau of Investigation, FY 2020 Budget Request a Glance (2020).

46. Department of Justice, *Criminal Resource Manual* § 163.

to use a monitor where a company does not have an effective internal compliance program, or where it needs to establish necessary internal controls."[47]

Monitors are selected by the DOJ and, to serve their intended purpose, must be independent from the corporation and the government. Recognizing that neither the corporation nor the public benefits from employing a monitor whose role is too narrowly or broadly defined, the DOJ instructs its prosecutors to tailor the scope of a monitor's duties to the facts of each case.[48] "A monitor generally works closely with a corporation and communicates with a corporation on a regular basis in the course of his or her duties. The monitor must also have the discretion to communicate with the Government as he or she deems appropriate."[49] "If the corporation chooses not to adopt recommendations made by the monitor within a reasonable time, either the monitor or the corporation, or both, should report that fact to the Government, along with the corporation's reasons. The Government may consider this conduct when evaluating whether the corporation has fulfilled its obligations under the agreement."[50]

Although selected by prosecutors, a monitor's fees are paid by the target company. This can be a massive additional expense on top of the direct monetary penalties in the accompanying DPA, and monitors can act as an ongoing hinderance to a company's operations and efforts to move past its wrongdoing. As such, disputes between monitors and the company they are overseeing often arise over, for example, the scope of the monitors' role and access to company files. According to a May 2010 memorandum from Acting Deputy Attorney General Gary Grindler, the DOJ created procedures to address such conflicts. The Grindler Memo suggested that DPAs include provisions specifying the DOJ's role in overseeing a monitor's performance and costs. Grindler wrote:

> With respect to any monitor recommendation that the company considers unduly burdensome, impractical, unduly expensive, or otherwise inadvisable, the company need not adopt the recommendation immediately; instead, the company may propose in writing an alternative policy, procedure, or system designed to achieve the same objective or purpose. As to any recommendation on which the company and monitor ultimately do not agree, the views of the company and monitor shall promptly be brought to the attention of the [DOJ]. . . .
>
> At least annually, and more frequently if appropriate, representatives of the company and the Department will meet together to discuss the monitorship and any suggestion, comments, or improvements the company may wish to discuss with or propose to the Department, including with respect to the scope or costs of the monitorship.[51]

1. Deferred Prosecution Agreements and the Attorney-Client Privilege

Pursuant to DOJ charging policies in place between 1999 and 2008, the availability of DPAs was permitted to be conditioned in part on a corporate defendant's willingness to waive the attorney-client and work product protections. In other words, businesses were strongly

47. *Id.*

48. *Id.*

49. *Id.*

50. *Id.*

51. *Id.* § 166.

encouraged, if not required, to turn over privileged materials to the government in order to be eligible for a DPA and avoid prosecution. In response to widespread backlash against this policy, in 2008 the DOJ revised its corporate charging guidelines to provide that credit for cooperation would no longer depend on a corporation's waiver of these protections.[52]

In keeping with this policy, which remains in force today,

> credit for cooperation will not depend on the corporation's waiver of attorney-client privilege or work product protection, but rather on the disclosure of relevant facts. Corporations that disclose relevant facts may receive due credit for cooperation, regardless of whether they waive attorney-client privilege or work product protection in the process. Corporations that do not disclose relevant facts typically may not receive such credit, like any other defendant.[53]

2. *Deferred Prosecution Agreements and Corporate Witnesses*

A company's cooperation with a DOJ investigation will often involve making its employees available for interviews with the FBI and prosecutors, and DOJ policy explicitly allows prosecutors to consider the extent to which a company has done so when evaluating the appropriateness of a DPA. This dynamic has raised a variety of legal issues about how a company's cooperation efforts may interfere with the rights of its employees.

In *United States v. Stein*, for example, Judge Kaplan of the Southern District of New York reviewed the cooperation record of accounting firm KPMG.[54] In the early 2000s, KPMG and many of its employees were under criminal investigation for their role in promoting allegedly illegal tax shelters. Although KPMG had a long-standing policy of covering the legal fees of any employees charged with crimes as a result of their job, the DOJ threatened to consider such payments as a factor weighing in favor of indicting the firm. Prosecutors made the same threat regarding any failure by KPMG to make full disclosure to the government.[55]

In response to this pressure, KPMG changed its policies. With respect to paying its employees' legal fees, KPMG agreed to do so only up to $400,000 and only on the condition that the employee cooperated with prosecutors. "In other words, KPMG told its personnel that it would cut off payment of legal expenses of any employee who refused to talk to the government or who invoked the Fifth Amendment. And it made crystal clear that it would cut off any payments of legal fees to anyone who was indicted."[56] The government took full advantage of this policy change. "It sought interviews with many KPMG employees and encouraged KPMG to press the employees to cooperate [by disclosing] any personal criminal wrongdoing. When individuals balked, the prosecutors told KPMG. In each case, KPMG reiterated its threat to cut off payment of legal fees [or be fired] unless the government were

52. United States v. HSBC Bank USA, N.A., 12-CR-763 at *11, n.10 (E.D.N.Y. July 1, 2013).

53. Press Release, U.S. Department of Justice, Justice Department Revises Charging Guidelines for Prosecuting Corporate Fraud (Aug. 28, 2008), *available at* http://www.justice.gov/opa/pr/2008/August/08-odag-757.html.

54. 440 F. Supp. 2d 315 (S.D.N.Y. 2006).

55. *Id.* at 317.

56. *Id.* at 318.

satisfied with the individual's cooperation."[57] The DOJ thereafter secured proffers with nine KPMG employees who were subsequently indicted.

During pretrial proceedings, these employees argued that their statements were coerced in violation of their Fifth Amendment privilege against self-incrimination and moved to preclude prosecutors from using their statements and any derivative evidence at trial. Relying on the Supreme Court's decision in *Garrity v. New Jersey*, 385 U.S. 493 (1967), Judge Kaplan noted that "[i]t no longer may be doubted that economic coercion to secure a waiver of the privilege against self incrimination, where it is attributable to the government, violates the Fifth Amendment if the pressure is sufficient to 'deprive [the accused] of his free choice to admit, to deny, or to refuse to answer.'"[58]

From this starting point, Judge Kaplan ruled that the statements of two of the defendants had been improperly coerced. As to the first, the vice chair of the firm, the evidence indicated that he had rejected his attorney's advice and agreed to proffer in direct response to KPMG's explicit threat "to fire him if he did not fall into line."[59] The second employee testified that his decision to participate in a proffer was driven by his fear of KPMG cutting off payment of his legal fees.[60] The court ultimately concluded that the undue pressure place upon these individuals was attributable to the government:

> Many companies faced with allegations of wrongdoing are under intense pressure to avoid indictment, as an indictment—especially of a financial services firm—threatens to destroy the business regardless of whether the firm ultimately is convicted or acquitted. That is precisely what happened to Arthur Andersen Co., one of the world's largest accounting firms, which collapsed almost immediately after it was indicted—and the Supreme Court's eventual reversal of its conviction did not undo the damage. So any entity facing such catastrophic consequences must do whatever it can to avoid indictment.
>
> The DOJ and other federal agencies have capitalized on this, in part by altering the manner in which suspected corporate crime has been investigated, prosecuted, and, when proven, punished. . . . In cases involving vulnerable companies, the pressure exerted by [DOJ charging policies] and by the prosecutors who apply it inevitably sets in motion precisely what occurred here—the exertion of enormous economic power by the employer upon its employees to sacrifice their constitutional rights.
>
> In this case, the pressure that was exerted on the Moving Defendants was a product of intentional government action. The government brandished a big stick—it threatened to indict KPMG. And it held out a very large carrot. It offered KPMG the hope of avoiding the fate of Arthur Andersen if KPMG could deliver to the USAO employees who would talk, notwithstanding their constitutional right to remain silent, and strip those employees of economic means of defending themselves. In two instances, that pressure resulted in statements that otherwise would not have been made. . . . The coerced statements and their fruits must be suppressed.[61]

---

57. *Id.*

58. *Id.* at 326.

59. *Id.* at 330.

60. *Id.* at 332.

61. *Id.* at 337–38.

In a subsequent decision in the same case, the court addressed defendants' motion to dismiss the indictment on the ground that the DOJ had interfered with their Sixth Amendment right to counsel by pressuring KPMG to stop paying their legal fees so that it could maintain a cooperative posture with prosecutors in accordance with its DPA.[62] Again finding that KPMG's decision was a "direct consequence" of pressure put on the company by prosecutors, Judge Kaplan determined that the DOJ had undermined the fairness of the proceedings by improperly influencing the manner in which the defendants defended the case against them.[63] Granting the motions to dismiss, he wrote: "Justice is not done when the government uses the threat of indictment . . . to coerce companies into depriving their present and even former employees defending themselves against criminal charges in a court of law."[64] Following a DOJ appeal, the Second Circuit affirmed Judge Kaplan's decision, finding that the government had "unjustifiably interfered with [employees'] relationship with counsel and their ability to mount a defense, in violation of the Sixth Amendment."[65]

3. Judicial Oversight of Deferred Prosecution Agreements

On December 11, 2012, the DOJ filed an information in the Eastern District of New York charging the U.S. entity of British bank HSBC with violations of the Bank Secrecy Act and the financial sanctions imposed by the U.S. government on Iran, Cuba, Sudan, Libya, and Myanmar. As a result of these violations, HSBC had, among other things, acted as a conduit for at least $881 million in drug trafficking proceeds belonging to the Sinaloa Cartel in Mexico and the Norte del Valle Cartel in Colombia.[66]

Simultaneously with the information, the DOJ filed a DPA requiring HSBC to pay a $1.92 billion penalty, serve five years' probation, and pay for a monitor. At a status conference several weeks later, District Judge Gleeson noted his authority to accept or reject the DPA under Fed. R. Crim. P. 11(c)(1)(A) and U.S.S.G. Section 6B1.2 depending on whether it adequately reflected the seriousness of the offense and was otherwise consistent with the goals of federal sentencing. Pursuant to these asserted supervisory powers, Judge Gleeson approved the DPA and granted the parties' request to toll application of the Speedy Trial Act for the five-year term of probation.[67] The government was further ordered to file a confidential report prepared by HSBC's compliance monitor with the court (which the government then did, under seal). Afterward, in November 2015, a private citizen moved to have the report unsealed. The district court granted the motion and HSBC and the DOJ filed a joint appeal arguing that the district court's involvement in the DPA's implementation was improper.

---

62. United States v. Stein, 435 F. Supp. 2d 330, 350 (S.D.N.Y. 2006).

63. *Id.* at 357–58.

64. *Id.* at 382.

65. United States v. Stein, 541 F.3d 130, 136 (2d Cir. 2008); *see also* Trent O. Bridges, *U.S. v. Stein: Federal Prosecutors Twisting the Arm of Corporate America While Its Employees Cry Uncle (Sam)*, 43 Tulsa L. R. 739 (Spring 2008) (discussing the *Stein* case in detail).

66. Spencer Woodman, HSBC Moved Vast Sums of Dirty Money after Paying Record Laundering Fine, (International Consortium of Investigative Journalists, Sept. 21, 2020).

67. United States v. HSBC Bank USA, N.A., 12-CR-763 (E.D.N.Y. July 1, 2013).

The Second Circuit agreed. Viewing the district court's oversight of the DPA as a violation of the fundamental separation of powers between the three branches of the federal government, the panel found that the district court had "impermissibly encroached on the Executive's constitutional mandate to 'take Care that the Laws be faithfully executed.'"[68] As such, they ruled that since the monitor's report was no longer relevant to the "performance of the judicial function" with respect to the DPA, it was not properly characterized as a "judicial document" subject to public assess, rendering the order to unseal erroneous.[69]

While this decision did not completely extinguish any judicial oversight of DPAs, it limited it to extraordinary situations. "[B]ecause the United States Attorneys are charged with taking care that the laws are faithfully executed, there is a 'presumption of regularity' support[ing] their prosecutorial decisions and, in the absence of clear evidence to the contrary, courts [must] presume that they have properly discharged their official duties."[70] Accordingly, if misconduct connected with a DPA comes to the attention of a district court, it may "well be justified in invoking its supervisory power sua sponte to monitor" the DPA's implementation. "The point is not that the court can or should disregard government misconduct, but rather that a federal court has no roving commission" to oversee prosecutors' decision to enter into DPAs or how such agreements are effectuated.[71] In the typical case, therefore, a district court's role is limited to determining whether the DPA "is *bona fide* before granting a speedy trial waiver—that is, that the DPA in question is genuinely intended to 'allow[ ] the defendant to demonstrate his good conduct,' and does not constitute a disguised effort to circumvent the speedy trial clock."[72]

II. CORPORATE CRIMINAL LIABILITY IN THE UNITED KINGDOM—THE LEGAL FRAMEWORK

Just as in the United States, criminal prosecution of corporate offenders is seen in the United Kingdom as providing a "deterrent effect, protecting the public and supporting ethical business practices" but not as "a substitute for the prosecution of criminally culpable individuals such as directors, officers, employees or shareholders." As stated in the CPS's guidance on corporate prosecutions, "prosecuting such individuals provides a strong deterrent against future corporate wrongdoing. Equally, when considering prosecuting individuals, it is important to consider the possible liability of the company where the criminal conduct is for corporate gain." Although their basic principles are the same, U.S. prosecutors have been far more aggressive in pursuing criminal remedies against business entities than their British

68. United States v. HSBC Bank USA, N.A., 863 F.3d 125, 129 (2d Cir. 2017).

69. *Id.*

70. *Id.* at 136.

71. *Id.*; *see also* United States v. Fokker Servs. B.V., 818 F.3d 733, 744 (D.C. Cir. 2016) ("[A]lthough charges remain pending on the court's docket under a DPA, the court plays no role in monitoring the defendant's compliance with the DPA's conditions."); In re U.S., 503 F.3d 638, 641 (7th Cir. 2007) ("[A] judicial effort to supervise [a prosecutor's] process of reaching a decision intrudes impermissibly into the activities of the Executive Branch of government.").

72. HSBC, 863 F.3d at 138.

counterparts. With the introduction of DPAs via the February 2014 addition of Schedule 17 to the Crime and Courts Act 2013, however, this is starting to change.

Unless a statute expressly creates criminal liability for companies, corporate criminal liability can be established under two theories: vicarious liability and the so-called "identification principle."

A. Vicarious Liability

The common law doctrine of vicarious liability can be used to make a company criminally liable for the acts of its employees and agents in the same way as an individual person can be. This concept is deemed implied in most acts of Parliament that define a criminal offense. As the High Court has recognized since at least the early twentieth century, "[I]t may [reasonably] be [inferred that] the intention of the Legislature, in order to guard against the happening of a forbidden thing, [is] to impose a liability upon a principal even though he does not know of, and is not a party to, the forbidden act done by his servant."[73]

Because of difficulties in establishing an entity's mens rea under English law (discussed in the following section), vicarious liability is normally reserved for strict liability offenses that do not have an intent element—for example, health and safety laws and environmental laws. The application of vicarious liability in the context of a strict liability statute is relatively straightforward: if the statute was violated by a company's employee or agent in the course of his or her employment, the company may also be criminally liable.

B. The Identification Principle

Under the identification principle, corporate entities can be guilty of criminal offenses requiring criminal intent if the evidence shows that the crime was perpetrated by individuals who represent "the directing mind and will" of the company.[74]

As this principle was described by Lord Diplock in *Tesco Supermarkets Ltd v. Nattras*: the answer to "the question [of] what natural persons are to be treated in law as being the company for the purpose of acts done in the course of its business . . . is to be found by identifying those natural persons who . . . are entrusted with the exercise of the powers of the company."[75] This does not mean that "every high executive or agent acting on behalf of a company can by his actions make the company criminally responsible." Rather, the key factor is "whether the natural person or persons in question have the status and authority which in law make their acts in the matter under consideration the acts of the company, so that the natural person is to be treated as the company itself."[76]

---

73. Mousell Bros Ltd v. London and North Western Railway Co [1917] 2 KB 836.

74. Lennard's Carrying Co v. Asiatic Petroleum Co [1915] A.C. 705; Bolton Engineering Co v. Graham [1957] 1 QB 159; R. v Andrews Weatherfoil [1972] 56 C App R 31 CA.

75. [1972] AC 153.

76. Meridian Global Funds Management Asia Ltd v. Securities Commission [1995] 2 A.C. 500, PC; Attorney General's Reference (No 2 of 1999) [2000] QB 796 ("it is impossible to find a company guilty unless its alter ego is identified").

In *R v. St Regis Paper Co Ltd* [2011] EWCA Crim 2527, for example, a paper manufacturer was criminally charged for an intentionally false entry in a record required for environmental pollution control made by one if its employees, Christopher Steer. The Crown Court made a preliminary ruling that the company could be held liable for Steer's conduct under the identification principle. The case then proceeded to trial and the company and Steer were convicted on all counts. On appeal, St Regis Paper argued that the identification principle had been misapplied because Steer was not, as a matter of law, the "controlling mind and will" of the company.

After concluding that the statute in question did not impose strict liability, the Court of Appeal agreed with St. Regis Paper because Steer was not senior enough:

> In our view, it was not open to the jury to conclude that Mr Steer fell within the category of one whose state of mind can be attributed to the company. . . . As technical and environmental manager, Mr Steer reported to the mill operations manager, who reported to the mill's managing director. The mill's managing director reported to divisional technical managers and a divisional environmental director, who formed part of the senior management team.[77]

The practical effect of the identification principle is that criminal acts by senior company officers will not only individually subject them to criminal charges, but also open up their employers to criminal charges. This is true even if the officers' crime consisted of a fraud on the company.[78] At the same time, the identification principle means that companies will not be able to be criminally charged if the wrongdoing was limited to lower-level employees.

CPS guidance provides that, in seeking to identify the "directing mind" of a company, prosecutors should "consider the constitution of the company concerned (with the aid of memoranda/articles of association/actions of directors or the company in general meeting), the governance of the company and any appropriate delegation of authority." Reflecting the lessons learned by the DOJ in the Arthur Andersen case, the CPS also mandates consideration of the broader effects of a corporate prosecution: "Where the evidence provides a realistic prospect of conviction, the prosecutor must consider whether or not a prosecution is in the public interest. . . . The more serious the offence, the more likely it is that prosecution will be needed in the public interest."

The identification principle has been widely criticized for creating too high a bar to secure corporate convictions. In a recent editorial published in *The Times*, for example, current SFO Director Lisa Osofsky said that the requirement to prove wrongdoing by a company's "directing mind" "enables bad behaviour because leaders can distance themselves from the actions of their company" through what she called a "culture of organized irresponsibility"—that is, "inappropriately heavily delegated decision-making; a lack of record-keeping; responsibility spread across different corporate entities; email trails petering out at board level and a culture at the top of 'don't raise that with me.'"[79]

---

77. [2011] EWCA Crim 2527, [16]–[17].

78. Meridian Global Funds Management Asia Ltd v. Securities Commission [1995] 2 A.C. 500, PC.

79. Lisa Osofsky, "We're Defending the UK as a Safe Place for Business," The Times, June 30, 2021.

Nevertheless, the English courts have reaffirmed that the *Tesco Supermarkets Ltd.* decision remains a controlling precedent absent legislative reforms by Parliament. As Lord Justice Davis noted in *SFO v. Barclays Plc & ANR*, "It is said that [the identification principle] would tend to render large companies with widely devolved management less exposed to criminal prosecution than small companies. . . . But as against that, the decision in *Tesco v Nattrass* can be said to give rise to a degree of certainty in the required approach. Moreover, it is to be borne in mind that the policy considerations which have driven the doctrine of vicarious liability in the law of tort simply do not apply in the same way in criminal law."[80]

III. DEFERRED PROSECUTION AGREEMENTS IN THE UNITED KINGDOM

Long a prominent feature of U.S. federal law, DPAs are a much more recent phenomenon in the United Kingdom. As noted, this form of criminal settlement was introduced into English law in 2014 with the addition of Schedule 17 of the Crime and Courts Act (CCA) 2013. The new law was announced by Justice Minister Damian Green in October 2012: "A new measure announced today will help prosecutors combat corporate offending including fraud, money laundering and bribery . . . Deferred Prosecution Agreements will give prosecutors an effective new tool to tackle [financial crime and] ensure that more unacceptable corporate behaviour is dealt with."[81]

Schedule 17 defines a DPA as an agreement between CPS or SFO prosecutors and a corporate investigation target whereby the target can avoid prosecution for certain financial crimes through negotiation.[82] Similar to the structure of the U.S. version, Schedule 17 DPAs include an agreed-upon statement of facts, an expiry date, and a series of requirements imposed on the defendant company—these can include various financial penalties, an obligation to cooperate in the investigation of any related offense, implementation of enhanced compliance procedures, and payment of the prosecutors' costs.[83]

These agreements are reached through the following process. Once an investigation obtains evidence indicating that an entity has committed a crime, prosecutors and defense counsel will begin discussions about a possible DPA. Before prosecutors can continue these negotiations, they must apply *ex parte* to the Crown Court for a declaration that the proposed

---

80. [2018] EWHC 3055 (QB), [67].

81. Press Release, Ministry of Justice, New Tool to Fight Financial Crime (Oct. 23, 2012), *available at* https://www.gov.uk/government/news/new-tool-to-fight-economic-crime.

82. As summarized by the Rt. Hon. Sir Brian Leveson in *SFO v. Rolls Royce PLC* (U20170036), "a DPA is potentially available for certain economic or financial offences to a body corporate, a partnership or an unincorporated association in respect of whom the only criminal sanction is financial: it does not cover (nor does it protect from prosecution) any individual. It provides a mechanism whereby, subject to the approval of the court, prosecution can be avoided by entering into an agreement on negotiated terms with a prosecutor designated by the 2013 Act."

83. Crime and Courts Act (CCA), Sch. 17, para.5.

DPA is in the interests of justice and "reasonable and proportionate."[84] If requested by the court, the parties must participate in a private hearing with the judge to discuss details of the offense and the proposed terms. Once the Crown Court has given preliminary sign off, the parties will then continue negotiations and finalize an agreement. Prosecutors must then submit a second application to the Crown Court for a declaration confirming that its earlier conclusions still stand.[85] The SFO or CPS prosecutor then will file an indictment directly in Crown Court, initiating proceedings that are then automatically suspended immediately. The DPA and the court's initial and final declarations must then be made public.

Like DPAs in the United States, authorities in the United Kingdom have the option of requiring a DPA target to install an independent third party—called an "external reviewer"—to monitor its compliance with the agreement. But whereas monitors are routinely imposed by the DOJ, to date, the SFO has required an external reviewer in only one instance.

A. Termination of the Deferred Prosecution Agreement

Suspension of an indictment pursuant to a DPA may only be lifted by application of the prosecutor and only when the DPA is no longer in force, either by way of a breach or expiry by its terms. If prosecutors believe the DPA has been breached, they must make an application to the Crown Court setting out the evidence for the defendant's failure to comply. If the court accepts the prosecution's position on the balance of probabilities, it may either invite the parties to negotiate a remedy or terminate the agreement (at which point the indictment can be resurrected).

In cases where the DPA expires on its own terms, prosecutors must notify the Crown Court that they no longer wish for the suspended proceedings to continue. Once this occurs, prosecutors are then barred from instituting any future proceedings against the defendant for the alleged offense.[86]

B. Use of Deferred Prosecution Agreement Material in Criminal Proceedings

If the DPA is breached and terminated, the statement of fact can be treated as a formal admission of guilt by the defendant company. All materials relating to the negotiation (e.g., any draft of the DPA and communications between the parties) can only be used in a prosecution for presenting knowingly inaccurate, misleading, or incomplete information, or on a prosecution for some other offense in which the company makes a statement that is inconsistent.[87]

84. CCA, Sch. 17, para.7.

85. CCA, Sch. 17, para.8.

86. CCA, Sch. 17, para.11.

87. CCA, Sch. 17, para. 13.

C. The Serious Fraud Office's Deferred Prosecution Agreement Code of Practice

Compared with the more ad hoc and confidential procedures used by the DOJ, the SFO's DPA Code of Practice, introduced in 2020, is more formulaic and transparent. The Code specifies that if the prosecution wishes to enter into DPA negotiations, it must "do so by way of a formal letter of invitation outlining the basis on which any negotiations will proceed." "The prosecutor is under no obligation to invite [the target company] P to negotiate a DPA and P is under no obligation to accept that invitation should it be made. The terms of the DPA are similarly voluntary, and neither party is obliged to agree any particular term therein."[88] Whether a resolution via DPA is appropriate in the circumstances of a particular case, prosecutors are directed to consider (i) the extent of the defendant company's cooperation, (ii) any past misconduct, (iii) the objective effectiveness of its compliance program, (iv) whether the company self-reported in a timely manner, and the (v) nature of the offense (including the degree of harm inflicted on victims).[89]

To ensure transparency, prosecutors must ensure that "a full and accurate record of negotiations is prepared and retained. It is essential that a full written record is kept of every key action and event in the discussion process, including details of every offer or concession made by each party, and the reasons for every decision taken by the prosecutor. Meetings between the parties should be minuted and the minutes agreed and signed."[90]

The Code "recognis[es] that there is a balance to be struck between encouraging all parties to be able to negotiate freely, and the risk that P may seek knowingly (or when it should have known) to induce the prosecutor to enter into a DPA on an inaccurate, misleading or incomplete basis." Accordingly, "if P provides inaccurate, misleading, incomplete information where P knew or ought to have known that the information was inaccurate, misleading or incomplete, the prosecutor may instigate fresh proceedings."[91] In such case, most materials disclosed to prosecutors during DPA negotiations may be used by prosecutors to establish liability.[92] The Code provides nonexhaustive examples of the types of documents that may be used when DPA negotiations fail or when the DPA has been breached: (i) all contemporaneous evidence of the crime (e.g., documents, financial records and emails); (ii) any internal or independent investigation report disclosed to prosecutors; (iii) interview notes or witness statements obtained from an employee of P; and (iv) any document or information obtained by the prosecutor at any time from any source.[93]

In terms of disclosure obligations placed on prosecutors during the DPA process, the Code requires only that "P should have sufficient information to play an informed part in the

---

88. DPA Code of Practice, para. 3.2; *see also Serious Fraud Office v. Rolls-Royce Plc* (U20170036), at [33] (setting forth relevant considerations for whether a DPA is in the interests of justice); Serious Fraud Office v. Tesco Stores Limited (U20170287), at [45] (same).

89. DPA Code of Practice, para. 2.8.

90. DPA Code of Practice, para. 3.4.

91. DPA Code of Practice, paras. 4.2–4.3.

92. *Id.* at paras. 4.4–4.5.

93. *Id.* at para. 4.6.

Table 11.1 The Serious Fraud Office's Deferred Prosecution Agreements, 2015 to 2021

Company	Year	Penalty	Offense
Standard Bank	2015	$32.3 million plus $330,000 in costs	Failure to prevent bribery
Sarclad Ltd	2016	£6.2 disgorgement plus £352,000 penalty	Failure to prevent bribery
Rolls-Royce	2017	£258 million disgorgement, £239 million penalty, plus £13 million costs	Conspiracy to corrupt Failure to prevent bribery False accounting
Tesco	2017	£129 million fine, £85 million victim compensation, plus £3 million costs	Market abuse False accounting
Serco Geografix Ltd	2019	£19.2 million fine plus £3.7 million costs	Fraud and false accounting
Gürlap Systems Ltd	2019	£2 million disgorgement	Foreign bribery
Airbus SE	2020	€398 million fine, €586 million disgorgement, plus €7 million costs	Failure to prevent bribery
G4S Care & Justice Services (UK) Ltd	2020	£38.5 million penalty plus £5.9 million costs	Fraud on the government
Airline Services Ltd	2020	£1 million disgorgement, £1.24 million penalty, plus £750,000 costs	Failure to prevent bribery
Amec Foster Wheeler Energy Ltd	2021	£99.9 million penalty, £210,610 victim compensation, plus £3.4 million costs	Conspiracy to corrupt Failure to prevent bribery
Two Undisclosed Companies	2021	£2,510,065 combined penalty and disgorgement	Failure to prevent bribery

negotiations." In contrast to the fair trial concerns underlying the broader discovery afforded criminal defendants who have already been charged, "the purpose of disclosure [in the DPA context] is to ensure that negotiations are fair and the P is not mislead as to the strength of the prosecution case. . . . For instance, disclosure ought to be made of information that might undermine the factual basis of conclusions drawn by P from material disclosed by P."[94]

To date, the SFO has entered into twelve DPAs (table 11.1). No DPAs have yet been filed by the CPS.

Although the SFO has brought criminal charges against individual executives on the back of four of these settlements, none have been found guilty: *Sarclad* (three charged, all acquitted after trial); *Gürlap* (three charged, all acquitted after trial); *Tesco* (three charged, prosecution dropped for insufficient evidence); *Serco* (two charged, prosecution dropped

94. *Id.* at para. 5.2.

because of SFO's failure to disclose relevant documents). This has opened the SFO to criticism that it is overly focused on generating revenue from DPAs at the expense of obtaining convictions in the public interest.[95]

CHAPTER 11: KEY DISTINCTIONS

United States	United Kingdom
Deferred prosecution agreements (DPAs) available to entities and individuals	DPAs only available to corporate entities
DPAs can be entered by the Department of Justice (DOJ) and civil regulators at the Securities Exchange Commission	DPAs only available to criminal prosecutors at the Serious Fraud Office (SFO) and Crown Prosecution Service
Presumption that a company that fully cooperates with an investigation will receive a DPA	No presumption is given to cooperating companies
Selective waiver not recognized	Internal investigation reports can be provided to prosecutor without broadly waiving privilege
Corporate criminal liability can be imposed for crimes requiring criminal intent under vicarious liability principles	Corporate criminal liability can only be imposed for strict liability offenses (including failure to prevent bribery)
Entities deemed to have the "collective knowledge" of their employees	Entities considered to only have the knowledge of senior executives who are effectively the entity's "directing mind"
DPAs are negotiated without any judicial oversight	DPAs are negotiated with direct judicial involvement
Courts can only reject a DPA if there is evidence of prosecutorial misconduct	Courts can deny approval of a DPA if it is substantively unfair, unreasonable, or contrary to the public interest
DOJ has entered into 600+ corporate DPAs since 2000	SFO has entered into 12 corporate DPAs since they became available under English law in 2014
DPAs have generated more than $64 billion for the U.S. government since 2010	DPAs have generated a total of £1.6 billion for the U.K. treasury

95. *See, e.g.*, Liam Naidoo et al., *SFO DPAs: Is the System Working?*, GLOBAL INVESTIGATIONS REVIEW (Nov. 15, 2021); Martin Coyle, "Amec Foster Wheeler Bribe Details Highlight Lack of UK Action against Executives," mLex (Feb. 8, 2022).

Index

F